COMPARATIVE POLITICS TODAY, AP* EDITION

CONTRIBUTORS

OLADIMEJI ABORISADE
Obafemi Awolowa University, Nigeria

GABRIEL A. ALMOND
Late, Stanford University

HOUCHANG E. CHEHABI
Boston University

WAYNE A. CORNELIUS
University of California, San Diego

RUSSELL J. DALTON
University of California, Irvine

ARANG KESHAVARZIAN
Connecticut College

THAD KOUSSER
University of California, San Diego

A. CARL LEVAN
American University

MELANIE MANION
University of Wisconsin

ROBERT J. MUNDT
Late, University of North Carolina at Charlotte

G. BINGHAM POWELL, JR.
University of Rochester

AUSTIN RANNEY
Late, University of California, Berkeley

THOMAS F. REMINGTON
Emory University

RICHARD ROSE
University of Aberdeen, Scotland

KAARE STRØM
University of California, San Diego

JEFFREY A. WELDON
Instituto Technologico Autónomo de Mexíco
(ITAM)

NINTH EDITION

COMPARATIVE POLITICS TODAY AP* EDITION

A WORLD VIEW

Gabriel A. Almond
Late, Stanford University

G. Bingham Powell, Jr.
University of Rochester

Russell J. Dalton
University of California, Irvine

Kaare Strøm
University of California, San Diego

PEARSON
Longman

New York   San Francisco   Boston
London   Toronto   Sydney   Tokyo   Singapore   Madrid
Mexico City   Munich   Paris   Cape Town   Hong Kong   Montreal

Acquisitions Editor: Vikram Mukhija
Supplements Editor: Brian Belardi
Associate Marketing Manager: Sasha Anderson-Smith
Production Manager: Eric Jorgensen
Project Coordination, Text Design, and Electronic Page Makeup: GGS Book Services, Inc.
Cover Design Manager: Wendy Ann Fredericks
Cover Image: VEER Geoff Graham/Photonica/Getty Images
Visual Researcher: Anita Dickhuth
Senior Manufacturing Buyer: Dennis J. Para
Printer and Binder: Courier Corp
Cover Printer: Coral Graphic Services, Inc.

Library of Congress Cataloging-in-Publication Data
Comparative politics today : a world view / Gabriel A. Almond . . . [et al.].—9th, Advanced Placement ed.
   p. cm.
 Includes bibliographical references and index.
 ISBN-13: 978-0-13-135854-6
 ISBN-10: 0-13-135854-5
 1. Comparative government—Textbooks. I. Almond, Gabriel A. (Gabriel Abraham), 1911–2002.
 JF51.C62 2008
 320.3—dc22

                         2007052870

Please visit us at www.ablongman.com

AP* Edition-High school Binding ISBN-13: 978-0-13-135854-6
                             ISBN-10: 0-13-135854-5

College Edition ISBN-13: 978-0-205-52931-5
                 ISBN-10: 0-205-52931-3

 2 3 4 5 6 7 8 9 10—CRK—11 10 09

The editors and coauthors of the ninth edition of
Comparative Politics Today, AP* Edition dedicate this
book to the memory of Austin Ranney—a colleague,
a friend, a leader in the study of American politics,
and for many years, a contributor to this book.
He passed away on July 24, 2006, at the age of 85.

BRIEF CONTENTS

DETAILED CONTENTS

CHAPTER 11

Politics in Mexico   298
*Wayne A. Cornelius and
Jeffrey A. Weldon*

CHAPTER 12

Politics in Iran   350
H. E. Chehabi and Arang Keshavarzian

CHAPTER 13

Politics in Nigeria   396
*Robert J. Mundt, Oladimeji Aborisade,
and A. Carl LeVan*

CHAPTER 14

Politics in the United States   448
Austin Ranney and Thad Kousser

A GUIDE TO COMPARING NATIONS

This analytic index provides a guide to where specific themes are addressed in each chapter.

Topics	Chapters 1–7	Britain	Russia	China
History	—	160–63	205–15	254–58
Social Conditions	10–23	156–60	239–41	258–59
Executive	103–07, 113–20	165–71	210–12, 217–22	262–63, 264–65
Parliament	103–07, 110–13	171–73	212–14	260–62, 263–64
Judiciary	107–09	165	214, 242–44	263
Provincial Government	107	156–57	214–17	—
Political Culture	43–52	173–76	218–21	272–73
Political Socialization	52–57	176–79	221–22	270–72
Participation/Recruitment	60–64	179–83	222–25	268, 273–78
Interest Groups	64–76, 80–81	183–86	225–30	278–80
Parties and Elections	81–98	186–91	230–37	263–68
Policy Process	31–38	191–96	213–14	280–86
Outputs and Outcomes	38–39, 127–45, 147–49	154–56, 196–99	204–05, 237–39, 241	252–53, 286–92
International Relations	145–47	155–56	245–46	292

Mexico	Iran	Nigeria	United States
305–10	353–58	398–402	451
310–13	385–89	402–06	452–53
323–27	358–60	418–19, 423–25	456–57
317–19, 320–23, 325–27	360–61	423–25	456–57
344	361	425–26	457
319–20	—	421–23	455–56
313–14	368–71	408–14	458–60
314–15	371–76	414–18	460–61
315–17, 327–28	365, 368, 371–76	418–20, 429	461–65
329–30	362–68	429–35	469–77
299–305, 330–38	362–68	429–35	469–77
321–23	361–62, 380–84	—	477–80
305, 338–45	352–53, 384–89	397–98, 436–42	449–51, 480–84
310–11	389–90	406–07, 442–43	449–50, 453–54

A BRIEF GUIDE TO ANALYZING VISUALS

We are used to thinking about reading written texts critically—for example, reading a textbook carefully for information, sometimes highlighting or underlining as we go along—but we do not always think about "reading" visuals in this way. We should, for images and informational graphics can tell us a lot if we read and consider them carefully. Especially in the so-called information age, in which we are exposed to a constant stream of images on television and the Internet, it is important for us to be able to analyze and understand their meanings. This brief guide provides information about the types of visuals you will encounter in *Comparative Politics Today: A World View* and offers some questions to help you analyze everything from tables to charts and graphs to news photographs.

TABLES

Tables are the least "visual" of the visuals we explore. They consist of textual information and/or numerical data arranged in columns and rows. Tables are frequently used when exact information is required and when orderly arrangement is necessary to locate and, in many cases, to compare the information. For example, Table 1.4 makes data on the income distribution of many nations organized and easy to compare. Here are a few questions to guide your analysis:

- What is the purpose of this table? What information does it show? There is usually a title that offers a sense of the table's purpose.
- What information is provided in the column headings (the table's top row)? How are the rows labeled? Are there any clarifying notes at the bottom of the table?
- Is a time period indicated, such as July to December 2005? Or, are the data as of a specific date, such as January 1, 2006? Are the data shown at multiple intervals over a fixed period or at one particular point in time?

Income Distribution for Selected Nations				TABLE 1.4
Country	**Year**	**Wealthiest 10%**	**Poorest 40%**	**Wealthy/Poor Gap**
Germany	2000	22.1	22.2	−0.1
Russia	2002	23.8	20.9	2.9
Japan	1993	21.7	24.8	3.1
France	1995	25.1	19.8	5.3
India	1999	28.5	21.2	7.3
Britain	1999	28.5	17.5	11.0
United States	2000	29.9	16.2	13.7
Iran	1998	33.7	19.5	14.2
China	2001	33.1	13.7	19.4
Nigeria	1996	35.4	12.6	22.8
Mexico	2000	43.1	10.3	32.8
Brazil	2001	46.9	8.3	38.6

Source: World Bank, *World Development Indicators 2005*, table 2–7 (www.worldbank.org); distribution of income or consumption.

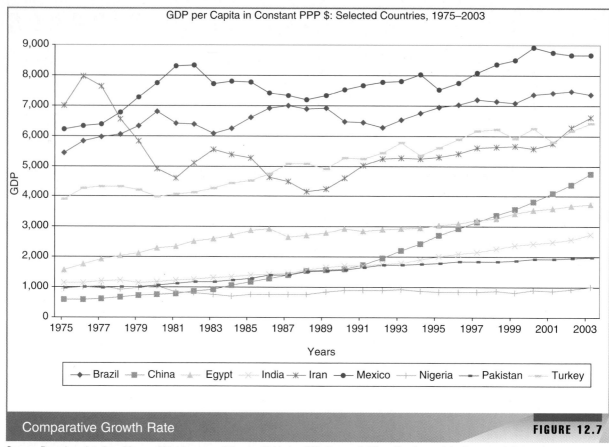

Comparative Growth Rate

FIGURE 12.7

Source: Based on data from Massoud Karshenas and Hassan Hakimian, "Oil, Economic Diversification and the Democratic Process in Iran," *Iranian Studies* 38, no. 1 (March 2005), 67–90.

- If the table shows numerical data, what do these data represent? In what units? Dollars spent on social service programs? Percentage of voters who support the British Labour Party? Projected population increases?
- What is the source of the information presented in the table? Is it government information? Private polling information? A newspaper? A corporation? The United Nations? An individual? Is the source trustworthy? Current? Does the source have a vested interest in the data expressed in the table?

CHARTS AND GRAPHS

Charts and graphs depict numerical data in visual forms. The most common kinds of graphs plot data in two dimensions along horizontal and vertical axes. Examples that you will encounter throughout this book are line graphs, pie charts, bar graphs, and timelines. These kinds of visuals emphasize data relationships: at a particular point in time, at regular intervals over a fixed period of time, or, sometimes, as parts of a whole. Line graphs show a progression, usually over time (as in Figure 12.7 comparative growth rate). Pie charts (such as Figure 9.6, 2006 Russian Federal Budget) demonstrate how a whole (total government spending) is divided into its parts (different types of government programs). Bar graphs compare values across categories, showing how proportions are related to each other (as in Figure 10.5, showing the male and female populations in China by age bracket). Bar graphs can present data either horizontally or vertically. Timelines show events and changes over a defined period of time (such as the list of Prime Ministers of Britain in Figure 8.2). You will also encounter charts that map out processes and hierarchies

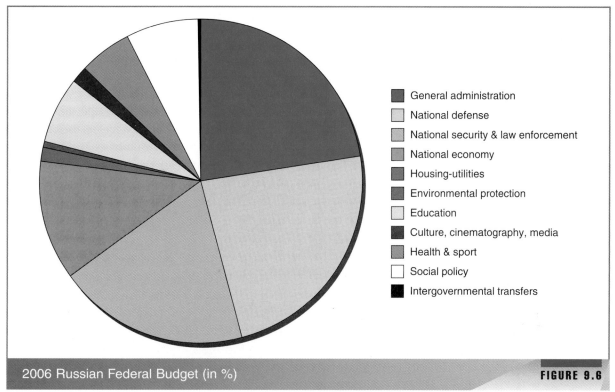

2006 Russian Federal Budget (in %)

FIGURE 9.6

Source: Russian press reports.

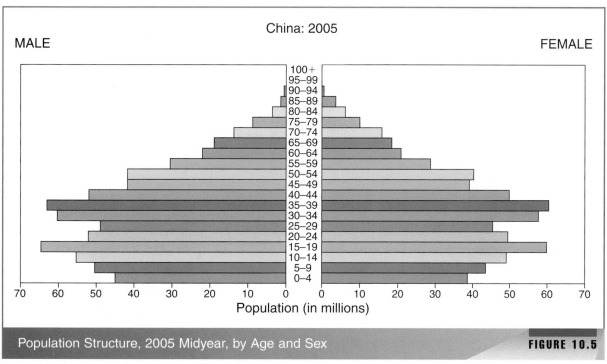

Population Structure, 2005 Midyear, by Age and Sex

FIGURE 10.5

Source: U.S. Census Bureau, International Data Base at http://www.census.gov/ipc/www/idbpyr.html.

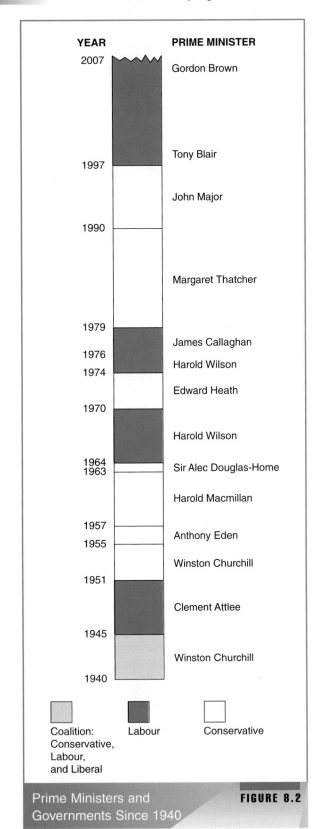

YEAR	PRIME MINISTER
2007	Gordon Brown
1997	Tony Blair
	John Major
1990	
	Margaret Thatcher
1979	
	James Callaghan
1976	
1974	Harold Wilson
	Edward Heath
1970	
	Harold Wilson
1964	
1963	Sir Alec Douglas-Home
	Harold Macmillan
1957	
1955	Anthony Eden
	Winston Churchill
1951	
	Clement Attlee
1945	
	Winston Churchill
1940	

Coalition: Conservative, Labour, and Liberal

Labour

Conservative

Prime Ministers and Governments Since 1940

FIGURE 8.2

throughout this book (as in the structure of the government of Nigeria shown in Figure 13.4)

Many of the same questions you ask about tables are important when analyzing graphs and charts also (see above). Here are more questions to help you:

- In the case of line and bar graphs, how are the axes labeled? Are symbols or colors used to represent different groups or units?
- Are the data shown at multiple intervals over a fixed period or at one particular point in time?
- If there are two or more sets of figures, what are the relationships among them?
- Is there distortion in the visual representation of the information? Are the intervals equal? Does the area shown distort the actual amount or the proportion? Distortion can lead you to draw an inaccurate conclusion on first sight, so it's important to look for it.

MAPS

Maps of countries, regions, and the world are very often used in political analysis to illustrate demographic, social, economic, and political issues and trends. See, for example, Figure 11.7 Levels of Social Well-Being by State, in 2000 (page xx). Though tables and graphs might sometimes give more precise information, maps help us to understand in a geographic context data that are more difficult to express in words or numbers alone. Here are a few more questions to add to those in the above sections:

- What does the map key/legend show? What are the factors that the map is analyzing? Are symbols or colors used to differentiate sections of the map? Maps can express information on political boundaries, natural resources, ethnic groups, and many other topics, so it is important to know what exactly is being shown.
- What is the region being shown? How detailed is the map?
- Maps usually depict a specific point in time. What point in time is being shown on the map?

NEWS PHOTOGRAPHS

Photos can have a dramatic—and often immediate—impact on politics and government. Think about some photos that have political significance. For example, do you remember the photos from the September 11, 2001,

The Structure of Government Under the 1999 Constitution   **FIGURE 13.4**

terrorist attacks? Visual images usually evoke a stronger emotional response than do written descriptions. For this reason, individuals and organizations have learned to use photographs to document events, to make arguments, to offer evidence, and even in some cases to manipulate the viewer into having a particular response. The photo of a student protester confronting tanks in Tiananmen Square (page xxi) captured the attention of the world and drew attention to the violent response of the Chinese government to the protesters. Here are a few questions to guide your analysis:

- When was the photograph taken? (If there is no date given for the photograph in its credit line or caption, you may be able to approximate the date according to the people or events depicted in the photo.)
- What is the subject of the photograph?
- Why was the photo taken?
- Is it spontaneous or posed? Did the subject know he or she was being photographed?
- Who was responsible for the photo (an individual, an agency, or an organization)? Can you discern the photographer's attitude toward the subject?
- Is there a caption? If so, what information does it provide? Does it identify the subject of the photo? Does it provide an interpretation of the subject?

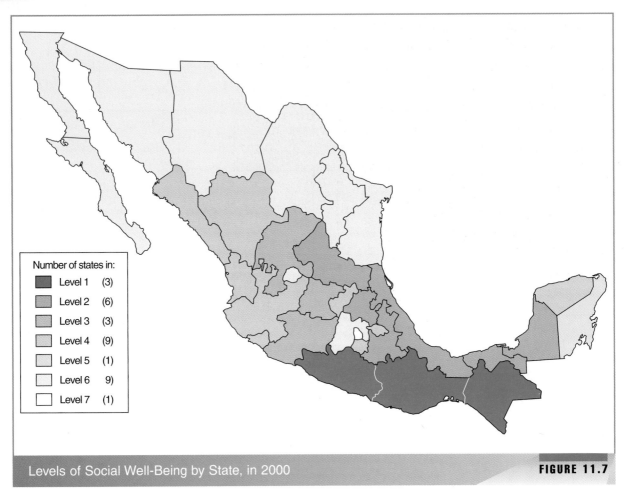

Levels of Social Well-Being by State, in 2000   FIGURE 11.7

Level 1: Chiapas, Guerrero, Oaxaca
Level 2: Campeche, Hidalgo, Puebla, San Luis Potosí, Tabasco, Veracruz
Level 3: Guanajuato, Michoacán, Zacatecas
Level 4: Colima, Durango, Jalisco, Morelos, Nayarit, Querétaro, Sinaloa, Tlaxcala, Yucatán
Level 5: Quintana Roo
Level 6: Aguascalientes, Baja California, Baja California Sur, Coahuila, Chihuahua, México, Nuevo León, Sonora, Tamaulipas.
Level 7: Distrito Federal

Note: Level of social well-being is measured by characteristics of dwellings (have electricity, refrigerator, television, concrete vs. dirt floors, sewerage connection, private bathroom; number of rooms; use something other than firewood or coal for cooking) and population characteristics (percentage economically active; literate; 6–19-year-olds who attend school; receive health care; live in urban area; average number of children born to women over age 12).

Source: Instituto Nacional de Estadística, Geografía e Informática, www.inegi.gob.mx.

In 1989, ordinary Chinese participated in the largest spontaneous protest movement the communists had ever faced. A lone protester shows defiance of regime violence in his intransigent confrontation with a Chinese tank.

AP Images

CORRELATION GUIDE

AP* COMPARATIVE GOVERNMENT AND POLITICS COURSE DESCRIPTION OUTLINE CORRELATED TO *COMPARATIVE POLITICS TODAY*, AP* EDITION

AP* Topics	*Comparative Politics Today*, AP* Edition
I. Introduction to Comparative Politics	Chapters 1 & 2
Purpose and methods of comparison and classification	10–12, 39–41
Why/ways to organize government	10–12, 23–25, 31–38
Normative and empirical questions	38–39, 39–41, 147–150
Concepts (state, nation, regime, government)	2–3, 8–10, 13–14
Process and policy (what is politics, purpose of government; what is political science/comparative common policy challenges)	1–3, 3–8, 13–26, 28, 127–150
II Sovereignty, Authority, and Power	Chapters 1, 3, 6, Country studies
Political culture, communication, and socialization	43–57, 173–179, 218–222, 270–273, 313–315, 368–376, 408–418, 458–461
Nations and states	8–14
Supranational governance (e.g., European Union)	8–10
Sources of Power	8–10
Constitutions (forms, purposes, application)	23–25, 101–103, 164–165, 210–212, 259–260, 317–319, 354–355, 361–363, 420–421, 454–455
Regime types	45–47, 103–110, 204, 351
Types of economic systems	130, 136–138
State building, legitimacy, and stability	3–5, 44–45, 173–174
Belief systems as sources of legitimacy	1–3, 16–17, 44–51, 51–53, 205–206, 259–260, 356–358, 373–375
Religion	16–17, 53, 206, 351, 353–358, 373–375, 411, 418
Ideology (liberalism, communism, socialism, conservatism, fascism)	1–3, 47–48, 206–208, 259–260
Governance and accountability	109–110
III. Political Institutions	Chapters 4–6, Country studies
Levels of government	Chapter 6, Country studies
Supranational/national/regional/local	214–218
Unitary/federal	107, 156–159, 214–218, 319–320, 421–424, 455–456
Centralization/decentralization	
Executives (head of state, head of government, cabinets)	109–110, 113–120, 165–170, 210–212, 263–265, 323–325, 358–360, 418–419, 423–425, 456–457
Single or dual	113–116

AP* Topics	*Comparative Politics Today,* AP* Edition
President	104–107, 210–212, 214, 263–265, 323–325, 358–360, 456–457, 479–480
Prime minister	104–107, 165–168
Legislatures	110–113, 171–172, 212–214, 260–264, 320–322, 360–361, 457, 473–475
Unicameral/bicameral (symmetric/asymmetric)	110–111, 214
Organization	110–111, 261–262
Membership (representation)	111–113
Parliamentary and presidential systems	104–107, 214, 325–327, 423–425
Institutional relations	104–107, 113–120, 457
Elections	83–86, 92–94, 177, 186–189, 211, 231–236, 274–276, 301–304, 361, 364–368, 431–435, 464–465, 469–471
Presidential	233–235, 301–304, 332–333, 364–366, 464–465, 469–471
Parliamentary	186–189, 211, 231–235, 320–321, 367–368
Referendums	463
Noncompetitive	92–94, 236, 274–276, 331–333, 361–62, 368
Electoral systems	85–86, 211, 320–321, 464–465, 485–486
Proportional representation	85–86, 189, 211, 320–321
Single member district (plurality, majority turnoff)	85, 188–189, 211, 320–321, 485–486
Political parties (organization, membership, institutionalization, ideological position)	79–90, 189–191, 230–237, 259–268, 330–338, 364, 429–435, 469–477
Party systems	81–94, 236–237
Leadership and elite recruitment	111–113, 116–118, 180–183, 223–225, 266–268, 327–328, 376–377, 418–420, 464
Interest groups and interest group systems	64–70, 74–76, 183–186, 225–230, 278–280, 329–330, 377–380, 426–428, 465–469
Bureaucracies	120–124, 170–171, 175, 182, 266–268, 382–385
Military and other coercive institutions	94–95, 243–244, 265–266, 418–419
Judiciaries	
Degrees of autonomy	108, 242–244, 324, 344, 382, 425–426
Judicial review (including European Union in relations to states and citizens)	107–109, 214, 243, 344, 457
Types of law	242–245, 268–270, 343–345, 357, 382, 485
IV. Citizens, Society, and the State	Chapters 1 & 3, Country studies
Cleavages and politics (ethnic, racial, class, gender, religious, regional)	13–17, 156–160, 215–216, 258–259, 305–307, 310, 353, 408–411, 432–433, 458, 472
Civil society and social capital	67–68, 222–223
Media roles	55, 71, 179, 244, 270, 315, 375, 416–417, 460–461
Political participation (forms/modes/trends) including political violence	60–74, 179–180, 222–223, 273–278, 315–317, 364–368, 380, 429, 461–464
Social movements	60–66, 74, 369
Citizenship and social representation	103, 111–113
V. Political and Economic Change	All chapters
Revolution, coups, and war	94–95, 106, 208–210, 255–258, 307–308, 310, 355–358, 418–421

AP* Topics	*Comparative Politics Today*, AP* Edition
Trends and types of political change (including democratization)	23–26, 30–31, 33–34, 35–38, 56–57, 74–76, 94–95, 95–97, 154–156, 160–163, 204–205, 208–210, 251–258, 268–270, 299–310, 355–358, 418–419, 444, 449–451
Components	58–59, 159–160, 208, 248, 367–368
Promoting or inhibiting factors	28, 58, 96, 153, 208, 367
Consequences	28–29, 58–59, 208, 248, 368–369
Trends and types of economic change (including privatization)	17–23, 57, 237–241, 252–253, 286–288, 310–313, 383–384, 402–407
Components	18–20, 57, 252–253
Promoting or inhibiting factors	57
Consequences	18–23, 57, 252–253
Relationship between political and economic change	8, 30–31, 57, 237–241
Globalization and fragmentation interlinked economics, global culture, reactions against globalization, regionalism	17, 25–26, 391
Approaches to development	17–23, 252–253, 328–340, 402–409
VI. Public Policy	Chapters 1 and 7, Country studies
Common policy issues	13–26, 38–39, 107–109, 147–149, 154–156, 203–205, 240–241, 252–253, 286–291, 304–305, 310–312, 338–345, 352–353, 383–390, 402–407, 435–442, 449–451, 480–484
Economic performance	17–23, 138–143, 194–195, 239, 286–288, 341–343, 403–409, 435
Social welfare (e.g., education, health, poverty)	128–132, 240, 341, 385–386, 437–438, 481–483
Civil liberties, rights, and freedoms	23–25, 137–138, 315, 362, 386–389, 441
Environment	22–23, 288–289, 483–484
Population and migration	13–15, 21–22, 289–291, 352–353, 458
Economic development	17–23, 338–340, 383–384, 403–407
Factors influencing public policymaking and implementation	127–150, 154–156, 198–199, 243–246, 280–286, 304–305, 384–385, 403–407, 442, 449–451, 480–484
Domestic	127–128, 138–145, 154–155, 243–245, 280–291, 403–407, 442, 444, 477–479
International	145–147, 155–156, 245–246, 291–292, 310–312, 389–390, 442–443, 449–450, 479–480

PREFACE TO THE 9E, AP*EDITION OF COMPARATIVE POLITICS TODAY

We are pleased to be able to offer this special AP* edition of *Comparative Politics Today: A World View* for use in high school Advanced Placement Program* courses. The first seven chapters of this edition offer the general introduction to the field of comparative politics. The country chapters, written by distinguished specialists on the politics of each country, include the countries that are in the AP* program: Great Britain, Russia, China, Mexico, Nigeria, and Iran. We have also included our chapter on the United States, which we think will help students understand some new concepts by presenting them in a familiar context.

Comparative Politics Today has long been used in AP* courses. We introduce the fundamental concepts of political system, political culture, political functions and structures, and policymaking that allow us to compare very different kinds of political systems. We discuss how governments try to achieve such goals as building community, providing security, promoting economic development, protecting rights, and enhancing social justice. We explain how sometimes government becomes part of the problem, rather than the solution. We describe the social, economic, and international conditions that make government more difficult. We also discuss the roles of different kinds of political organizations—interest groups, political parties—and political institutions—legislatures, executives, courts—in the policymaking process. All these concepts are applied and illustrated in the chapters on specific countries.

It may be helpful to indicate more specifically where the topics that are designated in the **AP* Comparative Government and Politics Course Description Outline** can be found in the Introductory and System, Process, and Policy chapters in this text. These topics are also covered, as appropriate, in the country chapters. The correlation between the **AP* Course Description Outline** and the presentation in our chapters is provided in a table on page xxiii. We recommend that users follow the logic of the book itself, taking the introductory chapters in order, taking special note of AP* content area topics when these arise. However, it is also possible to address them in the order of the AP* curriculum.

Each of the country chapters is organized following a common framework, making them easy to compare with each other, with the themes in the introductory and theoretical chapters and with the AP* curriculum. See "A Guide to Comparing Nations" on page xii. That common framework begins with current policy challenges and then discusses the unique historical origins of politics in that political system, as well as relevant features of the social and economic environment. The constitutional arrangements and main political institutions are introduced, usually followed by a discussion of the political culture and citizen participation. Interest groups and interest articulation are usually described next, followed by electoral system, parties, and party system. The policymaking process and the roles played by various institutions, with emphasis on the most important ones in the specific country, are the next section. The chapter generally concludes with an overview of public policy and policy performance, domestic and international.

The thematic chapters were substantially revised in 2007 to expand the number of illustrative example boxes, increase the comparisons of patterns across the

---

*AP, Advanced Placement, and Advanced Placement Program are registered trademarks of The College Board, which was not involved in the production of, and does not endorse, this product.

country chapters, and to make the material more accessible. The country chapters were revised and updated to include such recent events as the domestic and international problems facing the British Labour government under its new Prime Minister Gordon Brown. The revised Russia chapter discusses Vladimir Putin's rebuilding of a powerful government by eliminating opposition in civil society and the media and recentralizing executive power. It also covers Russia's economic resurgence and its dependence on the country's oil resources. In China we see the impact of China's booming economic growth on Communist Party control and policies. The Mexico chapter describes the bitterly fought presidential election of 2006 and the victory of Felipe Calderon. In Iran we see the politics of domination by religious theocracy, yet multiple power centers, in the volatile Middle East region. The Nigeria chapter describes the critical and scandal ridden 2007 presidential election, in a context of ethnic and religious conflicts. Finally, the U.S. chapter covers the controversial war in Iraq and the election of a new Democratic majority in Congress in November 2006.

We live in a dynamic and increasingly connected world, with important changes occurring across the globe. This makes it an interesting time to be a student of comparative politics. Events in far-flung capitals affect our own lives in many ways. At the same time, seeing the many different ways of running political systems and the impacts of different cultural and economic environments helps us understand the nature of our own political system. We hope that this special AP* edition will be helpful to AP* teachers of comparative politics, who have our greatest respect as they challenge their outstanding students to step outside the familiar bounds of American politics.

ACKNOWLEDGMENTS

We are pleased to acknowledge the contributions of some of the many people who helped us prepare the 9E, AP* Edition of *Comparative Politics Today*. But first we want to note that our new chapter on Iran has replaced the chapter on Egypt that appeared in previous editions. This was a painful decision, and we are

sincerely grateful to Ann Mosely Lesch for excellent contributions to many previous editions of this book.

We would like to thank the following individuals for their careful review and analysis of this book: Michael Brittingham, University of Louisville; Jon Jonassen, Brigham Young University-Hawaii; Jody Neathery-Castro, University of Nebraska at Omaha; Jim Peterson, Valdosta State; **Judi Newins, Freehold Township High School; Gray Pedersen, Lakeside School; and Stephen Popp, St. John's School.** We are also grateful to Farhat Popal for research assistance and to Sonal R. Desai for assistance in developing the index for this edition.

Our coauthors wish to acknowledge their gratitude to a number of individuals who have contributed to their respective chapters. Melanie Manion wishes to thank Russell Dalton for his helpful comments and Michel Oksenberg and Nina Halpern for their comments on an earlier version of the China chapter. Wayne A. Corenlius and Jeffery A. Weldon thank Claudia Y. Carmona and Luis Estrada for research assistance on the Mexico chapter. Oladimeji Aborisade and A. Carl LeVan thank Claire Christian of American University for research assistance. In addition, Aborisade thanks Robert LaGamma, Curtis Huff, Arlene Jacquerre, and Charlotte Peterson for bringing together himself and Robert J. Mundt under the auspices of the U.S. Information Agency. He also thanks John A. Ayoade, Cecil Brown, Roger Brown, Charles Coe., Alex Gboyega, Jim Mean, Aladosu Oyelakin, Gary Rassel, Jim Svara, and Deil Wright for their help on earlier versions of the Nigeria chapter. Thad Kousser would like to thank Mike Binder for research assistance and Nancy Ranney for facilitating communication between Austin Ranney and himself. Arang Keshavarzian thanks Adrian Dumitru, Nicola Gaye, and Katayon Kholdi-Haghighi for their research assistance.

Our thanks also go to the team at Longman and GGS Book Services: Eric Stano, Vikram Mukhija, Lucy Silberman, Eric Jorgensen, Dennis Para, Wendy Fredericks, Ann Stypuloski, Liz Hoens, and Saraswathi Muralidhar.

G. BINGHAM POWELL, JR.
RUSSELL J. DALTON
KAARE STRØM

AP* EDITION SUPPLEMENTS

Longman Publishers is pleased to be able to offer qualified adopters of this text, and their students, several ancillaries that will make teaching and learning from this text even more effective and enjoyable.

Most of the teacher supplements and resources for this book are available electronically for adoption preview and download on the IRC. Please go to www.pearsonschool.com/access_request and select "access to online instructor resources". You will be required to complete a one time registration subject to verification before being emailed access information for download.

AP* Test Prep ISBN: 0-13-135858-8

Specifically created to accompany *Comparative Politics Today*, this student guide contains an overview of the AP* program and the AP* Comparative Politics and Government exam. It also provides test taking strategies, correlations between key AP* test-topics and the textbook, practice study questions, guidelines for mastering multiple-choice and free response questions, commentary on taking AP* Comparative Politics and preparing for the AP* Comparative Politics exam, and practice tests.

AP* Instructor's Manual & Test Bank ISBN: 0-13-195999-9

This supplement provides chapter overview, chapter outlines, learning objectives, teaching suggestions, key terms, discussion and essay questions, and AP*-style multiple-choice questions for each chapter.

AP* TestGen ISBN: 0-13-196046-6

This easy-to-customize test generation software package contains all of the AP*-style multiple-choice questions from the printed Test Bank. This fully networkable, user-friendly program enables instructors to view and edit questions, and print tests in a variety of formats.

AP* Digital Transparency Masters

Organized around a lecture outline, this electronic presentation contains maps, tables, and figures from each chapter.

AP* Transparency Masters

This set of downloadable transparency masters contains all of the text's maps, tables, and figures.

AP* MyPoliSciKit for *Comparative Politics Today*

MyPoliSciKit is a premium online supplement that offers book-specific learning objectives, chapter summaries, weblinks, flashcards, and practice tests, as well as comparative exercises and mapping exercises to aid comprehension and critical thinking. To also help students make connections between concepts and country knowledge, MyPoliSciKit includes an hourly *New York Times* newsfeed and access to popular and academic journals through Research Navigator. With the Instructor Gradebook, instructors can easily track students work on the site and student progress on each activity. For more information visit www.mypoliscikit.com.

High school teachers can obtain teacher and student preview or adoption access in one of two ways:

- By registering online at www.pearsonschool.com/access_request

- Through the use of a physical pincode card. High school adopters will receive an adopter access pincode card (ISBN 0130343919) with their textbook order. Preview access pincode cards may be requested using ISBN 0131115989. Both adopter and preview pincode cards include follow-on directions and provide teacher and student access.

For questions concerning access, please contact your local Pearson sales representative or email PHwebaccess@pearsoned.com.

ISSUES IN COMPARATIVE POLITICS

WHAT IS POLITICS?

Some people love politics. They relish the excitement of political events, such as a presidential election, as they would an exciting athletic contest (the World Series of baseball or the World Cup of soccer, perhaps). Others are fascinated with politics because they care about the issues and their consequences for people in their own communities and around the world. Still others hate politics, either because it sets groups and individuals against each other, or because it involves abuse of power, deceit, manipulation, and violence. Finally, some people are indifferent to politics because it has little to do with the things that matter most to them. All of these reactions involve kernels of truth about politics. Indeed, most of us react to politics with a mixture of these sentiments. Politics has many faces and can be a force for good as well as evil. The core of politics, however, is about human beings making important decisions for themselves and for others.

This book is about the comparative study of politics. In order to make political comparisons, we need to understand what politics is as well as what it means to study politics comparatively. Comparative politics thus involves two separate elements:

- It is a subject of study—comparing the nature of politics and the political process across different political systems.
- It is a method of study—involving how and why we make such comparisons.

We address the first point in this chapter, and Chapter 2 discusses the second.

Politics deals with human decisions, and political science is the study of such decisions. Yet, not all decisions are political, and many of the social sciences study decisions that are of little interest to political scientists. For example, consider when you go with a friend to an event, such as a concert or a soccer match. You can spend your money on the tickets (to get the best seats possible) or on food and drink, or you can save your money for the future. Economists study the sorts of spending decisions people make, and perhaps how they reach them. Psychologists, on the other hand, might study why you went to the event with this friend and not another, or who suggested going in the first place.

Political scientists seldom examine such personal experiences, unless they have political consequences. Instead, we examine the political process and its impact on the citizens. Political decisions constantly touch our lives in many ways, our careers, and our families. Our jobs are structured by government regulations, our homes are built to conform to government housing codes, our public schools are funded and managed by the government, and even when we go to a concert or sporting event, we travel on roads maintained by the government and monitored by the police. We might not think of politics as omnipresent in our lives, but it affects us in many important ways. Therefore, it is important to study how political decisions are made and what their consequences are.

Political decisions are *public* and *authoritative*. There is no such thing as political solitaire, playing politics by yourself. Political decisions take place within some community that we call a *political system*, which we describe below. Yet, not all social decisions are public. Most of what happens within families, among friends, or in social groups belongs to the *private sphere*. Actions within this sphere do not bind anyone outside that group. In most societies, your choice of concert partners and food are private decisions.

The *public sphere* deals with collective decisions that extend beyond the individual, typically involving government action. In totalitarian societies, like Hitler's Third Reich and some communist nations, the public sphere is very large and the private sphere is very limited. The state tries to dominate the life of its people, even intruding into family life. On the other hand, in some less developed nations the private domain may almost crowd out the public one. People in many African nations, for instance, may be unaware of what happens in the capital city and untouched by the decisions made there. Western democracies have a more balanced mix of private and public spheres. However, the boundaries between the two spheres get redrawn all the time. A couple of decades ago, the sex lives of U.S. presidents or members of the British royal family were considered private matters, not to be discussed in public. These norms are changing in Britain and the United States, but the traditional standards remain in other countries. Similarly, at one time in British history certain religious beliefs were considered treasonous. Today, religious beliefs are considered private matters in most modern democracies, but not in many other parts of the world. Even though politics may be influenced by what happens in the private domain, it deals directly with only those decisions that are public.

Politics is also *authoritative*. Authority means that formal power rests in individuals or groups whose decisions are expected to be carried out and respected. Thus, political decisions are binding for members of that political system. Governments may use force to ensure compliance, although authority is not always backed up by force. For instance, a religious authority, such as the Pope, has few coercive powers. He can persuade, but rarely compel, the Catholic Church's followers. In contrast, tax authorities, such as the U.S. Internal Revenue Service, can both exhort and compel people to follow their rules.

Thus, politics refers to activities associated with the control of public decisions among a given people and in a given territory, where this control may be backed up by authoritative means. Politics involves the crafting of these authoritative decisions—who gets to make them and for what purposes.

We live in one of the most exciting times to study politics. The end of the Cold War created a new international order, although its shape is still uncertain. The democratic transitions in Eastern Europe and many developing nations have transformed the world, although it is unclear whether these new democracies will endure and what forms they might take. In Western nations, new challenges and choices have arisen that divide their citizens. Some of these problems—such as confronting global warming and achieving international peace—are transnational. Part of their solutions, we hope, lies in the political choices that people make about their collective future. Our goal in this book is to give you a sense of how governments and politics function to address these challenges.

GOVERNMENTS AND THE STATE OF NATURE

Governments are organizations of individuals who have the power to make binding decisions on behalf of a particular community. Governments thus have authoritative and coercive powers. Governments do many things. They can wage war or encourage peace; cultivate or restrict international trade; open their borders to the exchange of ideas and art or close them; tax their populations heavily or lightly and through different means; allocate resources for education, health, and welfare or leave such matters to others. People who are affected by such decisions may well agree with them and indeed welcome them, but there is also often heated disagreement about the proper role of government decisions.

Debates over the nature and appropriate role of government are far from new. They reflect a classic polemic in political philosophy. For centuries, philosophers have debated whether governments are a force for good or evil. In the seventeenth and eighteenth centuries—the time of the English, French, and American revolutions—much of this debate was couched in arguments concerning the **state of nature.**

Philosophers thought about the state of nature as the condition of humankind if no government existed. In some cases, they thought that such a situation existed before the first governments were formed. These philosophers used their ideas about the state of nature to identify an ideal social contract (agreement) on which to build a political system. Even today, many philosophers find it useful to make such a mental experiment to consider the consequences of having governments.

These debates have shaped our images of government, even to the present. The contrast between Thomas Hobbes' and Jean-Jacques Rousseau's ideas about the state of nature is most striking. Hobbes was the ultimate pessimist. He thought of the state of nature as mercilessly inhospitable, a situation of eternal conflict of all against all, and a source of barbarism and continuous fear. He pessimistically argued that "[i]n such condition, there is no place for Industry; because the fruit thereof is uncertain: and consequently no Culture of the Earth; no Navigation, nor use of the commodities that may be imported by Sea; no commodious Building, . . . no Arts; no Letters; no Society; and which is worst of all, continuall feare, and danger of violent death; And the life of man, solitary, poor, nasty, brutish, and short."[1]

Rousseau, in contrast, was more optimistic. For him, the state of nature represented humanity before its fall from grace, without all the corruptions that governments have introduced. "Man is born free," Rousseau observed in *The Social Contract*, "and yet everywhere he is in chains." Rousseau saw governments as the source of power and inequality, and these conditions in turn as the causes of human alienation and corruption. "The extreme inequality in our way of life," he argued, "excess of idleness in some, excess of labor in others; . . . late nights, excesses of all kinds, immoderate ecstasies of all the passions; fatigues and exhaustion of mind, numberless sorrows and afflictions . . . that most of our ills are our own work; that we would have avoided almost all of them by preserving the simple, uniform, and solitary way of life prescribed to us by nature."[2]

John Locke's ideas have been particularly important for the development of Western democracies. He took a position between those of Hobbes and Rousseau. Compared with Hobbes, Locke thought of human beings as more businesslike and less war prone. Yet, like Hobbes he proposed a social contract to replace the state of nature with a system of government. While Hobbes thought the main task for government is to quell disorder and protect against

violence and war, Locke saw the state's main role as protecting property and commerce and promoting economic growth. He believed government would do this by establishing and enforcing property rights and rules of economic exchange. Whereas Hobbes thought government needed to be a Leviathan—a benevolent dictator to whom the citizens would yield all their power—Locke favored a limited government.[3]

Although these debates began centuries ago, they still underlie current discussions on the appropriate role of government. To some, government is the solution to many human needs and problems—a theme that former U.S. President Bill Clinton often advocated. To others, the government is often part of the problem—a theme that former U.S. President Ronald Reagan articulately argued. To some, government exists to create the social order that protects its citizens; to others, the government's rules limit our freedoms. This tension is part of the political discourse in many contemporary nations, including the United States. We explore these contrasting views and different examples of government structures in this book.

WHY GOVERNMENTS?

A recent libertarian science fiction book begins with the scenario of a group of travelers landing at an airport after a long overseas flight. As they disembark from the plane, they notice there are no police checking passports, no customs officers scanning baggage, and no officials applying immigration rules.[4] They had landed in a society without government, and the puzzle was what having no government would mean for the citizenry. The answer is a lot (see Box 1.1). As philosophers have pointed out, there are many reasons why people create governments and prefer to live under such a social order. We shall discuss some of these, beginning with activities that help generate a stable community in the first place and then those that help this community prosper.

Community- and Nation-Building

One of the first purposes of governments is to create and maintain a community in which people can feel safe and comfortable. While humans may be social beings, it is not always easy to build a community in which large numbers of people can communicate, feel

U.S. Government's Top Ten List

BOX 1.1

Paul Light surveyed 450 historians and political scientists to assess the U.S. government's greatest achievements in the past half century. Their top ten list is as follows:

- Help rebuild Europe after World War II
- Expand the right to vote for minorities
- Promote equal access to public accommodations

- Reduce disease
- Reduce workplace discrimination
- Ensure safe food and drinking water
- Strengthen the nation's highway system
- Increase older Americans' access to health care
- Reduce the federal deficit
- Promote financial security in retirement

Source: Paul Light, *Government's Greatest Achievements of the Past Half-Century* (Washington, DC: Brookings Institution, 2000) (www.brookings.edu/comm/reformwatch/rw02.pdf).

at home, and interact constructively. Governments can help generate such communities in many different ways, for example, by teaching a common language, instilling common norms and values, creating common myths and symbols, and supporting a national identity. However, sometimes such actions create controversy because they threaten the values of minority groups.

Nation-building activities help instill common worldviews, values, and expectations. Using a concept discussed more in Chapter 3, governments can help create a national **political culture.** The political culture defines the public's expectations toward the political process and its role within the process. The more the political culture is shared, the easier it is to live in peaceful coexistence and engage in activities for mutual gain, such as commerce.

Security and Order

Government activities partially reflect Hobbes' belief that only strong governments can make society safe for their inhabitants. Providing security and law and order is among the most essential tasks that governments perform. Externally, security means protecting against attacks from other political systems. Armies, navies, and air forces typically perform this function. Internally, security means protecting against theft, aggression, and violence from members of one's own society. In most societies providing this protection is the function of the police.

Providing security and order is a critical role of modern governments. While governments worldwide have privatized many of the services they once performed—for example those involving post offices,

railroads, and telecommunications, few, if any, governments have privatized their police or defense forces. This shows how security is one of the most essential roles of government. The international terrorist attacks in New York City and Washington, D.C., on September 11, 2001, and subsequent attacks in London, Madrid, and other cities underscore the importance of security.

Protecting Rights

John Locke considered property rights to be particularly critical to the development of prosperous communities. Without effective protection of property rights, people will not invest their goods or energies in productive processes. Also, unless property rights exist and contracts can be negotiated and enforced, people will not trust their neighbors enough to engage in trade and commerce. Anything beyond a subsistence economy requires effective property rights and contracts. Therefore, Locke believed that the primary role of government is to establish and protect such rights. Similarly, contemporary authors argue that social order is a prerequisite for development and democratization.[5]

Effective property rights allocate ownership and provide security against trespass and violations. Such rights must also make the buying and selling of property relatively inexpensive and painless. Finally, people must have faith that their property rights can be defended. Thus, many analysts argue that one of the most restrictive limitations on development in the Third World is the government's inability (or unwillingness) to guarantee such rights. Peasant families who have lived for generations on a plot of land cannot claim ownership, which erodes their incentive and opportunity to invest in the future.

Although Locke was most concerned with economic property rights, governments also protect many other social and political rights. Among them are freedoms of speech and association and protection against various forms of discrimination and harassment. Indeed, the protection of these rights and liberties is one of the prime goals of government—with other factors such as nation-building, security, and property rights providing a means toward this goal. Governments also play a key role in protecting the rights of religious, racial, and other social groups. Human development stresses the expansion of these rights and liberties, and governments play a key role in this process.

Promoting Economic Efficiency and Growth

Economists have long debated the government's potential role in promoting economic development. Neoclassical economics shows that markets are efficient when property rights are defined and protected, when competition is rigorous, and when information is freely available. When these conditions do not hold, markets may fail and the performance of the economy may suffer.[6] At least in some circumstances, governments can lessen the results of market failure.

Governments may be especially important in providing **public goods,** such as clean air, a national defense, or disease prevention. Public goods have two things in common. One is that if one person enjoys them, they cannot be withheld from anyone else. The second is that one person's enjoyment or consumption of the goods does not detract from anyone else's. Consider clean air. For most practical purposes, it is impossible to provide one person with clean air without also giving it to his or her neighbors. Moreover, my enjoyment of clean air does not mean that my neighbors have any less of it. Analysts therefore argue that people in a market economy will not pay enough for public goods. They claim that only government can provide such public goods. Otherwise, people will not voluntarily pay for public goods because they can benefit from the goods that others provide, or they will not act until they are assured others will also contribute.

Governments can also benefit society by controlling the **externalities** that occur when an activity produces costs that are not borne by the producer or the user. For instance, many forms of environmental pollution occur when those who produce or consume goods do not pay all of the environmental costs. Polluting factories, waste dumps, prisons, and major highways can impose large costs on those who live near them. NIMBY ("not in my backyard") groups are an example of citizens complaining about these costs. Governments can help protect people from such unfair externalities or ensure that burdens are fairly shared.

Governments also can promote fair competition in economic markets. For example, governments can assure that all businesses follow minimum standards of worker protection and product liability. In other cases, the government may control potentially monopolistic parts of the economy to ensure that suppliers do not take advantage of their market power. This happened in the nineteenth century with railroad monopolies, and now in the twenty-first century with technology monopolies, such as Microsoft, or telecommunications companies. In these cases the government acts as the policeman to ensure that the economically powerful do not exploit their power. Sometimes, the government itself may become the monopolist. There are some markets in which very large start-up costs or prohibitive costs of coordination mean that there should be only one producer. The government may then set itself up as that monopolist, or it may decide to tightly control a private monopolist. Telecommunications have commonly been a government monopoly, as have mail services and strategic defense industries.

Social Justice

Governments can also play a role in dividing the fruits of economic growth in equitable ways. Many people argue that governments are needed to promote social justice by redistributing wealth and other resources among citizens. In many countries the distribution of income or property is highly uneven. Moreover, in many societies income and wealth inequalities worsen over time. Brazil, for example, has one of the most severe income inequalities in the world, an inequality that grew in every decade from the 1930s to the 1990s.

Under such circumstances, social justice may require a "new deal," especially if inequalities deprive many individuals of education, adequate health care, or other basic needs. Government can intervene to redistribute resources from the better-off to the poor. Some theorists argue that such transfers should attempt to equalize the conditions of all citizens. Others prefer governments to redistribute enough to equalize opportunities, and then let individuals be responsible for their own fortunes.

Many private individuals, organizations, and foundations attempt to help the poor, but they generally lack the capacity to effect large-scale redistribution. Governments do, at least under some circumstances. Many tax and welfare policies effectively redistribute income, although the degree of redistribution is often hotly disputed. Yet most individuals agree that governments should provide their citizens with the opportunities to reach certain minimum standards of living and a social safety net.

Protecting the Weak

We commonly rely on the government to protect individuals and groups that are not able to speak for themselves. Groups such as the poor or the homeless or future generations cannot effectively protect their own interests. Governments, however, can protect the interests of the unborn and prevent them from getting saddled with economic debts or environmental degradation. In recent decades, governments have become much more involved in protecting groups that are politically weak or disenfranchised, such as children, the old, and the infirm or disabled, as well as nonhumans—from whales and birds to trees and other parts of our natural environment.

WHEN DOES GOVERNMENT BECOME THE PROBLEM?

There are many reasons that governments may become involved in human affairs, but such intervention is not always welcomed. When and how government intervention is necessary and desirable are among the most disputed issues in modern politics. During the twentieth century, the role of governments expanded enormously in most nations. At the same time, criticisms of many government policies have persisted and sometimes intensified. Such skepticism is directed at virtually all government activities, especially the economic role of government.

Destruction of Community

Whereas some see governments as a way to build community, others argue that governments destroy natural communities. Government, they hold, implies power and inequality among human beings. And power corrupts. In Lord Acton's famous words, "Power corrupts, and absolute power corrupts absolutely."

While those who have power are corrupted, those without it are degraded and alienated. According to Rousseau, only human beings unfettered by government can form bonds that allow them to develop their full human potential. By imposing an order based on coercion, hierarchy, and the threat of force, governments destroy natural communities. The stronger government becomes, the more it creates inequalities of power that have negative consequences. Such arguments stimulated Western criticism of communism as limiting the potential and freedom of its citizens.

Others argue that strong governments create a "client society," in which people learn to be subservient to authorities and to rely on governments to meet their needs. In such societies, governments patronize and pacify their citizens, as seen in many developing nations today.

Violations of Basic Rights

Just as governments can help establish many essential rights, they can also use their powers to violate these rights in the most serious manner. The twentieth century witnessed enormous progress in the extension of political, economic, and social rights in societies worldwide. At the same time, however, some governments violated basic **human rights** on an unprecedented scale. The millions of lives lost to political persecution is the most serious example of this. Such horrors happened not only in Nazi extermination camps and during Stalin's Great Terror in the Soviet Union, but also on a huge scale in China, Cambodia, and Rwanda, and on a smaller scale in Iraq, Argentina, the Sudan, and Afghanistan.

These extreme abuses of government power illustrate a dilemma that troubled James Madison and other Founders of the American Revolution: the tension between creating a government strong enough to govern effectively but not so strong that it could destroy the rights of its citizens. They understood the irony that to protect individuals from each other, societies can create a government that has even more power to coerce the individual.

Economic Inefficiency

Governments can help economies flourish, but they also can distort and restrict a state's economic potential. President Robert Mugabe, for instance, has destroyed the economy of a once developing Zimbabwe, and similar examples exist in many struggling economies. Economic problems might arise even if government officials do not actively abuse their power. Government regulation of the economy may distort the terms of trade and lower people's incentives to produce. Further inefficiencies may arise when governments actually own or manage important economic enterprises. This is particularly likely if the government holds a monopoly on an important good, since monopolies generally cause goods to be undersupplied and overpriced. Moreover, government industries may be especially prone to inefficiency and complacency because management and workers often have better job protection than those in the private sector. Therefore, they may worry less about the economic performance of the firm. Such experiences stimulate calls to restrict the economic role of governments in both developing and advanced industrial economies.

Government for Private Gain

Society also may suffer if government officials make decisions to benefit themselves personally, or select policies to get themselves reelected regardless of whether those policies would be the best for the society. These actions are like a game in which one person's gain is another person's loss. A politician or political group may use the government to unfairly reap benefits at the public's expense—what is called "rent seeking." *Rents* are benefits created through government intervention in the economy—for example, tax revenue or profits created because the government has restricted competition. Rent seeking refers to efforts by individuals, groups, firms, or organizations to reap such benefits. The idea is really quite simple. For instance, a local mayor plans an economic development project that will benefit his friends who own land in the area or who will supply contracts for the project. Rent seeking can impose large net costs on society because policies are chosen for the private benefits that they produce rather than for their social efficiency and because groups may expend large amounts of resources to control the spoils of government. Rent seeking may turn into outright corruption when influence is traded for money or other advantage (see Box 1.2).

Political exploitation is a particularly serious problem in poor societies. Holding political office is often an effective way to enrich oneself when other political actors are too weak to constrain the abuse of government officials. Besides, many developing societies do not have strong norms against using government for private gain. On the contrary, people often expect those in government to use their power to benefit themselves, their families, and their neighbors. Even in many advanced democratic societies public officeholders are expected to appoint their supporters

---

The Case of Mobutu Sese Seko

BOX 1.2

What happens if politicians use their power in their own self-interest or to benefit individuals or groups that support them? President Mobutu Sese Seko (1930–1997) of Zaire offers a tragic example of the costs that rent-seeking politicians can impose on their societies. After seizing power in a 1965 coup, Mobutu ruled the large African state of Congo (which he renamed Zaire) for more than thirty years. During his long rule, President Mobutu used government funds, including aid from Western states such as the United States, to amass a huge personal fortune, which he invested abroad. In addition to large sums of money, he is reported to have owned about thirty luxury residences abroad, including a number of palatial estates on the French Riviera. Meanwhile, living standards in Zaire, a poor country despite significant natural resources, plummeted, and the country was racked with epidemic disease and civil war. Mobutu died of natural causes shortly after his ouster.

to ambassadorships and other public posts, constrained in part by civil service rules designed to reward merit over patronage. The temptations of officeholding are great. Despite formal rules, press scrutiny, and citizen concerns, few governments anywhere finish their terms of office untainted by some corruption scandal.

Vested Interests and Inertia

Government-created private gains are difficult to change or abolish once they have been established. Some people enjoy the benefits of government jobs, contracts, or other favors that they otherwise might not have had. The larger the government and the more attractive the benefits it provides, the more likely it is that such vested interests will resist change (unless change means even larger benefits). Therefore, any government will foster a group of people with a vested interest in maintaining or enlarging the government itself. Such groups may become a powerful force in favor of the status quo.

Vested interests make it difficult to change government policies or make them more efficient. Once established, agencies and policies can live on far beyond their usefulness. For example, when the Spanish Armada threatened to invade England in 1588, the government posted a military observation post at Land's End in southwest England. This observation post remained in place for four centuries! In the United States, the Rural Electrification Administration was created in 1935 to bring electricity to rural America; it persisted for almost sixty years until it was finally merged into the Rural Utilities Service in 1994.

Vested interests are particularly likely in political systems that contain a lot of safeguards against rapid political change. While the checks and balances in political systems as the United States are designed to safeguard individual rights, they may also protect the privileges of vested interests. Yet, even political systems that contain far fewer such checks may exhibit an excess of political inertia. Britain is an excellent example. Until recently, the House of Lords represented the social groups that dominated British society before the Industrial Revolution more than 200 years ago (noblemen, bishops, and judges). Only in the last few years has Britain begun reforming the House of Lords to eliminate features that reflect Britain's feudal and preindustrial past.

This debate and struggle over the proper role of government are an ongoing part of politics. In the past twenty-five years or so, there has been a clear trend away from extensive government regulation of many economic sectors. Since the 1970s especially, many societies have moved to privatize many economic sectors and to deregulate others. Government regulation has become less extensive in some areas, but it has grown in others—for example, through enacting laws to protect the environment or the rights of children. The overall size of governments in advanced industrial countries has not changed very much. In the former communist countries and in some developing countries, however, the government's size has shrunk quite dramatically. Yet, countries vary widely in the size of their governments, and they are likely to continue to do so.

POLITICAL SYSTEMS AND STATES

We began by discussing governments, but governments are only one part of a larger political system. Since the term **political system** is a main organizing concept of this book, it deserves a full explanation. A system necessarily has two properties: (1) it has a set of interdependent parts, and (2) it has boundaries between its environment.

Political systems are a particular type of social system that is involved in the making of authoritative public decisions. Central elements of a political system are the institutions of government—such as parliaments, bureaucracies, and courts—that formulate and implement the collective goals of a society or of groups within it.

Political systems also include important parts of the society in which governments operate. For example, political organizations, such as political parties or interest groups, are part of the political system. Such organizations do not have coercive authority, except insofar as they control the government. Likewise, the mass media only indirectly affect elections, legislation, and law enforcement. A whole host of institutions—beginning with the family and including communities, churches, schools, corporations, foundations, and think tanks—influence political attitudes and public policy. The term *political system* refers to the whole collection of related, interacting institutions and agencies.

The political systems that we compare in this book are all independent states. They represent some of the important countries in the contemporary world. At the same time, they reflect the diversity of political systems that exist today. A **state** is a particular type of political system. It has **sovereignty**—an independent legal authority over a population in a particular territory, based on the recognized right to self-determination. Sovereignty rests with those who have the ultimate right to make political decisions.

External sovereignty means the right to make binding agreements (treaties) with other states. For instance, France's external sovereignty means that it can enter into treaties with other states. The city of Bordeaux, however, does not have this right (nor do other subnational units of government in France). Internal sovereignty means the right to determine matters having to do with one's own citizens. For example, the French government has internal sovereignty so that it can impose taxes on French citizens.

Yet, states mold and are molded by a domestic environment and an international environment. The system receives inputs from these environments and shapes them through its outputs. The boundaries of political systems are defined in terms of persons, territory, and property. Most people have citizenship rights in only one country. Similarly, territory is divided between states. A given piece of land is supposed to belong to only one country. Of course, disputes over citizenship, territory, and property are by no means uncommon and are among the most frequent causes of international conflict.

Every state faces some constraints on its external and internal sovereignty. For example, with the increasing integration of France into the **European Union (EU),** the French government has given up parts of its sovereignty to the EU, and this loss of sovereignty is a major topic of political debate. In the United States, we confuse things a bit by calling the fifty constituent units "states," even though they enjoy much less sovereignty than France. The states of the United States share the power and authority of the "state" with the federal government in Washington, D.C.

We often think of the world as a patchwork of states with sizable and contiguous territories and a common identity shared by their citizens. A nation is a group of people, often living in a common territory, who have such a common identity. We call the cases in which national identification and sovereign political authority largely coincide **nation-states.** We have come to think of nation-states as the natural way to

organize political systems, and often as an ideal. The national right to self-determination—the idea that every nation has a right to form its own state if it wants to do so—was enshrined in the Treaty of Versailles signed at the end of World War I.

Nation-states are often a desirable way to organize a political system. However, the national right to self-determination is a relatively modern invention. Until the end of the Middle Ages, Europe consisted of many very small political systems and a few very large ones, whose territorial possessions were not always very stable or contiguous. Nor did states always consist of people with the same national identity. Gradually, a set of European nation-states evolved, and the 1648 Treaty of Westphalia established that principle for the political organization of Europe. The nation-state thus emerged as the dominant political system during the eighteenth and nineteenth centuries in Europe.

Since then, Europe has transformed itself into distinct nation-states. This did not happen accidentally— indeed, the governments of the emerging nation-states had a lot to do with it. They sought to instill a common national identity among the peoples they controlled. They did so, often heavy-handedly, by promoting a common language, a common educational system, and often a common religion. While this process of *nation-building* was often harsh, it produced a Europe in which the inhabitants of most states have a strong sense of community.

Many societies in the developing world today face similar challenges. Especially in Africa, the former colonial powers (particularly Britain and France) left the newly independent states with very weak national identities. In many parts of Africa, large-scale national communities simply did not exist at the time of colonization. Even where they did exist, they were rarely reflected in the boundaries that the colonial powers drew between their possessions. After independence, many new states have therefore faced huge nation-building tasks.

There are additional challenges to contemporary nation-states. After World War II, power in Western states began to shift downward from the state to local governments, and upward to supranational organizations, such as the EU. Most of the industrialized countries of Western Europe have gradually created a common market economy. Originally consisting of six countries—France, Germany, Italy, Belgium, the Netherlands, and Luxembourg—the EU has expanded to twenty-seven members with the addition of two members in 2006.

The **United Nations (UN),** formed at the end of World War II in 1945, has also acquired new responsibilities since the collapse of the Soviet Union in the 1990s. As of early 2006, UN forces were peacekeepers in fifteen countries. These operations—involving more than 100,000 peacekeepers—separate combatants in domestic and international conflicts, settle disputes, and form effective governing institutions. The UN has increased authority over world security, constraining, supporting, and sometimes replacing the unilateral actions of individual states. While the sovereignty of states may be diminishing, they are still the most important political systems. That, of course, is the main reason that they are the subject of our study.

THE DIVERSITY OF STATES

Just about the entire surface of the world today is covered by independent states. There were 192 UN "member-states" in 2006.[7] A few countries are not members of the UN (Taiwan, Switzerland, and the Vatican), and some independence movements would create even more states. When the United States declared its independence in 1776, most independent states were European (see Figure 1.1). Much of the rest of the world existed as colonies to one of the European empires. In the nineteenth and early twentieth centuries, the number of states increased, principally in Latin America, where the Spanish and Portuguese empires broke up into twenty independent states. In Europe, newly independent countries emerged in the Balkans, Scandinavia, and the Low Countries.

Between the two world wars, national proliferation extended to North Africa and the Middle East; and Europe continued to fragment as the Russian and Austro-Hungarian empires broke up. Since World War II, the development of new states has taken off. By 2006, 125 new countries have joined the sixty-eight states that existed in 1945. The largest group of new states is in Sub-Saharan Africa. More than twenty new countries formed in the 1990s—mostly the successor states of the Soviet Union, Yugoslavia, and Czechoslovakia.

All these countries—new as well as old—share certain characteristics. They have legal authority over their territories and people; most have armies, air forces, and

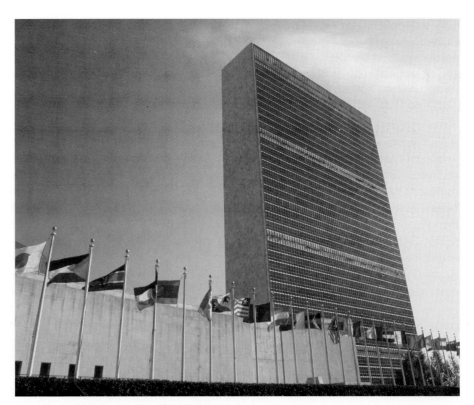

The United Nations is the most inclusive organization of states. As of 2006, the United Nations had 192 member states, represented by the flags flying outside its headquarters in New York City.

Joseph Sohm–ChromoSohm, Inc./Corbis

the Catholic Church, with less than half a square kilometer of turf and less than a thousand residents.

The contrasts between geographic size and population size can be graphically seen in the following two maps. Map 1.1 is the familiar global map in which countries are displayed according to their size. Russia, with its landmass extending over eleven contiguous time zones, is the world's largest state with more than 17 million square kilometers. The United States falls about midpoint in this range, with just more than 9 million square kilometers. Many of the established democracies in Europe are relatively small (Britain has 242,000 square kilometers and Germany 349,000).

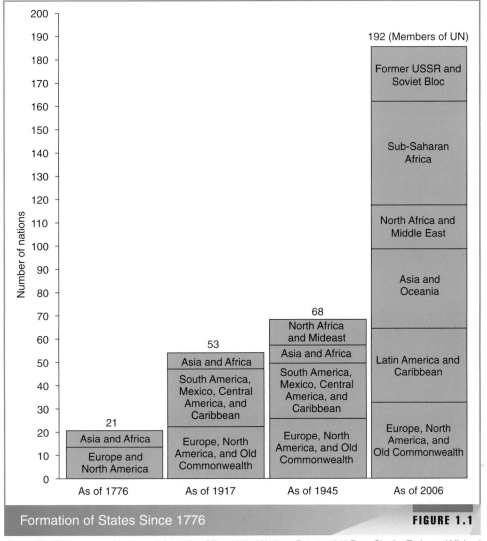

Formation of States Since 1776

FIGURE 1.1

Source: For Contemporary Members, Information Office, United Nations. Data to 1945 From Charles Taylor and Michael Hudson, *World Handbook of Political and Social Indicators* (New Haven, CT: Yale University Press, 1972), 26 ff.

in some cases navies; they collect taxes and spend money; they regulate their economies, maintain public order, and pursue their general welfare. Countries send and receive ambassadors; most belong to several international organizations. They also vary, often profoundly, in physical size, histories, institutions, cultures, religions, economies, and social structures—factors that shape their politics.

Big and Small States

Nations come in all sizes. The smallest legally independent political entity in both geographic extent and population is Vatican City, the headquarters of

Map 1.2 is more provocative because is displays nations by their population size. Instantly we see China and India balloon in size because of their large populations. China alone accounts for almost a quarter of the world's population (with 1.3 billion people), and India is not far behind (with 1.1 billion). The European democracies we compare—Britain, France, and Germany—look smaller in these comparisons because their populations range from about 60 million to 80 million. Even more dramatically, Australia shrinks from a continent in the first map to a small dot in the population map because of its small population size (20 million). The United States in this global perspective seems relatively small in population terms

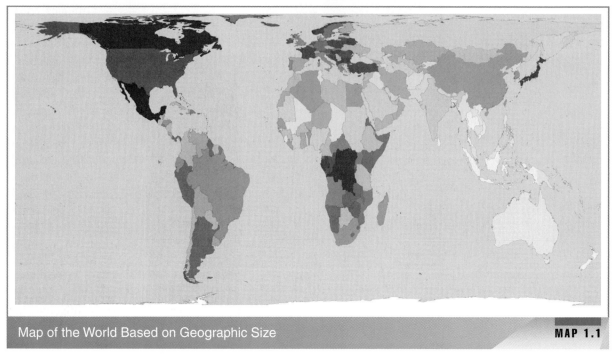

Map of the World Based on Geographic Size   MAP 1.1

Source: Copyright © *The Real World Atlas,* Thames & Hudson, Ltd., London, 2008.

(298 million), even though it has roughly the same area as China and is geographically larger than India. And even though Russia has almost twice as much land as any other country, it has a modest population size (142 million) that is barely half as large as the United States and Russia is shrinking.

The political implications of these striking contrasts in population size and geographic area are not always obvious. Big countries are not always the most important and do not always prevail over the small ones: Cuba has challenged the United States for almost forty years; Israel stands off the Arab world; and tiny Vatican City has great power and influence. Nor do area and population size determine a country's political system. Both little Luxembourg and large India are democracies. Authoritarian regimes are found in small, medium, and large countries. These enormous contrasts in size show only that the states now making up the world differ greatly in their physical and human resources.

A state's geographic location can also have important strategic implications. In the sixteenth through nineteenth centuries, European states typically required a large land army to protect themselves from the threats of their neighbors. These nations had difficulties developing free political institutions, since they needed a strong government to extract resources on a large scale and keep the population under control. Britain was protected by the English Channel and could defend itself through its navy, a smaller army, lower taxation, and less centralization of power—which aided political liberalization. Most peoples of Asia, Africa, and Latin America were colonized by the more powerful Western nations. Those that had the richest natural resources and the most benign climates tended to attract the largest numbers of settlers.

Whether they are old or new, large or small, most of the world's states face a number of common challenges. The first is building community. Most states do not have a homogeneous population, and instilling a sense of shared identity can be a serious challenge. Second, the ability to foster economic and social development is a challenge that is shared even by the wealthiest states. Finally, most states face significant challenges in advancing democracy and civil liberties. These challenges should be familiar from our discussion of the purposes and dangers of governments. In the remainder of this chapter, we discuss these challenges successively.

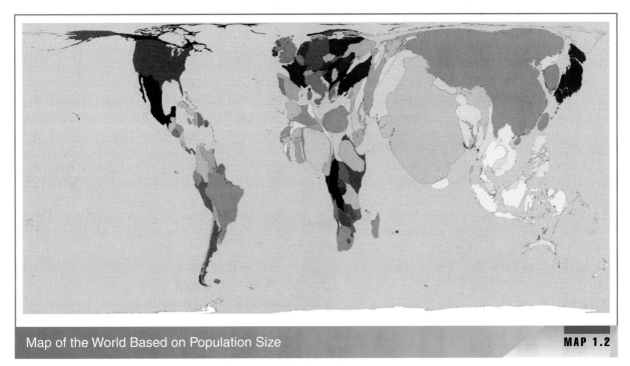

Map of the World Based on Population Size   MAP 1.2

Source: Copyright © *The Real World Atlas,* Thames & Hudson, Ltd., London, 2008.

BUILDING COMMUNITY

One of the most important challenges facing political systems worldwide is to build a common identity and a sense of community among the citizens. The absence of a common identity can have severe political consequences. Conflicts over national, ethnic, or religious identities are among the most explosive causes of political turmoil, as we have witnessed in Northern Ireland, the former Yugoslavia, Rwanda, and elsewhere. But while building community is a pervasive challenge, some countries are in a much better situation than others. Japan, for example, has an ethnically homogeneous population, a common language, and a long national political history. A large majority of the Japanese share in the religions of Buddhism and Shintoism, and the country is separated by miles of ocean from its most important neighbors. Nigeria, in contrast, is an accidental and artificial creation of British colonial rule and has no common precolonial history. The population is sharply divided between Muslims and Christians; the Christians are divided equally into Catholics and Protestants. There are some 250 different ethnic groups, speaking a variety of local languages, in addition to English. Obviously, the challenges of building community are much greater in Nigeria than they are in Japan. Although few countries face problems as complicated as those of the Nigerians, the community-building challenge is one of the most serious issues facing many states today.

States and Nations

The word *nation* is sometimes used to mean almost the same as the word *state,* as in the name the United Nations. Strictly speaking, however, we wish to use the term **nation** to refer to a group of people with a common identity. When we speak of a "nation," we thus refer to the self-identification of a people. That common identity may be built upon a common language, history, race, or culture, or simply upon the fact that this group has occupied the same territory. Nations may or may not have their own state or independent government. In some cases—such as Japan, France, or Sweden—there is a close correspondence between the memberships of the state and the nation. Most people who identify themselves as Japanese do in fact live in the state of Japan, and most people who live in Japan identify themselves as Japanese.

In many instances, the correspondence between the nation and the state is not so neat. Nor is it obvious that it should be. In some cases, states are *multinational*—consisting of a multitude of different nations. The Soviet Union, Yugoslavia, and Czechoslovakia were multinational states that broke apart. In other cases, some nations are much larger than the corresponding states, such as Germany for most of its history, or China. Some nations have split into two or more states for political reasons, such as Korea today and Germany between 1949 and 1990. Some groups with claims to be nations have no state at all, such as the Kurds, the Basques, and the Tamils. When states and nations do not coincide, it can cause explosive political conflict, as discussed later. At the same time, the presence of several nations within the same state can also be a source of diversity and cultural enrichment.

Nationality and Ethnicity

There is a fine line between nations and *ethnic groups,* which may have common physical traits, languages, cultures, or history. Like nationality, **ethnicity** need not have any objective basis in genetics, culture, or history. The German sociologist, Max Weber, defined ethnic groups as "those human groups that entertain a subjective belief in their common descent because of similarities of physical type or of customs or both, or because of memories of colonization and migration.... [I]t does not matter whether or not an objective blood relationship exists."[8] Similarly, groups that are physically quite similar, but differ by language, religion, customs, marriage patterns, and historical memories (for example, the Serbs, Croats, and Muslim Bosnians) may believe they are descended from different ancestors and hence are physically different as well. Over centuries, originally homogeneous populations may intermix with other populations, even though the culture may continue. This is true, for example, of the Jewish population of Israel, which has come together after more than two millennia of global dispersion.

Ethnic differences can be a source of political conflict.[9] Since the end of the Cold War, many states of the former Soviet bloc have come apart at their ethnic and religious seams. In the former Yugoslavia, secession by a number of provinces triggered several wars. The most brutal of these was in Bosnia-Herzegovina, where a Muslim regime faced rebellion and murderous "ethnic cleansing" by the large Serbian minority. Intervention by the UN, the North Atlantic Treaty Organization (NATO), and the United States contained Serbian aggression and led to an uneasy settlement, but considerable tension remains. Similar tensions and violent aggression occurred in Kosovo as well.

With the Chinese government encouraging economic growth and foreign investment, the Shanghai skyline is now a mix of highrises and construction cranes.

Wolf Kern/VISUM/The Image Works

In many developing countries, boundaries established by former colonial powers cut across ethnic lines. In 1947 the British withdrew from India and divided the subcontinent into a northern Muslim area—Pakistan—and a southern Hindu area—India. The most immediate consequence was a terrible civil conflict and "ethno-religious" cleansing. There still are almost 100 million Muslims in India. Similarly, thirty years ago the Ibo "tribe" of Nigeria fought an unsuccessful separatist war with the rest of Nigeria, resulting in the deaths of millions of people. The Tutsi and Hutu peoples of the small African state of Rwanda engaged in a civil war of extermination in the 1990s, with hundreds of thousands of people slaughtered, and millions fleeing the country in fear of their lives.

The migration of labor, forced or voluntary, across state boundaries is another source of ethnic differentiation. The American descendants of Africans forcefully enslaved between the seventeenth and the nineteenth centuries are witnesses of the largest coercive labor migration in world history. In contrast, voluntary migration takes the form of Indians, Bangladeshi, Egyptians, and Palestinians seeking better lives in the oil sheikhdoms around the Persian Gulf; Mexican and Caribbean migrant workers moving to

the United States; and Turkish and North African migrants relocating to Europe. Some migration is politically motivated, triggered by civil war and repression. Two scholars refer to the contemporary world as living through an "Age of Migration,"[10] comparable in scale to that of the late nineteenth and early twentieth centuries.

Table 1.1 provides examples of politically significant "ethnicity," broadly defined, in our selected twelve countries. Five sets of traits are included, beginning with physical differences, then language, norms against intermarriage, religion, and negative historical memories. The table illustrates the importance of each distinction to ethnic identity. The most important bases of distinction lie in intermarriage, religion, and historical memories. Language differences are of great importance in four cases and of some importance in six; and finally, and perhaps surprisingly, physical differences are of great importance in only two cases. Recent migration has made such previously homogeneous states as France, Japan, and Germany more multiethnic. Other countries, such as the United States and Canada, have long been multiethnic and have become even more so. Indeed, globalization and migration seem destined to increase the diversity of many societies worldwide.

Examples of Ethnicity: Its Bases and Their Salience*   TABLE 1.1

	Physical Differences	Language	Norms Against Intermarriage	Religion	Negative Historical Memories
Brazil: Blacks	XX	O	XX	X	X
Britain: South Asians	X	O	X	XX	X
China: Tibetans	X	XX	XX	XX	XX
France: Algerians	X	X	XX	XX	XX
Germany: Turks	X	XX	XX	XX	O
India: Muslims	O	X	XX	XX	XX
Iran: Kurds	X	XX	XX	XX	XX
Japan: Buraku-min	O	O	XX	O	XX
Mexico: Mayan	X	X	XX	X	XX
Nigeria: Ibo	O	X	XX	XX	XX
Russia: Chechens	X	XX	XX	XX	XX
United States:					
African-Americans	XX	X	XX	O	XX
Hispanics:	X	X	X	O	X

*Salience is estimated at the following levels: O = none or almost none; X = some; XX = much importance in affecting differences.

Language

Language can be a source of social division that may overlap with ethnicity. There are approximately 5,000 different languages in use in the world today, and a much smaller number of language families. Most of these languages are spoken by relatively small tribal groups in North and South America, Asia, Africa, or Oceania. Only 200 languages have a million or more speakers, and only eight may be classified as world languages.

English is the most truly international language. There are approximately 380 million people who speak English at home, and 1.8 billion who live in countries where it is one of the official languages. Other international languages include Spanish (more than 300 million home speakers), Arabic (200 million), Russian (165 million), Portuguese (165 million), French (100 million), and German (100 million). The language with the largest number of speakers, though in several varieties, is Chinese (1.2 billion). The major languages with the greatest international spread are those of the former colonial powers—Great Britain, France, Spain, and Portugal.[11]

Linguistic divisions can create particularly thorny political problems. Political systems can choose to ignore racial, ethnic, or religious differences among their citizens, but they cannot avoid committing themselves to one or several languages. Linguistic conflicts typically show up in controversies over educational policies, or over language use in the government. Occasionally, language regulation is more intrusive, as in Quebec, where English-only street signs are prohibited and large corporations are required to conduct their business in French.

Religious Differences and Fundamentalism

States also vary in their religious characteristics. In some—such as Israel, the Irish Republic, and Pakistan—religion is a basis of national identity for a majority of the population. Iran is a theocratic regime, in which religious authorities govern and religious law is part of the country's legal code. In other societies, such as Poland under communism, religion can be a rallying point for political movements. In many Latin American countries, the clergy have embraced a liberation theology that fosters advocacy of the poor and criticism of government brutality.

Table 1.2 indicates that Christianity is the largest and most widely spread religion, which is divided into three major groups—Roman Catholics, Protestants (of many denominations), and Orthodox (e.g., Greek and Russian). The Catholics are dominant in Europe and Latin America; there is a more equal distribution of Catholics and Protestants elsewhere. While the traditional Protestant denominations have declined in North America in the last decades, three forms of Protestanism—Fundamentalist, Pentecostal, and Evangelical—have increased.

The Muslims are the second largest religious group and the most rapidly growing religion. Muslims are primarily concentrated in Asia and Africa, as well as substantial numbers in Europe and North America, and are becoming revitalized in the Asian successor

TABLE 1.2

Adherents of All Religions by Six Continents (mid-2004, in millions)

Religion	Africa	Asia	Europe	Latin America	North America	Oceania	Total	Percentage
Christians	401.7	341.3	553.6	510.1	273.9	26.1	2,106.2	33.0
Muslims	350.4	892.4	33.2	1.7	5.1	.4	1,283.4	20.1
Nonreligious and Atheists	6.4	724.2	130.6	18.6	33.1	4.2	917.7	14.4
Hindus	2.6	844.5	1.4	.8	1.4	.4	851.2	13.3
Buddhists	.1	369.3	1.6	.7	3.0	.4	375.4	5.9
Jews	.2	5.3	1.9	1.2	6.1	.1	14.9	.2
Other	107.7	693.5	3.2	17.6	6.3	1.0	828.8	13.1
Total	869.1	3,870.5	725.5	550.7	328.9	32.6	6,377.6	100%

Source: Adherents as defined in *Encyclopedia Britannic 2006*.

states of the Soviet Union. Muslims have been particularly successful in missionary activities in Sub-Saharan Africa.

Religion can be a source of intense antagonism, since beliefs may take the form of deep personal convictions that are difficult to compromise. Religious groups often battle over such issues as the rules of marriage and divorce, childrearing, sexual morality, abortion, euthanasia, the emancipation of women, and the regulation of religious observances. Religious communities often take a special interest in educational policies in order to transmit their ideas of nature and humankind, right and wrong. On such issues, religious groups may clash with one another as well as with more secular groups. Although religious groups can coexist peacefully, and are often the source of exemplary acts of compassion and reconciliation, they may also commit acts of violence, cruelty, and terrorism.[12]

Even societies in which most people supposedly belong to the same community of faith may be split by conflicts between "fundamentalists" and those who are more moderate in their beliefs. **Religious fundamentalism** has recently emerged in some form in all major faiths in reaction to social modernization. Fundamentalists have frequently been technologically adaptive, even while militantly rejecting some elements of modernity (see Box 1.3).

Judaism, Christianity, and Islam are all "religions of the book," although not exactly the same book. The Jews believe only in the Old Testament; the Christians add on the New Testament; and the Muslims add the Koran to these two. While each religion disagrees over the interpretation of these texts, Jewish, Christian, and Muslim fundamentalists all believe in the truth of their respective sacred books and attack some of their own clergy for lukewarm defense of these sacred texts. There are also Hindu and Buddhist fundamentalists. The rise of fundamentalism has affected the entire world.

The extremist wings of fundamentalist movements employ violence in many forms: from threats and property destruction to assassination and destructive suicide, as young people turn themselves into bombs. The terrorism of these acts lies in their enormity. They stagger the imagination and are intended to weaken the will. From this point of view, the September 11, 2001, attacks on the World Trade Center and the Pentagon were acts of mega-terrorism, involving not only suicide pilot-hijackers but also aircraft filled with volatile fuel and innocent passengers converted into immense projectiles. (See Box 14.1 in Chapter 14.) These attacks were followed by terrorist assaults in Bali, Madrid, London, Riyadh, and other cities. Dealing with international terrorism by religious fundamentalists is now a challenge that faces many nations worldwide.

FOSTERING ECONOMIC DEVELOPMENT

Two major forces are transforming political systems and nations, and the lives of their citizens; they provide major sources of comparison across the nations in this book. The first is the process of economic development, and the second is political democratization.

The Origins of "Fundamentalism"

BOX 1.3

Fundamentalism got its name in the decades before World War I when some Protestant clergymen in the United States banded together to defend the "fundamentals" of religious belief against the secularizing influences of a modernizing society. This was a reaction to new biblical scholarship at the time that questioned the divine inspiration and authorship of the Bible, and to the expansion of science and Darwinist theories of evolution. These church leaders were also distressed by the apparent erosion of morality and tradition in the United States. In 1920, a journalist and Baptist layman named Curtis Lee Laws appropriated the term "fundamentalist" as a designation for those who were ready "to do battle royal for the Fundamentals." The fundamentalists affirmed the inerrancy (the absolute truth) of the Bible and formed enclaves to protect themselves from error and sin. Religious fundamentalism has recently emerged in some form in all major faiths in reaction to social modernization.

A political system cannot generally satisfy its citizens unless it can foster social and economic development. Thus, as significant as nation-building may be, the level of economic and social development and the rate of economic growth are exceptionally important. Economic development implies that citizens can enjoy new resources and opportunities. Many people are primarily concerned that government can improve their living conditions through economic growth, providing jobs, and raising income standards. However, development can also create social strains and damage nature. For better or worse, the social changes that result from economic development transform the politics of developing countries. The success of governments—both democratic and autocratic—is often measured in these terms.

For many affluent, advanced industrial societies, contemporary living standards provide for basic social needs (and much more) for most of the public. Indeed, the current political challenges in these nations often focus on problems resulting from the economic successes of the past, such as protecting environmental quality or managing the consequences of growth. New challenges to social welfare policies are emerging from the medical and social security costs of aging populations. For most of the world, however, substantial basic economic needs still exist, and governments focus on improving the socioeconomic conditions of the nation.

Over the past two decades, globalization, democratization, and marketization have begun to transform living conditions in many nations. The United Nations Development Program (UNDP) combines measures of economic well-being, life expectancy, and educational achievement into what it calls the Human Development Index (HDI).[13] The HDI shows dramatic improvements in life conditions in many regions of the world over the past three decades (Figure 1.2). East Asia and South Asia have made substantial improvements since 1975. For instance, in 1975 South Korea and Taiwan had

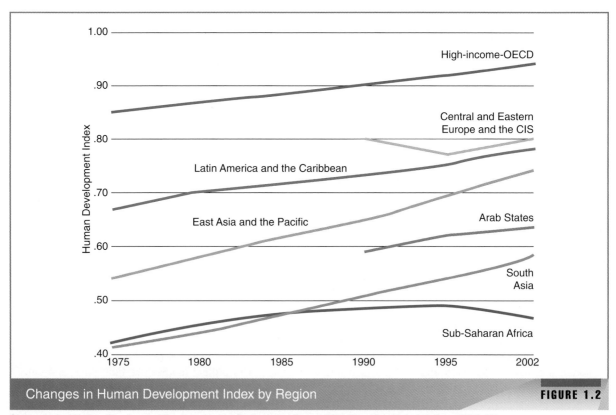

Changes in Human Development Index by Region

FIGURE 1.2

Source: United Nations Development Program, *Human Development Report 2004*. (New York: United Nations, 2004) 134.

a standard of living close to many poor African nations, and they are now affluent societies. Even more striking is the change in the two largest nations in the world. China improved from a HDI of .52 in 1975 (the same as Botswana or Swaziland) to .75 in 2003 (similar to the Philippines or Ecuador); India improved from an HDI of .41 to .60. These statistics represent improved living conditions for billions of people. At the same time, other regions of the world are not sharing in these advances. Living conditions have changed only marginally in Sub-Saharan Africa over this period—the poorest of the poor nations have not improved. In addition, many of the postcommunist nations of Central and Eastern Europe have suffered economically following the transition from communism to capitalism and democracy. The HDI for Russia, for instance, has stagnated since 1990.

The process of economic development typically follows a similar course. One element is a transformation of the structure of the labor force. The five advanced industrial countries in our comparisons all have agricultural employment as less than 10 percent of the labor force. The three poorest countries—China, India, and Nigeria—have more than two-thirds of their labor forces employed in agriculture. The middle-income countries—Mexico and Brazil—have about a third to a fifth of their labor forces in agriculture. In addition, economic development is typically linked to urbanization, as peasants leave their farms and move to the cities. In nations undergoing rapid economic development, such as China, urban migration creates new opportunities for the workers but also new economic and social policy challenges for the governments.

The UNDP's Human Development Index provides a means to compare the differences in current life conditions across the twelve comparison nations in this chapter (Table 1.3). Perhaps the most striking feature of this table is the wide gap in living standards that still exist across nations worldwide. For instance, the **gross national product (GNP)** per capita, which is a measure of national economic development, is nearly thirty times higher in the Western advanced industrial democracies than in Nigeria.[14] Similarly, there are notable gaps in life expectancy and educational opportunities between the affluent Northern societies and the developing nations in Africa and Asia. In highly industrialized countries, education is virtually universal and practically everyone over age 15 can read and write. In India and Nigeria, less than two-thirds of the adult population has this minimal level of education. Moreover, the countries with the fewest literate citizens also have the fewest radios and television sets—even

Human Development Indicators						TABLE 1.3
Nation	Life Expectancy	Percent Enrolled in School	GNP/Capita (ppp)	2003 HDI	1975 HDI	2003 World Rank
United States	77.4	93	37,562	.944	.867	10
Japan	82.0	84	27,967	.943	.857	11
United Kingdom	78.4	—	27.147	.939	.845	15
France	79.5	92	27,677	.938	.853	16
Germany	78.7	89	27,756	.930	—	20
Mexico	75.1	75	9,168	.814	.689	53
Russia	65.3	90	9,230	.795	—	62
Brazil	70.5	91	7,790	.792	.645	63
China	71.6	69	5,003	.755	.525	85
Iran	70.4	69	6,995	.736	.566	99
India	63.3	60	2,892	.602	.412	127
Nigeria	43.4	64	1,050	.453	.318	158

Source: United Nations Development Program, *World Development Report 2005* (New York: United Nations, 2005) (www.undp.org).

though these devices do not require literacy. Economic development is also associated with better nutrition and medical care. In the economically advanced countries, fewer children die in infancy, and the average citizen has a life expectancy at birth of over seventy-five years. Improvements in living conditions have substantially increased life expectancy in many low-income nations, such as Mexico and China. However, the average life expectancy of an Indian is sixty-three years; and the Nigerian little more than forty years. Material productivity, education, exposure to communications media, and longer and healthier lives are closely interconnected.

In order to become more productive, a country needs the resources to develop a skilled and healthy labor force and to build the infrastructure that material welfare requires. Preindustrial nations face most urgently the issues of economic development: how to improve the immediate welfare of their citizens yet also build and invest for the future. Typically, these are newer nations that also face the challenges of building community and effective political institutions. Political leaders and celebrities, such as Bono and Angelina Jolie, have mobilized public awareness that these differences in living conditions are a global concern—for those living in the developing world, the affluent nations and their citizens, and international organizations such as the United Nations and the World Bank.

Problems of Economic Development

The HDI or GNP per capita measure the overall wealth, income, and opportunity in a nation, but these factors are not evenly distributed within nations. The unequal distribution of resources and opportunities is among the most serious causes of political conflict. A large GNP may conceal significant differences in the distribution of resources and opportunities. A high rate of national growth may benefit only particular regions or social groups, leaving large parts of the population unrewarded or even less well off than before. The "inner cities" of the United States, the older parts of such Indian cities as Delhi and Calcutta, the peripheral ramshackle settlements around the cities of Latin America, many rural areas in China, and the arid northeast of Brazil all suffer from poverty and hopelessness. At the same time, other parts of the countries experience growth and improved welfare. Moreover, there is some evidence that rapid economic development tends to increase such inequalities.

A country's politics may be sharply affected by internal divisions of income, wealth, and other resources. Table 1.4 displays income distributions for our twelve comparison countries. Generally speaking, economic development improves the equality of income, at least past a certain stage of economic growth. Wealthy nations like Japan, Germany, and

Poverty in Third World cities is illustrated by this scene of a back street in Calcutta, India, where the poor make their beds in the street. Similar scenes, though on a lesser scale, are to be encountered in modern American cities where homeless people sleep on the sidewalks and in doorways.

Jehangir Gazdar/Woodfin Camp & Associates

Income Distribution for Selected Nations				**TABLE 1.4**
Country	**Year**	**Wealthiest 10%**	**Poorest 40%**	**Wealthy/Poor Gap**
Germany	2000	22.1	22.2	−0.1
Russia	2002	23.8	20.9	2.9
Japan	1993	21.7	24.8	3.1
France	1995	25.1	19.8	5.3
India	1999	28.5	21.2	7.3
Britain	1999	28.5	17.5	11.0
United States	2000	29.9	16.2	13.7
Iran	1998	33.7	19.5	14.2
China	2001	33.1	13.7	19.4
Nigeria	1996	35.4	12.6	22.8
Mexico	2000	43.1	10.3	32.8
Brazil	2001	46.9	8.3	38.6

Source: World Bank, *World Development Indicators 2005*, table 2-7 (www.worldbank.org); distribution of income or consumption.

France have relatively more egalitarian income distributions than middle- or low-income countries. Still, the wealthiest 10 percent in Japan receive about the same total income as the poorest 40 percent receive. This is a large gap in life conditions between rich and poor, but the gap is even wider in less affluent nations. In Mexico, a middle-income country, the ratio is closer to 10 to 1; and in Brazil it is more than 20 to 1. The table also suggests that a nation's political characteristics make a difference. India has consciously worked to narrow inequality, which places it higher in the table, while inequality in the United States is as great as several poor nations, such as China.

Although industrialization and high productivity may eventually encourage a more equal distribution of income, the first stages of industrialization may actually increase **income inequality.** As economies modernize they create a dual economy—a rural sector and an urban industrial and commercial sector, both with inequalities of their own. These inequalities increase as education and communication spread more rapidly in the modern sector, which may contribute to the political instability of developing countries. Moreover, there is no guarantee that inequality will diminish in later stages of development. In Brazil, for instance, income inequality has increased for decades, even as the economy has developed. In the United States, income inequality increased substantially from the 1970s to the mid-1990s because of changes in economic structure, the increase in single-parent families,

and a lowering of income taxes. In Russia and other postcommunist societies, the development of new capitalist markets was accompanied by new income inequalities. Inequality is an issue that many nations face.

Several studies have proposed various policy solutions to mitigate the hardships economic inequality causes in developing societies.[15] Taiwan and South Korea are models showing how early land reforms equalized opportunity at the outset of the developmental process. Investment in primary and secondary education, in agricultural inputs and rural infrastructure (principally roads and water), and in labor-intensive industries produced remarkable results for several decades. A comparative advantage in cheap and skilled labor enabled Taiwan and South Korea to compete effectively in international markets. Thus, some growth policies mitigate inequalities, but it can be very difficult to put them into practice, especially where substantial inequalities already exist.

Another correlate of development is population growth. The book *The Population Explosion* drew attention to the social burden that may follow from the population growth that typically accompanies economic development.[16] As health care improves, living standards increase, and life expectancies lengthen, population sizes grow. This is a positive development because it represents improved living conditions for these people, but rapid population growth also can pose policy challenges for many developing nations.

TABLE 1.5

Population by Economic Development Level in 1990 and Projected to 2015 (in millions)

Economic Development Level	In 1990		Projected to 2015	
	Number	Percentage	Number	Percentage
Low-income economies	1,777	33.9	2,794	39.4
Middle-income economies	2,588	49.3	3,299	46.5
High-income economies	887	16.8	1,007	14.1
Total	5,252	100	7,100	100

Source: World Bank, *World Development Report Indicators 2005*, table 2-1 (www.worldbank.org) population dynamics.

Table 1.5 puts this issue in sharp relief. The table divides the world population into three strata: low-income economies, middle-income economies, and high-income economies. In 1990 the low-income countries had a population total of almost 2 billion, or about a third of the total world population. In contrast, the high-income nations had about a sixth of the world's population.

Some projections estimate that the world population in 2015 will increase to 7 billion and that the poorer countries will see a more rapid rate of growth. In 2005, Hania Zlotnik of the UN population division estimated that "out of every 100 persons added to the [world's] population in the coming decade, 97 will live in developing countries."[17] Rapid economic growth in the developing world can create significant burdens for these nations.

These prospects have produced a development literature that mixes both light and heat. Economist Amartya Sen warns of a "danger that in the confrontation between apocalyptic pessimism on one hand, and a dismissive smugness, on the other, a genuine understanding of the nature of the population problem may be lost."[18] He points out that the first impact of "modernization" on population is to increase it rapidly, as new sanitation measures and modern pharmaceuticals reduce the death rate. As an economy develops, however, changing conditions tend to reduce fertility. With improved education (particularly of women), health, and welfare, the advantages of lower fertility become clear, and population growth declines.

Fertility decreased in Europe and North America as they underwent industrialization. Today, in many European nations the native populations are decreasing because fertility rates are below levels necessary to sustain a constant population size. This pattern appears to be occurring in the developing world. Thus annual population growth in the world has declined from 2.2 percent to 1.7 percent in the last two decades. The rate of population growth in India, for example, rose to 2.2 percent in the 1970s and has since declined. Latin America peaked at a higher rate and then came down sharply. The major problem area is Sub-Saharan Africa, with an average growth rate of more than 2.7 percent each year during the 1990s.[19] The fertility rate in Africa has recently dropped dramatically because of the tragically rising death rate from the AIDS epidemic.

While population growth rates appear to be slowing, governments are addressing this issue in different ways. China adopted a coercive policy of limiting families to a single child, which in urban areas produced dramatic results at great costs. India followed a collaborative approach involving governmental intervention and market and education to affect family choices.[20] Kerala in southern India is a dramatic example of what can be accomplished by the collaborative approach, where expanding education (particularly among women) and otherwise improving living conditions has reduced fertility more than in China.

Economic growth can have other social costs. For instance, advanced industrial societies are dealing with the environmental costs of their industrial development. Despoiled forests, depleted soils and fisheries, polluted air and water, nuclear waste, endangered species, and a threatened ozone layer now burden their legislative dockets. With increasing industrialization and urbanization in the developing world, many of these environmental problems could worsen. Thus, economic development can impose serious environmental costs as well as benefits. At the same time, some environmental problems are even more acute in less developed countries, where rapid increases in population and urbanization create shortages of clean air, clean water, and adequate sanitation.[21] Thus,

The world's increasing energy use is causing serious environmental challenges. The burning of fossil fuels—such as coal, oil, and gas—polllutes our air, water, and atmosphere, whereas nuclear power plants, such as this one in Northern Bohemia, pose the risk of nuclear radiation.

Sean Sprague/Panos Pictures

economic development generally improves living conditions of the public, but in the process it produces new policy problems that governments must address.

FOSTERING DEMOCRACY, HUMAN RIGHTS, AND CIVIL LIBERTIES

The second major force transforming contemporary political systems is the process of democratization, which includes the enhancement of human rights and the expansion of freedom. Democracy is the form of government to which most contemporary countries, more or less sincerely and successfully, aspire. A **democracy,** briefly defined, is a political system in which citizens enjoy a number of basic civil and political rights, and in which their most important political leaders are elected in free and fair elections and are accountable under a rule of law. Democracy literally means "government by the people."

In small political systems, such as local communities, it may be possible for "the people" to share directly in debating, deciding, and implementing public policy. In large political systems, such as contemporary states, democracy must be achieved largely through indirect participation in policymaking. Elections, competitive political parties, free mass media, and representative assemblies make some degree of democracy, some degree of "government by the people," possible. This indirect, or representative, democracy is not complete or ideal. But the more citizens are involved and the more influential their choices, the more democratic the system.

The most important general distinction in classifying political systems is between democratic systems and authoritarian systems. *Authoritarian* states lack one or several of the defining features of democracy. In democracies, competitive elections give citizens the chance to shape the policymaking process through their selection of key policymakers. In authoritarian systems the policymakers are chosen by military councils, hereditary families, dominant political parties, and the like. Citizens are either ignored or pressed into symbolic assent to the government's choices.

Authoritarian states can take several forms. (See Chapter 6.) In **oligarchies,** literally "rule by the few," important political rights are withheld from the majority of the population. South Africa, until the abolition of apartheid in the early 1990s, is a good example. Other authoritarian states, such as Egypt, are controlled by an individual dictator and his party or military supporters. **Totalitarian systems**—such as Nazi Germany, or the Soviet Union under Stalin, or North Korea today—are systems in which the government constricts the rights and privacy of its citizens in a particularly severe and intrusive manner.

As societies become more complex, richer, and more technologically advanced, the probability of citizen involvement and democratization increases. In the first half of the twentieth century most Western states were transformed from authoritarian regimes or oligarchies to democracies. After World War II, a second democratic wave—which lasted from 1943 until the early 1960s—saw both newly independent states (such as India and Nigeria) and defeated authoritarian powers (such as Germany and Japan) set up the formal institutions of democracy.[22]

Another round of democratic transitions began in 1974, involving Southern Europe, East Asia, Latin America, and a number of African states. The most dramatic changes came in Central and Eastern Europe, where in a few short years the Soviet empire collapsed, the nations of Eastern Europe rapidly converted to democracy, and many of these nations have now joined the European Union. The people power revolution in the Philippines, the end of the apartheid regime in South Africa, and the public protests for democratization in Indonesia were equally dramatic. Samuel P. Huntington speaks of this latest move toward democracy as a "Third Wave" of worldwide **democratization.**[23]

As a result of these three democratization waves, democracy has become a common goal of the global community (see Figure 1.3). As late as 1978, only a third of the world's independent countries had competitive party and electoral systems. Communist and other single-party governments and other authoritarian regimes dominated the landscape. By 2004, almost two-thirds of states had a system of electoral democracy, and human rights and liberties were similarly spreading to more of the world's population.[24] This democratization trend is continuing in the new millennium, with prospects for further progress in many nations.

This democratization process results from a combination of factors. Economic development transforms societies in ways that typically encourage democratization by creating autonomous political groups that demand political influence, by expanding the political skills of the citizenry, and by creating economic complexity that encourages systems of self-governance. Social modernization transforms the political values and political culture of the public, which increases demands for a more participatory system (see Chapter 3). New democracies are also much more likely to endure when founded in economically developed societies.[25]

Democracy is not an all-or-nothing proposition, however. No democracy is perfect, and we can speak of shades or gradations of democracy. Democracy typically does not come about overnight. It often takes time to establish democratic institutions and to have citizens recognize them and comply with the rules of the democratic process.

It can be especially difficult to consolidate democracy in less economically developed societies. Not all of the newly democratizing countries are succeeding beyond the first few years. In some, democratic processes fail to produce stable institutions and effective public policies and give way to some form of authoritarianism. In Nigeria, a democratic-leaning regime installed in 1979 was overthrown by a military coup in 1983, and a partial movement toward redemocratization was again aborted by the military in 1993 before being reestablished in 1999. Nigeria is by no

Growth in Free Governments over Time   **FIGURE 1.3**

Source: Freedom House, *Freedom in the World 2006* (www.freedomhouse.org).

Women and Political Development

BOX 1.4

If a poor nation could do one thing to stimulate its development, what should it do? Opening the fiftieth session of the United Nations Commission on the Status of Women in 2006, UN Deputy-Secretary General Louise Fréchette said the international community finally comprehends that empowering women and girls around the globe is the most effective tool for a country's development. She stated that studies have repeatedly shown that by giving women equal education and work opportunities and access to a society's decision-making processes, a country can boost its economic productivity, reduce infant and maternal mortality rates and improve the general population's nutrition and health. These results are achieved because women's education and participation in the labor force increase family output, increase the likelihood that children will be better educated and benefit from health care, improve nutrition in the family, and better the quality of life for women and their families.

Source: UN News Center, February 27, 2006.

means unique. Transition can move in either direction, toward or away from democracy. The recent wave of democratization is supported by the more favorable environments of more modernized societies and because there are now more democracies in the world to support new democracies. However, democracy is difficult to sustain when severe economic or political problems face a nation, or where the public remains uncertain about democracy.

Even when states democratize, there is no guarantee that they will grant human rights and civil liberties to all their people. In some countries, majority rule turns into a "tyranny of the majority" against ethnic or religious minorities. Therefore, democracies have to balance between respecting the will of the majority and protecting the rights of the minority. Even when political rulers sincerely try to promote human rights and civil liberties (which is by no means always the case), they do not always agree on the nature of those rights.

A good example of the spread of rights and liberties—and cultural differences in the definition of rights—involves gender issues. Governments in Western industrial societies favor gender policies that guarantee equality for women in society, the workplace, and politics. The United Nations and other international organizations have become advocates of women's rights. But gender norms often vary across cultural zones. The UN's statistics indicate that many developing nations hesitate to grant equal rights to women, restricting their education and involvement in the economy and politics.[26] Restrictions on women's rights are even starker in many Arab states. Ironically, other research indicates that improving the status of women is one of the most productive ways to develop a nation politically and economically (see Box 1.4). In short, expanding human rights is an ongoing process in the world today, and there is much room for further progress.

LOOKING FORWARD

The last several decades have been a period of tremendous social, economic, and political change in the world. Economic development, improved living standards, the spread of human rights, and democratization improved the life chances and life conditions of billions of individuals. In most of the world, the average child born today can look forward to a longer, better, and freer life than his or her parents—especially if she is a girl.

At the same time, continuing social, economic, and political problems remain. Progress in one area can create new opportunities, but also new problems in another. Economic development, for example, can sometimes stimulate ethnic strife and destabilize political institutions. Economic development can also disrupt social life. And the process of development has been uneven across and within nations. Many basic human needs still remain in too short supply.[27]

Even in the affluent democracies, as one set of policy issues is addressed, new issues come to the fore. Western democracies struggle to address issues of environmental quality, changing lifestyles, and the challenges of globalization and multiculturalism. A more affluent and information-driven citizenry can also limit the effectiveness of political parties, interest groups, parliaments, and political executives. Success in meeting these old and new challenges can improve the living conditions for the world's populations, decrease international conflict, and come closer to meeting the ideals of humankind.

Governments and politics have played a large role in promoting the successes and failures of the past. Just as we can point to governments whose actions improved life for their citizens, there are other governments that took regressive actions. Governments and their activities are central to our political futures. Our goal in this book is to examine the ways in which citizens, policymakers, and governments address the policy challenges that face them today.

REVIEW QUESTIONS

- What is politics?
- What are the contrasting images of the "state of nature" of humankind?
- What are the potential positive and negative outcomes of government activity?
- What are the main challenges that countries face in building a political community?
- What are the causes and consequences of economic development?
- What are the causes and consequences of democratization?

KEY TERMS

democracy
democratization
ethnicity
European Union (EU)
externalities
governments

gross national product (GNP)
human rights
income inequality
nation
nation-states

oligarchies
political culture
political system
public goods
religious fundamentalism
sovereignty

state
state of nature
totalitarian systems
United Nations (UN)

SUGGESTED READINGS

Chenery, Hollis et al. *Redistribution with Growth.* New York: Oxford University Press, 1981.

Cornelius, Wayne et al., eds. *Controlling Immigration: A Global Perspective.* Stanford, CA: Stanford University Press, 1995.

Dalton, Russell, and Doh Chull Shin, eds. *Citizens, Democracy, and Markets Around the Pacific Rim.* Oxford: Oxford University Press, 2006.

Diamond, Larry, ed. *Developing Democracy: Towards Consolidation.* Baltimore: Johns Hopkins University Press, 1999.

Ehrlich, Paul, and Anne Ehrlich. *The Population Explosion.* New York: Simon & Schuster, 1990.

Horowitz, Donald. *Ethnic Groups in Conflict.* Berkeley: University of California Press, 1985.

Huntington, Samuel. *The Third Wave: Democratization in the Late Twentieth Century.* Norman: University of Oklahoma Press, 1991.

———. *The Clash of Civilizations and the Remaking of World Order.* New York: Simon & Schuster, 1996.

Lijphart, Arend. *Patterns of Democracy.* New Haven, CT: Yale University Press, 1999.

Linz, Juan, and Alfred Stepan, eds. *Problems of Democratic Transitions and Consolidation.* Baltimore: Johns Hopkins University Press, 1996.

Marty, Martin, and Scott Appleby. *Fundamentalism Observed.* Chicago: University of Chicago Press, 1991.

Putnam, Robert. *Making Democracy Work: Civic Traditions in Modern Italy.* Princeton, NJ: Princeton University Press, 1993.

Przeworski, Adam et al. *Democracy and Development: Political Institutions and Well-being in the World 1950–1990.* New York: Cambridge University Press, 2000.

Sachs, Jeffrey. *The End of Poverty: Economic Possibilities for Our Time.* New York: Penguin, 2005.

United Nations. *World Development Report.* New York: Oxford University Press, annual editions.

Weiner, Myron. *The Global Migration Crisis: Challenge to States and to Human Rights.* New York: HarperCollins, 1995.

Zakaria, Fareed. *The Future of Freedom: Illiberal Democracy at Home and Abroad.* New York: Norton, 2003.

ENDNOTES

1. Thomas Hobbes, *Leviathan,* ed. C. B. Macpherson (New York: Penguin, 1968), 186.

2. J. J. Rousseau, *Second Discourse on Inequality, The First and Second Discourses* (New York: St. Martin's Press, 1964), pp. 109–10.

3. Two other philosophical groups are especially outspoken critics of government: libertarians and anarchists. Adherents of **libertarianism** are individualists who see society as composed of individual human beings with fundamental rights that must be protected. The main problem with government, libertarians argue, is that the more tasks it takes on, the more prone it is to violate such basic rights. Adherents of **anarchism** claim that governments produce undesirable effects; they see societies not as collections of individuals but as communities of people who in their natural condition are equal. Governments and power corrupt such communities and lead to oppression and alienation.

4. Martin Greenberg and Mark Tier, *Visions of Liberty* (New York: Baen Publishers, 2004).

5. See, for example, Fareed Zakaria, *The Future of Freedom: Illiberal Democracy at Home and Abroad* (New York: Norton, 2003).

6. See, for example, Douglas North, *Institutions, Institutional Change, and Economic Performance* (Cambridge: Cambridge University Press, 1990); Mancur Olson, "The New Institutional Economics: The Collective Choice Approach to Economic Development," in C. Clague, ed., *Institutions and Economic Development.* (Baltimore: Johns Hopkins University Press, 1997; S. Knack and P. Keefer, "Institutions and Economic Performance," *Economics and Politics* 7 (1995) 207–29.

7. The Vatican and Switzerland are not members of the UN but maintain permanent observer missions at the UN headquarters. Taiwan was expelled from the UN in 1971 to accommodate mainland China (the People's Republic).

8. Max Weber, *Economy and Society,* ed. Guenther Roth and Claus Wittich (Berkeley: University of California Press, 1978), 389.

9. Even before the end of the Cold War, ethnic autonomy movements in parts of old countries—such as the United Kingdom (the Scots and Welsh) and Canada (the Quebecois)—sought to break free or achieve greater autonomy.

10. Stephen Castles and Mark J. Miller, *The Age of Migration: International Population Movements in the Modern World* (New York: Guilford, 1994).

11. Erik V. Gunnemark, *Countries, Peoples, and Their Languages: The Geolinguistic Handbook* (Gothenburg: Lanstryckeriet, 1991).

12. A book dealing with this theme is R. Scott Appleby, *The Ambivalence of the Sacred* (Lanham, MD: Rowman & Littlefield, 2000).

13. United Nations Development Program, *Human Development Report 2005* (New York: United Nations). See also www.undp.org. for additional data and interactive presentations.

14. The per capita *gross national product (GNP)* is the total economic output per person. Rather than the traditional measures computed according to the exchange rates of the national currencies, the *purchasing power parity (PPP)* index takes into account differences in price levels from one country to another. Most analyses assume that the GNP/PPP statistics are more comparable measures of living conditions. The income gap increases, however, if one uses the traditional exchange rate measure of GNP.

15. For example, see Hollis Chenery et al., *Redistribution with Growth* (New York: Oxford University Press, 1981).

16. Paul Ehrlich and Anne Ehrlich, *The Population Explosion* (New York: Simon & Schuster, 1990).

17. Hania Zlotnik, "Statement to the Thirty-Eighth Session of the Commission on Population and Development," April 4, 2005 (www.un.org/esa/population/cpd/Statement_HZ_open. pdf).

18. Amartya Sen, "Population: Delusion and Reality," *New York Review of Books,* 22 Sept., 1994, pp. 62ff.

19. World Bank, *World Development Report, 1998–1999* (New York: Oxford University Press, 1999).

20. Sen, "Population: Delusion and Reality."

21. Regina Axelrod, David Downie, and Norman Vig, eds., *The Global Environment: Institutions, Law, and Policy* (Washington, DC: CQ Press, 2004)**;** Yale Center for Environmental Law and Policy and Center for International Earth Science Information Network, *2005 Environmental Sustainability Index: Benchmarking National Environmental Stewardship* (New Haven, CT: Yale University, 2005) (http://www.yale.edu/esi/).

22. While many countries became formally democratic in these years, most of them quickly lapsed into authoritarianism. Many of these would-be democracies failed in their first decade; another "reverse wave" in the 1960s and early 1970s swept away some older democracies (Chile, Greece, and Uruguay, for example) as well.

23. Samuel Huntington, *The Third Wave* (Norman: University of Oklahoma Press, 1991).

24. Freedom House, *Freedom in the World 2004* (Washington, DC: Freedom House, 2005) (www. freedomhouse. org).

25. Seymour Martin Lipset, "Some Social Requisites of Democracy," *American Political Science Review 53* (September 1959), 69–105; Larry Diamond, "Economic Development and Democracy Reconsidered," in G. Marks and L. Diamond, eds., *Reexamining Democracy* (Newbury Park, CA: Sage, 1992); Tatu Vanhanen, *Prospects of Democracy* (New York: Routledge, 1997); Adam Przeworski et al., *Democracy and Development: Political Institutions and Well-being in the World 1950–1990* (New York: Cambridge University Press, 2000).

26. See United Nations Development Program, *Human Development Report 2005* (New York: United Nations) (http://hdr.undp.org/reports/global/2005/), tables 25-30, and associated discussion.

27. Many of these issues are addressed by the United Nations' Millennium Development Goals. Visit the UN website (http://www. un. org/ millenniumgoals/) or see United Nations, *Millennium Development Goals Report 2005* (New York: United Nations) (http:/ /unstats. un. org/ unsd/ mi/ pdf/ MDGBook. pdf).

COMPARING POLITICAL SYSTEMS

WHY WE COMPARE

The great French interpreter of American democracy, Alexis de Tocqueville, while traveling in America in the 1830s, wrote to a friend explaining how his own ideas about French institutions and culture entered into his writing of *Democracy in America*. Tocqueville wrote: "Although I very rarely spoke of France in my book, I did not write one page of it without having her, so to speak, before my eyes."[1]

On a more general note about the comparative method, he offered this comment: "Without comparisons to make, the mind does not know how to proceed."[2] Tocqueville was telling us that comparison is fundamental to all human thought. We add that it is the methodological core of the humanistic and scientific methods. It is the only way we can fully understand our own political system. Comparing our experience with that of other countries deepens our understanding of our own institutions. Examining politics in other societies permits us to see a wider range of political alternatives. It illuminates the virtues and shortcomings of our own political life. By taking us beyond our familiar arrangements and assumptions, comparative analysis helps expand our awareness of the possibilities of politics.

Comparison is also at the methodological core of the scientific study of politics. Comparative analysis helps us develop explanations and test theories of the ways in which political processes work and in which political change occurs. The goals of the comparative methods used by political scientists are similar to those used in more exact sciences. But political scientists cannot normally design experiments, a major path to knowledge in many of the natural sciences. We cannot control and manipulate political arrangements and observe the consequences. We are especially limited when dealing with large-scale events that drastically affect many people. For example, researchers cannot and would not want to start a social revolution to see its effects.

We can, however, use the comparative method to describe and explain the different combinations of political events and institutions found in different societies. More than two thousand years ago, Aristotle in his *Politics* contrasted the economies and social structures of Greek city-states in an effort to determine how the social and economic environments affected political institutions and policies (see Box 2.1). More contemporary political scientists also try to explain differences between the processes and performance of political systems. They compare two-party democracies with multiparty democracies, parliamentary with presidential regimes, democracies in poor countries with those in rich countries, elections in new party systems with those in established democracies. These and many other comparisons have greatly enriched our understanding of politics.

HOW WE COMPARE

We study politics in several different ways: we describe it; we seek to explain it; sometimes we try to predict it. These are all parts of the scientific process. Each of them may use the comparative method.

Aristotle's Library

BOX 2.1

There is historical evidence that Aristotle had accumulated a library of more than 150 studies of the political systems of the Mediterranean world of 400–300 B.C. Many of these had probably been researched and written by his disciples.

While only the Athenian constitution survives of this library of Aristotelian polities, it is evident from the references to such studies that do survive that Aristotle was concerned with sampling the variety of political systems then in existence, including the "barbarian" (Third World?) countries, such as Libya,

Etruria, and Rome: "[T]he references in ancient authorities give us the names of some 70 or more of the states described in the compilation of 'polities.' They range from Sinope, on the Black Sea, to Cyrene in North Africa; they extend from Marseilles in the Western Mediterranean to Crete, Rhodes, and Cyprus in the East. Aristotle thus included colonial constitutions as well as those of metropolitan states. His descriptions embraced states on the Aegean, Ionian, and Tyrrhenian Seas, and the three continents of Europe, Asia, and Africa."

Source: Ernest Barker, ed., *The Politics of Aristotle* (London: Oxford University Press, 1977), 386.

The first stage in the study of politics is description. If we cannot describe a political process or event, we cannot really hope to understand or explain it. Much less can we predict what might happen next or in similar situations. In order to describe politics, we need a set of concepts that are clearly defined and well understood. We speak of this as a conceptual framework. The easier this set of concepts is to understand, and the more generally it can be applied, the more helpful it is to the study of politics. Conceptual frameworks are not generally right or wrong, but they may be more or less useful to the task at hand.

POLITICAL SYSTEMS: ENVIRONMENT AND INTERDEPENDENCE

Comparative Politics Today suggests that we compare political systems with a structural-functional systems framework. To do so, we need to discuss three general concepts that we use throughout this book: (1) system, (2) structure, and (3) function. **System,** as we defined it in Chapter 1, suggests an object having interdependent parts, acting within a setting or an **environment.** The **political system** is a set of institutions and agencies concerned with formulating and implementing the collective goals of a society or of groups within it. **Governments** are the **policymaking** parts of political systems. The decisions of governments are normally

backed up by legitimate coercion, and obedience may be compelled. (We discuss legitimacy at greater length in Chapter 3.)

Figure 2.1 tells us that a political system exists in both an international environment and a domestic environment. It is molded by these environments and it tries to mold them. The system receives **inputs** from these environments. Its policymakers attempt to shape them through its outputs. In the figure, which is quite schematic and simple, we use the United States as the central actor. We include other countries as our environmental examples—Russia, China, Britain, Germany, Japan, Mexico, and Iran.

Exchanges among countries may vary in many ways. For example, they may be "dense" or "sparse"; U.S.–Canadian relations exemplify the dense end of the continuum, while U.S.–Nepalese relations would be at the sparse end.

Relationships among political systems may be of many different kinds. The United States has substantial trade relations with some countries and relatively little trade with others. Some countries have an excess of imports over exports, whereas others have an excess of exports over imports. Military exchanges and support with such countries as the NATO nations, Japan, South Korea, Israel, and Saudi Arabia have been of significant importance to the United States.

The interdependence of countries—the volume and value of imports and exports, transfers of capital, international communication, the extent of foreign

FIGURE 2.1

travel and immigration—has increased enormously in the last decades. This increase is often called **globalization.** We might represent this process as a thickening of the input and output arrows between the United States and other countries in Figure 2.1. Fluctuations in this flow of international transactions and traffic attributable to depression, inflation, protective tariffs, international terrorism, war, and the like may wreak havoc with the economies of the countries affected.

The interaction of a political system with its domestic environment—the economic and social systems and the political culture of its citizens—is also depicted in Figure 2.1. We can illustrate this interaction in the U.S. case by the rise of the "high-tech information-based economy."

The composition of the U.S. labor force, and consequently its citizenry, has changed dramatically in the last century. Agriculture has declined to under 2 percent of the gainfully employed. Employment in heavy extractive and manufacturing industries has decreased substantially. Newer, high-technology occupations, the professions, and the service occupations have increased sharply as proportions of the labor force. The last half-century has also witnessed significant improvements in the educational level of the U.S. population. Many more young people complete high school and go on to college. Moreover, people move more easily from one region to another. These and other changes in the U.S. social structure have altered the challenges facing the U.S. system and the resources available to meet these challenges.

These changes in the economy and the citizenry are associated with changes in American **political culture.** (Political culture—the attitudes, beliefs, and values of the people in a country—is discussed at more length in Chapter 3.) People want different things from politics. For example, an educated and culturally sophisticated society is more concerned with quality of life, the beauty and healthfulness of the environment, and similar issues.

At the same time, the globalization of the economy leads to demands from firms and workers in some industries for protection of their jobs. Natural disasters, such as the hurricane that devastated New Orleans in 2005, spur calls for the national government to lead reconstruction. Local issues are seen as the responsibility of the entire country. People live longer. An aging population demands that governments do more to help with medical benefits. In input-output terms, socioeconomic changes transform the political demands of the electorate and the kinds of policies that it supports.

Thus a new pattern of society results in different policy outputs, different kinds and levels of taxation, changes in regulatory patterns, and changes in welfare expenditures. The advantage of the system-environment approach is that it directs our attention to the **interdependence** of what happens between and within countries. It provides us with a vocabulary to describe, compare, and explain these interacting events.

If we are to make sound judgments in politics, we need to be able to place political systems in their domestic and international environments. We need to recognize how these environments both set limits on and provide opportunities for political choices. This approach keeps us from reaching quick and biased political judgments. If a country is poor in natural resources and lacks the capabilities necessary to exploit what it has, we cannot fault it for having a low industrial output or poor educational and social services. Each country chapter in the second half of this book begins by discussing the current policy challenges facing the country and its social and economic environment.

POLITICAL SYSTEMS: STRUCTURES AND FUNCTIONS

Governments do many things—from establishing and operating school systems, to maintaining public order, to fighting wars. In order to carry on these disparate activities, governments have specialized agencies, or **structures,** such as parliaments, bureaucracies, administrative agencies, and courts. These structures perform **functions,** which in turn enable the government to formulate, implement, and enforce its policies. The policies reflect the goals; the agencies provide the means to achieve them.

Figure 2.2 locates six types of political structures—political parties, interest groups, legislatures, executives, bureaucracies, and courts—within the political system. These are formal organizations engaged in political activities. They exist in most contemporary political systems. This list is not exhaustive. Some structures, such as ruling military councils or governing royal families, are found in only a few countries. Some, such as Iran's Council of Guardians, are unique to their political system.

We might think that if we understand how such structures work in one political system, we can apply this insight to any other system. Unfortunately, that is not always the case. The sixfold classification will not carry us very far in comparing political systems with each other. The problem is that similar structures may have very different functions across political systems. For example, Britain and China have all six types of political structures. However, these institutions are organized differently in the two countries. More importantly, they function in dramatically different ways. They do different things in the political processes of their countries.

The political executive in Britain consists of the prime minister, the ministers assigned to the Cabinet, and the larger ministry, which consists of all the heads of departments and agencies. All these officials are usually selected from Parliament. There is a similar structure in China, called the State Council, headed by a premier and consisting of the various ministers and ministerial commissions. But while the British prime minister and Cabinet have substantial policymaking power, the State Council in China is closely supervised by the general secretary of the Communist Party, the Politburo, and the Central Committee of the party.

Both Britain and China have legislative bodies—the House of Commons in Britain and the National People's Congress in China. Their members make speeches to each other and vote on prospective public policies. But while the House of Commons is a key institution in the policymaking process, the Chinese Congress meets for only brief periods, ratifying decisions made mainly by the Communist Party authorities.

CHINA

RUSSIA

JAPAN

Output

Domestic environment

Input

Political parties   Executives
Interest groups   Bureaucracies
Legislatures   Courts

Input

Domestic environment

Output

BRITAIN

BRAZIL

The Political System and Its Structures

FIGURE 2.2

Usually the Chinese delegates do not even consider alternative policies.

There are even larger differences between political parties in the two countries. Britain has a competitive party system. The majority in the House of Commons and the Cabinet are constantly confronted by an opposition party or parties, competing for public support. They look forward to the next election when they may unseat the incumbent majority, as happened in 1997, when the Labour Party replaced the Conservatives in government. In China the Communist Party controls the whole political process. There are no other political parties. The principal decisions are taken in the Politburo and to some extent in the Central Committee of the Communist Party. The governmental agencies implement the policies, which are initiated or approved by the top Communist Party leaders.

Thus, an institution-by-institution comparison of British and Chinese politics that did not spell out their interdependence and the functions that they perform would not bring us far toward understanding the important differences in the politics of these two countries. Each country study in this book includes a figure that shows how some of the major structures select and control each other. Another figure illustrates how they fit into the policymaking process.

Figure 2.3 shows the functions of the political process that we can use to compare all political systems. The center of Figure 2.3 under the heading **"process functions"** lists the distinctive activities necessary for policy to be made and implemented in any kind of political system.

- **Interest articulation** involves individuals and groups expressing their needs and demands.
- **Interest aggregation** combines different demands into policy proposals backed by significant political resources.

This meeting of the National Assembly of the People's Republic of China in the Great Hall of the People in Beijing illustrates the importance of structural functionalism. While this is called the "National People's Congress" and the delegates are raising their hands in a vote, the vote is purely formal, since there is no real choice between alternatives.

Mark Avery/AP Images

- **Policymaking** decides which policy proposals are to become authoritative rules.
- **Policy implementation** carries out and enforces public policies; **policy adjudication** settles disputes about their application.

(We discuss each concept in greater detail in Chapters 4, 5, and 6.) We call these process functions because they play a direct and necessary role in the process of making policy.

Before policy can be decided, some individuals and groups in the government or the society must decide what they want and hope to get from politics. The political process begins as these interests are expressed or articulated. The many arrows on the left of the figure show these initial expressions.

To be effective, however, these demands must be combined (aggregated) into policy alternatives—such as higher or lower taxes or more or fewer social security benefits—for which substantial political support can be mobilized. Thus the arrows on the left are consolidated as the process moves from interest articulation to interest aggregation.

Governments then consider alternative policies. Whoever controls the government backs one of them and authoritative policymaking takes place. The policy must be enforced and implemented, and if it is challenged, there must be some process of adjudication.

Each policy may affect several different aspects of a society, as reflected in the three arrows for the implementation phase.

These process functions are performed by such political structures as parties, legislatures, political executives, bureaucracies, and courts. The **structural-functional approach** stresses two points. One is that *in different countries, the same structure may perform different functions.* A second is that while a particular institution, such as a legislature, may have a special relationship to a particular function, such as policymaking, *institutions often do not have a monopoly on any one function.* Presidents and governors may share in the policymaking function (veto powers), as do the higher courts (judicial review of statutes for their constitutionality).

The three functions listed at the top of the figure—socialization, recruitment, and communication—are not directly involved in making and implementing public policy but are of fundamental importance to the political system. We refer to these three functions as **system functions.** They determine whether or not the system will be maintained or changed. For example, will policymaking continue to be dominated by a military council or be replaced by competitive parties and a legislature? Will a sense of national community persist, or will it be eroded by new experiences?

The arrows leading from these three functions to all parts of the political process suggest their crucial

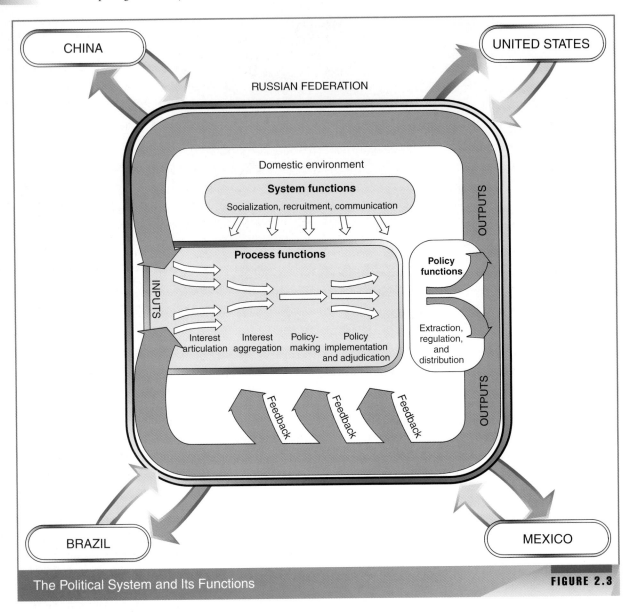

The Political System and Its Functions

FIGURE 2.3

role in underpinning and permeating the political process.

- **Political socialization** involves families, schools, communications media, churches, and all the various political structures that develop, reinforce, and transform the political culture, the attitudes of political significance in the society. (See Chapter 3.)
- **Political recruitment** refers to the selection of people for political activity and government offices. In a democracy, competitive elections play a major role in political recruitment. In authoritarian systems,

recruitment may be dominated by a single party, as in China, or unelected religious leaders, as in Iran.
- **Political communication** refers to the flow of information through the society and through the various structures that make up the political system. Gaining control over information is a key goal of most authoritarian rulers, as shown in the elaborate efforts of Chinese leaders to control content on the Internet.

Understanding the performance of the system functions is essential to understanding how political systems respond to the great contemporary challenges of building community, fostering economic development, and securing democracy that we discussed in Chapter 1.

On the right side of Figure 2.3 we see the consequences of the policy process. The **outputs** are the implementations of the political process. These are the substantive impacts on the society, the economy, and the culture. They include various forms of **extraction** of resources in the form of taxes and the like, **regulation** of behavior, and **distribution** of benefits and services to various groups in the population. The **outcomes** of all these political activities reflect the way the policies interact with the domestic and international environments. Sometimes these outcomes are the desired results of public policies. But sometimes the complexities of policy and society result in unintended consequences. Among these may be new demands for legislation or for administrative action, or increases or decreases in the amount of support given to the political system and incumbent officeholders. We shall return to the policy level, after providing an example of a structural-functional comparison.

The functional concepts shown in Figure 2.3 describe the activities carried on in any society regardless of how its political system is organized or what kinds of policies it produces. Using these functional categories, we can determine how institutions in different countries combine in making and implementing different kinds of public policy. Each country study in this book discusses the ways the different political functions are performed.

AN ILLUSTRATIVE COMPARISON: REGIME CHANGE IN RUSSIA

Figures 2.4 and 2.5[3] offer a simplified graphic comparison of structures and functions in Russia before and after the breakdown of communist rule in the Soviet Union. They illustrate the use of the comparative method to assess the way a political regime changed significantly in a short period of time. The point here is to illustrate how we can use the tools of political analysis, rather than provide the details of the Russian case (which are discussed in depth in Chapter 9).

The figures depict the changes in the functioning of the major structures of the political system brought about by the collapse of communism. These include two revolutionary changes. One is the end of the single-party political system dominated by the Communist Party of the Soviet Union, which held together the vast, multinational Soviet state. The other is the dissolution of the Soviet Union itself into its fifteen member republics. As a result of these two remarkable events, Russia, the republic that was the core republic of the old union, became an independent noncommunist state.

In June 1991, Boris Yeltsin, a bitter rival to the Soviet president, Mikhail Gorbachev, was elected president of Russia. Six months later, the Soviet Union collapsed and Gorbachev gave up his office. In December 1993, Russian voters were called on to ratify a new constitution, which provided for a powerful executive presidency and at the same time elected a new parliament dominated by a diverse range of political parties.

In the new Russia, democratic tendencies competed with pressures for authoritarian rule. Overall, the new system was a mixture of pluralism with vestiges of the old, bureaucratically run, state socialist order. New political parties were represented in Parliament and tried to develop national political bases of support for the next elections. A reborn Communist Party—called the Communist Party of the Russian Federation—regularly denounced Yeltsin and called for the restoration of a strong state and more social protection. Parliament had become a meaningful site for policy debate and decision making. The mass media were no longer tightly controlled by the Communist Party. New organized interest groups, such as business associations and labor unions, were actively involved in policymaking. The bureaucracy remained a powerful central player in the political process, however, with substantial continued control over the economy.

These and subsequent changes are reflected in the differences between the two figures. In 1985 (the year that the reform leader Mikhail Gorbachev came to power), the Soviet Union was a communist regime. Its Communist Party ruled the country. The top leader of the country was the general secretary of the Communist Party. Although the country had the formal trappings of democracy, power actually flowed downward from the decision makers at the top to government and society.

Figure 2.4 therefore shows how the basic functions of the political system were performed in 1985. The Communist Party was the dominant political institution of the country, overseeing schools and media, the arts and public organizations, the economy and

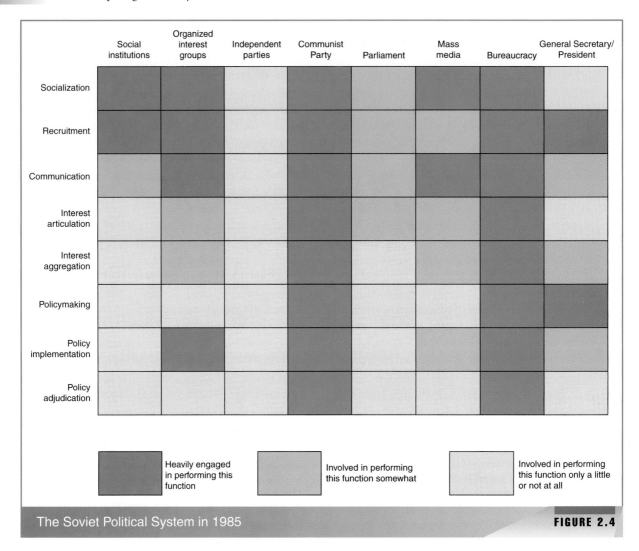

The Soviet Political System in 1985

FIGURE 2.4

the courts. For this reason, all the cells of the chart in the column marked "Communist Party" are shaded dark, as are the cells under the column marked "Bureaucracy." Although social institutions—such as the family, workplace, arts, and hobby groups—exercised some influence over such system-level functions as socialization, recruitment, and communication, it was the Communist Party and state bureaucracy that dominated process-level functions. Under their tutelage, the mass media in 1985 were a key agent of communist political socialization and communication. Parliament was a compliant instrument for ratifying decisions made by the party and bureaucracy. No other parties could exist beside the Communist Party. The only organized interest groups were those authorized by

the party. The party's general secretary was the most powerful official in the country, since there was no state presidency.

By 2000 the political system had undergone fundamental changes, as shown in Figure 2.5. Many more structures played a role in the political process, as is immediately evident by the larger number of cells that are heavily shaded. In particular, Parliament, independent political parties, and regional governments all acquired important new powers in policymaking. The freedom enjoyed by ordinary citizens to articulate their interests and to organize to advance them had expanded enormously. The Communist Party, no longer an official or monopolistic party, had declined substantially in power and

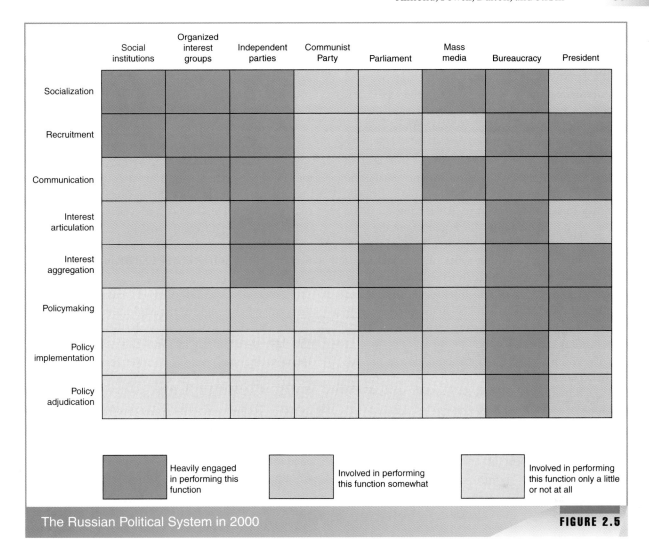

The Russian Political System in 2000

FIGURE 2.5

was playing by the rules of the parliamentary game. The lighter shading for the Communist Party in Figure 2.5 shows its diminished influence. The state bureaucracy remained an important element in the political system, although adapting itself to the new trend of movement toward a market economy by adopting quasi-commercial forms.

The presidency, now occupied by Vladimir Putin, has been a dominating policymaking institution in the new Russia, as shown in Figure 2.5. The Parliament, although fairly representative of the diversity of opinion in the country, was frustrated in its policymaking and oversight roles by the inertia of the vast state bureaucracy, by its inability to compel compliance with its laws, by its weak links with the electorate, and

by the president's power to make policy by decree. Nevertheless, it played a much greater role than before in aggregating interests and making policy, as shown when comparing Figures 2.4 and 2.5.

A further updating of Figure 2.5 would show the eclipse of independent parties and Parliament by President Putin after 2000. This movement in a more authoritarian direction, although not back to communism, would be shown by fewer dark shaded columns in the middle of the figure. These further developments are discussed in detail in Chapter 9.

The brief comparisons presented here illustrate the use of the structural-functional approach. This approach enables us to examine how the same functions are performed in different countries, or in the same country at two different points in time. Similarly, we may examine changes in the functions performed by the same structures over time or across different political systems. In a country undergoing as rapid and dramatic a transition as Russia in the 1990s, this framework helps us to analyze changes in the distribution of power among the major institutions making up the political system.

Neither the analysis of structures nor that of functions is complete without the other. A structural analysis tells us the number of political parties, or the organization of the legislature. It describes how the executive branch, the courts, the bureaucracy, the mass media, interest groups, and other structures of a political system are set up and by what rules or standards they operate. A functional analysis tells us how these institutions and organizations interact to produce and implement policies. This kind of analysis is especially essential when we are comparing very different kinds of political systems.

The country chapters of this book do not present formal structural-functional sketches like Figures 2.4 and 2.5. But at the core of each chapter is a set of discussions of these functions and the structures that perform them. We can see these in the section headings of the country studies and in the analytic guide at the beginning of this book. These tools make it possible to compare the workings of the very different political systems in this book.

THE POLICY LEVEL: PERFORMANCE, OUTCOME, AND EVALUATION

The important question is what these differences in structure and function do for the interests, needs, and aspirations of people. We call this the **policy level** of the political system.

Looking again at Figure 2.3, we see reflections of the relationships between the international environment, the domestic society, and the political system. At the left of Figure 2.3 are arrows signifying inputs of demands and supports from the society and the international system. Inputs also come from the independent initiatives of political leaders and bureaucrats. The structures performing the political process functions convert these inputs into the policies of the government. These policies extract resources, distribute benefits, and regulate behavior. They are designed

to achieve broad goals, such as welfare, justice, and freedom—or control and domination—as well as special benefits for groups and individuals. At the right are arrows signifying outputs and outcomes, the end products of the political process, the things a government does for and to its people.

We call the outputs of a political system—its extractions, distributions, regulations, and symbolic acts—its policy performance. We have to distinguish among these efforts, the things a government does, and the actual outcome of these efforts. Governments may spend equal amounts on education and health, or defense, but with different consequences. Government efficiency or corruption plays a role in the effectiveness of politics. But so do the underlying cultural, economic, and technological levels.

Americans spend more per capita on education than any other people in the world. But their children perform less well in some subjects, such as mathematics, than do children in some other countries that spend substantially less. The United States spent enormous sums and many lives on the war in Vietnam in the 1960s and 1970s, as did the Soviet Union on its war in Afghanistan in the 1980s. Yet, both countries were held at bay by small countries resolved to resist at all costs. Because of these costly failures, they were weakened internally. The outcome of public policy is never wholly in the hands of the people and their leaders. Conditions in the internal environment, conditions and events in the larger external world, and simple chance may frustrate the most thoughtfully crafted programs and plans. Each country study in this book concludes with a discussion of the country's performance, describing both policies and their outcomes.

Finally, we must step even further back to consider the whole situation of political system, process, and policy, and the environment in order to evaluate what political systems are doing. Evaluation is complex because people value different things and put different emphasis on what they value. We will refer to the different things people may value as political "goods." In Chapter 7, we discuss goods associated with the system level, such as the stability or adaptability of political institutions. We also discuss goods associated with the process level, such as citizen participation in politics. Finally, we consider goods associated with the policy level, such as welfare, security, and liberty. To evaluate what a political system is doing, we assess performance and outcomes in each of

The wall dividing California from Mexico illustrates the input-output model of comparative politics. The two men are trying to escape from the poverty of the Mexican economy. The wall is part of the output of the American political system, intended to frustrate illegal immigrants. The two figures illustrate the point that outputs do not necessarily produce the intended outcomes.

Les Stone/Sygma

these areas. We must also be aware of how outcomes affect individuals and subgroups in the society, of specific changes that may often be overlooked in presenting averages.

A particularly important problem of evaluation concerns building for the future as well as living today. The people of poor countries wish to survive and alleviate the suffering of today but also to improve their children's lot for tomorrow. The people of all countries, but especially rich ones, must deal with the costs to their children of polluted and depleted natural resources as the result of the thoughtless environmental policies of the past.

HOW WE EXPLAIN

Once we are able to describe politics with the help of the conceptual framework that we choose, the next task is to explain it. What we mean by explaining political phenomena is seeking to identify relationships among them. For example, we might be interested in the relationship between democracy and international peace (see Box 2.2). Are democratic states more peaceful than others? If so, are they peaceful because they are democratic, are they democratic because they are peaceful, or are they perhaps both peaceful and democratic because they are more prosperous than other states?

These questions show that we often want explanations to go beyond associating one thing with another. Ideally, we want to put many political relationships in causal terms, so that we can say that one political feature is the cause of another, and the latter is the effect of the former.

Theories are statements about causal relationships between general classes of events—for example, about what causes democracy, war, or welfare policies. Scientific theories are always tentative; they are always subject to modification or falsification as our knowledge improves. And theories need to be testable. A good theory is one that holds up after continued trials and experiments. Yet, it can be further confirmed or modified as we test the theory again and again. A well-tested theory allows us to explain confidently what happens in specific cases or groups of cases: these two countries have a peaceful relationship because they are democracies (see Box 2.2).

Researchers in political science distinguish between studies based on large numbers (large "n") and small numbers (small "n"). In large "n" studies, it is often possible and helpful to use statistical analysis. Such studies are usually referred to as *statistical studies;* small "n" studies are usually called *case studies.* Large "n" studies have a sufficient number and variety of cases to enable the researcher to examine the relation among the variables. Variables are the features on which our cases differ—for

Statistical Methods

BOX 2.2

A popular contemporary research program known as *democratic peace research* illustrates the pros and cons of statistical and case study research. It has been of primary interest to international relations scholars, who took the diplomatic history of the Cold War period and asked whether democratic countries are more peaceful in their foreign policy than authoritarian and nondemocratic ones. Many scholars in the democratic peace research group took the statistical route. They counted each year of interaction between two states as one case. With roughly half a century of diplomatic history involving a state system of 100 countries or more, they had a very large number of cases, even after eliminating the many irrelevant cases of countries that never, or rarely, had any relations with one another. Political scientists Andrew Bennett and Alexander George drew these conclusions after surveying the statistical research:

> Statistical methods achieved important advances on the issue of whether a nonspurious interdemocratic

peace exists. A fairly strong though not unanimous consensus emerged that: (1) democracies are not less war-prone in general; (2) they have very rarely if ever fought one another; (3) this pattern of an interdemocratic peace applies to both war and conflicts short of war; (4) states in transition to democracy are more war-prone than established democracies; and (5) these correlations were not spuriously brought about by the most obvious alternative explanations.

Yet, although much was learned from the statistical studies, they were not as successful at answering "why" questions. Case studies make clinical depth possible, revealing causal interconnections in individual cases. Careful repetition of these causal tracings from case to case strengthens confidence in these relationships. Thus Bennett and George concluded that the best research strategy uses statistical and case study methods together, with each method having its own strengths.

Source: Andrew Bennett and Alexander George, "An Alliance of Statistical and Case Study Methods: Research on the Interdemocratic Peace," APSA-CP: *Newsletter of the APSA Organized Section in Comparative Politics* 9 (1998) no. 1: 6.

example, "form of government: democracy or dictatorship." Statistical analysis enables us to consider possible alternative causes at the same time, accepting some and rejecting others. Small "*n*" studies permit investigators to go deeply into a case, identify the particularities of it, get the clinical details, and examine each link in the causal process. Most researchers recognize that these methods are complementary (see Box 2.2).

Large "*n*" statistical studies allow us to be more certain and precise in our explanations. On the other hand, we need the depth that case studies provide. They encourage us to formulate insightful hypotheses for statistical testing in the first place. They allow us to trace the nature of the cause-and-effect relations (sometimes called "causal mechanisms") better than large "*n*" studies. In this manner, political scientists may come to know not only whether democracies are more peaceful than dictatorships, but more precisely why democratic leaders behave in the way that they do.

We can also generate and test hypotheses about the causes and consequences of political change by comparing countries at different historical periods. Tocqueville's study of the French Revolution contributed to a general theory of revolution by comparing pre- and postrevolutionary France.[4] Theda Skocpol based her theories of the causes of revolution on a comparison of the "old regimes" of France, Russia, and China with their revolutionary and postrevolutionary regimes.[5]

An example may suggest how you might go about theorizing in comparative politics, going beyond "just mastering the facts." It is well known that rich countries are more likely to be democracies than are poor countries; democracy and economic development are strongly associated. But there are many possible reasons for this association. Some have suggested that this relationship comes about because democracy encourages education and economic development. Others have argued that as countries develop economically, their new middle classes or better organized working class are more likely to demand democratization. Yet others have seen that both democracy and economic development are commonly found in some regions of the world, such as Western Europe, while both tend to be scarce in the Middle East and Africa. This fact suggests that certain cultures may encourage or discourage both of them.

We want to understand the causal nature of this association, for reasons of both science and policy. Fostering economic development and securing democracy are two of the significant political challenges that we discussed in Chapter 1. It is vitally important that we understand how they relate to each other.

A work of Adam Przeworski and his associates examined the full experience of democracies, non-democracies, and transitions between them in all parts of the world between 1950 and 1990.[6] Their statistical analysis led them to conclude that the explanation for the association did not lie in regional effects or superior economic growth in democracy. Moreover, countries at any level of development seemed able to introduce democracy, although economically developed countries are somewhat more likely to do so. They argue that key to the relationship lies rather in the consistently greater fragility of democracies in societies at lower levels of economic development. Democracy can easily be introduced in poor societies with less educated populations. But in these social conditions it is often replaced by some kind of dictatorship. In rich countries, on the other hand, democracy tends to survive once it has been introduced. These democratic failures in poor countries produce a strong association between development and democracy. We still need to understand just why democracy is more precarious in less developed societies. But we are making progress in understanding the causal element in the relationship. We are better able to explain the relationship between development and democracy, as well as the failures of democratization in specific countries.

Comparative analysis is a powerful and versatile tool. It enhances our ability to describe and understand political processes and political change in any country by offering concepts and reference points from a broader perspective. The comparative approach also stimulates us to form general theories of political relationships. It encourages and enables us to test our political theories by confronting them with the experience of many institutions and settings.

REVIEW QUESTIONS

- How do the main elements in the environment of a political system affect the way it performs?
- Why can't we compare political systems by just describing the different structures we find in them?
- What are the functions performed in all political systems as policies are made?

- What is the difference between outputs and outcomes of policy?
- How do we use theories to explain political events?

KEY TERMS

distribution	interdependence	policy level	process functions
environment	interest aggregation	policymaking	regulation
extraction	interest articulation	political communication	structural-functional
functions	outcomes	political culture	approach
globalization	outputs	political recruitment	structures
governments	policy adjudication	political socialization	system
inputs	policy implementation	political system	system functions

SUGGESTED READINGS

Collier, David. "The Comparative Method," in Ada W. Finifter, ed., *Political Science: The State of the Discipline II.* Washington, DC: American Political Science Association, 1993.

Dogan, Mattei, and Dominique Pelassy. *How to Compare Nations: Strategies in Comparative Politics.* Chatham, NJ: Chatham House, 1990.

Goodin, Robert E., and Hans-Dieter Klingemann. Chapters 2 and 3, and Part 4 of *A New Handbook of Political Science.* New York: Oxford University Press, 1996.

King, Gary, Robert O. Keohane, and Sidney Verba. *Scientific Inference in Qualitative Research.* New York: Cambridge University Press, 1993.

Lichbach, Mark, and Alan Zuckerman. *Comparing Nations: Rationality, Culture, and Structure.* New York: Cambridge University Press, 1997.

Przeworski, Adam, and Henry Teune. *The Logic of Comparative Social Inquiry.* New York: Wiley, 1970.

ENDNOTES

1. Alexis de Tocqueville to Louis de Kergolay, 18 October 1847, in *Alexis de Tocqueville: Selected Letters on Politics and Society*, ed. Roger Boesche (Berkeley: University of California Press, 1985), 191.
2. Alexis de Tocqueville to Ernest de Chabrol, 7 October 1831, ibid, 59.
3. Figures 2.4 and 2.5 and the text of this section were contributed by Thomas Remington.
4. Alexis de Tocqueville, *The Old Regime and the French Revolution,* trans. Stuart Gilbert (New York: Doubleday, 1955).
5. Theda Skocpol, *States and Social Revolutions* (New York: Cambridge University Press, 1979).
6. Adam Przeworski et al., *Democracy and Development* (Cambridge: Cambridge University Press, 2000).

POLITICAL CULTURE AND POLITICAL SOCIALIZATION

Do you remember the first time you traveled to a foreign country? You probably were surprised by how many of the normal things in your life were different there. The food was different, people wore different clothes, houses were constructed and furnished differently, and the pattern of social relations differed (for instance, whether they talked to strangers or stood in queues). You were observing how social norms shape what people eat, how they dress, how they live, and maybe even on which side of the road they drive.

Similarly, each nation has its own political norms that influence how people think about and react to politics. Americans' strong feelings of patriotism, the Japanese deference to political elites, and the French proclivity for protest all illustrate how cultural norms shape politics. The way political institutions function at least partially reflects the public's attitudes, norms, and expectations. Thus, the English use their constitutional arrangements to sustain their liberty, while the same institutions were once used as a means of repression in South Africa and Northern Ireland. When a new regime forms, a supportive public can help develop the new system, while the absence of public support may weaken the new system. To understand the political tendencies in a nation, we must begin with public attitudes toward politics and their role within the political system—what we call a nation's political culture.

Chapter 1 stated that one main goal of any government, and a special challenge for a new government, is to create and maintain a political community. In part, this involves developing common structures and systems (such as a single economy), common political institutions, and common political processes. At the level of the public, this involves developing common worldviews, values, and expectations among the public that together comprise the nation's political culture. So studying political culture partially explains how a political community is created and sustained.

In this chapter we map the important parts of political culture. We then discuss political socialization: how individuals form their political attitudes and thus, collectively, how citizens form their political culture. We conclude by describing the major trends in political culture in world politics today.

MAPPING THE THREE LEVELS OF POLITICAL CULTURE

A nation's **political culture** includes its citizens' orientations at three levels: the political system, the political and policymaking process, and policy outputs and outcomes (Table 3.1). The *system* level involves how people view the values and organizations that comprise the political system. Do citizens identify with the nation and accept the general system of government? The *process* level includes expectations of how politics should function, and individuals' relationship to the political process. The *policy* level deals with the public's policy expectations for the government. What should be the policy goals of government and how are they to be achieved?

Aspects of Political Culture	Examples
TABLE 3.1 The Aspects of Political Culture	
System	Pride in nation National identity Legitimacy of government
Process	Role of citizens Perceptions of political rights
Policy	Role of government Government policy priorities

The System Level

Orientations toward the political system are important because they tap basic commitments to the polity and the nation. It is difficult for any political system to endure if it lacks the support of its citizens.

Feelings of national pride are considered an affective, emotional tie to a political system. National pride seems strongest in nations with a long history that has emphasized feelings of patriotism—the United States is a prime example (see Figure 3.1). Such a common sense of identity and national history often binds a people together in times of political strain. The figure indicates that high levels of pride exist in nations with very different political and economic systems, such as the United States and Poland. In contrast, national pride is low in Japan and Germany, two nations that have avoided nationalist sentiments in reaction to the World War II regimes and their excesses. In other cases, ethnicity, language, or history divide the public, which may strain national identities and ultimately lead to conflict and division.

Feelings of popular **legitimacy** are another foundation for a successful political system. When people believe that they ought to obey the laws, legitimacy is high. If they see no reason to obey or if they comply only from fear, legitimacy is low. Because it is much easier for government to function when citizens believe in the legitimacy of the system, virtually all governments, even the most brutal and coercive, try to encourage people to believe that they should obey the laws. A political system and a government with high legitimacy are typically more effective in carrying out policies and are more likely to overcome hardships and reversals.

Citizens may grant legitimacy to a government for different reasons. In a traditional society, legitimacy may depend on the ruler's inheriting the throne or on the ruler's commitment to religious customs. In a modern democracy, the legitimacy of the authorities depends on their selection by voters in competitive elections and on the government following constitutional procedures. In other political cultures, the leaders may base their claim to legitimacy on their special wisdom or ideology, which they claim will transform people's lives for the better, even though the government does not respond to specific public demands or follow prescribed procedures.[1] Theocratic regimes, such as Iran, base their legitimacy on adherence to religious principles. Thus, legitimacy also presumes an agreement on the broad form of government that defines the political system and thus the standards of legitimacy: monarchical rule, a tribal system, a communist order, or a democratic system.

Whether legitimacy is based on tradition, ideology, elections, or religion, feelings of legitimacy reflect a basic understanding between citizens and political authorities. Citizens obey the laws and in return the government meets the obligations set by the terms of its legitimacy. As long as the government meets its obligations, the public is supposed to be supportive and act appropriately. If legitimacy is violated—the line of succession is broken, the constitution is subverted, or the ruling ideology is ignored—the government may expect resistance and perhaps rebellion.

In systems with low legitimacy, people often resort to violence or extra-governmental actions to solve political disagreements. Legitimacy is lacking where the public disputes the boundaries of the political system (as in Northern Ireland or Kashmir), rejects the current arrangements for recruiting leaders and making policies (as when Indonesians took to the streets in 1998 demanding a new democratic regime), or loses confidence that the leaders are fulfilling their part of the political bargain (as when the Thai opposition forced the prime minister from office in 2006).

The Soviet Union disintegrated in the early 1990s because all three legitimacy problems appeared. After the communist ideology failed as a legitimizing force, there was no basis for a national political community in the absence of common language or ethnicity. Similarly, the loss of confidence in the Communist Party as a political organization led many people to

100	Egypt
	United States/Poland
	Mexico/Canada/Iran
	Peru/Finland
	India/Argentina
90	Nigeria
	France
	Britain/Hungary/Turkey
	Sweden/Italy
	Israel
	China
80	Latvia/Czech Republic
	Netherlands
	Germany (East)
70	
	Russia
	Estonia
	Germany (West)
60	
	Japan/Lithuania

Feelings of National Pride   **FIGURE 3.1**
(in percent)

Source: Selected nations from the 2000–2002 *World Values Survey* and the 1999 *European Values Survey*. Figure entries are the percent "proud" and "very proud"; missing data are excluded from the calculation of percentages.

call for institutional reform. Finally, shortages of food and consumer goods caused people to lose faith in the government's short-term economic and political policies. Soviet President Mikhail Gorbachev failed in his efforts to deal with all three problems at the same time.

The Process Level

The second level of the political culture involves what the public expects of the political process. Whether you are English or Nigerian, what do you think about the institutions of your political system and what is expected of you as a citizen?

Broadly speaking, three different patterns describe the citizen's role in the political process:[2]

- **Participants** are, or have the potential to be, involved in the political process. They are informed about politics and make demands on the polity, granting their support to political leaders based on performance.
- **Subjects** passively obey government officials and the law, but they do not vote or actively involve themselves in politics.
- **Parochials** are hardly aware of government and politics. They may be illiterates, rural people living in remote areas, or simply people who ignore politics and its impact on their lives.

As shown in Figure 3.2, in a hypothetical modern industrial democracy a majority are participants, a third are simply subjects, and a small group are parochials. This distribution provides enough political activists to ensure competition among political parties and sizable voter turnout, as well as critical audiences for debate on public issues by parties, candidates, and pressure groups. At the same time, not all citizens feel the need to be active in or concerned about the political system.

The second column in Figure 3.2 shows the pattern we expect in an industrialized authoritarian society, such as the former communist nations of Eastern Europe. A small minority of citizens are involved in a one-party system, which penetrates and oversees the society, as well as decides government policies. Most other citizens are mobilized as subjects by political institutions: political parties, the bureaucracy, and government-controlled mass media. People are encouraged and even forced to cast a symbolic vote of support in elections and to pay taxes, obey regulations, and follow the dictates of government. Because of the effectiveness of modern social organization and the efforts of the authoritarian power structure, few people are unaware of the government and its influence on their lives. If such a society suddenly attempts to democratize its politics, many people must learn to become democrats and participants.

The third column shows an authoritarian society that is partly traditional and partly modern, such as in Iran or China. In spite of an authoritarian political system, some participants—students and intellectuals, for example—oppose the system and try to change it

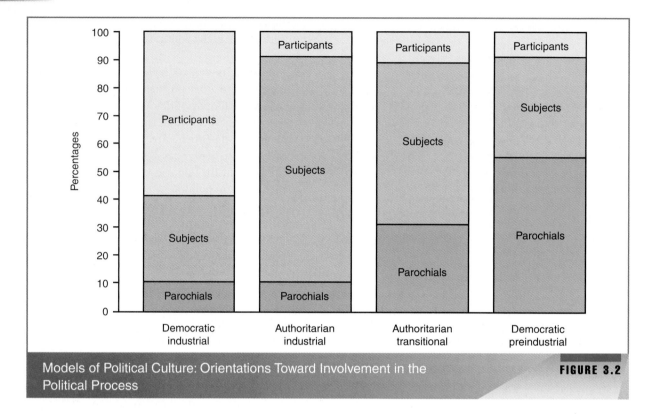

Models of Political Culture: Orientations Toward Involvement in the
Political Process

FIGURE 3.2

by persuasion or acts of protest. Favored groups, like business people and landowners, discuss public issues and engage in lobbying. Most people in such systems are passive subjects, aware of government and complying with the law but not otherwise involved in public affairs. The parochials—poor and illiterate urban dwellers, peasants, or farm laborers—have limited contact with the political system.

The fourth column shows the democratic preindustrial system, perhaps India or Nigeria, which has a predominantly rural, illiterate population. In such a country, the few political participants are chiefly educated professionals, business people, and landowners. A much larger number of employees, workers, and farmers are directly affected by government taxation and other official policies. The largest group of people are illiterate peasants, whose knowledge of and involvement with national politics are minimal. Such a society faces a significant challenge to create a more aware public that can participate meaningfully and shape government policies through democratic means.

Attitudes toward the citizen's role are also shaped by the political form of the regime. In the early 1900s, many different political systems existed worldwide.

Fascism was on the rise in Europe, communism was establishing itself in the Soviet Union, colonial administrations governed large parts of the world, and monarchical or authoritarian governments ruled other nations. All of these systems encouraged a restrictive role for the citizens. Western Europe and North America were the democracies in this sea of conflicting currents.

Today, many of these nondemocratic forms of governance are no longer widely accepted. Communism still has strongholds in China and Cuba, but it has lost its image as a progressive force for global change. Some nations still accept autocratic or religiously based systems of government. However, the global wave of democratization since the early 1990s has raised democratic principles to a position of prominence (see Figure 1.3 in Chapter 1). Democratic norms emphasize the importance of a participatory system, majority rule and minority rights, and the values of political tolerance. Most of the people in the world today seem to favor democratic principles even if they differ in how those principles should be applied.[3]

The distribution of these citizen types and political norms is affected by the process of social and

Becoming Modern

BOX 3.1

Alex Inkeles and David Smith report how one Nigerian worker replied to a question about how his new job in a factory made him feel. "Sometimes like 9 feet tall with arms a yard wide. Here in the factory I alone with my machine can twist any way I want a piece of steel that all the men in my home village together could not begin to bend at all." Such experiences—and the parallel changes in educational levels and access to information—can create a more modern political culture.

Source: Alex Inkeles and David Smith, *Becoming Modern* (Cambridge, Harvard University Press, 1974), 158.

economic **modernization** that we introduced in Chapter 1. Industrialization, urbanization, and improved living standards transform the social base of a nation. Exposure to modernity through work, education, and the media shapes an individual's personal experiences and sends messages about norms in other societies. It encourages citizen participation, a sense of individual equality, the desire for improved living standards and increased life expectancy, and government legitimacy based on policy performance. It also frequently disrupts familiar ways of life, traditional bases of legitimacy, and political arrangements that depend on citizens remaining parochials or subjects. In addition, the secularizing influences of science can alter economic and social systems, which then reshapes the political culture. This modernization trend has powerful effects as it penetrates societies (or parts of societies). Alex Inkeles and David Smith's classic study of modernization emphasized how factory experience can create an awareness of the possibilities of organization, change, and control over nature that empowers the individual (see Box 3.1).

This modernization process is spread unevenly across the globe. The advanced industrial societies have the largest proportion of citizens who are participants and cognitively engaged in politics. The recent economic growth in East Asia is similarly transforming the political culture and political behavior in these nations.[4] In contrast, modernization has proceeded more slowly and uncertainly in Africa and Arab nations. Some political leaders in these nations even reject the principles of modernization as incongruent with their national values. However, there is persuasive evidence that where social and economic modernization occurs, it transforms the political culture to emphasize self-expression, participatory values, and autonomy.[5]

The Policy Level

What is the appropriate role of government? If you ask political theorists, you get a wide range of answers—from the minimal state to the all-encompassing polity (see Chapter 1). And if you travel to other nations, you quickly realize that there is wide variation in how people answer this question.

The policy activities of a country are influenced by public images of what constitutes the good society and the government's role in achieving these goals. Should government manage the economy, or should private property rights and market forces guide economic activity? Should the state intervene in addressing social and moral issues, or should it follow a minimalist strategy? The ongoing debates over "big government" versus "small government" in democratic states, and between socialist and market-based economies reflect these different images of the scope of government.

We can illustrate differences in policy expectations with an opinion survey question that asks whether the government is responsible to provide for everyone (see Figure 3.3). The range in opinions is considerable, about three-quarters of respondents in Nigeria and Sweden believe this is a government responsibility compared with only a quarter of the French or West Germans. In general, people in developing nations and in the formerly communist nations of Eastern Europe are more supportive of a large government role—reflecting both their social condition and their past political ideologies. In some Western nations, such as Sweden and Finland, traditions include a large role for the government. In general, however, support for government action generally decreases as national affluence increases.[6]

Cubans wave flags at a pro-government rally organized by the Castro government.

AP Images

Policy expectations also involve specific issue demands.[7] Indeed, each country study in this book begins with a discussion of the policy challenges facing the nation and the public's issue concerns. This sets the agenda of politics that responsive governments should address.

Some policy goals, such as economic well-being, are valued by nearly everyone. Concern about other policy goals may vary widely across nations because of the nation's circumstances and because of cultural traditions. People in developing countries are more likely to focus on the government's provision of basic services to ensure public welfare. Advanced industrial societies have the resources to provide for basic needs. In these nations, people are often more concerned with quality-of-life goals, such as preservation of nature and even government support for the arts.[8] One basic measure of a government's performance is its ability to meet the policy expectations of its citizens.

Another set of expectations involves the functioning of government. Some cultures put more weight on the policy outputs of government, such as providing welfare and security. Other cultures also emphasize how the process functions, which involves values such as the rule of law and procedural justice. Among Germans, for example, the rule of law is given great importance; in many developing nations political relations are personally based, and there is less willingness to rely on legalistic frameworks.

Consensual or Conflictual Political Cultures

Although political culture is a common characteristic of a nation, values and beliefs can also vary within it. Political cultures may be consensual or conflictual on issues of public policy and, more fundamentally, on views of legitimate governmental and political arrangements. In some societies, citizens generally agree on the norms of political decisionmaking and their policy expectations. In other societies—because of differences in histories, conditions, or identities—the citizens are sharply divided, often on both the legitimacy of the regime and solutions to major problems.[9]

When a country is deeply divided in its political values and these differences persist over time, distinctive **political subcultures** may develop. The citizens in these subcultures may have sharply different points of view on some critical political matters, such as the boundaries of the nation, the nature of the regime, or the correct ideology. They may affiliate with different political parties

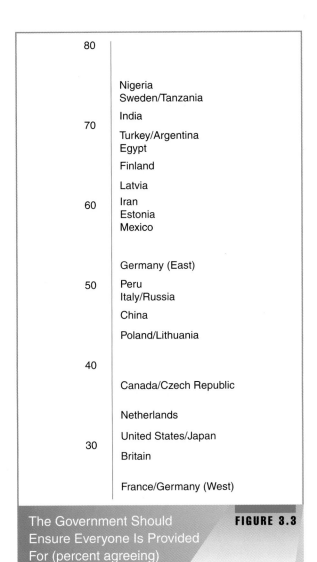

FIGURE 3.3

The Government Should Ensure Everyone Is Provided For (percent agreeing)

Source: Selected nations from the 2000–2002 *World Values Survey* and 1999 *European Values Survey*; missing data are excluded from the calculation of percentages.

of peoples into new areas—made possible by easier transportation and encouraged by wars, political conflicts, and the desire for economic betterment—can seem to threaten the way of life of the host society. The exposure to values from other cultures also may intensify one's own self-image, which may increase cultural tensions. Although such exposure may eventually lead to greater tolerance, that outcome is not guaranteed.

WHY CULTURE MATTERS

Political culture does not explain everything about politics. Even people with similar values and skills might behave differently from each other when they face different situations. Nor is political culture unchangeable. However, cultural norms typically change slowly and reflect stable values. Thus, political culture is important first because it encapsulates the history, traditions, and values of a society. To understand how most people in a nation think and act politically, we can begin by understanding their political culture. Political culture can create the common political community that is one goal of government.

In addition, the distribution of cultural patterns is typically related to the type of political process that citizens expect and support. This is the principle of *congruence theory*. For instance, support for a democratic system is typically higher in societies that have a more participatory political culture. Authoritarian states are more likely to endure when the public is characterized by subjects and parochials—where individuals lack the skills or motivations to participate and the state discourages their participation. These cultural norms represent the "rules of the game" for the political system, and the system works better when citizens accept these rules. Where political structures and political cultures are mutually reinforcing, a more stable political system is likely to emerge.

We can illustrate the logic of congruence theory in terms of the relationship between political culture and the democratic development of a nation (Figure 3.4). The horizontal axis of the figure displays the public's adherence to self-expressive values, reflecting the participatory norms we discussed earlier. The vertical axis represents the democratic development of the nation based on a variety of expert evaluations. You can see that as participatory values increase, so too does the democratic development of the nation. The nations

and interest groups, read different newspapers, and even have separate social clubs and sporting groups. Thus, they are exposed to different information about politics. For instance, such subcultural differences characterize the publics in India, Nigeria, and Russia today.

In some instances, historical or social factors generate different cultural trajectories. For instance, *ethnic*, *religious*, or *linguistic* identities in many parts of the world shape citizen values.[10] Moreover, as such groups increase their political skills and self-confidence, they may express their identities and demand equal treatment. In fact, the processes of globalization might actually heighten these cultural contrasts.[11] The migration

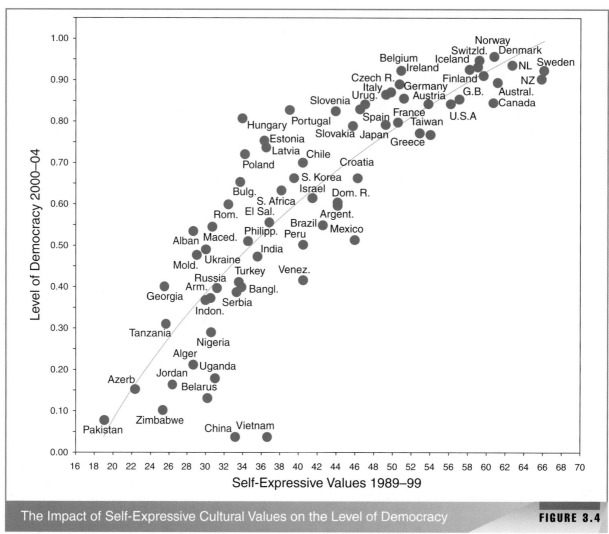

The Impact of Self-Expressive Cultural Values on the Level of Democracy

FIGURE 3.4

Source: The self-expressive values measure is from the *World Values Survey*; higher scores represent more citizen emphasis on self-expression. The level of democracy measure is a composite of the ranking of democracy by the Freedom House and other national rankings. Higher scores indicate a higher level of democratic development. For additional discussion of these measures see Ronald Inglehart and Christian Welzel, *Modernization, Cultural Change and Democracy: The Human Development Sequence* (New York: Cambridge University Press, 2005).

in this book that are included in these analyses show a clear differentiation between the established Western democracies, relatively new democracies (such as Russia and other East European nations), and nondemocracies (such as China and several Middle East nations). Structure and culture do overlap in these nations.[12]

Do democracies create a participatory democratic public or does such a political culture lead to a democratic political system? It works both ways. For example, immediately after World War II, Germans were less supportive of democracy, but political institutions and political experiences transformed their culture over the next generation.[13] At the same time, democracy

endured in Britain during the strains of the Great Depression and World War II, at least in part because the British public supported the democratic process. The important conclusion is that there is normally a relationship between political culture and political structures.

Beyond shaping the structure of the political system, a nation's political culture also influences the style of politics and the content of policymaking. We have stressed how the policy elements of a political culture can influence the content of policy. In addition, research suggests that cultural factors, such as social trust and engagement, influence the efficiency and effectiveness of government.[14]

Finally, while the political culture may help build a national community, it may also provide a basis of division. For instance, where political subcultures coincide with ethnic, linguistic, or religious differences—as in Northern Ireland, Bosnia, and Lebanon—the divisions can be enduring and threatening. The fragmentation of the Soviet empire, the breakup of Yugoslavia, and the impulses toward autonomy and secession among ethnically distinct regions (such as in Scotland or separatist movements in Africa) all reflect the lasting power of language, culture, and historical memory to create and sustain the sense of ethnic and national identity among parts of contemporary states. In broader international terms, Samuel Huntington has divided the world into different civilizations defined by their religious and cultural traditions.[15] He then predicted that these cultural differences will be a major source of international conflict in this century. While culture may have the power to divide, it is counterbalanced by its potential to build a common political community.

POLITICAL SOCIALIZATION

Political cultures are sustained or changed as people acquire their attitudes and values. *Political socialization* refers to the way in which political values are formed and the political culture is transmitted from one generation to the next. Most children acquire their basic political values and behavior patterns by adolescence.[16] Some of these attitudes will evolve and change throughout their lives, while other attitudes may remain part of their political self throughout life.

At any specific time, a person's political beliefs are a combination of various feelings and attitudes. At the deepest level, there are general identifications, such as nationalism, ethnic or class self-images, religious and ideological commitments, and a fundamental sense of rights and duties in the society. At the middle level, people develop attitudes toward politics and governmental institutions. Finally, there are more immediate views of current events, policies, issues, and personalities. All these attitudes can change, but those in the first level usually were acquired earliest, have been most frequently reinforced, and tend to be the most durable.

Three points about political socialization deserve mention. First, the socialization process can occur in different ways. Direct socialization involves an actor explicitly communicating information, values, or feelings toward politics. Examples of direct socialization include civics courses in the schools, public education programs of the government, and the political information campaigns of interest groups. Communist political systems also heavily use direct indoctrination programs (see Box 3.2). Indirect political socialization occurs when political views are inadvertently molded by our experiences. For example, children normally learn important political values by observing the behavior of their parents, teachers, and friends. Or, people may learn by observing the political and social

---

Socializing Values   BOX 3.2

Communist East Germany had a special ceremony for eighth graders to mark their passage to adulthood. The heart of the ceremony was the endorsement of the following four pledges:

- As young citizens of our German Democratic Republic, are you prepared to work and fight loyally for the great and honorable goals of socialism, and to honor the revolutionary inheritance of the people?
- As sons and daughters of the worker-and-peasant state, are you prepared to pursue higher education, to cultivate your mind, to become a master of

your trade, to learn permanently, and to use your knowledge to pursue our great humanist ideals?
- As honorable members of the socialist community, are you ready to cooperate as comrades, to respect and support each other, and to always merge the pursuit of your personal happiness with the happiness of all the people?
- As true patriots, are you ready to deepen the friendship with the Soviet Union, to strengthen our brotherhood with socialist countries, to struggle in the spirit of proletarian internationalism, to protect peace and to defend socialism against every imperialist aggression?

context that surrounds them, watching what governments do and how other citizens react.

Second, socialization is a lifelong process. Early family influences can create an individual's initial values, but subsequent life experiences—becoming involved in new social groups, moving from one part of the country to another, shifting up or down the social ladder, becoming a parent, finding or losing a job—may change one's political perspectives. More dramatic experiences—such as relocating to a new country or suffering through an economic depression or a war—can alter even basic political attitudes. Such events seem to have their greatest impact on young people, but people at any age are affected to some degree.

Third, patterns of socialization can unify or divide. Governments design public education systems, for instance, to create a single national political culture. Some events, such as international conflict or the death of a popular public figure, can affect nearly the entire nation similarly. In contrast, subcultures in a society can have their own distinctive patterns of socialization. Social groups that provide their members with their own newspapers, their own neighborhood groups, and perhaps their own schools can create distinctive subcultural attitudes. Divisive patterns of socialization can lead to a political gap among members of a nation.

AGENTS OF POLITICAL SOCIALIZATION

Individuals in all societies are affected by **agents of political socialization:** individuals, organizations, and institutions that influence political attitudes. Some, like civics courses in schools, are direct and deliberate sources of political learning. Others, like playgroups and work groups, affect political socialization indirectly.

The Family

The direct and indirect influences of the family—the first socialization source that an individual encounters—are normally powerful and lasting. The family has distinctive influences on attitudes toward authority. Participation in family decision making can increase a child's sense of political competence, providing skills for political interaction and encouraging active participation in the political system as an adult. Similarly, unquestioning obedience to parental decisions may lead a child toward a role as a political subject. The family also shapes future political attitudes by defining a social position for the child: establishing ethnic, linguistic, class, and religious ties; affirming cultural values; and influencing job aspirations.

The nature of the family is changing in many societies. Family sizes are generally decreasing, which changes the pattern of family life. In addition, there has been a marked rise of single-parent families, especially in the advanced industrial democracies. The impact of these structural changes on family socialization patterns is still unclear.

In addition, gender roles are changing in many industrial nations, although they persist in many less developed nations.[17] The rise of the women's movement and self-help groups has encouraged women to become politically active and change social cues about how women should relate to politics. The lessening of gender differences in self-images, in parental roles, and in relations to the economy and the political system is significantly affecting patterns of political recruitment, political participation, and public policy. A more open family, equality of parenting, and the early exposure of children to childcare and preschool group experiences have modified the impact of the family in the socialization process. Especially in the developing world, the changing role of women may have profound influences in modernizing the society.[18]

Schools

Schools educate children about politics and their role in the process, providing them with information on political institutions and relationships. Schools can also help shape attitudes about the political system, the rules of the political game, the appropriate role of the citizen, and expectations about the government. Schools typically reinforce attachments to the political system and reinforce common symbols, such as the flag and Pledge of Allegiance, that encourage emotional attachments to the system. When a new nation comes into being, or a revolutionary regime comes to power in an old nation, it usually turns immediately to the schools as a means to supplant "outdated" values and symbols with new ones more congruent with the new ideology.

In some nations, educational systems do not provide unifying political socialization but send starkly different messages to different groups. For instance, some Muslim nations segregate girls and boys within the school system. Even if educational experiences are intended to be equal, segregation creates different experiences and expectations. Moreover, the content of education often differs between boys and girls. Perhaps the worst example occurred under the Taliban in Afghanistan, where for several years young girls were prohibited from attending school. Such treatment of young girls severely limits their life changes, and ensures they will have restricted roles in society and the economy—which was the intent of the Taliban system. The new Afghanistan government reversed this policy, and now young girls are being included in the education system, and their future life prospects are improving as a result.

Education also affects the political skills and resources of the public. Educated people are more aware of the impact of government on their lives and pay more attention to politics.[19] The better educated have mental skills that improve their ability to manage the world of politics. They also have more information about political processes and participate in a wider range of political activities.

Religious Institutions

The religions of the world are carriers of cultural and moral values, which often have political implications. The great religious leaders have seen themselves as teachers, and their followers have usually attempted to shape the socialization of children through schooling, preaching, and religious services. In most nations, there are formal ties between the dominant religion and the government. In these instances, religious values and public policy often overlap. Catholic nations, for instance, are less likely to have liberal abortion policies, just as Islamic governments enforce strict moral codes.

Religious institutions of many kinds offer valuable moral and ethical guidance that individuals often need to make choices in complex societies. Religious affiliations are often important sources of partisan preferences and can guide people in making other political choices. Thus, even though church attendance is decreasing in many nations, the political relevance of religion continues.

Where churches teach values that may be at odds with the controlling political system, the struggle over socialization can be intense. These tensions can take a

wide variety of forms: the clash between secular and religious roles in the French educational system, the efforts of American fundamentalists to introduce prayer in the schools, or the conflict between Islamic fundamentalists and secular governments in Algeria and Egypt. In such cases, religious groups may oppose the policies of the state, or even the state itself.

The emergence of religious fundamentalism in recent decades has influenced the society and politics of countries as diverse as the United States, India, Israel, Lebanon, Iran, Pakistan, Algeria, and Nigeria. Such **fundamentalism** is often a defensive reaction against the spread of scientific views of nature and human behavior, and the libertarian values and attitudes that accompany these views.[20] The influence of fundamentalism has been most visible in the Middle East and in Muslim countries, but it is important in Christian countries as well. Both Protestant and Catholic versions of fundamentalism exist in the United States, Europe, and Latin America. Versions of fundamentalism also exist, combined with ethnic and nationalist tendencies, in the Confucian, Buddhist, and Hindu countries of Asia. Broadly speaking, fundamentalism seeks to raise conservative social, moral, and religious issues to the top of the contemporary policy agenda.

Peer Groups

Peer groups also shape political attitudes. They include childhood playgroups, friendship cliques, school and college fraternities, small work groups, and other groups in which members share relatively equal status and close ties. They can be as varied as a group of Russian mothers who meet regularly at the park, to a street gang in Brazil, to a group of Wall Street executives who are members of a health club.

A peer group socializes its members by motivating or pressuring them to conform to the attitudes or behavior accepted by the group. Individuals often adopt the views of their peers because they like or respect them or because they want to be like them. Similarly, an individual may become interested in politics or attend a political demonstration because close friends do so. One example of peer networks is the international youth culture symbolized by rock music, T-shirts, and blue jeans (and more liberal political values). Some observers claim that it played a major role in the failure of communist officials to mold Soviet and

Eastern European youth to the "socialist personality" that was the Marxist-Leninist ideal. Likewise, the "skinheads" groups that have sprouted up among lower-class youth in many Western countries have adopted political views that are based on peer interactions.

Social Class

Most societies have significant social divisions based on class or occupation. Individuals live in different social worlds defined by their class position. For instance, industrialization in Britain created a working class that was concentrated in particular neighborhoods. This working class developed its own forms of speech, dress, recreation, and entertainment, as well as its own social organizations (such as social clubs, trade unions, and political parties). Similarly, the life experience of the rural peasantry in many less developed nations is radically different from urban dwellers. Often, these social divisions are politically relevant: identifying yourself as a member of the working class or the peasantry leads to distinct political views about what issues are important and which political groups best represent your interest.

Interest Groups

Interest groups, economic groups, and similar organizations also shape political attitudes. In most industrial countries, the rise of trade unions transformed the political culture and politics, created new political parties, and ushered in new social benefit programs. Today, unions are active participants in the political process and try to persuade their members on political matters. Other professional associations—such as groups of peasants and farmers, manufacturers, wholesalers and retailers, medical societies, and lawyers—also regularly influence political attitudes in modern and modernizing societies. These groups ensure the loyalty of their members by defending their economic and professional interests. They can also provide valuable political cues to nonmembers, who might identify with a group's interests or political ideology. For instance, when a group that you like (or dislike) publicly supports a policy, it gives you information on the likely content of the policy.

The groups that define a civil society are also potential agents of socialization. These groups might include ethnic organizations, fraternal associations, civic associations (such as parent-teacher associations), and policy groups (such as taxpayers' associations, women's groups, and environmental groups). Such groups provide valuable political cues to their members and try to reinforce distinct social and political orientations. They also provide settings to learn about how making political choices in small groups can be extended to politics. For instance, Vietnam has an active network of social groups that socialize individuals into the norms of the communist regime; while civil society groups in the United States are treated as

The international press cover an emergency summit of the Organization of the Islamic Conference (OIC) called to discuss the Iraqi crisis in March 2003.

AP Images

democracy-building organizations.[21] In addition, these groups—using the media and other sources—send out large quantities of information on political, social, and economic issues to the public and elites.

Political Parties

Political parties normally play an important role in political socialization. In democratic systems, political parties attempt to mold issue preferences, arouse the apathetic, and find new issues to mobilize support. Party representatives provide the public with a steady flow of information on the political issues of the day. Party organizations regularly contact voters by mail or phone, and in many nations party activists visit voters at home. In addition, every few years there is an election in which parties present their accomplishments and discuss the nation's political future. Elections can serve as national civics lessons, and the political parties are the teachers.

In competitive democratic party systems, partisan socialization can be also a divisive force. In their efforts to gain support, party leaders may appeal to class, language, religion, and ethnic divisions and make citizens more aware of these differences. The Labour and Conservative parties in Britain, for example, use traditional symbols of class to attract supporters. Similarly, the Congress Party in India tries to develop a national program and appeal, but other parties emphasize the ethnic and religious divisions. Leaders of preindustrial nations often oppose competitive parties because they fear such divisiveness. Although this is sometimes a sincere concern, it is also self-serving to government leaders, and is increasingly difficult to justify against contemporary demands for multiparty systems.

Authoritarian governments often use a single party to inculcate common attitudes of national unity, support for the government, and ideological agreement. The combination of a single party and controlled mass media is potent: the media present a single point of view, and the party activities reinforce that perspective by directly involving the citizen. In a closed environment, single-party governments can be potent agents of socialization.

Mass Media

The mass media—newspapers, radio, television, magazines—are important in socializing attitudes and values in nations around the globe. The mass media are typically the prime source of information on the politics of the day. There is virtually no place so remote that people lack the means to be informed about events elsewhere: in affluent nations the public is wired to the Internet, satellite dishes sprout from houses in Iran, inexpensive transistor radios are omnipresent even in Third World villages far removed from urban centers.

There is one thing most people in the world share in common: we sit before our televisions to learn about the world.[22] Television can have a powerful cognitive and emotional impact on large public audiences by enlisting the senses of both sight and sound. Watching events on television—such as the broadcasts of government affairs or the war in Iraq—gives a reality to the news. Seeing the world directly can shape political attitudes. Today, the Internet provides another powerful source of news for those with access to it.

Access to information thus becomes an important political commodity in the contemporary world. Western democracies put a premium on freedom of the media, even if they frequently complain about what the media reports. In many European nations, the government still manages television and radio stations because it views the media as a public service. Autocratic governments typically seek to control the media and what they can report, as well as the public's access to information (see Box 3.3). Similarly, the communist regimes of Eastern Europe had tried to limit access to news reports from the West because they feared it would undermine their regimes, and the movements for democracy in the region were partially created by the image of the way of life in the West. In the contemporary world of Internet and satellite broadcasting, it is becoming increasingly difficult for governments to control the spread of information.

Direct Contact with the Government

In modern societies, the wide scope of governmental activities brings citizens into frequent contact with various bureaucratic agencies. One survey of Americans found that about a third had had contact with a government official (federal, state, or local) in the preceding year.[23] Citizens contacted a wide range of government offices, from federal officials, to state and local governments, to school boards and the police. In addition, the government touches our lives in a myriad of other ways, from running the public schools to providing retirement

BOX 3.3

The Great Firewall of China

The People's Republic of China currently has the largest number of Internet users of any nation in the world, except the United States, and this fact has government officials worried. Chinese "netizens" find themselves surfing in the shadow of the world's most sophisticated censorship machine. There is now an estimated 30,000-strong Internet police force, which—with the aid of Western-provided technology—is dedicated to monitoring websites and e-mails. On a technical level, the five gateways that connect China to the global Internet filter traffic coming into and going out of the country. Keyword blocking technology—much of it provided by U.S. companies such as Microsoft and Google—prevents access to offending sites. Even the country's 110,000 Internet cafes are now highly regulated and state-licensed, and all are equipped with standard surveillance systems.

Source: Richard Taylor, "The Great Firewall of China," *BBC News*, January 6, 2006.

checks to providing social services. The degree of government intervention in daily life, and hence the necessity for contacts with government, varies greatly across nations as a function of their political system and the role of government in the society.

These personal experiences are powerful agents of socialization, strengthening or undercutting the images presented by other agents. Does the government send retirement checks on time? Do city officials respond to citizen complaints? Are the schools teaching children? Do unemployment offices help people find jobs? Are the highways well maintained? These are very direct sources of information on how well the government functions. No matter how positive the view of the political system that people have learned as children, citizens who face a different reality in everyday life are likely to change their early-learned views. Indeed, the contradictions between ideology and reality proved to be one of the weaknesses of the communist systems in Eastern Europe.

In summary, the country chapters in this book all examine the patterns of political socialization for several reasons. The sources of political socialization often determine the content of what is learned about politics. If people learn about new events from their friends at church, they may hear different information than people who rely on their workplace or the television for information. The role of these different socialization agents and the content of their political messages also vary systematically across nations. In addition, the ability of a nation to re-create its political culture in succeeding generations is an important factor in perpetuating the political system. Finally, cultures change when new elements are added to the process of political learning.

Thus, socialization provides the feedback mechanism that enables a political culture to endure or change.

TRENDS SHAPING CONTEMPORARY POLITICAL CULTURES

A political culture exists uniquely in its own time and place. Citizens' attitudes and beliefs are shaped by personal experiences and by the agents of political socialization. Yet, in any historical period there may be trends that change the culture in many nations. The major social trends of our time reflect both general societal developments and specific historic events.

For the past two decades, a major new development is the trend toward democracy in Eastern Europe, East Asia, and other parts of the developing world. This **democratization** trend reflects long-term responses to modernity as well as immediate reactions to current events. Modernization gradually eroded the legitimacy of nondemocratic ideologies, while the development of citizens' skills and political resources made their claim to equal participation in policymaking (at least indirectly) more plausible. Thus, many studies of political culture in Eastern Europe and the former Soviet Union uncovered surprising support for democratic norms and processes among the citizenry as the new democratic system formed.[24]

Ironically, as democracy has begun taking root in Eastern Europe, citizens in many Western democracies are increasingly skeptical about politicians and political institutions. In 1964, three-quarters of Americans said they trusted the government; today only a third of the public say as much—and the malaise is spreading to

Western Europe and Japan.[25] At the same time, public support for democratic norms and values has strengthened over time in most Western democracies. Thus, these publics are critical of politicians and political parties when they fall short of these democratic ideals. Although this cynicism is a strain on democratic politicians, it presses democracy to continue to improve and adapt, which is ultimately democracy's greatest strength.

Another recent major trend affecting political cultures is a shift toward **marketization**—that is, an increased public acceptance of free markets and private profit incentives, rather than a government-managed economy. One example of this movement appeared in the United States and many Western European nations beginning in the 1980s, where economies had experienced serious problems of inefficiency and economic stagnation. Margaret Thatcher in Britain and Ronald Reagan in the United States rode to power on waves of public support for reducing the scale of government. Public opinion surveys show that people in these nations felt that government had grown too large (see again Figure 3.3).

Just as Western Europeans began to question the government's role in the economy, the political changes in Eastern Europe and the Soviet Union transformed the discussion. The command economies of Eastern Europe were almost exclusively controlled by state corporations and government agencies. The government set both wages and prices and directed the economy. The collapse of these systems raised new questions about public support for marketization. Public opinion

surveys generally find that Eastern Europeans support a capitalist market system and the public policies that would support such an economic system.[26]

Globalization is another trend affecting political cultures of many nations. Increasing international trade and international interactions tend to diffuse the values of the overall international system. Thus, as developing nations become more engaged in the global economy and global international system, the development of certain norms—such as human rights, gender equality, and democratic values—increases.[27] People in developing nations also learn about the broader opportunities existing in other nations, which can spur cultural change as well as economic change. Thus, although globalization has been a deeply divisive political issue for the past decade in many nations, the Pew Global Values Survey found broad support for globalization among citizens worldwide—especially in developing nations where it is seen as improving living standards and life chances.[28]

Clearly, political culture is not a static phenomenon, so our understanding of political culture must be dynamic. It must encompass how the agents of political socialization communicate and interpret historic events and traditional values. It must juxtapose these factors with the exposure of citizens and leaders to new experiences and new ideas. But it is important to understand the political culture of a nation, because these cultural factors influence how citizens act, how the political process functions, and what policy goals the government pursues.

REVIEW QUESTIONS

- What are the three key elements of a political culture?

- Why does political culture matter?

- Why is the process of political socialization important?

- What are the main agents of political socialization?

- What are the major trends in cultural change in the contemporary world?

KEY TERMS

agents of political
   socialization
democratization
fundamentalism

legitimacy
marketization
modernization

parochials
participants
political culture

political socialization
political subcultures
subjects

SUGGESTED READINGS

Almond, Gabriel A., and Sidney Verba. *The Civic Culture.* Princeton, NJ: Princeton University Press, 1963.

———, eds. *The Civic Culture Revisited.* Boston: Little Brown, 1980.

Barnes, Samuel, and Janos Simon, eds. *The Postcommunist Citizen.* Budapest: Erasmus Foundation, 1998.

Bratton, Michael, Robert Mattes, and E. Gyimah-Boadi. *Public Opinion, Democracy, and Market Reform in Africa.* Cambridge: Cambridge University Press, 2004.

Cleary, Matthew, and Susan C. Stokes. *Democracy and the Culture of Skepticism: Political Trust in Argentina and Mexico.* New York: Russell Sage, 2006.

Dalton, Russell. *Democratic Challenges, Democratic Choices: The Erosion of Political Support in Advanced Industrial Democracies.* Oxford: Oxford University Press, 2004.

Harrison, Lawrence, and Samuel P. Huntington, eds. *Culture Matters: How Values Shape Human Progress.* New York: Basic Books, 2000.

Horowitz, Donald. *Ethnic Groups in Conflict.* Berkeley: University of California Press, 1985.

Huntington, Samuel. *The Clash of Civilizations and the Remaking of World Order.* New York: Simon & Schuster, 1996.

Inglehart, Ronald, and Pippa Norris. *Sacred and Secular: Religion and Politics Worldwide.* Cambridge: Cambridge University Press, 2004.

Inglehart, Ronald, and Christian Welzel. *Modernization, Cultural Change, and Democracy: The Human Development Sequence.* New York: Cambridge University Press, 2005.

Inkeles, Alex, and David H. Smith. *Becoming Modern.* Cambridge: Harvard University Press, 1974.

Jennings, M. Kent. "Political Socialization," in Russell Dalton and Hans-Dieter Klingemann, eds, *Oxford Handbook of Political Behavior.* Oxford: Oxford University Press, 2007.

Jennings, M. Kent, and Richard Niemi. *Generations and Politics: A Panel Study of Young Adults and Their Parents.* Princeton, NJ: Princeton University Press, 1981.

Klingemann, Hans Dieter, Dieter Fuchs, and Jan Zielonka, eds. *Democracy and Political Culture in Eastern Europe.* London: Routledge, 2006.

Norris, Pippa, ed. *Critical Citizens: Global Support for Democratic Government.* Oxford: Oxford University Press, 1999.

Norris, Pippa, and Ronald Inglehart. *Rising Tide: Gender Equality and Cultural Change Around the World.* New York: Cambridge University Press, 2003.

Pharr, Susan, and Robert Putnam. *Disaffected Democracies: What's Troubling the Trilateral Democracies?* Princeton, NJ: Princeton University Press, 2000.

Putnam, Robert. *The Beliefs of Politicians.* New Haven, CT: Yale University Press, 1973.

———. *Making Democracy Work: Civic Traditions in Modern Italy.* Princeton, NJ: Princeton University Press, 1993.

Pye, Lucian W., and Sidney Verba, eds. *Political Culture and Political Development.* Princeton, NJ: Princeton University Press, 1965.

Rochon, Thomas. *Culture Moves: Ideas, Activism, and Changing Values.* Princeton, NJ: Princeton University Press, 1998.

Rose, Richard, Christian Haerpfer, and William Mishler. *Testing the Churchill Hypothesis: Democracy and Its Alternatives in Postcommunist Societies.* Cambridge, UK: Polity/Baltimore: Johns Hopkins University Press, 2000.

ENDNOTES

1. This concept of legitimacy and its bases in different societies draws on the work of Max Weber. See, for example, Max Weber, *Basic Concepts in Sociology*, trans. H. P. Secher (New York: Citadel Press, 1964), chs. 5–7.

2. These terms were developed in Gabriel A. Almond and Sidney Verba, *The Civic Culture: Political Attitudes and Democracy in Five Nations* (Princeton, NJ: Princeton University Press, 1963).

3. Ronald Inglehart and Christian Welzel, *Modernization, Cultural Change, and Democracy: The Human Development Sequence* (New York: Cambridge University Press, 2005); Pippa Norris, ed., *Critical Citizens: Global Support for Democratic Government* (Oxford: Oxford University Press, 1999).

4. Russell Dalton and Doh Chull Shin, eds., *Citizens, Democracy, and Markets Around the Pacific Rim* (Oxford: Oxford University Press, 2006).

5. Inglehart and Welzel, *Modernization, Cultural Change, and Democracy.*

6. Ronald Inglehart, *Modernization and Postmodernization* (Princeton, NJ: Princeton University Press, 1997), chs. 6–7.

7. Ole Borre and Elinor Scarbrough, eds., *The Scope of Government* (Oxford: Oxford University Press, 1995).

8. Ronald Inglehart, *Culture Shift in Advanced Industrial Societies* (Princeton, NJ: Princeton University Press, 1990).

9. Even within established Western democracies, there are internal differences in the appropriate role of government, the role of the citizen, and the perceived goals of government. See Max Kaase and Ken Newton, *Beliefs in Government* (Oxford: Oxford University Press, 1995).

10. W. Kymlicka and N. Wayne, eds., *Citizenship in Divided Societies* (Oxford: Oxford University Press, 2000); Donald Horowitz, *Ethnic Groups in Conflict* (Berkeley: University of California Press, 1985).

11. Amy Chua, *World on Fire: How Exporting Free Market Democracy Breeds Ethnic Hatred and Global Instability* (New York: Doubleday, 2003).

12. See also Inglehart and Welzel, *Modernization, Cultural Change, and Democracy*.

13. Kendall Baker, Russell Dalton, and Kai Hildebrandt, *Germany Transformed* (Cambridge: Harvard University Press, 1981).

14. Robert Putnam, *Making Democracy Work: Civic Traditions in Modern Italy* (Princeton, NJ: Princeton University Press, 1993); Robert Putnam, *Bowling Alone* (New York: Simon & Schuster, 2000).

15. Samuel P. Huntington, *The Clash of Civilizations and the Remaking of World Order* (New York: Simon & Schuster, 1996); see also Fareed Zakaria, *The Future of Freedom* (New York: Norton, 2003).

16. See Almond and Verba, *Civic Culture*, ch. 12; M. Kent Jennings, Klaus R. Allerbeck, and Leopold Rosenmayr, "Generations and Families," in Samuel H. Barnes, Max Kaase, et al., *Political Action* (Beverly Hills, CA: Sage, 1979), chs. 15–16.

17. Pippa Norris and Ronald Inglehart, *Rising Tide: Gender Equality and Cultural Change Around the World* (New York: Cambridge University Press, 2003).

18. Martha Nussbaum and Jonathan Glover, eds., *Women, Culture, and Development* (New York: Oxford University Press, 1995).

19. For example, see Sidney Verba, Norman H. Nie, and Jae-on Kim, *Participation and Political Equality* (New York: Cambridge University Press, 1978); Barnes, Kaase, et al., *Political Action*, ch. 4.

20. See Martin Marty and Scott Appleby, *Fundamentalism Observed* (Chicago: University of Chicago Press, 1991).

21. Robert Putnam, ed., *Democracies in Flux* (Oxford: Oxford University Press, 2002).

22. The Pew Global Attitudes Project found that over two-thirds of the public in most nations cited television as their main source of political information. Only in poor African nations did this statistic fall below 50 percent, and in these nations the radio provided an alternative. Pew Global Attitudes Project, *What the World Thinks in 2002* (Washington, DC: Pew Global Attitudes Project, 2002) (http://pewglobal.org/).

23. Sidney Verba et al., *The American Participation Study 1990* (Ann Arbor: Interuniversity Consortium for Political and Social Research, University of Michigan).

24. Arthur Miller, William Reisinger, and Vicki Hesli, eds., *Public Opinion and Regime Change* (Boulder, CO: Westview Press, 1993); William Mishler and Richard Rose, "Trajectories of Fear and Hope: Support for Democracy in Post-communist Europe," *Comparative Political Studies* 28 (1995): 553–81. Compare to Robert Rohrschneider, "Institutional Learning Versus Value Diffusion," *Journal of Politics* 58 (1996): 442–66.

25. Norris, *Critical Citizens*; Russell Dalton, *Democratic Challenges, Democratic Choices*.

26. See William Zimmerman, *The Russian People and Foreign Policy: Russian Elite and Mass Perspectives* (Princeton: Princeton University Press, 2002), ch. 2; Raymond Duch, "Tolerating Economic Reform," *American Political Science Review* 87 (1993): 590–608. Russian support for marketization noticeably lags behind that of most Eastern Europeans.

27. Wayne Sandholtz and Mark Gray, "International Integration and National Corruption," *International Organization* 57 (Autumn 2003): 761–800; Mark Gray, Miki Kittilson, and Wayne Sandholtz, "Women and Globalization: A Study of 180 Countries, 1975–2000," *International Organization* 60 (Spring 2006): 293–333.

28. Pew Global Attitudes Project, *Views of a Changing World, June 2003* (Washington, DC: Pew Global Attitudes Project, 2003): 71–81 (http://pewglobal.org/reports/display.php?ReportID=185).

INTEREST ARTICULATION

Every political system has some way for people and social groups to express their needs and demands to the government. This process, known as **interest articulation,** can take many forms. For example, a person might contact a city council member or in a more traditional system she might meet with the village head or tribal chieftain. Or, a group of people might work together on a common concern. In large, established political systems, formal interest groups are a primary means of promoting political interests.

As societies have become internally more complex and the scope of government activity has widened, the quantity and variety of methods to articulate public interests have grown proportionately. People work together to address local and national needs, ranging from providing clean water in a village to passing national clean water standards. Social movements involve the public in issues as diverse as protecting the rights of indigenous people in the Amazon to debating nuclear power. Formal, institutionalized interest groups develop to represent labor, farmers, businesses, and other social interests. Interest groups, in large numbers, work in capitals like London, Washington, D.C., and Tokyo. Some of these headquarter buildings are as imposing as those housing major governmental agencies. Today, Internet chatrooms or blogging provides another forum for expression. In countries with powerful local governments, interest groups are active at the provincial or local level as well.

This chapter considers the multiple ways that people can express their interests in contemporary political systems. First we discuss the means of interest articulation that are available to individual citizens. Then we describe how formal interest groups and associations provide another means of interest articulation. For example, in most countries that allow them, labor unions, manufacturers' associations, farm groups, and associations of doctors, lawyers, engineers, and teachers represent these interests. In the end, most political systems rely on many different forms of interest articulation to determine what the public and social groups want from their government.

CITIZEN ACTION

One aspect of interest articulation involves what you might do as an individual citizen. Suppose an unjust or unfair law was being passed by the government, what could you do to express your dissatisfaction and try to stop the legislation? Or suppose you see a need that the government is not addressing, what could you do to encourage government action? These are the questions that often face us as citizens—what choices do we have for making our interests and needs known to policymakers?

Individual citizens can use various methods to make requests and demands for policies (Table 4.1).[1] Each of these forms of citizen action has different characteristics, as described in the table. The most common form of citizen participation is voting in an election. When elections are free and meaningful, they enable people to express their interests and to make a collective choice about the government's past progress

Forms of Citizen Interest Articulation		**TABLE 4.1**
Form	**Scope of Interests**	**Degree of Pressure on Elites**
Voting, participation in elections	Broad, collective decision on government leaders and their programs	Modest pressure, but not policy focused
Informal group	Collective action focused on a common interest	High pressure
Direct contact on personal matter	Normally deals with specific, personal problem	Low pressure
Direct contact on policy issue	Action on a government policy	Modest pressure
Protest activity	Highly expressive support for specific interests	High pressure
Political consumerism	Focused on specific issues, activities	High pressure

and the future policies for the nation. Although elections select political elites, they often are a blunt policy tool because they involve many different issues, and between elections officeholders may stray from the voters' preferences.

People can also work with others in their community to address common needs, as when parents work to better the local schools or residents express their worries about how the community is developing. These activities are typically very policy focused and exert direct pressure on decision makers. Such group activity exists in both democratic and authoritarian systems, although nondemocracies may limit the methods of expression to ones that do not openly confront authorities.

Some interest articulation involves direct contact with government, such as writing a letter to an elected official or to a government bureaucracy (see Box 4.1, page 63). Some direct contact involves personal issues, such as when a veteran writes to his legislator for help in getting benefits approved, or when a homeowner asks the local party precinct leader to get her driveway snowplowed regularly. These forms of personal contact are universal across political systems, including the authoritarian ones. Other direct contact involves broader political issues facing the government, such as campaigns to support or block new legislation. Direct contact on policy issues occurs primarily in democratic systems, where citizen input is broadly encouraged. However, even in autocratic nations the public often finds ways to petition the government on policy matters.[2]

The expression of interests also may involve **protests** or other forms of contentious action. The spontaneous gathering of outraged ghetto dwellers,

the public protests that overthrew the communist governments of Eastern Europe, and the environmental protests of Greenpeace are all examples of how protest articulates policy interests. Protests and other direct actions tend to be high-pressure activities that can both mobilize the public and directly pressure elites; these activities can also be very focused in their policy content.

Recent participation studies found that political consumerism—buying or boycotting a product for political reasons—is another active form of participation, at least in Western democracies.[3] Such participation allows individuals to protest the activities of a firm that pollutes or has unfair labor practices. Several boycotts of American and Western products have been organized in Arab nations to protest Western policies toward the region. Such efforts are very focused. If they become politically visible, they can have broader policy effects as well.

In summary, people can take many routes to express their interests, and each of these routes has particular characteristics associated with it.

HOW CITIZENS PARTICIPATE

The amount of citizen political participation varies widely according to the type of activity and the type of political system. Table 4.2 shows examples of the types of citizen participation in several of the nations examined in this book.

The most frequent forms of political participation revolve around elections: turning out to vote, trying to convince others how to vote, or working with political

	United										
TABLE 4.2											
Citizen Participation Across Nations (percentage)											
Type of Participation	**States**	**Britain**	**France**	**Germany**	**Japan**	**Russia**	**Mexico**	**Brazil**	**China**	**Iran**	**Nigeria**
Voter turnout in most recent national elections	54%	61%	60%	78%	68%	56%	59%	78%	—	60%	49%
Discussed politics with others	74	46	65	84	64	75	58	58	70	69	74
Participated in political party activity	18	3	2	3	4	1	5	—	10	—	—
Participated in citizen interest group	36	7	6	7	9	2	11	—	3	—	—
Signed a petition	81	81	68	52	63	12	19	47	—	—	7
Participated in lawful protest demonstration	21	13	39	28	13	24	4	25	—	—	17

Sources: Election turnout data is percent of registered public for most recent national legislative election from the International Institute for Elections and Democracy, downloaded from www. idea.org; 2000–2002 *World Values Survey* and the 1999 *European Values Survey* for other statistics. Some of the participation questions were not asked in each survey, and these missing items are noted by a dash in the table.

parties. Because elections are the most common form of public involvement in the political process, they are important forms of interest articulation. During elections, citizens speak their minds on current issues by engaging in conversations, attending meetings, contributing to campaigns, and even expressing their opinions to pollsters. Ultimately, individuals decide their preferences in their ballot choices. At the same time, however, elections perform many other functions: aggregating political interests, recruiting political elites, and even socializing political values and preferences through the campaign process (see Chapter 2).

Among the democracies, the United States stands out for its rather low levels of national voting participation: both West Europeans (with their long democratic experience) and Russians (who are new to democratic elections) vote more frequently than Americans. However, as the table shows, Americans' low level of election turnout does not simply reflect apathy. Americans are much more likely than the British to try to discuss politics with others, and Americans are much more likely to work for a party or candidate than either the British or Germans.

Public efforts to express political interests and influence public policy extend beyond elections. Grassroots politics—people working together to address a common problem—is a very direct method for articulating political interests and attempting to

influence policy. Alexis de Tocqueville considered such grassroots community action as the foundation of democracy in America. Today, such activities are often identified with middle-class participation in affluent societies—such as parent-teacher association groups, community associations, and public interest groups—but group activity occurs in almost any nation.[4] Indian villagers working together to build a communal latrine or to develop rural electricity, and indigenous people protecting their land rights are other examples of community action.

Table 4.2 indicates that group action is frequent in the advanced industrial democracies. Nearly a third of Americans are members of a citizen interest group, and significant numbers are active in Europe as well.[5] Such activity is high in Mexico, perhaps because this survey overlaps with the politicization of Vicente Fox's election in 2000. However, surveys from the developing world suggest that these activities are regularly used, albeit less frequently than in more developed nations.

Perhaps the most expressive and visible form of citizen action involves participation in protests, demonstrations, or other direct actions (see Box 4.2). For instance, many environmentalists believe that direct actions—hanging an environmental banner from a polluting smokestack, staging a mass demonstration outside of parliament, or boycotting

---

The *Shangfang* System

BOX 4.1

In 1949, the communist government in China created the *Shangfang* system that allows individuals to formally petition the government to intervene on their behalf. This system was intended as a safety valve to allow disgruntled individuals to express their grievances, and as a method for the state to mobilize expression of support from the populace. The petitioners typically are concerned about personal problems or local issues, and this system allows them to bypass unresponsive local officials and petition Beijing.

Sometimes they even travel to the capital to present their petition in person. The use of *Shangfang* has ebbed and flowed over time, but it illustrates how even authoritarian governments seek input from their citizens. In 2004, the government's petition office received more than 10 million petitions, ranging from a complaint over an eviction notice to protests about the effects of the Three Gorges Dam. However, only a miniscule fraction of these petitions receive a government response.

Source: Kevin O'Brien. (See "Rightful Resistance," *World Politics* 49 (1996): 31–55.)

---

polluters—effectively generate media attention and public interest in their cause. Political protests arise for quite different reasons. On the one hand, protest and direct action is often used by individuals and groups that feel they lack access to legitimate political channels. The mass demonstrations in Eastern Europe in the late 1980s and the public rallies and marches of black South Africans against apartheid illustrate protests as the last resort of the disadvantaged. On the other hand, peaceful protests are also increasingly used by the young and better-educated citizens in Western democracies. To many democratic citizens, protest is the continuation of "normal" politics by other means.

A majority in most nations have signed a petition, a form of political action that has become so common that it no longer can be described as unconventional (see again Table 4.2). Roughly a fifth of Americans and Germans have at some time participated in a legal demonstration. Many different sectors of society now use protests and direct action.[6] The French have more protest involvement than most other established democracies, with nearly two-fifths of the population reporting participation at some point. These numbers reflect both French traditions of popular protest and the difficulties citizens often find in getting the attention of government. The Russian patterns are also striking. In 1990, only 4 percent of Russians reported participating in a protest, reflecting the communist government's repression of such activities. A decade later, nearly a quarter of Russians said they had participated in a legal demonstration—they are learning to express their grievances in a more democratic setting.

The table also indicates that protest activities are less frequent in developing societies, such as Mexico and Nigeria.

Citizen participation thus reflects the way that people use the opportunities existing within a political system. In nations with active political parties and competitive elections, many people participate in the electoral process. In nations where such activities are limited, people may turn to group-based activity or protest in order to express their preferences, but it is more likely that they are politically inactive. As we noted in Chapter 3, a participatory political culture—of all forms—is a by-product of political modernization.

Cross-national research shows that better educated and higher social status individuals are more likely to use the various opportunities for participation. These individuals tend to develop attitudes that encourage participation, such as feelings of efficacy and a sense of civic duty.[7] They also possess the personal resources and skills that are useful in becoming politically active when duty calls or a need arises. Skill and confidence are especially important for demanding activities, such as organizing new groups or becoming a leader in an organization. This inequality in participation is less for easier activities, such as voting. The tendency for the better-off to be politically active is more evident in societies (such as the United States) with weak party organizations, weak working-class groups (such as labor unions), and less party attention to lower-class interests. In nations with stronger working-class parties and labor unions, organizational networks encourage the participation of less affluent citizens.

Participation patterns are important for several reasons. For citizens to influence government policy, they first need to articulate their interests to the government. A wider choice of activities presumably increases the citizens' ability to express their interests and be heard. Moreover, the forms of action differ in their policy content and political pressure (see again Table 4.1). Finally, individuals differ in their level of political activities and the types of activities that they use. These differences in voice are likely reflected in policy outputs if the government responds to public pressures. In other words, those who are more active in articulating their interests are more likely to have their interests addressed by policymakers.

INTEREST GROUPS

Interest articulation can also occur through the actions of social or political groups that represent a set of people. Some groups are poorly organized and unfocused, and often short-lived. Other groups have a permanent organizational base, often with professional staffs to provide expertise and representation. In addition, interest groups often participate in the political process, serving on government advisory bodies and testifying at parliamentary hearings. Interest groups vary in structure, style, financing, and support base, and these differences may influence a nation's politics, its economics, and its social life. We begin by defining four types of interest groups: anomic, nonassociational, institutional, and associational.

Anomic Groups

Anomic groups are spontaneous groups that suddenly form when many individuals react to an event that stimulates frustration, disappointment, or other strong emotions. They are flash affairs, rising and subsiding suddenly. Without previous organization or planning, frustrated individuals may suddenly take to the streets to vent their anger as news of a government action touches deep emotions or as a rumor of new injustice sweeps the community. Their actions may lead to violence, although not necessarily. Particularly where organized groups are absent or where they have failed to get adequate political representation, smoldering discontent may be sparked by an incident or by the emergence of a leader. It may then suddenly explode in relatively unpredictable and uncontrollable ways.

Some political systems, including both developed and developing nations, report a rather high frequency of violent and spontaneous anomic behavior.[8] This behavior often involves spontaneous public demonstrations or acts of violence, rather than the planned and orchestrated protests of institutionalized political groups. Other countries are notable for the infrequency of such disturbances, which may reflect either the limited opportunities for action or the nation's political culture.

In France, for example, protests have become part of the tradition of politics (see again Table 4.2). In the late 1960s, the French government nearly collapsed as a result of protests that began when university students stimulated a mass protest against the government. In 2006, another wave of mass protests nearly brought the economy to a standstill and forced the government to withdraw unpopular labor regulations. In a typical year, Paris might experience protests by students, shopkeepers, farmers, homemakers, government employees, environmentalists, women's groups, and a host of other interest groups. Protest is almost a national political sport in France.

Anger over the assassination of a popular political leader or other catastrophic event can also stimulate a public outburst. For instance, one commonly sees relatively spontaneous public demonstrations when one nation makes a hostile action toward another nation. Wildcat strikes (spontaneous strike actions by local workers, not organized actions by national unions), long a feature of the British trade union scene, also occur frequently in such European countries as France, Italy, and Sweden.

Sometimes anomic groups are a subset of individuals drawn from a larger social grouping, such as a racial or an ethnic group. For instance, in 1992 there was rioting and looting by some residents in minority neighborhoods of Los Angeles following the acquittal of police officers accused of excessive violence in the beating of an African-American suspect. Similarly, in 1992, riots broke out in Algeria when some Muslim fundamentalists protested the government's invalidation of the recent election. We treat these as anomic group actions because there is no structure or planning to the event, and the people involved disperse after the protest ends.

We must be cautious, however, about calling something an anomic political behavior when it really

Attacks on Globalization

In July 2001 tens of thousands of protestors arrived in Genoa to demonstrate at the G8 Summit Meeting. Hundreds of different groups came to protest at the meetings, and several of the more radical groups engaged in running battles with the police. Many of the most violent clashes involved what became known as the "Black Block." The Block was comprised of several loosely organized anarchist and radical groups, wearing trademark black clothing, black hoods, and gas masks. Confrontations with police often appeared choreographed in advance, coordinated by cell phones, and videotaped by sympathetic activists—and subsequently distributed on the Internet. Many other protest groups in Genoa were worried that the radical anarchist goals of the Block detracted attention from their policy concerns about the economic and social impacts of globalization. After two days of violent clashes, the summit ended. Damage ran into the tens of millions of dollars, 200 protestors were arrested, and one protestor was shot in a clash with police. In the end, the violence in the streets overshadowed both the elected politicians at the summit and the policy goals of the nonviolent groups in Genoa.

Source: BBC World News.

is the result of detailed planning by organized groups. For instance, the demonstrations against the World Trade Organization in Seattle in 1999 and Genoa in 2001 owed much to indignation but little to spontaneity (see Box 4.2).

Nonassociational Groups

Like anomic groups, **nonassociational groups** rarely are well organized, and their activity is episodic. They differ from anomic groups because they are based on common interests and identities of ethnicity, region, religion, occupation, or perhaps kinship. Because of these economic or cultural ties, nonassociational groups have more continuity than anomic groups. Subgroups within a large nonassociational group (such as an ethnic minority or workers) may act as an anomic group, as in the 1992 Los Angeles riots, the 2005 Paris riots, and the Middle East protests against the Danish cartoons of Mohammed in 2006. Throughout the world, ethnicity and religion, like occupation, are powerful identities that can stimulate collective activity.

Two kinds of nonassociational groups are especially interesting. One is a large group that is not formally organized, although its members may perceive common interests. Many ethnic, regional, and occupational groups fit into this category. The members share a common interest or need, but there is no formal group to represent their interests.

It can be very difficult to organize such groups because although members share a common problem, none of them will undertake the effort to organize other members. This is commonly known as the **collective action problem.**[9] Moreover, if large collective benefits—for example, ending discriminatory legislation or cleaning up water pollution—are achieved, they will be shared even by those who did not work, the so-called free riders. This pattern of people waiting for the rewards without sharing the cost or risk of action affects other types of groups as well. For instance, students who might benefit from lower tuition fees are typically underrepresented because there is no organization to articulate their interests. Understanding the collective action problem helps us to see why some groups (including governments and revolutionary challengers) become organized and others do not, and under what circumstances the barriers to collective action are overcome.

A second type of nonassociational group is the small village, economic or ethnic subgroup whose members know each other personally. A small, face-to-face group has some important advantages and may be highly effective in some political situations. If its members are well connected or its goals unpopular or illegal, the group may remain informal or even inconspicuous. Such groups may undertake various actions, such as engaging in work stoppages, circulating student petitions to demand better support and training, requesting that a bureaucrat continue a grain tariff to benefit landowners, or asking a tax collector for favored treatment to benefit relatives. As the last example suggests, personal interest articulation may

The British Society of Civil Servants, a well-organized and unusually effective associational interest group, assembles for an orderly meeting in a London hall to plan a 24-hour work stoppage.

Les Wilson/Photri

often have more legitimacy and perpetuate itself by invoking group or personal ties.

Institutional Groups

Institutional groups are formal and have other political or social functions in addition to interest articulation. Political parties, business corporations, legislatures, armies, bureaucracies, and churches often have separate political groups with special responsibility for representing a group's interests. Either as corporate bodies or as smaller groups within these bodies (legislative blocs, officer cliques, groups in the clergy, or ideological cliques in bureaucracies), such groups typically express the interests of their members. The influence of institutional interest groups is usually drawn from the strength of their primary organizational base—for instance, the size of their membership or their income. A group based on a governmental institution has direct access to policymakers.

In industrial democracies, bureaucratic and corporate interests use their resources and special information to affect policy. In the United States, for instance, the military industrial complex consists of the combination of the U.S. Department of Defense and defense industries that support military expenditures. Similarly, the farm lobby and the U.S. Department of Agriculture often advocate agricultural policies. Political parties are among the most active institutional participants in the policy process of most democracies. And as in most societies, government bureaucracies do not simply react to pressures from the outside, they also can act as independent forces of interest representation.

Nonpolitical institutional groups can also participate in the political process. In Italy, for example, the Roman Catholic Church has exerted significant influence on the government. In electoral politics, the Church used to ask Catholics to vote against the Communists. Less overtly, the Church has members of the clergy call on officeholders to express opinions on matters of concern to the Church. In Islamic countries, fundamentalist clergy pursue a similar role, prescribing what morals public policy should follow, actively lobbying governmental officials, and sometimes participating in the governing process.

In authoritarian regimes, which prohibit or at least control explicit political groups, institutional groups can still play a large role. Educational officials, party officials, jurists, factory managers, officers in the military services, and government bodies representing other social units had significant roles in interest articulation in communist regimes.[10] In preindustrial societies, which usually have fewer associational groups and with limited popular support, military groups, corporations, party factions, and bureaucrats often play prominent political roles. Even where the military does not seize power directly, the possibility of such action often forces close government attention to military requests.

Associational Groups

Associational groups are formed explicitly to represent the interests of a particular group, such as trade unions, chambers of commerce, manufacturers' associations, and ethnic associations. These organizations have procedures for formulating interests and demands, and they usually employ a full-time professional staff. Associational groups are often very active in representing the interests of their members in the policy process. For instance, in recurring debates about health care in the United States there is an enormous mobilization of pressure groups and lobbyists—from representatives of doctors and health insurance organizations to consumer groups and the like—seeking to influence legislation.

Associational interest groups—where they are allowed to flourish—affect the development of other types of groups. Their organizational base gives them an advantage over nonassociational groups, and their tactics and goals are often recognized as legitimate in society. Labor unions, for example, are often central political actors because they represent the mass of the working class; in the same way, business associations often speak for the corporate interests of the nation.

A special subset of associational groups consists of citizens who are united not by a common economic or individual self-interest but by a common belief in a political ideology or a policy goal.[11] The environmental movement, many women's groups, and other civic groups are examples of this kind of associational group. In some of these issue groups, the members may seldom interact directly and not even share common social characteristics (such as employment or ethnicity), but are bound together by their support of a political organization, such as Greenpeace or Amnesty International. On the organizational side, many of these new social groups have fluid and dynamic organizations, with frequent turnover in both leadership and membership. On the tactical side, they use a wide range of approaches, often discounting

the value of partisan campaigning and conventional lobbying in favor of unconventional protests and direct actions.

Civic associations represent another way for citizens to articulate their policy goals by supporting groups that advocate their preferred policy positions. Such groups have proliferated in most advanced industrial democracies in the past generation, and they are now spreading to the developing world.

In summary, a social interest can manifest itself in many different groups. We can illustrate this point with examples of different groups that might involve members of the working class:

Anomic group: a spontaneous group of working-class individuals living in the same neighborhood

Nonassociational group: the working class as a collective

Institutional group: the labor department within the government

Associational group: a labor union

Distinguishing among the types of groups is important for several reasons. The nature of a group typically reflects the resources it can mobilize to support its political efforts. Perhaps one of the most important resources is an institutional structure that will sustain political efforts until the government responds to the group's interests. The nature of a group also may signify the tactics it uses to gain political access (see Table 4.3, page 75). Finally, since the articulation of interest is the first step in policy influence, the nature of groups suggests what types of interests are more likely to get a hearing in the political system and which interests may be underrepresented.

Civil Society and Social Capital

Political analysts have devoted increasing attention to whether an extensive network of interest groups and public participation in these groups creates a **civil society**—a society in which people are involved in social and political interactions free of state control or regulation. Community groups, voluntary associations, and even religious groups—as well as access to free communication and information through the mass media and the Internet—are important parts of a

Pakistanis in Karachi, Pakistan, protest publication in Europe of offensive cartoons depicting Muhammed.

Ilyas Dean/The Image Works

civil society.[12] Participation in associational and institutional groups can socialize individuals into the political skills and cooperative relations that are part of a well-functioning society. People learn how to organize, express their interests, and work with others to achieve common goals. These skills, norms, and networks are sometimes called **"social capital"** because they are assets that facilitate cooperation among people to solve economic and political problems. They also learn the important lesson that the political process itself is as important as the immediate results. Thus, a system of active associational groups can lessen the development of anomic or nonassociational activity. Group activity can help citizens to develop and clarify their own preferences, provide important information about political events, and articulate the interests of citizens more clearly and precisely than parties and elections.[13]

As political and economic conditions become interdependent across nations, there is also increasing attention directed toward the development of a global civil society. Individuals and groups in one nation are connected to groups with similar concerns in other nations, and jointly reinforce their individual efforts.

Environmental groups in the Western democracies, for example, assist environmental groups in developing nations with the expertise and organizational resources to address the issues facing their country. National groups meet at international conferences and policy forums, and the network of social relations, as well as Internet connections, extends across national borders.[14] This is another sign of how the international context of domestic politics is growing worldwide.

One problem facing the nations of Eastern Europe and other newly democratizing nations is building a rich associational group life in societies where the government had suppressed or controlled organized groups.[15] The Communist Party and the government bureaucracy dominated the nations of Eastern Europe for over forty years. The process of building new, independent associational groups to articulate the interests of different citizens is underway and will be important to the democratic process. Similarly, many less economically developed nations need to create a civil society of associational groups to involve citizens in the political process and represent their interests if democratization is to succeed.

INTEREST GROUP SYSTEMS

The nature of the connection between interest groups and government policymaking institutions is another important feature of the political process. Different types of connections create different interest group systems. All modern societies have large numbers of interest groups, but their relationships with government can follow different models. Interest group systems are classified into three major groupings: pluralist, democratic corporatist, and controlled.[16]

Pluralist interest group systems have several features involving both how interests are organized and how they participate in the political process:

- Multiple groups may represent a single societal interest.
- Group membership is voluntary and limited.
- Groups often have a loose or decentralized organizational structure.
- There is a clear separation between interest groups and the government.

For instance, not only are there different groups for different social sectors (such as labor, business, and professional interests), but there may be many multiple labor unions or business associations within each sector. These groups compete among themselves for membership and influence, and all simultaneously press their demands on the government. The United States is the best-known example of a strongly pluralist interest group system; Canada and New Zealand are also cited as examples. Despite its greater labor union membership and somewhat greater coordination of economic associations, Britain tends to fall on the pluralist side in most analyses, as do France and Japan.

Democratic **neo-corporatist interest group systems** are characterized by a much more organized representation of interests:

- A single peak association normally represents each societal interest.
- Membership in the peak association is often compulsory and nearly universal.
- Peak associations are centrally organized and direct the actions of their members.
- Groups are often systematically involved in making and implementing policy.

For instance, in a neo-corporatist system there may be a single peak association that represents all the major industrial interests; a pluralist system may have several different business groups that act autonomously. Equally important, interest groups in these systems often regularly and legitimately work with the government agencies and/or political parties as partners in negotiating solutions to policy problems.

The best-studied democratic neo-corporatist arrangements involve economic problems. Democracies with business and labor peak associations that negotiate with each other and the government have had better records than more pluralist countries in sustaining employment, restraining inflation, and increasing social spending.[17] In addition, there is also evidence that neo-corporatist systems are more effective in implementing other public policies, such as environmental protection.[18]

In many advanced industrial societies, however, membership in labor unions has decreased and some bargaining patterns have become less centralized. Thus, some countries that have relied on neo-corporatist patterns have adapted this system to these new consequences and applied corporatism in new ways.[19] In contrast, several nations in Eastern Europe had attempted to develop more corporatist structures to develop interest group politics, but the system of autonomous interest groups remained underdeveloped. The experience with neo-corporatist models in developing nations is even more varied.[20]

Because different sectors of a society may vary in their organized interest groups and in their government relations, we must be cautious about generalizing too much about interest group systems. Figure 4.1, however, shows the striking differences in organization of the labor movements across many of the nations in this book. Britain, the United States, France, and Japan are examples of more pluralist systems. Less than half the British labor force is unionized, but these unions are not as highly coordinated as those in corporatist countries. The member unions in the British Trades Union Congress have strong traditions of individual autonomy and are themselves relatively decentralized. Moreover, the influence of the labor unions on government policymakers has waned over the past few decades. In the United States and France, the labor movement is somewhat fragmented. These countries also lack a tradition of "social partnership" between government, unions, and employer associations. In the area of labor policy, at

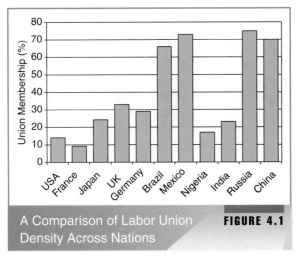

A Comparison of Labor Union Density Across Nations   **FIGURE 4.1**

Source: International Labor Organization, *World Labour Report 1997–1998,* The Statistical Annex, Table 1.2. (www.ilo.org). The figure plots union membership as a percentage of wage earners.

least, these are highly pluralist, not corporatist, interest group systems. However, corporatist-type arrangements among individual industries, trade associations, and governmental bureaucracies (without organized labor involvement) exist in Japan.

Germany is a closer fit to the neo-corporatist model. The most thoroughly corporatist interest group systems are in Austria, Finland, the Netherlands, Norway, and Sweden. These nations are characterized by a high level of union membership among the nonagricultural labor force, and a highly centralized and united labor movement. In addition, under the corporatist model interest groups such as labor unions often have special access to government. For instance, German labor unions have formal membership on many government commissions, special access to policy administration, and are very influential through informal channels of influence.

Mexico and Brazil are examples of another form of corporatist politics. Union membership in many Latin American nations is fairly high, and the trade unions and peasant associations are closely tied to political parties or religious interests. Usually, these groups mobilize support for the political parties or social institutions that dominate them, and are closely tied to the state when their party is in power. This system is changing in both Mexico and Brazil, as democratization encourages the unions to become more politically independent and influential (see Chapter 11).

Nigeria and India illustrate a pattern common in other developing democracies. Interest groups, such as unions, are often not well developed and have a limited mass membership. They are participants in the process, but without the mass membership or formal access that gives labor unions influence in established Western democracies of either the pluralist or corporatist model.

Finally, **controlled interest group systems** follow a different pattern:

- There is a single group for each social sector.
- Membership is often compulsory.
- Each group is normally hierarchically organized.
- Groups are controlled by the government or its agents in order to mobilize support for government policy.

The last point is the most important: Groups exist to facilitate government control of society. The best examples are the traditional communist systems in which the party penetrates all levels of society and controls all the permitted associational groups. For instance, Figure 4.1 shows that 70 percent of wage earners in China belong to a union.[21] Unions and other interest associations are subordinated to the Communist Party, and they are only rarely permitted to articulate the interests of their members. Russia also once followed this communist model, and the unions have large memberships as a result of this experience. Chapter 9 on Russia discusses how the unions are struggling to gain autonomy from the state and play an influential role in the postcommunist system. But they have made limited progress.

These nations limit interest articulation to leaders of institutional groups, who can use their positions in political institutions as a base for expressing their demands. Numerous institutional interest groups can also emerge in these societies, especially from parts of the party and bureaucracy, such as the military, as well as informal nonassociational groups.

ACCESS TO THE INFLUENTIAL

To be effective, interest groups must be able to reach key policymakers through **channels of political access.** Otherwise, groups may express their members' interests yet fail to have an impact on policymakers.

Political systems vary in the ways they respond to political interests. Interest groups vary in the tactics they use to gain access. Group tactics are partially shaped by the opportunities offered by the structure of policymaking, as well as by their own values and preferences.

There is a significant distinction between legitimate and constitutional channels of access (such as the mass media, parties, and legislatures) and illegitimate, coercive access channels. These two channels reflect the types of resources that groups can use to influence elites as well as the group's perceptions of which tactics will be most successful. Groups with substantial resources—money, members, or status—typically have an easier time working through legitimate constitutional channels. Groups with limited resources or legitimacy may feel they must act through coercive channels because they are not accepted by the political system. In democracies, groups tend toward legitimate channels because the system expects and allows group activity. In contrast, nondemocratic systems typically limit legitimate access, which might stimulate illegitimate or coercive activities.

Legitimate Access Channels

The legitimate channels of access can take many forms, and these are often seen in both democratic and nondemocratic systems. For instance, personal connections are an important means of reaching political elites in all societies—the use of family, school, local, or other social ties. An excellent example is the information network among the British elite based on old school ties originating at Eton, Harrow, or other "public" schools, or at Oxford and Cambridge universities. Similarly, in Japan many alumni of the University of Tokyo Law School hold top positions among the political and bureaucratic elites who interact because of these personal ties. Although personal connections are commonly used by nonassociational groups representing family or regional interests, they serve other groups as well. Face-to-face contact is one of the most effective means of shaping attitudes and conveying messages. Interests communicated by a friend or neighbor carry much more weight than a formal letter from a stranger. In modern nations, personal connections are usually cultivated with special care. In Washington, D.C., the business of advising interest groups and individuals on access to politicians

is an increasingly lucrative profession (and, increasingly a target of government regulation and potential corruption). These activities are often carried on by former officeholders who use their personal governmental contacts for their lobbyist clients.

The **mass media**—television, radio, newspapers, and magazines—are another important access channel in democratic societies. The mass media, and the Internet can mobilize support for interest group efforts, leading to donations of time and money, and encouraging sympathizers to support the group. Many interest groups thus hire skillful public relations specialists, purchase direct advertising, and seek favorable attention in the media. Interest groups encourage media reports on their needs as well as coverage of their views on specific policies. When a cause receives national media attention, the message to policymakers carries added weight if politicians know that millions of voters are interested in the issue. Moreover, groups believe that in an open society, "objective" news coverage has more credibility than sponsored messages. However, multiple conflicting messages and a lack of specific focus can limit the effectiveness of the mass media for many smaller groups.

The potential power of the media can be seen when the communist governments in Eastern Europe loosened control over the media in the late 1980s. This action gave a huge boost to democracy movements. For instance, when asked what caused the democratic revolution in Poland in the 1990s, Lech Walesa pointed to a television and said "that did." Media reports on the failures in communist government policy and the contrasting lifestyles in the West undermined the legitimacy of the regimes. As democratic protests spread across Eastern Europe, stories of successful protests in other parts of the country, or in other countries, enhanced the confidence of demonstrators. Citizen protests encouraged by mass media reports helped convince the ruling groups that their support had vanished.

Political parties are another important access point. Democratic political parties often rely on interest groups for financial and voter support, and act as representatives of these interests within government. In a nation like Germany, the various components of the party organization, particularly parliamentary committees, are important channels for transmitting demands to the cabinet and the party in power. In some cases, other factors limit the role of parties as interest representatives. For instance, highly ideological

Lobbying Behind the Scenes

BOX 4.3

British beer companies use a variety of means to support their industry. For example, the industry contributed funds to Labour MPs who recently voted for longer opening hours for British pubs. They also provide travel support for MPs who are favorable to the industry. A group of MPs who support the industry formed the All-Party Parliamentary Beer Group (APBG). The group's announced goal is "to promote the wholesomeness and enjoyment of beer and the unique role of the pub in UK society." The parliamentary group campaigned to have beer taxes reduced, conducted hearings on whether the government overregulates British pubs, and supported the extension of pub hours. The group hosts a series of functions at Westminster, giving industry chiefs the opportunity to meet MPs and showcase their products. The parliamentary group also selects a "beer drinker of the year," who receives an award at their annual dinner. The parliamentary group receives direct financial support from breweries, and the secretary for the group is paid by the alcohol industry.

Visit the APBG website: www.publications.parliament.uk/pa/cm/cmparty/memi140.htm.

parties with a hierarchical structure, such as most communist parties, are more likely to control affiliated interest groups than to communicate the interest groups' demands. Decentralized party organizations, like those in the United States, may be less helpful than individual legislators in providing access.

Legislatures are another common target of interest group activities (see Box 4.3). Standard lobbying tactics include making appearances before legislative committees and providing information to individual legislators. In the United States, political action committees raise campaign contributions for individual members of Congress and usually receive some political attention in exchange. In Britain and France, the strong party discipline in the legislature lessens the importance of individual members of Parliament (MPs) as access channels for interest groups. In contrast, in the United States the combination of loose party discipline and a decentralized legislative system makes the individual members of the Congress major targets of group efforts.

Government bureaucracies are also a major access point in most political systems. Contacts with the bureaucratic agencies may be particularly important where the bureaucracy has policymaking authority or where interests are narrow and directly involve few citizens. A bureaucrat sympathetic to a group may try to respond to its demands without leaving bureaucratic channels by exercising administrative discretion. A government official may also give public consideration to an issue or frame an issue in a way that receives a sympathetic hearing by policymakers. The bureaucracy may be an especially important access point in nondemocratic systems because other legitimate channels of citizen access do not exist.

Government officials may consider protest demonstrations, strikes, and other forms of dramatic and direct pressure on government as legitimate or illegitimate tactics, depending on the political system. Protests may be either spontaneous actions of an anomic group or a planned use of unconventional channels by an organized group. In democratic societies, demonstrations often mobilize popular support—or electoral support—or media attention for the group's cause. The mass demonstrations on immigration reform in 2006 are examples of efforts to shape and influence the U.S. public debate on legislation being considered by Congress. On a regular basis, the Mall in Washington, D.C., hosts other groups protesting other policy issues. In nondemocratic societies, such demonstrations are more hazardous and often represent more extreme dissatisfaction that cannot find voice through conventional channels of access.

Lawful protest can be a tactic of society's powerless, those who do not have access or resources to influence policymakers through conventional channels. As a political tactic, protest activity is especially attractive to young people and minority groups, who are not among the elite. Protests are also a favored tactic of groups whose ideological commitments focus on challenging the established social and political order. Yet, protests are increasingly used as a means of interest articulation by organized and accepted interests who feel that dramatic actions can heighten support for their cause. Protests can supplement other channels, especially in gaining the attention of the mass media in an age when television comes to every household. Thus we find doctors in New Delhi, farmers in Japan, and "gray panthers" (the elderly) in Germany using a tactic that once was limited to the poor and minorities.[22]

Coercive Access Channels and Tactics

Most scholars see the level of collective violence as closely associated with the character of a society and the circumstances in the nation. In his studies of civil strife, Ted Robert Gurr argued that feelings of relative deprivation motivate people to act aggressively. Gurr defined relative deprivation as a "discrepancy between people's expectations about the goods and conditions of life to which they are entitled, on the one hand, and, on the other, their value capabilities—the degree to which they think they can attain these goods and conditions."[23]

Feelings of relative deprivation are a source of frustration, discontent, and anger. The more such discontent and anger persist, the greater the chance of collective violence. People also tend to turn to violence if they believe it is justified and if they believe it will lead to success. If they think that their government is illegitimate and that the cause of their discontent is justified, they will more readily turn to political violence. To this end, it is the responsibility of the government and its institutions to provide peaceful alternatives to violence as a means of change.

This general description of political violence should not overlook the differences among the types of violent political activities. A riot, for example, involves the spontaneous expression of collective anger and dissatisfaction by a group of citizens. Though riots have long been dismissed as aberrant and irrational action by social riffraff, modern studies have shown that rioters vary greatly in their motivation, behavior, and social background.[24] Most riots seem to follow some fairly clear-cut patterns, such as confining destruction or violence to particular areas or targets. Relative deprivation appears to be a major cause of riots, but the release of the frustrations is not as aimless as is often supposed.

Although the 2005 riots in Paris were triggered by the accidental deaths of two teenagers, most analysts see their deaths as only a proximate cause, a "spark" that ignited already volatile factors. Gangs of minority youth burned thousands of automobiles, damaged shops, and attacked police who attempted to quell the violence. The French president and then the Parliament declared a state of emergency in reaction to the violent protests, establishing a curfew and limiting civil liberties. Even though much of the mayhem seemed poorly related to effective political action, it was a cry for attention. Youth from immigrant families had high levels of unemployment and felt that social and economic discrimination was limiting their life chances. Even in a democracy, the government sometimes overlooks the needs of its own citizens and allows such frustrations to explode into violence.

While deprivation may help fuel the discontent, strikes and obstructions are typically carried out by well-organized associational or institutional groups. For instance, violent protests in Seattle and Genoa against the World Trade Organization and globalization involved highly organized activities among some of the more radical groups participating in the protests (see again Box 4.2).

Historically, labor unions used the general strike to pressure the government or employers on fundamental issues. The influence of strikes and obstructions has varied, however, depending on the legitimacy of the government and coercive pressure from other groups. A massive truckers' strike helped bring down the government in Chile in 1972–1973, but student-inspired boycotts in Korea in the 1980s had only a modest impact on the government. Most spectacularly, the strikes, obstructions, and demonstrations in Eastern Europe in 1989 and 1990, like the earlier people's power movement in the Philippines, had massive success against regimes that had lost legitimacy.

Finally, **political terror tactics**—including deliberate assassination, armed attacks on other groups or government officials, and mass bloodshed—are sometimes used by radical groups. The tragedies in Northern Ireland; the suicide bombings by Palestinians in Israel; and the attacks of Jihadist terrorists in New York City, Madrid, London, Bali, and other cities demonstrate the use of such tactics. The use of terrorism typically reflects the desire of some group to change the rules of the political game or to destroy a political system, rather than to gain political access.

The use of political terror is more often likely to produce negative consequences rather than construct

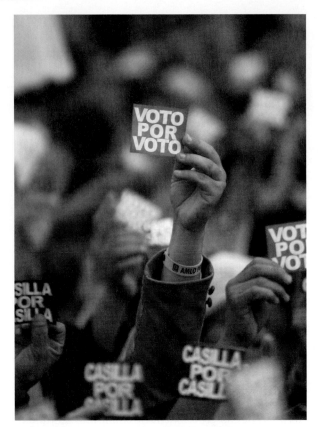

Protesters held a massive demonstration in front of Mexico's electoral court to demand a ballot-by-ballot recount of the disputed 2006 presidential election.

AP Images

positive policy change. Massive deadly violence may destroy a democratic regime, leading to curtailment of civil rights or even military intervention when many people and leaders feel that any alternative is preferable to more violence. For example, democratically elected governments justified their suppression of democratic institutions in Peru in 1992 and India in 1975 in response to the violent actions of terrorists. An authoritarian, repressive response often promises quick results against terrorists; however, small-group terrorism usually fails when confronted by united democratic leadership.[25] In a democratic society, violence often forfeits the sympathy that a group needs if its cause is to receive a responsive hearing. The current conflict between the West and jihadist terrorists has renewed the debate on how democratic governments should balance the need for security against the preservation of civil liberties.

POLICY PERSPECTIVES ON INTEREST ARTICULATION

As we pointed out in Chapter 2, we need to examine the structures performing political functions from both process and policy perspectives. In order to understand the formation of policies, we need to know which groups articulate interests and their policy preferences. Many associational interest groups specialize in certain policy areas. The concerns of other interest groups, such as anomic or institutional groups, may be less easily discerned, but they are equally important for the policy process.

Table 4.3 provides examples of legitimate and coercive interest articulation for different types of interest groups. Each case provides an example of the differences in legitimate access channels, such as informal meetings by Mexican business leaders lobbying their government to Greenpeace testifying before European Parliament committees. Similarly, coercive acts range from spontaneous outbursts by anomic groups to Hamas using terror tactics on the West Bank. This framework also helps us to think about how a single interest group might pursue its goals through multiple channels, including protests, representation by institutional groups, and lobbying by associational groups. For instance, honeybee farmers in the United States have lobbied their representatives in Congress to maintain federal price supports, and they have also used their allies in the U.S. Department of Agriculture to support their position (will honeybee protests be next?). This table presents examples from many nations in order to suggest the varied possibilities that exist in each nation. If we were studying interest articulation patterns in one nation, we could build a table showing the structures, policies, and channels involved during a particular period.

INTEREST GROUP DEVELOPMENT

One consequence of modernization is a widespread belief that the conditions of life can be altered through human action. Modernization normally involves education, urbanization, rapid growth in public communication, and improvement in the physical conditions of life. These changes are closely related to increases in political awareness, participation, and feelings of

TABLE 4.3

Process and Policy Perspectives on Interest Articulation

Examples of Interest Articulation

Channel of Access

Types of Interest Groups	Legitimate Channel	Coercive Channel
Anomic groups	Russian workers strike to protest price increases	Iranians attack Danish embassy to protest cartoons depicting Mohammed
Nonassociational groups	Mexican business leaders discuss taxes with president	Minorities in France riot in 2005 over their social conditions
Institutional groups	U.S. Department of Agriculture advocates subsidies for honey production	Indonesian army supports democracy movement to overthrow Suharto regime (1997)
Associational groups	Greenpeace lobbies the European Parliament to ban genetically modified foods	Palestinian Hamas launches terror attacks on Israel

political competence. Such participant attitudes encourage more diverse and citizen-based interest articulation.

At the same time, modernization produces an increasing diversity of life conditions and a specialization of labor as people work in many types of jobs—a process that leads to the formation of large numbers of special interests. The interdependence of modern life, the exposure provided by mass communications, and a larger policy role of government further multiply political interests. These interests are organized into different interest groups. Thus, the diversity of interest groups is another by-product of modernization.

Successful democratic development leads to the emergence of complex interest group systems that express the needs of groups and individuals in the society. Yet, this process is by no means automatic. The problems of organizing large groups for collective action are huge. Societies vary widely in the extent to which people engage in associational activity. One factor explaining participation is the level of trust shared among members of the society. Robert Putnam and his colleagues found that an active associational life in Northern Italian communities was associated with widespread trust in others. Furthermore, these qualities of the political culture were related to economic growth and a participant political life.[26] Ronald Inglehart has shown similar continuity in social trust across nations.[27] Alternatively, modernization may weaken traditional structures in some societies,

but then fail to develop effective associational groups in their place because of restrictive social attitudes. A nation's ability to achieve either stability or democracy will be hindered as a result.

In other cases, authoritarian parties and bureaucracies may control associational groups and choke off the channels of political access. Eastern Europe offers a situation in which forty years or more of authoritarian domination suppressed autonomous interest groups. Eventually, the processes of economic modernization pressured these authoritarian systems to allow more open organization and expression of political interests. In addition, social change led to an expansion of interest articulation activity and a need for associational groups to provide regular and organized expression for citizens' interests.

The recent development of organized interest groups in Eastern Europe should not, however, lead us to conclude that every conceivable group now has equal standing. Using the American experience as an example, the articulation of interests is frequently biased toward the goals of the better-off, who are also often better organized.[28] It is often pointed out that the American Association of Retired Persons (AARP) is an effective group that is not counterbalanced by a "Young Taxpayers Group," and that the traditional labor-management competition leaves consumers underrepresented.

We might test the breadth of citizen representation by evaluating systems in terms of their

An Italian environmentalist in front of Rome's U.S. Embassy protests the refusal of the United States to ratify the Kyoto Protocol on global warming.

AP Images

inclusiveness: what proportion of the population is represented to what degree in national-level politics? South Africa under apartheid illustrates the extreme case where the majority was prevented outright from forming associational groups. In the Third World, competing interests in the capital rarely involve the interests of rural peasants; sometimes peasant organizations are brutally suppressed, while urban middle- and upper-class groups can petition authorities. It seems to be no coincidence that the bias in group inclusion appears greatest where the gaps in income and education are widest. We previously suggested that, pushed to the extreme, those excluded from the process may engage in anomic activity or resort to

violence, a conclusion supported by statistical studies of inequality and violence.[29] Even in less extreme cases, the presence of different levels of political awareness means that every interest group system is somewhat biased. Democratization involves not only the provision of competitive elections but also the reduction of the bias in interest representation.

Another challenge faces the patterns of interest articulation and representation in advanced industrial democracies. There are claims that participation in associational groups is decreasing in the United States, and perhaps in other established democracies.[30] For instance, memberships in labor unions and formal church engagement have steadily trended downward in most Western democracies over the past several decades. Some scholars argue that this trend represents a growing social isolation in developed nations, as people forsake social and political involvement for the comfort of their favorite chair and their favorite television program. However, other researchers argue that we are witnessing a change in how citizens organize and express their interests, such as through public interest groups, Internet networks, and blogging.[31] Even in nations such as India and China, millions of people are now using the Internet to learn about politics and how they can articulate their interests.

What can be said for certain is that democratic politics rests on a participatory public that uses individual and group methods to express and represent its interests. Thus, developing of an active social and political life is an important standard for measuring the political development of a nation.

REVIEW QUESTIONS

- How do the different forms of citizen action vary in their potential influence on policy makers?
- What are the main types of interest groups?
- How does a "civil society" differ from a noncivil society?
- What are the key differences among pluralist, neo-corporatist, and controlled interest group systems?

- What are the consequences when an interest group works through legitimate channels of influence rather than coercive channels?
- What factors increase the diversity of interest groups and their efforts to influence the political process?

KEY TERMS

anomic groups

associational groups

channels of political access

civil society

collective action problem

controlled interest group
systems

institutional groups

interest articulation

mass media

neo-corporatist interest
group systems

nonassociational groups

pluralist interest group
systems

political terror tactics

protests

social capital

SUGGESTED READINGS

Dahl, Robert A. *Polyarchy: Participation and Opposition.* New Haven, CT: Yale University Press, 1971.

———. *Democracy and Its Critics.* New Haven, CT: Yale University Press, 1989.

Dalton, Russell J. *Citizen Politics: Public Opinion and Political Parties in Advanced Industrial Democracies,* 4th ed. Washington, DC: CQ Press, 2005.

Denardo, James. *Power in Numbers: The Political Strategy of Protest and Rebellion.* Princeton, NJ: Princeton University Press, 1985.

Hirschman, Albert. *Exit, Voice, and Loyalty.* Cambridge: Harvard University Press, 1970.

Howard, Marc Morjé. *The Weakness of Civil Society in Post-Communist Europe.* New York: Cambridge University Press, 2003.

Keck, Margaret, and Kathryn Sikkink. *Activists Beyond Borders: Advocacy Networks in International Politics.* Ithaca, NY: Cornell University Press, 1998.

Lichbach, Mark. *The Rebel's Dilemma.* Ann Arbor: University of Michigan Press, 1994.

Meyer, David, and Sidney Tarrow, eds. *The Social Movement Society: Contentious Politics for a New Century.* Lanham, MD: Rowman & Littlefield, 1998.

Norris, Pippa. *Democratic Phoenix: Reinventing Political Activism.* New York: Cambridge University Press, 2003.

Olson, Mancur. *The Logic of Collective Action.* Cambridge: Harvard University Press, 1965.

Putnam, Robert. *Bowling Alone: The Collapse and Revival of American Community.* New York: Simon & Schuster, 2000.

Putnam, Robert D., ed. *Democracies in Flux: The Evolution of Social Capital in Contemporary Society.* Oxford: Oxford University Press, 2002.

Richardson, Jeremy J., ed. *Pressure Groups.* New York: Oxford University Press, 1993.

Rootes, Christopher. *Environmental Movements: Local, National, and Global.* London: Frank Cass, 1999.

Shi, Tianjian. *Political Participation in Beijing.* Cambridge: Harvard University Press, 1997.

Tarrow, Sidney. *The New Transnational Activism.* New York: Cambridge University Press, 2005.

Thomas, Clive. *Political Parties and Interest Groups: Shaping Democratic Governance.* Boulder, CO: Lynn Rienner, 2001.

Van Deth, Jan et al. *Social Capital and European Democracy.* New York: Routledge, 1999.

Verba, Sidney, Norman H. Nie, and Jae-on Kim. *Participation and Political Equality.* Cambridge: Cambridge University Press, 1978.

Verba, Sidney, Kay Schlozman, and Henry Brady. *Voice and Equality.* Cambridge: Harvard University Press, 1996.

Wattenberg, Martin. *Where Have All the Voters Gone?* Cambridge: Harvard University Press, 2003.

Wiarda, Howard J. *Corporatism and Comparative Politics: The Other Great "ism."* Armonk, NY: Sharpe, 1997.

ENDNOTES

1. This framework draws on Sidney Verba, Norman N. Nie, and Jae-on Kim, *Participation and Political Equality* (Cambridge: Cambridge University Press, 1978), ch. 2.

2. See, for example, the range of activities of Beijing residents described in Tianjin Shi, *Political Participation in Beijing* (Cambridge: Harvard University Press, 1997).

3. Dietlind Stolle, Marc Hooghe, and Michele Micheletti, "Politics in the Supermarket: Political Consumerism as a Form of Political Participation," *International Political Science Review* 26 (2005): 245–70.

4. Pippa Norris, *Democratic Phoenix: Reinventing Political Activism* (New York: Cambridge University Press, 2003); Verba, Nie, and Kim, *Participation and Political Equality.*

5. Citizen interest group activity includes membership in groups working on local community issues, environmental interests, humans rights issues, women's issues, and the peace movement.

6. Russell Dalton, *Citizen Politics,* 4th ed. (Washington, DC: CQ Press, 2006, 2002), ch. 4; Norris, *Democratic Phoenix,* ch. 10.

7. See Verba, Nie, and Kim, *Participation and Political Equality;* and Barnes, Kaase, et al., *Political Action* (Beverly Hills: Sage Publications, 1979).

8. See the evidence in J. Craig Jenkins and Kurt Schock, "Political Process, International Dependence, and Mass Political Conflict: A Global Analysis of Protest and Rebellion, 1973–1978," *International Journal of Sociology* (2004) 33: 41–63.

9. Studies of these problems were stimulated by the now classic work of Mancur Olson, *The Logic of Collective Action* (Cambridge: Harvard University Press, 1965). See also Mark Lichbach, *The Rebel's Dilemma* (Ann Arbor: University of Michigan Press, 1994); Mancur Olson, "Dictatorship, Democracy, and Development," *American Political Science Review* 87, no. 3 (Sept. 1993): 567–76; Todd Sandler, ed., *Collective Action: Theory and Applications* (Ann Arbor: University of Michigan Press, 1992).

10. See G. F. Skilling and F. Griffiths, eds., *Interest Groups in Soviet Politics* (Princeton, NJ: Princeton University Press, 1971); the essays by Frederick C. Barghoorn and Skilling in Robert A. Dahl, *Regimes and Oppositions* (New Haven, CT: Yale University Press, 1973); Roman Kolkowicz, "Interest Groups in Soviet Politics," *Comparative Politics* 2, no. 3 (April 1970): 445–72.

11. Christopher Rootes, ed., *Environmental Movements: Local, National, and Global* (London: Frank Cass, 1999); Amrita Basu, ed., *The Challenges of Local Feminism: Women's Movements in Global Perspective* (Boulder, CO: Westview, 1995).

12. Jean Cohen and A. Arato, *Civil Society and Political Theory* (Cambridge: MIT Press, 1992); M. Walzer, ed., *Toward a Global Civil Society* (Oxford: Berghahn Books, 1995).

13. See Table 4.1; John Pierce et al., *Citizens, Political Communication, and Interest Groups: Environmental Organizations in Canada and the United States* (Westport, CT: Praeger, 1992).

14. Sidney Tarrow, *The New Transnational Activism* (New York: Cambridge University Press, 2005); Margaret Keck and Kathryn Sikkink, *Activists Beyond Borders: Advocacy Networks in International Politics* (Ithaca: Cornell University Press, 1998).

15. Marc Morjé Howard, *The Weakness of Civil Society in Post-Communist Europe* (New York: Cambridge University Press, 2003); Russell Dalton, "Civil Society and Democracy," in Russell Dalton and Doh Chull Shin, eds., *Citizens, Democracy, and Markets Around the Pacific Rim* (Oxford: Oxford University Press, 2006).

16. Philippe Schmitter, "Interest Intermediation and Regime Governability," in Suzanne Berger, ed., *Organizing Interests in Western Europe* (New York: Cambridge University Press, 1981), ch. 12; Arend Lijphart and Markus Crepaz, "Corporatism and Consensus Democracy in 18 Countries," *British Journal of Political Science* 21, no. 2 (April 1991): 235–46; Wyn Grant, ed., *The Political Economy of Corporatism* (New York: St. Martin's Press, 1985).

17. On the relative success of the corporatist systems in economic performance, see Miriam Golden, "The Dynamics of Trade Unionism and National Economic Performance," *American Political Science Review* 87, no. 2 (June 1993): 439–54; Arend Lijphart, Ronald Rogowski, and R. Kent Weaver, "Separation of Powers and Cleavage Management," in R. Kent Weaver and Bert A. Rockman, *Do Institutions Matter? Government Capabilities in the United States and Abroad* (Washington: Brookings Institution, 1993), 302–44.

18. Lyle Scruggs, "Institutions and Environmental Performance in Seventeen Western Democracies," *British Journal of Political Science* 29 (1999): 1–31.

19. Oscar Molina and Martin Rhodes, "Corporatism: The Past, Present and Future of a Concept," *Annual Review of Political Science* 2 (2002): 305–31.

20. Howard Wiarda, ed., *Authoritarianism and Corporatism in Latin America—Revisited* (Gainesville: University Press of Florida, 2004); Julius E. Nyang'Oro and Timothy M. Shaw, *Corporatism in Africa: Comparative Analysis and Practice* (Boulder, CO: Westview Press, 1990).

21. We should also note that most Chinese work and live in rural areas and are not wage earners. The figure is based on the share of the labor force that receives a regular salary, which in China means urban workers. But India has a comparable labor structure, and many fewer Indian wage earners are unionized.

22. Norris, *Democratic Phoenix.*

23. Ted Robert Gurr, "A Comparative Study of Civil Strife," in Hugh David Graham and Ted Robert Gurr, eds., *The History of Violence in America* (New York: Bantam Press, 1969), 462–63.

24. See Pippa Norris, Stefaan Walgrave, and Peter van Aelst, "Does Protest Signify Disaffection? Demonstrators in a Postindustrial Democracy," in Mariano Torcal and Jose Ramón Montero, eds., *Political Disaffection in Contemporary Democracies: Social Capital, Institutions and Politics* (London: Routledge, 2006): 279–307; Mark Baldassare, ed., *The Los Angeles Riots: Lessons for the Urban Future* (Boulder, CO: Westview, 1994).

25. On violence and democratic survival, see G. Bingham Powell, Jr., *Contemporary Democracies: Participation, Stability, and Violence* (Cambridge: Harvard University Press, 1982), ch. 8; see also the contributions to Juan J. Linz and Alfred Stepan, eds., *The Breakdown of Democratic Regimes* (Baltimore: Johns Hopkins University Press, 1978).

26. Robert D. Putnam, *Making Democracy Work: Civic Traditions in Modern Italy* (Princeton, NJ: Princeton University Press, 1993).

27. Ronald Inglehart, *Culture Shift in Advanced Industrial Societies* (Princeton, NJ: Princeton University Press, 1990), 34–36; see also Almond and Verba, *Civic Culture*, ch. 11.

28. Jeffrey M. Berry, *The Interest Group Society* (New York: Longman, 1997).

29. Many of these studies are reviewed by Mark I. Lichbach, "An Evaluation of 'Does Economic Inequality Breed Political Conflict' Studies," *World Politics* 41 (1989): 431–70. More recent references and analyses appear in T. Y. Wang et al., "Inequality and Political Violence Revisited," *American Political Science Review* 87, no. 4 (Dec. 1993): 979–93.

30. Robert Putnam, *Bowling Alone: The Collapse and Revival of American Community* (New York: Simon & Schuster, 2000); Robert Putnam, ed., *Democracies in Flux: The Evolution of Social Capital in Contemporary Society* (Oxford: Oxford University Press, 2002).

31. Cliff, Zukin et al., *A New Engagement? Political Participation, Civic Life, and the Changing American Citizen* (New York: Oxford University Press, 2006); Russell Dalton, *The Good Citizen* (Washington, DC: CQ Press, 2007), ch. 4.

INTEREST AGGREGATION AND POLITICAL PARTIES

Interest aggregation is the activity in which the political demands of individuals and groups are combined into policy programs. For example, in developing an economic policy program, politicians often have to balance farmers' desires for higher crop prices, consumers' preferences for lower prices and taxes, and environmentalists' concerns about water pollution and pesticides. Who prevails in such balancing acts depends in part on political institutions, which is the subject of Chapter 6. But interest aggregation depends also on political skills and resources, such as votes, campaign funds, political offices, media access, or even armed force.

How interests are aggregated is a key feature of the political process. The aggregation process determines which interests are heard, and what individuals and groups are allowed to participate. Interest aggregation can also help create a balanced government program out of competing policy goals. How stable and effective governments are also depend on their patterns of interest aggregation.

Interest aggregation can occur in many ways. An influential party leader or military dictator may have a considerable personal impact. Yet, large states usually develop more specialized organizations for aggregating interests. Political parties are just such organizations, and they play an important role in interest aggregation in democratic as well as in many nondemocratic systems. Each party (or its candidates) stands for a set of policies and tries to build a coalition of support for this program. In a democratic system, two or more parties compete to gain support for their alternative policy programs. In an authoritarian system, a single party or institution may try to mobilize citizens' support for its policies. In either type of system political parties may play a major role. In authoritarian systems the process is frequently covert and controlled, and the process is top-down rather than bottom-up. In other words, parties mobilize interests to support the government, rather than responding to demands by regular citizens or social interests.

It is important to remember that political parties may perform many different functions, and that different structures may aggregate interests. For instance, in addition to aggregating interests, parties frequently shape the political culture as they strive to build support for their ideologies, issue positions, and candidates. Parties recruit voters and select would-be officeholders. They articulate interests of their own and transmit the demands of others. Governing parties are also involved in making public policy and even in overseeing its implementation and adjudication. Yet, the distinctive and defining goal of a political party—its mobilization of support for policies and candidates—is especially related to interest aggregation. In this chapter we compare the role of parties in interest aggregation to those of other structures.

PERSONAL INTEREST AGGREGATION

One way to bring political interests together in policy-making is through personal connections. Virtually all societies feature **patron-client networks**—structures in which a central officeholder, authority figure, or group provides benefits (patronage) to supporters in exchange for their loyalty. It was the defining principle of feudalism. The king and his lords, the lord and his knights, the knight and his serfs and tenants—all were bound by ties of personal dependence and loyalty. The American political machines of Boss Tweed of New York or Richard Daley, Sr., of Chicago were similarly bound together by patronage and loyalty. Personal networks are not confined to relationships cemented by patronage only. The president of the United States, for instance, usually has a circle of personal confidants, a "brain trust" or "kitchen cabinet," bound to their chief by ideological and policy propensities as well as by ties of friendship.

The patron-client network is so common in politics that it resembles the cell in biology or the atom in physics—the primitive structure out of which larger and more complicated political structures are composed. Students of politics in all countries report such networks. When interest aggregation is performed mainly within patron-client networks, it is difficult to mobilize political resources behind unified policies of social change or to respond to crises. This is because political decisions depend on ever-shifting agreements among many factional leaders (patrons). Patron-client politics thus typically means a static political system.

Contemporary research on patron-client relationships was pioneered in studies of Asian politics, where this structure runs through the political processes of countries such as the Philippines, Japan, and India.[1] But parallels exist in Europe, the Middle East, Latin America, and most regions of the world. Patron-client relationships affect recruitment to political office, interest aggregation, policymaking, and policy implementation. Yet as Table 5.1 shows, patron-client networks are a particularly important means of aggregating political interests in poorer countries.

INSTITUTIONAL INTEREST AGGREGATION

In modern societies, as citizens become aware of larger collective interests and have the resources and skills to work for them, personal networks tend to be regulated, limited, and incorporated within broader organizations. Interest groups with powerful resources

Elections can stir strong feelings of joy or disappointment. Here, French protesters demonstrate against the election of President Nicolas Sarkozy in May 2007. The placard reads: "No to capitalism with a human face."

AFP/Getty Images

Country	Patron-Client Networks	Associational Groups	Competitive Parties	Authoritarian Parties	Military Forces
Brazil	Moderate	Moderate	Moderate	—	Moderate
Britain	Low	High	High	—	Low
China	Moderate	Low	—	High	High
France	Low	Moderate	High	—	Low
Germany	Low	High	High	—	Low
India	High	Moderate	Moderate	—	Low
Iran	High	Moderate	Low	—	Moderate
Japan	Moderate	High	High	—	Low
Mexico	Moderate	Moderate	Moderate	—	Low
Nigeria	High	Low	Moderate	—	Moderate
Russia	Moderate	Low	Moderate	—	Moderate
United States	Low	Moderate	High	—	Low

TABLE 5.1 Structures Performing Interest Aggregation in Selected Contemporary Nations*

Extensiveness of Interest Aggregation by Actor

*Extensiveness of interest aggregation rated as low, moderate, or high. Rating refers to broad-level performance issue areas and at different times. Blank implies that such actors do not exist.

can easily cross the subtle dividing line between interest articulation and aggregation. **Associational groups** (see Chapter 4) often support political contenders such as political parties. But they can occasionally wield sufficient resources to become contenders in their own right. For instance, the political power of the labor unions within the British Labour Party historically rested on the unions' ability to develop coherent policy positions and mobilize their members (who were formally represented in the party) to support those positions. As we discussed in Chapter 4, interest group systems of democratic corporatism empower both labor and business groups to get actively engaged in making economic policies. These arrangements include continuous political bargaining among organized labor, business interests, political parties, and government representatives. Such corporatist systems interconnect organizations that in other political systems play very different, often antagonistic, roles. Table 5.1 illustrates how associational groups tend to play a larger role in democratic politics that accept the independence of interest groups and their attempts to influence government policy.

Institutional groups, like bureaucratic agencies and military factions, can also be important interest aggregators. Indeed, the bureaucracy performs this function in most societies. Although established primarily to implement public policy, the bureaucracy may negotiate with interest groups to identify their preferences or to mobilize their support. Government agencies may even be "captured" by interest groups and used to support their demands. Bureaucrats often create client support networks to expand their organizations or to enhance their ability to solve problems in their areas of expertise. Military organizations, with their special control of physical force, can also be powerful interest aggregators. We shall have more to say about their role later in this chapter.

COMPETITIVE PARTY SYSTEMS AND INTEREST AGGREGATION

In many contemporary political systems, parties are the primary structures of interest aggregation. Political parties are *groups or organizations that seek to place candidates in office under their label.* In any given society, there may be one party, two parties, or as many as ten or twenty. We refer to the number of parties, and the relationships among them, as properties of the **party system.** The most critical distinction runs between **competitive party systems,** which primarily try to build electoral support, and noncompetitive or **authoritarian party systems,** which seek to direct society. This distinction does not depend on the closeness of electoral victory, or on the number of parties. It depends instead on the ability of political parties to freely form and compete for citizen support, and on this competition for citizen support as the key to government control. Thus a party system can be competitive even if one party wins most of the votes in a certain area, or even dominates several consecutive national elections, as long as other parties can challenge its dominance at the polls.

The role of competitive parties in interest aggregation depends not only on the individual party but also on the structure of parties, electorates, electoral laws, and policymaking institutions. Typically, interest aggregation in a competitive party system takes place

at several stages: within the individual parties, as the party chooses candidates and adopts policy proposals; through electoral competition; and after the election through bargaining and coalition building with other parties in the legislature or executive.

Political parties have been around as long as there have been elections and representative assemblies, but modern democratic parties began developing in Europe and the Americas from about the mid-nineteenth century. They have since emerged in all societies that have adopted free and fair elections and democratic government. Parties differ in their purposes and organization. Some have elaborate policy platforms, whereas others are little more than vehicles for ambitious politicians to get elected (or even to enrich themselves). Some parties are highly structured mass organizations, whereas others are loose, *personalistic* groups dominated by their leaders (see Box 5.1).

The first parties were typically *internally created;* their founders were politicians who already held seats in the national assembly or other political

---

Personalistic Parties

BOX 5.1

Political parties are typically formal organizations with officers, members, statutes, and official policy programs. Sometimes, however, parties can be much looser *personalistic* movements built around one political leader, or a small group of leaders. Personalistic parties are particularly common in new democracies. In Russia, for example, President Putin has been able to form a party (United Russia) with a strong personal following. But even India and France have highly personalistic parties. In India, the Congress Party has been dominated by the families of its most important founders, Gandhi and Nehru. In France, most presidents have come out of the Gaullist movement, which has had many names but has been dominated from the start by President Charles de Gaulle and later by some of his followers. Personalistic parties commonly do not have a very clear policy program. They are often susceptible to clientelistic politics and sometimes become vehicles for purely personal ambitions and rent seeking.

Shmuel Flatto-Sharon offers a blatant but extreme example. Flatto-Sharon is a French businessman of Jewish background. In 1977 he fled to Israel because the French authorities wanted to prosecute him for embezzling $60 million. To avoid extradition, he decided to run for election to the Knesset (the Israeli national assembly), which would give him immunity from prosecution. He formed a party, which he ran as a one-man operation—it had no other candidates or officers. Flatto-Sharon refused to identify himself as left, right, or center. He appealed for Jewish solidarity, arguing that Israel should not allow him to be imprisoned in a gentile country (France). He also promised a free television set to all Israeli households (this was before television sets became inexpensive and commonplace). And he promised to pay anyone who voted for him. Remarkably, he won two parliamentary seats, even though as his party's only candidate he could not fill the second seat. In 1981, however, Flatto-Sharon lost his bid for reelection. He was convicted of bribery for his vote-buying scheme and sent to jail in Israel, but never extradited to France.

offices. These parties were often committed to broad constitutional principles (such as republican government, universal suffrage, or separation of church and state), but otherwise they often had only loose policy programs and little organization outside the legislature. They often had colorful names which said little about their policies, such as Whigs and Tories in Britain, Whites ("Blancos") and Reds ("Colorados") in several Latin American countries, Hats and Caps in Sweden, or for that matter Democrats and Republicans in the United States. Some of the descendents of these parties have kept their original names; others now call themselves Liberals (such as the previous Whigs) or Conservatives (such as the previous Tories).

During the late nineteenth century and early twentieth century, a series of other types of parties emerged, as the democratic countries industrialized and urbanized, and as larger and larger segments of the adult population gained the right to vote. The growth of the industrial working class led to the formation of socialist, social democratic, communist, and other workers' parties. Farming interests gained representation through agrarian parties, and other parties emerged to represent religious communities (such as Catholics or Hindus) or ethnic or linguistic minorities. In countries that were not independent, parties of national independence often became a dominant force. All of these parties were typically *externally created*—they organized outside Parliament before they became a force inside those institutions. They often had much stronger mass membership organizations than their older competitors, and they often also had (and continue to have) closer ties to specific interest groups. Thus, social democrats and communists tended to have strong ties to labor unions, agrarian parties to farmers' organizations, and many Christian Democratic parties (at least Catholic ones) to the Vatican and religious organizations.

Most of these parties still exist and continue to play a leading role. They have settled into stable *party families* of Social Democrats, Conservatives, Christian Democrats, Liberals, Nationalists, etc., which often maintain close contacts across national boundaries. The party systems of most countries show a great deal of stability, and many of the most important parties of the early twenty-first century were also the dominant parties a hundred years ago. Yet, two important new types of parties have emerged in the past thirty or forty years, particularly in advanced industrial countries. One is the "new left," or Green parties, that in many countries emerged in the 1960s or 1970s. These parties tend to champion international peace and disarmament, ecological and environmental protection, gender equality, a large welfare state, and minority rights. They are often more supportive of alternative lifestyles than traditional working-class parties of the left (such as Social Democrats). The other important type of new party is the "populist right." These parties tend to be critical of existing parties and political leaders, whom they see as elitist, corrupt, and out of touch. They favor strict law-and-order policies but criticize what they see as "politically correct" government interventionism. They dislike the distortions that the welfare state sometimes creates, such as policies that make it unattractive to work and easy to live off of welfare benefits (see Chapter 7). And they typically oppose large-scale immigration (see Box 5.2).

The party systems of most democratic countries reflect a mix of these various party families. But no two party systems are exactly alike, and not all party families are represented in all countries. The variations in party systems reflect differences in demographics, economic development, and political histories. They also depend on differences in electoral systems, as we shall discuss below.

Elections

In democracies, political parties live and die by their performance in political elections. The act of voting, and giving support to a political candidate, party, or policy proposal, is one of the simplest and most frequently performed political acts. By aggregating these votes, the citizens can make a collective decision about their future leaders and public policies. Elections are one of the few devices through which diverse interests can be expressed equally and comprehensively.[2]

The simple act of voting can have profound implications. The voters' choice of parties and candidates helps aggregate political interests. Electoral outcomes determine who manages the affairs of government and makes public policy. And parties generally fulfill their electoral promises when they gain control of government.[3] When leftist governments come to power in Europe, they tend to expand the size and efforts of the government; whereas conservative parties generally slow the growth of government

BOX 5.2

Parties Just for Fun

Some political parties seem to have no other purpose than to make fun of politics and politicians. One example is Britain's Official Monster Raving Loony Party (OMRLP) formed in 1983. Its founding leader was musician David Sutch, who called himself Screaming Lord Sutch. Sutch and the other founders were apparently inspired by the television series *Monty Python's Flying Circus*. The OMRLP has never won any seat in Parliament, but has captured a few seats in local British government. Sutch died in 1999 and was replaced as party leader by Alan "Howling Laud" Hope. In 2005, the party ran on a platform of abolishing the income tax, inviting the rest of Europe to adopt the British currency, retraining "stupid traffic cops" as clergy, and introducing a ninety-nine-pence coin to "save on change." These proposals may be political longshots, but one of the party's early goals, for British pubs to stay open all day, has actually been achieved.

In Denmark, comedian Jacob Haugaard has since 1979 several times contested parliamentary elections as a candidate for the Association of Deliberate Work Avoiders. In 1994, he won election to the Danish Parliament. His election platform included demands for disability pensions for people who lack a sense of humor, tailwinds on all Danish bike paths, more generous Christmas presents, more renaissance furniture at IKEA, and more whales in Danish waters. Haugaard also promised his voters free beer, and he used the public funds his party received from the Danish government to fulfill this campaign commitment (he bought beer and hot dogs for his supporters after the election).

programs and promote private enterprise. Republicans and Democrats in the United States also have been fairly responsible in keeping their promises. However, parties that want radical change or have not recently been in office often find it difficult to implement their programs when they eventually come to power. When, for example, the German Greens came to power in 1998 as part of a coalition government, they had to modify their promise to shut down Germany's nuclear power plants immediately. Instead they negotiated a phase-out over many years. But by and large, parties try hard to implement their programs, and citizens can therefore influence interest aggregation and policymaking through their role in selecting elites.

When they aggregate interests and make policy, party leaders are often caught between the demands of their party activists and the voters. Party activists often want policies that are more radical than those that most voters prefer. At any rate, activists will typically insist more vigorously that the party program should be implemented, whereas ordinary voters are often happier when governments try to compromise and listen to opinions outside their own parties. There is a broad and ongoing debate about the extent to which democracy requires political parties to be internally democratic. Advocates of participatory democracy strongly support

this idea, as do parties such as the European Greens. On the other hand, the famous Austrian economist Joseph A. Schumpeter argued that vigorous competition *between* parties is what matters for a healthy democracy and that democracy within parties is irrelevant or even harmful.[4] (See also Box 5.3.)

Elections often have other functions as well (see also Chapter 4). The communist nations of Eastern Europe and elsewhere utilized elections to legitimize their governments. They routinely reported turnout that exceeded 98 percent of the electorate. But the outcome was given in advance. Until 1990, voters in the Soviet Union were given only one candidate to vote for, and this person was always a nominee of the Communist Party. Voter participation was very high in these nations because the government pressured people to participate and express their symbolic support for the regime, not because the elections actually decided anything. Elections played a role in socializing and shaping citizens' attitudes, but had little to do with interest articulation or aggregation.[5]

In most democratic countries, voters can freely choose whether or not to vote. Some democratic countries, though, require citizens to vote and impose penalties on those who do not. Voting choices reflect a mix of motivations.[6] Many citizens try to judge the parties' policy promises. For others, elections are a

The Iron Law of Oligarchy

BOX 5.3

Can political parties be the main vehicles of democratic representation if they do not govern themselves democratically? This has been a main concern among students of modern political parties. In 1911, the young German sociologist Robert Michels published a study of the German Socialist Party in which he formulated the "iron law of oligarchy," which states that all modern organizations tend towards oligarchy (rule by the few) rather than democracy. "Who says organization says oligarchy," Michels famously observed. He identified several forces that push organizations such as political parties towards oligarchy. One is the need for specialization and differentiation that exists in all large, modern organizations. A second cause of oligarchy lies in the fact that most ordinary members do not have the time or resources to hold their leaders accountable and that they often crave strong leadership. A third reason is that parties foster leaders who live "off" politics rather than "for" politics. They exploit their leadership positions to advance their own ambitions for wealth or power, often to the detriment of their followers. (In contemporary terms, we would refer to such self-interested pursuit of power as rent seeking.) Michels' study was particularly troubling because he found these tendencies even in a party, the German Socialist Party, with which he sympathized and which was considered particularly strongly committed to democratic ideals.

Source: Robert Michels, *Political Parties* (New York: Free Press, 1962).

simple referendum on government performance. They vote to throw the rascals out if times are bad, and to reelect them if times are good. In other cases, elections can be dominated by the charisma of a strong leader or the incompetence of a weak one. In each case, however, elections aggregate these diverse concerns to make a collective decision on the composition of government.

Electoral Systems

The rules by which elections are conducted are among the most important structures that affect political parties. We refer to these rules as the **electoral system.** They determine who can vote, how people vote, and how the votes get counted. The rules that determine how voter choices are translated into election outcomes, how votes are converted into seats, are especially important. In the United States, Britain, and many countries influenced by Britain (such as India and Canada), the legislative election rules divide the country into many election districts. In each district, the candidate who has more votes than any other—a *plurality*—wins the election in the district. This simple, **single-member district plurality (SMDP) election rule** is often called "first past the post," a horse-racing term, because the winner need only finish ahead of the others but not win a majority of the votes. This system seems obvious and natural to Americans, but it is rarely used in continental Europe or in Latin America. Another version of single-member district elections is the **majority runoff** (or **double-ballot**) system used in France and in presidential elections in Russia. In this system, voting happens in two stages, normally separated by a couple of weeks. In the first round, it takes a majority of all votes (50 percent + 1) to win. The winning candidate, then, has to win not just more votes than any other candidate, but more votes than all other candidates combined. If there is no majority winner in the first round, then only a smaller number of candidates (in French and Russian presidential elections the top two) make it into the second round, in which whoever gets the largest number of votes is elected.

In contrast to the single-member district system, most democracies use some form of **proportional representation (PR)** in multimember districts. In these systems the country is divided into a few large districts, which may elect as many as twenty or thirty members apiece. These districts are often the states or provinces that make up the country. In the Netherlands and Israel, the entire country is a single electoral district with more than 100 members. The competing parties offer lists of candidates for the slots in each district. The number of representatives a party wins depends on the overall proportion of the votes it receives, though no system is perfectly proportional. A party receiving 4 percent of the vote would be awarded approximately 4 percent of the legislative seats. Sometimes parties must achieve a minimum threshold of votes, usually 3 to 5 percent nationally, to receive any seats at all. If so many parties compete that a lot of them fall below this threshold, many voters may be left unrepresented, as happened in Russia in 1995.

In order to compete effectively, parties must formulate appealing policy programs and nominate attractive candidates for office. They must anticipate the offerings of their competitors and the preferences of the voters. The procedure that parties use to develop policy positions varies greatly from country to country and from party to party. In the United States the national party conventions held at each presidential election formalize the party's policy positions, both by adopting a party platform and by selecting a slate of candidates. In other countries, parties have more regular congresses, and centralized party organizations issue party programs (also known as platforms or manifestos).[7] Whatever the system, a successful program must both spell out policy positions that are popular with the voters and aggregate interests within the party.

Parties must also offer candidates for office. In the United States, voters directly select these candidates through **primary elections.** But primaries are an unusually open form of candidate selection. In most other countries with **single-member district (SMD)** elections, party officials select the candidates, either locally or nationally. In proportional representation elections, the party draws up a list of candidates for each district. In **closed-list PR systems,** the elected representatives are then simply drawn from the top of this list, in declining order, and ordinary voters have no say about their candidates. In **open-list systems,** on the other hand, voters can give preference votes to individual candidates, and these votes are counted when it is decided which candidates will represent the party in that district. Besides adopting programs and selecting candidates, parties also attempt to publicize them and mobilize electoral support through rallies, media advertising, door-to-door campaigning, and other activities.

Patterns of Electoral Competition

In democratic party systems, the electoral system is a major determinant of the patterns of electoral competition. Two famous political science theories help us understand this connection: Duverger's Law and Downs' median voter result. **Duverger's Law,** which is named after the French political scientist Maurice Duverger, is one of the best-known theories in political science.[8] It states that there is a systematic relationship between electoral systems and party systems, so that plurality single-member district election systems tend to create two-party systems in the legislature, while proportional representation electoral systems generate multiparty systems. Duverger identified two mechanisms behind this regularity. He called them the mechanical effect and the psychological effect. The **mechanical effect** is to be found in the way that different electoral systems convert votes into seats. In single-member district systems, parties get no representation unless they finish first in at least one district. Therefore, smaller parties that run second, third, or fourth across many districts receive little or no representation. In the 2005 election in Britain, for example, the Liberal Democratic Party (Britain's third largest party) received 22 percent of the votes, but less than 10 percent of the seats in Parliament. The **psychological effect** lies in the fact that both voters and candidates anticipate the mechanical effect. Therefore, voters do not throw their support behind "hopeless" parties and candidates. Instead, they may support their second-best (or even third-best) option in order to keep a party that they strongly dislike from winning. And knowing that the voters will not support them, minor party candidates are reluctant to run. Giving your support to a party or candidate that is not your first choice in order to avoid an even worse outcome is known as **strategic voting.** Duverger argues that strategic voting tends to work to the advantage of parties that are already large and to the disadvantage of small ones. In U.S. elections, it has been fairly common for third-party candidates to run well in the polls until close to the election date, when voters realize that these candidates are not going to win. Their support then often declines rapidly.

Anthony Downs examined the effects of the number of parties on their policy positions. He showed that in two-party systems in which the parties are competing along a left-right (or other) policy dimension and are interested only in winning elections, and where all voters choose the party closest to their policy preferences, the parties will moderate their policies so as to try to win the support of the median voter (the voter who is at the midpoint of the vote distribution, with as many other voters to the right as to the left). Downs' contribution is known as the **median voter result.** According to this theory, two-party systems will exhibit a centrist pull or "convergence." In systems with only two parties, parties have to try to win a majority, so targeting the "center" of the electorate is critical. In PR systems with many political parties, however, no one group has much chance of winning a

majority, and parties can survive with much less support. Therefore, there is not the same centrist pull and parties may instead spread themselves out across the policy spectrum.[9]

Figure 5.1 offers a comparative "snapshot" of parties and voters in several democratic countries. It shows where citizens in each country placed the parties on a left-right scale in public opinion surveys in the early

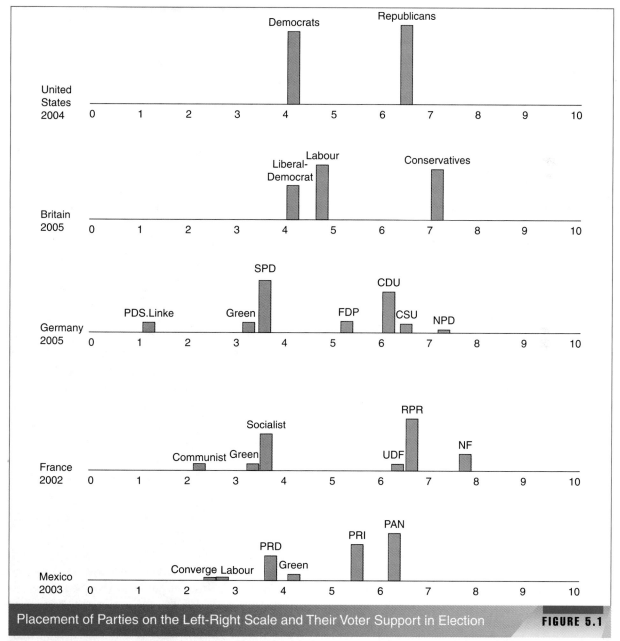

Placement of Parties on the Left-Right Scale and Their Voter Support in Election   **FIGURE 5.1**

Source: Party positions from placements by all voters. The height of the bar represents the percentage of the total vote won by that party in the legislative election identified on the left.

2000s, with zero identified as Left (or liberal in the United States) and 10 identified as Right (or conservative in the United States). Note that although the left-right placements reflect the relative positions of the parties in their respective societies, the meaning of left, right, and center can be different in different societies. The height of the columns above the scale shows what percentage of the electorate voted for each party. The two countries at the top of the figure, the United States and Britain, use SMDP electoral systems, whereas France uses a majority runoff system, Mexico a mixed system, and Germany in practice a PR system. According to Duverger, we should expect the United States and Britain to have only two serious parties and the others more. Following Downs, we should expect the two-party systems to be centrist and clustered in policy space and the multiparty systems to be more dispersed.

By and large, Figure 5.1 supports both Duverger and Downs. In the countries at the top of the figure, especially in the United States, there are only two large parties. Moreover, the parties are fairly close to the center. Democrats are somewhat to the left and Republicans somewhat to the right, with a lot of overlap. The left-right "gap" between the average party supporters, although larger than it was twenty years ago, is still fairly small. In France, toward the bottom of the figure, many parties receive voter support. There is a very large distance between the left-most party (the Communists) and right-most party (the National Front), and even between the two largest parties (Socialists and RPR).

Britain and Germany fall between these more extreme cases. As Duverger would predict, Britain looks more like the United States, but the parties are farther apart and the smaller Liberal Democratic Party falls between the two major ones. Mexico shows that even systems with proportional representation and more than two parties (though only three significant ones) can have convergent and centrist electoral politics. Yet, in the most recent years, for example in the 2006 presidential election, the Mexican parties have seemed to pull apart and become less centrist.

Table 5.2 presents additional information on electoral and party systems. It displays data on the **effective number of parties** in each country. This measure takes into account both the overall number of parties and their relative sizes. For example, if there are two parties and they are exactly the same size, the effective number of parties is 2.0. If, however, one

party has 80 percent of the votes and the other 20 percent, the effective number of parties is just below 1.5.[10] The effective number of parties can be calculated for either votes or seats, as we have done in Table 5.2. If Duverger's Law is correct, then the effective number of parties should be lower in countries that have SMDP electoral systems than in those that have other systems (particularly PR). Table 5.2 shows that this is largely true, as three of the four countries that have the lowest effective number of parties do indeed have SMDP elections. At the same time, India is an exception; it has a large number of parties despite an SMDP electoral system. But a closer look at India shows that even though the country has many parties overall, most electoral districts feature only two serious parties.[11] Thus, India helps us understand one limitation of Duverger's Law, which is that while SMDP systems tend to sustain only two parties in each election district, these two parties need not be the same throughout the country.

Table 5.2 also gives us a measure of the mechanical effect in Duverger's Law, the consequences of the counting rules themselves. By comparing the effective number of parties among the voters (vote shares) with the effective number of parties in the national assembly (seat shares), we can see how much the electoral system helps the large parties and disfavors the small ones. This bias exists in all countries and electoral systems, as the numbers in the column for seat shares are always consistently lower than those in the column for vote shares. Duverger's Law suggests that this difference should be greater in "first past the post" (SMDP) systems than elsewhere, but it is not clear that our data bear that out.

Competitive Parties in Government

If a competitive party wins control of the legislature and the executive, it will (if unified) be able to pass and implement its policies. Sometimes this control emerges directly from the electoral process, as a single party wins a majority of the vote. But in many countries the election laws help the largest party gain a governing majority even if it does not enjoy majority support among the voters. Thus, less than 50 percent of the vote may be converted into more than 50 percent of the legislative seats. Such "artificial" or "manufactured" legislative majorities have been the rule in countries with "first past the post" (SMDP) electoral systems, such as Britain.[12]

Elections—Lower House of National Legislature

TABLE 5.2

Country	Electoral System	Effective Number of Parties— Vote Shares	Effective Number of Parties— Seat Shares	How Are Individual Candidates Selected?
Brazil	PR open list	10.63	9.30	Candidate preference vote
Britain	SMD plurality	3.56	2.45	Nominated by local constituency association
China	No contested elections	No contested elections	No contested elections	No contested elections
France	SMD majority run-off	3.37	2.25	Nominated by local constituency association
Germany	Mixed system: SMD plurality + PR closed list	3.75*	3.44*	National party + state party conventions
India	SMD plurality	7.50	6.55	Nominated by local constituency association
Iran	MMD majority run-off	No available data	2.66	Must be approved by Council of Guardians
Japan	Mixed system: SMD plurality + PR closed list	3.72	2.26	National party
Mexico	Mixed system: SMD plurality + PR closed list	3.60	3.02	Nominated by local constituency association + national party
Nigeria	SMD plurality	2.62	2.34	Nominated by local constituency association
Russia	PR closed list	4.71 (under previous electoral system with SMD plurality + PR closed list)	3.18	National party
United States	SMD plurality	2.17	2.00	Primary elections

Note: Data from the most recent national elections, as of October 1, 2006.

MMD = Multimember district

SMD = Single-member district

PR = Proportional representation

*Calculated using proportional representation results.

Sources: Arend Lijphart, *Patterns of Democracy* (New Haven: Yale University Press, 1999); www.Electionguide.org; www.Wikipedia.org.

For example, since 1974 either the Conservative Party or the Labour Party has consistently won a majority of seats in the British House of Commons, even though neither party has ever been supported by a majority of the voters in any of these elections. Margaret Thatcher's Conservative Party won a solid majority in the House of Commons in 1983 and 1987 with only about 42 percent of the vote. With almost exactly the same level of support, Tony Blair and the Labour Party won nearly two-thirds of the seats in 1997 and 2001. In 2005, Labour's share of the vote fell to about 35 percent, but the party still got a solid majority of the seats. In all these elections, the quarter of the electorate supporting the smaller British parties received only a handful of parliamentary seats.

In other countries, multiparty elections do not yield single-party majorities, but party coalitions formed before the election may still offer the voters a direct choice of future governments. Before the election, a group of parties may join forces, agree to coordinate their election campaigns, or agree to govern together if they jointly win a parliamentary majority. When such coalitions form, as they have in many (but not all) elections in France and Germany, it is almost like a two-party system. Voters can clearly identify the potential governments and reward or punish the incumbents if they so choose. They thus have the ability to choose the direction of government policy through their party choice.

When elections do not create a majority party, and there is no preelectoral coalition, the political parties and their leaders must negotiate a new government after the election. This is common in many multiparty parliamentary systems, such as the India and Italy.[13] In these nations interests are not aggregated through elections, because the election does not determine the government. Instead, the aggregation of interests occurs in government when a coalition is negotiated. (See also Chapter 6, and Figure 6.2.)

The aggregation of interests at the executive rather than electoral level can have both costs and benefits. On the one hand, when elite party coalitions determine government policy, voters may feel that the government is not accountable to them. And because interest aggregation occurs among political elites, different elite coalitions can form on different issues. This can be confusing to citizens (and even informed observers). It may be difficult for voters to assign clear responsibility for government policy, and it may seem unfair that the electoral losers sometimes get to decide. This situation lessens the value of the vote as an instrument to shape future policy or to punish parties responsible for bad policy choices in the past.

On the other hand, there may be benefits for minority interests when all parties, not just the election winners, are represented in policymaking. All citizens hold minority opinions on some issues, and some are in the minority on many issues. If even minority representatives can influence policy between elections, they may feel that they have more political protection. Finally, even governments that win a majority of votes typically do not have majority support for all of their policy proposals. So there may be benefits for the nation as a whole when even the winners have to negotiate the different parts of their programs. Such bargaining may even increase the likelihood that policies reflect different majorities on different issues. The value of elections as instruments of representation may increase when interests are aggregated within a government coalition, though the value of elections as instruments of accountability may diminish.[14]

Cooperation and Conflict in Competitive Party Systems

Competitive party systems can be classified by the number of parties as well as by the patterns of competition or cooperation among them. **Majoritarian**

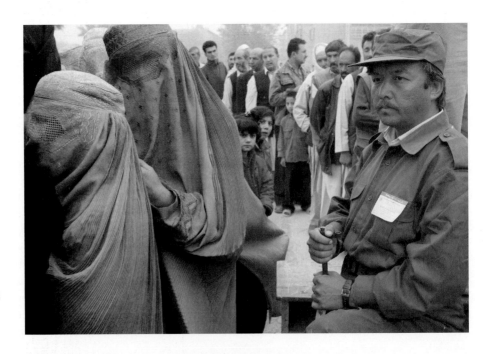

Democratization means new political rights and, often, social change. Here, women line up to vote in Afghanistan's first democratic elections.

Caren Firouz/Reuters/Corbis

two-party systems are either dominated by just two parties, as in the United States, or they have two dominant parties and election laws that usually create legislative majorities for one of them, as in Britain. In **majority-coalition systems,** parties establish preelectoral coalitions so that voters know which parties will attempt to work together to form a government. Germany and France have in most elections been in this category. Purely **multiparty systems** have election laws and party systems that virtually ensure that no single party wins a legislative majority and no tradition of preelection coalitions. Interest aggregation then depends on a coalition of parties bargaining and coming to agreement after the election.

The degree of antagonism or polarization among the parties is another important party system characteristic. In a **consensual party system,** the parties commanding most of the legislative seats are not too far apart on policies and have a reasonable amount of trust in each other and in the political system. These are typically party systems like those shown toward the top of Figure 5.1 Bargaining may be intense and politics exciting, but it seldom threatens the system itself. In a **conflictual party system,** the legislature is dominated by parties that are far apart on issues or are antagonistic toward each other and the political system, such as the Russian party system in the 1990s.

Some party systems have both consensual and conflictual features. Arend Lijphart has used the term **consociational** (or **accommodative**) to describe party systems in which political leaders are able to bridge the intense differences between antagonistic voters through power-sharing, broad coalitions, and decentralization of sensitive decisions to the separate social groups.[15] A consociational system can enable a deeply divided nation to find a way to peaceful democratic development. In Austria and Lebanon after World War II, suspicious and hostile groups—the socialists and Catholics in Austria, and the Christians and Muslims in Lebanon—worked out a set of consociational understandings that made stable government possible. Austria's accommodation was based on a two-party system and Lebanon's on many small, personalistic religious parties. Austria's consociationalism was largely successful, but the Lebanese experiment was not. After 1975, the country fell victim to civil war.

South Africa also adopted consociational practices in its transition to democracy. Leaders of the major political parties of the white minority and two major segments of the black majority negotiated (with great difficulty) arrangements for a democratic transition. The "Interim Constitution" guaranteed a share in power and government—cabinet posts—to all parties winning over 5 percent of the vote. Later, this feature was abandoned.

As the contrasting examples of Austria and Lebanon suggest, consociational practices (and the ability even to agree to attempt them) offer deeply divided democracies hope but no guarantees of long-term success. One critical aspect of consociationalism is that many important decisions are taken by small groups of politicians behind closed doors. If these politicians are able to work together more constructively than their supporters, then consociationalism can be a happy solution. But if the politicians are intransigent or self-interested, it may not be the best option.

The number of parties does not always tell us much about the degree of antagonism. The United States and Britain are relatively consensual majoritarian party systems. They are not perfect two-party systems because minor parties exist in both countries, especially in Britain. Yet, one or the other of the two major British parties usually wins majority control and governs through disciplined party voting. In the United States, the degree of consensus changes from election to election because of the shifting programs of presidential candidates. Moreover, the looser cohesion of American parties and the frequency of divided government lead to postelection bargaining that is similar to consensual multiparty systems.

But not all majoritarian party systems are consensual. Austria between 1918 and 1934 is the best example of a conflictual majoritarian party system. Antagonism between the Socialist Party and the other parties was so intense that in the mid-1930s it produced a brief civil war. The Austrian experience also illustrates how party systems can change. After World War II, the leaders of the two major parties negotiated an elaborate coalition agreement of mutual power sharing—checks and balances—to contain the country's conflicts. After some twenty years of the consociational "Grand Coalition," party antagonism had greatly declined.

Consensual multiparty systems are found in Norway and Sweden, among other countries. France (1946–1958), Italy (1945–1992), and Weimar Germany (1919–1933), on the other hand, are historical examples of conflictual multiparty systems, with powerful communist parties on the left and conservative or fascist movements on the right. Cabinets had to form out of centrist movements, which were themselves divided on many issues. This resulted in instability, poor government performance, and loss of citizen confidence in democracy. These factors contributed to the collapse of the French Fourth Republic, to government instability and citizen alienation from politics in Italy, and to the overthrow of democracy in Weimar Germany.

New democracies, especially those divided by language or ethnicity, sometimes face similar challenges. Some of the emerging party systems in Central and Eastern Europe have fallen into the pattern of conflictual, multiparty competition. For instance, in the 1995 parliamentary elections in Russia, forty-three parties appeared on the ballot—ranging from unreformed communists on the left to nationalist parties on the right—and seven parties won representation in Parliament. But later elections greatly reduced the number of parties.

Thus, although the number of parties affects political stability, the degree of antagonism among parties is more important. Two-party systems are stable and effective, but they may be dangerous if society is too deeply divided. Multiparty systems consisting of relatively moderate parties can often offer stability and fairly effective performance, especially if the parties are willing to commit themselves to preelectoral coalitions. Pure multiparty systems without preelectoral coalitions are more prone to ineffectiveness, but some have worked well over long periods. Where social groups and parties are highly antagonistic, however, collapse and civil war are ever-present possibilities, regardless of the number of parties. When crises develop, the most critical factor is typically how committed party leaders are to working together to defend democracy. Sometimes party leaders in a multiparty, representative setting are more accustomed to such cooperation.[16]

AUTHORITARIAN PARTY SYSTEMS

Authoritarian party systems can also aggregate interests. They deliberately attempt to develop policy proposals and to mobilize support for them, but they do so in a completely different way from competitive party systems. In authoritarian party systems, aggregation takes place within the party or in interactions with business groups, unions, landowners, and institutional groups in the bureaucracy or military. Although there may be sham elections, the citizens have no real opportunity to shape aggregation by choosing between party alternatives.

Authoritarian party systems can be distinguished according to the degree of top-down control within the party and the party's control over other groups in society. At one extreme is the **exclusive governing party,** which insists on almost total control over political resources. It recognizes no legitimate interest aggregation by groups within the party. Nor does it permit any free activity, much less opposition, from interest groups, citizens, or other government agencies. In its most extreme form, sometimes called totalitarianism, it penetrates the entire society and mobilizes support for policies developed at the top. Its policies are legitimated by a political ideology, such as communism or national socialism (Nazism) that claims to know the true interests of the citizens, regardless of what the citizens themselves believe.[17] At the other extreme is the **inclusive governing party,** which recognizes and accepts at least some other groups and organizations, but may repress those that it sees as serious challenges to its own control.

Exclusive Governing Parties

In a purely totalitarian society, there is only one party with total top-down control of society, and no autonomous opposition parties or interest groups. Totalitarian single-party systems can be impressive vehicles of political mobilization. A clear ideology provides legitimacy and coherence, and the party penetrates and organizes society in the name of that ideology and in accordance with its policies. But totalitarianism is difficult to sustain. Although the ruling communist parties of the Soviet Union before 1985, of Eastern Europe before 1989, and of North Korea, Vietnam, and Cuba today resemble this model, few parties have long maintained such absolute control. China is an interesting mixed case. While the Chinese government has withdrawn from the direct administration of much of the economy, it still does not recognize the legitimacy of any opposition groups. The ruling party permits, within bounds, some interest articulation by individuals, but not mass mobilization against government policy.[18]

Not all exclusive governing parties are totalitarian, however. Many leaders committed to massive social change—for example national independence from colonialism—have used the exclusive governing party as a tool for mass mobilization. Such exclusive governing parties may experience more internal dissent than is commonly recognized. Within the party, groups may unite around such interests as their region or industry, or behind leaders of different policy factions. Beneath the supposedly united front, power struggles may erupt in times of crisis. Succession crises are particularly likely to generate such power struggles, as at the death of Stalin in the Soviet Union and Mao Zedong in China. The Chinese Communist Party has several times had to rely on the army, even on coalitions of regional army commanders, to sustain its control.

It is difficult to build an exclusive governing party as an agent for social transformation. The seduction of power regularly leads to rent seeking or other abuses of power that are not checked by competitive democratic politics and that may distort the original party objectives. The exclusive governing parties in some African states also had limited capacity to control society. Furthermore, the loss of confidence in Marxist-Leninist ideology and in the Soviet model led all eight of the African regimes that had once invoked it to abandon that approach by the early 1990s.

As exclusive governing parties age, many enter a stage in which they maintain control but place less emphasis on mobilization. Some, such as North Korea, may degenerate into vehicles for personal rule and exploitation by the ruler's family and supporters.[19] Finally, as shown by the collapse of communism in the former Soviet Union and Eastern Europe, if and when the party leaders lose faith in the unifying ideology, it may be difficult to maintain party coherence.

Inclusive Governing Parties

Among the preindustrial countries, especially those with notable ethnic and tribal divisions, the more successful authoritarian parties have been *inclusive*. These systems recognize the autonomy of social, cultural, and economic groups and try to incorporate them or bargain with them, rather than control and remake them. The more successful African one-party systems, such as Kenya and Tanzania, permitted aggregation around personalistic, factional, and ethnic groups within a decentralized party.

Inclusive party systems have sometimes been labeled *authoritarian corporatist systems*. Like the

democratic corporatist systems (see Chapter 4), some of these systems encourage the formation of large organized interest groups that can bargain with each other and the state. Unlike the democratic corporatist systems, however, these authoritarian systems provide no political resources directly to the populace. Independent protest and political activity outside of official channels are suppressed. The party leaders permit only limited autonomous demands within the ranks of the party and by groups associated with it.

The inclusive authoritarian systems may permit substantial amounts of autonomous interest aggregation, which may take many forms. The party typically tries to gather various social groups under the general party umbrella and negotiate with outside groups and institutions. Some inclusive parties have attempted aggressive social change. Others have primarily been arenas for interest aggregation. Many inclusive party governments permit other parties to offer candidates in elections, as long as these opposition candidates have no real chance of winning. Indeed, one interesting feature of politics in the last thirty years or so, along with the increasing number of liberal democracies, has been the growth of **electoral authoritarianism.** This is where there is a facade of democracy providing "some space for political opposition, independent media, and social organizations that do not seriously criticize or challenge the regime."[20] The Mexican PRI was long a successful example of an inclusive governing party featuring electoral authoritarianism (see Box 5.4).

The fact that some inclusive authoritarian parties have been impressively durable does not necessarily mean that they are strong or successful. In many countries these parties coexist in uneasy and unstable coalitions with the armed forces and the civilian bureaucracy. In some countries the party has become window dressing for a military regime or personal tyranny. Seldom have these parties been able to solve the economic or ethnic problems that face their country.

These political systems were often created in a struggle against colonialism, and as colonialism becomes more distant, they may implode. As memories of the independence struggle fade and the leaders die off or retire, the ties of ideology and experience that hold these parties together weaken. These developments, in conjunction with the worldwide expansion of democracy, have led to a general loss of legitimacy for the single-party model. In some cases (as in Tanzania), they have adjusted by permitting

BOX 5.4

Mexico's PRI

One of the oldest and the most inclusive authoritarian parties was the Partido Revolucionario Institucional (PRI) in Mexico. For more than fifty years the PRI dominated the political process and gave other parties no realistic chances of winning elections. The PRI attained this dominance after President Lázaro Cárdenas turned it into a "big-tent" coalition in the 1930s; it was also careful to control the counting of the ballots. It did not have to fear electoral competition, at least until the 1990s. The PRI incorporated many social groups, with separate sectors for labor, agrarian, and middle-class interests. The party dealt with its opponents in carefully designed ways. While some political dissidents were suppressed, others were deliberately enticed into the party. The party also gave informal recognition to political factions grouped behind such figures as former presidents. Various Mexican leaders mobilized their factions within the PRI and in other important groups not directly affiliated with it, such as big business interests. Bargaining was particularly important every six years when the party had to choose a new presidential nominee, since the Mexican Constitution limits presidents to one term. This guaranteed some turnover of elites. In recent decades, however, rising discontent made it difficult to aggregate interests through a single party. The urban and rural poor who had not shared in Mexico's growth joined with reformers to demand a more fully democratic system. An armed uprising of peasant guerrillas in early 1994 shocked the political establishment and led to promises of genuine democratic competition. Legislative elections in 1997 were more open than earlier contests, and ended the seventy-year rule of the PRI, which then lost the presidency to the National Action Party (PAN) in 2000. After that election, the PRI has quickly diminished as a political force, even though it still controls many state and local governments. In 2006, its candidate ran a distant third in Mexico's presidential election. (See Chapter 11.)

real party competition. More frequently, they have resorted to electoral authoritarianism with varying degrees of manipulation to provide a veneer of domestic and international legitimacy. In more than a few cases, they have turned to naked coercion, with the military serving as final arbiter.

THE MILITARY AND INTEREST AGGREGATION

After independence, most of the nations of the Third World adopted at least formally democratic governments. But in many countries these civil governments lacked effectiveness and authority, which often led to their breakdown and replacement by **military governments.** The military had instruments of force and organizational capacity, and in the absence of a strong constitutional tradition, it was an effective contender for power. Even under civilian rule, the military had substantial political influence and often constituted a significant power contender. In Brazil, for example, the military played a crucial role in interest aggregation even under the civilian government prior to the coup of 1964. After that intervention, it was the dominant actor for the next twenty years. In many other countries, the military has long been a similarly important interest aggregator.

The military's virtual monopoly on coercive resources gives it great potential power. Thus, when aggregation fails in democratic or authoritarian party systems, the military may emerge by default as the only force able to maintain orderly government. If the legitimacy of the government is weak and the social order threatens to break down, a united military may be the only force that can sustain political cohesion. The military may also intervene for more self-interested reasons, such as protecting its autonomy or budgets from civilian interference. About two-fifths of the world's nations have confronted military coup attempts at some time, and in about a third of the nations these coups were at least partially successful in changing leaders or policy. Fewer than half of these coup attempts, however, focused on general political issues and public policy. Most coups seemed motivated by the professional interests of the military.

What happens after the military intervenes can vary. The soldiers may support the personal tyranny of

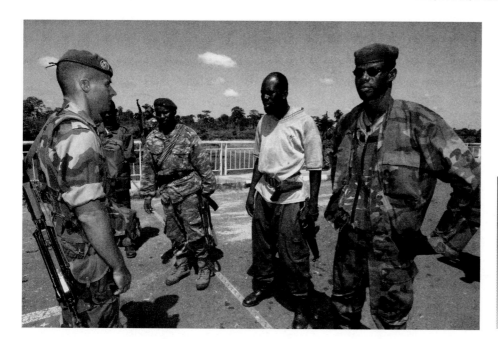

Rebel soldiers (on right), who staged an uprising against the Ivory Coast government and took over large areas of the country, meet with French troops monitoring a cease-fire in 2002.

Pascal Le Segretain/Getty Images

a civilian president or a dominant party. Or the armed forces may use their power to further institutional or ideological objectives. Military rulers may try to create military and/or bureaucratic versions of authoritarian corporatism, linking organized groups and the state bureaucracy with the military as final arbiter. They may undertake "defensive" modernization in alliance with business groups or even more radical modernization. In Latin America almost all the corporatist versions of authoritarian aggregation have had a strong military component and only rarely a dominant authoritarian party.

The major limitation of the military in interest aggregation is that its internal structures are not designed for interest aggregation. The military is primarily organized to have an efficient command structure. It is not set up to aggregate internal differences, to build compromise, to mobilize popular support, or even to communicate with social groups outside the command hierarchy. Nor do military regimes have the legitimacy in the international community that elections provide. Thus the military lacks many of the advantages held by party systems. These internal limitations may be less serious when the military is dealing with common grievances and putting pressure on—or seizing power from—unpopular authorities. The same limitations become a major problem, however, when a military government needs to stake out its own course

and mobilize support for it. For these reasons military governments frequently prove unstable and are often forced to share power with other institutions, or they simply voluntarily withdraw from politics.

TRENDS IN INTEREST AGGREGATION

As we have previously noted, the democratic trend in the world has gained momentum since the end of the 1980s. Figure 5.2 classifies the world's regimes by their degree of freedom at four points: the end of the 1970s, the end of the 1980s, the late 1990s, and 2005–2006. The percentages should be viewed as estimates, often based on limited information. But the figure provides a rough idea of the importance of competitive interest aggregation across the world.

In 1978 fewer than one-third of the world's almost 200 independent countries were classified as free. These regimes, which tended to have competitive party systems as their predominant interest aggregation structures, were dominant in Western Europe and North America (including the Caribbean), not uncommon in Latin America and Asia, but rare in Africa and the Middle East. Nearly as many countries had some versions of a single-party regime, and about 40 percent were classified as not free. In slightly less than a quarter of all countries the military dominated

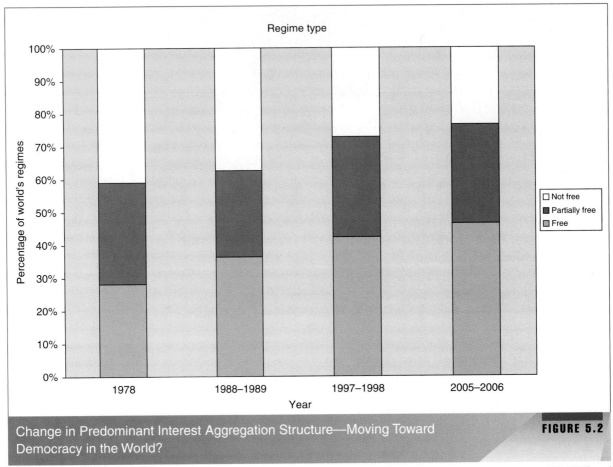

Change in Predominant Interest Aggregation Structure—Moving Toward Democracy in the World?

FIGURE 5.2

Source: Adapted from Raymond D. Gastil, *Freedom in the World 1979, 1988–1989, 1997–1998* (New York: Freedom House, 1979, 1989, 1998), and other data from www.freedomhouse.org.

interest aggregation, either formally (military governments) or in practice (military-dominated civilian governments). The military-dominated regimes accounted for about a third or more of the countries in Africa and Latin America. Single-party systems were the main form in Eastern Europe and relatively common in Africa and Asia and accounted for most of the remaining unfree countries.

A decade later, the trend was away from single-party governments. Across the world they declined from 30 to 24 percent of the world's nations, although still accounting for nearly 40 percent of African nations. As we already know, the decline of exclusive governing party regimes is even more striking. The proportion of military governments actually increased slightly, from 23 to 26 percent of the world's countries. There was a minor democratic trend toward competitive party and electoral systems, with

more than one-third of the world's governments now classified as free.

The trend toward democracy took off more dramatically beginning in 1989 in Eastern Europe, and with new pressures for democracy in the developing world. By the late 1990s, for the first time in world history there were more free than unfree states. The collapse of communism in Europe and elsewhere was in large part responsible, but the number of military dictatorships also declined. The declining acceptance of authoritarian governments, as well as the withdrawal of Soviet support, contributed to this trend, especially in Africa. Many African nations moved toward a more democratic and free system during the 1990s. Yet a few authoritarian party systems with exclusive governing parties are still around, such as China and Cuba. Most of the remaining unfree states are in the Middle East, Central Asia, and Africa. Many African nations still

Trying to Make Democracy Work

BOX 5.5

Nigeria is in many ways typical of the rough road to democracy that many developing countries have traveled. The Nigerian military government, which had ousted an ineffective civilian government in 1983, responded to the democratization wave of the early 1990s by introducing careful and measured reforms. It initiated state-level elections in 1991 and federal legislative elections in 1992. Finally, after presidential elections scheduled for June 1993, the transition to civilian rule would be complete. But the military kept strict control of the electoral process and disqualified politicians who had held office under previous civilian regimes (because they were considered to be tainted by corruption). Voters were left with a choice of only two parties, both created by the government. Voting turnout was low because many voters became cynical about the process. These doubts were confirmed when the

military annulled the presidential election, even before the results were announced, and installed an interim government instead. In November 1993, Defense Minister General Sani Abacha launched a military coup which overturned the interim government, banned all political activity, dissolved the legislature, dismissed the elected state governments, and thus ended Nigeria's cautious experiment with elections. In 1998, President Abacha suddenly died of a heart attack, and the reform process could begin anew. In spring 1999, the military government held a presidential election. The victor was a former army general, Olusegun Obasanjo, who went on to try to implement democratic reforms. He was reelected four years later. But continuing ethnic and religious violence, corruption, and abuses of power have made the Nigerian transition to democracy fragile. (See Chapter 13.)

feature some variety of the "electoral authoritarianism" discussed previously, with severe constraints on civil freedom and electoral opposition. A few remain unabashed authoritarian systems (as in Zimbabwe) or are mired in deadly civil war (as in Sudan and Somalia).

Perhaps in deference to the decline in the legitimacy of authoritarianism, the military throughout the world is now more likely to dominate from behind the scenes than through direct rule. Latin America also has experienced the genuine replacement of military regimes by competitive party regimes in such important countries as Argentina, Brazil, Chile, and Uruguay. Although the era of confidence in the military as a solution to development seems to have passed, military domination remains likely when other types of government are unsuccessful.

Where there has been "backsliding" on the road to democracy, the military has often played a part. So we cannot assume that the democratizing trend will continue relentlessly. Multiparty regimes that seem unable to cope with economic and social problems often lose their legitimacy. Such is now the challenge facing parts of Eastern Europe, as well as much of the Third World. In many of these countries, competitive party systems exist, but citizens have very little trust in them and often consider them to be corrupt. And military coups continue to occur, as in Thailand and Fiji in the fall of 2006.

SIGNIFICANCE OF INTEREST AGGREGATION

How interests are aggregated is an important determinant of what a country's government does for and to its citizens. Successful public policy depends on effective interest aggregation. One importance function of interest aggregation is to narrow policy options, so that the desires and demands of citizens are converted into a few policy alternatives. Many possible policies are eliminated in the process. Those that remain typically have the backing of significant sectors of society. For instance, even though such policies have been adopted in other nations, there has never been a "serious" proposal that the United States government take over the country's steel industry, because no powerful group has ever favored it.

In democratic countries, competitive party systems narrow down and combine policy preferences. Through elections, voters throw their support behind some of these parties and thus shape party representation in the legislature. Even at the legislative stage, further consolidation and coalition building takes place. At some point, however, most policy options have been eliminated from consideration. Either no party backed them or the parties supporting them fared badly in the elections.

In noncompetitive party systems, military governments, and monarchies, aggregation works differently, but with the similar effect of narrowing policy options. On some issues, aggregation virtually determines policy, as when a military government or a faction of an authoritarian party can decide the government's program. In other cases the legislative assembly, military council, or party politburo may contain several factions that must negotiate over policy. The narrowing of policy choices also affects the influence and access of social interests.

But politics shapes its environment as well as reflecting it. Interest aggregation often alters the polarization that the political culture projects into policymaking. That is one reason why politics is so fascinating. Well-organized and well-led political parties might, at least for a while, be able to dominate politics and limit the strength of extremist groups in the legislature. Conversely, well-organized extremists might be able to appeal to the fears and prejudices of some groups and get their support at the polls, thus gaining more legislative strength in an otherwise consensual country.

Aggregation ultimately affects the government's adaptability and stability. Authoritarian interest aggregation tends to create political power structures that do not reflect popular opinion. In highly divided and conflict-ridden societies, rulers may portray such lack of representation as a virtue. Leaders of military coups often justify their overthrow of party governments by claiming to depolarize politics and rid the nation of conflict it cannot afford. Similarly, heads of authoritarian parties typically claim that their nation must concentrate all its energies and resources on common purposes and that party competition would be too polarizing.

In contrast, most proponents of democratic interest aggregation argue that the best hope for accommodating conflicting social and political interests lies in free and fair electoral competition, followed by negotiation among those groups that gain the voters' favor. Democracy thus leads policymakers to act as the people wish. In a polarized political culture, the division and uncertainty that interest aggregation implies may be seen as a high price to pay for citizen control. As the frequent instability in authoritarian governments indicates, however, it may be easier to do away with the appearance of polarization than with the reality. Competing demands may find their way to the surface anyway, and the citizens may end up without either freedom and participation or stability.

REVIEW QUESTIONS

- What structures other than political parties aggregate interests?

- What is Duverger's Law? Which two effects does it imply?

- What is the median voter result, and why does it pertain only to two-party systems?

- What are the differences between totalitarian parties and other single-party systems?

- Why do many countries turn to military governments, and why are military governments often short-lived?

KEY TERMS

accommodative party systems	effective number of parties	majority-coalition systems	primary elections
authoritarian party systems	electoral authoritarianism	majority runoff	proportional representation (PR)
closed-list PR systems	electoral system	mechanical effect	psychological effect
competitive party systems	exclusive governing party	median voter result	single-member district (SMD)
conflictual party system	inclusive governing party	military governments	single-member district plurality (SMDP) election rule
consensual party system	institutional groups	multiparty systems	
consociationalism	interest aggregation	open-list systems	
double-ballot	majoritarian two-party systems	party system	strategic voting
Duverger's Law		patron-client networks	
		plurality election rules	

SUGGESTED READINGS

Cox, Gary W. *Making Votes Count: Strategic Coordination in the World's Electoral Systems.* Cambridge: Cambridge University Press, 1997.

Dalton, Russell J., and Martin P. Wattenberg. *Parties Without Partisans: Political Change in Advanced Industrial Democracies.* New York: Oxford University Press, 2000.

Decalo, Samuel. *Coups and Army Rule in Africa,* 2nd ed. New Haven, CT: Yale University Press, 1990.

Downs, Anthony. *An Economic Theory of Democracy.* New York: Harper & Row, 1957.

Farrell, David. *Electoral Systems: A Comparative Introduction.* New York: St. Martin's Press, 2001.

Farrell, David, Ian Holliday, and Paul Webb, eds. *Political Parties in Democratic States.* Oxford: Oxford University Press, 2002.

Jackson, Robert H., and Carl G. Rosberg. *Personal Rule in Black Africa.* Berkeley: University of California Press, 1982.

Kitschelt, Herbert. *The Transformation of European Social Democracy.* New York: Cambridge University Press, 1994.

Laver, Michael, and Norman Schofield. *Multiparty Government.* New York: Oxford University Press, 1990.

Lijphart, Arend. *Electoral Systems and Party Systems.* New York: Oxford University Press, 1994.

———. *Patterns of Democracy.* New Haven, CT: Yale University Press, 1999.

Linz, Juan J. *Totalitarian and Authoritarian Regimes.* Baltimore: Johns Hopkins University Press, 2002.

Mainwaring, Scott. *Rethinking Party Systems in the Third Wave of Democratization.* Stanford, CA: Stanford University Press, 1999.

Michels, Robert. *Political Parties.* New York: Free Press, 1962.

Nordlinger, Eric A. *Soldiers in Politics: Military Coups and Governments.* Englewood Cliffs, NJ: Prentice-Hall, 1976.

Powell, G. Bingham, Jr. *Contemporary Democracies: Participation, Stability, and Violence.* Cambridge: Harvard University Press, 1982.

———. *Elections as Instruments of Democracy.* New Haven, CT: Yale University Press, 2000.

Riker, William H. *Liberalism Against Populism.* San Francisco: W. H. Freeman, 1982.

Strøm, Kaare, Wolfgang C. Müller, and Torbjörn Bergman, eds. *Cabinets and Coalition Bargaining: The Democratic Life Cycle in Western Europe.* Oxford: Oxford University Press, 2008.

ENDNOTES

1. See, for example, Luis Roniger and Ayse Gunes-Ayata, eds., *Democracy, Clientelism, and Civil Society* (Boulder, CO: Lynne Rienner, 1994); S. Eisenstadt and L. Roniger, *Patrons, Clients, and Friends* (Cambridge: Cambridge University Press, 1984); Lucian W. Pye, *Asian Power and Politics* (Cambridge: Harvard University Press, 1985); and Martin Shefter, "Patronage and Its Opponents," in *Political Parties and the State* (Princeton, NJ: Princeton University Press, 1994).

2. Unfortunately, elections cannot solve all the problems of aggregating interests fairly. For example, giving each citizen one vote does not take into account the varying intensities with which different people may hold their opinions. Moreover, economists and political scientists have found that when there are three or more alternatives in any decision, there is no fair way to aggregate votes to select a single, best outcome ("Arrow's Paradox"). See Duncan Black, "On the Rationale of Group Decision Making," *Journal of Political Economy* 56 (1948): 23–34; Kenneth Arrow, *Social Choice and Individual Values* (New Haven, CT: Yale University Press, 1951). For an accessible discussion of some political implications, see William H. Riker, *Liberalism Against Populism* (San Francisco: W. H. Freeman, 1982); Kenneth A. Shepsle and Mark S. Bonchek, *Analyzing Politics: Rationality, Behavior, and Institutions* (New York: Norton, 1997), Part II.

3. Hans-Dieter Klingemann, Richard Hofferbert, and Ian Budge, eds., *Parties, Policy, and Democracy* (Boulder, CO: Westview, 1995); Michael, Gallagher, Michael Laver, and Peter Mair, *Representative Government in Western Europe,*

4th ed. (New York: McGraw-Hill, 2005); Richard Rose, *Do Parties Make a Difference?* (Chatham, NJ: Chatham House, 1984), ch. 5.

4. Joseph A. Schumpeter, *Capitalism, Socialism, and Democracy* (New York: Harper, 1943).

5. However, in Communist China semicompetitive elections for village leadership positions since 1987 has in some areas brought the opinions of local leaders and ordinary citizens closer together. See Melanie Manion, "The Electoral Connection in the Chinese Countryside," *American Political Science Review* 90 (1996): 736–48.

6. See Russell J. Dalton, *Citizen Politics: Public Opinion and Political Parties in Advanced Industrial Democracies,* 4th ed. (Washington, DC: Congressional Quarterly Press, 2005).

7. Ian Budge, David Robertson, and Derek Hearl, eds., *Ideology, Strategy, and Party Change: Spatial Analyses of Post-War Election Programmes in 19 Democracies* (New York: Cambridge University Press, 1987); Richard Katz and Peter Mair, eds., *How Parties Organize: Change and Adaptation in Party Organizations in Western Democracies* (Thousand Oaks, CA: Sage 1994).

8. Maurice Duverger, *Political Parties: Their Organization and Activity in the Modern State,* [1954] trans. Barbara and Robert North (New York: Wiley, 1963). For a more contemporary contribution, see Gary W. Cox, *Making Votes Count* (Cambridge: Cambridge University Press, 1997).

9. Anthony Downs, *An Economic Theory of Democracy* (New York: Harper & Row, 1957).

10. The effective number of parties is calculated as follows: first calculate the proportion of seats (or votes) held by each party. Square each of these proportions and then add them all up. Finally, divide one by the sum of all the squared proportions. See Markku Laakso and Rein Taagepera, "'Effective' Number of Parties: A Measure with Application to West Europe," *Comparative Political Studies* 12 (1979): 3–27.

11. See Pradeep Chhibber and Kenneth Kollman, *The Formation of National Party Systems* (Princeton, NJ: Princeton University Press, 2004).

12. For analyses of the consequences of election laws, see Douglas Rae, *The Political Consequences of Election Laws* (New Haven, CT: Yale University Press, 1967); Arend Lijphart, *Electoral Systems and Party Systems: A Study of Twenty-seven Democracies, 1945–1990* (Oxford: Oxford University Press, 1994).

13. On government coalitions, see especially Michael Laver and Norman Schofield, *Multiparty Government: The Politics of Coalition in Europe* (New York: Oxford University Press 1990); Kaare Strøm, Wolfgang C. Müller, and Torbjörn Bergman, eds., *Cabinets and Coalition Bargaining: The Democratic Life Cycle in Western Europe* (New York: Oxford University Press, 2008).

14. On elections and the representation of votes and preferences, as well as the trade-off with accountability, see G. Bingham Powell, Jr., *Elections as Instruments of Democracy* (New Haven, CT: Yale University Press, 2000), chs. 5–10.

15. See Arend Lijphart, *Democracy in Plural Societies* (New Haven, CT: Yale University Press, 1977); Arend Lijphart, *Patterns of Democracy* (New Haven, CT: Yale University Press, 1999).

16. See Lijphart, *Patterns of Democracy*; G. Bingham Powell, Jr., *Contemporary Democracies* (Cambridge: Harvard University Press, 1982), chs. 8 and 10; Juan J. Linz and Alfred Stepan, eds., *The Breakdown of Democratic Regimes* (Baltimore: Johns Hopkins University Press, 1978).

17. Juan Linz, *Totalitarian and Authoritarian Regimes* (Boulder, CO: Lynne Rienner, 2000); Amos Perlmutter, *Modern Authoritarianism: A Comparative Institutional Analysis* (New Haven, CT: Yale University Press, 1981), especially 62–114.

18. See Melanie Manion, "Politics in China," Chapter 10 below; for the earlier period, see, for example, Franz Schurman, *Ideology and Organization in Communist China* (Berkeley: University of California Press, 1966).

19. Juan Linz calls these "sultanistic" regimes; see *Totalitarian and Authoritarian Regimes* (Boulder, CO: Lynne Rienner, 2000), 151–157; Houchang Chehabi and Juan Linz, eds., *Sultanistic Regimes* (Baltimore: Johns Hopkins University Press, 1998); Robert H. Jackson and Carl G. Rosberg, *Personal Rule in Black Africa* (Berkeley: University of California Press, 1982).

20. Larry Diamond, "Thinking About Hybrid Regimes," *Journal of Democracy* 13 (2002): 26; the articles by Andreas Schedler; Steven Levitsky and Lucan Way; Nicolas van de Walle in the same issue.

GOVERNMENT AND POLICYMAKING

Policymaking is the pivotal stage in the political process, the point at which bills become law or edicts are issued by the rulers. Later, policies are implemented and enforced. To understand public policy, we must know how decisions are made. Where is power effectively located in different political systems? What does it take to change public policy: a simple majority vote in the legislature or approval also by an independently elected executive? Or is it a decree issued by the military commanders or the party central committee? Or is it merely the whim of the personal dictator?

This chapter focuses on decision rules and on the policymaking role of government agencies, such as legislatures, chief executives, bureaucracies, and courts. Government agencies are at the core of policymaking. While parties, interest groups, and other actors may be very active in articulating and aggregating interests, government officials do most of the actual initiation and formulation of policy proposals. Interest group demands for tax relief or for the protection of endangered species cannot succeed unless they are transformed into policy by government officials according to some accepted decision rules. They cannot be effective until these policies are appropriately implemented by other officials.

Yet, government action does not flow in one direction only. The interaction between government and citizens is a two-way process. It includes an upward flow of influence and demands from the society, as well as a downward flow of decisions from the government. (See Figure 2.2 in Chapter 2.)

CONSTITUTIONS AND DECISION RULES

A constitution establishes the basic rules of decision making, rights, and the distribution of authority in a political system. We sometimes use the term "constitution" to refer to a specific document laying out such principles—for example, the one adopted by the Founders of the United States in 1787. But a constitution need not be embodied in a single document. In fact, it rarely is. We should therefore think of a constitution as a set of rules and principles, whether it is a specific written document, a set of customs or practices, or, as is usually the case, both. Even a military or party dictatorship typically sets procedures for having decrees proposed, considered, and adopted.

Written constitutions are particularly important in political systems based on the *rule of law*. This means that government should take no action that has not been authorized by law and that citizens can be punished only for actions that violate an existing law. Under the rule of law, the constitution is the supreme body of laws.

A constitution thus contains a set of **decision rules**—the basic rules governing how decisions are made. Policymaking is the conversion of social interests and demands into authoritative public decisions. Constitutions establish the rules by which this happens. They confer the power to propose policies on specific groups or institutions. They may give others the right to amend, reject, or approve such proposals, or to implement, police, or adjudicate them. They may specify how many resources are needed to make policies, as well as what these resources are.

Decision rules affect political activity because they determine what political resources are valuable in influencing decisions and how to acquire and use these resources. For example, in a federal and decentralized system such as the United States, a pressure group may have to approach both the legislative and the executive branches, and it may have to be active both at the state and the federal levels. If instead decisions are made by decree from the commander of the armed forces or the central committee of a single-party state, groups will need to influence these crucial policymakers.

Different decision rules have different attractions. More inclusive rules about policymaking—such as those that require the cooperation of several institutions or the support of over 50 percent of voters—can protect against hasty decisions. They can also prevent decisions that disadvantage large minorities (perhaps close to half) of the voters. At the same time, more inclusive rules can give a minority the power to block proposals favored by a majority. The more inclusive the voting rules are, as the percentage to approve approaches unanimity, the less likely it is that any decision can be made at all. Less inclusive decision rules make it easier to reach a policy, but many interests may be ignored.

Both the government as a whole and its institutions have decision rules. Decision rules may be simple or complex and apply to different circumstances. For example, the U.S. Congress has many different decision rules that apply under different circumstances, such as a simple majority in each house to pass a bill initially, but a two-thirds majority to override a presidential veto. The British House of Commons uses a much smaller set of rules (mainly simple majority rule). Decision rules may be more or less formal and precise. Most legislatures have formal and precise decision rules, whereas cabinets at the head of the executive branch often have informal and flexible rules.

Within any given branch of government or other political institution, numerous rules affect the policymaking process. In most modern assemblies the decision rules about voting are *egalitarian*, which is to say that each member has the same voting power. Simply speaking: one person, one vote. That is hardly ever true in government departments (ministries), however. Or in dictatorships. There, decision making is *hierarchical.* Everybody is supposed to defer to his or her superior. In a pure hierarchy, only the vote of a person at the very top (for example, the minister) counts. Such a decision rule makes it easy to respond quickly in a policymaking emergency, but few interests or ideas may be taken into account.

Even when decisions are made through equal voting, the inclusiveness of the decision rules still shapes the outcomes. Many institutions operate through simple majority voting: in a choice between two options, whichever option gets the larger number of votes wins. Alternatively, more inclusive rules—such as "qualified" majorities of three-fifths, two-thirds, or even three-fourths—are sometimes required for particularly consequential decisions. For example, the U.S. Constitution requires two-thirds majorities in both houses of Congress in order to amend the Constitution or override a presidential veto. The most inclusive voting rule is unanimity, which means that any one member can block any decision.

It is important that decision rules in a democracy be transparent and stable. If they are not, citizens will not know what to expect from government. That may in turn cause them to be less trusting and less willing to invest or make other commitments. It may also lead to serious conflicts, and ultimately government may break down and issues be decided by force. The importance of having predictable decision rules was suggested by Thomas Jefferson in his introduction to the first Manual of the House of Representatives: "A bad set of rules is better than no rules at all."

Making Constitutions

Making a constitution is a fundamental political act: it creates or transforms decision rules. Most current constitutions were formed as the result of some break, often violent, with the past—war, revolution, or rebellion against colonial rule. New decision rules were made to accommodate new internal or external powers. Thus, the defeated powers and the successor states of World Wars I and II all adopted new constitutions or had new constitutions imposed on them.

Britain is unusual in having not a formal written constitution but only a long accepted and highly developed set of customs and conventions, buttressed by important ordinary statutes. This reflects the British record of gradual, incremental, and (on the whole) peaceful political change. Nevertheless, the major changes in British decision rules—such as the shift of power from the Crown to Parliament in the seventeenth century, and the Reform Acts of 1832 and 1867, which established party and cabinet government and vastly extended the right to vote—followed on periods of civil war or unrest.

Perhaps the most significant exception to the association between disruptive upheavals and constitution creation is the peaceful development over the last fifty years of the constitution of the European Union, whose growing powers are altering the decision rules affecting about 460 million Europeans in twenty-seven countries. While there has been no violence associated with the formation and growth of the EU, its origins lie in the bitter lessons of World Wars I and II.

The decades since World War II have seen much constitutional experimentation. Not only the defeated powers, but many new states—such as India and Nigeria, which achieved independence with the breakup of colonial empires—introduced new political arrangements. Some of the new states in the developing areas, such as Nigeria, have subsequently changed their form of government several times. In the last two decades the worldwide trend toward democracy, the end of the Cold War, and the dissolution of the Soviet Union have produced a new round of constitutional design. The recent constitutional crafting in Eastern Europe, Russia, and the other Soviet successor states as well as in South Africa and elsewhere have reignited old debates about the virtues and faults of different constitutional arrangements, or about the very wisdom of constitutional engineering.[1]

DEMOCRACY AND AUTHORITARIANISM

The most important distinction in policymaking is between democratic and authoritarian systems. **Democracy** means "government by the people." In small political systems, such as local communities, "the people" may share directly in debating, deciding, and implementing public policy. In large political systems, such as contemporary states, democracy must be achieved largely through indirect participation in policymaking. Policymaking power is delegated to officials chosen by the people.

Elections, competitive political parties, free mass media, and representative assemblies are political structures that make some degree of democracy, some "government by the people," possible in large political systems. Competitive elections give citizens a chance to shape policy through their selection and rejection of key policymakers. Such indirect democracy is not complete or ideal. Moreover, the democratic opportunities in less economically developed societies are often meaningful to educated elites or to those living near the centers of government, but less relevant to the average citizen in the countryside. But the more citizens are involved and the more influential their choices, the more democratic the system.

In **authoritarian regimes,** in contrast, the policymakers are chosen by military councils, hereditary families, dominant political parties, and the like. Citizens are either ignored or pressed into symbolic assent to the government's choices.

The basic decision rules of political systems—both democratic and authoritarian—differ along three important dimensions:

1. the separation of powers among different branches of government;
2. the geographic distribution of authority between the central (national) government and lower levels, such as states, provinces, or municipalities; and
3. limitations on government authority.

We shall discuss these dimensions in order, beginning with the separation of authority between executive and legislative institutions.

SEPARATION OF GOVERNMENT POWERS

The theory of **separation of powers** between different institutions of government has a long and venerable history going back at least to the work of Locke and Montesquieu.[2] Separation of powers, they argued, has the virtue of preventing the injustices that might result from an unchecked executive or legislature. Madison and Hamilton elaborated this theory in *The Federalist*,[3] which described and defended the institutional arrangements proposed by the U.S. Constitutional Convention of 1787.

Political theorists in the course of the nineteenth and first part of the twentieth centuries drew upon the two successful historical cases of representative democracy—Britain and the United States—to create the "classic" separation of powers theory. This theory argued that there are essentially two forms of

Distinguishing Features[a]	Parliamentary Democracies	Presidential Democracies
		TABLE 6.1
	Distinguishing Features of Parliamentary and Presidential Democracies	
Title of chief executive	Prime minister (head of government)	President (head of state and government)
Selection of assembly	By citizens in competitive election	By citizens in competitive election
Selection of chief executive	By assembly after election or removal	By citizens in competitive election
Removal of chief executive before fixed term?	By assembly: (No) confidence vote	Fixed terms
Dismissal of assembly before fixed term?	Prime minister may call for early election[b]	Fixed terms
Authority to legislate	Assembly only	Assembly plus president (e.g., veto)
Party relations in assembly and executive	Same parties control both; cohesive party voting	Different party control possible; less cohesive party voting

[a]These define the pure parliamentary and presidential types; as discussed in the text, many constitutional systems, especially in Eastern Europe, "mix" the features of the two types.
[b]Some constitutional systems that are parliamentary in all other ways do not allow for early legislative elections. All parliamentary democracies provide for legislative elections after some maximum time (from three to five years) since the last election.

representative democratic government: the presidential and the parliamentary.

The **democratic presidential regime** provides two separate agencies of government—the executive and the legislative—separately elected and authorized by the people. (See Table 6.1, column 3.) Each branch is elected for a fixed term; no one branch can by ordinary means unseat the other; and each has specific powers under the constitution. Ultimate power to authorize legislation and approve budgets in modern democracies resides with the legislature, whose relationships with the executive are then critical for concentration or dispersal of power. Different presidential regimes provide their presidents with a variety of different powers over government appointments and policymaking. For example, some presidents have the authority to veto legislation or to make policy by executive decree under some conditions.[4] In the United States, both the legislature and executive (Congress and the presidency) have large and significant roles in policymaking. In some other democratic presidential systems, such as Brazil, the president may have such a variety of constitutional powers (including the power to make laws through "emergency" decrees) that he or she can reduce the role of the legislature. But coordination between the separate institutions of executive and legislature must somehow be achieved to make policy.

The **parliamentary regimes,** in contrast, make the executive and legislative branches interdependent. (See Table 6.1, column 2.) First of all, only the legislative

branch is directly elected. The prime minister and his or her cabinet (the collective leadership of the executive branch) emerge from the legislature. The cabinet is chaired by the prime minister, who is the head of government and selects the other cabinet members.[5] Typically, neither branch has a fixed term of office. The cabinet can be voted out of office at any time, and most often this is true of the legislature (the parliament) as well.

The critical feature that makes this possible is the **confidence relationship** between the prime minister and the parliamentary majority. In a parliamentary system, the prime minister and his or her cabinet must at all times enjoy the confidence of the parliamentary majority. Whenever the parliamentary majority for whatever reason votes a lack of confidence, the prime minister and all the other cabinet members have to resign. At the same time, the prime minister typically has the power to dissolve parliament and call new elections at any time. These two powers—the parliamentary majority's dismissal power and the prime minister's dissolution power—make the two branches mutually dependent. This structure induces agreement between them by forcing each branch to be acceptable to the other.

Prime ministers in parliamentary democracies lead precarious political lives. Unlike presidents in presidential systems, prime ministers can be voted out of office at any time, and for any reason, by a parliamentary majority. There are two ways in which this

BOX 6.1

The Confidence Vote in Britain

British prime ministers can resort to the confidence motion in order to bring rebellious party members into line. Usually, the mere threat of a confidence motion is sufficient. But in 1993, Conservative Prime Minister John Major faced a parliamentary crisis over the ratification of the Maastricht Treaty, which expanded the powers of the European Union. Major had only a slim majority in the House of Commons. Many "Euroskeptics" in his own party were opposed to the Maastricht Treaty. About twenty of these Conservative dissidents voted with the Opposition and helped defeat the Maastricht Treaty in the House of Commons.

Immediately after this embarrassing defeat, however, Major introduced a confidence motion on his Maastricht policy. He announced that if he lost this vote, he would dissolve the House of Commons and hold new elections. Many of the Conservative dissidents feared that their party would do poorly in such an election and that they might personally lose their seats. Prime Minister Major's confidence motion passed by a vote of 339 to 299, and the House of Commons approved the Maastricht Treaty.

Thus, the confidence vote, which is generally available to prime ministers in parliamentary systems, helps explain why party discipline tends to be stronger in parliamentary than in presidential systems.

---

can happen. One is when parliament passes a motion expressing a lack of confidence in the prime minister—a no-confidence motion. The other possibility is when parliament defeats a motion expressing confidence in the prime minister—a confidence motion. No-confidence motions are typically introduced by the parliamentary opposition in the hope of bringing down the prime minister. Confidence motions, on the other hand, are normally introduced by prime ministers themselves.

Since one possible result of a confidence motion is being kicked out of office, it may seem like a form of Russian roulette. In reality, however, the confidence vote can be a powerful weapon in the hands of the prime minister. It is typically attached to a bill (a policy proposal) the prime minister favors, but the parliamentary majority does not. By attaching a confidence motion to the bill, the prime minister forces the members of parliament to choose between the bill and the fall of the cabinet. This can be a particularly painful choice for dissident members of the prime minister's own party. If they vote for the bill, they may bring down their own government, and perhaps immediately have to face the voters to boot (see Box 6.1). Thus, the possibility of a confidence motion actually helps explain why party discipline tends to be stronger in parliamentary than in presidential systems.

Thus parliamentary democracies do not experience the form of divided government that is common under presidentialism, when the party that controls the presidency does not control the legislature, or vice versa. Instead, the chief executive (prime minister and cabinet) becomes the agent of the parliamentary majority. In most parliamentary systems the cabinet consists largely of members of parliament. Conflicts between parliament and the executive are less likely to occur and decisionmaking tends to be more efficient than under presidentialism. Since the same party (or parties) controls both branches of government, the cabinet tends to dominate policymaking, and the legislature may be less influential than under a presidential constitution.

Not all democracies fit neatly into the presidential or parliamentary category. Some, such as France, are often characterized as mixed, or **"semipresidential."** In some of these mixed types, the president and the legislature are separately elected (as in presidential systems), but the president then has the power to dissolve the legislature (as in parliamentary systems). In such systems, the cabinet may be appointed by the president (as under presidentialism), but subject to dismissal by the legislature (as under parliamentarism). A variety of arrangements exist for such shared control. Their consequences are often sharply affected by which party or coalition controls the presidency and legislature. Many of the new constitutions of the emergent democracies of Eastern Europe and Asia are of this mixed type.

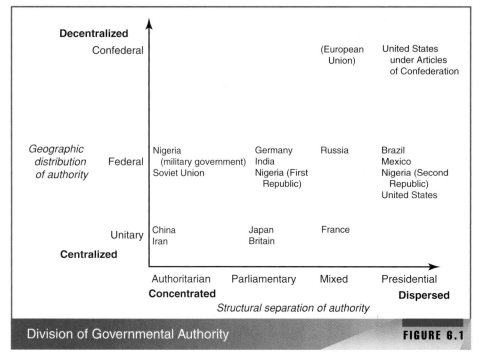

Division of Governmental Authority

FIGURE 6.1

Reading across Figure 6.1, we see political systems classified by the separation of policymaking powers between executive and legislative institutions, from concentrated to dispersed. The vertical dimension of the table shows geographic division of power, which is discussed in the next section. In authoritarian governments on the left of the figure, executive, legislative, and judicial power are typically concentrated. Two of the seven countries discussed in this book—China and Iran—have authoritarian governments not chosen in competitive elections. Britain, Germany, Japan, and India are parliamentary systems in which executive and legislative powers are concentrated in cabinets responsible to the popularly elected lower houses of parliament. At the extreme right of Figure 6.1 are pure presidential systems, such as Brazil, Mexico, and the United States. Nigeria seems to be in transition to a presidential democracy. In between, we find mixed systems, such as France and Russia.

In the debate over the best system of representative democracy, many political theorists traditionally favored the British-style parliamentary system. This version of parliamentarism—coupling plurality voting rules that usually create clear single-party majorities in parliament with a cabinet and prime minister responsible to parliament—can result in fairly stable governments responsible to the public will. Parliamentarism

coupled with proportional representation—as in Germany and France between the two world wars—seemed more crisis prone. Such crises occurred because of the emergence of large extremist political parties, which resulted in cabinet instability and even breakdown. However, the Scandinavian countries demonstrated that parliamentary systems with proportional representation can be quite stable when ideological conflict between the political parties remains moderate. Moreover, dominating parliamentary majorities, as in Northern Ireland, can sometimes threaten minority groups and intensify conflict.[6] In comparison to both versions of parliamentary government, the U.S. presidential system has often been criticized for periodically producing divided government, which could result in stalemate or "grid lock."

The third wave of democratization reopened these parliamentary-presidential debates. Advocates of parliamentarism, particularly of the proportional variety, argue that it provides a consensual framework in which different economic, ethnic, and religious groups can find representation and negotiate their differences. Parliamentary systems also have the flexibility to change governments between elections if the people disapprove of actions of the executive. Since many of the current transitional democracies are deeply divided, a parliamentary, proportional representation system may be particularly suitable. Presidentialism, they argue, is more susceptible to social conflict and democratic breakdown. Under conditions of divided government, a confrontation between the two legitimately elected institutions representing the people can tear a political system apart. Or, a strong president can use executive powers to repress competition.

Other scholars point out that practical politics is producing presidential systems with significant executive power.[7] Even in the domain of the former British empire (such as in Nigeria) and in most of Eastern Europe and the Soviet successor states, the constitutions provide for powerful presidents. Latin America has been dominated by presidential regimes for more than a century. A 1993 referendum in Brazil reaffirmed its commitment to presidentialism. Presidentialism also offers the citizens a more direct choice of chief executive, and it puts more effective checks on the power of the majority in the legislature.

GEOGRAPHIC DISTRIBUTION OF GOVERNMENT POWER

Another distinction between governmental structures is the geographic division of power: confederal systems at one extreme, unitary systems at the other extreme, and **federal systems** in the middle. (See the vertical dimension of Figure 6.1.) The United States under the Articles of Confederation was confederal. Ultimate power rested with the states. The central government had authority over foreign affairs and defense but depended on financial and other support from the states. Under the Constitution of 1787, the U.S. government changed from confederal to federal, which is to say that both central and state governments had separate spheres of authority and the means to implement their power. Today, the United States, Germany, Russia, India, Nigeria, Mexico, and Brazil are federal systems in which central and local units each have autonomy in particular spheres of public policy. These policy areas and powers are, however, divided among central and local units in varying ways. Britain, France, China, Japan, and Iran are unitary systems with power and authority concentrated in the central government. Regional and local units have only those powers specifically delegated to them by the central government, which may change or withdraw these powers at will.

Most of the world's states are unitary. In fact, only eighteen states are federal, or fewer than one in ten. Although the federal states are relatively few in number, they tend to be large and politically important. Thus, federal states account for more than one-third of the world's population and 41 percent of its land area. In general, the larger and the more diverse a state is, the more likely it is to be federal.

Federalism is commonly thought to have several advantages. In culturally divided societies, it may help protect ethnic, linguistic, or religious minorities, particularly if they are geographically concentrated. It may serve as a check on overly ambitious rulers and thus protect markets and citizen freedoms. Moreover, federalism may allow subunits (such as states) to experiment with different policy programs. Governments may thus learn from the experiences of others. In addition, citizens may be free to "vote with their feet" and choose the policy environment that best fits their preferences.

While federalism promotes choice and diversity, however, it does so at the expense of equality. Federalism allows local governments to pursue different policies. One implication is that citizens may get systematically different treatments and benefits from different local governments. Unitary governments may also be in a better position to redistribute resources from richer regions to poorer regions, if that is desirable.

In comparing confederal, federal, and unitary systems, we must distinguish between formal and actual distributions of power. In unitary systems, in spite of the formal concentration of authority at the center, regional and local units may acquire power that the central government rarely challenges. In federal systems, centralized party control may overcome apparent regional autonomy. Thus, the real differences between federal and unitary systems may be considerably less significant than their formal arrangements suggest.

Mexico is an example of the discrepancy between formal and actual federalism. Until recently the Partido Revolucionario Institucional (PRI) had centralized control in this formally federal system. Recent developments in Mexico, with oppositional parties winning ground in some states and the PRI power monopoly under challenge, have produced some "real" federalism to go along with the formalities.

LIMITATIONS ON GOVERNMENT POWER

Unlike authoritarian regimes, democracies are characterized by some legal or customary limitation on the exercise of power. Systems in which the powers of various government units are defined and limited by a written constitution, statutes, and custom are called **constitutional regimes.** Civil rights—such as the right to a fair trial and freedom to speak, petition, publish, and assemble—are protected against government interference except under specified circumstances.

	TABLE 6.2
Judicial Limitation of Governmental Authority	

Unlimited		Limited
Nonindependent Courts	**Independent Courts**	**Judicial Review**
China	Britain	United States
Iran		India
Nigeria		Germany
		France
		Brazil
		Japan
		Russia

The courts are crucial to the limitations on governmental power. As illustrated in Table 6.2, governments may be divided into those, at one extreme, in which the power to coerce citizens is relatively unlimited by the courts, and those, at the other extreme, in which the courts not only protect the rights of citizens but also police other parts of the government to see that their powers are properly exercised. The United States, Germany, and India are systems in which high courts rule effectively on challenges that other parts of the government have exceeded the powers allocated by the constitution. This practice of **judicial review** is authorized to various degrees in about half of the world's democracies and seems to be growing in popularity. But judicial review is often weakened by lack of independence of the appointment or tenure of judges, as in Japan, or by their ineffectiveness in overcoming executive power, as in Russia.

Some other constitutional regimes have independent courts that protect persons against the improper implementation of laws and regulations, but cannot legally overrule the assembly or the political executive, as in Britain. The substantive rights of people in these systems are protected by statute, custom, self-restraint, and political pressure—which are also essential to the effectiveness of courts even where judicial review is authorized. In authoritarian systems, policymakers do not usually allow courts to constrain their use and abuse of power, even where brave judges attempt to rule against them.

Arend Lijphart characterizes only four of the thirty-six democratic systems he examines as having "strong" judicial review: Germany, India, the United States, and Canada after 1982.[8] The Supreme Court of India is most similar to the U.S. Supreme Court, having successfully overruled the prime minister and assembly by declaring over 100 national laws and ordinances to be unconstitutional.[9] The German Constitutional Court also has a substantial impact on national and state policymaking, both through its rulings and through government's anticipation of those rulings.

About a quarter of Lijphart's democracies had either strong or medium-strength judicial review. In both France and Germany, new legislation may be challenged in court by opposition members of parliament even before it takes effect, a process called "abstract" judicial review. Lijphart classified a little over half of his democracies as having "weak judicial review," with the powers of courts constrained by very limited constitutional authority (as in Sweden) or limited independence of government-appointed judges (as in Japan). In the remaining democracies, including Britain, courts enjoyed no power of judicial review of legislation, although, as suggested in Table 6.2, they may still protect individuals from government abuse not specifically authorized by law.

In many of the new democracies of Eastern Europe judicial review was proclaimed in the constitution, but proved harder to implement in practice. There have been striking successes in constraining governments in some countries, as in Bulgaria, but failures in others, such as Albania and Belarus. In Nigeria, the courts long retained a striking degree of judicial independence under a succession of otherwise undemocratic military regimes, but were shown little respect under the Abacha regime of the mid-1990s, which established special military tribunals to prosecute its perceived enemies.

China, in contrast, after explicit rejection of any limits on "mass justice" from the late-1950s to the 1970s, has gradually attempted to introduce a very limited "rule by law." This is seen by Chinese rulers as a way to encourage stability and economic growth and control corruption. However, the practice falls far short of the promise of limitation on governmental authority.

All written constitutions provide for amending procedures. Most framers of constitutions have recognized that basic decision rules must be adaptable, because of potential ambiguities, inefficiencies, changes in citizen values, or unforeseen circumstances. But if amendments are too easy to make, they may jeopardize important constitutional protections. Therefore, many constitutions provide that certain arrangements may not be amended (for example, the provision in the U.S. Constitution granting each state equal representation in the Senate).

Amending procedures vary widely, ranging from the complex to the simple. Perhaps the simplest case is that of the United Kingdom, where an ordinary parliamentary statute may alter the constitution. In some cases, constitutional amendments must be approved by a popular vote. The U.S. Constitution has the most difficult formal procedure.

One of the main points of Figure 6.1 and Tables 6.1 and 6.2 is that constitutions may concentrate or disperse government power along several dimensions.[10] There are necessary trade-offs involved in making such constitutional choices. Probably no one who favors democracy and individual liberties would argue for extreme centralization of power in an omnipotent dictator, as in Thomas Hobbes's *Leviathan* (see Chapter 1). However, constitutional democracies that concentrate power to a somewhat lesser degree, such as the British system, have some important advantages. Their governments tend to be effective and efficient, and by relying on majority rule, they tend to treat all citizens equally. No small group can hold up a decision favored by a solid majority. On the other hand, constitutions that disperse power, like more inclusive decision rules, have their own advantages. They are more likely to check potential abuses of power, such as the tyranny of a majority, and policies will tend to be more stable over time.

CHECKING THE TOP POLICYMAKERS

One challenge of government is to control the excesses of top political leaders. In many authoritarian systems, there is no legal and institutionalized way to remove the top political leaders if they become unpopular or overstep whatever bounds they may face. Moreover, authoritarian leaders can usually change or simply ignore the constitution when it restricts their desires. Democracies have various procedures for keeping the leaders in check, but the procedures vary among the types of systems. In parliamentary systems, chief executives can be removed virtually at any time through a vote of no confidence if they lose the support of a parliamentary majority. In Germany, for example, Social

Democratic Party Chancellor Helmut Schmidt was ousted by Helmut Kohl of the Christian Democratic Party in October 1982.

Democratic presidential systems fall somewhere in between. Unlike prime ministers under parliamentary constitutions, presidents have fixed terms of office. Most presidential systems provide for the removal of presidents before their term is up, but typically only if they are guilty of serious criminal or other wrongdoing. This procedure is called **impeachment.** Impeachment typically involves three components: (1) impeachable offenses are usually identified as presenting unusual danger to the public good or safety; (2) the penalty is removal from office (sometimes with separate criminal penalties); and (3) impeachment cases are decided by the legislature, but require more than ordinary majorities and may also involve the judiciary in some way. The positive value of impeachment is that it provides a way of legally mobilizing political power against a threat to the constitutional or legal order. At the same time, the danger is that it can be used for mere partisan or personal goals.

In the U.S. system, impeachment procedures can be used against the incumbents in top offices, even the president (as in the cases of Presidents Nixon and Clinton) or a Supreme Court justice, if their activities stray too far beyond legal bounds. No U.S. president has yet been convicted by the Senate and removed from office, although that fate has befallen other federal officials, such as judges.

Impeachment is associated with constitutions having powerful presidencies with fixed terms of office, such as those in the United States, Brazil, South Korea, and the Philippines. Impeachment rules have also been adopted in the constitutions of semipresidential regimes, such as Russia, and even in purely parliamentary regimes.

In the long run, the ultimate control of democratic order is periodic and competitive elections. This need to achieve and regularly renew their mandates is the fundamental device that leads politicians to respond to the needs and demands of citizens. It is deeply imperfect. It may be difficult to tell when elected officials are incompetent, deceitful, or just unlucky. The complexities of policymaking may baffle the attempt of even trained observers to assign responsibility for successes or failures. The multiplicity of political issues may leave citizens torn between their candidate choices. Or, none of the choices may seem very palatable. Yet, deeply

BOX 6.2

Impeachment in Latin America

Brazil, Mexico, and many other Latin American nations with strong presidents have impeachment rules and traditions. These were often modeled on the U.S. Constitution. In Mexico, the president, the state governors, and federal judges are subject to impeachment. Brazil has an impeachment process similar to that of the United States, except that it takes a two-thirds vote in the lower house of the assembly to charge the president and other high civil officers with impeachable offenses. A two-thirds vote is also required in the Senate to convict. The clause was invoked in 1992 when Brazil's President Fernando Collor was impeached on charges of large-scale corruption. He resigned before trial in the Senate. Impeachment procedures also forced presidents from office in Venezuela in 1993 and Paraguay in 1999.

imperfect as it is, this remarkable recruitment structure gives every citizen some influence on the policymaking process. For this reason, we consider it the most significant democratic structure.

ASSEMBLIES

Legislative **assemblies** have existed for thousands of years. Ancient Greece and Rome had them, as did many other ancient societies. Indeed, the Roman Senate has given its name to modern assemblies in the United States and many other countries.

Almost all contemporary political systems have assemblies, variously called senates, chambers, diets, houses, and the like. Assemblies are also known as "legislatures" (regardless of what role they actually play in legislating) or as "parliaments" (mainly in parliamentary systems). Their formal approval is usually required for major public policies. They are generally elected by popular vote, and hence are at least formally accountable to the citizenry. Today, more than 80 percent of the countries belonging to the United Nations have such governmental bodies. The almost universal adoption of legislative assemblies suggests that in the modern world a legitimate government must formally include a representative popular component.

Assembly Structure

Assemblies vary in their size—from less than 100 to more than 1,000—and their organization. They may consist of one (in which case they are called unicameral) or two (bicameral) chambers. Most democracies, and some authoritarian systems, have bicameral (two-chamber) assemblies. Federal systems normally provide simultaneously for two forms of representation: often representation in one chamber is based on population and representation in the second chamber is based on geographic units. Even in unitary systems (such as France or Japan), **bicameralism** is common, but the purpose of the second chamber is to provide a check on policymaking rather than to represent subnational units. The bicameral U.S. Congress grew out of both federalism and the desire to separate the power of the federal government.

The U.S. system, in which the two chambers have roughly equal powers, is unusual. In most bicameral systems, one chamber is dominant, and the second (such as the Russian Council of the Federation or the French Senate) has more limited powers that are often designed to protect regional interests. While representatives in the dominant chamber are popularly elected, those in the second chamber are sometimes chosen by the regional governments (as in Germany) or in other indirect ways. The prime minister in most parliamentary systems is responsible only to the more popularly elected chamber, which therefore has a more important position in policymaking than the second chamber. (See the discussion of the vote of confidence procedure earlier in this chapter and in Box 6.1.) In such systems members of the prime minister's cabinet are usually chosen from the majority party or parties' leadership in this chamber.

Assemblies also differ in their internal organization in ways that have major consequences for policymaking. There are two kinds of internal legislative organization: party groups and formal assembly subunits (presiding officers, committees, and the like). There is often an inverse relationship between the strength of parties versus other subunits (such as committees). The stronger parties are, the weaker are committees, and vice versa. British members of Parliament vote strictly along party lines much more consistently than members of the U.S. Congress. As in most parliamentary systems, British members of Parliament rarely vote against the instructions of their party leaders. Because cabinets generally hold office only as long as they can command a parliamentary majority, deviating from the party line means risking the fall of the government and new elections.

In presidential systems, the president and the legislators are independently elected for fixed terms of office. Thus the fate of the governing party is less directly tied up with voting on legislative measures. In U.S. legislatures, party discipline operates principally on procedural questions, such as committee assignments or the selection of a presiding officer. On substantive policy issues, Democratic and Republican legislators are freer to decide whether or not to vote with their party leaders.

All assemblies have a committee structure, some organized arrangement that permits legislators to divide up their labor and to specialize in particular issue areas. Without such committees, it would be impossible to handle the large flow of legislative business. As we have seen, however, the importance of committees varies. In some legislatures—such as those in the United States, Japan, and Germany—committees are very influential. This is partially because they are highly specialized, have jurisdictions that match those of the executive departments, and have large staff resources. Strong committees tend to have a clear legislative division of labor that matches the executive branch, allowing for specialized oversight of executive activity. They are often arenas in which the opposition can be influential. British committees are much weaker than their opposite numbers in the United States, since they have small staffs, are dominated by the governing party, and get appointed for one bill at a time. Hence, they cannot accumulate expertise in a particular policy area. German and Japanese committees are stronger than those of Britain but weaker than their American counterparts.[11]

Assembly Functions

Assembly members deliberate, debate, and vote on policies that come before them. Most important policies and rules must be considered and at least formally approved by these bodies before they have the force of law. Assemblies typically also control public spending decisions, so that control of the purse strings (budgeting) is one of their major functions. In addition, some assemblies have important appointment powers, and some (like the British House of Lords in criminal cases) may serve as a court of appeals. Although laws typically need assembly approval, in most countries legislation is actually formulated elsewhere, usually by the political executive and the upper levels of the bureaucracy.

When we compare the importance of assemblies as policymaking agencies, the U.S. Congress, which plays a very active role in the formulation and enactment of legislation, is at one extreme. The other extreme is represented by the National People's Congress of the People's Republic of China, which meets infrequently and does little more than listen to statements by party leaders and rubber-stamp decisions made elsewhere. Roughly midway between the two is the House of Commons in Britain. There, legislative proposals are sometimes initiated or modified by ordinary members of Parliament, but public policy is usually initiated and proposed by members of the Cabinet (who are, to be sure, chosen from the members of the parliamentary body). The typical assembly provides a deliberating forum, formally enacts legislation, and sometimes amends it.

Assemblies should not be viewed only as legislative bodies. All assemblies in democratic systems have an important relationship to legislation, but not necessarily a dominant role. Their political importance is based not just on this function, but also on the great variety of other political functions they perform. Assemblies can play a major role in elite recruitment, especially in parliamentary systems where prime ministers and cabinet members typically serve their apprenticeships in parliament. Legislative committee hearings and floor debates may be important sites for interest articulation and interest aggregation, especially if there is no cohesive majority party. Debates in assemblies can be a source of public information about politics and thus contribute to the socialization of citizens generally and elites in particular.

Representation: Mirroring and Representational Biases

Contemporary legislative assemblies, especially in democratic systems, are valued particularly because they represent the citizens in the national policymaking process. It is not obvious, however, what the ideal linkage between citizens and government officials should be. Some argue that government officials should mirror the characteristics of the citizens as far as possible. This principle, also known as *descriptive representation*, is held to be particularly important with respect to potentially conflictual divisions (such as race, class, ethnicity, gender, language, and perhaps age).

However, descriptive representation is not the only concern in recruiting public officials. The limits of mirroring were inadvertently expressed by a U.S. senator. In defending a U.S. Supreme Court nominee who was accused of mediocrity, the senator lamely contended, "[E]ven if he were mediocre, there are a lot of mediocre judges and people and lawyers. They are entitled to a little representation, aren't they?"[12] Most people would probably not argue that government officials should mirror the general population in their abilities to do their jobs. Instead, we generally want political elites to be the best possible *agents* for their constituents. In this view, government officials should be selected for their ability to serve the interests of the citizens, whether or not they share the voters' background characteristics.

For politicians to be good agents, they need to have similar *preferences* to the citizens they represent *and* they need the appropriate *skills* to do their jobs. In democracies, political parties are the most important mechanism by which the preferences of citizens and leaders get aligned. As far as skills are concerned, education and experience are the most important factors. Political and governmental leadership—particularly in modern, technologically advanced societies—requires knowledge and skills that are hard to acquire except through education and training. Natural intelligence or experience may, to a limited degree, take the place of formal education.

Hence, it might be a good thing for government officials to be better informed, more intelligent, more experienced, and perhaps better educated than the people who they serve. Just as medical patients tend to look for the most capable physician rather than the one who is most like them, so, one could argue, citizens should look for the best qualified officeholder. In this view, selecting government officials, including representative policymakers, is like delegating to experts. It may be a hopeful sign that citizens in many modern democracies are increasingly willing to select leaders who do not share their background characteristics.

As in the case of so many other political choices, there is no obvious or perfect way to choose between mirroring and expert delegation. This is an old debate, and in many situations it is necessary to make a trade-off between the two. And different offices may require different considerations. Most people would, for example, probably put a higher emphasis on mirroring in their local assembly than in a regulatory agency overseeing nuclear technology.

The bad news is that political elites, even democratically elected members of legislative assemblies, hardly ever mirror the citizens they represent on any of the standard social characteristics. Even in democracies such as the United States, Britain, and France, political leaders tend to be of middle- or upper-class background or unusually well-educated and upwardly mobile individuals from the lower classes. There are exceptions. In some countries, trade unions or leftist political parties may serve as channels of political advancement for people with modest economic or educational backgrounds. These representatives acquire political skills and experience by holding offices in working-class organizations. Thus the Labour Party delegation in the British House of Commons and the Communist delegation in the French National Assembly have included substantial numbers of workers. And during the long domination of the executive by the Norwegian Labor Party (1935–1981), none of its prime ministers had even completed secondary school. But these are rare and vanishing examples. In most contemporary states, the number of working-class people in high office is small and declining.

Women have also been poorly represented in political leadership positions in most countries. History certainly offers examples of strong and influential female rulers, such as Queen Elizabeth I of England (who ruled from 1558 to 1603). Yet in most countries women did not have the right to vote until well into the twentieth century and have not held many political leadership positions.

That situation has changed significantly in the last twenty-five years. In 1980, women on average held fewer than 10 percent of the parliamentary seats in the advanced industrial democracies. By 1990, that figure was up to about 15 percent, and by 1997 women had surpassed 20 percent. Women have also held the chief executive office in a growing number of countries, particularly in Europe and Asia. (See Box 6.3.)

BOX 6.3

Women as Chief Executives

From about 1970 on, women have gained chief executive office in a growing number of countries. Interestingly, many of them have been from Asian and Middle Eastern countries, where women's roles in public life traditionally have been limited. Sinmavo Bandaranaike of Sri Lanka (1960–1965 and 1970–1977), Indira Gandhi of India (1966–1977 and 1980–1984), and Golda Meir of Israel (1969–1974) were among the pioneers. In the 1980s and 1990s, women also came to power in the Philippines, Pakistan, Bangladesh, and again in Sri Lanka. In Burma, Nobel Peace Prize winner Aung San Suu Kyi won the elections of 1990 but the military prevented her from taking office.

Women have also made inroads in leadership positions in Europe and North America, though they are still few and far between in Africa and Latin America. The first female leader in a major European country was Prime Minister Margaret Thatcher of Britain (1979–1990). Her strong and decisive leadership made her one of Europe's most influential politicians in the 1980s. Women have come to power in other western countries as well. Ireland and Iceland have had female presidents. Canada, France, and Switzerland have had brief stints with female prime ministers. Angela Merkel is chancellor of Germany. In Norway, Gro Harlem Brundtland held the prime ministership for a total of about ten years between 1981 and 1996. Brundtland, a physician and environmentalist, later headed the World Health Organization.

The career paths of Asian women leaders have tended to differ from those in Europe. Many of the former have come from prominent political families, such as the Gandhi family in India and the Bhuttos in Pakistan. In several cases, they have been the widows or daughters of important political leaders. In Europe, women leaders are more likely to have made independent political careers, and they can rely on stronger women's interest groups.

Angela Merkel, for example, became chancellor of Germany in 2005.

But women's advancement has been uneven, and their representation remains low in the developing world. In many Northern European countries, such as Sweden, women by the late 1990s accounted for 30 to 40 percent of the legislators and a similar proportion of cabinet members. But in Russia, Mexico, Brazil, and Japan, women still accounted for fewer than one legislator in ten in the 1990s.[13]

Political elites also tend to be unrepresentative with respect to age. In many countries, legislators (much less chief executives) under age 40 are a rarity, whereas a large proportion of leading politicians are past normal retirement age. Japan is an extreme example. In 1990, there were about eight legislators over age 60 for every one member under age 40. In many countries, university graduates—and often lawyers and civil servants in particular—are vastly overrepresented, whereas ethnic, linguistic, and religious minorities are often underrepresented. Representational biases are thus numerous and pervasive. And while women's representation is increasing, class biases are getting worse.

POLITICAL EXECUTIVES

In modern states, the executive branch is by far the largest, the most complex, and typically the most powerful branch of government. It is not easy to describe executives in simple ways, but it is sensible to start at the top. Governments typically have one or two **chief executives,** officials who sit at the very top of the often-colossal executive branch. Such executives have various names, titles, duties, and powers. They are called presidents, prime ministers, chancellors, secretaries general, or even leader (in Iran.) There are even a few kings who still have genuine power. Titles may mislead us as to what functions these officials perform, but they tend to be the main formulators and executors of public policy.

Structure of the Chief Executive

Democratic governments typically feature either a single chief executive (in presidential systems) or a split chief executive of two offices: a largely ceremonial head of state (who represents the nation on formal occasions) and a more powerful head of government,

		TABLE 6.3
Bases of Legislative Power of Chief Executives		
Authoritarian	**Democratic: Partisan Influence**	**Democratic: Constitutional Powers**
	Effective	
General Secretary, China	British Prime Minister	
	French Prime Minister	
	German Chancellor	
	Indian Prime Minister	
	Japanese Prime Minister	
	(Russian Prime Minister)	
	Ceremonial	
Chinese President		British Queen
		German President
		Indian President
		Japanese Emperor
	Ceremonial and Effective	
Iranian Leader	French President	Brazilian President
		Mexican President
		Nigerian President
		Russian President
		U.S. President

(who determines public policies). Table 6.3 distinguishes among executives according to the bases of their power to affect policymaking. In the left column we see the chief executives in authoritarian systems, whose power ultimately rests on coercion. The middle and right columns show the chief executives in democratic countries. The middle column shows executives whose power rests primarily on their partisan influence in the legislature, which is the case of the prime ministers in most parliamentary systems. The right column includes chief executives whose ability to influence legislation resides in powers directly granted them by the constitution, rather than partisan connection alone. Strong presidents may be able to veto legislation, for example, issue legal decrees, or introduce the budget. They usually have the power to appoint and dismiss members of the cabinet.

Reading down the table, we see the distinction between executives with effective power over policy, purely ceremonial roles, or both effective and ceremonial power. Political executives are effective only if they have genuine discretion in the enactment and implementation of laws and regulations, in budgetary matters, or in important government appointments. Where they do not have these powers, they are symbolic or ceremonial. In presidential systems, the ceremonial and effective roles are almost always held by the same person, the president, as we see in both authoritarian and democratic systems at the bottom of Table 6.3. In parliamentary democratic systems, and in some authoritarian systems, the two roles are separated between the "head of state," who is primarily a ceremonial official, and a "head of government," who makes and implements the decisions. The British, German, Indian, and Japanese prime ministers appear in column two at the top right of the table, while their ceremonial counterparts appear at the center right.

These distinctions are not absolute. Some constitutions, such as the German, give substantial formal powers to their prime ministers. At the same time even largely ceremonial presidents can exert important influence if the parties are divided or by exercising special constitutional powers (or both, as has recently happened in India). Moreover, partisan influence in the legislature is useful even to the strongest democratic presidents. Still, it is usually easy to determine the primary sources of legislative power, even where the formal names may be misleading.

As noted earlier, a few countries, such as France and Russia, have both significant presidents and prime ministers. The balance of power between them depends on the constitutional powers of the president and on the partisan division in the legislature. In Russia, the constitutional powers of veto and decree of the president are very great, and the legislature has seldom been unified against him; the prime minister is mostly just another administrator, with little effective power. In France, however, the president's formal powers are much weaker; when the legislature is unified under opposition parties it has elected a prime minister who has effectively dominated policy-making, greatly reducing the president's political influence.

In China the chairman of the Communist Party is the most powerful political figure and the effective chief executive. The Chinese president is the head of state, which is a purely ceremonial role, without associated powers. However, in recent years the same individual (Jiang Zemin and now Hu Jintao) has held both offices, and also a key role as chairman of the party military commission. A third role was the premier, or head of government, which was a largely administrative position.

Monarchies are much more rare at the beginning of the twenty-first century than they were at the beginning of the twentieth. Some monarchs, such as the king of Saudi Arabia and some other Arab monarchs, still exercise real power. Most contemporary monarchs, however, have little or no actual political influence. Monarchs like the British queen or the Scandinavian kings are principally ceremonial and symbolic officers with very occasional political powers. They are living symbols of the state and nation and of their historical continuity. Britain's queen may bestow honors or peerages (appointments to the nobility) with a stroke of her scepter, but these are recommended by the prime minister. The Japanese monarchy has also traditionally been dignified and exalted and played an important role as a national symbol. In contrast, the Scandinavian and Low Country monarchies are more humdrum. Because members of these royal families occasionally use more humble means of transportation, these dynasties are sometimes called "bicycle monarchies." In republican democracies with parliamentary systems, presidents perform the functions that fall to kings and queens in parliamentary monarchies. Thus German presidents give speeches on important anniversaries and designate prime ministers after elections or when a government has resigned.

World leaders attend a meeting during the G8 Summit on July 16, 2006, in St. Petersburg, Russia.

Getty Images News

A system in which the ceremonial executive is separated from the effective executive has a number of advantages. The ceremonial executive symbolizes unity and continuity and can be above politics. The U.S. presidency, which combines both effective and ceremonial functions, runs the risk that the president will use his ceremonial and symbolic authority to

Queen Beatrix of the Netherlands rides her bicycle on a visit in East Holland, thus illustrating why the Scandinavian and Low Country monarchies are called "bicycle monarchies."

Hulton-Deutsch/Hulton-Getty

enhance his political power or that his involvement in politics may make him a less effective symbolic or unifying figure.

Recruitment of Chief Executives

Historically, finding generally acceptable ways to select the individuals to fill the top policymaking roles has been critical to political order and stability. A major accomplishment of stable democracies is regulating the potential conflict involved in leadership succession and confining it to the mobilization of votes instead of weapons. When we refer generally to "recruitment structures," we are thinking of how nations choose their top policymakers and executives. Table 6.4 shows the recruitment structures in twelve selected countries.

The most familiar structures are the presidential and parliamentary forms of competitive party systems. In presidential systems, as in Brazil and the United States, parties select candidates for nomination, and the electorate chooses among them. Russia and France have directly elected presidents but also give an important role to the prime minister, who is appointed by the president but can be removed by the legislature.

Mexico appears similar to other presidential systems. But for half a century the Partido Revolucionario Institucional (PRI) had such control over the electoral process that the voters merely ratified the party's presidential nominee. That nomination itself was announced by the outgoing president after complex bargaining between party factions and other powerful groups. Mexico seemed to be moving to give the voters an honest role in choosing between alternative candidates, but until the remarkable July 2000 election many voters remained skeptical that a non-PRI president could really come to power. As the table shows, Mexico now seems a newly democratic presidential system, with parties nominating candidates and voters genuinely choosing among them, as in the very close election of 2006.

In both presidential and parliamentary democracies the tenure of the chief executive is limited, directly or indirectly. In the presidential system this is usually directly, through fixed terms of office for the chief executive. In the parliamentary system there is a maximum term for the parliament, which then indirectly

TABLE 6.4

Recruitment of Chief Executive

Country	Chief Executive Structure	Recruitment Structures	How Often Has This Type of Government Survived Succession?[b]
Brazil	President	Party and voters	Often
Britain	Prime minister	Party, House of Commons, voters	Very often
China	Party secretary[a]	Party and military	Often
France	President/Prime minister	Party, (Assembly) voters	Often
Germany	Chancellor	Party, Bundestag, voters	Often
India	Prime minister	Party, Lok Sabha, voters	Often (one interruption)
Iran	Leader, President	Religious elites, voters	Once
Japan	Prime minister	Party, Diet, voters	Often
Mexico	President	Party and voters	Twice
Nigeria	President	Military, party, voters	Never
Russia	President	Party and voters	Once
United States	President	Party and voters	Very often

[a] "Party secretary" refers to that position or to a similar one as head of party in a communist regime.
[b] "Often" means that at least three successions have taken place under that type of government.

also limits the life of the cabinet, since the prime minister is accountable to the new parliamentary majority and can be removed by it.

Table 6.4 also illustrates the role of noncompetitive parties and military organizations in China, the military in Nigeria, and nonelected religious elites in Iran. The important role played by political parties illustrates the great need to mobilize broad political support behind the selection of chief executives. The frequent appearance of parties also reflects, no doubt, the modern legitimacy of popular sovereignty: the promise that the rulers' actions will be in the interest of the ruled.

Authoritarian systems rarely have effective procedures for leadership succession. The more power is concentrated at the top, the riskier it is to transfer it from one person to the next. Very often, authoritarian leaders do not dare to relinquish their power, and leadership succession occurs only when they die or are overthrown. In communist regimes, the Communist Party selected the general secretary (or equivalent), who was the controlling executive force. Individual succession was not a simple matter. These systems did not limit the terms of incumbents, who were difficult to oust once they had consolidated their supporters into key party positions. Nonetheless, they always had to be aware of

the possibility of a party coup of the type that ousted Nikita Khrushchev from the Soviet leadership in 1964. As a system, however, the Soviet leadership structure seemed quite stable until the dramatic 1991 coup attempt against Gorbachev. Although he was briefly restored to power, the events surrounding the coup stripped the Soviet presidency of power, and legitimacy passed to the presidencies and legislatures of the fifteen constituent republics, most importantly to President Boris Yeltsin of Russia. Russia managed its first democratic transition surprisingly smoothly, from Yeltsin to his chosen successor Vladimir Putin, who was elected as the new president in April 2000 and reelected in 2004.

The poorer nations show substantially less stability, and the regimes have usually had less experience at surviving succession crises.[14] Nigeria is typical. It experienced a succession of military coups and governments from 1966 until 1979, then introduced a competitive presidential system, which was overthrown by a military coup shortly after its second election in 1983. The military government again moved toward civilian rule in the early 1990s but then annulled the 1993 presidential election before the results were announced. The military rulers finally allowed a return to civilian rule in 1999.

Many African nations experienced repeated coups. Military governments, stable or unstable, have also been common in Latin America and the Middle East, although they are now more likely to dominate in coalition or from behind the scenes. (See Chapter 5.) The Chinese Communist Party has remained in power for fifty years but has suffered several periods of internal strife, and the army has been involved in recruitment at all levels. India's democracy, having persisted through assassinations and other crises, has been an exception to the rule among poorer nations. It has provided a number of democratic successions with a single interruption (authoritarian emergency rule that postponed elections for several years) in the 1970s.

The Cabinet

In many political systems, the **cabinet** is the most important collective decision-making body. Its power can be particularly great in parliamentary systems, where its formation is closely linked to selection of the prime minister. It typically contains the leaders (often called "ministers" or "secretaries of state") of all the major departments (sometimes called "ministries") into which the executive branch is divided. The cabinet meets frequently, often several times per week. It is typically selected and led by the head of government: the president in presidential systems and the prime minister in parliamentary ones. In some parliamentary systems, the entire cabinet is collectively responsible to the legislature. The prime minister may be little more than "first among equals," especially under conditions of multiparty coalition governments. In other parliamentary systems, such as Germany, the constitution confers much more authority on the prime minister.[15]

How does the cabinet get selected? In presidential systems, selecting cabinet members is typically a presidential prerogative, though sometimes (as with the U.S. Senate), the legislature has to give its approval. The president can typically also dismiss cabinet members at will, whereas the legislature's ability to do so is most often severely limited.

In parliamentary systems, in contrast, the process is very different, since the prime minister and his or her cabinet need to maintain the confidence of the parliamentary majority. Therefore, cabinet formation depends on the result of parliamentary elections and on the composition of parliament. If a competitive

Coalition partners emphasize their solidarity before the German Bundestag in February 2003: Chancellor Gerhard Schroeder of the Social Democratic Party (right) welcomes Foreign Minister Joschka Fischer of the Green Party. Their two parties had campaigned together in a preelection coalition in the 2002 parliamentary election and formed a majority coalition cabinet afterwards.

AP Images

party wins a parliamentary majority by itself, it will (if unified) be able to form a cabinet of its own members and can then pass and implement its policies. Sometimes the election directly determines who controls the majority. This will always be the case in pure two-party systems, where one party or the other will always have a parliamentary majority. It can also happen in multiparty systems, whenever one party gets more seats than all its competitors combined. But the more parties there are, the less likely it is that one of them will have a majority on its own. We call the outcome in which one party controls a parliamentary majority by itself—a majority situation. Whenever majority situations occur in parliamentary systems, the majority party almost always forms a *majority single-party cabinet* by itself.

Far more often, no party wins a majority of votes. In most multiparty countries, the typical election result is that no party has a parliamentary majority by itself—a minority situation. Most commonly under such circumstances, several parties (two, three, or as many as six or seven) join forces and form a *coalition cabinet* in which they are all represented. Sometimes, parties anticipate this need to form coalitions before the election. They may then make a formal agreement with one another and inform the voters that they intend to govern together if they collectively get enough votes. The allied parties may thus encourage their voters to support the coalition partners' candidates where their own party's candidates seem weak and often take advantage of special provisions of voting laws. Many German and French governments have come to power in this fashion. In such cases, the voters can have a direct voice in the choice of the future cabinet, much as they do in two-party systems. Voters are thus given a major role in choosing the direction of government policy.

But parties often do not make such preelection commitments. Even when they do, they often fail to get the support they would need to control a parliamentary majority. If no party or preelection coalition wins control of the legislature through the election, then parties may bargain after the election, or between elections, to form a new cabinet. In the Netherlands, such bargaining took four months after the 2003 election. In Germany, about three weeks of bargaining was necessary to form a "grand coalition" of the two largest parties after the 2005 parliamentary election.

Whether bargaining takes place before or after the elections, the parties in parliamentary systems typically have a lot of options concerning the composition of the cabinet. In minority situations, the result can be either a minority government or a majority coalition of several parties. In some cases, a single party decides that it can form a minority cabinet alone, often because the other parties disagree too much among themselves to offer any alternative. Figure 6.2 illustrates these various possibilities. In the minority case, the parties in the cabinet must continually bargain with other parties to get policies adopted and even to remain in office. In majority coalitions, bargaining will take place primarily among coalition partners represented in the cabinet. In both of these circumstances, the power of the prime minister may depend on the bargains he or she can strike with leaders of other parties.

These complications illustrate two of the problems of combining parliamentary government with electoral systems of proportional representation. Such systems tend to produce minority situations, which do not give the voters a very clear choice about who will control the executive branch. Instead, the parties may determine this behind closed doors after the election. Sometimes, the results are paradoxical, as when parties that have just lost votes in the elections are able to negotiate their way into a governing coalition. The second problem is that under minority situations, cabinets are sometimes

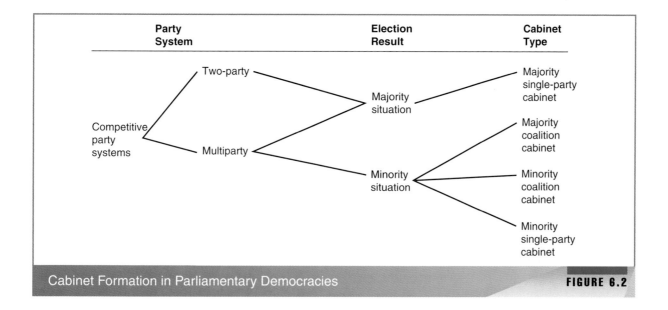

Cabinet Formation in Parliamentary Democracies   **FIGURE 6.2**

unstable. Italy, for example, has had on average more than one change of government per year since World War II. Yet, such problems need not always emerge. In Germany, for example, cabinets have been quite stable, and the voters have generally been given fairly clear options ahead of elections.

Functions of the Chief Executive

Typically, the chief executive is the most important structure in policymaking. The executive normally initiates new policies. Depending on the division of powers with the legislature and the partisan balance, the executive also has a substantial part in their adoption. In presidential systems, the president very often has veto powers. Thus the chief executive not only has the first word in policymaking, he or she also typically has the last word. In parliamentary systems, on the other hand, the chief executive is less likely to be able to exercise a veto.

The political executive also oversees policy implementation and can hold subordinate officials accountable for their performance. The central decisions in a foreign policy crisis are generally made by the chief executive: the president (George W. Bush in the Iraq War) or the prime minister (Tony Blair in the Iraq War). Political initiatives and new programs typically originate in the executive. A bureaucracy without an effective executive tends to implement past policies, rather than to initiate new ones. Without politically motivated ministers, bureaucracies tend toward inertia.

The decision of a president, prime minister, cabinet, or central party committee to pursue a new foreign or domestic policy is usually accompanied by structural adaptations—the appointment of a vigorous minister, an increase in staff, the establishment of a special cabinet committee, and the like. Where the political executive is weak and divided, as in Fourth Republic France or contemporary Italy (at least until recently), this dynamic force is missing. Initiative then passes to the bureaucracy, legislative committees, and powerful interest groups—and general needs, interests, and problems may be neglected. In a separation-of-powers system when the presidency and the congress are controlled by different parties, even a strong president may be hampered in carrying out an effective policy. And if the president is hamstrung, the assembly is rarely able to fill the gap.

Chief executives also perform important system functions. Studies of childhood socialization show that the first political role perceived by children tends to be the chief political executive—the president, prime minister, and king or queen. In early childhood the tendency is to identify the top political executive as a parent figure. As the child matures, he or she begins to differentiate political from other roles, as well as to differentiate among various political roles (see Chapter 3). The conduct of the chief executive affects the trust and confidence that young people feel in the whole political system and they carry that with them into adulthood. The role of the chief executive in recruitment is obviously important, appointing the cabinet and other officials. The political executive also plays a central role in communication, in explaining and building support for new policies, or in improving performance in various sectors of the society and economy.

THE BUREAUCRACY

Modern societies are dominated by large organizations, and the largest contemporary organizations are government **bureaucracies,** or their systems of public administration. These agencies, by which we mean all the members of the executive branch below the top executive (president/monarch, prime minister, and cabinet) are generally in charge of implementing government policy. The size of government bureaucracies increased over the course of the twentieth century. This is partly due to the efforts of governments to improve the health, productivity, welfare, and security of their populations. It may also be partly due to the tendency for government agencies, once they have been established, to seek growth for its own sake. In reaction to this tendency, and as part of the concern about government inefficiencies, there has been a recent movement to reduce government budgets and to downsize the bureaucracy (see Chapter 7).

Structure of the Bureaucracy

The most important officials in bureaucracies are the experienced and expert personnel of the top **civil service.** The British "government," which we can think of as its top executive positions, consists of approximately 100 "frontbench" members of Parliament, some twenty of whom serve in the Cabinet, with the remainder named as ministers, junior ministers, and parliamentary secretaries. This relatively small group of political policymakers oversees some 3,000 permanent members of the **higher civil service,** largely recruited directly from the universities. They spend their lives as an elite corps, moving about from ministry to ministry, watching governments come and go, and becoming increasingly important as policymakers as they rise in rank. Below the higher civil service are a huge body of more than half a million permanent public employees, ordinary civil servants, organized into about twenty government departments and a number of other agencies. The total number of British civil servants rose from 100,000 in 1900 to more than 700,000 in 1979, but it then declined to under 500,000 under Conservative governments of the 1980s and 1990s.

The importance of the permanent higher civil service is not unique to Britain, though perhaps it has been most fully institutionalized there. In France, too, the higher civil service is filled with powerful generalists who can bring long tenure, experience, and technical knowledge to their particular tasks. In the United States, many top positions go to presidential appointees rather than to permanent civil servants. Despite this difference and a greater emphasis on technical specialization, there are permanent civil servants in the key positions just below the top appointees in such agencies as the Internal Revenue Service, the Federal Bureau of Investigation, the Central Intelligence Agency, the National Institutes of Health, and all the cabinet departments. These people tend to be specialists—such as military officers, diplomats, doctors, scientists, economists, and engineers—who exert great influence on policy formulation and execution in their specialties. Below these specialists and administrators are the vast numbers of ordinary government employees, postal workers, teachers, welfare case agents, and so forth, who see that governmental policies are put into practice. In 2004, the United States had 22 million public employees of all kinds, federal, state, and local, or about 17 percent of the total labor force. In many European countries, that proportion is even higher, approaching a third of the labor force in Norway, Denmark, and Sweden.

The Functions of the Bureaucracy

Bureaucracies have great significance in most contemporary societies. One reason is that the bureaucracy is almost alone in implementing and enforcing laws and regulations. In so doing, they may have quite a bit of discretion. Most modern legislation is general and can be effectively enforced only if administrative officials work out its detail and implementation. Policy implementation and enforcement usually depend on bureaucrats' interpretations and on the spirit and effectiveness with which they put policies into practice. But the power of bureaucracies is not restricted to their implementation and enforcement of rules made by others. In Chapters 4 and 5 we discussed how bureaucratic agencies may articulate and aggregate interests. Departments like those for agriculture, labor, defense, welfare, and education may be among the most important voices of interest groups. Moreover, administrative agencies in modern political systems do a lot of adjudication. Tax authorities, for example, routinely determine whether citizens have faithfully reported their income and paid their taxes, and these authorities assess penalties accordingly. While citizens may in principle be able to appeal such rulings to the courts, relatively few actually do.

Finally, bureaucracies are involved in communication. Political elites, whether executives or legislators, base many of their decisions on the information they obtain from the public administration. Similarly, interest groups, political parties, the business elites, and the public depend on such information. Most major agencies in modern governments have spokespersons whose job it is to inform and influence the media. With the increasing media power in modern societies, top government executives are eager to present their versions of events. Increasingly, however, large parts of the journalistic professions refuse to recognize any limits on the publication of private as well as political information. Leaks of secret or confidential information and intelligence have become a veritable flood. Thus political executives and bureaucracies can no longer control information in the ways that they formerly did. In dealing with the media, top administrators now must have more complex strategies and professional assistance. The art of "spin control" has replaced their reliance on classification and "executive privilege."

Bureaucracy and Performance

We commonly use the term "bureaucracy" to refer to all systems of public administration. Strictly speaking, however, bureaucracy refers to a particular way of organizing such agencies, a practice that gained favor in the latter part of the nineteenth century and the beginning of the twentieth century. According to the classical German sociologist Max Weber, bureaucracies have the following features:

1. Decision making is based on fixed and official jurisdictions, rules, and regulations.
2. There are formal and specialized educational or training requirements for each position.
3. There is a hierarchical command structure: a firmly ordered system of super- and subordination, in which information flows upward and decisions downward.
4. Decisions are made on the basis of standard operating procedures, which include extensive written records.
5. Officials hold career positions, are appointed and promoted on the basis of merit, and have protection against political interference, notably in the form of permanent job tenure.[16]

No organization is perfectly bureaucratic in this sense, but professional armies come reasonably close, as do tax revenue departments.

These features of bureaucracies have a number of desirable effects. They promote competence, consistency, fair treatment, and freedom from political manipulation. Imagine what life could be like without bureaucracies. Before the advent of modern bureaucracy, public officials were often a sorry lot. Some of them inherited their jobs; others got them through family or political connections. Yet others bought their posts and used them either to enrich themselves or gain social status (or both). Many saw their jobs strictly as a sideline and devoted little time to their duties. No wonder, then, that public officials were often incompetent, uninterested in their jobs, corrupt, or all of the above. They often used their powers arbitrarily, to favor friends and neighbors, and to the disadvantage of others. Given the lack of rules and records, aggrieved citizens typically had few recourses.

But the negative connotations that the word "bureaucracy" has taken on suggest that such organizations have liabilities as well. Bureaucratic organizations can become stodgy, rule-bound, inflexible, and insensitive to the needs of their clients. In many cases, bureaucrats also have few incentives to be innovative and efficient, or even to work very hard. Although bureaucracies are supposed to be politically and ideologically neutral, in fact they tend to be influenced by the dominant ideologies of the time, to have conservative propensities, and to pursue institutional interests of their own.[17] Many citizens are exasperated with bureaucracy and its propensities for inefficiency and lack of responsiveness. This frustration is reflected in popular cynicism as well as in periodic attempts to reform government.

Mark Nadel and Francis Rourke suggest a variety of ways that government and societal agencies may influence and control bureaucracies, externally or internally.[18] The major external government control is the political executive. Although presidents, prime ministers, and ministers formally command subordinate officials and may have the power to remove them for nonperformance of duty, executives and bureaucracies actually depend on one another. Top executives typically try to persuade; rarely do they go to the extreme of dismissing or transferring civil servants. Centralized budgeting and administrative reorganization are other means of executive control. The threat to take away resources or authority may bring bureaucratic implementation into greater conformity with the aims of the political executive.

Modern authoritarian systems discovered that the bureaucracy was an essential tool of government control. Thus, recruitment of the bureaucracy was part of a larger pattern of control. Bureaucratic selection in the former Soviet Union, as in China today, was controlled through a device called *nomenklatura*. Under this procedure important positions were kept under the direct supervision of a party agency whose officials had the final word on recruitment. Moreover, the party offered a complicated set of inducements to control the behavior of the chosen officials. These inducements made it difficult for any but the topmost officials to have much freedom of action. Soviet leaders used normative incentives (such as appeals to party, ideology, and national idealism), financial incentives (such as better salaries, access to finer food and clothing, better housing, and freedom to travel), and coercive control (such as reporting by police, party, and bureaucrats). They used demotion or imprisonment, even execution, as penalties. To avoid a coup by police or military forces, the varied layers of command and inducement structures were interwoven, so that no layer could act independently.

In democracies, assemblies and courts also help control the bureaucracy. Legislative committee hearings or judicial investigations may bring bureaucratic performance into line with political desires. Sweden invented the institution of the **ombudsman** to prevent bureaucrats from doing injury or injustice to individuals.[19] This invention has been copied by other states. In the Scandinavian countries, Britain, Germany, and elsewhere ombudsmen now investigate citizen claims that they have suffered injury or damage as a result of government action. Ombudsmen typically have no power of their own, but report to the legislature for remedial action. Their cases rarely lead to criminal conviction, but often government officials change their policies as a result of embarrassing publicity. Thus, ombudsmen offer a more expeditious and less costly procedure than court action. Among the extragovernmental forces that constrain bureaucracies are public opinion and the mass media, as well as interest groups of various kinds.

All such controls on civil servants tend to be less effective outside the advanced industrial democracies. Authoritarian systems lack many of these controls, particularly external ones, such as elected political executives and legislators, independent courts, free mass media, and interest groups. Therefore, authoritarian regimes are particularly prone to bureaucratic inefficiency and inertia. Moreover, in many nonindustrial countries, mass media are neither independent nor influential, few citizens participate in politics, and lower-level government employees are poorly trained and paid—all conditions that encourage bribery, extortion, and bureaucratic mismanagement.[20]

Successful democracy requires that public policies made by national assemblies and chief executives be implemented fairly and effectively; democracy depends on the rule of law. When ruling parties demand kickbacks of public money from construction firms seeking public works contracts, the democratic process is subverted by rent-seeking politicians. (See Chapter 1 and Box 1.2.) Similarly, when tax officials and border authorities are open to cash payments to overlook tax deficiencies and customs violations, democratic law making is undermined. Citizens who must bribe teachers to get education for their children or health officials to get immunizations are deprived of the benefits of democratic public policies. Such practices are all too common in the poorer nations of the world.

Failure of the rule of law is difficult to study systematically, but some comparative insight into corruption in public bureaucracies is provided by the surveys of perceptions of corruption on the part of businesspeople, academics, and analysts in different countries. These have been combined into the Corruption Perceptions Index, which rates about one hundred countries each year on a scale from 0 ("highly corrupt") to 10 ("highly clean"). Figure 6.3 shows on the vertical dimension the ratings for 2005 (based on a three-year moving average) of the twelve countries studied in this book. As we see, all of the countries experience some levels of corruption. The world's top-rated country in 2005 was Iceland at 9.7. But Britain, Germany, the United States, France, and Japan (despite individually notorious cases in each), rated in the top half of the scale. Brazil, Mexico, China, Iran, and India are far more corrupt, with scores in the low range of the scale. Russia, plagued by many problems of its dual economic and political transitions, scores even worse. Nigeria, despite its recent efforts at democratic transition, is perceived as one of the world's most corrupt countries.

Perceived Corruption and Economic Development Level, 2005*   **FIGURE 6.3**

*Economic development level from World Bank, downloaded from www.worldbank.org/data on July 6, 2006; Corruption Perception, Index from Transparency International, downloaded from www.transparency.org/cpi/index on July 6, 2006.

We can compare the perceived corruption scores with the purchasing power parity (PPP) measure of economic wealth and productivity on the horizontal dimension of Figure 6.3. This comparison shows that corruption and the failure of the rule of law are very strongly associated with poverty and underdevelopment, as well as with direct indicators of widespread misery (see also Table 1.3 in Chapter 1).[21] However, some individual countries do better or worse than we might expect. For example, Russia is somewhat more corrupt than we would expect from its middle-level income.

The ills of bureaucracy, including inefficiency and inertia, are pandemic. This is truly a dilemma because we are unlikely to invent any schemes for carrying out large-scale social tasks without the organization, division of labor, and professionalism that bureaucracy provides. Its pathologies can only be mitigated. The art of modern political leadership consists not only of defining and communicating appropriate goals and policies, but also of getting them implemented by a massive and complex bureaucracy—how and when to press and coerce it, reorganize it, reward it, teach it, or be taught by it.

REVIEW QUESTIONS

- What are the advantages of more inclusive decision rules in making policies? What are the disadvantages?
- Why is the confidence relationship so important in parliamentary democracies?
- In what different ways can policymaking power be dispersed and limited by constitutional arrangements?

- What are the advantages and disadvantages of assembly representation that mirrors the characteristics of citizens?
- How are cabinets formed after national elections in parliamentary systems?
- Why are bureaucracies necessary but sometimes liabilities in policymaking?

KEY TERMS

assemblies
authoritarian
    regimes
bicameralism
bureaucracies
cabinet
chief executives

civil service
confidence relationship
constitutional regimes
decision rules
democracy
democratic presidential
    regime

federal systems
higher civil service
impeachment
judicial review
ombudsman
parliamentary
    regimes

policymaking
semipresidential
    regime
separation of powers

SUGGESTED READINGS

Aberbach, Joel, Robert D. Putnam, and Bert A. Rockman. *Bureaucrats and Politicians in Western Democracies.* Cambridge: Harvard University Press, 1981.

Döring, Herbert, ed. *Parliaments and Majority Rule in Western Europe.* New York: St. Martin's Press, 1995.

Huber, John D. *Rationalizing Parliament.* Cambridge: Cambridge University Press, 1996.

Laver, Michael, and Norman Schofield. *Multiparty Government: The Politics of Coalition in Europe.* Ann Arbor: University of Michigan Press, 1998.

Lijphart, Arend. *Democracy in Plural Societies.* New Haven, CT: Yale University Press, 1977.

———. *Patterns of Democracy: Government Forms and Performance in Thirty-Six Countries.* New Haven, CT: Yale University Press, 1999.

Linz, Juan, and Arturo Valenzuela, eds. *The Failure of Presidential Democracy: Comparative Perspectives.* Baltimore: Johns Hopkins University Press, 1994.

Mainwaring, Scott, and Matthew Shugart, eds. *Presidentialism and Democracy in Latin America.* New York: Cambridge University Press, 1997.

North, Douglass. *Institutions, Institutional Change, and Economic Performance.* Cambridge: Cambridge University Press, 1990.

Powell, G. Bingham. *Contemporary Democracies.* Cambridge: Harvard University Press, 1982.

Riker, William H. *Federalism: Origin, Operation, and Significance.* Boston: Little, Brown, 1964.

Sartori, Giovanni. *Comparative Constitutional Engineering.* New York: New York University Press, 1997.

Secondat, Charles de, Baron de Montesquieu. *The Spirit of the Laws.* London: Hafner, 1960.

Shugart, Matthew, and John Carey. *Presidents and Assemblies: Constitutional Design and Electoral Dynamics.* Cambridge: Cambridge University Press, 1992.

Stone-Sweet, Alec. *Governing with Judges: Constitutional Politics in Europe.* Oxford: Oxford University Press, 2002.

Strøm, Kaare. *Minority Government and Majority Rule.* Cambridge: Cambridge University Press, 1990.

Tsebelis, George. *Veto Players: How Political Institutions Work.* Princeton, NJ: Princeton University Press, 2002.

Weaver, Kent, and Bert Rockman, eds. *Do Institutions Matter? Government Capabilities in the United States and Abroad.* Washington, DC: Brookings Institution, 1993.

Weber, Max. "Bureaucracy." In H. H. Gerth and C. Wright Mills, eds., *From Max Weber.* New York: Oxford University Press, 1976, pp. 196–244.

Weingast, Barry R. "Political Foundations of Democracy and the Rule of Law." *American Political Science Review* 91, no. 2 (June 1997): 245–63.

ENDNOTES

1. For a skeptical view of constitutional design, see James G. March and Johan P. Olsen, *Rediscovering Institutions: The Organizational Basis of Politics* (New York: Free Press, 1989), 171–72. For a more sanguine argument, see Giovanni Sartori, *Comparative Constitutional Engineering* (New York: New York University Press, 1995).

2. John Locke, *Two Treatises of Government*, ed. Peter Laslett (Cambridge: Cambridge University Press, 1960); Charles de Secondat, Baron de Montesquieu, *The Spirit of the Laws* (London: Hafner, 1960).

3. *The Federalist: A Commentary on the Constitution of the United States* (Washington: National Home Library Foundation, 1937).

4. On presidential decree powers, see John M. Carey and Matthew S. Shugart, *Executive Decree Authority* (New York: Cambridge University Press, 1998); for more general discussions of presidential powers, see Matthew S. Shugart and John M. Carey, *Presidents and Assemblies: Constitutional Design and Electoral Dynamics* (Cambridge: Cambridge University Press, 1992); Scott Mainwaring and Matthew S. Shugart, eds., *Presidentialism and Democracy in Latin America* (New York: Cambridge University Press, 1997).

5. It is important to avoid confusion between the formal titles of government officials and the source of their selection and bases of their powers—which determine the type of political system. For example, Germany is a parliamentary system, whose executive is headed by a prime minister, although his official title is chancellor; and as in many parliamentary systems the German head of state is a ceremonial president, chosen by the legislature, with little policymaking power. See also Table 6.3.

6. Arend Lijphart, *Democracy in Plural Societies* (New Haven, CT: Yale University Press, 1977); G. Bingham Powell, *Contemporary Democracies* (Cambridge: Harvard University Press, 1982); Arend Lijphart, *Patterns of Democracy: Government Forms and Performance in Thirty-Six Countries* (New Haven, CT: Yale University Press, 1999).

7. Donald Horowitz, "Comparing Democratic Systems," in Larry Diamond and Mark F. Plattner, eds., *The Global Resurgence of Democracy* (Baltimore: Johns Hopkins University Press, 1993), 127 ff.

8. Arend Lijphart, *Patterns of Democracy*, 226.

9. George H. Gadbois, Jr., "The Institutionalization of the Supreme Court of India," in John R. Schmidhauser, ed., *Comparative Judicial Systems* (London: Butterworth Enterprises, 1987), 111–42.

10. A major trend in the division and limitation of policymaking powers in recent years has been the growth of independent central banks. Central banks, such as the Federal Reserve in the United States, have the critical task of regulating the supply of money and the interest rates, as well as many financial transactions for government and society. In most countries, such bank policy was long controlled by the chief executive as part of the government bureaucracy. But in the last 20 years, and especially since the early 1990s, many countries have given their central banks substantial independence and set for them the primary task of using monetary policy to maintain price stability and limit inflation. Their independence from the executive is encouraged by giving bank governors long terms of office free from the possibility of dismissal, as well as stipulated policy objectives and responsibilities. Such independence reassures investors, domestic and foreign, and seems to constrain inflation, but it limits the economic policy alternatives of the chief executive and cabinet.

11. For a survey of parliamentary committees in Europe, see Ingvar Mattson and Kaare Strøm, "Parliamentary Committees," in Herbert Doring, ed., *Parliaments and Majority Rule in Western Europe* (New York: St. Martin's Press, 1995), 249–307.

12. Senator Roman Houska quoted in *Time* magazine March 30, 1970.

13. See Pippa Norris, "Legislative Recruitment," in Lawrence LeDuc, Richard G. Niemi, and Pippa Norris, eds., *Comparing Democracies* (London: Sage, 1996), 184–215; Richard E. Matland, "Women's Representation in National Legislatures: Developed and Developing Countries," *Legislative Studies Quarterly* 23, no. 1 (February 1998): 109–125.

14. Adam Przeworski, et al., *Democracy and Development* (New York: Cambridge University Press, 2000).

15. See the relevant chapters in Michael Laver and Kenneth A. Shepsle, *Cabinet Ministers and Parliamentary Government* (New York: Cambridge University Press, 1994).

16. See the discussion in Julien Freund, *The Sociology of Max Weber* (NY: Random House, 1969), 234–35.

17. See Joel Aberbach, Robert D. Putnam, and Bert A. Rockman, *Bureaucrats and Politicians in Western Democracies* (Cambridge: Harvard University Press, 1981).

18. Mark V. Nadel and Francis E. Rourke, "Bureaucracies," in Fred Greenstein and Nelson Polsby, eds., *Handbook of Political Science*, vol. 5 (Reading, MA: Addison-Wesley, 1975), 373–440.

19. See Frank Stacey, *The British Ombudsman* (Oxford: Clarendon Press, 1971); Roy Gregory and Peter Hutchesson, *The Parliamentary Ombudsman: A Study in the Control of Administrative Action* (London: Allen & Unwin, 1975).

20. On the difficulties involved in reducing administrative corruption in developing countries, see Robert Klitgard, *Controlling Corruption* (Berkeley: University of California Press, 1989).

21. For a statistical analysis explaining scores on the Corruption Perceptions Index, see Daniel Triesman, "The Causes of Corruption: A Cross-National Study," *Journal of Public Economics* 76 (June 2000): 399–457, who suggests lower levels of economic development, shorter exposure to democracy, and federalism to be among the factors encouraging more perceived corruption.

PUBLIC POLICY

Public policy consists of all the authoritative public decisions that governments make—the outputs of the political system. Policies or outputs are normally chosen for a purpose: they are meant to promote end results that we refer to as political outcomes. Different policies may be more or less efficient ways to reach the outcomes that policymakers want. But whether a particular outcome is good or bad ultimately depends on political goods and values. And whatever values and goals policymakers and citizens have will surely affect their evaluation of the political outcomes they actually reach. Since politicians and citizens often disagree over political goods and values, it is important to keep these goals in mind when we study public policy. In this chapter, we shall discuss these aspects of public policy in order, but we begin by considering what governments actually do.

GOVERNMENT AND WHAT IT DOES

Governments do many things. Some things they do are timeless. In the days of the Roman Empire, for example, defense against external and internal enemies was a major government responsibility. It continues to be so in most societies today. In other ways, governments today do things that were unthinkable in the past. For example, contemporary governments regulate telecommunications and air traffic, policy areas that were unknown until the twentieth century.

Governments produce many goods and services, though exactly which ones vary a great deal from country to country. In most societies, governments provide law enforcement, roads, and postal services, and in many countries they do much more. In the former Soviet Union and other communist states, governments owned and operated most major industries and produced everything from military equipment to such consumer goods as clothing and shoes. In a capitalist society, such as the United States, most consumer goods are produced in the private sector. In much of Europe, the government produces more than in the United States, but far less than in the former Soviet Union. In some developing countries, the government produces very few goods or services.

The range of government involvement varies not just among countries, but also among different economic sectors within the same country. For example, one study showed that the U.S. government employed only 1 percent of the people engaged in mining and manufacturing, but 28 percent of those working for the utilities that supply gas, water, and electrical power; in France, the corresponding figures were 8 percent and 71 percent, respectively. Compared with socialist countries, governments in capitalist free-market societies tend to leave more production to private firms. Yet, there is no society in which the government produces no goods or services, and conversely no state in which all industries are run by the government. Even in the former Soviet Union, part of the agricultural sector was private, as were many simple consumer services, such as babysitting. Other ostensibly communist societies, such as China today, feature a lot of private enterprise, particularly in the consumer goods sector.

Public Policies

The importance of governments goes far beyond their role as producers of goods and services. Indeed, this may not even be their most important role in most contemporary states. Governments also engage in various forms of public policy. In Chapter 1, we discussed three important challenges facing contemporary states: building community, fostering development, and securing democracy and human rights. Many **public policies** are wholly or in part directed at these challenges. Public policies are designed to strengthen national identity and community by reinforcing a common language or culture, or by promoting allegiance to a shared political heritage. A host of economic policies aims to promote economic and social development and to make its benefits broadly accessible. Finally, government policies establish or enhance democratic institutions that enable citizens to control political decisions. In the past century, most Western nations have been transformed from authoritarian, or oligarchic (systems ruled by the few), regimes to democracies. Government policy has increasingly been used to meet popular needs and demands. Even so, we cannot always assume that what democratic governments do is what is in the best interest of their citizens.

Public policies may be summarized and compared according to outputs—the actions that governments take to accomplish their purposes. We classify these actions or outputs under four headings:

1. **distribution**—of money, goods, and services—to citizens, residents, and clients of the state;
2. **extraction** of resources—money, goods, persons, and services—from the domestic and international environments;
3. **regulation** of human behavior—the use of compulsion and inducement to bring about desired behavior; and
4. **symbolic outputs**—political speeches, holidays, rites, public monuments and statues, and the like—used to exhort citizens to engage in desired forms of behavior, build community, or celebrate exemplary conduct (see Chapter 1).

Political systems have different policy profiles. Some governments produce a lot of goods and services but regulate little. Elsewhere, the government may be heavily engaged in extraction and distribution, but rely on the private sector to produce most goods and services. In the next sections, we shall discuss these four types of policies, beginning with distribution.

DISTRIBUTION

The political scientist Harold D. Lasswell famously argued that the essence of government is deciding "who gets what, when, and how." Politics, he thought, is essentially about distribution. Whether or not we agree with Lasswell's point of view, there is no question that distributive policies are very important in contemporary societies. Whether or not they are democratic, all governments have to distribute resources in order to survive. Distributive policies include transfers of money, goods, services, honors, and opportunities to individuals and groups in the society. Such policies generally consume more government resources and employ more government officials than anything else that modern governments do.

Distributive Policy Profiles

Health, education, and national defense are among the policy areas that consume the largest proportions of government spending worldwide. Figure 7.1 reports central governmental expenditures in these policy areas as a percentage of gross domestic product (GDP). Clearly, central government expenditures depend heavily on economic development. Developed countries generally allocate from one-half to two-thirds of their central government expenditures to education, health, and welfare. France, Germany, and Britain spend more than two-thirds of their budgets in these areas, compared with just under one-half in the United States, where a larger share of health care spending is in the private sector. Before 1989, the Soviet Union and the communist countries of Eastern Europe spent less on education, health, and welfare than the democracies of Western Europe. But as these Eastern European countries have introduced market economies, their expenditure patterns have become more similar to the West.

Since World War II especially, governments have greatly expanded their spending on education. Developing societies have made large efforts to provide at least primary education for all their citizens,

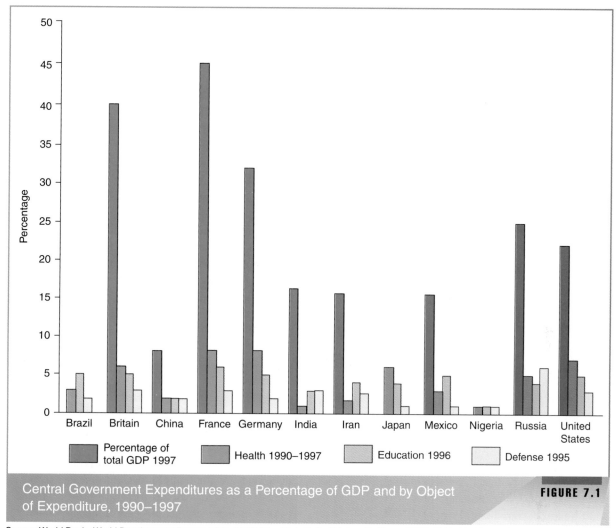

Central Government Expenditures as a Percentage of GDP and by Object
of Expenditure, 1990–1997

FIGURE 7.1

Source: World Bank, *World Development Report: 1999–2000* (New York: Oxford University Press, 2000), Table 14, 256–57; Table 7, 242–43; Table 6, 240–41; Table 17, 262–63.

while most of the richer societies have also experienced a huge increase in secondary and university (tertiary) enrollments. A few decades ago, fewer than 5 percent of young adults in most European countries were able to get a college education. Today, those numbers have risen to 40 percent or more (see Table 7.4). Since most of these colleges and universities are public, government spending on secondary and higher education has risen substantially.

Public health is another major spending category. Some developing countries, such as India and Nigeria, typically spend less on health than on education. The government in Nigeria seems to have little impact on its people in these areas. India's efforts are only slightly better. Sadly, the countries that need them most have

the least to spend on education and health. Poor nations, with limited budgets and many pressing demands, cannot easily spare the resources for health and education. Also, social security expenditure in poor nations tends to be low, because shorter life expectancies and high birth rates mean that there are comparatively few older people. But part of the explanation of the low social expenditures in poor countries may also have to do with poor measures. Just as our GDP measures fail to include the subsistence economy and therefore underreport the wealth of the poorest countries (see Chapter 1), our measures of health expenditures may similarly underreport the efforts of the poorest states. In these societies the aged and the infirm typically receive some care through the extended family, and these services go unreported in our statistics.

National security spending shows a different pattern. Particularly among less developed countries, spending varies as much with the international environment as with overall economic means. Some states that are locked in tense international confrontations (such as those in the Middle East) or that are trying to exert international influence make extraordinary defense efforts. Because of its worldwide security commitments, the United States is by far the heaviest military spender, although between the end of the Cold War and September 11, 2001, U.S. defense spending actually decreased. Japan, which spends as much as most Western countries on health and education, has spent relatively little on defense since World War II.

From the Night Watchman State to the Welfare State

The importance of distributive policies has grown enormously over the past century or so, particularly in industrialized societies. Much of this growth has come about because the government performs more functions today than it did in the past. The **night watchman state** that was common in the nineteenth century was very different from the more expansive governments that emerged later. The night watchman state was a Lockean state (see Chapter 1), which primarily sought to regulate just enough to preserve law, order, a good business climate, and the basic security of its citizens.

With the twentieth century came the **police state,** the **regulatory state,** and the **welfare state.** The police state regulates much more intrusively and extracts resources more severely than the night watchman state. The most oppressive forms of the police state have been associated with the totalitarian ideologies (Nazism, fascism, and communism) that also left their mark on the past century. Fascist and communist governments typically call on their citizens to devote a lot of time to military or other community service and try to control their lives. But the twentieth century also produced more benign forms of big government. The regulatory state has evolved in all advanced industrial societies as they face the complexities of modern life. Finally, the welfare state, which is found particularly in prosperous and democratic societies, distributes resources extensively to provide for the health,

education, employment, housing, and income support of its citizens.

The main reason that distribution has become such a dominant concern in modern governments lies in the welfare state. The welfare state refers to a set of government, and sometimes private, policies involving old age pensions (known in the United States as social security), health, sickness, and accident insurance, unemployment benefits, and the like. Over time, welfare state policies have also come to include public education, housing subsidies, child and childcare benefits, and other distributive policies.

The first modern welfare state programs were introduced in Germany in the 1880s. In response to rapid industrialization and urbanization, the German government under Chancellor Bismarck began offering social insurance programs that protected workers against unemployment, accidents, sickness, and poverty during old age. During the twentieth century, and particularly from the Great Depression of the 1930s until the 1970s, most industrialized states adopted and greatly expanded such welfare state policies. As developing countries become wealthier, they also tend to spend more of their resources on welfare state services.

Figure 7.2 shows that the welfare state in advanced capitalist—**Organization for Economic Cooperation and Development (OECD)**—countries continued to grow during the 1980s and 1990s, albeit at a somewhat slower rate. As the figure shows, welfare state spending consists of two major categories: cash transfers to individuals and families, and direct government spending on services. Though both categories have grown, the transfer programs remain the largest. Among the individual programs that make up the welfare state, old-age pensions (social security) and health care loom particularly large. In many European countries with jobless rates of up to 10 or 15 percent, unemployment benefits are another major government outlay.

The welfare state is a mixture combining a social insurance scheme and a program of social redistribution. It is in part paternalistic (forcing people to put away money for their old age and potential illnesses) and in part Robin Hood (taking from the rich and giving to the poor). The balance between these two functions depends in part on which programs a particular country emphasizes and in part on how it finances them. Thus, not all welfare states are alike. Even among the advanced industrial countries, some welfare states are larger than others, and different programs traditionally took precedence over education. Americans began spending on social security and welfare programs much later, and the U.S. government still does less in these areas than the governments of most other advanced democracies. And in many areas of welfare provision, U.S. programs are needs-based, whereas those in some European countries, such as Sweden, are entitlement-based (universalistic). For example, in the United States child benefits ("welfare") are given only to needy recipients for a limited period of time. In Scandinavia, on the

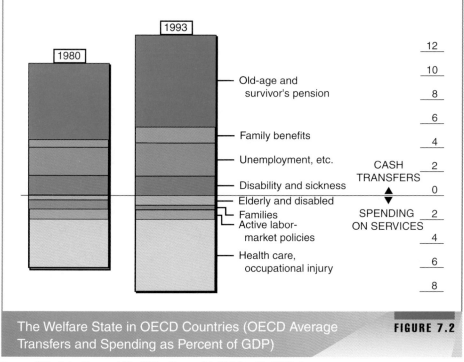

The Welfare State in OECD Countries (OECD Average Transfers and Spending as Percent of GDP)

FIGURE 7.2

Source: "Privatising Peace of Mind," *The Economist,* (October 24, 1998), 4.

political systems emphasize different benefits. All the wealthier nations try to assist the aged, the disabled, and the unemployed; but differences in expenditures reflect contrasts in priorities and historical experiences.

Because welfare benefits can be expensive and governments have limited funds, three principles govern most welfare state provisions. One is *need*: help and services are provided to those who need them the most. Social assistance is most commonly based on this idea. A second principle is *contribution*: benefits should go to those that have contributed to the program, for example, by paying taxes or insurance premiums. This is the basic idea behind social security in the United States, though other criteria also enter in. A third principle is *entitlement*, or *universalism*: everyone should have the benefit, regardless of specific circumstances. This is the principle that most countries apply to primary education or to treatment for life-threatening diseases.

The U.S. model stresses equality of opportunity through public education. Especially in higher education, the United States made a much greater and earlier effort than did most European nations. In contrast, on the European continent, social security and health

other hand, all parents (billionaires as well as paupers) get the same payment from the government. In addition, they get generous parental leave at close to full pay. In sum, compared with Europeans, Americans have historically put more emphasis on equality of opportunity and less on welfare obligations. This may reflect the U.S. heritage as a nation of immigrants, many of whom arrived poor and have been expected to prosper by their own efforts.

Also, it is important to keep in mind that many welfare services in the United States are provided by private foundations, churches and other religious organizations, and individuals. In recent years, multi-billionaires, such as Warren Buffett and Bill and Melinda Gates, have made huge donations to charitable causes in the United States and abroad. And they are not alone. In 2005 Americans gave $260 billion to charitable organizations. More than three-fourths of these gifts came from living individuals, many of them people of very limited means. The nonprofit sector of the U.S. economy now accounts for 9 percent of the GDP, more than twice as much as in 1960. It employs close to 10 percent of the American workforce, more than the federal and state governments combined. This nonprofit sector exists in other

A seriously injured man is wheeled on a gurney into the emergency room of a Detroit, Michigan, hospital. He must sign the Medicaid form in order to activate his health benefits.

Leonard Freed/Magnum Photos, Inc.

developed states as well, but generally on a much smaller scale.

Challenges to the Welfare State

Welfare states have many beneficial consequences. The Western European countries that pioneered these programs have virtually eradicated dire poverty, and they have created a much more "level playing field" for their citizens. Crime rates tend to be low in countries with extensive welfare states, and most of the programs are popular with ordinary citizens. Yet, the welfare state is also expensive. As government expenditures have grown to between one-third and one-half of GDP in most industrial democracies, they have caused serious concern about the ability of future generations to pay. One of the most serious problems is that at the same time that senior citizens are qualifying for greater pension benefits and health care costs are rising rapidly, the ranks of the elderly are swelling relative to those in the workforce. This is reflected in the dependency ratio, which is the proportion of those outside the workforce (because they are too young or too old) to those in the working-age population. Over the next decades, dependency ratios will increase in all advanced industrial societies, and particularly in such countries as Japan where the fertility rate is low and life expectancy high. Therefore, fewer working people

will have to pay higher taxes just to support existing health and welfare programs. In the United States, Medicare and social security may incur large deficits in the future. In other countries, social welfare programs are already costing more than their designated taxes are bringing in.

Another problem is that some welfare state policies give citizens few incentives to work. Norway and Sweden are among the leading countries in the world in life expectancy and public health statistics. Yet, workers in these countries are on sick leave about twice as often as those elsewhere in Europe, as the average Swedish worker misses about five or six weeks of work per year. In Norway, more than 10 percent of the working-age population is on disability pensions. This is because generous sick leave benefits let workers keep virtually their entire pay from the first day they miss work, and because it is fairly easy to qualify for disability benefits. But these policies are costly. In Sweden, sick pay and disability benefits account for more than 10 percent of the government's total spending.

These problems with the welfare state have stirred efforts to prevent further increases in spending obligations (entitlements) and to contain the costs of those already in effect. Thus the gradual expansion of welfare benefits that characterized most of the twentieth century can no longer be taken for granted.

EXTRACTION

Since distribution means that governments spend, there must also be ways for governments to collect money and other resources. All political systems *extract* resources from their environments and inhabitants. When simple societies go to war, for example, individuals of specific age groups (most commonly young men) may be called on to fight. Anthropologists have estimated that in some hunter-gatherer societies, such obligations have been so onerous that about half of all males have died in warfare. (Thomas Hobbes would not have been surprised.) Such direct extraction of services is still found in modern states, in the form of compulsory military service, jury duty, or compulsory labor imposed on those convicted of crime.

The most common contemporary forms of resource extraction, however, are taxation and borrowing. *Taxation* is the extraction for governmental purposes of money or goods from members of a political system, for which they receive no immediate or direct benefit. Tax policies are designed to meet many different objectives, which sometimes conflict. On the one hand, governments often want to collect as much tax revenue as possible from their citizens in order to finance various services. On the other hand, they do not want to kill the goose that lays the golden egg. The more governments tax their citizens, the less these people are inclined to work, and if the tax burden becomes too onerous, they may try to evade taxes or even leave the country altogether. Another common trade-off in tax policies is between efficiency and equity. *Efficiency* means extracting the most tax revenue possible at the lowest cost to economic production. *Equity* means taxing in such a way that, as much as possible, no one is unfairly burdened, and particularly so that those who have the least are spared. In most societies, the tax system is designed to redistribute wealth in favor of the less well-off. Therefore, income taxes are generally progressive, which means that citizens with greater incomes are taxed at higher rates than those who earn less. Yet, there is a limit to how progressive income taxes can be. Highly progressive income taxes can reduce people's incentive to work and thus hurt capital formation. Therefore, they are often inefficient.

Personal and corporate income taxes and taxes on capital gains and wealth are called **direct taxes,** since they are directly levied on persons and corporations. Such taxes, as well as property taxes, tend to be progressive. But although corporate income taxes are meant to be progressive, corporations often avoid them through creative accounting or by moving their

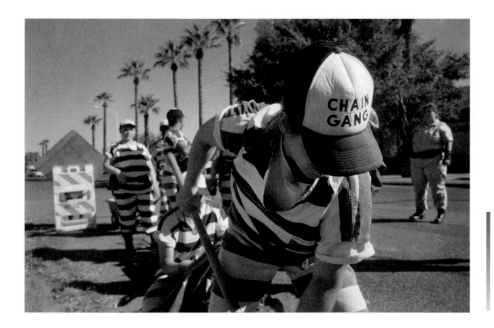

Prison labor and community service are important forms of government extraction. This photo shows a female chain gang in the United States.

Jack Kurtz/The Image Works

operations to countries where taxes are lower. If personal income taxes become too high, similar things can happen. **Indirect taxes** include sales and value-added taxes, excise taxes, and customs duties. Their distributive effects depend on who purchases the relevant commodities and services. Since the poor spend more of their income on food and clothing than do those who are better off, sales (or value-added) taxes on such necessities are regressive (which means that the poor pay relatively more than the rich). But indirect taxes on luxury goods may be progressive, since the poor rarely purchase yachts, fine jewelry, or private planes. Payroll taxes, which are often used to finance pensions (for example, social security in the United States), tend to hit the middle class, since the wealthy often receive a larger share of their income from dividends, interest, or capital gains. Taxes on wages also penalize people in the labor force relative to retirees and homemakers and can therefore hurt employment or drive businesses into the "underground economy" in which they do not report their incomes.

Political systems that rely heavily on sales and payroll taxes are less likely to attain a progressive tax structure overall. On the other hand, such taxes are less "visible" than income taxes and seem to generate less resentment and tax avoidance. In many countries, particularly where the government does not have good financial records, indirect taxes are easier to collect. Finally, the more mobile a tax object is, the more difficult it is to tax. Financial investments tend to be highly mobile, which makes them difficult to tax. Land and buildings, on the other hand, are not very mobile, and many states tax them substantially.

Besides redistribution and efficiency, tax policies are often designed to promote such values as charity, energy conservation, or home ownership. For example, many countries stimulate home ownership by making mortgage interest payments tax deductible. The rationale is that home ownership promotes stable families who take an active interest in their neighborhoods. If such tax incentives are too generous, however, they can cause economic distortions. Families may put all their savings into housing, so that businesses are starved of capital. Moreover, mortgage deductions are primarily a middle-class benefit of little use to the truly poor, who rarely own their own homes.

Figure 7.3 shows the central government revenues as a percentage of **gross domestic product (GDP)**, the total value of goods and services produced by a country's residents in a year. For the average country, about a fifth of the GDP is extracted by the central government's taxes, but in some countries the proportion is much higher. Regional and local taxes add to the tax burden. In federal systems—such as Brazil, Germany, India, Russia, and the United States—these taxes can increase the total tax burden by a third or more.[1] Governments also derive revenues from nontax sources (the lighter columns in Figure 7.3), such as administrative fees and income from business enterprises that they run.

The tax profiles of different countries vary both in their overall tax burdens and in their reliance on different types of taxes. Sweden has the highest tax rates overall, as it extracts more than 50 percent of its GDP in taxes. France comes close to the 50-percent mark. Britain and Germany are among a number of advanced industrial societies that collect about 40 percent of GDP, while the United States and Russia extract about a third. Outside the European and North American areas, central government revenue rarely exceeds 20 percent of GDP. The central government revenue of India is under 15 percent, or about 20 percent more if we add state and local governments.

Countries also differ in how they collect their revenues. Some advanced industrial countries (including Germany and France) rely heavily on social security taxes imposed on both employers and employees. In both Germany and Britain, most of the revenue comes from social security and income taxes, but whereas Germany relies far more heavily on social security payments, Britain relies more on income taxes. The United States and Japan, which fall below average in total tax burden, depend to a large extent on direct income taxes rather than on sales and consumption taxes.[2] Poorer countries, such as Iran, India, and Mexico, receive most of their revenue from indirect taxes.

Although overall tax burdens continue to grow, income tax rates have decreased in Western countries since the early 1980s, as there has been a shift from direct income taxes to less visible indirect consumption taxes. Growing tax burdens led to taxpayer revolts and some scaling back of government extraction. From 1975 to 1990, British top marginal income tax rates declined by 43 percentage points, Swedish rates by 35 points, and Japanese rates by 25 points. During the same time period in the United States, federal rates

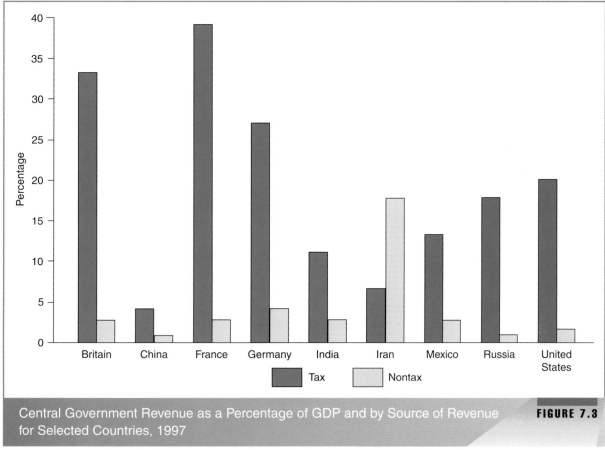

Central Government Revenue as a Percentage of GDP and by Source of Revenue for Selected Countries, 1997

FIGURE 7.3

Source: World Bank, *World Development Report, 1999–2000* (New York: Oxford University Press, 2000), Table 14, 256–57.

BOX 7.1

Balancing the Books

In the long run, governments cannot spend more money than they raise. If governments fail to balance their books and instead run budget deficits, they have to borrow money, which creates debt that future generations of taxpayers have to pay off. Yet, even rich governments are notoriously bad at balancing their books, and many run budget deficits year after year. In 2004, nineteen of the twenty-eight (highly developed) Organization for Economic Cooperation and Development (OECD) countries ran budget deficits, and the average deficit was equal to 3.5 percent of gross domestic product (GDP). The United States, which had run deficits most of the time since the Vietnam War, briefly balanced its budget in the late 1990s, but then slid back into fiscal imbalance due to the stock market crash in 2000, the terrorist attacks of September 11, 2001, increased spending on homeland security, the invasion of Iraq, and tax cuts. As of 2006, however, the United States had reduced its deficit to 1.9 percent of GDP, well below European countries such as France, Germany, and Italy. When these countries in the 1990s decided to adopt a common currency, the euro, they also committed themselves to keeping their respective national deficits smaller than 3 percent of GDP. In practice, however, they have often been unable to keep that promise.

declined by 42 points (although they then rose by about 13 points by the end of the Clinton administration, but have come down by about 4.5 points under President George W. Bush). The average decline in top tax rates for all OECD countries was 18 percent.[3] In Russia, President Putin cut income taxes drastically shortly after he came to power. Tax rates have come down because of the spread of economic views that stress the importance of entrepreneurial incentives for productivity. Lower marginal income tax rates stimulate economic activity and lessen incentives for tax evasion, but they may cause income inequalities to grow.

REGULATION

Regulation is the exercise of political control over the behavior of individuals and groups in the society. Most contemporary governments are not only welfare states, they are also regulatory states. Governments regulate for many reasons, as we discussed in Chapter 1. As social contract theorists such as Hobbes and Locke realized, regulation can facilitate many beneficial activities.

Economic production and commerce, for example, rely on government regulation to establish and protect property rights and to enforce contracts. There need to be rules to keep traffic moving smoothly on the freeways, in the air, and on the airwaves. Citizens and consumers often demand protections against fraud, manipulation, and obnoxious externalities, such as toxic waste and pollution. And governments are increasingly involved in setting product standards, particularly for pharmaceuticals and food, to make sure that these products are safe. Governments also regulate to shield their citizens, and often particularly children and women, from physical and other abuse, and to some extent they protect animals and plants against cruelty and environmental degradation.

Government regulation has proliferated enormously over the last century. Industrialization and urbanization have caused problems in traffic, health, and public order. Industrial growth has also generated concerns about industrial safety, labor exploitation, and pollution. Moreover, the growth of science and the belief that humanity can harness and control nature have led to increased demands for government action. Finally, changes in citizen values have led to

---

Regulation and Development   BOX 7.2

In the advanced industrial countries of North America, Japan, and Western Europe, regulation has grown enormously along with their industrial and postindustrial economies. It is easy to think, therefore, that there is more regulation in wealthy countries than in poor ones. But this is not always true. In fact, low-income countries sometimes regulate more than rich ones. This is particularly true of regulations of business entry and competition. In many less developed countries, it is cumbersome and time consuming, for example, to get the permits necessary to start a new business. Such regulations often mainly serve to create *rents* that government officials can exploit for their own benefit (see Chapter 1). They protect existing businesses by giving them monopolies or other protections. Many politicians expect the businesspeople who benefit from these regulations (often their family members, friends, or

business associates) to show their gratitude through kickbacks and other favors. Or business owners pay off politicians or civil servants to get around onerous regulations or to avoid long delays in handling their applications. Overregulation of this kind tends to hurt economic productivity and keep out foreign investment.

The Peruvian economist Hernando de Soto reports a sobering experience with abusive government regulation. As an experiment, he registered a small clothing factory in Lima, Peru, and decided in advance not to pay bribes. While he was waiting for his business to be registered, government officials asked him for bribes no fewer than ten times. Twice he broke his own rule and paid the bribe so that he would not be forced to give up his experiment. After ten months, his factory was finally registered. In New York, a similar procedure takes four hours.

Source: World Bank, *World Development Report 2005*, Chapter 5; William Easterly, *The Elusive Quest for Growth: The Economists' Adventures and Misadventures in the Tropics* (Cambridge: MIT Press, 2001) 233.

demands for new kinds of regulation. Thus, government regulation in the United States has extended to include gun control, protection of voting rights, prohibition of discrimination in employment, pollution abatement, and the like. At the same time, however, at least most Western societies have lessened their regulation of birth control, abortion, divorce, blasphemy, obscenity, and sexual conduct.

Governments regulate the lives of their citizens in many ways. Although we often associate regulation with legal means, there are other ways to regulate as well. Governments may control behavior by offering material or financial inducements or by persuasion or moral exhortation. For example, many governments try to reduce tobacco use by a combination of methods: bans on smoking, tobacco sales, or advertising; sales ("sin") taxes; and information campaigns to convince people of the hazards of smoking.

But even though there are many similarities in regulative policies across the world, states often differ substantially in their policy profiles. Patterns of regulation vary not only with industrialization and urbanization, for example, but also with cultural values. In the study of public policy, we describe and explain such differences among political systems by asking the following questions:

1. What aspects of human behavior and interaction are regulated and to what degree? Does the government regulate such domains as family relations, economic activity, religious activity, political activity, geographic mobility, professional and occupational qualifications, and protection of person and property? These questions have to do with the *domain* of government regulation.
2. What social groups are regulated, with what procedural limitations on enforcement, and what rights? Are these sanctions applied uniformly, or do they affect different individuals or groups differently? Are there rights of appeal? Such questions help us identify the *subjects* of regulation.
3. What sanctions are used to compel or induce citizens to comply? Does the government use exhortation and moral persuasion, financial rewards and penalties, licensing of some types of actions, physical confinement or punishment, or other

forms of coercion? These questions help us map the *instruments* or *mechanisms*, of regulation.

Although all modern states use sanctions, they vary in their goals and strategies. Yet, one aspect of regulation is particularly important politically: government control over political participation and communication. Recall from earlier chapters that democracy requires political competition. Governments in authoritarian systems often suppress political competition by prohibiting party organization, voluntary associations, and political communication. Government regulation in this area therefore has a crucial effect on democracy. Yet, governmental regulation is not always negative. Our civilization and amenities depend on regulation. Government regulation commonly promotes such values as the safety of persons and property, sanitation, prevention of environmental pollution, safe disposal of toxic wastes, maintenance of occupational safety, and equal access to housing and education.

Table 7.1 shows the political rights and civil liberties ratings for twelve countries, based on expert

Political and Economic Rights and Liberties, 2004–2005			**TABLE 7.1**
Country	**Political Rights**	**Civil Liberties**	**Economic Freedom**
Brazil	2	3	5.9
Britain	1	1	8.1
China	7	6	5.7
France	1	1	7.3
Germany	1	1	7.6
India	2	3	6.7
Iran	6	6	6.1
Japan	1	2	7.5
Mexico	2	2	6.6
Nigeria	3	3	5.6
Russia	6	5	5.6
United States	1	1	8.2

Note: Expert ratings of political rights and civil liberties for each country on a 1 (highest) to 7 (lowest) scale. Economic freedom scored on summary scale from 0 (low) to 10 (high).

Source: Freedom House website, www.freedomhouse.org (downloaded February 3, 2006); James Gwartney and Robert Lawson with William Easterly, *Economic Freedom of the World: 2006 Annual Report* (Vancouver: Fraser Institute, 2006), 13.

judgments. Political rights refers to citizen opportunities to participate in the choice of political leaders—voting rights, the right to run for office, and the like. Civil liberties refers to protections in such areas as freedom of speech, press, assembly, and religion, as well as to procedural rights, such as trial by a jury of peers and bans on arbitrary or cruel treatment. The rich democratic countries all have ratings of 1 or 2 for both political and civil rights. India, Brazil, and Mexico, which have improved significantly in recent years, follow next. At the other extreme, China, Iran, and most recently Russia substantially suppress both political rights and civil liberties. China in particular has tried to control the media comprehensively and sets few limits on government regulation vis-à-vis the individual. Nigeria is rated in the middle. These rankings, of course, vary over time. Rights and liberties in the United States have improved since the civil rights movement of the 1960s. Nigeria's military governments of the 1990s were repressive and frequently brutal, but things have improved there since power was turned over to an elected civilian president in 1999.

There is a strong correlation between political and civil rights. No country that scores high on participatory rights also scores very low on civil liberties, and no country low on participatory rights is high on civil liberties. This suggests a strong relationship between popular participation and the rule of law and equitable procedure. In a study of governmental repression in 153 countries during the 1980s, Steven C. Poe and C. Neal Tate found that positive civil and political rights records were best explained by democratic political institutions and conditions of peace and social order. Authoritarian states and those involved in internal or international war were the most frequent civil rights violators. A high level of economic development also helps explain a strong rights record.[4]

Table 7.1 also reports the level of economic freedom in each country. It is not always true that countries that are politically free also foster economic freedom, or vice versa. For example, China provides a lot less political freedom than Nigeria, but the level of economic freedom in the two countries is about the same. And even though Britain and France score the same on political rights and liberties, Britain has a higher level of economic freedom. On the whole, though, political and economic freedoms tend to go together.

COMMUNITY-BUILDING AND SYMBOLIC OUTPUTS

A fourth type of output is symbolic policies. Much communication by political leaders takes the form of appeals to the courage, wisdom, and magnanimity embodied in the nation's past; or appeals to values and ideologies, such as equality, liberty, community, democracy, communism, liberalism, or religious tradition; or promises of future accomplishment and rewards. Political leaders appeal to such values for different reasons—for example, to win elections or to push their own pet projects. But at the same time many symbolic appeals and policies have the purpose of building community—for example, by boosting people's national identity, civic pride, or trust in government.

Symbolic outputs are also intended to enhance other aspects of performance: to make people pay their taxes more readily and honestly; comply with the law more faithfully; or accept sacrifice, danger, and hardship. Such appeals may be especially important in times of crisis. Some of the most magnificent examples are the speeches of Pericles in the Athenian Assembly during the Peloponnesian War, or those of Franklin D. Roosevelt in the depths of the Great Depression, or of Winston Churchill during Britain's darkest hours in World War II. But symbolic policies are important even in less extreme circumstances. Public buildings, plazas, monuments, holiday parades, and civic and patriotic indoctrination in schools all attempt to contribute to the population's sense of governmental legitimacy and its willingness to comply with public policy.

OUTCOMES: DOMESTIC WELFARE

While we can describe different government policies, it is not always clear what their consequences will be. How do extractive, distributive, regulative, and symbolic policies affect the lives of citizens? Unexpected economic, international, or social events may frustrate the purpose of political leaders. Thus a tax rebate to stimulate the economy may be nullified by a rise in the price of oil. Increases in health expenditures may

TABLE 7.2

Welfare Outcomes, 1990–2005

Country	Private Household Consumption Annual (%) Growth 1990–2003	Population Below $2 per Day %, ca. 2000	Access to Safe Water (%) 1990/2002	Access to Sanitation (%) 1990/2002
Brazil	3.4	22.4	83/89	70/75
Britain	3.1	ND	100/100	100/100
China	8.5	46.7	70/77	23/44
France	1.6	ND	100/100	96/ND
Germany	1.5	ND	100/100	ND/ND
India	4.9	80.6	68/86	12/30
Iran	3.5	7.3	91/93	83/84
Japan	.4	ND	100/100	100/100
Mexico	2.8	26.3	80/91	66/77
Nigeria	3.7	90.8	49/60	39/38
Russia	.9	7.5	94/96	87/87
United States	3.7	ND	100/100	100/100

Source: World Bank, *World Development Indicators 2005*, Tables 2.5, 2.15, 4.10 (downloaded February 3, 2006), from http://devdata.worldbank.org/wdipdfs/tab2_5.pdf, 2_15.pdf, from http://devdata.worldbank.org/wdi2005/Table4_10.htm; and previous editions.

have no effect because of unexpected epidemics or rising health costs, or health services may not reach those most in need. Sometimes policies have unintended and undesirable consequences, as when the introduction of benefits for troubled social groups lead others to simulate the same troubles to get the same favors. Consequently, to estimate the effectiveness of public policy, we have to examine actual welfare outcomes as well as governmental policies and their implementation.

Table 7.2 compares a number of welfare indicators. The first two columns report measures of economic well-being or its lack: growth in private consumption and the share of the population living on less than $2 per day. The severe problems of Nigeria and India are particularly notable: the vast majority of those populations live on less than $2 a day. The latter columns report the availability of critical public facilities: safe water and sanitation. While most of the people of the developed world have access to safe water, this is true for less than half of the population of many less advantaged countries. In Nigeria, for example, only 49 percent of the population had access to safe water in 1990, though by 2002 this percentage had risen to 60. The good news

is that most of the poorer countries in our sample experienced solid progress over the past decade or so, although that progress may be more secure in China and India than in oil-dependent Nigeria.

In Chapter 1, we saw how income distribution tends to be most unequal in medium-income developing societies, such as Brazil, and more equal in advanced market societies as well as in low-income developing societies, such as India (see Table 1.4 in Chapter 1). In his studies of European economic history, Simon Kuznets showed that in the early stages of industrialization income distribution became more unequal, whereas in later stages of industrialization income distribution again came closer to equality.[5] This "Kuznets curve" reflects the fact that in the early stages of modernization, traditional farmers tend to be left behind as industry and commercial agriculture begin to grow. At higher levels of economic attainment, however, the number of poor farmers is reduced compared with the industrial and service sectors. In addition, when trade unions and democratic political parties emerge, they tend to make the income distribution more equal through taxation, wage policy, and welfare state policies.

BOX 7.3

Government and the Rural Poor

Visitors from rich countries are often shocked and appalled at the poverty they see in the fast-growing cities of the developing world. Poverty in these teeming metropolises is often exacerbated by crime, violence, homelessness, and pollution. Yet, poverty is even more of a problem in the countryside than in the cities. The poorest countries in the world are overwhelmingly rural, and in most poor countries poverty rates in the countryside are much higher than in the cities. In Brazil, for example, only 15 percent of the urban population fell below the country's (modest) poverty line in 1998, whereas 51 percent of the rural population did so. There are many reasons that rural poverty is often so dire. In rural areas, there is often less investment in education and infrastructure. Farmers in poor countries often find it difficult to obtain title to their land or credit (see Box 7.4). And rural dwellers are more susceptible than city-dwellers to the vagaries of the climate.

But part of the problem of rural poverty can also result from government policy. In many African states, for example, the rulers tend to favor the urban population because they want the country to modernize and industrialize. Sometimes politicians also worry that a starving urban population might riot and bring down the government. For these reasons, governments tend to keep food prices artificially low, which hurts farmers. Governments also tend to prefer targeted government agricultural programs (often subsidies), which help particular groups of farmers (often wealthy ones). Such targeted programs help governments gain political supporters but are often wasteful. Even in democratic countries where the majority of voters are poor farmers, government policies often do little for them. Many voters do not trust politicians who promise to deliver broad public goods (such as health care and education), but instead support candidates who promise targeted private goods (such as jobs and subsidies). Thus, even spending on schools becomes a way to create jobs rather than to educate children. In India, teachers' salaries account for 96 percent of recurrent expenditures in primary education. Even so, teacher absenteeism is rampant. When inspectors made unannounced visits to rural schools, about two-thirds of the teachers were absent.

Sources: Robert H. Bates, *Markets and States in Tropical Africa* (Berkeley: University of California Press, 1981); Philip Keefer and Stuti Khemani, "Why Do the Poor Receive Poor Services?" *Economic and Political Weekly*, 28, February 2004, 935–43; World Bank, *World Development Report 2002*, 31–32.

Table 7.3 reports on health outcomes. During the 1990s, the average public health expenditure per capita for the economically developed countries was $2,505, compared with $182 for the developing countries. The average number of physicians per 1,000 people in the developed world was 2.8, compared with 1.3 in the developing world. But in Nigeria the number was only 0.2 in 1990 and 0.3 in 2004. The country has a high birth rate, but almost one out of ten infants fails to survive the first year of life; and more than one-third of Nigerian children under age 5 suffer from malnutrition. Nigerian citizens have a life expectancy at birth of just 45 years (compared with 75–80 years in advanced industrial countries).

Nigeria demonstrates the ills of poverty, but some poor countries cope more successfully than others. Consider the difference between China and India. With similar levels of GDP per capita, Chinese average life expectancy is 71 years and infant mortality is 30 per 1,000 live births, while those of India are 63 years and 63 per 1,000, respectively. China has three times as many physicians as India relative to its population. Almost half of India's children under age 5 are undernourished, compared with a sixth of those in China. Fortunately, however, health conditions are improving in most of the poor countries, including India.

While the incidence of infant mortality and malnutrition is much lower in advanced economies, these problems are still serious among the poor in advanced industrial countries, such as the United States. The United States spends the largest proportion of its GDP on health care (approximately 15 percent) of any country. At the same time, however, the United States has a somewhat higher infant death rate than Japan and Western Europe due to more widespread poverty, drug abuse, and unequal access to health care. As Table 7.3 shows, Japan has an exceptional health record. It has the longest life expectancy and the

BOX 7.4

Microcredit

One of the greatest obstacles to economic growth in many poor areas is the difficulty of obtaining credit. In advanced industrial countries, property owners (for example, farmers or home owners) typically have a recognized title to their property. If they want to invest to expand their business or start a new one, they can borrow against this collateral. People in poor countries rarely have this opportunity, and it is especially difficult for poor farmers and women to obtain loans. As a result, they often cannot get the funds they need to tide them over hard times or to take advantage of promising business opportunities.

Muhammad Yunus, a U.S.-educated professor of economics, had noticed these problems in his native country of Bangladesh. In 1974, he began extending small loans to poor people to help them out of these circumstances. His first loan amounted to $27 from his own pockets, which he lent to forty-two people, including a woman who made bamboo furniture, which she sold to support herself and her family. In 1976, Yunus founded Grameen Bank to make loans to poor Bangladeshis. The bank has since then given out more than $5 billion in loans. To secure its loans, the bank sets up a system of "solidarity groups," which meet on a weekly basis and support each other's efforts. As of May 2006, Grameen Bank had almost 7 million borrowers, 97 percent of whom were women. Their repayment rate is 98 percent. In 2006, Muhammad Yunus and the Grameen Bank received the Nobel Peace Prize for these efforts to help poor people improve their lives.

TABLE 7.3

Health Outcomes, 1990–2004

Country	Total Health Expenditure as % of GDP, 2002	Physicians per 1000 Citizens, 1990/2004	Life Expectancy at Birth 2003	Infant Mortality per 1,000 Live Births 2003	Fertility Rate, 2003
Brazil	7.9	1.3/2.1	69	33	2.1
Britain	7.7	1.4/1.7	78	5	1.6
China	5.8	1.5/1.6	71	30	1.9
France	9.7	2.6/3.3	79	4	1.9
Germany	10.9	3.1/3.6	78	4	1.3
India	6.1	0.5/0.5	63	63	2.9
Iran	6.0	0.3/1.0	69	33	2.0
Japan	7.9	1.7/2.0	82	3	1.3
Mexico	6.1	1.1/1.7	74	23	2.2
Nigeria	4.7	0.2/0.3	45	98	5.6
Russia	6.2	4.1/4.2	66	16	1.3
United States	14.6	2.4/5.5	77	7	2.0

Source: World Bank, *World Development Indicators 2005*, Tables 2.14, 2.16, 2.17, 2.19 (downloaded February 7, 2006), from http://devdata.worldbank.org/wdi2005/Table2_14.htm, Table2_16.htm, Table2_17.htm, Table2_19.htm.

lowest infant mortality rate among all the twelve countries in this survey. But its fertility rate of 1.3 means a declining population. (With no net migration, a fertility rate of approximately 2.1 results in a steady-state population.)

Table 7.4 tells us about access to education and information technologies, such as newspapers and personal computers. As we can see, many more people are reached by newspapers in rich and well-educated countries, such as Japan, than in the developing world. Yet even in poorer countries, communications have become much easier. Television has become widely available even in countries at middling development levels (e.g., Brazil and Mexico). Personal

Education and Information					TABLE 7.4
Country	Public Education Expenditure as Percent of Gov't Spending, 2002–03	Gross Percentage of Relevant Age Group Enrolled, Tertiary, 2002–03	Percentage 15 Years and Above Illiterate, Male/Female, 2002	Female Share of Labor Force, 1998	Newspapers per 1,000 Inhabitants, 2000	Personal Computers per 1,000 Inhabitants, 2003
Brazil	12	18	14/13	35	46	75
Britain	11	64	ND	44	326	406
China	ND	13	5/13	45	59	28
France	11	54	ND	45	143	347
Germany	10	49	ND	42	291	485
India	13	11	32/55	32	60	7
Iran	18	21	16/30	ND	28	91
Japan	11	49	ND	41	566	382
Mexico	24	21	7/11	33	94	82
Nigeria	ND	8	26/41	36	25	7
Russia	12	70	0/1	49	105	89
United States	17	81	ND	46	215	659

Source: World Bank, *World Development Indicators 2005*, Tables 2.10, 2.11, 2.13; 5.10, 5.11 (downloaded February 7, 2006), from http://devdata. worldbank.org/wdi2005/Table2_10.htm,Table2_11.htm,Table2_13.htm, Table5_10.htm, Table5_11.htm; also World Bank, *World Development Indicators 2000* (for data on female labor force participation).

computers, however, are much rarer outside the advanced industrial economies. Compared with people in Brazil, people in the United States are three times more likely to own a television, but ten times more likely to own a personal computer. In the developed countries, most adults and many children have a cell phone, but in India and Nigeria there are about twenty-five people to a phone. Even so, the advent of cellular phones has made it much easier to connect the rural population in developing countries where there are often very few land lines.

Table 7.4 also provides a picture of educational attainment. The first column, showing public education expenditure as a percentage of GDP, gives a rough measure of the "priority" given to education. Remember, however, that private schools, which in some countries are very common, are not counted here. There are differences in educational requirements: Nigeria requires only children from ages 6 to 12 to attend school. And the differences in dollar expenditures per student are very large. The outcomes are predictable enough. At the high end in educational outcomes, France, Germany, Japan, and Britain have virtually all of their primary and secondary school-age

children in schools, and about half of the college-age population is in some form of advanced education. In the United States, college education is even more common. Nigeria has only 8 percent of the appropriate age cohort in tertiary education, by far the poorest record of these countries. India's figure is 11 percent.

The payoffs of development and education are clearly reflected in literacy rates: 30 to 40 percent of all adult Indians and Nigerians are unable to read or write. Yet China has less than 10 percent illiteracy. But because they are often based on the number of school years completed, not on actual reading ability, literacy figures are a crude measure of skill and competence and must be treated with caution. The high official literacy figures in the United States, for example, conflict with studies showing substantial functional illiteracy among American adults.

Women in developing countries often lag behind in literacy. For example, fewer than half of all adult females in India are reported to be literate. The discrepancy between male and female literacy rates tells us something of the status of women. Where women make up a smaller proportion of the labor force, female illiteracy also tends to be higher. Faced with

BOX 7.5

Women and the Informal Economy

Parmila is an Indian widow in her thirties with two young children. Although she comes from a wealthy family, her husband's death forced her to take various part-time jobs. She collects wood from local forests, dries it, and then twice a week walks five miles to sell it at a local market. In the winter (November to January), she works on farms dehusking rice. She gets to keep some of the rice she produces. Outside of the rainy season, she also works as a laborer on a construction site, where her boss pays her about half of the Indian minimum wage. Parmila's total income is very low by Western standards, but it is enough to allow her to send her two children to school. Parmila does not ask for sympathy or for financial support from her relatives. "Even in times of acute crisis, I held my nerves and did not give in to circumstances," she says. "My God has always stood with me."

Women make up an increasing share of the world's workers. In most non-Islamic countries, they now make up 40 percent or more of the labor force. But in many parts of the world, most women work in the informal economy, where their work is often poorly paid. It commonly also escapes taxation and regulation. In India and in many African countries, for example, more than four out of five women who work outside of agriculture are in the informal economy. Many women choose such jobs voluntarily. They may do childcare for others or produce arts and crafts, often for local consumption. These jobs may be attractive because they can be performed at home while the women also take care of their own children or relatives. But many women also work in the informal sector because they face discrimination elsewhere. And some are enticed or forced into exhausting, dangerous, or degrading work in sweatshops or in the sex industry. While the informal economy can offer job flexibility, it can also be a place where there is little protection against abusive working conditions.

Source: William Easterly, *The Elusive Quest for Growth: The Economists' Adventures and Misadventures in the Tropics* (Cambridge: MIT Press, 2001), 45.

poverty, disease, and the absence of a social safety net, parents in poor countries traditionally want to have many children, to ensure that some survive and can support them in old age. But in large families mothers usually have few opportunities to educate themselves or hold jobs outside the home. Modernizing the status of women generally makes them better informed and more capable of making choices that lead to a more stable and healthy population. As women are educated and/or enter the labor force, they recognize the advantages of smaller families and become more aware of the importance of education and adequate health care.

Table 7.4 also reveals the sobering difficulties of trying to change societies, even in an area such as literacy, where modern technologies are available. It is hard for a poor country to spend a high percentage of its GDP on education, because it must then make sacrifices elsewhere. And the effects are limited if much of the country's productive effort has to go into feeding a rapidly growing population. No matter how large the educational effort may be, it does not translate into much per child, because the resource base is small and the population is growing rapidly. Moreover, since most older people are illiterate, the net effect on literacy is slow. And in many poorer countries, their best-educated young people often leave the country to take jobs in the big cities of the rich countries.

All of these data show how governmental and private efforts, in societies at different levels of economic development and of differing social structures and cultures, affect human life chances. Economic development affects economic prosperity; public health provisions, such as sanitation and the availability of potable water; and access to the outside world through telephone and television, roads, and other infrastructure. But although natural resources and socioeconomic structure constrain these outcomes, government and private efforts can make a big difference.

OUTCOMES: DOMESTIC SECURITY

As Thomas Hobbes would have reminded us, maintaining domestic law and order and protecting persons and property are among the most basic government responsibilities. Without them the conduct of personal, economic, and civic life are impossible. It is therefore worrisome that until recently crime rates have been on the increase in many advanced industrial countries, as well as in the developing world. Thus in the United States the crime rate increased by almost 15 percent between 1982 and 1991. In France the 1990 incidence of crimes against persons and property was almost twice that of 1975. In Russia the crime rate doubled between 1985 and 1993, as the moral and legal order collapsed. The country now has a murder rate almost five times as high as the United States. Brazil and Mexico also have considerably higher murder rates than the United States, while those of such European countries as England, France, and Germany are a small

fraction of the U.S. numbers. China has similarly low murder rates, whereas Japan is even lower.

High crime rates are primarily a problem of the larger urban areas where much of the population of modern countries resides. The causes of urban crime are complex. Rapidly increasing migration into the major cities, from the domestic countryside or from poorer foreign countries, increases diversity and often conflict. The pace of urbanization is particularly explosive in many developing countries, such as Brazil and Nigeria, where there are severe problems of poverty and infrastructure. The newly arrived city-dwellers often find themselves uprooted from their cultures, unwelcome, without a job, and living in squalor far apart from their families and traditional communities. Also, inequality of income and wealth, unemployment, and drug abuse, lie behind this general decline in public order and safety. In some former communist countries, the situation is compounded by the fact that traditional authorities and law enforcement have collapsed.

Yet, crime rates have recently come down significantly in the United States and some other countries. The number of murders per 100,000 inhabitants in the United States peaked at 9.4 in 1994, and declined to 5.7 in 2003 (see Figure 7.4). There are several reasons that crime rates have recently come down in the United States and elsewhere. One is a strong economy, in which more young people have been able to find jobs. A second reason is stricter law enforcement. This is reflected in part in the number of police officers relative to total population, which ranges from one police officer for every 350 persons in the United States, to 820 in India, and 1,140 in Nigeria. In the United States, both federal and state governments have also sought to reduce crime by increasing the length of

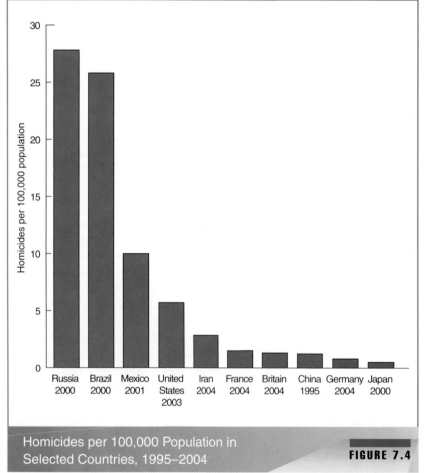

Homicides per 100,000 Population in Selected Countries, 1995–2004

FIGURE 7.4

Source: *United Nations Demographic Yearbook, 2002* (New York: United Nations, 2002) and "United Nations Surveys on Crime Trends and the Operations of Criminal Justice Systems" downloaded from http://www.unodc.org/unodc/en/crime_cicp_surveys.html.

imprisonment. By removing the criminally prone from the streets, these authorities have succeeded in cutting the crime rate, but at the cost of an exploding prison population. The United States now imprisons more people than any other country, including communist China. The total prison population in the United States in 2004 was around 2.2 million, including 1.3 million in state prisons, and 700,000 in local jails awaiting sentencing or serving short sentences. The total U.S. prison population has for the past ten years been increasing at a rate of about 50,000 per year. Similarly, the French prison population almost doubled between 1983 and 1990.[6] A third cause of lower crime rates has been a decrease in the number of youth at the age at which most crimes are committed. Yet, as the 15- to 25-year-old male population in the United States is now on the rise, violent crime may increase once again.

INTERNATIONAL OUTPUTS AND OUTCOMES

Most states engage in a great variety of international activities. Such economic, diplomatic, military, and informational activities may result in prosperity or depression, war or peace, secularization or the spread of particular beliefs.[7] The most costly outcome of the interaction among nations is warfare. Table 7.5 reports the numbers of deaths from international and internal collective violence for almost the entire twentieth century (1900–1995). The figures are mostly civilian and military deaths from interstate warfare, but they also include the slaughter of civilians in the efforts to implement communism in the Soviet Union, the holocaust of European Jews under the German Nazis (Hitler's National Socialist Party), many "ethnic cleansing" episodes in Europe and Africa, and civil wars in all parts of the world.

Over the long haul, the deadly costs of international warfare have gradually escalated. One authority estimates that more than 90 percent of the war deaths since 1700 occurred in the twentieth century. Civilian deaths caused by war have increased even more rapidly than military ones. In the last decades of the twentieth century, more than three-quarters of the war deaths were civilian.[8]

Table 7.5 shows that the people of USSR/Russia, by a margin of more than two-to-one, were the most numerous victims of the tormented history of the twentieth century. The enormous Russian casualties during World War I destroyed the czarist regime. Its

TABLE 7.5

Deaths from Collective Civilian-Military Violence, 1900–1995

Country	Civilian Deaths	Military Deaths	Unspecified Deaths	Total Deaths
Brazil	—	1,000	2,000	3,000
Britain	131,000	1,350,000	—	1,481,000
China	4,047,000	2,671,000	818,000	7,536,000
France	490,000	1,830,000	—	2,320,000
Germany	2,232,000	7,150,000	—	9,382,000
India	889,000	71,000	37,000	997,000
Iran	120,000	468,000	1,000	589,000
Japan	510,000	1,502,000	—	2,012,000
Mexico	125,000	125,000	10,000	260,000
Nigeria	1,005,000	1,000,000	6,000	2,011,000
Soviet Union/Russia	12,028,000	11,901,000	96,000	24,025,000
United States	—	524,000	—	524,000
TOTALS	21,577,000	28,593,000	970,000	51,140,000

Source: Adapted from Ruth Leger Sivard, "Wars and War Related Deaths, 1900–1995," *World Military and Social Expenditures 1996* (Washington, DC: World Priorities, 1996), 18–19. U.S. deaths add Korean and Vietnam war totals, from U.S. Department of State figures, to Sivard report of World War I and II deaths.

collapse was followed by the 1917 Bolshevik Revolution, the Civil War (1918–1921), and Stalin's Great Terror (particularly in the 1930s), each of which cost the lives of millions. Soviet suffering climaxed in World War II with a total of 17 million civilian and military dead. All told, the USSR/Russia suffered more than 24 million civilian and military deaths in the wars and political horrors of the twentieth century.

Germany suffered the second-largest number of deaths from twentieth-century collective violence. More than 3 million deaths, mostly military, occurred in World War I. In World War II, Germany suffered almost 5 million military and another 1.75 million civilian deaths. Other countries with huge losses include China (7 to 8 million) and Japan, whose more than 2 million deaths include half a million civilians, notably many residents of Hiroshima and Nagasaki. French and British sufferings were of roughly similar magnitude. Both countries took horrendous military casualties in the trench warfare of World War I. Since the Civil War, the United States has largely avoided the horrors of large-scale fighting on its own soil, but it still suffered over 120,000 deaths in World War I and close to half a million in World War II. While in the Korean and Vietnam wars, America suffered only moderate losses by these terrible standards, Korean and Vietnamese casualties were in the millions.

After World War II, the most devastating conflicts have occurred in the Third World. The partition of formerly British India into India, Pakistan, and Bangladesh has been associated with numerous deadly conflicts within and between the three countries. Some two million lives, mostly civilian, have been lost. In recent years, much of the world's media focus has been on conflicts in the Middle East, but conflicts in Africa have in fact been more frequent and devastating. Many African countries, newly independent from about 1960, but with borders arbitrarily drawn by colonial powers, have serious problems of national cohesion and have suffered from chronic civil war. Large-scale civil war in Nigeria (1967–1970) cost perhaps more than a million lives, and more sporadic conflict has continued to the present time. In 2002, for example, when the country hosted an international beauty contest, violent clashes erupted between Muslims and Christians that resulted in hundreds of deaths.

The end of the Cold War around 1990 witnessed a wave of instability and conflict in Eastern Europe and Central Asia. The breakup of the Soviet Union and Yugoslavia resulted in bloody border wars and secessional conflicts (for examples, in Bosnia and Kosovo in the former Yugoslavia, and Chechnya in Russia). These conflicts brought another wave of ethnic slaughter, religious clashes, and struggles for power among different warlords. But since 1992, the number of wars and casualties has gradually and steadily declined. And although recent years have seen horrific acts of terrorism, its annual human toll has not changed much. Some students of international conflict see hope in what they call the "democratic peace," the fact that democratic countries hardly ever fight wars against one another. As more countries become democratic, will the world also become more peaceful?

The Uppsala Conflict Data Project reports of 118 armed worldwide conflicts (defined as involving at least twenty-five battle deaths) from 1989 through 2004. In 2004, there were thirty ongoing conflicts, of which seven involved more than 1,000 deaths.[9] Each was a civil war occurring within state boundaries, although a few were internationalized in that foreign powers were also involved. In every year since the end of World War II in 1945, there have been more civil wars than interstate conflicts (wars between countries), and the civil wars have also caused more casualties than interstate wars. There are many reasons for the high incidence of civil war. Some are related to ethnic or religious conflicts. But others seem mainly due to struggles between warlords over lootable resources, such as diamonds, gold, or oil. External actors—such as the United Nations (UN), the United States, NATO, or strong regional powers—can sometimes help end civil wars, but in some cases (such as Angola) civil wars have been prolonged because foreign powers have been engaged on both sides of the conflict.

The UN in the post–Cold War world has intervened in some of these conflicts by providing peacekeeping missions when the parties to conflicts are ready to accept these mediations. More rarely the UN intervenes as a peacemaker, as in Bosnia and later in neighboring Kosovo in the 1990s, or when the peacekeeping mission in Sierra Leone (West Africa) was converted into a peacemaking effort. The UN's effectiveness in controlling domestic and international collective violence depends on consensus among the great powers. How tenuous this consensus can become is illustrated in the troubled efforts of the UN to disarm Iraq after the Gulf War of 1990–1991 and later to

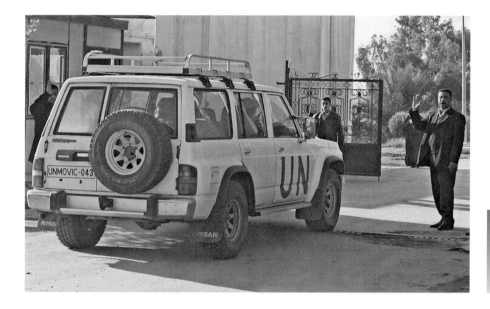

United Nations weapons inspectors arrive at the Al-Rasheed missile propellant compound in Iraq in January 2003.

AP Images

prevent Saddam Hussein's government there from producing weapons of mass destruction, leading to the U.S.-led invasion of 2003.

The economic costs of national security can be high. Many countries face a massive national debt that often includes large deferred costs of borrowing for earlier wars and the maintenance of national defense. Many states, particularly in conflict-prone regions, feel that they need to spend significantly on national defense because of the "security dilemma"—they have to "take out insurance" against the possibility that their neighbors might be aggressive. While military expenditures in the world have declined since the collapse of the Soviet Union, the horrors of September 11, 2001, have led to a new costly mobilization of resources against international terrorism.

POLITICAL GOODS AND VALUES

If we are to compare and evaluate public policy in different political systems, we need to consider the political goods that motivate different policies. That leads us back to the issues we discussed in Chapters 1 and 2, to the functions and purposes that governments serve. This book is organized around the concepts of system, process, and policy. We can think about values as "political goods" related to each of those levels of analysis.

At the system level, there is a long tradition in political analysis that emphasizes order, predictability,

and stability. Citizens are most free and most able to act purposefully when their environment is stable, transparent, and predictable. We call these conditions **system goods,** since they reflect the functioning and effectiveness of the whole political system. While people generally want some measure of change and new opportunities, most prefer stability to abrupt and unforeseeable change. Political instability—constitutional breakdowns, frequent leadership changes, riots, demonstrations, and the like—upsets most people's plans and can cost lives and cause material destruction. System goods have to do with the regularity and predictability with which political systems work, but also with their ability to adapt to environmental challenges.

Regularity and adaptability are typically somewhat in conflict. Sometimes order and stability are at the top of the agenda. In the United States, the administration of Warren Harding after World War I was such a period, called "a return to normalcy." There was a similar withdrawal from mobilization after World War II and the Korean War. On the other hand, the 1930s and the 1960s were periods of change and adaptation, in which the reach of governmental powers was extended. But the stress on change and adaptation can also be a call for reductions in the scope in government, as in the Thatcher administration in Britain or the Republican "Contract With America" of 1994–1995.

Another school of thought emphasizes goods associated with the political process—citizen participation and free political competition. Democracy is good and authoritarianism is bad, according to this school of thought, because of the way citizens are treated in the process, and not because democracy, for example, produces better economic results. Democratic procedures and various rights of due process, then, are **process goods.** Process goods include participation, compliance, and procedural justice. We value participation not merely as a means to responsive government, but for its own sake, since it enhances citizen competence and dignity. Compliance with authority can also be a good, as individuals respond to the impulse to serve others, which can be one of humanity's most gratifying experiences. U.S. President John F. Kennedy in his inaugural address called on such impulses to serve and sacrifice when he said, "Ask not what your country can do for you; ask what you can do for your country." Procedural justice (trial by jury, habeas corpus, no cruel and unusual punishment) is another crucial process value, without which citizens would have much greater reasons to fear their governments.

Procedural goods also include *effectiveness* and *efficiency*. A preference for effectiveness means that we prefer policies that actually lead to their desired purpose over policies that do not. Efficiency means that policies should attain their objectives at the lowest possible cost. If two alternative policies would lead to the same result but at very different costs, we would prefer the policy with the lower cost. In designing government agencies, most of us would prefer lean and inexpensive institutions to bloated agencies that produce no better results.

A third and final focus is on **policy goods,** such as economic welfare, quality of life, freedom, and personal security. We value a political system that improves welfare, decreases inequalities, enhances public safety, enables people to live lives they want for themselves, and cleans up its environment, whatever the political process that produces these results. Well-meaning people do not always agree which of these policy goods are most important. Yet, there are at least two important criteria that most of us would agree that government policy should meet. The first is *fairness.* The problem is that people often disagree over what is fair. In some situations, we believe that fairness requires all people to be treated equally (as when family members attempt to divide a tempting pie). In other situations, fairness demands that individuals be treated according to performance (as when grades are

given in a college course). And in yet other situations, fairness means that people are treated according to their needs (for example, in cases of medical treatment). Thus fairness can imply *equal treatment* in some cases, *just desserts* (reward in proportion to merit or contribution) in others, and *treatment according to need* in yet others. Many distributive policies—for example, pension systems such as social security in the United States—rely on some combination of these criteria.

The debate over these various conceptions of fairness is never settled. In most cases, however, fairness would rule out practices that are *arbitrary* or *partial.* Few of us would find it fair if government officials threw dice to determine who would be imprisoned or be given pensions, or if they made such decisions solely on the basis of their personal prejudices or connections. We can think of fairness in this sense as reflected in the process good of *procedural justice.*

The second consideration is the promotion and preservation of *freedom.* As anarchists, libertarians, and other government skeptics would remind us, public policies should promote and protect freedom and basic human and political rights. If two policies are equally efficient and fair, then we would prefer the one that respects the rights and liberties of the citizens to the greater extent. But even in a democratic society, freedom is not always chosen over other political goods. The right to bear arms, protected in the Second Amendment to the U.S. Constitution, is a hotly contested issue, as many Americans would like to prevent those most likely to cause harm from carrying lethal weapons. Similarly, freedom of speech is a constitutional guarantee, but many people want to prohibit speech that is insulting, blasphemous, or offensive.

Liberty is sometimes viewed only as freedom from governmental regulation and harassment. Freedom is more than inhibition of government action, however, because even private individuals and organizations may violate the liberty and privacy of others. In such cases, liberty may be fostered by government intervention. Much legislation against racial segregation and discrimination generally has been impelled by this purpose. Liberty to act, organize, obtain information, and protest is an indispensable part of effective political participation. Nor is it irrelevant to social, political, and economic equality. Prior to the breakdown of

Levels of Political Goods	Classes of Goods	Content and Examples
System level	System maintenance	The political system features regular, stable, and predictable decision-making processes.
	System adaptation	The political system is able to adapt to environmental change and challenges.
Process level	Participation in political inputs	The political system is open and responsive to many forms of political speech and action.
	Compliance and support	Citizens fulfill their obligations (e.g., military service and tax obligations) to the system and comply with public law and policy.
	Procedural justice	Legal and political procedures are orderly and fair (due process) and there is equality before the law.
	Effectiveness and efficiency	Political processes have their intended effects and are no more cumbersome, expensive, or intrusive than necessary.
Policy level	Welfare	Citizens have access to health care, learning, and material goods, which the government seeks to distribute broadly.
	Security	The government provides safety of person and property, public order, and national security.
	Fairness	Government policy is not discriminatory and recognizes individuals from different ethnic, linguistic, or religious groups; vulnerable or disadvantaged citizens are protected.
	Liberty	Citizens enjoy freedom from excessive regulation, protection of their privacy, and respect for their autonomy.

TABLE 7.6 Political Goods

communism in Eastern Europe and the Soviet Union, it was a common view that the communist countries were trading liberty for equality. In contrast, capitalism was said to trade off equality for liberty. But one important thing that came to light after the collapse of communism was the extent of corruption and privilege in communist societies. While they had surely traded off liberty for a basic security of employment, it was not clear that the communists had otherwise gained much in the way of equality.

Table 7.6 draws on our three-level analysis of political systems to present a checklist of political goods or values. There is no simple way to say which value should prevail when they conflict. In fact, different preferences among such values as freedom, fairness, and efficiency set different cultures, parties, and political philosophies apart. One society or group of citizens may value fairness over liberty; another may make the opposite choice, as in Patrick Henry's famous exclamation, "Give me liberty or give me death!"

TRADE-OFFS AND OPPORTUNITY COSTS

One of the hard facts about political goods is that we cannot always have them all simultaneously. A political system often has to **trade off** one value to obtain another. Spending funds on education is giving up the opportunity to spend them on welfare, or to leave them in the hands of those who earned them. **Opportunity costs** are what you lose in one area by committing your resources to a different good. They often arise when politicians have to decide how much to invest for the future rather than spend today (for example, when they determine future retirement benefits). Even more difficult are the trade-offs between security and liberty. Extreme liberty, as Hobbes would tell us, would give us a highly insecure world where the strong might bully the weak and where collective action would be difficult. Yet, without liberty, security may be little more than servitude or imprisonment. The trade-offs between political goods are not the same under all circumstances. Sometimes increasing liberty will also increase security (for example, because riots against censorship will end). And under some conditions investment in education will be paid back many times in health and welfare, because trained citizens can better care for themselves and work more productively. These are positive trade-offs in which there may be no opportunity costs. But often you cannot "have your cake and eat it, too." One of the important tasks of social science is to discover the conditions under which positive and negative trade-offs occur.

Regrettably, political science has no way of converting units of liberty into units of safety or welfare. And we can never calculate the value of a political outcome gained at the cost of human life. Political decision makers often have to make such conversions, but as political scientists we can only point to value judgments that they are willing to make. The weight given to various goods differs across cultures and contexts. A religious faith or a political ideology may tell us how one value should be traded against another, and thus offer an orderly basis for choice. Such schemes may be invaluable for those pressed into action in the terrible circumstances of war, revolution, and famine. But when people do not share these underlying schemes and values, there may be serious conflicts. Sadly, there is no ideology, just as there is no political science, that can solve all these problems objectively.

REVIEW QUESTIONS

- What explains the growth of the welfare state?
- What are the advantages and disadvantages of different types of taxes?
- Do some governments tend to promote political rights and others civil rights, or do civil and political rights tend to go together?
- How is the welfare outcome for women changing in developing countries today?
- What sorts of armed conflicts are most common in today's world, and what problems do they cause?

KEY TERMS

direct taxes
distribution
extraction
gross domestic product (GDP)
indirect taxes
night watchman state
opportunity costs
Organization for Economic Cooperation and Development (OECD)
outcomes
police state
policy goods
political goods and values
process goods
public policies
regulation
regulatory state
symbolic outputs
system goods
trade off
welfare state

SUGGESTED READINGS

Bates, Robert H. *Markets and States in Tropical Africa*. Berkeley: University of California Press, 1981.

Bratton, Michael, and Nicholas van de Walle. *Democratic Experiments in Africa: Regime Transitions in Comparative Perspective*. New York: Cambridge University Press, 1997.

Castles, Francis G., ed. *The Comparative History of Public Policy*. Cambridge, UK: Polity Press, 1989.

Dahl, Robert. *Democracy and Its Critics*. New Haven, CT: Yale University Press, 1989.

Diamond, Larry, ed. *Democracy in Developing Countries*. Boulder, CO: Lynne Rienner, 1992.

Easterly, William. *The Elusive Quest for Growth: The Economists' Adventures and Misadventures in the Tropics*. Cambridge: MIT Press, 2001.

Flora, Peter, and Arnold Heidenheimer. *The Development of Welfare States in Europe and America*. New Brunswick, NJ: Transaction Books, 1981.

Gourevitch, Peter. *Politics in Hard Times*. Ithaca, NY: Cornell University Press, 1986.

Harbom, Lotta, and Peter Wallensteen. "Armed Conflict and Its International Dimensions, 1946–2004." *Journal of Peace Research* 42, no. 5 (2005): 623–35.

Jackson, Robert, and Carl Rosberg. *Personal Rule in Black Africa*. Berkeley: University of California Press, 1982.

Keefer, Philip, and Stuti Khemani. "Why Do the Poor Receive Poor Services?" *Economic and Political Weekly*, 28 February 2004, 935–43.

Lijphart, Arend. *Patterns of Democracy*. New Haven, CT: Yale University Press, 1999.

Lindblom, Charles E. *Politics and Markets*. New Haven, CT: Yale University Press, 1978.

Olson, Mancur. *The Rise and Decline of Nations*. New Haven, CT: Yale University Press, 1982.

———. *Power and Prosperity*. New York: Basic Books, 2000.

Putnam, Robert D. *Making Democracy Work*. Princeton, NJ: Princeton University Press, 1993.

Tsebelis, George. *Veto Players: An Introduction to Institutional Analysis*. Princeton, NJ: Princeton University Press, 2002.

Wilensky, Harold. *Rich Democracies: Political Economy, Public Policy, and Performance*. Berkeley: University of California Press, 2002.

Wilson, James G. *The Politics of Regulation in the United States*. New York: Basic Books, 1980.

ENDNOTES

1. See World Bank, *Entering the 21st Century: World Development Report 1999–2000* (New York: Oxford University Press, 2000), Table A.1, 216–17.

2. Peter Flora and Arnold Heidenheimer, *The Development of Welfare States in Europe and America* (New Brunswick, NJ: Transaction Books, 1981); Arnold Heidenheimer, Hugh Heclo, and Carolyn Teich Adams, *Comparative Public Policy*, 3rd ed. (New York: St. Martin's Press, 1990).

3. Heidenheimer, Heclo, and Adams. *Comparative Public Policy*, 211–19.

4. Steven C. Poe and C. Neal Tate, "Repression of Human Rights to Personal Integrity in the 1980s: A Global Analysis," *American Political Science Review* 88, no. 4 (December 1994): 853–72.

5. Simon Kuznets, "Economic Growth and Income Equality," *American Economic Review* 45 (1955):1–28.

6. World Bank, *World Development Report: Infrastructure for Development* (New York: Oxford University Press, 1994), Overview, 1 ff.

7. Peter Gourevitch, in his book *Politics in Hard Times* (Ithaca, NY: Cornell University Press, 1986), analyzes the policy responses of five Western industrial nations—Britain, France, Germany, Sweden, and the United States—to the three world depressions of 1870–1890, 1930–1940, and 1975–1985. Gourevitch shows how these crises affected business, labor, and agriculture differently in each country; consequences for political structure and policy varied greatly. Thus the world depression of the 1930s resulted in a conservative reaction in Britain (the formation of a "National" government), a moderate left reaction in the United States (the "New Deal"), a polarization and paralysis of public policy in France ("Immobilisme"), a moderate social democratic reaction in Sweden, and a radical right and left polarization in Germany, leading to a breakdown of democracy and the emergence of National Socialism. While the causes of World War II were complex, the pacifism of Britain, the demoralization and defeatism in France, the isolationism of the United States, and the nihilism and aggression of Germany were all fed by the devastating worldwide economic depression of the 1930s.

8. Ruth Leger Sivard, *World Military and Social Indicators* (Washington, DC: World Priorities, 1993), 20.

9. See Lotta Harbom and Peter Wallensteen, "Armed Conflict and Its International Dimension, 1946-2004," *Journal of Peace Research*, 42, no. 5 (2005), 623–35.

POLITICS IN BRITAIN

Richard Rose

Country Bio

UNITED KINGDOM

Population
59.6 million

Territory
94,525 square miles

Year of Independence
from twelfth century

Year of Current Constitution
unwritten; partly statutes, partly common law and practice

Head of State
Queen Elizabeth II

Head of Government
Prime Minister Gordon Brown

Language(s)
English, Welsh (about 600,000), and Scottish form of Gaelic (about 60,000)

Religion
Anglican 26.1 million, Roman Catholic 5.7 million, Presbyterian 2.6 million, Methodist 1.3 million, Other Christian 2.6 million, Muslim 1.5 million, Hindu 500,000, Sikh 330,000, Jewish 260,000, Other 300,000, no religion 8.6 million; did not state a religion 4.4 million.

In a world of new democracies, Britain is different because it is an old democracy that has evolved over many centuries. In medieval times, the English monarch claimed to rule France and Ireland as well as England. From the end of the fifteenth century onwards, the territory of the king of England changed. The claim to rule France was abandoned and sovereignty was gained over Wales and Scotland. Unlike new democracies in Eastern Europe, Latin America, and Asia, Britain did not become a democracy overnight after a dictatorship fell. It became a democracy by evolution rather than revolution. Democratization was a slow process. The rule of law was established in the seventeenth century; the accountability of the executive to Parliament was established by the eighteenth century; and national political parties organized in the nineteenth century. Even though competitive elections had been held for more than a century, the right of every adult man and woman to vote was not recognized until the twentieth century.

This evolution of democracy contrasts to the dominant European practice of countries switching between democratic and undemocratic regimes. Whereas older British people have lived under the same constitution all their lives, the oldest Germans have lived under four or five constitutions, two democratic and two or three undemocratic.[1]

The gradual evolution of political institutions means that at no point in history did representatives of the British peoples meet together to decide what kind of government they would like to have, as happened in America and France at the end of the eighteenth century, and in many democracies since. British politicians have been socialized to accept institutions and rules of the game that are a legacy from distant predecessors. Ordinary citizens have been socialized to accept established institutions, too.

The influence of British government can be found in places as far-flung as Australia, Canada, India, and the United States. Just as Alexis de Tocqueville travelled to America in 1831 to seek the secrets of democracy, so might we journey to Britain to seek secrets of stable representative government. Yet its limitations as a model are shown by the failure of attempts to transplant its institutions to countries gaining independence from the British Empire, and even more by the failure of its constitutional conventions institutions to bring political stability to Northern Ireland.

POLICY CHALLENGES FACING BRITAIN

When Tony Blair became prime minister in 1997, he declared a desire to create a New Britain, a "cool Britannia." Yet rebranding a country is not as easy as rebranding pop groups or designer fashions. Blair has recognized: "In opposition announcement is the reality. For the first period of time in government, there was a tendency to believe the same situation applied. It doesn't. The announcement is only the intention."[2] When Gordon Brown replaced Blair as prime minister in 2007, the Labour government faced many challenges.

The readiness of the government to open up Britain to international trade has forced the British economy to become more competitive. For centuries, Britain has depended on world trade, importing much food and many raw materials. To pay for imports, it has exported manufactured goods and "invisible" services provided by financial institutions in London. The British pound sterling (£) is an international currency but speeches by the prime minister and chancellor of the exchequer do not determine the foreign exchange value of the pound. This is decided in international markets in which currency speculators play a significant role. Since 1997, the value of the British pound in exchange for the dollar has ranged from above $2.50 to less than $1.25.

Maintaining economic growth is important not only for British consumers, who borrow heavily, but also to finance increased government spending. An aging population requires more health care, an educated population demands better education for their children, and a more prosperous society wants a better environment as well as better housing. However, the means of raising additional revenue without raising visible taxes are few. Moreover, any increase in deficit spending threatens inflation and a rise in interest rates by the independent Bank of England. The fiscal dividend of economic growth makes it much easier to meet these challenges.

There are some problems, such as fighting crime, that cannot be resolved solely by spending money. Successive Conservative and Labour governments have spent more money on the police and built more prisons, measures that have led to an increase in the prison population. There has also been an increase in crimes of violence, and the use of guns in robberies and in shootings of policemen and women.

Multiculturalism is another problem that cannot be met just by spending more money. The Blair government sought to promote a sense of Britishness among immigrants, giving lessons about the rights and obligations of British people to immigrants wanting citizenship. British-born offspring of immigrants automatically gain citizenship. Whether they choose to adopt British ways is much influenced by family and ethnic background and, in the case of a few Moslems, by jihadist activists.

Within government there is a need to restore the traditional British practices of deliberating carefully about the pros and cons of an issue before making decisions. In the words of the former head of the civil service, the Blair government put "too much emphasis on selling" and too little on careful deliberation. In the words of this senior civil servant, "Just because ministers say to do something does not mean that we ignore reality, which is what seems to have happened on issues I've been involved in, until things were supposed to happen and then reality could not be ignored any longer."[3]

Blair initially enjoyed a high level of political trust, but this eroded after the start of the war in Iraq. Official inquiries into the "spin" that Blair gave for going to war in Iraq showed that he had exaggerated or misread intelligence briefings. In addition, revelations about shadowy and potentially corrupt tactics that Blair has approved to obtain donations of millions of dollars to finance his political campaigns have led to widespread popular cynicism. Since early 2002, less than half the British public has expressed satisfaction with him as prime minister, and in a September 2006 MORI (Market & Opinion Research International) poll only 23 percent did so.

Blair's decision to retire in the middle of a Parliament left the selection of his successor Gordon Brown, in the hands of the **Labour Party** rather than the British electorate. Whether Brown remains in office however, will depend on the outcome of the next general election. The Labour government is vulnerable to losing its parliamentary majority then, since Blair's victory in 2005 was achieved with only 35.2 percent of the popular vote. This was a lower share than that of any majority government in the twentieth century.

After losing three successive elections under three different leaders, the chief Opposition Party, the Conservatives Party, has accepted the challenge to change by electing a youthful new leader, David Cameron. His strategy has much in common with that of Tony Blair in Opposition: to move the party from its Thatcherite base to the political center. This means abandoning rightwing policies and seeking support from advocates of the environment, gay rights, and other liberal issues. Cameron has been a member of Parliament (MP) only since 2001, hence he cannot be identified with unpopular policies that led to his party's defeats. However, since neither he nor his principal associates has ever held office in government, their inexperience raises questions about what a Cameron-led government would actually do if it were to win an election.

The **Liberal Democratic Party,** led by Menzies Campbell, is now the closest approximation to a "left" party that Britain has today. It is prepared to consider raising taxes slightly to have more money to spend on health, education, and environmental programs. It also attacks government proposals that encroach on civil liberties. In addition, it was the only major party to oppose the Iraq war. Because it comes third in votes, the Liberal Democrats have no chance of forming a government on their own. But because the **Conservative Party** faces an uphill struggle to win an absolute majority of seats in the House of Commons, it could become a partner in a coalition government. However, a general election is not expected until 2009 or May 2010 at the latest.

In a changing world, the big question is: where does Britain belong? When a public opinion poll asked whether Britain should act like a leading world power or a small neutral country (like Sweden or Switzerland), 49 percent favored being a small power while 34 percent wanted the country to be a world power.[4] However, prime ministers from Churchill to Blair have claimed that Britain is a major power because of its close ties with Commonwealth countries, the United States, and Europe. The British Empire was transformed into the Commonwealth, a free association of fifty-four sovereign states with members on every continent, after World War II. The independent status of its chief members is shown by the absence of the word "British" from the name of the Commonwealth. Commonwealth countries from Antigua and Australia to Zambia and Zimbabwe differ from each other in wealth, language, culture, and religion. They also differ in their commitment to democracy.

Since Churchill's time, every British prime minister has claimed a special relationship with the United States. In the words of one diplomat, "America provides the brawn and we provide the brains." After the end of the Cold War, the emergence of the United States as a unique global force has made the relationship more attractive to Britain. However, the number of countries with which the U.S. president claims a special relationship keeps expanding and the unilateralist policy of the Bush administration has reduced the influence that another country may have on U.S. foreign policy.

When President George W. Bush sought a coalition of the willing for the war in Iraq, Blair was more than willing, believing that the war was desirable to make the world, including Britain, a safer place. In response to doubts raised in the House of Commons, Blair argued that allying with President Bush in the war in Iraq would give Britain greater influence by strengthening ties with Washington. However, both British MPs and public opinion have increasing doubts. In a June 2006 Populus poll, only three in five thought it important for Britain to maintain a special relationship with the United States, and two-thirds said Britain's future lies more with Europe than with the United States.

As Britain's world position has declined and European countries, such as Germany and France, have gained importance, the British government has looked to Europe. In a jet age, the English Channel is no longer a barrier to travel to the European continent and a tunnel under the Channel provides a shorter rail and road link to Paris than to the north of England or Scotland. Manufacturers such as the Ford Motor Company link their plants in Britain with factories across Western Europe, just as Ford links factories across American states.

The European Community—now the European Union (EU)—was established in 1957, but Britain did not join until 1973. Today, its single European market enables the EU to impose regulations affecting British businesses and limiting the British government's power to subsidize industries. British ministers spend an increasing amount of their time negotiating with other EU countries on matters ranging from political fundamentals to whether British beer should be served in metric units or by the traditional measure of a British pint.

Although an EU member, Britain's commitment to the European Union remains limited. British public opinion is divided among those who endorse strengthening the EU, those who want to leave it as it is, and those who want to reduce its powers or to leave the EU. Blair has described the consequence thus:

> The dilemma of a British prime minister over Europe is acute to the point of the ridiculous. Basically, you have a choice: co-operate in Europe and you betray Britain; be unreasonable in Europe, be praised back home and be utterly without influence in Europe. It's sort of isolation or treason.[5]

The British government cannot insulate the country from the rest of the world. It is not possible for Britain to become a small, rich country like Switzerland or Sweden. The effective choice today is between Britain being a big, rich country or a big relatively poor European country. In small countries, which have always recognized the influence of bigger neighbors, exchanging nominal sovereignty to participate in the EU presents no problems. However, it is a shock to British governors who pride themselves on having a major role in three different international settings.

THE ENVIRONMENT OF POLITICS

One Crown but Five Nations

The Queen of England is the best known monarch in the world, yet there is no such entity as an English state. In international law, the state is the United Kingdom. The **United Kingdom** of Great Britain and Ireland was created in 1801 as the climax of centuries of expansion begun in the twelfth century. Great Britain, the principal part of the United Kingdom, is

divided into England, Scotland, and Wales; the fourth part is Northern Ireland. **Wales** was joined with England in the sixteenth century and administered thereafter as part of England. Its most distinctive feature is that one-quarter of its populace speak an old Celtic language, Welsh, as well as English. **Scotland** was once an independent kingdom. Since the 1707 Act of Union, there has been a common Parliament and monarch for all of Great Britain. Even so, the Scots retained separate legal, religious, and educational institutions. The fourth part of the United Kingdom, **Northern Ireland,** consists of the six counties of Ulster. The remainder of Ireland rebelled against the **Crown** in 1916 and a separate Irish state with its capital in Dublin was recognized in 1921. The current boundaries of the United Kingdom of Great Britain and Northern Ireland, colloquially known as Britain, were fixed in 1921.

The United Kingdom is a union—that is, a political system having only one source of authority, the British Parliament. However, institutions governing the United Kingdom are not uniform. Distinct administrative institutions exist in Scotland and Wales, and devolution has increased their legitimacy by creating popularly elected assemblies. Northern Ireland has always been subject to exceptional legislation. There are differences too in the parties competing for seats in each nation of the United Kingdom. Northern Ireland is extreme, for British parties do not contest seats there, and one party, Sinn Fein, also contests seats in the Republic of Ireland.

In national identity, the United Kingdom is a multinational state, for its citizens differ in how they describe themselves (see Table 8.1). In England, people often are confused about the difference between being English or British and use the terms interchangeably. This does not happen elsewhere in the United Kingdom. In Scotland, three-quarters see themselves as Scots. In Wales, three-fifths identify themselves as Welsh. In Northern Ireland, people divide three ways: almost half see themselves as British and another fifth identify with Ulster (that is, Northern Ireland). Catholics are divided with just over half seeing themselves as Irish and most of the rest as Ulster, an identity different from being Irish or British.

Historically, Scotland and Wales have been governed by British Cabinet ministers accountable to the Westminster Parliament. After decades of campaigning by nationalist parties seeking independence, in 1997 a

National Identities				**TABLE 8.1**
	England	**Scotland**	**Wales**	**Northern Ireland**
		(% identifying)		
British	51	19	27	47
English, Scots, Welsh, Irish	38	75	60	27
Other, don't know	11	6	13	26*

*Includes 21 percent identifying as Ulster

Source: England: British Social Attitudes Survey, 2004; Scotland: Scottish Social Attitudes Survey, 2004; Wales: Life and Times Survey, 2003; Northern Ireland: Life and Times Survey, 2004.

British Labour government introduced measures to devolve some of its responsibilities to elected assemblies in Scotland and in Wales. In referendums on devolution in September 1997, the policy was endorsed by 74 percent in Scotland. Welsh voters narrowly endorsed devolution by 50.3 percent against 49.7 percent.

In May 1999, the Scottish Parliament, with powers to legislate, tax, and spend, was established in Edinburgh. Election to the 129-seat Parliament is by a system mixing the traditional British "first-past-the-post" and proportional representation (PR) ballots. In the first two elections the Labour Party won the most seats, but not an absolute majority, and it governed in a coalition with the Liberal Democractic Party. At the May 2007 Scottish Parliament election, the unpopularity of the Labour government in London resulted in the pro-independence Scottish National Party (SNP) winning the most seats (47) and the largest share of the vote. Its leader, Alex Salmond, became the first minister in a minority government. The opposition is divided between the Labour Party (46 seats), Conservatives (17 seats), Liberal Democrats (16 seats), and the Green Party and others (3 seats). The SNP wants a national referendum about whether Scotland should become independent, but it lacks the votes in the Scottish Parliament to legislate for a referendum, and opinion polls suggest that the majority of Scots prefer devolution to independence.

Labour has been the biggest party in the Welsh Assembly (60 seats). In the first Assembly election in 1999, an electoral system mixing first-past-the-post and PR ballots resulted in no party having a majority, and Labour formed a coalition with the Liberals. In the May 2003 election, Labour's share of the vote went up to 37 percent and it took half the Assembly seats. At the May 2007 Assembly election, Labour won 26 seats, the Welsh Nationalist Party—Plaid Cymru—(15 seats),

the Conservatives (12 seats), Liberal Democrats (6 seats), and others (1 seat). Labour and the Welsh National Party formed a coalition. There is no demand in the Assembly for a referendum on independence and powers over Welsh legislation and total public expenditure remain in the hands of a British Cabinet minister. However, the optional or compulsory use of the Welsh language in schools and public places can be affected by the Assembly, and it is a contentious issue.

Northern Ireland is the most un-English part of the United Kingdom. Formally, it is a secular polity, but differences between Protestants and Catholics about national identity dominate its politics. Protestants, comprising about three-fifths of the population, want to remain part of the United Kingdom. Until 1972 the Protestant majority governed through the home-rule Parliament at Stormont, a suburb of Belfast. Many of the Catholic minority did not support this regime, wanting to leave the United Kingdom and join the Republic of Ireland, which claimed the territory of Northern Ireland.

Since 1968, when Catholics launched nonviolent protests against discrimination, Northern Ireland has been in turmoil. Demonstrations turned to street violence in August 1969, and the British Army intervened. The illegal **Irish Republican Army (IRA)** was revived and in 1971 began a military campaign to remove Northern Ireland from the United Kingdom. In response, Protestants organized illegal armed forces too. More than 3,200 people have been killed in political violence. After adjusting for population differences, the deaths from political violence are equivalent to more than 120,000 political deaths in Britain or more than 550,000 deaths in America.

British policy in Northern Ireland has been erratic. In 1969 the British Army went into action to protect Catholics. In 1971 it helped intern hundreds of

Parliament has met in London by the River Thames for more than 700 years, and the clock tower of Big Ben is famous as a symbol of democracy in Canada and Australia as well as in Europe.

Steve Vidher/Leo de Wys, Inc.

Catholics without trial in an unsuccessful attempt to break the IRA. In 1972 the British government abolished the Stormont Parliament, placing government in the hands of a Northern Ireland Office under a British Cabinet minister. In 1985 the British government took the unprecedented step of inviting the Dublin-based government of the Republic of Ireland to participate in institutions affecting the governance of part of the United Kingdom.

A stable settlement in Northern Ireland requires the support of paramilitary organizations on each side of the religious divide as well as of political parties. In 1994 the IRA announced a cessation of its military activity, and Sinn Fein, the party political wing of the Irish Republican movement, agreed to talks. Protestant paramilitary forces also announced a cessation of activities. On Good Friday 1998, an agreement was reached for an elected power-sharing executive and cross-border institutions involving both Dublin and Belfast.

The basic principle of the Good Friday agreement, power-sharing, is the opposite of British government practice, which gives leaders of a party commanding a majority in the Commons the right to form a government on its own. However, in Northern Ireland, whatever the outcome of an election, by law, government must be a coalition of representatives of both the pro-British Protestant majority and the pro-Irish Republic Catholic minority. This arrangement was endorsed in a referendum by a majority of Northern Ireland Catholics and of Protestants.

The election of the Northern Ireland Assembly in June 1998 led to a power-sharing executive consisting of the Ulster Unionist Party; the nonviolent Social Democratic and Labour Party (SDLP); and Sinn Fein, a party linked politically with the IRA. The Democratic Unionist Party, led by Dr. Ian Paisley, refused to join the administration. After the IRA failed to produce sufficient tangible evidence to convince representatives of the skeptical Protestant majority that it was giving up its weapons, in 2002 the power-sharing executive collapsed. Northern Ireland once again came under direct rule.

An Assembly election in March 2007 gave the most seats to the Democratic Unionist Party, and Sinn Fein came second. Confronted with a British government ultimatum that failure to agree would lead to greater influence being given to Dublin, Dr. Ian Paisley agreed to become the first minister in a power-sharing executive in which representatives of Sinn Fein, including convicted IRA bombers, also served.

While there is no agreement about national identity within Britain, there is no doubt about which nationality is the most numerous. England dominates the United Kingdom. Its population constitutes five-sixths of the total and the remainder is divided among three different nations. Hence, previous editions of this chapter have been called politics in England on the grounds, to quote former Prime Minister Tony Blair, "Sovereignty rests with me, as an English MP, and that's the way it will stay."[6] However, changes in the institutions of the United Kingdom have also begun to affect politics in England. For example, in the 2005 British general election, the Conservative Party won the most votes in England but the Labour Party, thanks to its dominance in Scotland and Wales, won the most votes in the United Kingdom and a majority in the British Parliament.

A Multiracial Britain

Throughout the centuries England has received a relatively small but noteworthy number of immigrants from other parts of Europe. The Queen herself is descended from a titled family that came from Hanover, Germany, to assume the English throne in 1714. Until the outbreak of anti-German sentiment in World War I, the surname of the royal family was Saxe-Coburg-Gotha. By royal proclamation, George V changed the family name to Windsor in 1917.

The worldwide British Empire was multiracial but not democratic; it is now a multiracial Commonwealth. Since the late 1950s job seekers have been arriving from the West Indies, Pakistan, India, Africa, and other parts of the Commonwealth and settling in Britain. In addition, many people from the United States, Australia, New Zealand, Canada, and the European Union flow into and out of Britain as students or as workers. A strong British economy is attracting many temporary workers from Central and East European countries.

The new Commonwealth immigrants have only one characteristic in common: they are not white. Beyond that, immigrants share neither culture nor religion. West Indians speak English as their native language and have a Christian tradition; immigrants from India and Pakistan are Hindus, Muslims, or Sikhs and most speak English as a second language. The smaller number of African immigrants are divided by nationality and sometimes by tribe as well. Chinese from Hong Kong have a distinctive culture. Altogether, more than half of new Commonwealth immigrants have come from the Indian subcontinent, a quarter are black people from the Caribbean or Africa, and about a tenth are Asian.

The 2001 census estimated that the nonwhite population of the United Kingdom had risen from 74,000 in 1951 to 4.6 million, almost 8 percent of the total. Public opinion has opposed unlimited immigration, and both Labour and Conservative governments have passed laws trying to limit the number of immigrants. However, these laws contain many exceptions, for example, people can claim political asylum. By 2006 the Home Office minister responsible for immigration control admitted that its administration was a shambles and there were hundreds of thousands of illegal immigrants in Britain.

With the passage of time, the nonwhite population is becoming increasingly British-born and educated, which raises the important question: what is the position of British-born offspring of immigrants? Whatever their country of origin, they differ in how they see themselves: 64 percent of Caribbean origin identify as British; as do more than three-fifths of Pakistanis, Indians, and Bangladeshis; and two-fifths of Chinese.

Since the 9/11 terrorist attacks in the United States in 2001, the Labour government has shifted from promoting multiculturalism to stressing the integration of immigrant families into the British way of life. On July 7, 2005, a coordinated terrorist attack in London killed more than fifty passengers on buses and underground trains. The organizers were British-born offspring of Pakistani immigrants and had been converted to jihadism at British mosques. In August 2006, police arrested two dozen British Moslems on charges of attempting to blow up trans-Atlantic flights. This group too was led by British-born Moslems who had converted to jihadism.

The government's response to terrorist attacks has been to increase greatly police powers, justifying shoot-to-kill policies even when people wrongly suspected of being terrorists are the victims. Its program of cooperating with people it identifies as leaders of the Moslem community has also been challenged. Those cooperating with British government have not been effective in preventing some of their co-religionists from supporting transnational terrorist networks. Moreover, they have criticized police methods used in surveillance of the Moslem community and British military actions in Afghanistan and Iraq.

Political disturbances worldwide have resulted in an increasing number of immigrants who claim to be refugees from troubled areas in the Balkans, the Middle East, and Africa. Some have valid credentials as refugees whereas others have been smuggled and arrive with false papers. In response to popular concern, the government has promised to bring in laws imposing restrictions on asylum-seekers and making deportation easier.

Many immigrants and their offspring are being integrated into electoral politics, since residential concentration makes their votes conspicuous in some constituencies. There are now hundreds of elected nonwhite councillors in local government. In some constituencies, candidates from different immigrant groups fight each other. The fifteen nonwhite MPs in the Commons today come from diverse backgrounds—India, Pakistan, the West Indies, Ghana, and Aden—and sit for the Labour, Liberal Democrat, and Conservative parties. A disproportionate number of immigrant voters and elected representatives are Labour.

THE LEGACY OF HISTORY

The legacy of the past limits current choices, and Britain has a very long past. Much of its legacy is positive, for many fundamental problems of governance were resolved centuries ago. The Crown was established as the central political authority in medieval times. The supremacy of the state over the church was settled in the sixteenth century when Henry VIII broke with the Roman Catholic Church to establish the Church of England. The power struggle between Crown and Parliament was resolved by a civil war in the seventeenth century in which Parliament triumphed and a weakened monarch was then restored. The Parliament chosen by an unrepresentative franchise was able to hold the Crown accountable in the eighteenth century.

The continuity of England's political institutions through the centuries is remarkable. Prince Charles, the heir to an ancient Crown, pilots airplanes, and a medieval-named Chancellor of the Exchequer pilots the British economy through the deep waters of the international economy. Yet symbols of continuity often mask great changes in English life. The Parliament was once a supporter of royal authority. Today the Parliament is primarily an electoral college deciding which party leader is in charge of government.

There is no agreement among political scientists about when England developed a modern system of government.[7] The most reasonable judgment is that modern government developed during the very long reign of Queen Victoria from 1837 to 1901, when government institutions were created to cope with the problems of a society that was increasingly urban, literate, industrial, and critical of unreformed institutions. The creation of a modern system of government does not get rid of the problems of governing. Developments since World War II can be divided into five stages.

First of all, an all-party wartime coalition government led by Winston Churchill laid the foundations

A tunnel under the English Channel between England and France, opened in 1994, provides a physical link between Britain and the Continent. In political geography, however, England remains an "offshore" member of the European Union, seeking weak rather than strong ties with its continental neighbors.

Reuters Bettmann/Corbis

for a *mixed economy Keynesian welfare state*. From this coalition emerged the Beveridge Report on social welfare, John Maynard Keynes's Full Employment White Paper of 1944, and the Butler Education Act of 1944. These three measures—the first two named after Liberals and the third after a Conservative—were landmarks in the development of the British welfare state. In 1945 Britain emerged on the winning side of World War II, but its political influence was reduced. The 1945 British general election was won by a Labour government led by Clement Attlee. It combined the promotion of social welfare policies, establishing the comprehensive National Health Service and socialist economic policies. Many basic industries were taken into state ownership, and wartime rationing was maintained as part of the Labour government's policy of a planned economy and fair shares.

Second, between 1951 and 1964 the Conservatives under Winston Churchill, Sir Anthony Eden, and Harold Macmillan maintained a consensus about the welfare state. Food rationing was completely ended in 1954 and Keynesian techniques for promoting economic growth, full employment, and low inflation led to an era of consumer prosperity. However, Eden's abortive attempt to seize the Suez Canal from Egypt in 1956 failed for lack of international support.

The third stage commenced in the early 1960s with a flood of books on the theme "What's wrong with Britain?" Continuities with the past were attacked as the dead hand of tradition. Politicians of all parties denounced "stagnation" and competed in what Michael Moran has described as an age of "hyper-innovation." The Labour Party under Harold Wilson won the 1964 election campaigning with the vague activist slogan, "Let's Go With Labour." New names were given to government department offices, but behind their entrances many officials went through the same routines as before. The economy did not grow as predicted, and in 1967 the government was forced to devalue the pound and seek a loan from the International Monetary Fund (IMF). Labour lost the 1970 election.

The major achievement of Edward Heath's 1970–1974 Conservative government was to make Britain a member of what was then the European Community and is now the European Union. Doing so divided his own party and the opposition. In trying to limit unprecedented inflation by controlling wages, Heath risked his authority in a confrontation with the left-wing-led National Union of Mineworkers, which struck for higher wages in what was then the state-owned coal industry.

When Heath called the "Who Governs?" election in February 1974, many voters rejected both major parties. Labour won the most seats in the House of Commons, but no party had an absolute majority there. Labour formed a minority government, with Harold Wilson again becoming prime minister. A second election in October 1974 gave Labour a bare majority. Inflation, rising unemployment, and a contraction in the economy undermined Labour's program. James Callaghan succeeded Wilson as prime minister in 1976. Keynesian policies were abandoned in 1977 after Labour relied on a loan from the IMF to stabilize the value of the pound in international currency markets.

The Conservatives, led by Margaret Thatcher, won the 1979 election and she became the first woman prime minister of a major European country. Thatcher's radical break with both the Wilson and Heath policies launched the fourth stage. She regarded the economic failures of previous governments as arising from too much compromise: "The Old Testament prophets did not say 'Brothers, I want a consensus.' They said: 'This is my faith. This is what I passionately believe. If you believe it too, then come with me.'"[8]

Divisions among opponents enabled Thatcher to lead her party to three successive election victories, although never winning more than 43 percent of the total vote. Militant left-wing activists seized control of the Labour Party. Under Michael Foot, its 1983 election manifesto was described by a Labour MP as the longest suicide note in history. In 1981 four former Labour Cabinet ministers formed a centrist Social Democratic Party (SDP) and made an alliance with the Liberal Party. After Thatcher's third successive election victory in 1987, the SDP leadership merged with the Liberals to form the Liberal Democratic Party.

While proclaiming the virtues of the market and attacking big government, Thatcher did not court electoral defeat by radically cutting the biggest spending and most popular programs of government (see Box 8.1). In consequence, public spending continued to grow in the Thatcher era. It was 40 percent of the gross domestic product in her last full year in office. While the Conservative majority in the Parliament endorsed Thatcher's policies, it did not win the hearts and minds of the electorate. When polled on the tenth

BOX 8.1

The Meaning of Thatcherism

Among British prime ministers, Margaret Thatcher is unique in giving her name to a political ideology, **Thatcherism.** Thatcher's central conviction was that the market offered a cure for the country's economic difficulties. She rejected the mixed-economy welfare state philosophy of her Conservative and Labour predecessors. As Milton Friedman, the Nobel Prize-winning monetary economist, noted: "Mrs. Thatcher represents a different tradition. She represents a tradition of the nineteenth-century Liberal, of Manchester Liberalism, of free market free trade."[†]

The Thatcher administration experienced both successes and frustrations in economic policy. Her anti-inflation policies succeeded but unemployment doubled. Industrial relations acts gave members the right to elect their union's leaders and vote on whether to hold a strike. State-owned industries and municipally owned council houses were sold to private owners. What were described as "businesslike" methods were introduced into managing everything from hospitals to museums.

As long as it was in her hands, Thatcher believed in strong government. In foreign policy she was a formidable proponent of what she saw as Britain's national interest in dealings with the European Union and in alliance with President Ronald Reagan. The 1982 Argentine invasion of the Falkland Islands, a remote British colony in the South Atlantic, led to a brief and victorious war. Thatcher also quickly asserted her personal authority against colleagues in the Cabinet and against civil servants.[*] The autonomy of local government was curbed and a property tax on houses was replaced by a poll tax on each adult.

[*]"Thatcher Praised by Her Guru," *The Guardian* (London), March 12, 1983.
[†]Cf. Margaret Thatcher, *The Downing Street Years* (New York: HarperCollins, 1993); Dennis Kavanagh, *The Reordering of British Politics* (Oxford: Oxford University Press, 1997).

anniversary of Thatcher's period as prime minister whether or not they approved of "the Thatcher revolution," less than one-third responded yes.[9]

Within the Conservative Party, Thatcher's increasingly autocratic treatment of Cabinet colleagues created resentment, and during her third term of office this resentment was reinforced by unpopularity in opinion polls. In autumn 1990, disgruntled Conservative MPs forced a ballot for the party leadership that caused her to resign. Conservative MPs elected a relatively unknown John Major as party leader.

In 1992 John Major won an unprecedented fourth consecutive term for the Conservative government. A few months later, however, his economic policy of a strong British pound crashed under pressure from foreign speculators. A division opened up within the Conservative Party as Thatcherites criticized Major for agreeing to the Maastricht Treaty, expanding the powers of the European Union. By 1993 Major reached the lowest popularity rating in the history of the Gallup Poll. Even so, the Major government held onto office and Thatcherite economic policies, such as the **privatization** of the coal mines and railways, were pursued.

A fifth stage in postwar British politics opened after Tony Blair became Labour leader in 1994. Blair was elected leader because he did *not* talk or look like an ordinary Labour Party member. Instead of being from a poor background, he was educated at boarding school and studied law at Oxford. Instead of having grown up in the Labour movement, his parents were Conservatives, and he joined the **Labour Party** due to the encouragement of a girlfriend, Cherie Booth (now his wife and a very successful lawyer).

Blair first won office proclaiming that he represented New Labour, a vague Third Way philosophy modeled on the strategy of U.S. President Bill Clinton. In setting out Labour's manifesto, Blair proclaimed, "We are proud now to be the party of modern, dynamic business, proud now to be the party of law and order, proud now to be the party of the family, and proud now to be the party pledged not to increase income tax."[10] He pledged a pragmatic government that would do "what works," and appealed to the voters to "trust me" (see Box 8.2).

BOX 8.2

Accomplishments and Frustrations of Tony Blair

Tony Blair became leader of the Labour Party with the goal of winning elections. To make the party electable, he abandoned Labour's traditional commitments to the trade unions and to socialist values. Blair appealed to middle-class voters whose support Labour needed to win elections. The strategy produced an unprecedented series of three straight Labour wins in the 1997, 2001, and 2005 elections.

Once prime minister, Blair centralized power in 10 Downing Street. The number of political advisers greatly increased and, like Blair, they usually had no prior governing experience. They used the prime minister's authority to produce good headlines rather than developing sustainable policies. Far more attention was given to media publicity, where a sound bite or a clever phrase is sufficient to catch sympathetic attention, than to the House of Commons, where MPs can challenge what is said.

The government implemented Labour's long-standing program of constitutional reforms, including the devolution of powers to elected assemblies in Scotland and Wales, and achieved a power-sharing government in Northern Ireland. It also adopted major laws protecting individual human rights. However, in the wake of terrorist attacks the government has sought to limit human rights in ways that draw protests from civil liberties groups.

In international affairs, Blair gave priority to close working relationships with Bill Clinton and with George W. Bush. After the 9/11 terrorist attacks in 2001, he committed British troops to action in Afghanistan and Iraq. In addition, Blair talked about the need for initiatives to bring peace to the Middle East and to end poverty in Africa. In 2006 Blair was out of the country for a total of fifty-eight days on trips to more than two dozen different nations. One consequence of giving priority to trans-Atlantic relations is that Blair has failed in his declared goal of placing Britain at the heart of Europe, for example, by adopting the euro as Britain's currency.

Blair also promoted policies to change the delivery of state-financed health, education, and pensions by introducing more market mechanisms and offering citizens a measure of "consumer" choice for publicly funded services.* Many doctors, teachers, and public employees have been demoralized or angered by these government measures; for example, in 2006 university teachers staged their first nationwide strike. Given that it takes years to deliver changes in social policies, the full effects of these measures can become evident only years after Blair has left office.

*Cf. Tony Blair, *New Britain: My Vision of a Young Country* (London: Fourth Estate, 1996); Anthony Seldon, *Blair* (New York: Free Press, 2004); Simon Jenkins, *Thatcher and Sons* (London: Allen Lane, 2006).

After eighteen years of Labour being of an opposition party, Blair devoted his first term (1997–2001) to demonstrating that Labour was fit for government. Reacting against his party's record of devaluing the pound and maintaining high taxes, Blair and his Chancellor of the Exchequer, Gordon Brown, committed the New Labour government to carry on the Thatcherite program of reducing the services government delivered. Five months after reelection in 2001, Blair responded to the 9/11 attacks in the United States by closely aligning himself with the United States. Along with other NATO allies of the United States, Britain sent troops to Afghanistan. This action was followed by Blair's commitment of a substantial number of British troops to President George W. Bush's military action in Iraq in 2003. However, this policy lacked the full support of his party. It was only endorsed in Parliament with the support of Conservative MPs.

In 2005 Labour again won a majority of seats in the House of Commons. Victory enabled Blair to become Britain's second-longest serving prime minister of the past century, and he announced a full agenda of domestic policy measures. Since a prime minister does not have a fixed term of office, when Blair subsequently became very unpopular and Labour support plummeted in the opinion polls, he came under pressure from his most likely successor, Gordon Brown (see Box 8.3), to name a date when he would deliver his public pledge not to lead Labour into a fourth election. In June 2007, Tony Blair retired and Gordon Brown was chosen as Labour leader and thus became prime minister.

BOX 8.3

Frustrations and Accomplishments of Gordon Brown

Gordon Brown's career has followed the classic path of a Labour leader. Born in 1951 as the son of a Church of Scotland clergyman, he grew up in a home where duty was stressed more than making money. His strict Scot's upbringing kept him aloof from the show business glitter that surrounds Blair. At Edinburgh University, Brown was very active in student politics. After receiving a Ph.D., he became a college lecturer and published books on Labour Party history and socialism. After Brown became a Labour MP in 1983, his abilities quickly gained him prominence. He became Labour's chief spokesperson on economic affairs, a position just below the party leader, John Smith.

When Smith unexpectedly died in 1994, Brown believed he should become Labour's leader and looked to his junior colleague, Tony Blair, for support. Instead, Blair said he would seek election as leader because Brown represented the traditional and election-losing Labour Party. Blair and Brown made a tacit agreement that Brown would be in charge of economic policy and Blair would eventually resign so that Brown could become the prime minister. This understanding was not committed to paper and has been a recurring source of friction since.

When Labour entered government in 1997, Brown became Chancellor of the Exchequer. In his decade as Chancellor the economy grew at 2.8 percent annually, inflation averaged 2.4 percent, and unemployment fell. Brown also opposed replacing the British pound with the European Union's euro currency. Brown has also influenced domestic policy in health, education, transportation, and local government, for departmental ministers knew that Blair's policy promises could be met only if money was provided by Brown. To finance increased spending without raising income tax, Brown has relied on "stealth" taxes, such as raising employers' social security tax. In addition, he has extended government control of education, the health service, and other public agencies by setting targets to be met as a condition of getting increased public funds.

For a decade, the one thing that Gordon Brown could not control was the prime minister's office. There was a continuing war of acrimonious and anonymous press briefings by the prime minister's aides against Brown, and Brown's staff retorted in kind. It was fueled by uncertainty over when Blair would finally leave. Blair's retirement enabled Brown to become prime minister—an ambition frustrated since 1994. It also meant that he inherited a decade of Blair's policy commitments.

Sources: William Keegan, *The Prudence of Mr. Gordon Brown* (Chichester: Wiley, 2003); Tom Bower, *Gordon Brown* (London: HarperCollins, 2004); Simon Jenkins, *Thatcher and Sons* (London: Allen Lane, 2006).

THE STRUCTURE OF GOVERNMENT

We must understand what government is as a precondition of evaluating what it does. Descriptions of a government often start with its constitution. However, England has never had a written constitution. At no time in the past was there a break with tradition that forced politicians to write down how the country should be governed.

The **unwritten constitution** is a jumble of acts of Parliament, judicial pronouncements, customs, and conventions about the rules of the political game. The vagueness of the constitution makes it flexible, a point that political leaders such as Margaret Thatcher and Tony Blair have exploited to increase their own power. Instead of giving written guarantees to citizens, as the U.S. Bill of Rights does, the rights of English people are

meant to be secured by trustworthy governors. In the words of a constitutional lawyer, J. A. G. Griffith, "The Constitution is what happens."[11]

Comparing the written United States constitution and the unwritten English constitution emphasizes how few are the constraints of an unwritten constitution (see Table 8.2). The U.S. Constitution gives the U.S. Supreme Court the final power to decide what the government may or may not do. By contrast, in Britain the final authority is Parliament, where the government of the day commands a majority of votes. The Law Lords and the Judicial Committee of the Privy Council can resolve disputes about the interpretation of Acts of Parliament but not declare an act unconstitutional. The Bill of Rights in the U.S. Constitution allows anyone to seek redress in the courts for

	Britain (unwritten)	United States (written)
Origins	Medieval customs	1787 Constitutional Convention
Form	Unwritten, indefinite	Written, precise
Final power	Majority in Parliament	U.S. Supreme Court
Bill of individual rights	No	Yes
Amendment	Ordinary vote in Parliament; unprecedented action by government	More than majority vote in Congress, states
Policy relevance	Low	High

TABLE 8.2 Comparing an Unwritten and a Written Constitution

infringement of personal rights. In Britain, an individual who believes his or her personal rights are infringed on by an act of Parliament had no redress through the courts until the Blair government incorporated the European Convention of Human Rights into the country's laws. Whereas amendments to the U.S. Constitution must receive the endorsement of well over half the states and members of Congress, the unwritten constitution can be changed by a majority vote in Parliament, or by the government of the day choosing to act in an unprecedented manner.

English courts claim no power to declare an act of Parliament unconstitutional. Courts ask whether the executive acts within its statutory powers. Many statutes delegate broad discretion to a Cabinet minister or public authority; the courts hesitate to question how the executive exercises this delegated discretion. Even if the courts rule that the government has improperly exercised its authority, the effect of such a judgment can be annulled by a subsequent act of Parliament retroactively authorizing an action.

The Crown and Government

The **Crown** rather than a constitution symbolizes the authority of government. However, the monarch is only a ceremonial head of state. The public reaction to the accidental death of Princess Diana was a media event but not a political event like the assassination of U.S. President John F. Kennedy. Queen Elizabeth II does not influence the actions of what is described as Her Majesty's government. While the queen gives formal assent to laws passed by Parliament, she may not publicly state any opinion about legislation. The queen is expected to respect the will of Parliament, as communicated to her by the leader of the majority party in Parliament, the prime minister.

No simple answer can be given to the question: what constitutes the Crown? The Crown is a symbol to which people are asked to give loyalty. It does not refer to a particular community of people. The idea of the Crown combines the dignified parts of the constitution, which sanctify authority by tradition and myth, with the efficient parts, which carry out the work of government.

In everyday political conversation, British people talk about government, not the constitution. The term **government** is used in many senses (see Figure 8.1). People may speak of the Queen's government, to emphasize enduring and nonpartisan features, or they may refer to Tony Blair's government to stress its personal and transitory features, or to a Labour or Conservative government to emphasize partisanship. The term *government officials* usually refers to civil servants. Collectively, the executive agencies of government are often referred to as **Whitehall,** after the London street in which many major government offices are located. **Downing Street,** where the prime minister's residence is located, is a short and narrow street off Whitehall. **Parliament**—that is, the popularly elected House of Commons and the nonelected House of Lords—is at the bottom end of the street called Whitehall. Collectively, these institutions are often referred to as **Westminster,** after the district in London in which they are located.

The Prime Minister

Within the Cabinet, the **prime minister** occupies a unique position, sometimes referred to as *primus inter*

| Electorate, Local and Regional | Legislature | Executive |

Structure of the British Government

FIGURE 8.1

pares (first among equals). But as Winston Churchill once wrote, "There can be no comparison between the positions of number one, and numbers two, three or four."[12] However, the preeminence of the prime minister is ambiguous. A politician at the apex of government is remote from what is happening on the ground. The more responsibilities attributed to the prime minister, the less time there is to devote to any one task. Like a president, a prime minister is the prisoner of the law of first things first. The imperatives of the prime minister are as follows.

1. **Winning Elections.** To become prime minister, a politician must first be elected leader of his or her party. The only election that a prime minister must win is that as party leader. Six of the eleven prime ministers since 1945—Winston Churchill, Anthony Eden, Harold Macmillan, Alec Douglas-Home, James Callaghan, and John Major—initially entered Downing Street during the middle of a Parliament rather than after a national election. In the seventeen elections since 1945, the prime minister of the day has ten times led the governing party to victory and seven times to defeat.

2. **Campaigning Through the Media.** A prime minister does not need to attract publicity; it is thrust upon him or her by the curiosity of television and newspaper reporters. Media eminence is a double-edged sword. When the news is bad, it puts the prime minister in an unfavorable light. While the personality of a prime minister remains relatively constant, during a term of office his or her popularity can fluctuate by more than 45 percentage points in public opinion polls.[13]

3. **Using Patronage.** To remain prime minister, a politician must keep the confidence of a party. Potential critics can be silenced by appointing a quarter of MPs to posts as government ministers, who sit on front bench seats in the House of Commons. MPs not appointed to a post are backbenchers; many ingratiate themselves with the party leader in hopes of becoming a government minister. In making ministerial appointments, a prime minister can use any of four different criteria: (1) personal loyalty (rewarding friends); (2) co-option (silencing critics by giving them an office so that they are committed to support the government); (3) representativeness (for example, appointing a woman or someone from Scotland

or Wales); and (4) competence in giving direction to a government department.

4. ***Exhibiting Strong Parliamentary Performances.*** The prime minister appears in the House of Commons weekly for half an hour of questions from MPs, engaging in rapid-fire repartee with a highly partisan audience. Unprotected by a speechwriter's script, the prime minister must show that he or she is a good advocate of government policy or suffer a reduction in confidence. He or she occasionally makes statements to the Commons.

5. ***Making and Balancing Policies.*** Leading government is a political rather than a managerial task. If a prime minister tries to tell a minister well informed about a department what to do, he or she risks exposing ignorance. To ask an awkward question or to give advice to a minister puts the person in charge of a department on the spot. The overriding concern of a prime minister is foreign affairs, because of the need to deal with heads of governments around the world. When there are conflicts between international and domestic policy priorities, the prime minister is the one person who can strike a balance between pressures from the world "out there" and pressures from the domestic electorate. The number of "intermestic" policies (that is, problems combining both an international and domestic element) is increasing and with it the balancing role of Downing Street.

While the formal powers of the office remain constant, individual prime ministers have differed in their electoral success (see Figure 8.2), how they view their job and in their impact on government. Clement Attlee, Labour prime minister from 1945 to 1951, was a nonassertive spokesperson for the lowest common denominator of views within a Cabinet consisting of very experienced Labour politicians. When an aging Winston Churchill succeeded in 1951, he concentrated on foreign affairs and took little interest in domestic policy; the same was true of his successor, Anthony Eden. Harold Macmillan intervened strategically on a limited number of domestic and international issues, while giving ministers great scope on everyday matters. Alec Douglas-Home was weak because he lacked knowledge of economic affairs, the chief problem during his administration.

Prime Ministers and Governments Since 1940

FIGURE 8.2

During the Iraq War, Tony Blair was the foreign leader closest to President Bush.

AP Images

Both Harold Wilson and Edward Heath were initially committed to an activist definition of the prime minister's job. However, Wilson's major initiatives in economic policy were unsuccessful. In 1974 the electorate rejected Heath's aggressive direction of the economy, and Wilson won office promising to replace confrontation between management and unions with political conciliation. James Callaghan, who succeeded Wilson in 1976, also emphasized consensus.

Margaret Thatcher had strong views about many major policies; associates gave her the nickname TINA because of her motto: There Is No Alternative. Thatcher was prepared to push her views against the wishes of Cabinet colleagues and civil service advisors by any means necessary. In the end, her "bossiness" caused a revolt of Cabinet colleagues that helped bring about her downfall. Her former colleagues welcomed John Major in place of a hectoring leader. However, his conciliatory manner was often interpreted as a sign of weakness, and sniping from ministers led Major to refer to his Cabinet colleagues as "bastards."

Tony Blair carried into Downing Street the priority he gave to campaigning while in Opposition. Blair's innovations led to criticisms that he was creating a presidential system. However, by comparison with a U.S. president, a British prime minister has less formal authority. The president is directly elected for a fixed four-year term. A prime minister is chosen by his or her party for an indefinite term and is thus vulnerable to losing office if its confidence wanes. The president is the undoubted leader of the federal executive and can dismiss Cabinet appointees with little fear of the consequences; by contrast, senior colleagues of a prime minister are potential rivals for leadership and may be kept in Cabinet to prevent them from challenging from the outside.

With the support of the Cabinet and the majority of the governing party's MPs, a prime minister can be far more confident than a president that major legislative proposals will be enacted into law. Although the president is the chief of the executive branch of the federal government, the White House is without authority over Congress, state and local government, and the judiciary. The prime minister is at the apex of a unitary government, with powers not limited by the courts or by a written constitution.[14]

THE CABINET AND CABINET MINISTERS

The **Cabinet** consists of senior ministers appointed by the prime minister: they must be either members of the House of Commons or of the House of Lords. As ministers are leading figures in the majority party in Parliament, they contribute to what Walter Bagehot described as "the close union, the nearly complete fusion of the executive and legislative powers."[15]

The Cabinet has historically been the forum in which the prime minister brought together leading members of the governing party—many with competing departmental interests and personal ambitions—to ensure agreement about major government policies. This was possible because the convention of Cabinet responsibility requires that all Cabinet ministers and their deputies give public support, or at least refrain from public criticism, of what the government is doing, even if they have opposed a policy in private. A minister who is unwilling to share responsibility has been expected to resign office. However, it is rare for a minister to resign because of policy differences.

The Cabinet is no longer a place for collective deliberation about policies. A half century ago there were almost two Cabinet meetings a week and many took several hours to arrive at a political consensus. By the time of John Major, shorter meetings occurred less than once a week. Tony Blair further reduced the frequency of meetings and cut their average length to under an hour. Instead of being a forum for consultation, Blair's Cabinet meetings became a forum in which Number Ten exhorts ministers to produce good news and bury bad news.

Cabinet ministers remain important as department heads, for most decisions of government are made within departments, and departments are responsible for overseeing all the services of government, which are usually delivered by public agencies subordinate to and distant from Whitehall (see Box 8.4).

Major Whitehall departments differ greatly from each other. For example, the Home Office supervises a much larger staff than the Treasury. However, because of the importance of the economy, the Treasury has more senior civil servants. The Home Office staff tend to be at lower levels, being involved in such everyday tasks as policing, fire prevention, prison work, control of obscene publications, and so on. The Treasury concentrates on one big task, the management of the economy. The varied tasks of the Home Secretary make him or her much more vulnerable to adverse publicity if, for example, a convicted murderer escapes from prison. But the job of the Chancellor of the Exchequer is more important politically, insofar as economic performance affects the governing party's electoral fate.

Departmental Organization and Reorganization

BOX 8.4

British government departments are multipurpose administrative units created as a result of the growth of government and brought together through a series of reorganizations justified by efficiency, policy, fashion, or political expediency.* For example, since 1964 responsibilities for trade, industry, and technology have been placed in departments labeled Trade and Technology, then Trade and Industry, then separate departments for Trade and for Industry, and once again reunited as a single Trade and Industry department. Each time that the title on the front door of the department was changed, most officials and programs continued as before. When Gordon Brown formed his first Cabinet in 2007, it had the following departments:

1. *External affairs:* foreign and commonwealth office; defense; international development

2. *Economic affairs:* treasury; business, enterprise and regulatory reform; transport

3. *Law:* Lord chancellor; justice; law Officer's department; home office

4. *Social services:* health; social security; innovation, universities and skills; work and pensions; culture, media and sport; children, schools, and families

5. *Territorial:* environment, food, and rural affairs; communities and local government; the Northern Ireland Office

6. *Managing government business:* Leader of the House of Commons; Chief Whip in the House of Commons; Leader of the House of Lords; Chancellor of the Duchy of Lancaster

*See Richard Rose, *Ministers and Ministries: A Functional Analysis* (Oxford: Clarendon Press, 1987).

A minister has many roles: initiating policies, selecting among alternatives brought forward from within the department, avoiding a difficult or unpopular decision. A minister is responsible for actions taken by thousands of civil servants nominally acting on the minister's behalf and must answer for agencies to which Whitehall is increasingly contracting out responsibility for delivering public services. In addition, a minister is a department's ambassador to the world outside, including Downing Street, Parliament, the mass media, and pressure groups. Not least, Cabinet ministers are individuals with ambitions to rise in politics. The typical minister is not an expert in a subject but an expert in parliamentary politics, willing to deal with any department that offers opportunities to further his or her political career.

The political reputation of Cabinet ministers depends on their success in promoting the interests of their department in Parliament, in the media, and in battles within Whitehall. Cabinet ministers are willing to go along silently with their colleagues' proposals in exchange for endorsement of their own measures. However, ministers often have to compete for scarce resources, making conflict inevitable among departments. Regardless of party, the Defense and Education ministers will press for increased spending while Treasury ministers oppose such moves. Cabinet ministers sometimes resolve their differences in Cabinet committees that include ministers whose departments are most affected by an issue.

Tony Blair has sought to exercise control over ministers through his personal staff. However, Blair does not have any more time during the week to go into the details of policy, and because he has never been a departmental minister, his public remarks sometimes show naivete about how government actually works—and the same can be even more true of his staff.[16]

The Civil Service

Although government could continue for months without new legislation, it would collapse overnight if hundreds of thousands of civil servants stopped administering laws and delivering public services. The largest number of civil servants are clerical staff with little discretion; they carry out routine activities of a large bureaucracy. Only if these duties are executed satisfactorily can ministers have the time and opportunity to make new policies.

The most important group of civil servants is the smallest: the few hundred higher civil servants who advise ministers and oversee the work of their departments. Top British civil servants deny they are politicians because of the partisan connotations of the term. However, their work is political because they are involved in formulating, revising, and advising on policies. A publication seeking to recruit bright graduates for the higher civil service declares: "You will be involved from the outset in matters of major policy or resource allocation and, under the guidance of experienced administrators, encouraged to put forward your own constructive ideas and to take responsible decisions."[17]

Top civil servants are not apolitical; they are bipartisan, being ready to work for whichever party is the winner of an election. Their style is not that of the professional American athlete for whom winning is all-important. English civil servants have grown up playing cricket; its motto is that winning is less important than how one plays the game.

The relationship between ministers and higher civil servants is critical. Ministers expect higher civil servants to be responsive to their political views and to give advice consistent with their outlook and that of the governing party and Downing Street. Civil servants like working for a political heavyweight who can carry the department's cause to victory in interdepartmental battles. A busy politician does not have time to go into details; he or she wants a brief that can catch a headline or squash criticism. Civil servants prefer to work for a minister who has clear views on policy, but they dislike it when the views proclaimed will get the department into trouble later because they are impractical.

In the traditional Whitehall model, both ministers and civil servants concentrated on political management rather than administrative concerns. High-level civil servants were expected to be able to think like politicians, anticipating what their minister would want and objections that would be raised by Parliament, pressure groups, and the media. Ministers were expected to be able to think like civil servants as well as politicians, recognizing the obstacles to achieving desirable goals, and scaling down their ambitions when ways could not be found to overcome these obstacles.

The Thatcher government introduced a new phenomenon in Whitehall: a prime minister who believed civil servants were inferior to business people because they did not have to "earn" their living, that is, make a profit. Management was made the buzzword in Whitehall, and departments were supposed to be run in a businesslike fashion, achieving value for money so that the government could profit politically by cutting taxes. Parts of government departments were "hived off" to form separate public agencies, with their own accounts and performance targets. However, when an agency's task is politically sensitive, such as the marking of national school examinations, the education minister cannot avoid blame if there are major errors in arriving at the examination marks sent to pupils.

The Blair government continued Thatcherite attempts to make the civil service more businesslike, in hopes of providing more public services without raising taxes. In addition, it has made political advisors important in formulating policy. Some civil servants fear that efforts to "modernize" the civil service are a mask for appointing officials who are pliable in the hands of ministers. The head of the trade union of higher civil servants has argued, "There is a danger of descending into a search for scapegoats when problems emerge."[18]

After years in office, Tony Blair recognized the consequences of government by political advisors and spin doctors. In a leaked memo to Cabinet ministers, he complained of "too often" rushing out policies "in ignorance of the risks," thus making the government look bad.[19]

The Role of Parliament

The principal division in Parliament is between the party with a majority of seats in the House of Commons and the opposition party. The government expects to get its way because its members are the leading politicians in the party with a majority in the Commons. If a bill or a motion is identified as a vote of confidence in the government, the government will fall if it is defeated. MPs in the majority party almost invariably vote as the party leadership instructs, because only by voting as a bloc can their party maintain control of government.

The government's state of mind is summed up in the words of a Labour Cabinet minister who declared, "It's carrying democracy too far if you don't know the result of the vote before the meeting."[20] In nine out of ten votes in the Commons, voting is 100 percent along party lines. If a handful of MPs votes against the party whip or abstains, this is headlined as a rebellion. Major differences of opinion between Tony Blair and old Labour MPs and divisions between Thatcherite and post-Thatcherite Conservatives have increased the size and frequency of rebellions.

Whitehall departments draft bills presented to Parliament and only a small percentage of amendments to legislation are carried without government backing. Moreover, the government rather than Parliament sets the budget for government programs. The weakness of Parliament is in marked contrast to the U.S. Congress, where each house controls its own proceedings independent of the White House and can be at loggerheads when different parties control each branch. A U.S. president may ask Congress to enact a bill but cannot compel a favorable vote. The first function of the Commons is to weigh political reputations. MPs continually assess their colleagues as ministers and potential ministers. A minister may win a formal vote of confidence but lose status if his or her arguments are demolished in debate.

In the second function of the Commons, MPs in the governing party have private access to government ministers. The whip is expected to listen to the views of dissatisfied backbench MPs and to convey their concerns to ministers. In the corridors, dining rooms, and committees of the Commons, backbenchers can tell ministers what they think is wrong with government policy. However, MPs are unwilling to vote against their party if it threatens to bring down the government. The opposition cannot expect to alter major government decisions because it lacks a majority of votes in the Commons. The opposition accepts the frustrations going with its minority status for the life of a Parliament, because it hopes to win a majority at the next election.

Publicizing issues is a third function of Parliament. Debates in the House of Commons have limited importance; only one-sixth of backbenchers regularly listen to their colleagues' speeches in the House of Commons. An MP can get the attention of the media by voicing a distinctive opinion and television cameras are now in Parliament. However, news programs usually show only sound bites.

Scrutinizing legislation is a fourth function of the House of Commons. Backbench MPs can demand that the government do something about an issue. The procedures of the Commons force a minister to explain and defend a bill in detail. In theory a government bill can be substantially amended or even withdrawn as a consequence of criticism in Parliament—but such incidents are rare. Laws are described as acts of Parliament, but it would be more accurate if they were stamped "Made in Whitehall."

Fifth, MPs can examine how Whitehall departments administer public policies. An MP may write to a minister questioning a departmental decision called to his or her attention by a constituent or pressure group. MPs can request the parliamentary commissioner for administration (also known as the ombudsman, after the Scandinavian prototype) to investigate complaints about maladministration. Committees scrutinize administration and policy, interviewing civil servants and ministers. However, as a committee moves from discussing details to questions of political principle, it raises the question of confidence in the government and this can divide a committee along party lines, with MPs in the governing party in the majority.

A newly elected MP contemplating his or her role as one among 646 members of the House of Commons is faced with many alternatives. An MP may decide to be a party loyalist, voting as the leadership decides without participating in deliberations about policy. The MP who wishes more attention can make a mark by brilliance in debate, by acting as an acknowledged representative of a pressure group, or in a nonpartisan way—for example, being known for making amusing remarks. An MP is expected to speak for constituency interests, but constituents accept that their MP will not vote against party policy if it is in conflict with local interests. The only role that an MP rarely undertakes is that of lawmaker.

The limited influence of both houses of Parliament encourages proposals for reform. Backbench MPs perennially demand changes to make their jobs more interesting and to give them more influence. Labour MPs, especially women elected since 1997, have criticized procedures inherited from past centuries as inappropriate for the new millennium. However, the power to make major changes rests with the government rather than the House of Commons. Whatever criticisms MPs made of Parliament while in opposition, once in Cabinet party leaders have an interest in existing arrangements that greatly limit the power of Parliament to influence or stop what ministers do.

Among modern Parliaments, the **House of Lords** is unique as a second chamber because it was initially composed of hereditary peers, supplemented by lords appointed for life. However, in 1999 the Labour government abolished the right of all but ninety-two hereditary peers to sit in the House of Lords. Today, a big majority of its members are life peers who have been given a lifelong title for achievement in one or another public sphere, including membership in the House of Commons or being a prominent donor of money to a party. No party has a majority there. As of March 2007, among its nearly 750 members, 29 percent were Labour, 28 percent Conservative, 11 percent Liberal Democrats, 28 crossbenchers who reject a party identification, and the remainder in a miscellany of categories, such as Church of England bishops.

The government often introduces relatively noncontroversial legislation in the Lords if it deals with technical matters, and it uses the Lords as a revising chamber to amend bills. In addition, the Lords can discuss public issues on matters of partisan controversy or on such cross-party topics as pornography or the future of hill farming. The Lords cannot veto legislation, but it can and does amend or delay the passage of some government bills.

Although all parties accept the need for some kind of second chamber to revise legislation, there is no agreement about how the chamber should be composed or what its power should be. The hereditary principle is often criticized as an undemocratic legacy from an earlier era. An appointed second chamber raises concerns about the prime minister of the day abusing appointing powers, following the Scotland Yard police investigation of Blair's offer of peerages to donors of very large sums to the Labour Party. Many argue for an elected upper house, but the last thing the government of the day wants is an electoral reform that gives the upper chamber enough legitimacy to challenge government legislation. In an advisory vote in March, 2007, the House of Commons endorsed the principle of a 100 percent elected upper chamber, but the resolution approved left open many issues about how the chamber should be elected.

Government as a Network

The ship of state has only one tiller, but direction is given by more than one pair of hands. In an era of big government, power does not rest in a single individual or office; it is manifest in a network of relations within and between a network of institutions. Policymaking involves interactions among the prime minister, ministers, and leading civil servants, all of whom share in what has been described as the "village life" of Whitehall. This English village is far smaller and more intimate than the city full of politicians inside the Washington, D.C., beltway.[21]

Within the Whitehall network, a core set of political figures are especially important in determining policies. The prime minister is the single most important person in government. Since there is no written constitution, a determined prime minister can challenge the status quo and turn government to fresh ends. For example, Margaret Thatcher entered office with a large agenda of market-oriented policies that she wished to promote, and the determination and stamina to push through policies against opposition from a number of Cabinet colleagues and civil servants.

To say that the prime minister makes the most important decisions and departmental ministers the secondary decisions begs the question: what is an important decision? Decisions in which the prime minister is not involved, such as those involving transport or agriculture, are more numerous, require more money, and affect more lives than most decisions taken in Downing Street. Scarcity of prime ministerial time is a major limitation on the influence of the prime minister. In the words of one Downing Street official, "It's like skating over an enormous globe of thin ice. You have to keep moving fast all the time."[22]

The head of the Treasury, the Chancellor of the Exchequer, makes many decisions with broad political ramifications for economic growth, taxation, and public expenditure. Within each department, the permanent secretary, its highest-ranking civil servant, usually has much more knowledge of a department's problems than does a transitory Cabinet minister.

Tony Blair has sought to increase the role of Downing Street as the central node in the network. However, his style of governing has also increased the risk of policy errors. An inquiry by a former head of the civil service into events leading to Britain's involvement in the Iraq War concluded of Blair's method of government: "We are concerned that the informality and circumscribed character of the government's procedures which we saw in the context of policy-making towards Iraq risks reducing the scope for informed collective political judgment."[23]

POLITICAL CULTURE AND LEGITIMACY

The importance of cultural values is illustrated by the statement of a British judge: "In the constitution of this country, there are no guaranteed or absolute rights. The safeguard of British liberty is in the good sense of the people and in the system of representative and responsible government which has been evolved."[24] However, politics involves the expression of conflicting beliefs about who should govern and what government should do. In Britain there are three different views about who should be involved when important political decisions are made.

The **trusteeship theory of government** assumes that leaders should take the initiative in deciding what is collectively in the public interest. It is summed up in the epigram, "The government's job is to govern." The trusteeship doctrine is always popular with the party in office because it justifies doing whatever the government wishes. The opposition party rejects this theory because it lacks the power of government.

The **interest group theory** sees government's role as balancing the demands of competing groups and classes in society. From this perspective, parties and pressure groups advocating group or class interests are more authoritative than individual voters.[25] Traditional Conservatives emphasized harmony between different classes in society, each with its own responsibilities and rewards. To socialists, group politics is about class divisions between trade unions and business, seeking to use government to their own ends. With changes in British society, party leaders have distanced themselves from organized interests as they realize that votes are cast by individuals rather than business firms or trade unions.

The **individualist theory** of representation postulates that political parties should represent people rather than organized group interests. In the 1980s Margaret Thatcher was an outspoken advocate of economic individualism, regarding each person as responsible for his or her welfare through the marketplace. She even went so far as to declare, "There is no such thing as society."

Liberal Democrats emphasize individual freedom from collective constraints. Similarly, Tony Blair has endorsed more choice in public services. However, individuals are rarely offered a referendum allowing them to vote directly on what government does.

In addition, decisions about holding a referendum and the question put are in the hands of the government of the day.

The Legitimacy of Government

The great majority of British people find it inconceivable that there should be a fundamental change in the way the country is governed. Even Nationalist parties in Scotland and Wales do not reject parliamentary institutions; what they want is an independent Parliament for Scotland and for Wales.

The unresponsiveness of government to Parliament has encouraged popular protest—but the legitimacy of government means that protest is usually kept within lawful bounds. For example, while the World Values Survey finds that nearly every Briton says they might sign a petition and half said they might participate in a lawful demonstration, only one-sixth said they might consider an illegal occupation of a building or factory.

The legitimacy of government is evidenced by the readiness of the British people to comply with basic political laws. The crimes that occur are antisocial actions (such as street violence) rather than political crimes against the state (such as assassinations). The one notable exception is Northern Ireland, where many major crimes, from murder to bank robbery, are carried out with the political objective of overturning an elected government.

The legitimacy accorded to British government is not the result of economic calculations about whether parliamentary democracy "pays" best, as rational choice theories propound. During the depression of the 1930s, British Communist and Fascist parties received only derisory votes, while their support was great in Germany and Italy. Likewise, inflation and unemployment in the 1970s and 1980s failed to stimulate extremist politics.

The symbols of a common past, such as the monarchy, are sometimes cited as major determinants of legitimacy. But surveys of public opinion show that the Queen has little political significance; her popularity derives from the fact that she is nonpolitical. The popularity of a monarch is a consequence, not a cause, of political legitimacy. In Northern Ireland, where the minority denies the legitimacy of British government, the Queen is a symbol of divisions between British Unionists and Irish Republicans who reject the Crown.

Habit and tradition appear to be the chief explanations for the persisting legitimacy of British government. A survey asking people why they support the government found that the most popular reason was "It's the best form of government we know." Authority is not perfect or trouble free. Winston Churchill made this point when he told the House of Commons:

> No one pretends that democracy is perfect or all wise. Indeed, it has been said that democracy is the worst form of government, except all those other forms that have been tried from time to time.[26]

Abuses of Power

The government of the day can claim its authority is legitimate only if it acts within the rule of law. In constitutional theory, Parliament can hold ministers accountable for abuses of power by the government. In practice, Parliament is an ineffective check on executive power, because the executive consists of the leaders of the majority party in Parliament. When a member of the government is under attack, the tendency of MPs in the governing party is to close ranks in defense of a colleague.

The power of the government to get away with mistakes is supported by official secrecy and the doctrine of collective Cabinet responsibility. The Whitehall view is that information is a scarce commodity that should not be given out freely. Publicity about policymaking is not seen in the "public (sic)" interest, for it can make government appear uncertain or divided about what should be done. The Whitehall view is restrictive: "The need to know still dominates the right to know."[27] Secrecy remains strong because it serves the interests of the most important people in government, Cabinet ministers and civil servants. The Freedom of Information Act has reduced but not ended the executive's power to keep secret the exchange of views within the Whitehall network. For example, in response to a request for information about its operation, a civil servant at the Histories, Openness and Records Unit of the Cabinet Office wrote: "Releasing information which would allow analysis of policy decisions affecting the operation of the Act would of itself be detrimental to the Act's operation because it may reveal sensitivities."[28]

Both ministers and senior civil servants are prepared to mislead Parliament and the public. William

Waldegrave, the Conservative minister nominally responsible for open government, told a Commons select committee in 1994 that "in exceptional cases it is necessary to say something that is untrue in the House of Commons."

When accused in court of telling a lie about the British government's efforts to suppress an embarrassing memoir by an ex-intelligence officer, the then head of the civil service and secretary to the Cabinet, Robert Armstrong, described the government's statements as "a misleading impression, not a lie. It was being economical with the truth."

Abuses of executive power have created tensions for civil servants who believe that their job is not only to serve the elected government of the day but also to maintain the integrity of government. This has led civil servants at times to leak official documents with the intention of preventing government from carrying out a policy that the leaker believes to be unethical or inadvisable (see Box 8.5).

Citizens have reacted to changing standards of political behavior by distrusting their elected representatives. Only a third of Britons report that they have a great deal or quite a lot of confidence in Parliament. The press and trade unions—institutions that theories of civil society describe as important in holding government accountable—are trusted by even fewer people. The most trusted public institutions today are those that maintain authority, led by the armed forces and the police (see Figure 8.3).

The decline of ministerial accountability to Parliament has encouraged the courts to become more active in making rulings against the elected government of the day. Judges today are ready to find grounds to nullify actions of ministers that go beyond broad grants of power made by Acts of Parliament. Britain's membership in the European Union and adherence to the European Convention of Human Rights offer additional ways in which actions of ministers can be challenged. When judges act in ways that Labour ministers do not like, ministers have publicly attacked the decisions that judges have made about applying laws for which ministers are responsible. The result is a conflict between the principle that elected politicians should make decisions and the principle that government actions should be in accord with the rule of law.

Terrorist activities challenge conventional norms about the use and abuse of power. In Northern Ireland the British government has had to deal with the Irish Republican Army and illegal armed Protestant groups that regard violence as legitimate for use in liberating Northern Ireland from British rule. Their violence was met by Crown forces "bending" the law, including shoot-to-kill policies and fabricating evidence to produce convictions of IRA suspects that have years later been overturned by the courts as falsely obtained.

In response to Moslem terrorist bombs in London, the police have been ready to use harsh measures against suspects. Such measures have led to

---

Conflicting Loyalties Among Civil Servants   BOX 8.5

The inability of Parliament to hold the government of the day accountable for palpable misdeeds disturbs senior civil servants who know what is going on and risk becoming accessories before the fact if they assist ministers in producing statements that mislead Parliament. Some even challenge the doctrine that a civil servant must support a minister, whatever the official's personal opinion.

In one well-publicized case, a Ministry of Defense official, Clive Ponting, leaked to the House of Commons evidence that questioned the accuracy of government statements about the conduct of the Falklands War. He was indicted and tried for violating the Official Secrets Act. The judge asked the jury to think about the issue this way: "Can it then be in the interests of the state to go against the policy of the government of the day?" The jury concluded that it could be; Ponting was acquitted.

However, most senior civil servants are unwilling to become whistle-blowers challenging actions of ministers, thereby jeopardizing their own careers.

See Graham Wilson and Anthony Barker, "Whitehall's Disobedient Servants? Senior Officials' Potential Resistance to Ministers in British Government Departments," *British Journal of Political Science* 27, no. 2 (1997): 223–46.

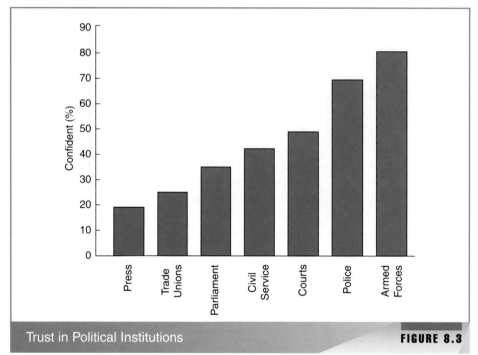

Trust in Political Institutions

FIGURE 8.3

Source: Ronald Inglehart et al., World Values Survey and European Values Survey, 1999–2001. (Ann Arbor: Interuniversity Consortium for Political and Social Research). Interviews conducted in Great Britain, October–November 1999 (N = 1000).

shooting people suspected of being terrorists, but who turned out to have no connection with such activities.

Culture as a Constraint on Policy

British people simultaneously value their form of government while making many specific criticisms about how it works. In the phrase of the English writer E. M. Forster, people give "two cheers for democracy."

The values of the political culture impose limitations on the scope of public policy. Cultural norms about freedom of speech prevent political censorship. In the "swinging 1960s," laws against homosexual relations were repealed and abortion legalized. AIDS has been treated as a disease rather than as a cause of shame or moralizing. Cultural expectations also influence what politicians must do. Regardless of party preference, the great majority of British people believe that government ought to provide education, health services, and social security.

Today, the most significant limits on the scope of public policy are practical and political. Public expenditure on popular policies such as the health service is limited by the extent to which the economy grows and the reluctance of Labour or Conservative governments to raise more money for health care by increasing taxes or by imposing limited charges of some sort for the use of health services.

POLITICAL SOCIALIZATION

Socialization influences the political division of labor. At an early age children learn about social differences relevant to politics; a small proportion become interested in politics, a larger proportion become apathetic, and the median person takes some but not that much interest in politics. The predispositions that a young person forms by the time she or he is old enough to vote are modified by adult experience. A middle-aged person has voted in five or six general elections and is likely to evaluate subsequent political events in the light of what has already been learned.

Family and Gender

The family's influence comes first chronologically; political attitudes learned within the family become intertwined with primary family loyalties. A child may not know what the Labour or Conservative party stands for, but if it is the party of Mom and Dad this can be enough to create identification with a party.

The influence of family on voting is limited; 36 percent do not know how one or both of their parents usually voted, or that their parents voted for opposing parties. Among those who report knowing which party both parents supported, just over half vote as their parents have done. In the electorate as a whole, only 35 percent say that they know how both parents voted and that they vote for the same party.[29]

Children also acquire a religious identification from their parents but, except in Northern Ireland, religion no longer has a substantial influence on voting, and there are no groups comparable to the American religious right.

Children learn different social roles according to gender, yet as adult citizens men and women have the same legal right to vote and participate in politics. Bipartisan interest in appealing to women is illustrated by the 1976 Sex Discrimination Act, prohibiting discrimination in employment. It was enacted by a Labour government following a report by a Conservative government.

Today, all political parties seek the votes of women, since women are a majority of the electorate. However, parties do not want to offend men, for men are 48 percent of the electorate. Whether politicians are talking about economic, social, or international issues, they usually stress concerns common to both men and women. At each general election, women divide between parties in much the same way as men, and apparent differences can reflect differences in life expectancy producing more older women in the electorate.

Men and women tend to have similar political attitudes. On most political issues women divide into two contrasting groups, and the same is true of men.

For example, more than half of women and half of men favor capital punishment and a substantial minority in each group oppose it. Gender differences are less important than class, age, or education as influences on party loyalties (see Table 8.3).

Gender differences do, however, lead to differences in political participation. Even though women constitute more than half the electorate, men are almost twice as likely as women to be local government councillors. Women constitute almost half the employees in the civil service, but are heavily concentrated in lower-level clerical jobs; women hold about 10 percent of the top appointments in the civil service. A record number of women candidates stood for the Commons in 2005, but male candidates still outnumbered women by a margin of more than four to one. A total of 128 women were elected to the House of Commons; it remains four-fifths male.

Education

The majority of the population was once considered fit for only a minimum of education; in today's electorate the oldest voters left school at 14 and the median voter by age of 17. The highly educated are a small fraction of the population; they expect and are expected to play a leading role in politics. Within the

	Labour	Conservative	Liberal Democrat	Other
Gender				
Women	39	34	22	5
Men	40	29	23	8
Difference	−1	5	−1	−3
Age				
18–29	44	20	30	6
30–59	40	30	23	7
60 plus	36	41	18	5
Difference	8	−21	12	1
Class				
Middle	36	36	23	5
Lower middle	32	39	24	5
Skilled manual	48	27	18	7
Unskilled manual	52	18	20	10
Difference	−16	18	3	−5

TABLE 8.3

Social Differences in Voting (percentage of voters in 2005)

Source: British Election Survey, 2005; number of reported voters—2,787.

state system, the great majority of pupils attend comprehensive secondary schools, which recruit students at all levels of ability. Within the school, pupils are often divided into an academic stream being taught at an advanced level and many being given only a basic education. Less than 6 percent of young persons attend "public" schools, that is, fee-paying schools that are actually private. Whereas half a century ago England had few universities, today almost one-half of young persons are in postsecondary institutions, many of which lack the facilities of established research universities.

The stratification of English education used to imply that the more education a person had, the more likely a person would be Conservative. This is no longer so. People with a university degree or its equivalent are more likely to vote Labour than Conservative. The minority who are most educated now divide their vote between all three big parties, and the Liberal Democrats also attract a disproportionate share of more educated voters.

Education is strongly related to active participation in politics. The more education a person has, the greater the possibility of climbing the political ladder. People with a minimum of education constitute half the electorate but less than 2 percent of all MPs. Whereas at one time graduates of Eton, Harrow, and other leading public schools predominated in Cabinet, today less than a third of MPs have attended public schools.

The relatively small percentage of university graduates in the country contribute more than two-thirds of the members of the House of Commons. The expansion of universities has broken the dominance of Oxford and Cambridge; barely one-quarter of MPs went to these two institutions. The concentration of graduates from many different British universities in top jobs is a sign of a meritocracy, in which governors qualified by education replace an aristocracy based on birth and family.

Class

The concept of **class** can refer to occupational status or serve as a shorthand term for the social status conferred by income and education. Occupation is the most commonly used indicator of class. Manual workers are usually described as the working class and non-manual workers as the middle class.

Historically, party competition has been interpreted in class terms; the Conservative Party has been described as a middle-class party, and Labour as a working-class party. One reason why class has appeared as relatively important in England is the absence of big divisions on race, religion, or language, as in the United States,

Schools and street scenes in big cities show that Britain is now a multi-racial society.

J. C. Tordai/Panos Pictures

Canada, or Northern Ireland. Today, the upper class no longer commands deference and celebrities owing their prominence to television and achievements in sports, rock music, or making money are better known than dukes or earls.

Most Britons have a mixture of middle-class and working-class attributes. The mixed-class group has been increasing, as changes in the economy have reduced the number of manual jobs and increased the number of middle-class jobs. Many occupations, such as computer technicians and office workers, now have an indeterminate social status. Today, the Registrar-General classifies two-thirds of the population in one or another level of the middle class. However, when British people are asked what class they belong to, 57 percent reject placing themselves in either the middle or the working class.

The relationship between class and party has become limited. No party now wins as much as half the vote of middle-class electors. In working-class occupations, just over half of unskilled workers voted Labour and just under half of skilled workers did so (see Table 8.3). Due to the cross-class appeal of parties, only two-fifths of voters conform to the stereotypes of middle-class Conservatives or working-class Labour voters. Socioeconomic experiences other than occupation also influence voting. At each level of the class structure, people who belong to trade unions are more likely to vote Labour than Conservative. Housing creates neighborhoods with political relevance. People who live in local government-owned council houses tend to vote Labour, while Conservatives do relatively well among homeowners.

Mass Media

The mass media tends to reenforce differences arising from class and education. The British press is sharply divided into a few quality papers—such as *The Times, The Guardian, Daily Telegraph, The Independent,* and *The Financial Times*—that carry news and comment at an intellectual level higher than American newspapers, and mass circulation tabloids that concentrate on trivia and trash, such as *The Sun,* Britain's biggest selling newspaper. Most papers tend to lean toward one party but not uncritically so. For example, when the Conservatives became unpopular with the electorate in the 1990s, some newspapers that were previously pro-Conservative sought to follow their voters in admiring Tony Blair. He actively courted the support of right-wing newspapers but following his fall in popular approval during the Iraq War former press allies became vocal critics.

Historically, radio and television were a monopoly of the British Broadcasting Corporation (BBC). Seeking to educate and to elevate, the BBC was also very respectful of all forms of authority, including government. The introduction of commercial television in the 1950s and commercial radio in the following decade has made all broadcasting channels populist in competing for audiences. There are now many television channels and a great variety of radio stations. The law forbids selling advertising to politicians, parties, or political causes.

Current affairs programs often seek audiences by exposing alleged failings of government, and TV personalities make their names by the tough cross-examination of politicians of all parties. However, the government of the day controls the renewal of the licenses of broadcasting companies and it sets the annual fee that every viewer must pay for noncommercial BBC programs, currently about $250 a year. Broadcasters try to avoid favoring one party because over a period control of government is likely to shift between parties and with it the power to make decisions that affect the revenue and licenses of broadcasting companies. Public opinion polls show that television is the primary source of political news, and it is much more trusted than the press.

Since political socialization is a lifetime learning process, the loyalties of voters are shaped by an accumulation of influences. In the course of a lifetime, an individual develops values expressing what government ought to do. These political values are independent of family and socioeconomic interests. Economic values concerned with trade unions, the welfare state, business, and privatization influence choices between parties. The judgments that people make about government reflect their preexisting values, and this is particularly true of popular evaluations of party and leaders.

POLITICAL PARTICIPATION

If political participation is defined as paying taxes and drawing benefits from public programs, then everyone is involved, for public policies provide benefits at every stage of life, from maternity allowances to mothers through education, employment and unemployment benefits, health care, and pensions in old age.

An election is the one opportunity people have to influence government directly. Every citizen age 18 or older is eligible to vote. Local government officials register voters, and the list is revised annually, ensuring that nearly everyone eligible to vote is actually registered. Turnout at general elections has averaged 77 percent since 1950. However, in the 2001 election it fell to 59.4 percent.

In an attempt to boost turnout, the Labour government has experimented with voting by mail rather than in person. When postal ballots were mailed out in several North of England constituencies during the 2004 European Parliament election, three-fifths of those receiving a ballot did not bother to return it. In the 2005 general election postal voting on demand led to serious allegations of fraud in several inner-city constituencies. Even then, turnout was no more than 61 percent.

The wider the definition of political participation, the greater the number who can be said to be at least indirectly or intermittently involved in politics (see Figure 8.4). Two-fifths have signed a petition on a public issue and a third say that they feel close to a political party. Political values can also be reflected in refusing to buy a product: one-quarter say that politics has affected their shopping by leading them to boycott a product. The most politically involved are no more than one-tenth of the electorate, those who say they are very interested in politics, take part in a demonstration or are active in a party or pressure group.

Although political activists are a minority of the electorate, their actions are the focus of much political news. Because of the concentration of the media and politics, a London-based protest with a few thousand people can get press coverage, even though those participating are only one–one-hundredth of 1 percent of the electorate.

Political Recruitment

We can view recruitment into politics deductively or inductively. The deductive approach defines the job to be done and individuals are recruited with skills appropriate to the task; this practice is favored by management consultants. Alternatively, we can inductively examine the influences that lead people into politics and ask: given their skills and motives, what can such people do? The constraints of history and institutions make the inductive approach more realistic.

The most important political roles in Britain are those of Cabinet minister, higher civil servant, partisan advisers, and intermittent public persons analogous to inside the beltway experts in Washington, D.C. Each group has its own recruitment pattern. To become a Cabinet minister, an individual must first be

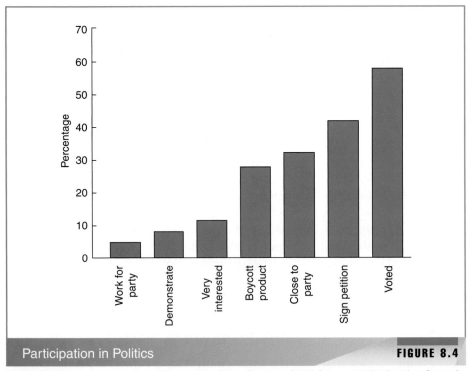

Participation in Politics

FIGURE 8.4

Source: Roger Jowell and the Central Coordinating Team, European Social Survey 2002/03 (London: Centre for Comparative Social Surveys, City University). Interviews conducted in the United Kingdom, September 24, 2002 to February 4, 2003 (N = 1908).

elected to Parliament and spend years attracting positive attention there. Shortly after leaving the university, partisan advisers become assistants to politicians and then "graduate" to careers as MPs, journalists, or lobbyists. Individuals enter the civil service shortly after leaving the university by passing a highly competitive entrance examination; promotion is based on achievement and approval by seniors. Intermittent public persons gain access to ministers and civil servants because of their expertise or position in organizations outside politics, or because they are personally trusted by leading politicians.

In all political roles, starting early in a political career is usually a precondition of success, because experience is positively valued. But aspiring Cabinet ministers are not expected to begin in local politics and work their way gradually to the top at Westminster. Instead, at an early age an individual becomes a "cadet" recruit to a junior position, such as a parliamentary assistant to an MP or a "gofer" for a Cabinet minister. This path can lead to a central political role after gaining skill and seniority.

Geography is a second major influence on recruitment. Ministers, higher civil servants, and other public persons spend their working lives in London. A change at Downing Street does not bring in policymakers from a different part of the country, as can happen in the White House when a president from Texas succeeds a president from Arkansas. Since London is atypical of the cities and towns in which most British people live, there is a gap between the everyday lives of policymakers and the majority on whose behalf they act.

Cabinet Ministers

For a person ambitious to be a Cabinet minister, becoming an MP is the necessary first step. Nomination for a winnable or safe seat in the House of Commons is in the hands of local party selection committees. A candidate does not have to be resident in the constituency in which he or she is nominated. Hence, it is possible for a young person to go straight from the university to a job in the House of Commons or party headquarters, and then look around the country for a nomination for a winnable seat, a process that takes years. Once selected for a constituency in which his or her party has a big majority, the MP can then expect to be reelected routinely for a decade or more. After entering the

House of Commons, an MP seeks to be noticed. Some ways of doing so—for example, grabbing headlines by questioning the wisdom of the party leadership—make it difficult to gain promotion to ministerial rank. Other approaches assist promotion, such as successfully attacking opposition leaders in debate or being well informed about a politically important topic. So, too, does showing loyalty to the party leader.

Experience in the Commons does not prepare an individual for the work of a minister. An MP's chief concerns are dealing with people and talking about what government ought to do. A minister must also be able to handle paperwork, relate political generalities to specific technical problems facing his or her department, and make hard decisions when all the alternatives are unpopular.

The restriction of ministerial appointments to MPs prevents a nationwide canvass for appointees. A prime minister must distribute about 100 jobs among approximately 200 MPs in the governing party who are experienced in Parliament and are not ruled themselves out of consideration on grounds of parliamentary inexperience, old age, political extremism, personal unreliability, or lack of interest in office. An MP has a better than even chance of a junior ministerial appointment if he or she serves three terms in Parliament. Exceptionally, Tony Blair has given ministerial posts to personal supporters who he has made life peers; they owe their posts to their patron, Tony Blair, rather than to voters and to the Labour Party.

A minister learns on the job. Usually, an MP is first given a junior post as an under secretary and then promoted to Minister of State before becoming a full member of the Cabinet. In the process, an individual is usually shuffled from one department to another, having to learn new subject matter with each shift between departments. The average minister can expect to stay in a particular job for about two years, and never knows when the accidents of politics—a death or an unexpected resignation—will lead to a transfer to another department. The rate of ministerial turnover in Britain is one of the highest in Europe. The minister who gets a new job as the result of a reshuffle usually arrives at a department with no previous experience of its problems. It takes time to learn how to deal with the particular problems of a department. Anthony Crosland, an able Labour minister, reckoned: "It takes you six months to get your head properly above water, a year to get the general drift of most of the field, and two years really to master the whole of a department."[30]

Higher Civil Servants

Whereas MPs come and go from ministerial office with great frequency, civil servants have a job in Whitehall for the whole of their working lives. Higher civil servants are recruited without specific professional qualifications or training. They are meant to be the "best and the brightest"—a requirement that has traditionally meant getting a prestigious degree in history, literature, or languages. The Fulton Committee on the Civil Service recommended that recruits should have "relevant" specialist knowledge, but members could not decide what kind of knowledge was relevant to the work of government.[31] The Civil Service Commission tests candidates for their ability to summarize lengthy prose papers, resolve problems by fitting specific facts to general regulations, draw inferences from a simple table of social statistics, and perform well in group discussions about problems of government.

Because bright civil service entrants lack specialized skills and need decades to reach the highest posts, role socialization into Whitehall by senior civil servants is especially important. The process makes for continuity, since the head of the civil service usually starts there as a young official under a head who had himself entered the civil service many decades before.

In the course of a career, civil servants become specialists in the difficult task of managing political ministers and government business. As the television series, *Yes, Minister* shows, they are adept at saying "yes" to a Cabinet minister when they mean "perhaps" and saying "up to a point" when they really mean "no." Increasingly, ministers have tended to discourage civil servants from pointing out obstacles to what the government wants to do; they look to "can do" advisors from outside the civil service.

Political Advisors and Intermittent Public Persons

The Blair government has greatly expanded the appointment of two types of political advisors. The largest number are aptly called "political" advisors, for their job is to mobilize political support for the government and for the Cabinet minister to whom they are assigned. Because their background is in party politics and the media, they bring skills that civil servants often lack. But because they have no prior experience of the civil service, they are often unaware of its conventions and legal obligations. The methods used by political appointees to put a desirable spin on what the government is doing can backfire and cause public controversy.

Another category of political advisors are experts with specialist knowledge about such problems as environmental pollution or cloning. While they may be inexperienced in the ways of Whitehall, they can contribute expertise that is often lacking in government departments, and they are often long-time supporters of the governing party too.

Most leaders of institutions such as the universities, banks, churches, and trade unions do not think of themselves as politicians and have not stood for public office. They are principally concerned with their own organization. But when government actions impinge on their work, they become involved in politics, offering ministers advice and sometimes criticism. They are thus intermittent public persons.

Selective Recruitment

Nothing could be more selective than a parliamentary election that results in one person becoming prime minister of a country. Yet nothing is more representative, because an election is the one occasion when every adult can participate in politics with equal effect.

Traditionally, political leaders had high social status and wealth before gaining political office. Aristocrats, business people, and trade union leaders can no longer expect to translate their high standing in other fields into an important political position. Today, politics is a full-time occupation. As careers become more specialized, professional politicians become increasingly distant from other spheres of British life.

The greater the scope of activities defined as political, the greater the number of people actively involved in government. Government influence has forced company directors, television executives, and university heads to become involved in politics and public policy. Leadership in organizations outside

Whitehall gives such individuals freedom to act independently of government, but the interdependence of public and private institutions, whether profitmaking or nonprofit, is now so great that sooner or later they meet in discussions about what constitutes the public interest.

ORGANIZING GROUP INTERESTS

Civil society—that is, institutions independent of government—has flourished in Britain for centuries. So confident are leaders of civil society that they discuss public affairs with government officials in expectation that they can exert pressure on behalf of interests they represent.

The scope of group demands varies enormously from the narrow concerns of an association for single parents to the encompassing economic policies of organizations representing business or trade unions. Groups also differ in the nature of their interests; some are concerned with material objectives, whereas others deal with single causes, such as television violence or race relations.

The Confederation of British Industries is the chief representative organization of British business. As its name implies, its membership is large and varied. The Institute of Directors represents the highest paid individuals at the top of large and small businesses.

The biggest businesses in Britain usually have direct contacts with Whitehall and with ministers, whatever their party, because of the importance of their activities for the British economy—and for Britain's role in the international economy. For example, British Petroleum is one of the world's largest oil companies. Most of the oil it drills is found outside the United Kingdom. Government deems the success of such a company as important for national security as well as the national economy. The construction industry has access to government because home-building is important for the national economy and Whitehall's tight control over land use influences where houses can be built.

The chief labor organization is the Trades Union Congress (TUC); its members are trade unions that represent many different types of workers, some white collar and some blue collar, and some unions have competing interests. Most member unions of the TUC are affiliated with the Labour Party, and some leading trade unionists have been Communists or Maoists. None has ever been a supporter of the Conservative Party.

Changes in employment patterns have eroded union membership; less than one-third of the British labor force now belongs to unions. Over the years, the membership of trade unions has shifted from workers in such heavy industries as coal and railways to white-collar workers in the public sector. Three-fifths of trade union members are now public-sector workers, such as teachers and health service employees. Today, less than one-third of trade union members are manual workers and more than half are women. Trade unions have a special relationship with government, for more than half their members are employed by the public sector; elected representatives thus control their wages, and strikes or go-slow actions by teachers, police, or firemen can cause political embarrassment to the government.

Britain has many voluntary and charitable associations, ranging from clubs of football team supporters to the Automobile Association. It is also home to a number of internationally active nongovernmental organizations, such as Oxfam, concerned with the problems of poorer developing countries, and Amnesty International, concerned with political prisoners. The latter organizations try to bring pressure not only on Westminster but also on organizations such as the World Bank and on repressive governments around the world.

Unlike political parties, interest groups do not seek influence by contesting elections; they want to influence policies regardless of which party wins. Nonetheless, there do remain ties between interest groups and political parties. Trade unions have been institutionally part of the Labour Party since its foundation in 1900. The connection between business associations and the Conservatives is not formal, but its traditional commitment to private enterprise is congenial to business. Notwithstanding common interests, both trade unions and business groups demonstrate their autonomy by criticizing partisan allies acting against the group's interest and seeking to work with whichever party is in government.

Party politicians seek to distance themselves from pressure groups. Conservatives appreciate that they can win an election only by winning the votes of ordinary citizens, including some trade union members. Tony Blair has succeeded in attracting big donations from multimillionaire businessmen to finance his campaigning activities. However, this has led union leaders to attack his government as unsympathetic and threaten to withdraw cash contributions vital to Labour Party finance. A few small unions have left the Labour Party.

To lobby successfully, interest groups must be able to identify those officials most important in making public policy. They concentrate their efforts on Whitehall. When pressure groups were asked to rank the most influential offices and institutions, they named the prime minister first by a long distance; Cabinet ministers came second, the media third, and senior civil servants fourth (see Figure 8.5). Less than 1 percent thought MPs outside the ministerial ranks were of primary importance. However, pressure groups do not expect to spend a

lot of time in Downing Street. Most pressure group contacts are with sections within a government department concerned with issues of little public concern but of immediate interest to the group. Groups that stir up confrontational media publicity make it difficult to gain a sympathetic private hearing from government departments.[32]

What Interest Groups Want

Most interest groups pursue four goals:

1. Information about government policies and changes in policies
2. Sympathetic administration of established policies
3. Influence on policymaking
4. Symbolic status, such as being given the prefix "Royal" in their title

Whitehall departments are happy to consult with interest groups insofar as they can provide government officials with reciprocal benefits:

1. Cooperation in administering and implementing policies
2. Information about what is happening in their field
3. Evaluation of the consequences of policies under consideration
4. Support for government initiatives

As long as the needs of Whitehall and interest groups are complementary, they can bargain as professionals sharing common concerns. Both sides seek a negotiated agreement. This avoids contested decisions being made by politicians who know less and care less about details than interest groups and civil servants involved in departmental administration.

Organizing for Political Action in Civil Society

The more committed members are to a pressure group's goals, the more confidently leaders can speak for a united membership. Consumers are more difficult to organize because they have no social contacts with people who have the same taste in consumer goods. Drivers of Ford cars are a category rather than

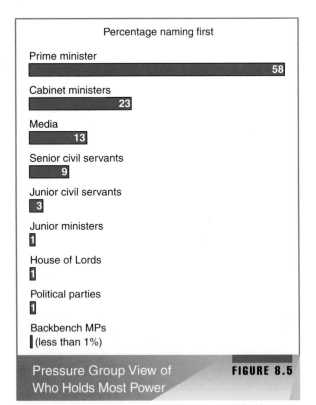

Percentage naming first

Prime minister
58

Cabinet ministers
23

Media
13

Senior civil servants
9

Junior civil servants
3

Junior ministers
1

House of Lords
1

Political parties
1

Backbench MPs
(less than 1%)

Pressure Group View of Who Holds Most Power   **FIGURE 8.5**

Source: Survey of officials of business, labor, and campaign groups, as reported in Rob Baggott, "The Measurement of Change in Pressure Group Politics," *Talking Politics* 5, 1 (1992): 19.

a social group. Changes in the economy, in class structure, and in the life styles of generations have resulted in a decline in the "dense" social capital networks of villages. Individuals are now free to choose among a variety of networks.

Whitehall civil servants find it administratively convenient to deal with united interest groups that can implement agreements. But decades of attempts to plan the British economy demonstrate that business and union leaders cannot guarantee that their nominal followers will carry out bargains that leaders make. Group members who care about an issue may also disagree about what their leaders ought to do.

Individuals usually have a multiplicity of identities that often conflict—for example, as workers desiring higher wages and as consumers wanting lower prices. The spread of mass consumption and decline in trade union membership has altered the balance between these priorities. As a trade union leader has recognized, "Our members are consumers too."[33]

Even if a pressure group is internally united, its demands may be counteracted by opposing demands from other groups. This is normally the case in economic policy, where interests are well defined, well organized, and competing. Ministers can play off producers against consumers or business against unions to increase their scope for choice and present their policies as "something for everybody" compromises. The more a group's values are consistent with the cultural norms of society as a whole, the easier it is to equate its interest with the public interest. But in an open society such as Britain the claims of one group to speak for the public interest can easily be challenged by competing groups.

The centralization of authority in British government means that interest groups must accept as given the political values and priorities of the governing party. **Insider pressure groups** usually have values in harmony with every party. These groups are often noncontroversial, such as the Royal National Institute for the Blind. Insiders advance their case in quiet negotiations with Whitehall departments. Demands tend to be restricted to what is politically possible in the short term, given the values and commitments of the government of the day.[34]

Outsider pressure groups are unable to negotiate because their demands are inconsistent with the party

in power. If they are inconsistent with the views of the opposition as well, then outsider groups are completely marginalized. Outsider groups without any influence in Whitehall often campaign through the media. To television viewers, their demonstrations appear as evidence of their importance; in fact, they are often signs of a lack of political influence. Green pressure groups face the dilemma of campaigning for fundamental change in hopes that eventually Whitehall departments will turn their way or of becoming insiders working within the system to improve the environment to some extent but not as much as some ecologists would like.

Keeping Pressure Groups at a Distance

For a generation after World War II ministers endorsed the corporatist philosophy of bringing together business, trade union, and political representatives in tripartite institutions to discuss such controversial issues as inflation and unemployment, and the restructuring of declining industries. Corporatist bargaining assumed a consensus on political priorities and goals and that each group's leaders could deliver the cooperation of those they claimed to represent. In practice, neither Labour nor Conservative governments were able to maintain a consensus. Nor were interest group leaders able to deliver their nominal followers. By 1979, unemployment and inflation were both out of control.

The Thatcher administration demonstrated that a government firmly committed to distinctive values can ignore group demands and lay down its own pattern of policy. It did so by dealing at arm's length with both trade unions and business groups. Instead of consulting with interest groups, it practiced state-distancing, keeping the government out of everyday marketplace activities, such as wage bargaining and deciding prices and investment.

A state-distancing strategy concentrates on policies that government can implement without the agreement of interest groups. It emphasizes the use of legislation to achieve goals, since no interest group can defy an act of Parliament. Laws have reduced the capacity of trade unions to frustrate government policies through industrial action. The sale of state-owned industries has removed government from immediate responsibility for the operation of major

Labour Prime Minister
Tony Blair and Labour
Chancellor of the
Exchequer Gordon Brown
were the two most power-
ful individuals in British
government for a decade.
However, they often did
not see eye to eye.

Corbis

industries. Labour Chancellor Gordon Brown transferred to the Bank of England responsibility for
monetary policy.

State-distancing places less reliance on negotiations with interest groups and more on the independent authority of the Crown. Business and labor are
free to carry on as they like—but only within the pattern imposed by the government's policy and legislation. Most unions and some business leaders do not
like being "outside the loop" when government makes
decisions. Education and health service pressure
groups like it even less, because they depend on government appropriations to fund their activities and
cannot effectively turn to the market as an alternative
source of revenue.

While in opposition, Tony Blair often spoke
about the need to achieve "the reinvention of community,"[35] implying endorsement of corporatist
institutions of cooperation between representatives
of different groups in society. As prime minister,
however, Blair has made sure that meetings with
groups are on terms laid down by Downing Street.
When conflicts are apparent between pressure
groups, he has often avoided getting involved to broker agreements. However, once Blair has laid down a
pattern of policy, he has demanded acceptance by
pressure groups with the claim that he speaks in the
name of the public interest.

PARTY SYSTEM AND
ELECTORAL CHOICE

British government is party government, for parties
nominate parliamentary candidates and elect a leader
who is prime minister or in charge of the opposition.
An election gives voters the choice of deciding
between parties competing for the right to govern.

A Multiplicity of Choices

A general election must occur at least once every five
years; within that period, the prime minister is free to
call an election at any time. Although every prime minister tries to pick a date when victory is likely, often this
goal is denied. An election offers a voter a very simple
choice between several candidates wanting to represent one of the 646 constituencies of the House of
Commons. The party leader's name is not on the ballot.
Within each constituency, the winner is the candidate
who is **first past the post,** that is, the person who has
a plurality (the largest number) of votes even if this is a
not an absolute majority of more than half the vote.

If only two parties contest a constituency, the candidate with the most votes will have an absolute
majority. But since at least four candidates now contest most constituencies, a candidate can often win
with less than half the vote, thanks to the division of

the vote among multiple competitors. For example, in a hard-fought contest between four parties in Inverness in 1992, the Liberal Democrats won the seat with only 26 percent of the vote.

The winner nationally is the party that gains the most constituency seats. In 1951 and in February 1974, the party winning the most votes nationally did not win the most seats and thus did not form the government. At the next general election, the Labour Party would be able to win an absolute majority in the House of Commons with a smaller share of the vote than the Conservative Party because its electoral strength is concentrated rather than spread evenly throughout the country.

Between 1945 and 1970 Britain had a two-party system; the Conservative and Labour parties together took an average of 91 percent of the popular vote and in 1951 as much as 97 percent (Figure 8.6). The Liberals had difficulty fielding candidates to contest most seats and even more difficulty in winning votes and seats. Support for the two largest parties was evenly balanced; Labour won four elections and the Conservatives won four.

In a two-party system the failure of one party tends to benefit its opponent. However, when both the largest parties are discredited, other parties have an opportunity to gain support. A **multiparty system** emerged in the elections of 1974. The Liberals won nearly one-fifth of the vote, and Nationalists did well in Scotland, Wales, and Northern Ireland. Together, the Conservative and Labour parties took only 75 percent of the vote. The 1980s saw the Labour Party vote plummet as the Alliance of Liberals and Social Democrats won almost a quarter of the popular vote. Although the Alliance broke up after the 1987 election, the fragmentation of voters and parties has continued since.

Whether Britain can be described as having a two-party system depends on the priority given to the following points:

1. The number of parties competing for votes varies from three to five in different parts of the United Kingdom. In England, three parties—Labour, Conservatives, and Liberal Democrats—compete for votes. In 2005 the United Kingdom Independence Party fought a majority of seats too, campaigning in opposition to the European Union. In Scotland and Wales there are normally four parties, and the Scottish National and Plaid Cymru (Welsh Nationalist) parties win seats too.

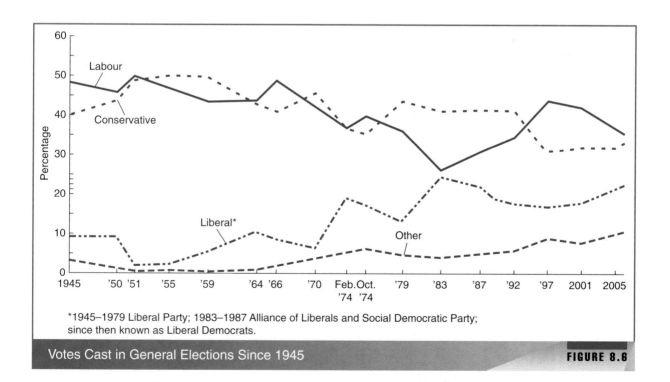

*1945–1979 Liberal Party; 1983–1987 Alliance of Liberals and Social Democratic Party; since then known as Liberal Democrats.

Votes Cast in General Elections Since 1945   **FIGURE 8.6**

In Northern Ireland, at least five parties normally contest seats.

2. The two largest parties do not monopolize votes. Since 1974, the Conservative and Labour parties together have won an average of three-quarters of the vote and in the 2005 election gained just 67.6 percent of the total vote.

3. At the constituency level, the two largest parties in Westminster are often not the two leading parties. At the 2005 election, in more than one-quarter of constituencies one or both of the two front-running parties was neither Labour nor Conservative.

4. More than half a dozen parties consistently win seats in the House of Commons. In 2005 "third" parties won ninety-three seats in the Commons.

5. Significant shifts in voting usually do not involve individuals moving between the Labour and Conservative parties but in and out of the ranks of abstainers or between the Liberal Democrats and the two largest parties.

To win a substantial number of seats in the House of Commons, a party must either gain at least one-third of the popular vote nationally or concentrate its votes in a limited number of constituencies. For this reason, the distribution of seats in the House of Commons is different from the distribution of the share of votes. The Labour Party wins more than 55 percent of the seats in the House of Commons with 35 percent of the popular vote (see Figures 8.6 and 8.7).

Opposing the Labour government in the House of Commons are MPs from parties that have collectively won almost two-thirds of the popular vote. However, they have less than half the MPs because that vote is divided among more than eight different parties plus independents. The variety of opposition parties makes the left-right classification an oversimplification. Nationalist parties in Scotland, Wales, and Northern Ireland win seats because they concentrate their candidates in one part of the United Kingdom from which they seek independence. Although the Liberal Democrats often win more than one-fifth of the popular vote, because their support is spread relatively evenly across the country, their candidates are far more likely to finish second or third rather than first. In a totally proportional system of representation, the party's vote share in

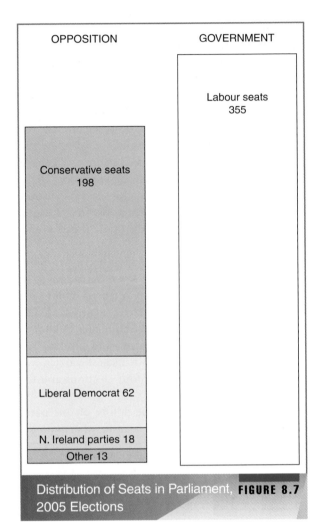

Distribution of Seats in Parliament, **FIGURE 8.7** 2005 Elections

2005 would have given it 142 seats, more than twice the sixty-two seats it received.

Britain's system of disproportional representation can manufacture a House of Commons majority for a party with as little as 35 percent of the popular vote. If Britain had a proportional representation system, a majority government would require a coalition between at least two parties, since no party has come close to winning half the popular vote for half a century.

Defenders of the British electoral system argue that proportionality is not a goal in itself. The first-past-the-post system is justified because it places responsibility for government in the hands of a single party. This justification is used in the United States, where the president can be described as representing all the people, even though he wins about half the vote. In continental European countries using proportional representation, coalition or minority governments are the norm. When a coalition is necessary, a party finishing third in the popular vote can determine who governs by choosing either the party second or first in the popular vote as its partner in government.

The strongest advocates of proportional representation are the Liberal Democrats, the party that would benefit most from a change in the electoral system. A change is also supported by those who believe that a coalition government is a better government because it encourages broader interparty consensus.

Successive British governments have altered the electoral system for contests that do not affect the composition of the Westminster Parliament. In Northern Ireland proportional representation has been used for more than three decades. The Scottish Parliament and the Welsh Assembly are elected by a system involving proportional representation and so are British members of the European Parliament. The mayor of Greater London is elected by the alternative vote, ensuring that the winner is the first or second choice of more than half the voters. The Westminster system remains unaltered because the decision about what kind of voting system to have is not determined by reasoning from abstract principles but by the interests of the party in power.

Control of Party Organization

Political parties are often referred to as machines, but this description is very misleading, for parties cannot manufacture votes. Nor can a political party be commanded as an army can be commanded. Parties are like universities; they are inherently decentralized, and people belong to them for a variety of motives.

Much of the work of party organizations is devoted to keeping together three disparate parts of the party: those who vote for it, the minority who are active in its constituency associations, and the party in Parliament. If the party has a majority in Parliament, there is a fourth group, the party in government. Whether the party leader is the prime minister or the leader of the opposition, he or she must try to keep all parts of the party together in support of his or her position, or risk well-publicized intraparty disputes that can alienate voters.

Each British party leader is elected by rules that differ from party to party. The Labour Party leader is determined by an electoral college composed of three groups: Labour MPs, constituency party members, and trade unions. Each group has a very different number of members and method of deciding which candidate to back. In order to create a ballot when the party leader is in place, one-fifth of Labour MPs must sign nomination papers for a challenger, and if there is a vacancy due to the resignation of the leader, one-eighth must sign the nomination paper.

The Conservative Party in Parliament has been separate from the campaigning arm of the party, the Conservative Central Office, and local constituency associations. Until 1965, the party leader was not elected but "emerged" as the result of consultation among senior MPs and peers. Since then, the Conservatives have elected their leader. There is now a ballot among Conservative MPs and the two MPs with the most votes are then voted on by the party membership at large, whose choice is decisive. The current Conservative leader, David Cameron, was chosen by this method in 2005 because of his youth, and with it distance from past Conservative defeats, was seen as most likely to appeal to middle-of-the-road voters whose support is necessary for the party to win the next general election.

The Liberal Democrats have a small central organization, in keeping with their relatively few MPs. Liberal Democrats have sought to build up the party's strength by winning council seats at local government elections. At parliamentary elections, it targets seats where the party is strong locally. This strategy has paid off; it has more than trebled its number of MPs from twenty in 1992 to sixty-two in 2005 while its share of the vote was only 0.5 percent higher. The candidates for leadership are nominated by Liberal MPs and the leader, currently Menzies Campbell, is determined by vote of the party's membership.

A party leader is strongest when he or she is also prime minister. Constitutional principles and Cabinet patronage strengthen a prime minister's hand. Moreover, an open attack on a prime minister threatens electoral defeat as a result of conflict within the party. However, Margaret Thatcher lost the prime ministership by a vote of Conservative MPs, and by 2006 Labour MPs were threatening to force a vote on Tony Blair's tenure if he did not commit himself to a date for leaving office before the next election.

The headquarters of each party provides more or less routine organizational and publicity services to constituency parties and to the party in Parliament. Each party has an annual conference to debate policy and to vote on some policy resolutions. Constituency parties are nationally significant because each selects its own parliamentary candidate. The **decentralization** of the selection process has allowed the choice of parliamentary candidates with a wide variety of political outlooks and abilities. The Thatcher era encouraged an ideological litmus test on both the right and the left. Under Tony Blair, the Labour Party has introduced more central direction in choosing candidates. Blair has justified centralization on the grounds it would promote the adoption of more women candidates in constituencies electing Labour MPS, and this has been the case. New women MPs have also disproportionately supported Blair against critics within the Labour Party.

Party Images and Appeals

Differences of ideology are often simplified in terms of a left-right scale, with the left representing socialist values and the right the values of Conservatives. While the terminology of left and right is part of the language of elite politicians, it is rejected by the great majority of British voters. When asked to place themselves on a left-right scale, the median voter chooses the central position, and only a tenth place themselves on the far left or far right. Consequently, parties that veer to one or another extreme risk losing votes.

When public opinion is examined across a variety of issues—such as inflation, protecting the environment, spending money on the health service, and trade union legislation—a majority of Conservative, Labour, and Liberal Democratic voters tend to agree. However, Tony Blair has gone too far in proclaiming the goal of making Labour a party that is "the political arm of none other than the British people as a whole." This view denies the existence of politics; that is, debate about what the government of the day ought to do—and which party and which MP ought to be prime minister.

Big divisions in contemporary British politics often cut across party lines, for example, attitudes toward the European Union divide both Labour and Conservative MPs. So has the Iraq War. Any attempt to impute a coherent ideology to a political party is doomed to failure, for institutions cannot think, and parties are not organized to debate philosophy but to fight elections.

Instead of campaigning in ideological terms or by appealing to collectivist economic interests, parties increasingly stress consensual goals, such as promoting prosperity and fighting crime. They compete in terms of which party or party leader can best be trusted to do what people want—or whether it is time for a change because one party has been in office for a long time. The titles of election manifestos are virtually interchangeable between the Conservative and Labour parties—and so too is much of their content (see Table 8.4).

TABLE 8.4

Consensual Title of Party Election Manifestos

Year	Conservatives	Labour
1964	Prosperity With a Purpose	Let's Go With Labour
1966	Action, not Words	Time for Decision
1970	A Better Tomorrow	Now Britain's Strong—Let's Make It Great to Live In
1974	Firm Action for a Fair Britain	Let Us Work Together
1974	Putting Britain First	Britain Will Win With Labour
1979	The Conservative Manifesto	The Labour Way Is the Better Way
1983	The Challenge of Our Times	The New Hope for Britain
1987	The Next Moves Forward	Britain Will Win
1992	The Best Future for Britain	Time to Get Britain Working Again
1997	You Can Only Be Sure	Because Britain Deserves Better Than the Conservatives
2001	Time for Common Sense	Ambition for Britain
2005	It's Time for Action	Britain Forward not Back

In office, the governing party has the votes to enact any parliamentary legislation it wishes, regardless of protests by the opposition. However, most of the legislation introduced by the government is noncontroversial or popular, so the opposition dare not vote against the bill's principle. For every government bill that the opposition votes against on principle in the House of Commons, three are adopted with interparty agreement.[36]

Most policies of the government are not set out in its party manifesto; they are inherited from predecessors of the same or a different party. When the Thatcher administration entered office in 1979, it inherited hundreds of programs enacted by preceding governments, including some on the statute books since 1760. The median law was more than half a century old.[37] In more than a decade, the Thatcher administration introduced dozens of new programs. It repealed programs inherited from its predecessors— and it repealed some of its own programs that were quickly recognized as mistakes. When Thatcher left office, two-thirds of the programs for which the government was responsible, such as the national health service, were those inherited from previous administrations. When public expenditure is analyzed, the influence of the "dead hand" of the past is greater still. Only 11 percent of public expenditure was devoted to programs that Thatcher started and almost three-quarters went to programs based on laws enacted before the end of World War II.

Prior to the 1997 general election, the Labour Party pledged that it would not immediately alter the spending limits of the Conservative government. It spent much of its first term seeking to maintain pledges on controlling public expenditure and introducing devolution and other constitutional reforms that Blair had inherited as commitments made before he became leader. The Blair government started major measures to reform the delivery of public services in the second term. But after ten years in office, Blair has complained that he still has a lot to do to alter the legacy of domestic policy commitments made by previous Labour and Conservative governments.

The freedom of action of the governing party is limited by constraints embedded in the obligations of office. Once in office, ministers find that all the laws enacted by their predecessors must be enforced, even if the government of the day would not have enacted them. A newly elected government also inherits many commitments to foreign countries and to the European Union. As a former Conservative minister said of his Labour successors, "They inherited our problems and our remedies."[38]

CENTRAL AUTHORITY AND DECENTRALIZED DELIVERY OF POLICIES

A unitary state is characterized by the **centralization** of political authority. Decisions made by central government are of fundamental importance; they are binding on all public agencies through acts of Parliament and regulations prepared in Whitehall. In addition, Whitehall controls taxation and public expenditure to a degree unusual among other member states of the European Union, where coalition government and federalism encourage territorial and functional decentralization.

For ordinary individuals the actions of government are tangible only when services are delivered to them in local schools, in a doctor's office, or to their home. However, Whitehall departments usually do not deliver policies themselves. Most public goods and services are delivered by public agencies outside the framework of Whitehall ministries and five-sixths of public employees work for non-Whitehall agencies.[39] Thus, making and delivering public policies involves *intra*governmental politics.

Ministers do not want to be in charge of delivering services for many reasons. Ministers may wish to avoid charges of political interference (tax collection is placed in the Office of Revenue and Customs). They may want to allow flexibility in the market (the Bank of England), lend an aura of impartiality to quasi-judicial activities (the Monopolies Commission), show respect for the extragovernmental origins of an institution (Oxford and Cambridge universities), allow qualified professionals to regulate technical matters (the Royal College of Physicians and Surgeons), or remove controversial matters from Whitehall (the Family Planning Association). Ministers, and above all the prime minister, prefer to focus on the glamorous "high" politics of foreign affairs and economic management. Since "low level" services remain important to most voters' lives, however, ministers are under pressure to do something when there is evidence of declining standards in schools, lengthening queues for hospital admission, and increasing crime on the streets.

While politicians can make headlines by announcing a good intention, turning popular intentions into a program that delivers services to citizens requires scarce resources of time and money. Running *the Whitehall obstacle race* is the first step in intragovernmental politics. Interdepartmental negotiations are required to get ministers to agree how credit and responsibility are to be divided up; how a new program relates to existing commitments; which agency should administer the program and how much money is needed. Since most new policies must take into account the effects of existing policies in a crowded policy "space," negotiations are often time consuming. From the point of view of a prime minister who believes that popular election makes it desirable to take many actions and take them quickly, the process of turning headline statements of intention into practical programs is often frustrating.

Treasury control of public expenditure means that before a bill can be put to Parliament the Treasury must authorize the additional expenditure required, since increased spending implies increased taxation. Ministers in charge of spending departments dislike constant Treasury reminders that there are strict cash limits on what they can spend. In the words of a veteran Treasury official, "the Treasury stands for reality."[40]

A departmental minister must pilot a bill through Parliament. If a matter is controversial, a minister will face attacks from the opposition and a host of amendments designed to test the minister's understanding of a policy. While the governing party can usually count on having the votes needed to secure passage of a bill, the pro-market policies of Blair have led some Labour MPs to rebel, a major embarrassment to the prime minister and the minister in charge of a bill.

In addition to running the Whitehall obstacle race, a minister often must negotiate agreement with public agencies outside Whitehall and with affected interest groups. The formally centralized authority of the Crown co-exists with a maze of institutions with varying and overlapping territorial and functional responsibilities. *Local government* is subordinate to central government: in Scotland and in Wales, to devolved representative assemblies. Westminster has

the power to write or rewrite the laws that determine what locally elected governments do and spend, or even to abolish local authorities and create new units of government with different boundaries. Changes in boundaries have reflected a vain search to find a balance between efficiency (assumed to correlate with fewer councils delivering services to more people spread over a wider geographical area) and responsiveness (assumed to require more councils with a smaller territory and fewer people).

Local council elections are fought on party lines. In the days of the two-party system, many cities were solidly Labour for a generation or more, while leafy suburbs and agricultural counties were overwhelmingly Conservative. The Liberal Democrats now win many seats in local elections and when no party has a majority introduce coalition government into town halls. However, being a councillor is usually a part-time job.

The Blair government has assumed that elected mayors are a good way of holding government accountable and incidentally, destroying the local power base of Labour veterans skeptical of Blair's new Labour Party. Downing Street introduced the direct election of the mayor of Greater London, citing New York and Chicago as positive examples. However, it refuses to give local governments the independence in taxing and spending that American local government enjoys.[41] This initiative backfired when a left-wing Labour populist, Ken Livingstone, won election as London's first mayor running as an independent against an official Labour candidate.

Local government is usually divided into two tiers of county and district councils, each with responsibility for some local services. The proliferation of public-private initiatives and special-purpose agencies has reduced the services for which local government is exclusively or primarily responsible. For example, it has promoted city academics under private as well as public sponsorship as an alternative to local government schools.

Today there is a jumble of more or less local institutions delivering such public services as education, police protection, refuse collection, housing, and cemeteries (see Box 8.6). Collectively, local institutions account for about a fifth of total public expenditure.

Central government financial grants are the largest source of local government revenue. There is

Delivering Public Services on the Doorstep

BOX 8.6

The growth of government has caused the primary activities of government to shift from debates in Westminster to the delivery of public services, such as health care, education, and rubbish collection. Government on the scale that we know today could not exist if all its activities were concentrated in London, for five-sixths of the country's population lives elsewhere. As the demand for public services has increased, government has grown chiefly through pluralization—that is, the multiplication of familiar institutions, such as schools and hospitals. Devolution to Scotland and Wales has added to decentralization. Edinburgh and Cardiff are responsible for delivering many everyday services, while overall financial control remains in London.

Education illustrates the combination of central authority and localized service delivery. Educational policy is authorized by an act of Parliament, financed principally by central government, and the minister of education is a member of Parliament and of the Cabinet. However, the delivery of primary and secondary education is the responsibility of classroom teachers. Dissatisfaction with local government's responsibility for managing schools has led Whitehall to establish secondary schools independent of local government but dependent on Whitehall.

Increasingly, central government seeks to monitor the performance of schools in nationwide examinations. But since the Department of Education employs only 1 percent of the people working in education, success depends on actions taken by others.*

*See Richard Rose, "From Government at the Center to Government Nationwide," in Y. Meny and V. Wright, eds., *Center-Periphery Relations in Western Europe* (London: George Allen & Unwin, 1985), 13–32; Richard Rose, "The Growth of Government Organizations," in C. Campbell and B. G. Peters, eds., *Organizing Government, Governing Organizations* (Pittsburgh: University of Pittsburgh Press, 1988), 99–128.

no local income tax, since the central government does not want to give local authorities the degree of fiscal independence that U.S. local governments have. The Thatcher government replaced the local property tax with a poll tax on every adult resident of a local authority, believing it would make voters more aware of the costs of local government and keep spending down. The tax produced a political backlash and was replaced by a community charge (tax) on housing, which the central government tends to control.[42] The continued squeeze on central government grants to local authorities under the Blair government has pushed up the community charge tax and controversy about local government finance.

Both Conservative and Labour parties are centralist. Centralization is justified in terms of **territorial justice**—that is, the same standards of public policy ought to apply everywhere in the country. For example, schools in inner cities and rural areas should have the same resources as schools in prosperous suburbs. This can be achieved only if tax revenues are collected by central government and then redistributed from well-to-do to poorer parts of the country. In addition, ministers

emphasize that they are accountable to a national electorate of tens of millions of people, whereas local councillors are accountable only to those who vote in their ward. Instead of small being beautiful, a big nationwide electorate is assumed to be better. The statement, "Local councillors are not necessarily political animals; we could manage without them," was made by a left-wing law professor.[43]

Devolution has given a degree of autonomy to the delivery of public services in Scotland, Wales, and Northern Ireland. The Scottish Executive, accountable to a parliament in Edinburgh, can enact legislation affecting a large range of social and public services of direct concern to individuals and communities, such as education, health, and roads. It also determines spending priorities within the limits set by its block grant of money from the British Treasury. The Welsh Assembly has administrative discretion, but no legislative or taxing powers. Northern Ireland is exceptional because the key service is police and security—which are kept under the control of British ministers, with the Army and intelligence services in the background.

Executive agencies are functional institutions headed by nonelected officials responsible for delivering many major public services. The biggest, the National Health Service (NHS), is not one organization but a multiplicity of institutions. Access to the national health service is free to every citizen. But health care is not costless. The government allocates public money to hospitals and to doctors and dentists who must work to its guidelines and the targets it sets. Because central government picks up the bill, the Treasury perennially seeks to cut costs in providing health care in order to limit the increase in health expenditure. The Treasury tries to drive down prices for supplies, which it can do because it is a monopoly purchaser of drugs and many health goods and services. It also tries to restrict the supply of medical services by limiting the number of hospital beds and the number of doctors that it trains and must pay for.

Public demand for more and better health care rises with the aging of the population and the development of new forms of medical treatment. The government's rationing of supply produces lengthening queues, involving months of waiting before a person can see a medical specialist and months of additional waiting before a hospital operation. The Blair government has dealt with this problem by management changes. It has not adopted the common practice of most European Union countries: asking patients to pay a limited part of the cost of seeing a doctor or getting hospital treatment.

Quangos

British government sponsors more than a thousand **quasi-autonomous nongovernmental organizations (quangos).** Some quangos simply advise on policy, while others deliver public services. All are created by an act of Parliament or by an executive decision; their heads are appointed by a Cabinet minister; public money can be appropriated to finance their activities; and, when things go wrong, Parliament has difficulty in assigning responsibility for decisions.

Advisory committees draw on the expertise of individuals and organizations involved in programs for which Whitehall departments are nominally responsible. Ministry of Agriculture officials can turn to advisory committees for detailed information about farming practices; the Department of Trade and Industry can turn to business associations on

matters of trade and to industrial associations for information about a particular industry. Because they have no executive powers, advisory committees usually cost very little to run. Representatives of interest groups are glad to serve because doing so gives them privileged access to Whitehall and an opportunity to influence government in matters in which they are directly interested.

Administrative tribunals are quasi-judicial bodies that make expert judgments in such fields as medical negligence or that handle a large number of small claims, such as disputes about whether the rent set for a rent-controlled flat is fair. Ministers may use tribunals to avoid involvement in politically controversial issues, such as decisions about deporting immigrants. Tribunals normally work much more quickly and cheaply than the courts. However, the quasi-judicial role of tribunals creates a demand for independent auditing of their procedures to ensure that they are fair to all sides. The task of supervising some seventy tribunals is in the hands of a quango, the Council on Tribunals.

Turning to the Market

The 1945–1951 Labour government turned away from the market because its socialist leaders believed that government planning was better able to promote economic growth and full employment. It nationalized many basic industries, such as electricity, gas, coal, the railways, and airlines. State ownership meant that industries did not have to run at a profit; some consistently made money while others consistently lost money and required big subsidies. Government ownership politicized wage negotiations and investment decisions.

The Thatcher government promoted privatization, selling shares of nationalized industries on the stock market. Profit-making industries—such as telephones, oil, and gas—were sold without difficulty. Selling council houses to tenants at prices well below their market value was popular with tenants. Companies and industries that were losing money—such as British Airways, British Steel, and the coal mines—had to be reorganized, and unprofitable activities were shed to make them attractive to buyers. Industries needing large public subsidies to maintain public services, such as the railways, have continued to receive subsidies after privatization.

Privatization is justified on grounds of economic efficiency (the market is better than civil servants in determining investment, production, and prices); political ideology (the power of government is reduced); service (private enterprise is more consumer-oriented than are civil servants); and short-term financial gain (the sale of public assets can provide billions in revenue for government). Although the Labour Party initially opposed privatization, it quickly realized that it would be electorally disastrous to take back privatized council houses and shares that people had bought at bargain prices.

Since many privatized industries affect the public interest, the government created new regulatory agencies to regulate telephones, gas, electricity, broadcasting, and water. Where there is a substantial element of monopoly in an industry, the government regulatory agency promotes competition and often has the power to fix price increases at a lower rate than inflation. Even though it no longer owns an industry, when things go wrong government does not ignore what has happened. An extreme example of government intervention occurred when several fatal accidents occurred on railway track maintained by a privatized transport company. The Blair government took it back into public ownership.

From Trust to Contract

Historically, the British civil service has relied on trust in delivering policies. British civil servants are much less rule-bound than their German counterparts and less threatened with being dragged into court to justify their actions than are U.S. officials. Intragovernmental relations between Whitehall departments and representatives of local authorities traditionally arrived at consensual understandings upheld by all sides as much on the basis of trust as of law. However, the Thatcher government preferred to rely on law to set targets and constraints on local government and to establish new agencies or contracts with private sector agencies. The Blair government continued this practice.

Trust has been replaced by contracts with agencies to undertake the day-to-day delivery of such central government services as automobile licenses, patents, and social security benefits. In addition, the government has sought to keep capital expenditure for building public facilities from visibly increasing public debt through private finance initiatives. Banks and other profit-making companies loan money to build facilities that will be leased by government agencies or even operated by profit-making companies. The theory is that government can obtain the greatest value for money by buying services from the private sector, ranging from operating staff canteens in government offices to prison services.

Government by contract faces political limits because the departmental minister must answer to Parliament when something goes wrong. The Prison Service is a textbook example. It was established as an executive agency separate from the Home Office in 1993 to bring in private management to reduce unit costs in the face of a rising "demand" for prison services due to changes in crime rates and sentencing policies. However, when prisoners escaped and other problems erupted, the Home Secretary blamed the business executive brought in to head the Prison Service. The Prison Service head replied by attacking the minister's refusal to live up to the terms of the contract agreed between them.

The proliferation of many agencies, each with a distinctive and narrow responsibility for a limited number of policies, tends to fragment government activities. For example, a single parent may have to deal with half a dozen different agencies to secure all the public services to which she or he is entitled.

The Blair government endorsed the idea of "joined up" government, that is, linking the provision of related services by different public agencies so that they can more easily be delivered to citizens. In order to achieve this goal, Whitehall must centralize powers that were contracted out. Moreover, it must centralize powers *within* Whitehall, a measure consistent with Blair's creation of a large staff in Downing Street but inconsistent with the responsibility of individual Cabinet ministers for running their own departments. It must also have the administrative competence to computerize records of individuals now held by many different agencies. However, Whitehall's efforts to promote e-government have resulted in billions of pounds being spent on unsuccessful computerization.

The Contingency of Influence

The theory of British government is centralist: All roads lead to Downing Street, where the prime minister and the Chancellor of the Exchequer have their homes and offices. The Treasury and the Foreign

Office buildings are only a few steps away. In practice, policymaking is multidimensional, for those involved can be divided horizontally between ministries, executive agencies, and other forms of quangos, and vertically between central government and local authorities and other nondepartmental public bodies that deliver services locally and functionally.

Influence is contingent: it varies with the problem at hand. Decisions about war and peace are taken at the very center by the highest ranking political and military officials. By contrast, decisions about whether a particular piece of land should be used for housing are normally made by local authorities.

Most political decisions involve two or more government agencies, and therefore require discussion and bargaining before a decision can be implemented. The making of policy is constrained by disputes within government much more than by differences between the governing party and its opponents. Many tentacles of the octopus of government work against each other, as each public agency claims to represent conflicting definitions of the public interest.

While the center of central government has been pressing harder on other parts of British government, Whitehall itself has been losing influence because of its obligations in the European Union. The Single Europe Act promotes British exports, but it also increases the scope for EU decisions to regulate the British economy. Whitehall has adopted a variety of strategies in its EU negotiations, including noncooperation and public dispute. Ironically, it is just these tactics that local government and British executive agencies use when they disagree with Whitehall.

Why Public Policy Matters

However citizens vote, they do not need to look far to see the outputs of government: if there is a school-age child or a pensioner in the house, the benefits to the family are continuous and visible. If a person is ill, the care provided by doctors and hospitals is an important output of public policy; so too is police protection and tight controls of land use that maintain greenery even in urban landscapes. Today, the average household annually receives two significant welfare state benefits, such as education, health care, or a pension.

To produce the benefits of public policy, government relies on three major resources: laws, money, and personnel. Most policies involve a combination of these resources, but they do not do so equally. Policies regulating individual behavior, such as marriage and divorce, are law-intensive; measures that pay benefits to millions of people, such as social security, are money-intensive; and the delivery of such public services as health care are labor-intensive.

Laws are the unique resource of government, for private enterprises cannot enact laws and contracts operate only if the laws of the land are respected. The British executive centralizes within it the power to draft laws and regulations that can be approved without substantial amendment by Parliament. Moreover, many laws give ministers significant discretion in administration. For example, an employer may be required to provide "reasonable" toilet facilities rather than having all features of lavatories specified down to the size and height of a toilet seat.

Public employees are needed to administer laws and deliver major services. Privatizing public services has reduced the number of people counted as civil servants or public employees, but it has not reduced to the same extent the number who depend on public spending for their job. In total, more than a fifth of the entire British labor force depends on government for their job.

To meet the costs of public policy, British government collects almost two-fifths of the gross national product in taxation. Income tax accounts for 28 percent of tax revenue; the top rate of taxation is 40 percent. Social security taxes are paid by deductions from wages and additional contributions of employers; these account for an additional 17 percent of revenue. Since there are no state or local income taxes, a well-to-do British person can be taxed at a lower total rate than a well-off person living in New York City.

Taxes on consumption are important too. There is a value-added tax of 17.5 percent on the sale of almost all goods and services, and gasoline, cigarettes, and alcohol are taxed very heavily too. In total, taxes on consumption account for one-quarter of all tax revenue.

Since profits fluctuate from year to year, the government prefers businesses to pay taxes on their gross revenues through value-added tax and on their total wages bill through the employer's contribution to social security. Taxes on the profits of corporations

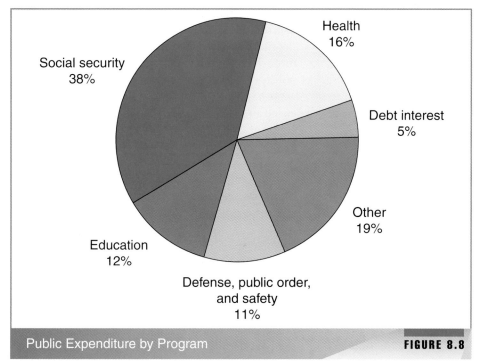

Social security
38%

Health
16%

Debt interest
5%

Other
19%

Defense, public order,
and safety
11%

Education
12%

Public Expenditure by Program

FIGURE 8.8

Source: Office for National Statistics, *United Kingdom National Accounts: The Blue Book* (London: The Stationary Office 2004), 276ff.

education are second and third in their claims on the public purse. Together, these three social welfare programs account for two-thirds of total public expenditure. A classic commitment of government—defense and maintaining public order and safety through the police, fire service, courts, and prisons—are fourth in spending importance.

Since there is no item in the public budget labeled "waste," any government wanting to reduce public spending must squeeze existing programs—and big savings can be made only by squeezing popular programs, such as those involving health, education, or pensions. But doing so would go against public opinion. When Margaret Thatcher entered office in 1979, the public divided into three almost equal groups: those wanting to spend more and tax more, those wanting to cut taxes even if it meant a reduction in public services, and a large middle group wanting to leave things as they were. Thatcher's campaign to cut taxes and public spending produced a reaction in favor of public expenditure. By the time she left office, a majority favored taxing and spending more on social programs and this has remained the position since (see Table 8.5).

claim an eighth of tax revenue. Additional revenue is generated by the National Lottery, launched in 1993; more people play the lottery than vote in a general election.

Social security is the most costly program of British government. It accounts for 38 percent of public expenditure (see Figure 8.8). It is also the most popular, for it transfers money from government to more than 10 million older people receiving pensions, plus millions of invalids, the unemployed, women on maternity leave, and poor people needing to supplement their limited resources. Spending on health and

TABLE 8.5

Public Preference for More Taxing and Spending Rather Than Less (in percentages)

	1983	1987	1991	1995	2001
Increase taxes and spending on health education and social benefits	32	50	65	61	59
Keep taxes and spending the same as now	54	42	29	31	34
Reduce taxes and spending	9	3	3	5	3
Don't know	5	5	3	3	4

Source: British Social Attitudes surveys, as reported in Alison Park et al., eds., *British Social Attitudes: The 19th Report* (Thousand Oaks, CA: Sage, 2002), 76.

Tony Blair's government entered office pledged not to increase income taxes. However, in order to finance increased expenditure on social programs that are popular with the electorate, it has put up less visible "stealth taxes," such as taxes on pension funds. The effects of these tax increases are passed on to voters—but often in a form that is not noticed at the time.

POLICY OUTCOMES AND CHANGES IN SOCIETY

Although living conditions reflect public policy, only a totalitarian regime claims responsibility for everything that happens in society. In an open society such as Britain, social conditions are a consequence of the interaction of public policies, the national and international economy, the not-for-profit institutions of civil society, and individual and household activities free of state control. The term "welfare state" is misleading. Total welfare in society is the sum of a "welfare mix," combining actions of government, the market, and the nonmonetized production of welfare in the household.[44]

Defending the population against threats to security at home and abroad is a unique responsibility of government. In an interdependent world, British government seeks to guarantee national security by participating in international alliances. It has been a founder member of NATO, and has fought alongside the United States from the Korean War to the Iraq War. Maintaining order at home requires the cooperation of others. This is clearest in Northern Ireland, where Whitehall negotiates with leaders of armed paramilitary organizations as well as with elected representatives. In England it depended on the "self-policing" of immigrant communities until terrorist attacks in 2005 showed that these communities could spawn British-born Moslem terrorists.

Crime prevention depends not only on policing but also on whether there are a lot of unemployed youths ready to violate the laws in pursuit of money. Over the decades the crime rate has been rising, including crimes of violence, but it remains lower than in the United States.

Both Conservative and Labour governments accept responsibility for the economy. Most firms are profit making, consumers can spend money as they like, and wages and prices are principally decided in the marketplace. Government influences the market through taxing and spending policies, interest rates, and policies for growth and unemployment. Increasingly, what happens to the British economy is also influenced by what happens elsewhere in the European Union and on other continents too, for British government cannot isolate the country from what happens in the global economy.

In each decade since World War II, the British economy has grown; compounding a small annual rate of growth over many decades cumulatively results in a big rise in living standards. Per capita national income has more than tripled since 1945. Many consumer goods that were once thought of as luxuries, such as owning a car or one's own home or enjoying holidays abroad, are now mass consumption goods. Things unknown in 1945, such as home computers or mobile phones, are now commonplace. In the past decade the British economy has grown by one-third. Its growth rate has been higher than the average for the European Union or advanced industrial societies.

Poverty can be found in Britain; the extent depends on the definition used. If poverty is defined in relative terms—such as having less than half the average wage—then about 10 percent of Britons are living in relative poverty. If poverty is defined as being trapped at a low-income level for many years, then less than 4 percent are long-term poor.

On all the major indicators of social well-being, the British people enjoy a higher standard of living today than a generation ago. Infant mortality has declined by more than four-fifths since 1951. Life expectancy for men and for women has risen by 12 years. A gender gap remains, as women on average live four years longer than men. The postwar expansion of schools has significantly raised the quantity of education available. Classes are smaller in size, and upwards of one-half of British youths go on to some form of further education, usually in institutions that did not exist in 1950. More than two-thirds of families now own their own home, and nine-tenths report satisfaction with their housing.

The outputs of public policy play a significant part in the everyday life of all Britons. Everyone makes major use of publicly financed health and education services. Children at school and patients seeing a doctor do not think of themselves as participating in politics. Yet the services received are controlled and paid for by government. Welfare state benefits—such as free education, health care, and the guarantee of an income in old age or unemployment—are so taken for granted today that most people see them as nonpolitical. People do not want a change in government after an election to result in radical changes in major social policies.

Popular Expectations

For a century commentators on British society have bemoaned the relative global decline in the country's achievements compared with America and leading continental European countries. But ordinary people do not compare their lives with other countries; the most important comparison is with their own past. Evaluating change across time shows great improvements in the living conditions of most people compared with their parents or grandparents. The longer the time span, the greater the improvement. Furthermore, in the production of such political "goods" as freedom from the state, confidence in the honesty of public officials, and administrative flexibility, British government remains an international leader. The great majority of people are proud of the achievements of Britain and would not want to be a citizen of any other country.

Frustration with government arises only if people expect it to be consistently very successful. But British people tend to have low expectations of government. Decades of economic difficulties lowered expectations of what government can do to make the economy grow or prevent unemployment. When there are low expectations, any time in which the economy does not get worse can be considered a reprieve from bad news.

British people do not hold government responsible for what is most important in their lives; personal circumstances are evaluated very differently from public policy. When opinion polls ask people each year whether they think next year will be better or worse personally than the preceding year, nine-tenths of the time a majority say they expect the coming year to be all right for themselves, even when many expect economic difficulties for the country as a whole. When people are asked to evaluate their lives, they are most satisfied with their family, friends, home, and job, and least satisfied with major political institutions of society.[47]

Satisfaction with the present goes along with acceptance of the principle of political change. However, there are disagreements about the direction of change, for example, whether Westminster should take more responsibility for public services or devolve more responsibilities to regions and municipalities, and whether Britain should align itself more closely with the United States or with countries in the European Union. Even when goals are agreed upon, there are differences about the particular policy that can best achieve a given goal. Politics in Britain is thus an ongoing debate about the direction, the means, and the tempo of adapting old institutions and inherited policies to new circumstances in the twenty-first century.

KEY TERMS

Cabinet
centralization
class
Conservative Party
Crown
decentralization
devolution
Downing Street
first past the post [electoral system]
government
House of Lords
individualist theory
insider pressure groups
interest group theory
Irish Republican Army (IRA)
Labour Party
Liberal Democrat Party
multiparty system
Northern Ireland
outsider pressure groups
Parliament
prime minister
privatization
quasi-autonomous nongovernmental organizations (quangos)
Scotland
territorial justice
Thatcherism
trusteeship theory of government
United Kingdom
unwritten constitution
Wales
Westminster
Whitehall

SUGGESTED READINGS

Bulmer, Simon et al. *British Devolution and European Policymaking.* Basingstoke: Palgrave Macmillan, 2002.

Butler, D. E., and Geraint Butler. *Twentieth Century British Political Facts, 1900–2000*, 8th ed. Basingstoke: Macmillan, 2000.

———. *British Political Facts Since 1979.* Basingstoke: Palgrave Macmillan, 2006.

Cowley, Philip. *The Rebels: How Blair Mislaid His Majority.* London: Politico's, 2005.

Flinders, Matthew. *The Politics of Accountability in the Modern State.* Aldershot: Ashgate, 2001.

Grant, Wyn. *Pressure Groups and British Politics.* New York: St. Martin's Press, 2000.

Hazell, Robert, ed. *The English Question.* London: Manchester University Press, 2006.

Hayward, Jack, Brian Barry, and Archie Brown, eds. *The British Study of Politics in the Twentieth Century.* Oxford: Oxford University Press, 1999.

Kavanagh, Dennis, and David Butler. *The British General Election of 2005.* Basingstoke: Palgrave Macmillan, 2005.

Moran, Michael. *The British Regulatory State: High Modernism and Hyper-Innovation.* New York: Oxford University Press, 2003.

Norris, Pippa, and Christopher Wlezien, eds. *Britain Votes 2005.* Oxford: Oxford University Press, 2005.

Norris, Pippa, and Joni Lovenduski. *Political Recruitment: Gender, Race, and Class in the British Parliament.* New York: Cambridge University Press, 1995.

Oliver, Dawn. *Constitutional Reform in the United Kingdom.* New York: Oxford University Press, 2003.

Page, Edward C., and Bill Jenkins. *Policy Bureaucracy: Government With a Cast of Thousands.* Oxford: Oxford University Press, 2005.

Park, Alison, ed. *British Social Attitudes: The 22nd Report.* Thousand Oaks, CA: Sage, 2005.

Pattie, Charles, Patrick Seyd, and Paul Whitely. *Citizenship in Britain.* New York: Cambridge University Press, 2004.

Rallings, Colin, and Michael Thrasher. *British Electoral Facts, 1832–2006.* Aldershot: Ashgate, 2007.

Rose, Richard. *Ordinary People in Public Policy.* Newbury Park, CA: Sage, 1989.

———. *The Prime Minister in a Shrinking World.* Boston: Polity Press, 2001.

Rose, Richard, and Phillip L. Davies. *Inheritance in Public Policy: Change Without Choice in Britain.* New Haven, CT: Yale University Press, 1994.

Schmidt, Vivien. "Adapting to Europe: Is It Harder for Britain?" *British Journal of Politics and International Relations*, 8, no. 1 (2006), 15–33.

Seldon, Anthony. *Blair.* New York: Free Press, 2004.

Smith, Martin J. *The Core Executive in Britain.* London: Macmillan, 1999.

Social Trends. London: Stationery Office, annual.

Webb, Paul. *The Modern British Party System.* Thousand Oaks, CA: Sage, 2003.

Whitaker's Almanack. London: J. Whitaker, annual.

Wilson, David, and Game, Chris. *Local Government in the United Kingdom*, 3rd ed. Basingstoke: Palgrave, 2002.

INTERNET RESOURCES

www.ucl.ac.uk/constitution-unit

www.gov.uk

www.parliament.uk

www.pm.gov.uk

www.news.bbc.co.uk

www.ipsos-mori.com/polls

www.psa.ac.uk

ENDNOTES

1. See Richard Rose, *What Is Europe? A Dynamic Perspective* (New York: Addison Wesley Longman, 1996), ch. 3.

2. Quoted in Krishna Guha, "Labour Escapes From Its Bloody Tower," *Financial Times*, 24 August 2002.

3. Quoted by David Leppard, "ID Cards Doomed, Say Officials," *Sunday Times* (London), 9 July 2006. See also interview with Sir Robin Butler, "How Not to Run a Country," *The Spectator* (London), 11, December 2004.

4. *Gallup Political and Economic Index*, London: Gallup Poll, No. 390 (February 1993), 42.

5. Quoted from the text of a speech at Oxford, 2 February 2006.

6. John Kampfner and David Wighton, "Reeling in Scotland to Bring England in Step," *Financial Times*, 5 April 1997.

7. See Richard Rose, "England: A Traditionally Modern Political Culture," in Lucian W. Pye and Sidney Verba, eds., *Political*

Culture and Political Development (Princeton, NJ: Princeton University Press, 1965), 83–129.

8. Quoted in Richard Rose, *Do Parties Make a Difference?* 2nd ed. (Chatham, NJ: Chatham House, 1984), xv.

9. Cf. Andrew Dilnot and Paul Johnson, eds., *Election Briefing 1997* (London: Institute for Fiscal Studies, Commentary 60, 1997), 2.

10. John Kampfner and David Wighton, "Blair Seals Labour's Switch to Low Tax Party," *Financial Times*, 27, March 1997.

11. Quoted in Peter Hennessy, "Raw Politics Decide Procedure in Whitehall," *New Statesman* (London), 24 October 1986, p. 10.

12. Winston Churchill, *Their Finest Hour* (London: Cassell, 1949), 14.

13. See Richard Rose, "A Crisis of Confidence in the Party System or in Individual Leaders," *Contemporary Record* 9, no. 2 (1995): 273–93.

14. For trans-Atlantic comparisons of presidents and prime ministers, see Richard Rose, "Giving Direction to Government in Comparative Perspective," in Joel Aberbach and Mark A. Peterson, eds., *The Executive Branch* (New York: Oxford University Press, 2005), 72–99.

15. Walter Bagehot, *The English Constitution* (London: World's Classics, 1955), 9.

16. See Richard Rose, *The Prime Minister in a Shrinking World* (Boston: Polity Press, 2001).

17. *Careers in the Civil Service—an Alternative View*. London: First Division Association, 1987, p. 12, a publication of the trade union of higher civil servants.

18. Quoted in "Whitehall Remains Closed to Outsiders and Needs Radical Change, Report Says," *The Times* (London), 7 August 2006.

19. David Leppard and Robert Winnett, "Blair Blames Ministers for Policy Gaffes," *Sunday Times*, 18 April 2004.

20. Eric Varley, quoted in A. Michie and S. Hoggart, *The Pact* (London: Quartet Books, 1978), 13.

21. Hugh Heclo and Aaron Wildavsky, *The Private Government of Public Money* (London: Macmillan, 1974).

22. Bernard Ingham, press secretary to Margaret Thatcher, quoted in Richard Rose, "British Government: The Job at the Top," in R. Rose and E. Suleiman, eds., *Presidents and Prime Ministers* (Washington, DC: American Enterprise Institute, 1980), 43.

23. Lord Butler, *Review of Intelligence on Weapons of Mass Destruction*. House of Commons Document 898 (London: The Stationery Office, 2004) 160.

24. Lord Wright, in *Liversidge v. Sir John Anderson and Another*, 1941, quoted in G. Le May, *British Government, 1914–1953* (London: Methuen, 1955), 332.

25. See Samuel H. Beer, *Modern British Politics*, 3rd ed. (London: Faber & Faber, 1982).

26. House of Commons, *Hansard* (London: Her Majesty's Stationery Office), 11, November 1947, col. 206.

27. Cf. Colin Bennett, "From the Dark to the Light: The Open Government Debate in Britain," *Journal of Public Policy* 5, no. 2 (1985): 209.

28. Quoted by Sean O'Neill, "Too Sensitive to Reveal, Minister," *The Times* (London), 3 October 2005.

29. See Richard Rose and Ian McAllister, *The Loyalties of Voters* (Newbury Park, CA: Saje, 1990), ch. 3.

30. Quoted in Maurice Kogan, *The Politics of Education* (Harmondsworth: Penguin, 1971), 135.

31. See the Fulton Committee, *Report on the Civil Service* (London: Her Majesty's Stationary Office, 1966) vol. 1, 27ff., and Appendix E, especially 162.

32. See Rob Baggott, "The Measurement of Change in Pressure Groups," *Talking Politics* 5, no. 1 (1992): 18–22.

33. Sir Ken Jackson, quoted by Krishna Guha, "Engineers and Electricians Turn Away from Moderate Traditions," *Financial Times*, 19 July 2002.

34. See W. A. Maloney, G. Jordan, and A. M. McLaughlin, "Interest Groups and Public Policy: The Insider/Outsider Model Revisited," *Journal of Public Policy* 14, no. 1 (1994): 17–38.

35. Tony Blair, *New Britain: My Vision of a Young Country* (London: Fourth Estate, 1996), 299.

36. For details, see Denis Van Mechelen and Richard Rose, *Patterns of Parliamentary Legislation* (Aldershot, England: Gower, 1986), table 5.2; and more generally, Rose, *Do Parties Make a Difference?*

37. Richard Rose and Phillip L. Davies, *Inheritance in Public Policy: Change without Choice in Britain*. New Haven: Yale University Press, 1994.

38. Reginald Maudling, quoted in David Butler and Michael Pinto-Duschinsky, *The British General Election of 1970* (London: Macmillan, 1971), 62.

39. See *Better Government Services: Executive Agencies in the 21st Century* (London: Office of Public Service Reforms and the Treasury, 2002).

40. Sir Leo Pliatzky, quoted in Peter Hennessy, "The Guilt of the Treasury 1000," *New Statesman*, 23 January 1987.

41. See Paul Peterson, "The American Mayor: Elections and Institutions," *Parliamentary Affairs*, 53, no. 4 (2000): 667–79.

42. David Butler, Andrew Adonis, and Tony Travers, *Failure in British Government: The Politics of the Poll Tax* (Oxford: Oxford University Press, 1994).

43. J. A. G. Griffith, *Central Departments and Local Authorities* (London: George Allen & Unwin, 1966), 542; Cf. Simon Jenkins, *Accountable to None: The Tory Nationalization of Britain* (Harmondsworth: Penguin, 1996).

44. See Richard Rose, "The Dynamics of the Welfare Mix in Britain," in Richard Rose and Rei Shiratori, eds., *The Welfare State East and West* (New York: Oxford University Press, 1986), 80–106.

45. Rose, *Ordinary People in Public Policy*, 175ff.

POLITICS IN RUSSIA

Thomas F. Remington

Country Bio

Population
142.4 million

Territory
6.593 million square miles

Year of Independence
1991

Year of Current Constitution
1993

Head of State
President Vladimir Vladimirovich Putin

Head of Government
Premier Viktor Zubkov

Language(s)
Russian, other languages of ethnic nationalities

Religion
Russian Orthodox 70–80%; other Christian 1–2%; Muslim 8–9%; Buddhist 0.6%; Jewish 0.3%

RUSSIA

REBUILDING THE RUSSIAN STATE

Russian President Vladimir Putin hosted the annual summit of the leaders of the world's major industrial democracies, the Group of Eight, in his native city of St. Petersburg from July 15 to 17, 2006. Inclusion of Russia in this group, bringing it from the Group of Seven to the Group of Eight, was controversial, but the United States and its allies hoped that by making Russia a full partner in this body they would strengthen Russia's integration into the international community. For his part, Putin used the occasion of the G-8 meeting to showcase Russia's importance as a great power. The summit represented a symbolic victory for Putin's consistent efforts to rebuild Russian power at home and abroad following nearly two decades of political upheaval. Over that period, Russia's political and economic institutions collapsed; the Soviet federal state fell apart into its constituent parts; bloody ethnic conflicts erupted in several regions on Russia's periphery; and people's high expectations for a smooth transition to democracy and capitalism were dashed. Putin took understandable

satisfaction from the fact that during his presidency, political order in Russia had been restored, economic output was growing steadily, and Russia's role as a major oil and gas exporter gave it significant international leverage. The other members of the G-8, recognizing that too much was at stake to allow a new Cold War between Russia and the West to develop, implicitly endorsed Russia's claim to membership in the club of major powers.

The sustainability of Russia's great-power status is tenuous, however. Indeed, in several respects Russia's transformation from a communist state into a stable capitalist democracy has gone into reverse. Putin's policies are far from reestablishing a communist state, but they harken back to an older Russian political pattern in which Russia's rulers seek to restore the power of a weakened state by diminishing the realm of free association outside the state. Moreover, Russia's dependence on oil and gas revenues to fuel its economy leaves it vulnerable to the "resource curse," characteristic of states that become dependent on their abundant natural resources for their exports. Such states typically exhibit high levels of corruption, low accountability, and low investment in human capital. Finally, Russia continues to experience a severe demographic crisis. Mortality rates, particularly among adult males, shot up in the early 1990s and have improved little since then. High mortality combined with low birthrates are resulting in a net loss of close to a million people per year, posing a grave threat to Russia's national security and economic viability. In view of these deeper structural dilemmas, the long-term viability of Russia's political and economic recovery will require far-reaching institutional reform.

CURRENT POLICY CHALLENGES

Vladimir Putin took office as president in dramatic fashion. His predecessor, Boris Yeltsin, had served as president of Russia since 1991. On December 31, 1999, Yeltsin appeared on national television to announce that, as of midnight, he was resigning as president. Although his term was not due to expire until June 2000, he had decided to resign early to allow his chosen successor, Vladimir Putin, to take over. Putin was Yeltsin's prime minister and enjoyed Yeltsin's confidence, as well as strong public support. As acting president, Putin had a substantial advantage in the presidential elections, which under the constitution had to be held within three months of the president's departure. Putin's first move was to issue a decree guaranteeing Yeltsin and his family lifetime immunity from criminal prosecution. Although the manner in which the succession occurred was not illegal, it appeared to reflect an unseemly bargain: Yeltsin gave the presidency to Putin in return for security for himself.

Putin went on to win election as president in his own right in March 2000 and to exercise the powers of the presidential office forcefully. Enjoying a strong base of popular confidence, Putin undertook a steady effort to rebuild state power. He attacked the power of the so-called **oligarchs**—the small group of extremely wealthy figures who held controlling shares of Russia's major natural resource, manufacturing, financial, and media companies and exercised disproportionate influence over government— through prosecutions of two particularly prominent ones. He systematically weakened the independence of the chief executives of the country's regions—the **governors**—by establishing new federal districts

overseen by presidentially appointed representatives, securing the power to dismiss governors for violations of the law, and removing them as ex-officio members of the upper chamber of Parliament. He placed people whom he had worked with closely in the past into positions of responsibility in the government and the presidential administration.

Putin has continued to enjoy exceptionally high levels of public approval. This has given him considerable latitude in choosing policies to achieve his goals. Although Putin was not well known to the Russian public or to the international community at the point he assumed the presidency, with time, his general objectives have become clearer (see Box 9.1). In foreign policy, he seeks to restore Russia to its place as a major world power, a status it lost with the collapse of the Soviet Union. In the economy, he wants to achieve high, sustained growth by attracting substantial private investment, both domestic and foreign. At the same time he seeks direct state ownership and control of strategically important sectors, especially oil and gas. In politics, he seeks to preserve a framework of democratic institutions but to control the exercise of power through them. Elections are held, but their outcomes are predetermined; civil society is allowed to exist within certain highly restricted limits; individual rights are honored to the extent they do not conflict with the prerogatives of the state.

Many have termed Putin's model of political order "managed democracy," but more recently, Putin's associates have taken to using the slogan "sovereign democracy." Putin seeks to integrate Russia into the international economic system but at the same time to maintain a wide sphere of control for the state in the polity and economy. A strong state, for Putin, is one with an unbroken chain of executive authority stretching from the president down to the head of each region and district, with accountability running upward to the center rather than downward to the citizenry or society. He sees the president as the central figure directing the flow of power within the state. Putin accepts that Russia forms part of Europe and European civilization, but regards democratic principles as subordinate to, and potentially at odds with, the principle of state sovereignty. Possibly he believes that in a generation or two, Russia will be ready for a system featuring democratic accountability and separation of powers. For now, however, he appears to believe that the capacity and sovereignty of the state

Who Is Mister Putin?

Vladimir Putin's rise to power was so rapid that when he succeeded to the presidency, he was virtually unknown. A question often asked by Russians and foreigners alike was: "Who is Mr. Putin?"

Vladimir Vladimirovich Putin was born on October 7, 1952, in Leningrad (called St. Petersburg since 1991), and grew up in an ordinary apartment. From early on, he took an interest in martial arts and became expert at judo. Inspired by heroic tales of the secret world of espionage, at age 16 he visited the local headquarters of the KGB, hoping to become an agent. There he was told that he needed to go to university first. In 1970, he entered Leningrad State University and specialized in civil law. Upon graduation in 1975, Putin went to work for the KGB and was first assigned to work in counterintelligence, and then in its foreign intelligence division. Proficient in the German language, he was sent to East Germany in 1985. In 1990, after the Berlin Wall fell, Putin went back to Leningrad, working at the university but in the employ of the KGB. When a former law professor of his, Anatolii Sobchak, became mayor of Leningrad in 1991, he went to work for Sobchak. In the mayor's office he handled external relations, dealing extensively with foreign companies interested in investing in the city, and rose to become deputy mayor.

In 1996, Putin took a position in Yeltsin's presidential administration. He made a rapid career. In 1998, Yeltsin named Putin head of the FSB (the Federal Security Service—successor to the KGB), and in March 1999, secretary of the Security Council as well. In August 1999, President Yeltsin appointed him prime minister. Thanks to his decisive handling of the military operation in Chechnia, Putin's popularity ratings quickly rose. On December 31, 1999, Yeltsin resigned, making Putin acting president. Putin ran for the presidency and, on March 26, 2000, won with an outright majority of the votes.

Over time, Putin's political persona has become somewhat clearer. Uncomfortable with the give and take of public politics, he prefers the hierarchical style of organization used in the military and police. He is a pragmatist with no particular affection for either the Soviet or tsarist order. He recognizes that Russia must participate in the contemporary world economy rather than burden itself with new international conflicts. Skilled at projecting an affable, relaxed demeanor, he is also self-possessed and disciplined, and reveals little of himself in dealing with others. Like many previous Russian rulers, he has made the consolidation of his own political power his first priority.

require the centralization of executive authority, with the president as the linchpin of the entire political system.

Putin has only been partially successful in realizing his goals. Much of the credit for Russia's economic recovery goes to the high world market prices for oil and gas. Most of the ambitious fiscal and administrative reforms he has introduced have been blunted in implementation. Some of Putin's actions—such as the suppression of independent media and the state's takeover of the assets of the oil company **Yukos**— have discouraged business investment and fueled capital flight. Putin's heavy reliance on the country's "power structures" (the interior ministry with its police and security troops, the regular armed forces, the law enforcement system, and the secret services) to remove or intimidate his rivals has chilled open public discourse. This makes it harder for the center to monitor bureaucratic performance. Actual improvements in

the quality of governance under Putin have been modest. Putin has been much more successful in undercutting democratic checks and balances on central power than in making the new authoritarian system work effectively. However, history suggests that administrative over-centralization usually ends up not strengthening but weakening state capacity.

HISTORICAL LEGACIES

The Tsarist Regime

The Russian state traces its origins to the princely state that arose around Kiev (today the capital of independent Ukraine) in the ninth century. For nearly a thousand years, the Russian state was autocratic. That is, it was ruled by a hereditary monarch whose power was unlimited by any constitution. Only in the first decade of the twentieth century did the Russian tsar agree to grant a constitution calling for an elected legislature—and even then, the tsar soon dissolved the legislature and arbitrarily revised the constitution. In addition to autocracy, the historical legacy of Russian statehood includes *absolutism, patrimonialism*, and *Orthodox Christianity*. Absolutism meant that the tsar aspired to wield absolute power over the subjects of the realm. *Patrimonialism* refers to the idea that the ruler treated his realm as property that he owned rather than as a society with its own legitimate rights and interests.[1] This concept of power continues to influence state rulers today.

Finally, the tsarist state identified itself with the Russian Orthodox Church. In Russia, as in other countries where it is the dominant religious tradition, the Orthodox Church ties itself closely to the state, considering itself a national church. Traditionally, it has exhorted its adherents to show loyalty and obedience to the state in worldly matters, in return for which the state treated it as the state church. This legacy is still manifested in the postcommunist rulers' efforts to associate themselves with the heritage of Russia's church, and in many Russians' impulse to identify their state with a higher spiritual mission.

Absolutism, patrimonialism, and orthodoxy have been recurring elements of Russian political culture. But alternative motifs have been influential as well. At some points in Russian history, the country's rulers—have sought to modernize its economy and society. Russia imported Western practices in technology, law, state organization, and education in order to make the state competitive with other great powers. Modernizing rulers—such as Peter the Great (who ruled from 1682–1725) and Catherine the Great (1762–1796) had a powerful impact on Russian society, bringing it closer to West European models. The imperative of building Russia's military and economic potential was all the more pressing because of Russia's constant expansion through conquest and annexation of neighboring territories, and the ever-present need to defend its borders. The state's role in controlling and mobilizing society rose with the need to govern a vast territory. By the end of the seventeenth century, Russia was territorially the largest state in the world. But for most of its history, Russia's imperial reach exceeded its actual grasp.

Compared with other major powers of Europe, Russia's economic institutions remained backward well into the twentieth century. However, the trajectory of its development, especially in the nineteenth century, was toward that of a modern industrial society. By the time the tsarist order fell in 1917, Russia had a large industrial sector, although it was concentrated in a few cities. The country had a sizable middle class, although it was greatly outnumbered by the vast and impoverished peasantry and the radicalized industrial working class. As a result, the social basis for a peaceful democratic transition was too weak to prevent the Communists from seizing power in 1917.

The thousand-year tsarist era left a contradictory legacy. The tsars attempted to legitimate their absolute power by appealing to tradition, empire, and divine right. They treated law as an instrument of rule rather than a source of authority. The doctrines that rulers should be accountable to the ruled and that sovereignty resides in the will of the people were alien to Russian state tradition. Throughout Russian history, state and society have been more distant from each other than in Western societies. Rulers and populace regarded one another with mistrust and suspicion. This gap has been overcome at times of great national trials, such as the war against Napoleon and later World War II. Russia celebrated victory in those wars as a triumphant demonstration of the unity of state and people. But Russia's political traditions also include a yearning for equality, solidarity, and community, as well as for moral purity and sympathy for the downtrodden. And throughout the Russian heritage runs a deep strain of pride in the greatness of the country and the endurance of its people.

The Communist Revolution and the Soviet Order

The tsarist regime proved unable to meet the overwhelming demands of national mobilization in World War I. Tsar Nicholas II abdicated in February 1917 (March 1917, by the Western calendar). He was replaced by a short-lived provisional government, which in turn fell when the Russian Communists—Bolsheviks, as they called themselves—took power in October 1917 (November, by our calendar). Their aim was to create a socialist society in Russia and, eventually, to spread revolutionary socialism throughout the world. Socialism, the Russian Communist Party believed, meant a society without private ownership of the means of production, where the state owned and controlled all important economic assets, and where political power was exercised in the name of the working people. **Vladimir Ilyich Lenin** was the leader of the Russian Communist Party and the first head of the Soviet Russian government. (Figure 9.1 lists the Soviet and post-Soviet leaders since 1917.)

Under Lenin's system of rule, the Communist Party controlled all levels of government. At each level of the territorial hierarchy of the country, full-time Communist Party officials supervised government. At the top, final power to decide policy rested in the CPSU (Communist Party of the Soviet Union) Politburo. Under **Joseph Stalin,** who took power after Lenin's death in 1924, power was even further centralized. Stalin instituted a totalitarian regime intent on building up Russia's industrial and military might. The state survived the terrible test of World War II, ultimately pushing back the German army all the way to Berlin. But the combined cost of war and terror under Stalin was staggering. The institutions of rule that Stalin left behind when he died in 1953 eventually crippled the Soviet state. They included personalistic rule, insecurity for rulers and ruled alike, heavy reliance on the secret police, and a militarized economy. None of Stalin's successors could reform the system without undermining communist rule itself.

As vast as the Soviet state's powers were, they were frustrated by bureaucratic immobilism. As in any organization, overcentralization undermined the leaders' actual power to enact significant policy change—or even to recognize when serious policy change was needed. The center's ability to coordinate bureaucratic agencies in order to execute its initiatives was frequently undermined by tacit resistance to the center's orders by officials at lower levels, distortions in the flow of information up and down the hierarchy, and the force of inertia. Bureaucratic officials were generally more devoted to protecting and advancing their own personal and career interests than in serving the public interest. By the time **Mikhail Gorbachev** was elected General Secretary of the CPSU in 1985, the political system of the Soviet Union had grown top heavy, unresponsive, and corrupt. The regime had more than enough power to crush any political opposition. However, it was unable to modernize the economy or improve living standards for the population. By the early 1980s, the economy had stopped growing, and the country was unable to compete militarily or economically with the advanced countries of the West.

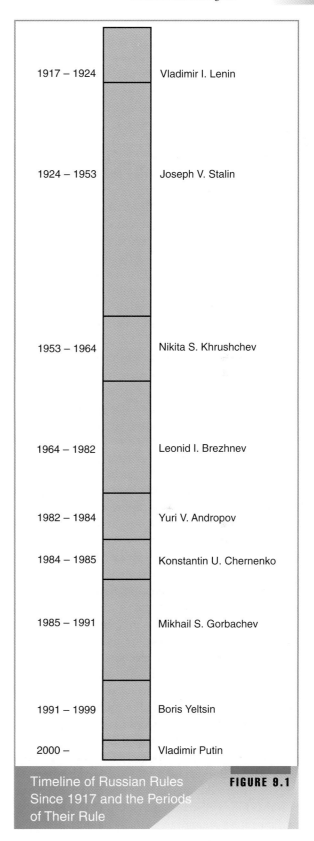

1917 – 1924	Vladimir I. Lenin
1924 – 1953	Joseph V. Stalin
1953 – 1964	Nikita S. Khrushchev
1964 – 1982	Leonid I. Brezhnev
1982 – 1984	Yuri V. Andropov
1984 – 1985	Konstantin U. Chernenko
1985 – 1991	Mikhail S. Gorbachev
1991 – 1999	Boris Yeltsin
2000 –	Vladimir Putin

FIGURE 9.1

Timeline of Russian Rules Since 1917 and the Periods of Their Rule

The youngest member of the Politburo at the time he was named party leader—he was age 54—Gorbachev quickly grasped the levers of power that the system granted the General Secretary. He moved both to strengthen his own political base, and to carry out a program of reform.[2] Emphasizing the need for greater openness—**glasnost**—in society, Gorbachev stressed that the ultimate test of the party's effectiveness lay in improving the economic well-being of the country and its people. By highlighting such themes as the need for market relations, pragmatism in economic policy, and less secretiveness in government, he identified himself as a champion of reform. Gorbachev not only called for political democratization, but he pushed through a reform bringing about the first contested elections for local soviets in many decades. He legalized private enterprise for individual and cooperative businesses and encouraged them to fill the many gaps in the economy left by the inefficiency of the state sector. He called for a "law-governed state" (*pravovoe gosudarstvo*) in which state power—including the power of the Communist Party—would be subordinate to law. He welcomed the explosion of informal social and political associations that were formed. He made major concessions to the United States in the sphere of arms control, which resulted in a treaty which, for the first time in history, called for the destruction of entire classes of nuclear missiles.

Gorbachev's early initiatives in the economic sphere failed to generate improvements in either competitiveness or living standards, and instead began fueling inflation. In 1988 he therefore turned to the political realm, hoping that democratization—a more open and competitive political arena—would unleash pressures for better bureaucratic performance. Using to the full the General Secretary's authoritarian powers, Gorbachev railroaded his proposals for democratization through the legislature. In 1989 and 1990, Gorbachev's plan for free elections and a working Parliament was realized as elections were held and new deputies were elected at the center and in every region and locality. When nearly half a million coal miners went on strike in the summer of 1989, Gorbachev declared himself sympathetic to their demands.

Gorbachev's radicalism received its most dramatic confirmation through the astonishing developments of 1989 in Eastern Europe. All the regimes making up the Socialist bloc collapsed and gave way to multiparty parliamentary regimes in virtually bloodless popular revolutions. The Soviet Union stood by and supported the revolutions. The overnight dismantling of communism in Eastern Europe meant that the elaborate structure of party ties, police cooperation, economic trade, and military alliance that had developed with Eastern Europe after World War II vanished. Divided Germany was allowed to reunite.

In the Soviet Union itself, meantime, the Communist Party faced a critical loss of authority. The newly elected governments of the national republics making up the Soviet state one by one declared that they were sovereign. The three Baltic republics declared their intention to secede from the union. Between 1989 and 1990, throughout the Soviet Union and Eastern Europe, Communist Party rule crumbled.

Political Institutions of the Transition Period: Demise of the USSR

Gorbachev's reforms had consequences he did not intend. The 1990 elections of deputies to the Supreme Soviets in all fifteen republics and for local soviets stimulated popular nationalist and democratic movements in most republics. In the core republic—Russia itself—Gorbachev's rival Boris Yeltsin won election as chairman of the Russian Supreme Soviet in June 1990. As chief of state in the Russian Republic, Yeltsin was well positioned to challenge Gorbachev for preeminence.

Yeltsin's rise forced Gorbachev to alter his strategy. Beginning in March 1991, Gorbachev sought terms for a new federal or confederal union that would be acceptable to Yeltsin and the Russian leadership, as well as to the leaders of the other republics. In April 1991, he reached an agreement on the outlines of a new treaty of union with nine of the fifteen republics, including Russia. A weak central government would manage basic coordinating functions. But the republics would gain the power to control the economies of their territories.

Gorbachev had underestimated the strength of his opposition. On August 19, 1991, his own vice president, prime minister, defense minister, head of the security police, and other senior officials preempted the signing ceremony of the treaty by placing Gorbachev under house arrest and seizing state power. This was a fateful moment for Russia. In Moscow and St. Petersburg, thousands of citizens rallied to the cause of democracy and Russian sovereignty. The coup collapsed on the third day and Gorbachev returned to office again as president. But his power had become fatally weakened. Neither union nor Russian power structures heeded his commands. Through the fall of 1991, the Russian government took over the union government, ministry by ministry. In November 1991, President Yeltsin issued a decree formally outlawing the Communist Party of the Soviet Union. By December, Gorbachev was president without a country. On December 25, 1991, he resigned as president and turned the powers of his office over to Boris Yeltsin.[3]

Political Institutions of the Transition Period: Russia 1990–1993

The Russian Republic followed the example of the Soviet Union and adopted its own constitutional amendments creating the Congress of People's Deputies and Supreme Soviet, and soon after, a state presidency.

Boris Yeltsin was elected president of the Russian Federation in June 1991. Unlike Gorbachev, Yeltsin was elected in a direct, popular, competitive election, which gave him a considerable advantage in mobilizing public support against Gorbachev and the central Soviet Union government (see Box 9.2).

Like Gorbachev before him, Yeltsin demanded extraordinary powers from Parliament to cope with the country's economic problems. Following the August 1991 coup attempt, he sought from the Russian Congress of People's Deputies, and was given, the power to carry out a program of radical market-oriented reform by decree. Yeltsin named himself acting prime minister and formed a government led by a group of young, Western-oriented leaders determined to carry out a decisive economic transformation. The new government's economic reforms took effect on January 2, 1992. Their first results were felt immediately as prices skyrocketed. Quickly many politicians

Boris Yeltsin: Russia's First President

BOX 9.2

Boris Yeltsin, born in 1931, graduated from the Urals Polytechnic Institute in 1955 with a diploma in civil engineering, and worked for a long time in construction. From 1976 to 1985, he served as first secretary of the *Sverdlovsk oblast* (provincial) Communist Party organization.

Early in 1986 Yeltsin became first secretary of the Moscow city party organization, but he was removed in November 1987 for speaking out against Mikhail Gorbachev. Positioning himself as a victim of the party establishment, Yeltsin made a remarkable political comeback. In the 1989 elections to the Congress of People's Deputies, he won a Moscow at-large seat with almost 90 percent of the vote. The following year he was elected to the Russian republic's Parliament with over 80 percent of the vote. He was then elected its chairman in June 1990. In 1991, he was elected president of Russia, receiving 57 percent of the vote. Thus, he had won three major races in three successive years. He was reelected as president in 1996 in a dramatic, come-from-behind race against the leader of the Communist Party.

Yeltsin's last years in office were notable for his lengthy spells of illness, and for the carousel of prime ministerial appointments he made. The entourage of

family members and advisers around him, dubbed colloquially "the Family," seemed to exercise undue influence over him. Yet, infirm as he was, he judged that Russia's interests and his own would be safe in Vladimir Putin's hands. Instead of turning against Putin when Putin gained in power and popularity, Yeltsin chose to resign and turn the presidency over to Putin. His resignation speech was full of contrition for his failure to bring a better life to Russians. After retiring, Yeltsin stayed out of the public eye. He died of heart failure on April 23, 2007, and was buried in Moscow with full honors.

Yeltsin's legacy is mixed. He was most effective when engaged in political battle, whether he was fighting for supremacy against Gorbachev or fighting against the communists. Impulsive and undisciplined, he was gifted with exceptionally keen political intuition. He regarded economic reform as an instrument in his political war with the communist opposition, and used privatization to make it impossible for any future rulers to return to state socialism. Imperious and willful, he also regarded the adoption of the 1993 constitution as a major achievement and willingly accepted the limits on his presidential power that it imposed.

began to distance themselves from the program: even Yeltsin's vice president denounced the program as "economic genocide." Through 1992, opposition to the reforms grew stronger and more intransigent. Increasingly, the political confrontation between Yeltsin and the reformers on the one side, and the opposition to radical economic reform on the other, became centered in the two branches of government. President Yeltsin demanded broad powers to carry out the reform program, but Parliament refused to adopt a new constitution that would give him the powers he demanded. In March 1993, a motion to remove the president through impeachment nearly passed in the Parliament.

On September 21, 1993, Yeltsin declared the Parliament dissolved, and called for elections to a new Parliament. Yeltsin's enemies barricaded themselves inside the Parliament building. After a ten-day standoff, the dissidents joined with some loosely organized paramilitary units outside the building and attacked the Moscow mayor's offices adjacent to the Russian White House. They even called on their followers to "seize the Kremlin." Finally, the army

agreed to back Yeltsin and suppress the uprising by force.

The circumstances of the December 1993 parliamentary elections were hardly auspicious. Yeltsin's decree meant that national elections were to be held for a legislature that did not, constitutionally, exist, since the constitution establishing these institutions was to be voted on in a referendum held in parallel with the parliamentary elections. Yet for all the violence surrounding its inception, the constitution approved in the December referendum has stayed in force since then.

THE CONTEMPORARY CONSTITUTIONAL ORDER

The Presidency

The 1993 constitution combined elements of presidentialism and parliamentarism. (See Figure 9.2 for a schematic overview of the Russian constitutional structure.) Although it provided for the separation of executive, legislative, and judicial branches and for a federal division of power between the central and

Structure of Russian Government

FIGURE 9.2

regional levels of government, it gave the president wide power. The president is directly elected for a four-year term and may not serve more than two consecutive terms. The president names the prime minister to head the government. Yet the government must have the confidence of parliament to remain in power. Although the constitution does not call the president the head of the executive branch, he is so in fact by virtue of his power to appoint the prime minister and the rest of the government and his right to issue **presidential decrees** with the force of law. (The decree power is somewhat limited in that decrees may not violate existing law and can be superseded by legislation.)

Over the decade since the constitution was approved, some informal practices have come to govern the exercise of central power. For example, the president and government divide executive responsibility. The government, headed by the prime minister, is primarily responsible for economic and social policy. The president directly oversees the ministries and other bodies directly concerned with coercion, law enforcement, and state security—the "power ministries." These include the Foreign Ministry, Defense Ministry, Ministry of Internal Affairs (which controls the regular police and security troops), Federal Security Service (FSB—formerly the KGB), and several other security and intelligence agencies. The president and his staff set overall policy in foreign and domestic domains, and the government develops the specific proposals and rules carrying out this policy. In practice, the government answers to the president, not Parliament. The government's base of support is the president rather than a particular coalition of political forces in Parliament.

Despite the asymmetrical constitutional balance, the Parliament does have some power. Its ability to exercise this power, however, depends on the composition of political forces represented in Parliament and the cohesiveness of the majority. Parliament's approval is required for any bill to become law. The State Duma (the lower house of Parliament) must confirm the president's nominee for prime minister. If, upon three successive votes, the Duma refuses to confirm the nomination, the president must dissolve the Duma and call new elections. Likewise, the Duma may vote to deny confidence in the government. If a motion of no confidence carries twice, the president must either dissolve Parliament or dismiss the government. During

Yeltsin's tenure as president, the Duma was able to block some of Yeltsin's legislative initiatives. Under Putin, however, it has largely been a rubber stamp. Conceivably, future presidents may have less of a free hand in their dealings with Parliament than Putin has. The constitution allows for wide ranging of types of relationships among the president, government, and Parliament, depending on the degree to which the president dominates the political system.

In addition to these powers, the president has a large array of other formal and informal powers in his constitutional capacity as "head of state," "guarantor of the constitution," and commander-in-chief of the armed forces. He oversees a large presidential administration, which supervises the federal government and keeps tabs on regional governments. Informally, the administration also manages relations with the Parliament, the courts, big business, the media, political parties, and major interest groups.

The president also oversees many official and quasi-official supervisory and advisory commissions, which he forms and regulates by presidential decree. One of the most important is the **Security Council,** chaired by the president. The Security Council consists of a permanent secretary, the heads of the power ministries and other security-related agencies, the prime minister, and chairs of the two chambers of Parliament. Its powers are broad but shadowy. Putin has used it to formulate policy proposals not only in matters of foreign and defense policy, but also on selected issues having to do with the organization of the executive branch.

Another prominent advisory body is the **State Council,** which comprises the heads of regional governments and thus parallels the Federation Council. In 2005 Putin created the **Public Chamber,** which is made up of 126 members from selected civic, sports, artistic, and other nongovernmental organizations (NGOs). Its purpose is to deliberate on matters of public policy, make recommendations to Parliament and the government on pending policy issues, and link civil society with the state. Like the State Council, it is a quasi-parliamentary deliberative body that the president can consult at will. All three bodies duplicate some of the deliberative and representative functions of Parliament, and therefore weaken Parliament's role. They illustrate the tendency, under both Yeltsin and Putin, for the president to create and dissolve new structures answering directly to the president. These improvised structures can be politically useful for the president as counterweights to constitutionally mandated bodies (such as Parliament), as well as providing policy advice and feedback. They help ensure that the president is always the dominant institution in the political system, but they undermine the authority of other formal institutions.

The Government

The *government* refers to the senior echelon of leadership in the executive branch. It is charged with formulating the main lines of national policy (especially in the economic and social realms) and overseeing its implementation. (The president oversees the formulation and execution of foreign and national security policy.) Here, the government corresponds to the Cabinet in Western parliamentary systems. But in contrast to most parliamentary systems, the makeup of the Russian government is not directly determined by the party composition of the Parliament. Indeed, there is scarcely any relationship between the distribution of party forces in the Duma and the political balance of the government. Nearly all members of the government are career managers and administrators rather than party politicians. Overall, the government's composition reflects the president's calculations about how to balance personal loyalty, professional competence, and the relative strength of major bureaucratic factions. When President Putin chose Viktor Zubkov to be prime minister on September 12, 2007, the political establishment was taken by surprise. Zubkov has headed the Federal Financial Monitoring Service, but he had a reputation as an effective manager and he is personally close to Putin. His very obscurity underscored the fact that Putin would continue to be the main source of policy direction for the country—perhaps even after leaving the presidency.

A major restructuring in 2004 reduced the number of ministries to sixteen. The goal was to simplify and rationalize the organization of the government by cutting down the number of ministries and state committees that were responsible for specific governmental functions and economic sectors and instead giving the ministries broader authority to oversee specialized agencies and services. However, although the aim was to streamline the structure of government, the total number of federal-level executive bodies rose from fifty-seven to seventy-two.[4]

The Parliament

The Parliament—called the Federal Assembly—is bicameral. The lower house is called the **State Duma,** and the upper house, the **Federation Council.** Legislation originates in the Duma. As Figure 9.3 shows, upon passage in the State Duma, a bill goes to the Federation Council for consideration. The Federation Council can only pass it, reject it, or reject it and call for the formation of an agreement commission (consisting of members of both houses) to iron out differences. If the Duma rejects the upper house's changes, it can override the Federation Council by a two-thirds vote and send the bill directly to the president.

When the bill has cleared Parliament, it goes to the president for signature. If the president refuses to sign the bill, it returns to the Duma. The Duma may pass it with his amendments by a simple absolute majority or it may override the president's veto, for which a two-thirds vote is required. The Federation Council must then also approve the bill, by a simple majority if the president's amendments are accepted or by a two-thirds vote if it chooses to override the president. On rare occasions, the Duma has overridden the president's veto; it has overridden Federation Council rejections more frequently. In other cases, the Duma has passed bills rejected by the president after accepting the president's amendments. Under President Yeltsin, political forces opposed to Yeltsin, particularly communists and nationalists, held the majority in the Duma. But Parliament and the president generally worked to head off major confrontations.

Until recently, the Duma's 450 members were equally divided between deputies elected in 225 single-member districts under a first-past-the-post (plurality) rule, and 225 deputies elected through proportional representation (PR) in a single national electoral district. A party receiving at least 5 percent of the vote on the party-list ballot is entitled to as many of the party-list seats in the Duma as its share of the party-list vote. As in other PR systems, votes cast for parties that fail to clear the 5 percent threshold are redistributed to winning parties. The electoral system has been reformed, however. Starting with the 2007 election, all 450 deputies will be elected proportionally from party lists in a single nationwide district, and the threshold for winning seats has been raised to 7 percent.[5]

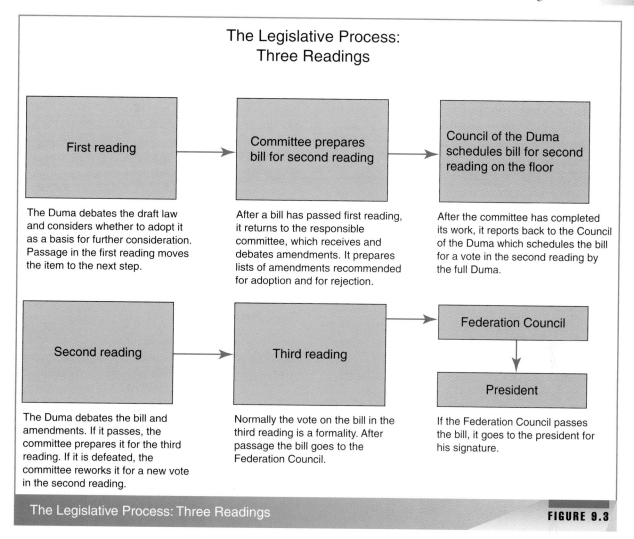

The Legislative Process: Three Readings

FIGURE 9.3

Nearly all Duma deputies either join party factions or form their own groups. Factions and groups enjoy desirable privileges in the Duma, including the right to committee chairmanships, office space, and recognition in floor debate. Faction leaders are represented on the governing body of the Duma, the Council of the Duma.

The December 2003 elections gave the forces aligned with President Putin an overwhelming majority in the Duma, which they have used to centralize power. The pro-Putin party, **United Russia,** holds two-thirds of the seats in the Duma. About 80 percent of all single-member district deputies joined the United Russia faction—a good indication of its drawing power. United Russia took nearly all committee chairmanships, and eight out of the eleven seats of the Council of the Duma, which is the steering body for the chamber. Since United Russia votes with a high degree of discipline, the Duma consistently delivers the president legislative majorities. Other factions have very little opportunity to influence the agenda, let alone the outcomes of legislative deliberations. United Russia's control over the agenda and voting has turned the Duma into a rubber stamp for Putin.

Each deputy is a member of one of twenty-nine standing committees with specific policy jurisdictions. As bills are submitted to the Duma, they are assigned to particular committees, which collect and review proposed amendments before reporting out the bills for votes by the full chamber with the committee's recommendations.

The Federation Council is designed as an instrument of federalism in that (as in the U.S. Senate) every constituent unit of the federation is represented by two representatives. Thus the populations of small ethnic-national territories are greatly overrepresented compared with more populous regions. The Federation Council has important powers. Besides acting on bills passed by the lower house, it also approves presidential nominees for high courts, such as the Supreme Court and the Constitutional Court. It must approve presidential decrees declaring martial law or a state of emergency, or any acts altering the boundaries of territorial units. It must consider any legislation dealing with taxes, budget, financial policy, treaties, customs, and declarations of war.

Until a major reform pushed through by President Putin in the spring of 2000, the Council's members were the heads of the executive and legislative branches of each constituent territory of the federation. Now, however, each governor and each regional legislature names a representative to the Federation Council to serve on a full-time basis. The governors appoint their representatives, who are then confirmed by the legislatures. The regional legislatures elect their representatives. They can recall their representatives at any time.

There is a great deal of dissatisfaction over the current role of the Federation Council. Many believe that the composition of the chamber should be replaced with one providing that the members are popularly elected. This must be reconciled, however, with the constitutional requirement that the two members of the chamber from each of Russia's eighty-nine territorial subjects must represent the executive and legislative branches.

Executive-Legislative Relations

Relations between president and Parliament during the Yeltsin period were often stormy. The first two Dumas, elected in 1993 and in 1995, were dominated by the communist and other leftist factions hostile to President Yeltsin and the policies of his government. This was particularly true in areas of economic policy and privatization. On other issues, such as matters concerning federal relations, the Duma and president often reached agreement—sometimes against the resistance of the Federation Council, whose members fought to protect regional prerogatives.

The 1999 election produced a Duma with a pro-government majority. President Putin and his government built a reliable base of support in the Duma for their legislative initiatives comprising a coalition of four centrist political factions. The 2003 election produced a still wider margin of support for the president in the Duma and an overwhelming majority for the United Russia party—which means that the president does not need to expend much effort in bargaining with the Duma to win its support for his policies. Generally speaking, the pro-presidential deputies in the Duma need the Kremlin much more than the Kremlin needs them. As a result, the balance of power in the political system under Putin has shifted steadily away from the Parliament and toward the president. A major shift in the alignment of political forces in the society, however, could lead to a different relationship between executive and legislative power.

The Constitutional Court

The 1993 constitution provides for judicial review by the **Constitutional Court.** Its nineteen members are nominated by the president but are subject to confirmation by the Council of the Federation. The court is empowered to consider the constitutionality of actions of the president, the Parliament, and lower-level governments. The court has carefully avoided issuing any decisions restricting presidential powers in any significant way. However, it has decided a number of thorny constitutional issues, including the relations between the two chambers of Parliament and the delineation of powers between the central and regional governments. It has also consistently defended the rights of individual defendants in the criminal justice system. The court has also tended to uphold the sovereignty of federal law over the rights of the constituent territories of the federation.

Under Putin, the court has taken care to avoid crossing the president. Nevertheless, even the possibility that it might exert a measure of independent political influence has led Putin to propose moving the seat of the court to St. Petersburg. This is an ingenious way of distancing the court from the tight web of governing bodies located in Moscow and thus of marginalizing it politically.

Central Government and the Regions

Following the breakup of the Soviet Union, many Russians feared that Russia would also break up into a patchwork of independent fiefdoms. Certainly Russia's territorial integrity was subjected to serious strains. Under President Yeltsin, the central government granted wide autonomy to regional governments in return for political support. Yeltsin went so far as to sign a series of bilateral treaties with over forty regions to codify the respective rights and responsibilities of the federal government and the individual regional government. Under Putin, however, the pendulum of federal policy has swung back sharply toward centralization.

The demographic factor is one reason that Russia did not break up. Eighty percent of Russia's population is ethnically Russian. None of its ethnic minorities accounts for more than 4 percent of the total (the Tatars form the largest of the ethnic minorities, constituting about 5.5 million of the 142 million total population). Rebuilding national community in post–Soviet Russia has been helped by Russia's thousand-year history of statehood. Yet until 1991, Russia was never constituted as a nation-state: under the tsars it was a multinational empire, and under Soviet rule it was nominally a federal union of socialist republics. State policy toward nationality has also varied over the centuries. In some periods, Russia recognized a variety of distinct ethnic-national communities and tolerated cultural differences among them. In other periods, the state pressured non-Russian groups to assimilate to Russian culture.

Russia was formally established as a federal republic under the Soviet regime. In contrast to the Soviet Union, of which it was the largest component, only some of Russia's constituent members were ethnic-national territories.[6] The rest were pure administrative subdivisions, populated mainly by Russians. The non-Russian ethnic-national territories were classified by size and status into autonomous republics, autonomous provinces, and national districts. In many of them, the indigenous ethnic group comprised a minority of the population. As of 2007, Russia comprises 85 constituent territorial units, officially termed the "subjects of the federation." They represent 6 different types of units. Republics, autonomous districts (all but one of them located within other units), and the one autonomous *oblast* give formal political representation to ethnic minorities; *oblasts* (provinces), *krais* (territories), and two cities of federal status (Moscow and St. Petersburg) are treated as ordinary administrative subdivisions with no special constitutional status.

One of the centralizing measures President Putin has pursued is the absorption of smaller ethnic districts into larger neighboring units. Two such mergers have

been approved and are being implemented. Several more such mergers are now being prepared. Most observers believe that the Putin administration seeks to eliminate most or all of the smaller ethnic units by merging them into their surrounding regions, thus reducing the patronage rights and political voice that come with their status as constituent members of the federation.[7]

The ethnic republics jealously guard their special status. From 1990 to 1992, all the republics adopted declarations of sovereignty, and two made attempts to declare full or partial independence from Russia. Only one, however, the Chechen Republic (**Chechnia**), resorted to arms to back up its claim. Chechnia is one of a belt of predominantly Muslim ethnic republics in the mountainous region of the North Caucasus, between the Black and Caspian Seas. Chechnia's president declared independence of Russia in 1991, an act Russia refused to recognize but did not initially overturn by force. When negotiations failed, however, in December 1994 Russian forces attacked the republic directly, subjecting its capital city, Groznyi, to devastating bombardment. This forced tens of thousands of Chechen and Russian residents to flee and led to a protracted, destructive war. Fighting ceased in summer 1996 but resumed in 1999. Federal forces had established control over most parts of Chechnia by early 2000, but Chechen guerrillas continue to carry out ambushes and suicide attacks against federal units.

Over time, the influence of radical fundamentalist Islam has increased among the Chechen rebels and they have resorted to terrorist attacks against civilian targets both in the North Caucasus region and in Moscow. One of the most shocking of these incidents was the seizure of a school in the town of Beslan, near Chechnia, in September 2004 (see Box 9.3). The brutal methods used by federal forces to suppress the uprising have fueled continuing hatred on the part of many Chechens against the federal government, which in turn facilitates recruitment by the terrorists. Observers hoped, however, that the death of the most notorious Chechen terrorist leader, Shamil Basaev, in July 2006, would weaken the guerrilla movement.

Chechnia, fortunately, is an exceptional case. In the other twenty ethnic republics, Moscow reached an accommodation granting the republics a certain amount of autonomy in return for acceptance of Russia's sovereign power. All twenty-one ethnic republics have the constitutional right to determine their own form

BOX 9.3

Beslan

September 1 is the first day of school each year throughout Russia. Children, accompanied by their parents, often come to school bringing flowers to their teachers. A group organized by the Chechen warlord Shamil Basaev chose September 1, 2004, to carry out one of the most horrific incidents in the history of the Chechen wars. A group of heavily armed militants stormed a school in the town of Beslan, located in the republic of North Osetia, next door to Chechnia. Over 1,000 schoolchildren, parents, and teachers were taken hostage. The terrorists crowded the captives into the school gymnasium, which they filled with explosives to prevent any rescue attempt. The terrorists refused to allow water and food to be brought into the school to relieve the hostages' suffering. Negotiations over the release of the hostages failed.

On the third day of the seige, something triggered the detonation of one of the bombs inside the school. In the chaos that followed, many of the children and adults rushed to escape. The terrorists fired at them. Federal forces stormed the school, trying to rescue the escaping hostages and to kill the terrorists. Many of the bombs planted by the terrorists exploded. Ultimately, about 350 of the hostages died, along with all but one of the terrorists, and an unknown number of security troops.

The media covered the events extensively. The Beslan tragedy had an impact on Russian national consciousness comparable to that of September 11 in the United States. While there had been a number of previous attacks tied to Chechen terrorists, none had cost so many innocent lives. Although many Russians blamed corruption and poor organization among the police for allowing the terrorists to take over the school initially and for failing to prevent the destruction at the end, they also recognized that the terrorists had made it risky for the security forces to attempt a rescue for fear of provoking a massacre of the children.

Putin and other senior government officials claimed that the terrorists were part of an international terrorist movement aimed ultimately at the dismemberment of Russia itself. Putin studiously avoided linking the incident to Russian policy in Chechnia. In response to the crisis, Putin called for measures to reinforce national security. He also demanded increased centralization of executive power, including an end to the direct election of governors. Most observers assumed that Putin had wanted to make these changes anyway, and that the Beslan tragedy simply gave him a political opening to enact them. Beslan was a tragic indication that the insurgency that began in Chechnia may be spreading throughout the North Caucasus region.

of state power so long as their decisions do not contradict federal law. All twenty-one have established presidencies. In many cases, the republic presidents have constructed personal power bases around appeals to ethnic solidarity and the cultural autonomy of the indigenous nationality. Often, they have used this power to establish personalistic dictatorships in their regions.

President Putin made clear his intention to reassert the federal government's authority over the regions. The reform of the Federation Council in 2000 was one step in this direction. Another was Putin's decree of May 13, 2000, that created seven new "federal districts." He appointed a special presidential representative to each district who monitors the actions of the regional governments within that district. This reform sought to strengthen central control over the activity

of federal bodies in the regions. Often, in the past, local branches of federal agencies had fallen under the influence of powerful governors.

Still another, very important, measure was the abolition of direct popular election of governors, including the presidents of the ethnic republics. Before 2005, regional chief executives were chosen by direct popular election. Since 2005, however, the president nominates a candidate to the regional legislature, which then approves the nomination (no legislature has dared to oppose one of Putin's appointments). Many citizens supported this change, believing that the institution of local elections had been discredited by corruption and fraud and that elections were more often determined by the influence of wealthy insiders than by public opinion. Critics of the reform accused Putin of creating a hypercentralized, authoritarian system of rule. Putin clearly hopes that appointed governors will be more accountable and effective, but past experience suggests that centralizing power by itself is unlikely to improve governance in the regions in the absence of other mechanisms for monitoring government performance and for enforcing the law.

Below the tier of regional government are units that are supposed to enjoy the right of self-government—municipalities and other local government units. Under new legislation, the right of local self-government has been expanded to a much larger set of units—such as urban and rural districts and small settlements—which has raised the total number of locally self-governing units to 24,000. In principle, local self-government is supposed to permit substantial policymaking autonomy in the spheres of housing, utilities, and social services (and to reduce the federal government's burden in providing such services). However, the new legislation—which is being phased in gradually—provides no fixed independent sources of revenue for these local entities. They thus depend for the great majority of their budgets on the regional governments. For their part, regional governments resist allowing local governments to exercise any significant powers of their own. In many cases, the mayors of the capital cities of regions are political rivals of the governors of the regions. Moscow and St. Petersburg are exceptional cases because they have the status of federal territorial subjects like republics and regions. Other cities lack the power and autonomy of Moscow and St. Petersburg, and they must bargain with their superior regional governments for shares of power.

Russia's postcommunist constitutional arrangements are still evolving. The political system allows considerable room for the arbitrary exercise of power and even, as under President Putin, the evisceration of democracy. Both Yeltsin and Putin have interpreted their presidential mandates broadly. Yeltsin used his decree power to carry out a massive privatization program. He also launched a brutal military campaign against the independence movement in the Chechen Republic without seeking parliamentary approval. In one eighteen-month period between 1998 and 1999, he named and dismissed his prime minister four times.

Putin has also used his presidential powers expansively. In 2000 he issued a decree creating seven federal superdistricts to facilitate central supervision of regional governments, and he appointed representatives to oversee them. By decree he also created a new consultative structure of regional governors called the State Council. This was an effort to mollify the governors, whom he had deprived of seats in the Federation Council. Both institutional changes were not envisioned by the constitution, but also were not specifically prohibited by it. The constitutional arrangements established under President Yeltsin had the potential to evolve toward democracy. A successful democratic transition, however, depends on more than a democratic constitution. The web of political institutions surrounding formal constitutional rules strongly shapes the way officeholders wield power and determines how effectively institutions hold leaders accountable for their actions. Informal rules can be far more important than formal rules. If rulers can circumvent formal limits on their power, constitutional structures may become irrelevant to the actual exercise of power.

Putin's style of rule resembles the pattern that political scientist Guillermo O'Donnell has called "delegative democracy."[8] In such a system, common in Latin America, a president may win an election and then proceed to govern as if he were the sole source of authority in the country. The president exercises so much power over other political structures, thanks to his control of the police and military and his access to patronage, that he can negate the nominal separation of powers written into the constitution. In such a system, parliamentarians may use their positions not to represent constituents or craft legislation but to trade favors and enrich their friends and family. Judges may deem it safer to tailor their decisions to the wishes of powerful state officials. The editors of major newspapers bury stories unfavorable to the authorities. Interest groups curry favor with officials rather than mobilizing their supporters around particular policy positions. The leaders of opposition parties learn to accept their role on the sidelines.

Under Putin this pattern of "hollowed-out democracy" has become evident. Without explicitly violating any constitutional limits on his power, and without abolishing elections or other democratic institutions, Putin has effectively negated the constitutional limits on his power built into the constitution. Using the president's extensive powers over the executive branch, he has neutralized and marginalized nearly all independent sources of political authority, while observing formal constitutional procedures. For

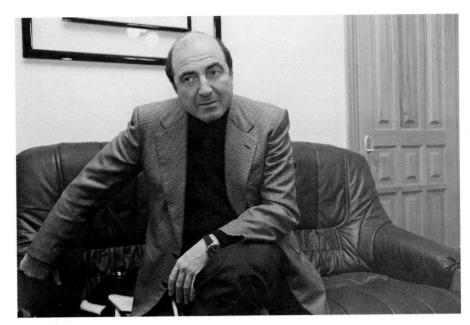

Boris Berezovsky was one of the most prominent oligarchs of the Yeltsin era. Today he lives in exile in Great Britain and faces criminal charges if he returns to Russia.

East News/Getty Images

example, he usually enacts his policy program by passing legislation through Parliament rather than by relying on his decree power. But having used his control over electoral processes to secure overwhelming majority support in both chambers, parliamentary approval of his agenda is assured. As observers have pointed out, Putin appears to dislike the open give and take of democratic politics, preferring more familiar methods of behind-the-scenes bureaucratic maneuvering. Putin's use of presidential power presents a sharp contrast to the Yeltsin period. Yeltsin used his presidential powers erratically and impulsively. But Yeltsin respected certain limits on his power: he did not suppress media criticism, and he tolerated political opposition. Faced with an opposition-led parliament, Yeltsin was willing to compromise with his opponents to enact legislation. However, Yeltsin grew dependent on a small group of favored oligarchs for support and allowed them to accumulate massive fortunes and corrupt influence. Likewise, Yeltsin allowed regional bosses to flout federal authority with impunity because he found it less costly to accommodate them than to fight them.

The loss of state capacity under Yeltsin illustrates one danger of an overcentralized political system. When the president does not effectively command the powers of the office, power drifts to other centers of power. Putin's presidency illustrates the opposite danger. When Putin took over, he was faced with the task of reversing the breakdown of political control and responsibility that had accelerated under Yeltsin. Although he has repeatedly called for a system based on respect for the rule of law, he has also steadily restored authoritarian rule. He captured the contradictory quality of this vision in his 2004 message to Parliament, when he said that creating "a free society of free people is the very most important of our tasks," but at the same time he warned that any attempts to effect a significant change in policy "could lead to irreversible consequences. And they must be absolutely excluded."[9]

RUSSIAN POLITICAL CULTURE IN THE POST-SOVIET PERIOD

Russian political culture is the product of centuries of autocratic rule, rapid but uneven improvement of educational and living standards in the twentieth century, and rising exposure to Western standards of political life. The result is a contradictory bundle of values in contemporary political culture: a sturdy core of belief in democratic values is accompanied by a firm belief in the importance of a strong state and sharp disillusionment with the way democratization and market reform worked out in Russia. In a 2005 survey, 66 percent of Russians agreed that "Russia needs democracy," but 45 percent said that the kind of democracy Russia needs is "a completely special kind corresponding to Russian specifics."[10] Fifty percent of the public regard Stalin as a positive figure in Russian history; only 36 percent assess him negatively.[11] Russians rate the Soviet regime before perestroika positively as a time of relative security and prosperity, but reject the notion of bringing back communism. Nearly half of the population (48 percent) agrees with the statement that it would have been better if perestroika had never been attempted, but 40 percent disagree.[12] Over 70 percent of Russians regret the breakup of the Soviet Union, but 72 percent say that restoring it is neither possible nor necessary.[13]

James Gibson sums up the findings of a number of studies by drawing three conclusions: one, there is rather extensive support in Russia for democratic institutions and processes so long as people see these as rights for themselves; two, there is much less support for extending rights to unpopular minorities; and three, the segments of the population who are the most exposed to the influences of modern civilization (younger people, more educated people, and residents of big cities) are also those most likely to support democratic values. These observations suggest that as Russia becomes more open to the outside world, support for democratic values will grow.[14]

Contemporary values and beliefs have been shaped by both long-term factors (such as the rise in educational levels over the decades of Soviet rule) and by short-term factors (such as the powerful impact of glasnost in raising popular aspirations for a standard of living close to that of the developed West). Public values were also shaped by the wrenching loss of familiar bearings as the old regime collapsed and with it, the very Soviet Union.

In his struggles with the communist opposition, Yeltsin encouraged people to imagine that his leadership would usher in a new era of prosperity and freedom. Instead, poverty, unemployment, and inequality rose sharply, and privation led to the enrichment of a small class of ultra-rich tycoons who flaunted their quickly amassed fortunes. Organized crime flourished. The modest but universal social safety net of the communist regime disintegrated. Little wonder that many Russians came to regard "democracy" as a bitter

joke and the market economy as a mechanism for exploitation—just as communist propaganda had taught. Democratization and economic liberalization became associated in Russians' minds with the breakdown of social and economic order since the late 1980s. Although Russians generally value the idea of democratic rights and freedoms, most people tend to consider them remote and unattainable in Russia.

Both nostalgia for the old order and aspirations for a better future set standards by which people judge the current regime harshly. Most Russians are highly critical of the performance of the current regime—apart from Putin. Russians think that the country's leaders are mainly concerned with their own power and wealth rather than with the country's well-being.

Surveys show that citizens have little faith in the current political system, although, as Table 9.1 shows, there is a good deal more confidence in Putin than in any other individual leader or institution.

Trust in Institutions, 2004	TABLE 9.1
	Percent Responding "fully merits confidence"
President of Russia	56
Church, religious organizations	43
Army	30
Press, radio, TV	26
Security organs	21
Regional (krai, oblast, republican) organs of power	19
Local (city, district) organs of power	19
Government of Russia	17
Courts	14
Procuracy	12
Federation Council	12
State Duma	11
Trade Unions	11
Police	10
Political Parties	5

Note: Question—"To what degree, in your view, does each of the following merit confidence?" Survey conducted September 2004. N = 2107. Margin of error 3%.

Source: Levada Center, Analiticheskii tsentr Yuriia Levady. http://www.levada.ru/press/2004092702.html (accessed 30 September 2004).

Moreover, as Figure 9.4 shows, the public distinguishes sharply between Putin and the government. Russians give Putin credit above all for reversing the deterioration of living standards: 24 percent of the population cite this as his main achievement. These figures show how successful Putin has been at taking credit for positive developments in the country and allowing the government to take the blame for continuing problems. Not surprisingly, Putin's popularity leads Russians to want to give him sweeping power over the political system. After the March 2004 presidential election, a nationwide survey found that 68 percent agreed with the statement that concentrating nearly all state power in Putin's hands "would be beneficial to Russia."[15] In 2005, 51 percent agreed with the proposition that the kind of president Russia needs is one "able to direct the work of the government, parliament, judiciary and regional organs of power with a firm hand"; 44 percent preferred one "who strictly

observes the Constitution and is able to cooperate with other state bodies on the basis of the law."[16]

Russians' impatience with a separation of powers system (and their faith in Putin) does not mean that they do not also want democratic rights and freedoms for themselves. Indeed, paradoxically, many associate Putin with democracy. Over half of the population (55 percent) thought that following Putin's reelection as president in 2004 the country would develop as a democracy; the comparable figure in 2000 was only 35 percent. Russians prize their right to criticize the authorities: 76 percent of respondents think it is permissible to criticize Putin, and 86 percent think criticism of the government is permissible.[17] And a clear majority of Russians believe that Russia needs a political opposition (see Table 9.2).

The political culture thus combines contradictory elements. Russians do value democratic rights, but experience has taught them that under the banner of

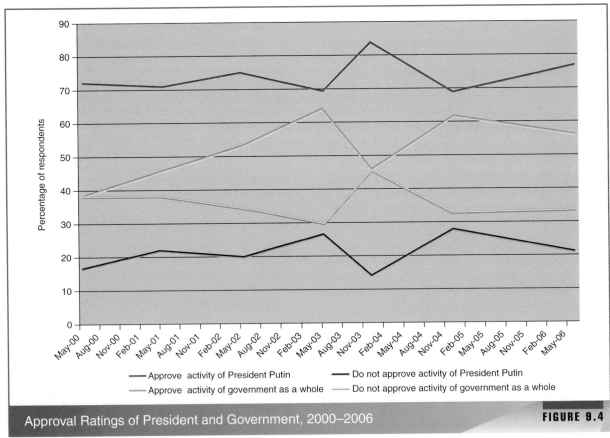

Approval Ratings of President and Government, 2000–2006   **FIGURE 9.4**

Source: Surveys of Russian population conducted by Levada Center (Moscow), reported on website: www.levada.ru.

Support for Principle of Democratic Opposition (in %)				TABLE 9.2
	Dec. 2002	Oct. 2004	Dec. 2005	June 2006
Definitely needed/ more needed than not	56	66	61	56
Definitely not needed/more not	24	21	25	20
Hard to say	20	13	14	24

Note: Question—"Is a political opposition to the authorities needed now in Russia?" Survey conducted 19–22 June 2006. N = 1600, 18 years old and older, in 128 towns and 46 regions.

Source: Levada Center, http://www.levada.ru/press/2006062901.html (accessed 13 July 2006).

democracy, politicians can abuse their power to the detriment of the integrity of the state and the well-being of society. They also feel powerless to affect state policy. Little wonder that a leader such as Putin can command such widespread support despite the general mistrust Russians have for the post-Soviet political institutions. Russians see him as restoring order following a protracted period of social and political breakdown. As Richard Rose and his colleagues argue, the reason Russians generally approve the current regime is not because they consider it to be ideal, but because it has improved economic well-being and they see little prospect for changing it.[18]

Surveys also reveal considerable continuity with the past in support for the idea that the state should ensure society's prosperity and the citizens' material security. More than in Western Europe or the United States, Russians believe that the state is responsible for providing a just moral and social order, with justice being understood as social equality more than as equality before the law. This pattern reflects the lasting influence of traditional conceptions of state and society on Russian political culture. Still, few would support the reestablishment of Soviet rule or a reversion to a military dictatorship. Most people think that the tremendous upheavals they have experienced since the late 1980s will result in an improved life—not soon, but "eventually."[19]

Political culture is also shaped by slower acting but more lasting influences, including the succession of generations, rising educational levels, and urbanization.[20]

The shift in values and beliefs has accelerated as new generations of young people are exposed to fundamentally different influences than those to which their parents were exposed. To a large extent, these differences are mutually reinforcing: the older generations tend to have lower levels of education and less exposure to the more cosmopolitan way of life of cities.

Political Socialization

The Soviet regime devoted enormous effort to political indoctrination and propaganda. The regime controlled the content of school curricula, mass media, popular culture, political education, and nearly every other channel by which values and attitudes were formed. The heart of Soviet doctrine was the Marxist belief that the way in which a society organizes its production—feudalism, capitalism, socialism, and so forth—determines the structure of values and beliefs prevalent in the society. The idea was that the ruling class in each society determines the basic ideology of the society. Therefore, Soviet propaganda and indoctrination emphasized that Soviet citizens were part of a world-wide working-class movement to overthrow capitalism and replace it with socialism, in which there would be no private property. Needing to knit together a highly diverse multinational state, the Soviet regime downplayed national feeling and replaced it with a sense of patriotic loyalty to the Soviet state and to the working class's interests in the worldwide class struggle.

Today the ideological content of Russian education has changed significantly, and there is much less overt political control over the formation of attitudes and values. In place of the idea of the class struggle and the international solidarity of the working class, textbooks stress love for the Russian national heritage. Historical figures who in the communist era were honored as heroes of the struggle of ordinary people against feudal or capitalist masters are now held up as great representatives of Russia's national culture.[21] Schoolbooks and mass media place heavy emphasis on loyalty to Russia as a state, tying it to Russian national and patriotic pride rather than to international working-class solidarity. This theme underlies Russia's effort to create a new sense of national community within the country's post-Soviet state boundaries.

State leaders also play on the strong undercurrent of desire for some sort of restored union among at least some of the former Soviet republics. Russian television broadcasts pay considerable attention to activities in the "near abroad," as Russians term the other former Soviet republics. Russians continue to feel tied to the other republics by decades of shared social, economic, cultural, and political experience. Putin and other politicians actively play on this sentiment, calling for the reinforcement of ties between Russia and its neighbors in the Commonwealth of Independent States (CIS). Sergei Shoigu, the relatively popular minister for Emergency Situation, noted during the Parliament election campaign in November 2003 that he hoped "to live to see the day when we have one big country within the borders of the [former] Soviet Union." A former KGB chairman went so far as to say that "if we do not reassemble the Soviet Union, we have no future at all."[22] The neoimperial currents running through Russian political culture undercut the effort to create a new post-Soviet national community based on democratic values.

The authorities have also turned to the Orthodox Church as an aid in political socialization. They regard the Church as a valuable ally in building patriotic loyalty, national pride, and a framework of ethical behavior. The Church in turn seeks to protect its traditional status as Russia's state church, enabling it to block other Christian denominations from proselytizing in Russia. As of the fall of 2006, a required course on the fundamentals of Orthodox culture had been introduced into the school curriculum in nearly twenty regions, and about 20,000 Orthodox priests were serving as chaplains in the armed forces.[23]

Although the Putin regime has gone far to impose political controls over the mass media, it has not constructed the kind of comprehensive political socialization system that the Soviet state employed to indoctrinate citizens with the desired attitudes, values, and beliefs. Nevertheless, the authorities under Putin have promoted a particular political message intended to build support for their foreign and domestic policies. Print and broadcast media consistently emphasize the principles of sovereignty and a strong state along with those of democracy, market economics, and the rule of law. Putin's team works to create the impression that they are finding a moderate middle ground between the extremes of the past—totalitarian communism on the one hand, and unbridled oligarchic capitalism, on the other—and to restore continuity with the best traditions of Russia's political history.

Political socialization in Russia is much less subject to direct state control than it was in the Soviet era, and even then, awareness of the political and economic standards of the outside world filtered into the consciousness of the Soviet population. Today, the authorities seek to build loyalty to the state, confidence in the future, and acceptance of a highly centralized regime, while at the same time spurring Russians to modernize the economy. As time passes, Russians' support for Putin's model of "sovereign democracy" will depend on the regime's performance in meeting its own goals.

POLITICAL PARTICIPATION

In a democracy, citizens take part in public life both through direct forms of political participation (such as voting, engaging in party work, organizing for a cause, demonstrating, and lobbying) and indirect forms of participation (such as membership in civic groups and in voluntary associations). Both kinds of participation influence the quality of government. By means of collective action citizens signal to policymakers what they want government to do. Through these channels of participation activists rise to positions of leadership. But, despite the legal equality of citizens in democracies, levels of participation in the population vary with differences across groups in resources, opportunities, and motivations. The better-off and better-educated are disproportionately involved in political life everywhere, but in some societies the disproportion is much greater than in others. And where deep inequalities in the distribution of wealth and income reinforce differentials in political voice between rich and poor, democracy itself is at risk.[24]

The Importance of Social Capital

A healthy fabric of voluntary associations has been recognized since de Tocqueville's time as an important component of democracy. As Robert Putnam has shown, participation in civic life builds social capital—reciprocal bonds of trust and obligation among citizens that facilitate collective action. Where social capital is significant, people treat one another as equals rather than as members of social hierarchies. They are more willing to cooperate in ways that benefit the society and improve the quality of government by sharing the burden of making government accountable and effective.[25] For example, where people feel less distance from and mistrust toward government, governments are better able to float bonds to provide improvements to community infrastructure. People are more willing to pay their taxes, so that government has more revenue to spend on public goods—and less ability and less incentive to divert it into politicians' pockets. Both capitalism and democratic government rest on people's ability to cooperate for mutual benefit.

In Russia, however, social capital has historically been scarce compared with West European societies, and participation in civic activity has been extremely limited. Moreover, state and society have generally been separated by mutual mistrust and suspicion. State authorities have usually stood outside and above society, extracting what resources they needed from society but not cultivating ties of obligation to it. The communist regime further depleted the stock of social capital by coopting associations useful for the state and repressing those that threatened its interests. For this reason, social capital not only in Russia, but throughout the former communist bloc, is significantly lower than in other parts of the world.[26]

The weakness of intermediate associations linking political elites to ordinary citizens widens the mutual distance between state and society. Thus, although Russians turn out to vote in elections in relatively high numbers, participation in organized forms of political activity is low. Opinion polls show that most people believe that their involvement in political activity is futile, and they have little confidence that they can influence government policy through their participation.

Since the late 1980s, political participation, apart from voting, has seen a brief, intense surge followed by a protracted ebb. Membership in voluntary associations in contemporary Russia is extremely low. According to survey data, 91 percent of the population do not belong to any sports or recreational club, literary or other cultural group, political party, local housing association, or charitable organization. Four percent belong to sports or recreation groups, and 2 percent each say that they belong to a housing bloc, neighborhood association, or cultural group. Only half a percent report being a member of a political party. About 9 percent report attending church at least once a month, and about 20 percent say that they are members of trade unions. Attending religious services and trade union membership are very passive forms of

participation in public life. Yet even when these and other types of participation are taken into account, almost 60 percent of the population still are outside any voluntary public associations.[27]

This is not to say that Russian citizens are *psychologically* disengaged from public life or that they are socially isolated. Half of the Russian adult population reports reading national newspapers "regularly" or "sometimes" and almost everyone watches national television "regularly" (81 percent). Sixty-nine percent read local newspapers regularly or sometimes. Sixty-six percent discuss the problems of the country with friends regularly or sometimes, and 48 percent say that people ask them their opinions about what is happening in the country. A similar percentage of people discuss the problems of their city with friends.[28] Russians do vote in high proportions in national elections—higher, in fact, than their American counterparts.[29]

Moreover, Russians prize their right *not* to participate in politics. Today's low levels of political participation are a reflection of the low level of confidence in political institutions and the widespread view that ordinary individuals have little influence over government. In one 2000 survey, 85 percent of the respondents expressed the opinion that they have no influence to affect the decisions of the authorities.[30] In the 2003 Duma elections, 4.7 percent of the voters expressed their dissatisfaction with the array of choices offered by checking the box marked "against all" on the party list ballot.[31]

The withdrawal from active political participation today results from the shattering of the expectations for change that rose to unrealistic levels in the late 1980s and early 1990s. Gorbachev's policy of relaxing controls on political expression and political participation stimulated a short-lived surge of involvement in many forms of public activity, including mass protests, such as strikes and demonstrations, as well as the creation of thousands of new informal organizations. But this wave subsided in the early 1990s. The disengagement and skepticism reflected in public life today reflects disillusionment with how conditions have turned out.

Elite Recruitment

Elite recruitment refers to the institutional processes in a society by which people gain access to positions of influence and responsibility. Elite recruitment is closely tied to political participation, because it is through participation in community activity that people take on leadership roles, learn civic skills (such as organization and persuasion), develop networks of friends and supporters, and become interested in pursuing political careers.

In the Soviet regime, the link between participation and elite recruitment was highly formalized. The Communist Party recruited the population into a variety of officially sponsored organizations—such as the Communist Party, youth leagues, trade unions, and women's associations. Through such organizations, the regime identified potential leaders and gave them experience in organizing group activity. The party reserved the right to approve appointments to any position that carried high administrative responsibility or that was likely to affect the formation of public attitudes. The system for recruiting, training, and appointing individuals for positions of leadership and responsibility in the regime was called the **nomenklatura** system. Those individuals who were approved for the positions on nomenklatura lists were informally called "the nomenklatura." Many citizens regarded them as the ruling class in Soviet society.

The democratizing reforms of the late 1980s and early 1990s made two important changes to the process of elite recruitment. First, the old nomenklatura system crumbled along with other Communist Party controls over society. Second, although most members of the old ruling elites adapted themselves to the new circumstances and stayed on in various official capacities, the wave of new informal organizations and popular elections brought many new people into elite positions. Today, the contemporary Russian political elite consists of a mixture of career types: some people have worked their way up through the state bureaucracy while others have entered politics through other channels, such as elective politics or business.

As in other areas of political life, old Soviet institutional mechanisms for recruitment are being restored under Putin. In the communist regime, the party maintained schools for training political leaders, where rising officials were given a combination of management education and political indoctrination. Today, most of those schools serve a similar function as academies for training civil servants and are overseen by Putin's presidential administration. Moreover, elements of the old nomenklatura system are being restored with a view to ensuring that competent and politically reliable cadres are available for recruitment not only to state bureaucratic positions but even for management positions in major firms.[32]

There are two major differences between elite recruitment in the communist regime and the present. The nomenklatura system of the Soviet regime ensured that in every walk of life, those who held positions of

President Vladimir Putin offers a reassuring word to Russian citizens.

AFP/Corbis

power and responsibility were approved by the party. They thus formed different sections of a single political elite and owed their positions to their political loyalty and usefulness. Today, however, there are multiple elites (political, business, scientific, cultural, etc.), reflecting the greater degree of pluralism in post-Soviet society.

Second, there are multiple channels for recruitment to today's *political* elite. Many of its members come from positions in the federal and regional executive agencies. Putin in particular has recruited officials for his administration heavily from among the police (the regular police and the security services) and from the military.[33] Other prominent political figures climbed the ladder by winning local or national elections, or after making successful business careers.

The formation of a business elite, in fact, is one of the most remarkable phenomena since the end of the Soviet regime. Many of today's successful businesspeople came out of the old Soviet nomenklatura, as old guard bureaucrats discovered ways to cash in on their political contacts and get rich quickly. Money from the Communist Party found its way into the establishment of many new business ventures, including several of the first commercial banks. As early as 1987 and 1988, officials of the Communist Youth League (**Komsomol**) saw the possibilities of using the organizations' assets to set up lucrative business ventures, such as video salons, banks, discos, tour agencies, and publishing houses.[34] They took advantage of their insider contacts, obtaining business licenses, office space, and exclusive contracts with little difficulty. Some bought (at bargain basement prices) controlling interests in state firms that were undergoing privatization, and a few years later found themselves millionaires or billionaires.

Other members of the new business elite rose through channels outside the state. Many, in fact, entered business in the late 1980s, as new opportunities for legal and quasi-legal commercial activity opened up. A strikingly high proportion of the first generation of the new business elite comprised young scientists and mathematicians working in research institutes and universities. The new commercial sector sprang up very quickly. By the end of 1992, there were nearly 1 million private businesses registered, with some 16 million people working in them.[35]

The new business elite are closely tied to the state, sometimes in order to capture benefits, and sometimes because state officials keep business on a short leash.

Financial-industrial conglomerates often cultivate strategic alliances with well-placed officials in the government. Both under Yeltsin and Putin, bureaucratic factions form around particular enterprises and industries. Businesses need licenses, permits, contracts, exemptions, and other benefits from government. Political officials, in turn, need financial contributions to their campaigns, political support, favorable media coverage, and other benefits that business can provide. In the 1990s, the close and collusive relations between many businesses and government officials nurtured widespread corruption and the meteoric rise of a small group of business tycoons, popularly known as oligarchs. The oligarchs took advantage of their links to President Yeltsin's administration to acquire control of some of Russia's most valuable companies. The prominence of the newly rich fed a strong public backlash that made it politically viable for President Putin to suppress some of them and destroy their business empires by police methods. The notion that businesspeople can make money honestly and benefit society by doing so strikes many people as a hopelessly naive proposition. Many therefore welcome a heavy-handed state to protect them from the power of the wealthy. But often when the state cracks down on a particular business firm, it is a maneuver by one bureaucratic faction to acquire control of a lucrative business asset from another, not a step toward the rule of law.

INTEREST ARTICULATION: BETWEEN STATISM AND PLURALISM

The political and economic changes of the last decade in Russia have had a powerful impact on the way social interests are organized. A far more diverse spectrum of interest associations has developed than existed under the communist regime. There are tens of thousands of nongovernmental organizations (NGOs)—a phenomenon that could not exist in the communist society, when the Communist Party oversaw all organizations. The pattern of interest articulation, however, still reflects the powerful impact of state control over society, as well as the sharp disparities in wealth and power that formed during the transition period. A few organizations have considerable influence in policymaking, while other groups have little. Patron-client networks between state officials and their patrons and their clients remain a persistent feature of political life.

The old regime did not tolerate the open pursuit of any interests except those authorized by the state. Interest organizations—such as trade unions, youth groups, professional societies, and the like—were closely supervised by the Communist Party. This statist model of interest articulation was upset by glasnost. Glasnost stimulated an explosion of political expression, which in turn prompted groups to form and to make political demands and participate in elections. It is hard today to imagine how profound was the impact of glasnost on Soviet society. Suddenly it opened the floodgates to a growing stream of startling facts, ideas, disclosures, reappraisals, scandals, and sensations. Gorbachev was clearly surprised by the range and intensity of the new demands that erupted. In loosening the party's controls over communication sufficiently to encourage people to speak and write freely and openly, Gorbachev also relinquished the controls that would have enabled him to limit political expression when it went too far.

As people voiced their deep-felt demands and grievances, others recognized that they shared the same beliefs and values, and made common cause with them, sometimes forming new, unofficial organizations. Therefore, one result of glasnost was a wave of participation in "informal"—that is, unlicensed and uncontrolled—public associations. Daring publications in the media allowed people with common interests to identify one another and encouraged them to come together to form independent associations. When the authorities tried to limit or prohibit such groups, they generated still more frustration and protest. Associations of all sorts formed: groups dedicated to remembering the victims of Stalin's terror, ultra-nationalists who wanted to restore tsarism, and nationalist movements in many republics. The devastating explosion of the nuclear reactor at Chernobyl in 1986 had a tremendous impact in stimulating the formation of environmental protest, linked closely to nationalist sentiment in Belarus and Ukraine.[36]

The elimination of the state's monopoly on productive property resulted in the formation of new interests, among them those with a stake in the market economy. No longer does the state demand that organized groups serve a state-defined political agenda, as was the case under the old regime. Now groups can form freely to represent a diversity of interests, compete for access to influence and resources, and define their own agenda. The Justice Ministry estimates that there are nearly half a million NGOs, although probably no more than a quarter of them are active at any given time.[37]

In some cases, NGOs are the successors of recognized associations of the old regime, such as official trade unions. Often these groups cling to their inherited organizational assets and continue to seek "insider" access to the state. Other groups sprang up during the glasnost period or later, but must work closely with legislative and executive authorities in order to gain access to meeting places and media attention.

There are elements of corporatism in the state's relations with interest groups under Putin because of the regime's preference for dealing directly with controllable umbrella organizations representing particular segments of society. Overall, however, the pattern of interest group activity is more pluralist than corporatist because in most cases, interest associations are too numerous, too weak internally, and too competitive for corporatism to succeed. But under Putin, interest articulation is becoming more statist as the regime has gradually increased political controls on nongovernment associations.

Although the pattern of comprehensive Communist Party control over nongovernmental associations that was characteristic of the Soviet regime is gone, the state still exercises substantial influence over NGOs. Under Putin, the rules governing their operation have tightened. A law enacted at the beginning of 2006 imposed new restrictions on NGOs, making it easier for the authorities to deny them registration and to shut them down. At the same time, the authorities warned that foreign intelligence services were sponsoring Russian NGOs for the purposes of intelligence-gathering and subversion. The political atmosphere for NGOs became considerably chillier.

Let us consider three examples of associational groups: the **Russian Union of Industrialists and Entrepreneurs (RUIE)**, the **League of Committees of Soldiers' Mothers,** and the **Federation of Independent Trade Unions of Russia (FITUR)**. They illustrate different strategies for organization and influence and different relationships to the state.

The Russian Union of Industrialists and Entrepreneurs

Most formerly state-owned industrial firms are now wholly or partly privately owned. More and more industrial managers respond to the incentives of a market economy rather than to those of a state socialist economy. Under the old regime, managers were told to fulfill the plan regardless of cost or quality. Profit was not a relevant consideration.[38] Now, more managers seek to maximize profits and increase the value of their firms. Although many still demand subsidies and protection from the state, more and more would prefer an environment where laws and contracts are enforced by the state, regulation is reasonable and honest, taxes are fair (and low), and barriers to foreign trade are minimized. These gradual changes are visible in the changing political interests of the association that represents the interests of big business in Russia, the Russian Union of Industrialists and Entrepreneurs, or RUIE. The RUIE is the single most powerful organized interest group in Russia. Its members comprise both the old state industrial firms (now mostly private or quasi-private) and the newer financial-industrial conglomerates headed by the oligarchs.

In the early 1990s, the RUIE's lobbying efforts were aimed at winning continued state support of industrial firms and planning for a slow transition to a market economy. The RUIE also helped broker agreements between business and labor, and it was a source of policy advice for government and Parliament. In 2000, the Putin administration let it be known that it wanted the oligarchs to join the RUIE and the RUIE to become the unified voice of big business. The Putin leadership also sponsored two other business associations to articulate the interests of small and medium-size business.

Over time, the RUIE's role has changed according to the opportunities and limits set by the state authorities. Under Putin, it has been a loyal, subordinate, and useful source of policy advice and political support for the government. It has expanded its in-house capacity for working with the government and the Parliament in drafting legislation. On a wide range of issues—from land reform; tax law; pension policy; bankruptcy legislation; reform of the natural gas, energy, and railroad monopolies; regulation of the securities market; and the terms of Russia's entry to the World Trade Organization—the RUIE has been active and influential in shaping policy.

Yet the limits of RUIE's power as the collective voice of big business are clear. When the Putin regime began its campaign to destroy the Yukos oil firm starting in July 2003 (see Box 9.4), RUIE confined itself to mild expressions of concern. Its members, evidently fearful of crossing Putin, chose not to defend Yukos' head, Mikhail Khodorkovsky, or to protest the use of police methods to destroy one of Russia's largest oil companies. Instead, they promised to meet their tax obligations and to do more to help the country fight poverty. Putin pointedly avoided meeting with RUIE and other business association leaders from November 2003 to July 2004—and then agreed to meet with them only on the condition that the subject of Yukos not be discussed. Perhaps if big business had taken a strong and united stand, they could have influenced state policy. But the desire by each individual firm to maintain friendly relations with the government and fear of government reprisals undercut big business's capacity for collective action.

The League of Committees of Soldiers' Mothers

The Soviet regime sponsored several official women's organizations, but these mainly served propaganda purposes. During the glasnost period, a number of unofficial women's organizations sprang up. One such group was the Committee of Soldiers' Mothers. It formed in the spring of 1989 when some 300 women in Moscow rallied to protest the end of student deferments from military conscription. Their protest came hard on the heels of Gorbachev's withdrawal of Soviet forces from the decade-long war in Afghanistan, where over 13,000 Soviet troops were killed in bitter and demoralizing fighting. In response to the Soldiers' Mothers' actions, Gorbachev agreed to restore student deferments. Since then Soldiers' Mothers' movement has grown, with local branches forming in hundreds of cities, joining together in the League of Committees of Soldiers' Mothers. Their focus has expanded somewhat but remains centered on the problems of military service. The league presses the military to eliminate the use of soldiers' labor in its construction battalions and to end the brutal hazing of recruits, which results in the deaths (in many cases by suicide) of hundreds of soldiers each year. The league also advises young men on how to avoid being conscripted.[39]

The onset of large-scale hostilities in Chechnia in 1994–1996 and 1999–2000 stimulated a new burst of activity by the league. It helped families locate soldiers who were missing in action or captured by the Chechen rebel forces. It sent missions to Chechnia to negotiate for the release of prisoners and to provide

One of the most widely publicized episodes of the Putin era was the state takeover of the powerful private oil company, Yukos, and the criminal prosecution of its Chief Executive Officer Mikhail Khodorkovsky. At the time of his arrest in October 2003, Khodorkovsky had been the wealthiest of Russia's new postcommunist magnates. His career began in the late 1980s when he was a young Komsomol activist working in the Moscow city government, and used his Komsomol resources and connections to start a bank and later to acquire—at a bargain basement price—80 percent of the shares of the Yukos oil company when the government privatized it. At first, like some of the other newly wealthy business tycoons, Khodorkovsky sought to squeeze maximum profit from the firm by stripping its assets. Soon, however, his business strategy changed, and he began to invest in the productive capacity of the firm. He made Yukos the most dynamic of Russia's oil companies. Khodorkovsky discovered that by emulating Western business practices, the company could increase its net worth and productive capacity. He reformed corporate governance practices and sought to have Yukos's shares listed on foreign stock exchanges. By improving the efficiency and transparency of the firm, Khodorkovsky found that share prices rose, and with them Khodorkovsky's own net worth. At its peak in 2002, the company's assets were estimated to be worth about $20 billion, of which Khodorkovsky owned nearly $8 billion. He was Russia's wealthiest citizen.

Meantime, seeking to improve his public image, Khodorkovsky created a foundation and launched several charitable initiatives. He recruited some distinguished international figures to his foundation's board. He became active in Russian politics, helping to fund the parties Yabloko and the Union of Rightist Forces, and sponsoring the election campaigns of several deputies to the State Duma. Critics accused him of wanting to control parliament and even of wanting to change the constitution to turn it into a parliamentary system. There was talk that he intended to seek the presidency.

Khodorkovsky himself refused to kowtow to the authorities. Without consulting with the Kremlin he began talks with foreign oil companies on selling a significant share of Yukos stock and signed an agreement with China under which Yukos would build a major oil pipeline from Siberia to China that would supply a quarter of China's oil imports.

By spring 2003, the Putin administration decided that Khodorkovsky and Yukos had grown too independent. In a series of actions beginning in July 2003, several top figures in Yukos and companies associated with it were arrested and charged with fraud, embezzlement, tax evasion, and even murder. The police raided the offices of the company and of a number of its affiliates, and even one of the orphanages its foundation sponsored.

At the end of December 2003, the government began issuing claims against the company for billions of dollars in back taxes and froze the company's bank accounts as collateral against the claims. When Yukos failed to pay the full tax bill, the government seized Yukos' main production subsidiary, and auctioned it off to a cut-out firm, which three days later sold it to Russia's only state-owned oil company, Rosneft. Rosneft's board chairman, Igor Sechin, is deputy head of Putin's presidential administration and a long-time associate of Putin from St. Petersburg.

In October 2003, Khodorkovsky was arrested and charged with fraud and tax evasion. The courts refused to release him on bail. In May 2004, he was sentenced to nine years imprisonment and sent to a prison camp in Siberia. In 2006, the last remnants of the company were forced into bankruptcy.

Many reasons have been suggested for the government's campaign against Yukos and Khodorkovsky. Some have argued that Khodorkovsky, through his open involvement in party politics, violated Putin's rule that big business stay out of politics. Another explanation is that Yukos was a pawn in a struggle among intra-bureaucratic factions over the distribution of control over profitable business assets. Certainly Yukos's independence was at odds with Putin's policy of placing all major oil and gas companies under direct state control in order to use energy policy to advance the state's global interests.

Whatever the regime's motives, the Yukos affair shows that the authorities are willing to manipulate the legal system for political purposes when it suits them, that many of the most important political contests in Russia are fought out within the state bureaucracy rather than in the open arena of public politics, and that the fight to redistribute control of Russia's most lucrative natural resource assets continues to be a driving force in politics.

proper burial for the dead. It collected information about the actual scale of the war and of its casualties. It also continued to advise families on ways to avoid conscription and to lobby for decent treatment of recruits. Through the 1990s, it became one of the most sizable and respected civic groups in Russia. It can call on a network of thousands of active volunteers for its work. They visit wounded soldiers in hospitals and help military authorities identify casualties. One of the movement's greatest assets is its moral authority as mothers defending the interests of their children. This stance makes it hard for their opponents to paint them as unpatriotic or power-hungry.

The league plays both a public political role (for instance, it lobbied to liberalize the law on alternative civil service for conscientious objectors) and a role as service-provider. Much of its effort is spent on helping soldiers and their families deal with their problems. Recently the league formed a political party in order to build a broader base of public support for its policy goals in the area of military reform, conscription, health care, and human rights. Although it has continued its efforts to reform conditions within the military, its leaders clearly believe that reform requires open political pressure on policymakers. How successful it will prove in attracting votes remains to be seen.

Like many NGOs, the League of Committees of Soldiers' Mothers cultivates ties with counterpart organizations abroad, and it has won widespread international recognition for its work. For some groups, such ties are a source of dependence, as organizations compensate for the lack of mass membership with aid and know-how from counterpart organizations abroad. However, the league enjoys a stable base of public support in Russia. Its international ties have also probably helped protect the group in the face of the sometimes-hostile attitude of the authorities.[40]

The Federation of Independent Trade Unions of Russia

The Federation of Independent Trade Unions of Russia (FITUR) is the successor of the official trade union federation under the Soviet regime. Unlike RUIE, however, it has poorly adapted itself to the postcommunist environment even though it inherited substantial organizational resources from the old Soviet trade union organization. In the Soviet era, virtually every employed person belonged to a trade union. All branch and regional trade union organizations were part of a single labor federation, called the All-Union Central Council of Trade Unions. With the breakdown of the old regime, some of the member unions became independent, while other unions sprang up as independent bodies representing the interests of particular groups of workers. Nonetheless, the nucleus of the old official trade union organization survived, and it is called the Federation of Independent Trade Unions of Russia. It remains by far the largest trade union federation in Russia. Around 95 percent of all organized workers belong to unions, which at least formally are members of FITUR. The independent unions are much smaller. By comparison with big business, however, the labor movement is fragmented, weak, and unable to mobilize workers effectively for collective action.

FITUR inherited valuable real estate assets from its Soviet-era predecessor organization, including thousands of office buildings, hotels, rest homes, hospitals, and children's camps. It also inherited the right to collect workers' contributions for the state social insurance fund. Control of this fund enabled the official trade unions to acquire enormous income-generating property over the years. These assets and income streams give leaders of the official unions considerable advantages in competing for members. But the FITUR no longer has centralized control over its regional and branch members. In the 1993 and 1995 parliamentary elections, for instance, member unions formed their own political alliances with parties. Thus internal disunity is another major reason for the relative weakness of FITUR as an organization. Much of its effort is expended on fighting other independent unions to win a monopoly on representing workers in collective bargaining with employers rather than in joining with other unions to defend the interests of workers generally.[41]

The ineffectiveness of the FITUR is also illustrated by the tepid response of organized labor to the severe deterioration in labor and social conditions in the 1990s, when there was much less labor protest than might have been expected. There were some strikes and protests, mainly over wage arrears. Surveys found that in any given year in the 1990s three-quarters of all workers received their wages late at least once.[42] Teachers were particularly hard hit by the problem of unpaid wages and organized numerous local strikes.

Waves of strikes by teachers shut down thousands of schools in the late 1990s. After 1999, protests subsided as the economy began to recover.[43]

Why was there not more labor protest? One reason is that workers depend on the enterprises where they work for a variety of social benefits that are administered through the enterprise, such as pension contributions, cheap housing, and access to medical clinics and day care facilities.[44] Another, however, is the close, clientelistic relationship between the leadership of the FITUR and government authorities. Like business, organized labor for the most part prefers to cultivate a clientelistic relationship with the political authorities rather than to stand independently of them. As a result, it is very difficult for labor to mount collective actions.

New Sectors of Interest In a time when people's interests are changing rapidly, interest groups search for new roles. Some old groups decline, while new organizations form. In Russia, many new associations have formed around the interests of new categories of actors. Bankers, political consultants, realtors, mayors of small cities, mayors of large cities, judges, attorneys, auditors, television broadcasters, political consultants, and numerous other professional and occupational groups have all formed associations to seek favorable policies or regulate professional standards. Environmental groups, women's organizations, human rights activists, and many other cause-oriented groups have organized. Most of these operate in a particular locality, but a few have national scope.

The rules of the game for interest articulation changed sharply after the communist regime fell, and are continuing to change more slowly as the new postcommunist regime defines a new framework for relations between state and society. In the Yeltsin period, lobbying frequently took corrupt forms, including bribery of parliamentary deputies and government officials. By the end of the 1990s, more collective action by business and other sectors of interest was evident, and there was more open bargaining over the details of policy. Under Putin, however, policymaking is more centralized again, and interest groups are more dependent on the goodwill of the president for access. Still, organized interests still press their demands through the mass media, the parliament, and the government, and public pressure does have some impact on policymaking.

PARTIES AND THE AGGREGATION OF INTERESTS

Interest aggregation refers to the process by which the demands of various groups of the population are combined into programmatic options for government. Although other political institutions also aggregate interests, parties in most countries are the quintessential structure performing this vital task. How well parties aggregate interests, define choices for voters, and hold politicians accountable is of critical importance to democracy.

In Russia, despite over a decade of postcommunist political development, the party system remains tenuous and fluid. There is considerable turnover in the parties that run in parliamentary elections from election to election. Politicians are constantly starting new parties, only to abandon them after the election. Voters have little sense of attachment to parties and more often associate them with particular politicians' personalities than with specific ideological stances. In the Duma, deputies do organize their political activity around party factions, but most of these parties have very weak roots in society. Party activity in Russia is organized more around *patronage*—the delivery of particularistic benefits to favored client groups—than around mobilizing support for the achievement of *programmatic* goals.[45]

Russia's party system has undergone a major transformation from the 1990s to the 2000s. In the first half of the 1990s, the struggle between democratic reformers and their communist opponents dominated party competition. Some parties allied themselves with the democratic movement, while others remain wedded to Marxist-Leninist ideology. There were also parties that sought to identify themselves with Russian nationalism. But although all three tendencies—democratic, communist, and nationalist—can still be found in the spectrum of Russia's political parties today, ideological differences have become much less central to party competition.

Instead, beginning in the mid-1990s and continuing into the 2000s, the authorities have made repeated efforts to create dominant parties built around patronage rather than programmatic appeals. Such a party is known as a **party of power.** To the voters, such a party presents an image of continuity and stability. For officeholders, a party of power is a vehicle for career advancement. In the 1990s there were several short-lived attempts to form parties of power, but under Putin the party United Russia has become *the* unquestioned party of power. United Russia presently casts such a long and commanding shadow over the political system that some observers believe that the Kremlin seeks to turn it into a replica of the ruling Communist Party of the Soviet era.

The party system in Russia is shaped by the rules of the electoral system as well as by the direct efforts of the Kremlin, big business, and regional officials to manipulate parties for their own purposes. The party list system used in parliamentary elections encourages ambitious politicians to join parties in order to run for office. But presidential elections have not stimulated party competition to the same degree. Because Russia's presidential system encourages the president to avoid making commitments to parties, presidential elections

have tended to concentrate attention on the candidates' personalities rather than on their policy programs, and therefore have undermined party development. Yet even in parliamentary elections, each new election presents voters with a substantially new set of party choices, making it hard for voters to develop any lasting attachments to parties or to make sensible judgments about parties' past or future performance.

Elections and Party Development

Table 9.3 indicates the results of the party-list voting in the 1993, 1995, 1999, and 2003 elections. The table groups parties into five categories: *democratic* (those espousing liberal democratic principles), *leftist* (those

TABLE 9.3

Party-List Vote in Duma Elections, 1993, 1995, 1999, and 2003

Party	1993	1995	1999	2003
Democratic Parties				
Russia's Choice	15.51	3.90	—	—
Union of Rightist Forces (SPS)	—	—	8.52	4.00
Yabloko	7.86	6.89	5.93	4.37
Party of Russian Unity and Concord (PRES)	6.76	—	—	—
Democratic Party of Russia (DPR)	5.52	—	—	.20
Centrist Parties				
Women of Russia	8.13	4.60	2.04	—
Civic Union[a]	1.93	1.60	—	—
Parties of Power				
Our Home Is Russia	—	10.10	1.20	—
Fatherland—All Russia (OVR)	—	—	13.33	—
Unity/United Russia[b]	—	—	23.32	38.20
Nationalist Parties				
Liberal Democratic Party of Russia (LDPR)[c]	22.92	11.20	5.98	11.60
Congress of Russian Communities (KRO)[d]	—	4.30	.62	—
Motherland (Rodina)	—	—	—	9.20
Leftist Parties				
Communist Party of the Russian Federation (CPRF)	12.40	22.30	24.29	12.80
Agrarian Party	7.99	3.80	—	3.69
Other parties failing to meet 5% threshold	10.98	26.81	12.55	11.10
Against all	4.36	2.80	3.34	4.80

[a]In 1995, the same alliance renamed itself the Bloc of Trade Unionists and Industrialists.
[b]In 2003, Unity ran under the name United Russia following a merger with the Fatherland Party.
[c]In 1999, the LDPR party list was called the Zhirinovsky bloc.
[d]In 1999, this party was called "Congress of Russian Communities and Yuri Boldyrev Movement."

Source: Compiled by author from reports of Central Electoral Commission.

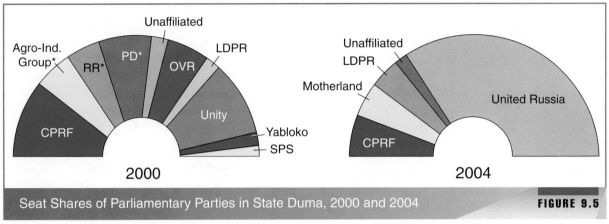

Seat Shares of Parliamentary Parties in State Duma, 2000 and 2004

FIGURE 9.5

Note: Figures taken as of January 2000 and May 2004. Percentages shift with time as members change factional affiliations. Note that United Russia was the result of a merger of the Fatherland Party with Unity.

* These were groups made up of deputies elected in single-member districts who chose not to affiliate with any of the party-based factions, but were registered as official deputy groups on the basis of having at least 35 members. In the 2004 Duma, there were no such groups.

Source: Compiled by author from reports of State Duma.

advocating socialist and statist values), *centrist* (mixing leftist and liberal democratic appeals), *nationalist* (highlighting ethnic nationalism, patriotism and imperialism), and "*parties of power.*"

Figure 9.5 shows how the election results translated into the distribution of seats in the Duma to various party factions following the 1999 and 2003 elections. Under the mixed electoral system that was in force from 1993 through 2006, parliamentary factions varied in their composition. A few had substantial numbers of both list and single-member district (SMD) deputies, but most were composed predominantly of one type of member or the other. Some factions were "start-up" groups made up of independents elected in SMD races who did not wish to affiliate themselves with the party factions, while for others, the core of their membership were deputies elected on the party list. In the United Russia faction in the 2003–2006 Duma, about 60 percent of the members were from single-member districts—which means that 80 percent of SMD deputies elected in 2003 chose to join the United Russia faction. This is a good indication of the power of the United Russia bandwagon.

The 1989 and 1990 Elections The development of parties began with the elections under Gorbachev to the reformed Soviet Union and Russian Republic parliaments. Democratically oriented politicians coalesced to form legislative caucus in the Soviet Union's Congress of People's Deputies in 1989, and in turn helped a broad coalition of democratic candidates run for the Russian Congress in 1990. In parliament, democratic factions competed for influence with communist, nationalist, agrarian, and other political groups. These parliamentary factions became the nuclei of political parties in the parliamentary election of December 1993.

The 1993 and 1995 Elections The 1993 election produced a shock—the proreform, pro-Yeltsin party, Russia's Choice, did unexpectedly poorly, while Vladimir Zhirinovsky's Liberal Democratic Party of Russia (LDPR) did unexpectedly well. Zhirinovsky's party is misleadingly named, because the flamboyant, extremist Zhirinovsky appeals to xenophobia, authoritarianism, and the nostalgia for empire rather than liberal or democratic values. The party's strong showing in the 1993 election was a signal of widespread popular discontent with the Yeltsin economic reforms.

The Communists (**Communist Party of the Russian Federation,** or **CPRF**) took about 10 percent of the seats. Altogether, the democratic factions received about 38 percent of the seats in the Duma, the left about 20 percent, and centrist factions about 20 percent. No political camp had a majority, but Zhirinovsky's oppositional stance meant the anti-Yeltsin forces had a narrow majority.

In the 1995 elections a wide array of political groups competed—far more than could possibly be accommodated given that the same 5 percent threshold rule was kept. Forty-three organizations registered and won a spot on the ballot. In the end, only four parties crossed the 5 percent threshold: the communists, Zhirinovsky's LDPR, the "Our Home Is Russia" bloc formed around Prime Minister Chernomyrdin, and the Yabloko party. Of these, the communists were the most successful, winding up with nearly a third of the seats in the Duma. Altogether, half of the votes were cast for parties that failed to win any seats on the party-list ballot.

The 1996 Presidential Election The 1995 parliamentary election was a test of strength for Russia's parties and leaders. The big unknown was how Yeltsin would perform in the 1996 presidential race. At the beginning of 1996 his approval was in the single digits.[46] During the campaign, Yeltsin succeeded in persuading voters that the election was about a choice between him and a return to communism.

This strategy worked. Yeltsin's displays of vigor during the campaign, his lavish promises to voters, and his domination of the media, all contributed to a surge in popularity and a victory over Gennadii Ziuganov, his communist rival (see Table 9.4).[47] The campaign took its toll on Yeltsin, however. Soon afterward he had major heart surgery and for much of his second term he was in poor health.

The 1999 Election The 1999 election was dominated by the question of who would succeed Yeltsin as president. Many federal and regional officeholders wanted to rally around a new "party of power" in order to protect their positions. A group of backroom Kremlin strategists formed a movement called Unity in late summer 1999. They wanted to create a political movement that state officials throughout the country could rally around in the parliamentary election. The party would serve as a political vehicle for Vladimir Putin, whom Yeltsin had just named prime minister and anointed as his successor. Conveniently for Putin, at the same time as Unity's formation and Putin's appointment, Chechen rebels launched raids into the neighboring region of Dagestan. Bombings of apartment buildings attributed to Chechen terrorists also occurred in Moscow and other cities. Putin's decisive handling of the military operations against the Chechen guerrillas gave him and the Unity movement a tremendous boost in popularity during the campaign. Unity, which had not even existed until late August, won 23 percent of the party-list vote.

Presidential Election Results, 1996 (in %)	**TABLE 9.4**	
	First Round (June 16, 1996)	**Second Round (July 3, 1996)**
Boris Yeltsin	35.28	53.82
Gennadii Ziuganov	32.03	40.31
Alecksandr Lebed	14.52	—
Grigorii Yavlinskii	7.34	—
Vladimir Zhirinovsky	5.70	—
Svyatoslav Fedorov	0.92	—
Mikhail Gorbachev	0.51	—
Martin Shakkum	0.37	—
Yurii Vlasov	0.20	—
Vladimir Bryntsalov	0.16	—
Aman Tuleev	0.00	—
Against all candidates	1.54	4.83

Putin and the 2000 Presidential Race The presidential election of 2000 occurred ahead of schedule due to President Yeltsin's early resignation. Under the constitution, the prime minister automatically succeeds the president upon the premature departure of the president, but new elections for the presidency must be held within three months. Accordingly, the presidential election was scheduled for March 26, 2000. The early election gave the front-runner and incumbent, Putin, an advantage because he could capitalize on his popularity and the country's desire for continuity. Putin ran the Russian equivalent of a "rose garden" campaign, preferring to be seen handling the normal daily business of a president rather than going out on the hustings and asking for people's votes. He counted on the support of officeholders at all levels, a media campaign that presented a "presidential" image to the voters, and the voters' fear that change would only make life worse. His rivals, moreover, were weak. Several prominent politicians prudently chose not to run against him. As Table 9.5 shows, Putin's strategy worked brilliantly.

The 2003 and 2004 Elections Under Putin the ideological divide between communists and democrats that had marked the transition era disappeared. The political arena was dominated by the president and his supporters. The loyal pro-Putin party Unity was renamed United Russia after it absorbed a rival party, Fatherland

Gennadii Ziuganov rallies the Communist Party faithful under a portrait of Vladimir Lenin at a November 1998 anniversary celebration of the October Revolution.

Sergey Chirkov/AFP/Corbis

Presidential Election Results, March 26, 2000 (in %)	TABLE 9.5
Vladimir Putin	52.94
Gennadii Ziuganov	29.21
Grigorii Yavlinskii	5.80
Aman Tuleev	2.95
Vladimir Zhirinovsky	2.70
Konstantin Titov	1.47
Ella Pamfilova	1.01
Stanislav Govorukhin	0.44
Yuri Skuratov	0.43
Alexei Podberezkin	0.13
Umar Dzhabrailov	0.10
Against all candidates	1.88

(headed by Moscow mayor Yuri Luzhkov). United Russia held a near-monopoly in the party spectrum, squeezing other parties to the margins. The magnetic attraction of a successful party of power was demonstrated vividly in the 2003 parliamentary election, when United Russia won 38 percent of the party-list vote and wound up with two-thirds of the seats in the Duma. The communists suffered a severe blow, losing almost half their vote share, and the democrats did even worse. For the first time, none of the democratic parties won seats

on the party-list vote. The result underscored Putin's drive to eliminate any meaningful political opposition. Such an impressive showing for United Russia assured Putin's reelection as president. The March 2004 race was a landslide. Putin won easily with 71.31 percent of the vote (see Table 9.6). European observers commented that the elections were "well administered" but hardly constituted "a genuine democratic contest" in view of the president's overwhelming control of media coverage of the race and the absence of genuine competition.[48]

As Russia enters the 2007–2008 electoral cycle, two closely related questions hang over the political system. First, as President Putin's second presidential term comes to an end, will he commit the power and prestige of his presidency to United Russia in order to make it a vehicle for his political legacy? Second, will United Russia become a long-lasting dominant party along the lines of Mexico's Partido Revolucionario Institucional (PRI)? For United Russia to survive as a party of power in the post-Putin era, it will need to control the channels of access to power for political officials at all levels, as well as win commanding majorities in federal and regional elections. This will require that the Kremlin—the large body of officials based in the presidential administration—commit its resources to United Russia to make it a long-term ruling party, something that it may not be willing to do.

Russian Presidential Election Results, 2004 (as % of valid vote)	**TABLE 9.6**
Vladimir Putin	71.31
Nikolai Kharitonov	13.74
Sergei Glaz'ev	4.10
Irina Khakamada	3.84
Oleg Malyshkin	2.02
Sergei Mironov	.75
Against all	3.45
Turnout	64.40

Source: Central Electoral Commission.

Party Strategies and the Social Bases of Party Support

Survey researchers have found some systematic differences in the bases of social support for parties. Such factors as household income, age, urban or rural residence, and education levels are related to differences in party preferences. These factors reflect the different types of images and appeals that parties present to voters.

Table 9.7 indicates how the parties differed in the social composition of their support in the 2003 Duma elections. Note that the table should be read downward. For example, it tells us that 64.5 percent of the

Social Bases of Support for Parties, Duma Parliamentary Election, December 2003 (in %)								**TABLE 9.7**
Party Support by Age Group	**Motherland**	**LDPR**	**United Russia**	**CPRF**	**Other Party**	**Against All**	**Did Not Vote**	**Total**
18–24	3.8	19.2	13.9	1.8	9.6	10.3	17.3	13.7
25–39	14.1	31.3	22.8	9.1	23.9	33.8	36.1	28.5
40–54	37.2	38.4	29.3	24.5	31.4	33.8	25.5	28.7
55+	44.9	11.1	34.0	64.5	35.1	22.1	21.2	29.1
Total	100	100	100	100	100	100	100	100
By Sex								
Male	43.6	60.6	38.0	49.5	44.1	43.3	46.6	45.3
Female	56.4	39.4	62.0	50.5	55.9	56.7	53.4	54.7
Total	100	100	100	100	100	100	100	100
By Education								
Incomplete secondary	35.9	20.2	29.9	43.1	25.1	16.7	26.8	28.0
Secondary, specialist	47.4	65.7	55.6	45.9	49.2	65.2	58.4	56.0
Incomplete higher, higher	16.7	14.1	14.5	11.0	25.7	18.2	14.9	16.0
Total	100	100	100	100	100	100	100	100
By Household Economic Situation								
Barely make ends meet	12.7	14.1	12.1	24.8	12.9	9.0	17.2	15.4
Enough for food	38.0	38.4	36.5	45.0	36.0	28.4	36.8	37.0
Enough for clothes	38.0	37.4	40.6	24.8	37.1	47.8	35.5	36.8
Enough for durables	11.4	10.1	10.8	5.5	14.0	14.9	10.4	10.8
Total	100	100	100	100	100	100	100	100

Key: LDPR: Liberal Democratic Party of Russia (Zhirinovsky's party) CPRF: Communist Party of the Russian Federation

Note: In each table, figures read downward. Each cell entry is the share of a given party's supporters represented by a given social category. Thus, of the supporters of the party Motherland, 3.8% were in the 18–24 age group; 29.1% of all voters were in the 55 years or older age group, but of Communist voters, 64.5% were in this age category.

Source: New Russia Barometer XII, 12–22 December 2003. www.russiavotes.org (accessed 19 July 2004). N = 1601.

communist voters were 55 and over. The table shows that age, gender, education, and economic situation all influence party choice. For example, the communists depended much more on older voters than do other parties, and on voters with lower levels of education and lower income levels. In contrast, United Russia drew its support from across the political spectrum. United Russia voters are distinctive because women predominate: 62 percent of their supporters were female. This fact is consistent with the observation that female voters in Russia tend to support parties promising stability and continuity in policy. In other respects, however, United Russia's base of social support is strikingly broad, suggesting that the party is successful in positioning itself as a nonideological catch-all party. It has benefited especially from its association with President Putin. As vague as its policy stances are, it has emphasized the message that it supports Putin unreservedly. Table 9.8 shows how much more popular United Russia is than any of its rivals.

For other parties, the 2003–2004 elections shattered their assumptions about their sources of support and forced them to rethink their strategies in an era when the Kremlin dominated the political stage so fully. For example, the communists traditionally relied on their inherited organizational networks, their habits of party discipline, a clear-cut ideological profile, and their association with the socialist legacy of the old regime to attract voters. Some party strategists, however, believe that they must change their message and their leadership in view of their dismal showing in 2003. Likewise, the democratic parties, such as the Union of Rightist Forces and Yabloko, both of which have fallen below the 5 percent threshold in national support, have joined forces in several regional elections. The nationalists found it difficult to identify any winning issues in the face of Putin's skillful manipulation of the idea of a strong state and continuity with Russia's past. Moreover, the Kremlin's ability to conjure up new parties overnight to peel off support from the existing nationalist and leftist parties made most politicians unwilling to commit themselves to any but the dominant party of power—United Russia.

Evolution of the Party System

Development of a viable competitive party system in Russia has been hampered by institutional factors, such as the powerful presidency, as well as by the

Duma election results and resulting seat shares, 2007*			TABLE 9.8
	Party list vote share (%)	No. of seats	% seats
United Russia	64.1	315	70
CPRF	11.6	57	13
LDPR	8.2	40	9
A Just Russia	7.8	38	8
Yabloko	1.6		
SPS	1.0		
Agrarian Party	2.3		
Other	3.4		
Against all	not allowed		

Note: Election was marked by unusually widespread fraud and manipulation.
*The reported figures are preliminary, pending release of final official results.

authorities' practice of manipulating the political arena. Strong presidentialism undermines the ability of parties to promise that electoral success will translate into policy influence, since the president can choose a government largely of his own liking. Moreover, both Yeltsin and Putin have avoided party affiliations, preferring to remain above the partisan fray. Under these circumstances, politicians have little incentive to invest their efforts in building up party organizations.

In addition, the authorities have directly undermined party competition by a number of manipulative tactics. These include sponsoring shadow leftist or nationalist parties to divide the opposition, denying their opponents access to the media, applying intense administrative pressure in state institutions to ensure that government employees vote as instructed, and, in some cases, resorting to outright fraud in tallying votes.[49] Ultimately the authorities seek to persuade voters that casting a vote for any but the party of power is futile. Putin's administration has been explicit about its goal of creating a party system in which United Russia enjoys a dominant but not exclusive position. Other parties on the right and left are allowed to exist as outlets for opposition sentiment, but are denied the ability to win elections or influence policy. Party competition is more nominal than real as a result. It does not serve to aggregate the interests of citizens or give voters meaningful choices over policy alternatives.

Some believe that Putin is restoring a political system similar to that of the old Soviet regime, where the ruling party suppressed all other political forces and ideologies. The model that Putin is constructing, however, allows limited rights for opposition parties and accepts that elections are a useful mechanism for conferring democratic legitimacy on rulers so long as United Russia wins. But the dependence of United Russia on Putin's popularity and administrative support means that its dominance of the political system beyond Putin's presidency is not assured. A future president may find it expedient to base his support on a different party, or no party at all. And over time, opposition parties may gradually gain political strength.

THE POLITICS OF ECONOMIC REFORM

The Dual Transition

Russia's transition was so wrenching because the country had to remake both its *political* and *economic* institutions following the end of communism. The move to a market economy created opportunities for some, and hardships for many more. Democratization opened the political system to the influence of groups that could organize to press for exclusive economic benefits for themselves. Many people who had modest but secure livelihoods under the communist regime were ruined by inflation and unemployment when the planned economy broke down. A smaller number took advantage of opportunities for entrepreneurship or exploited their connections with government to amass sizable fortunes. The Russian case illustrates the danger that a transition to democracy and a market economy can get stuck partway, as power is captured by powerful entrenched interests that take advantage of the initial steps toward reform, only to block any further steps toward competition and an open economy.

Stabilization Russia pursued two major sets of economic reforms in the early 1990s, macroeconomic stabilization and privatization. Stabilization, sometimes called **shock therapy,** is a program intended to staunch a country's financial breakdown. The government seeks to restore a macroeconomic balance between what society consumes and what it produces.

It requires a painful dose of fiscal and monetary discipline by radically cutting government spending and tightening the money supply. Stabilization gives the national currency real value, which requires eliminating chronic sources of inflation by cutting state spending, raising taxes, lifting price controls, and ending protectionism. Structural reform of this kind always lowers the standard of living for some groups of the population, at least in the short run.

Initially it was believed stabilization would be opposed by those whose living standards suffered as a result of the higher prices and lower incomes, such as workers in state enterprises, government employees, and pensioners. In practice, however, those who benefited from the early steps to open the economy and privatize state assets then opposed any subsequent measures to carry economic reform through to its conclusion. This includes officials who acquired ownership rights to monopoly enterprises and then worked to shut out potential competitors from their markets. It also includes state officials who benefited from collecting "fees" to issue licenses to importers and exporters or permits for doing business, and entrepreneurs whose firms monopolize the market in their industry.[50] A fully competitive market system, with a level playing field for all players, would threaten their ability to profiteer from their privileged positions.

From Communism to Capitalism Communist systems differed from other authoritarian regimes in ways that made their economic transitions more difficult. This was particularly true for the Soviet Union and its successor states. For one, the economic growth model followed by Stalin and his successors concentrated much production in large enterprises. This meant that many local governments were entirely dependent on the economic health of a single employer. The heavy commitment of resources to military production in the Soviet Union further complicated the task of reform in Russia, as does the country's vast size. Rebuilding the decaying infrastructure of a country as large as Russia is staggeringly expensive.

The economic stabilization program began on January 2, 1992, when the government abolished most controls on prices, raised taxes, and cut government spending sharply. Almost immediately, opposition to the new program began to form. Economists and politicians took sides. The "shock therapy" program was an easy target for criticism, even though there was no consensus among critics about what the alternative should be. It became commonplace to say that the program was all shock and no therapy.

By cutting government spending, letting prices rise, and raising taxes, the stabilization program sought to create incentives for producers to increase output and to look for new niches in the marketplace. In theory, increases in production should have driven down prices. But Russian producers did not respond by raising productivity. As a result, society suffered from a sharp, sudden loss in purchasing power. People went hungry, bank savings vanished, and the economy fell into a protracted slump. Firms that were politically connected were able to survive by winning cheap credits and production orders from government, which dampened any incentive for improving productivity. Desperate to raise operating revenues, the government borrowed heavily from the International Monetary Fund (IMF) and issued treasury bonds at ruinously high interest rates. IMF loans came with strings attached—the government pledged to cut spending further and step up tax collections as a condition of accepting IMF assistance, which fueled the depression further. Communists and nationalists got a rise out of audiences by depicting the government as the puppets of a malevolent, imperialist West.

Privatization Stabilization was followed shortly afterward by the mass **privatization** of state firms. In contrast to the shock therapy program, privatization enjoyed considerable public support, at least at first. Privatization transfers the legal title of state firms to private owners. Economic theory holds that under the right conditions, private ownership of productive assets is more efficient for society as a whole than is state ownership because in a competitive environment owners are motivated by an incentive to maximize their property's ability to produce a return. Under the privatization program, every Russian citizen received a voucher with a face value of 10,000 rubles (around $30 at the time). People were free to buy and sell vouchers, but they could be used only to acquire shares of stock in privatized enterprises or shares of mutual funds investing in privatized enterprises. The program sought to ensure that everyone became a property owner instantly. Politically, the program aimed to build support for the economic reforms by giving citizens a stake in the outcome of the market transition.

Economically, the government hoped that privatization would eventually spur increases in productivity by creating meaningful property rights. Beginning in October 1992, the program distributed 148 million privatization vouchers to citizens. By June 30, 1994, when the program ended, 140 million vouchers had been exchanged for stock out of 148 million originally distributed. Some 40 million citizens were, in theory, share owners. But these shares were often of no value, because they paid no dividends and shareholders could not exercise any voting rights in the companies.

The next phase of privatization auctioned off most remaining shares of state enterprises for cash. This phase was marked by a series of scandalous sweetheart deals in which banks owned by a small number of Russia's wealthiest tycoons—the so-called oligarchs—wound up with title to some of Russia's most lucrative oil, gas, and metallurgy firms for bargain basement prices. The most notorious of these arrangements became known as the **"loans for shares"** scheme. It was devised by a small group of magnates in 1995. They persuaded the government to auction off management rights to controlling packages of shares in several major state-owned companies in return for loans to the government. If the government failed to repay the loans in a year's time, the shares would revert to the banks that made the loans. The government, not surprisingly, defaulted on the loans, letting a small number of oligarchs acquire ownership of some of Russia's largest and most valuable companies.[51]

Consequences of Privatization On paper, privatization was a huge success. By 1996, privatized firms produced about 90 percent of industrial output, and about two-thirds of all large and medium-sized enterprises had been privatized.[52] In fact, however, the actual transfer of ownership rights was far less impressive than it appeared. For one thing, the dominant pattern was for managers to acquire large shareholdings of the firms they ran. As a result, management of many firms did not change. Moreover, many nominally private firms continued to be closely tied to state life-support systems, such as cheap state-subsidized loans and credits.[53]

The program allowed a great many unscrupulous wheeler-dealers to prey on the public through a variety of financial schemes. Some investment funds promised truly incredible rates of return. Most investors in Western companies would have regarded these claims as outrageous and fraudulent. Many people lost their savings by investing in funds that went bankrupt or turned out to be simple pyramid schemes. The Russian government lacked the capacity to protect the investors. Many people were disenchanted with the entire program as a result. Privatization was carried out before the institutional framework of a market economy was in place. Markets for stocks, bonds, and commodities were, and still are, small in scale and weakly regulated. The legal foundation for a market economy has gradually emerged, but only after much of the economy was already privatized. Banks do a very poor job of mobilizing private savings into investment in Russian companies. For much of the 1990s, the lack of liquidity in the economy meant that enterprises failed to pay their wages and taxes on time, and they traded with one another using barter. By 1998, over half of enterprise output was being "sold" through barter trade.

The government fell into an unsustainable debt trap. Unable to meet its obligations, it grew increasingly dependent on loans. As lenders became increasingly certain that the government could not make good on its obligations, they demanded ever higher interest rates, deepening the trap. Ultimately the bubble burst. In August 1998, the government declared a moratorium on its debts and let the ruble's value collapse against the dollar. Overnight, the ruble lost two-thirds of its value and credit dried up.[54] The government bonds held by investors were almost worthless. The effects of the crash rippled through the economy. The sharp devaluation of the ruble made exports more competitive and gave an impetus to domestic producers, but also significantly lowered people's living standards.

As Table 9.9 shows, economic output in Russia fell for a decade before beginning to recover in 1999.

The recovery is not due to a structural reform of the economy. There has not been a substantial overhaul of the banking system or the way industry is managed. The economy is still vulnerable to a downturn in the international economic situation, because Russia remains highly dependent on exports of natural resources: exports of oil and gas make up over half of Russian exports and a fifth of Russian gross domestic product (GDP).[55] Still, a number of industries are showing real vigor. The oil industry has increased investment and output sharply and several oil companies have expanded their international distribution and marketing efforts. They have even invested in the agriculture and food processing sectors, which are also recovering. Following the 1998 crash, several domestic industries got a boost from the drop in the ruble's exchange value as their prices became competitive and imported products became sharply more expensive. In an economy that was as deeply depressed as Russia's, even a small infusion of cash has a multiplier effect, as enterprises are able to pay off arrears in back wages and taxes. In turn, these taxes allowed government to pay off its backlog of wages and pensions, in turn allowing consumer demand for industry's products to rise, and so on. These trends have raised living standards noticeably. Unemployment has fallen since the August 1998 crisis and the number of people living in poverty has declined by about one-third. President Putin has expressed satisfaction with the favorable trends in the economy, but has warned that they are not sufficient to achieve sustained and balanced development. He has called for doubling GDP in ten years, which would require average annual economic growth of 7 percent per year for the next decade.[56] However, some of Putin's actions—such as the moves to drive the oil firm Yukos into bankruptcy and imprisonment of its founder, Khodorkovsky—are having a chilling

	1991	1992	1993	1994	1995	1996	1997	1998	1999	2000	2001	2002	2003	2004	2005
TABLE 9.9 Russian Annual GDP Growth and Price Inflation Rates, 1991–2005 (in %)															
GDP	−5.0	−14.5	−8.7	−12.6	−4.3	−6.0	0.4	−11.6	3.2	7.6	5.0	4.0	7.3	7.1	6.4
Inflation	138.0	2323.0	844.0	202.0	131.0	21.8	11.0	84.4	36.5	20.2	18.6	15.1	12.0	11.7	10.9

Note: GDP is measured in constant market prices. Inflation is measured as the percentage change in the consumer price index from December of one year to December of the next.

Source: Press reports of Russian State Statistical Service (www.gks.ru).

effect on business investment and make it that much harder for Russia to achieve high sustainable economic growth.

Social Conditions Living standards fell deeply during the 1990s. A small minority became wealthy, and some households improved their lot modestly. Most people, however, suffered a net decline in living standards as a result of unemployment, lagging income, and nonpayment of wages and pensions.

A much larger share of the populace lives in poverty than during the Soviet era. As of 2005, about 30 million people, or about 20 percent of the population, lived in poverty. High poverty rates are the result of unemployment and the lag of incomes behind prices. Unemployment, at about 7 percent, is much lower than its crisis level of 13 percent, but still is high for a country that was accustomed to nearly full employment in the Soviet period, and where the state-funded social safety net is weak.

As elsewhere in the former communist countries, unemployment has affected women more severely than men. Also vulnerable to the economic shock of the 1990s are groups whose incomes are paid directly out of the state budget, such as those living on pensions and disability payments, as well as teachers, scientists, and health care workers. Although they receive periodic increases in pay, these raises usually are insufficient to keep up with increases in prices.

Inequality has grown sharply since the end of the Soviet era. One commonly used measure of inequality is the Gini index, which is an aggregate measure of the total deviation from perfect equality in the distribution of wealth or income. In Russia, the Gini index nearly doubled during the early 1990s, rising from 26 in 1987–1990 to 48 in 1993–1994. Inequality in Russia was higher than any other postcommunist country except for Kyrgyzstan.[57] As the economy began to recover and poverty has declined, the gap between rich and poor has closed somewhat. Today, Russia's Gini index is just under 40, slightly lower than the level of the United States. The richest fifth of the population receive eight times as much income as do the poorest fifth in Russia, and the ratio is similar in the United States. But although Russia's total level of inequality is similar to that of the United States, the rapid growth of the gap between rich and poor since the end of the communist regime is a severe shock to a society brought up on the socialist doctrine of class equality.

An especially disturbing dimension of the social effects of transition has been the erosion of public health. Although public health had deteriorated in the late communist period, the decline worsened after the regime changed. Mortality rates have risen sharply, especially among males. Life expectancy for males in Russia is at a level comparable to poor and developing countries. At present, life expectancy at birth for males is just under fifty-nine years and for females seventy-two years. The disparity between male and female mortality—enormous by world standards—is generally attributed to the higher rates of abuse of alcohol and tobacco among men. Demographers have warned that at the present rate of mortality, 40 percent of Russia's 16-year-old boys will not reach their sixtieth birthday.[58]

Other demographic indicators are equally grim. Prime Minister Fradkov told a cabinet meeting in July 2006 that only 30 percent of newborn children "can be described as healthy," and that "there are more than 500,000 disabled children in need of various forms of treatment, and also some 730,000 orphans or abandoned children."[59] Rates of incidence of HIV and other infectious diseases, murders, suicides, drug addiction, and alcoholism are rising. Russia's leaders consider the demographic crisis to pose a grave threat to the country's national security both because of the growing shortage of labor in some regions and the army's inability to recruit enough healthy young men.[60] Every year Russia's population declines by about three-quarters of a million people due to the excess of deaths over births. Demographers estimate that Russia's population could fall by over one-third by 2050. In his 2006 message to parliament, President Putin called for a series of measures to raise birthrates, reduce mortality, and stimulate immigration.

Setting the country on a path of self-sustaining economic growth, where workers and investors are confident in their legal rights, requires a complete overhaul of the relationship of the state to the economy. The Soviet state used central planning to direct enterprises on what to produce and how to use resources. Much of the economy was geared to heavy industry and defense production, and government ministries directly administered each branch of the economy. The postcommunist state must have an entirely different relationship to the economy in order to stimulate growth. It must set clear rules for economic activity, regulate markets, enforce the law, supply public goods and services, and promote competition. Shifting the structure of the state bureaucracy and the attitudes of state officials has been a Herculean task.

We can get some idea of the legacy of the communist system in the way the state was intertwined with the economy by looking at the structure of the state budget. Figure 9.6 shows the breakdown graphically for the 2006 federal budget. Total spending was set at 28.4 trillion rubles, or about $100 billion U.S. dollars. The share spent on national defense (at 23.5 percent) is higher than in the United States (19.8 percent of federal spending in 2006). The high shares of spending on general administration (22.5 percent) and law enforcement (19.1 percent) make it difficult for Russia to maintain an adequate social safety net or to rebuild its education and health care systems. The budget surpluses of the last several years have made it possible for the government to meet its obligations, but spending was pared back so severely in the 1990s that many critical needs continue to go unmet.

Putin's government has recognized that the oil- and gas-fueled budget surpluses pose a serious danger of creating inflationary pressures in the economy. For this reason, like some other oil-rich states, Russia has created a "stabilization fund" that removes some of the revenues generated by high world energy prices from circulation and uses them to pay off external debt. By the beginning of 2006, the stabilization fund had accumulated some $44 billion, and political pressure was rising to spend it on social needs. President Putin also announced an ambitious program of spending on four high-priority projects to improve conditions in education, health care, housing, and agriculture. In addition to meeting some of the needs of these long-starved sectors, the spending should benefit Putin's allies in United Russia in the 2007 parliamentary elections.

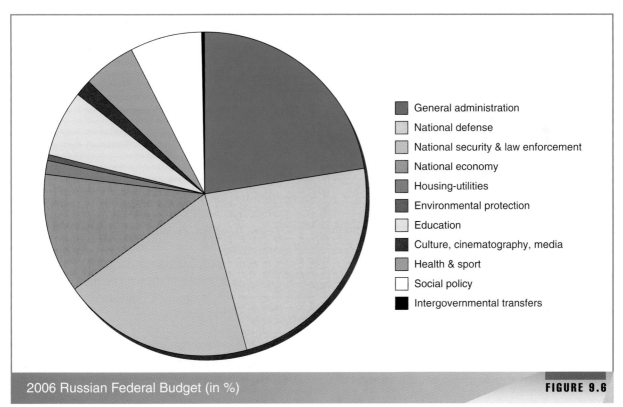

2006 Russian Federal Budget (in %)   **FIGURE 9.6**

Source: Russian press reports.

RULE ADJUDICATION: TOWARD THE RULE OF LAW

The Law-Governed State

One of the most important goals of Gorbachev's reforms was to make the Soviet Union a **law-governed state (pravovoe gosudarstvo)** rather than one in which state bodies and the Communist Party exercised power arbitrarily. Since 1991, the Russian leaders have asserted that the state must respect the primacy of law over politics—even when they took actions grossly violating the constitution. The difficulty in placing law above politics testifies to the lingering legacy of the old regime's abuse of the legal system. President Putin too has emphasized the rule of law (in a strange but memorable phrase, he once called for the "dictatorship of law") even while his actions have sometimes flagrantly infringed on the independence of the judiciary.

The struggle for the rule of law began well before Gorbachev. After Stalin died, his successors ended mass terror and took significant steps to reduce the use of law for political repression. Still, throughout the late Soviet era, the Communist Party and the KGB often used legal procedures to give the mantle of legal legitimacy to acts of political repression. Although the prosecution of political dissidents has ended, the use of the legal system for political purposes by state authorities continues. Changes since 1991 represented some movement toward establishing an independent judicial branch, but under Putin political control over the legal system has started to grow again.

The major institutional actors in the legal system are the **procuracy,** the *judiciary*, and the **bar.** Each has undergone substantial change in the postcommunist period.

The Procuracy Russia's legal system traditionally vested a great deal of power in the procuracy; the procuracy was considered to be the most prestigious branch of the legal system. The procuracy is comparable to the system of federal and state prosecuting attorneys in the United States, but has more wide-ranging responsibilities and is organized as a centralized hierarchy headed by the procurator-general. The procuracy is charged with fighting crime, corruption, and abuses of power in the bureaucracy. It investigates crimes and official malfeasance and seeks to ensure that all state officials and public organizations observe the law. Moreover, the procuracy oversees the entire system of justice. The procuracy has traditionally been the principal check on abuses of power by state officials. But it is inadequately equipped to meet the sweeping responsibilities that the law assigns to it, because of the difficulty of effectively supervising the vast state bureaucracy and overcoming the entrenched political machines of party and state officials.

The Judiciary In contrast to the influence that the procuracy has traditionally wielded in Russia, the bench has been relatively weak. Trial judges are usually the least experienced and lowest paid of the members of the legal profession, and the most vulnerable to external political and administrative pressure. Successful judicial reform requires greater independence and discretion on the part of courts. Judges are being asked to raise their standards of professionalism at a time of rapid change in law, legal procedure, and social conditions. In a few instances, judges have been murdered when they attempted to take on organized crime. Many judges have left their positions to take higher paying jobs in other branches of the legal profession, but caseloads have risen substantially.

State officials pay lip service to the principle of judicial independence but often violate it in practice by pressuring judges to render particular judgments in politically sensitive matters. At the same time, many reforms since the end of communism are intended to make the administration of justice more effective, and some increase the rights of defendants in criminal cases. For example, in the 1990s, trial by jury in major criminal cases was introduced in several regions on an experimental basis. Putin has backed its use nationwide. It is opposed by the procuracy because the prosecution has to work much harder to present a convincing case. It is also expensive, because court facilities must be expanded and jurors must be selected and paid. The goal of the jury system, however, is to make the judicial system more adversarial, so that the prosecution and the defense have equal status in the courtroom, and the judge becomes a neutral arbiter between them.[61]

The Russian judiciary is a unitary hierarchy. All courts of general jurisdiction are federal courts. There are also other specialized types of courts in addition to federal courts of general jurisdiction, among them the supreme courts of ethnic republics, local municipal courts (equivalent to justices of the peace), and military courts. Most criminal trials are held in district and city courts of general jurisdiction, which have original jurisdiction in most criminal proceedings. Higher-level courts, including regional and republic-level courts, hear appeals from lower courts and have original jurisdiction in certain cases. At the pinnacle of the hierarchy of courts of general jurisdiction is the Russian Supreme Court, which hears cases referred from lower courts and also issues instructions to lower courts on judicial matters. The Supreme Court does not have the power to challenge the constitutionality of laws and other official actions of legislative and executive bodies. The constitution assigns that power to the Constitutional Court. Under the constitution, the judges of the Supreme Court are nominated by the president and confirmed by the Federation Council.

There is a similar hierarchy of courts hearing cases arising from civil disputes between firms or between firms and the government called **commercial courts (arbitrazhnye sudy).** Like the Supreme Court, the Supreme Commercial Court is both the highest appellate court for its system of courts as well as the source of instruction and direction to lower commercial courts. As with the Supreme Court, the judges of the Supreme Commercial Court are nominated by the president and confirmed by the Federation Council. In recent years, the Supreme Commercial Court has handed down a number of major decisions that clarify the rules of the economic marketplace.

The Ministry of Justice oversees the court system and provides for its material and administrative needs. Its influence over the judiciary is limited, however, because it lacks any direct authority over the procuracy.

The Bar Change of another sort has been occurring among those members of the legal profession who represent individual citizens and organizations in both criminal and civil matters: "advocates" (*advokaty*). They are comparable to defense attorneys in the United States. Their role has expanded considerably with the spread of the market economy. They have long enjoyed some autonomy through their self-governing associations, through which they elect officers and govern admission of new practitioners. In the past, their ability to effectively use their rights was limited, but in recent years their opportunities have risen markedly. Private law firms are proliferating. The profession is attractive for the opportunities it provides to earn high incomes. A number of lawyers have become celebrities by taking on high-profile cases.

Constitutional Adjudication One of the most important reforms in postcommunist Russia's legal system is the establishment of a court for constitutional review of the official acts of government. The Constitutional Court has authority to interpret the constitution in a variety of areas. It has ruled on several ambiguous questions relating to parliamentary procedure. It has overturned some laws passed by national republics within Russia, and struck down several provisions of the Russian Criminal Code that limited individual rights. Generally, in disputes between individuals and state authorities, the court finds in favor of individuals, thus reaffirming the sphere of individual legal rights. It has consistently upheld the sovereignty of the federal constitution over regional governments.

The most important challenge for the court, however, is the huge domain of presidential authority. The court has been reluctant to challenge the president. One of its first and most important decisions concerned a challenge brought by a group of communist parliamentarians to President Yeltsin's decrees launching the war in Chechnia. The court ruled that the president had the authority to wage the war through the use of his constitutional power to issue decrees with the force of law. In other, less highly charged issues, the court established legal limits to the president's authority. For instance, the court ruled that Yeltsin could not refuse to sign a law after parliament had overridden his veto. However, in the more authoritarian climate under Putin, the court has not issued any rulings restricting the president's powers. Generally the court is sensitive to the political climate surrounding it and takes care not to issue a ruling that would be ignored or opposed by the president.

Obstacles to the Rule of Law

Movement toward the rule of law continues to be hampered by the abuse of legal institutions by the political authorities and endemic corruption in state and society.

In the post-Soviet state the security police continue to operate autonomously. In the Soviet period, the agency with principal responsibility for maintaining domestic security was called the KGB (State Security Committee). The KGB exercised very wide powers, including responsibility for both domestic and foreign intelligence. Since 1991 its functions have been split up among several agencies. The main domestic security agency is called the Federal Security

A family in Chechnia surveys the damage to their home from the war.

Malcolm Lintron/Getty Images

Service (FSB). Although the structure and mission of the security agencies have changed, they have never undergone a thorough purge of personnel. No member or collaborator of the Soviet-era security services has been prosecuted for violating citizens' rights.

The security police are regarded as one of the more professionally competent and uncorrupted state agencies. However, despite being assigned new tasks, such as fighting international narcotics trafficking and terrorism, they still demonstrate a Soviet-style preoccupation with controlling the flow of information about the country. For example, in 2001 the security police sent a directive to the Academy of Sciences demanding that scholars report all contacts with foreigners. Many similar Soviet-era police practices have been revived under Putin.

Also under Putin, the legal system has been used as an instrument for suppressing potential political opposition. An example is the series of legal maneuvers taken against the owners of independent media. These included police harassment and criminal prosecution, as well as civil actions such as bankruptcy proceedings. For example, the owners of two television companies were forced to divest themselves of their media holdings and transfer ownership to companies loyal to the administration. As a result, Russia's two relatively autonomous national television companies lost their political independence; one respected liberal newspaper was shut down; and the entire media

establishment was sent a strong signal that it would be wise to avoid crossing the current administration. Under Putin, only a small number of print media have retained a measure of political independence.

The heavy-handed use of procuracy, the police, and courts against the Yukos firm in a coordinated campaign to arrest the company's top leaders and dismantle the company represents another, particularly visible, instance of using the legal system for political ends.

Corruption Another serious obstacle to the rule of law is endemic corruption. Corruption increased substantially after the Soviet period. It is widespread both in everyday life and in dealings with the state. A large-scale survey by a Moscow research firm gives some indication of the nature and scale of corruption. At least half the population of Russia is involved in corruption in daily life. For instance, the probability that an individual will pay a bribe to get an automobile inspection permit is about 60 percent. The likelihood of paying a bribe to get one's child into a good school or college, or to get good grades, is about 50 percent. There is a 26 percent chance of paying a bribe to get a favorable ruling in a court case. The areas where the largest sums are spent are health care, education, courts, and automobile inspections; these alone account for over 60 percent of the money paid in bribes.[62]

Bribery in the dealings between business and the state is of a far larger magnitude. The survey's authors estimate that 82 percent of business firms engage in giving bribes to government officials, particularly those involved in licensing, taxation, and regulation. They calculated that the total annual cost of such corruption is $33.5 billion, a sum equivalent to about half of the federal budget.[63]

Corruption is hardly unique to Russia or to the former communist world. However, it is especially widespread in Russia and the other former Soviet states. Corruption on this scale imposes a severe drag on economic development, both because it diverts resources away from public needs, and because it undermines people's willingness to invest in productive activity.[64] Moreover, much corruption is tied to organized crime, which bribes government officials for protection and drives out legal businesses. For example, in a number of cases, criminal organizations have forced owners of legitimate businesses to sell out. The payment of protection money by businesses to organized crime groups is very widespread. The corruption of the police and courts ensures that such crimes go unpunished and forces legal businesses to compete in the corruption market with illegal ones.

Corruption in Russia has deep roots, and many Russians assume that it is ineradicable. Comparative studies of corruption demonstrate, however, that a culture of corruption can be changed by changing the expectations of the public and the government.[65] The key is for the political leadership to make a serious effort to combat corruption and to back up their commitment with institutional reform and sustained attention to the problem. In Russia, corruption is so pervasive that it is a significant drag on the economy and the political system.

Reforms of the legal system have made some progress toward realizing the goal of the rule of law. Since the early 1990s there have been a number of reforms that have the potential to strengthen the judiciary's independence from both political pressure and corruption. However, the authorities' habitual use of the procuracy and the courts for political purposes and the powerful corrosive effect of corruption continue to subvert the integrity of the legal system. In the long run, movement toward the rule of law will require that power be sufficiently dispersed among groups and organizations in the state and society so that neither private nor state interests be powerful enough to subordinate the law to their own purposes.

RUSSIA AND THE INTERNATIONAL COMMUNITY

Russia's thousand-year history of expansion, war, and state domination of society has left behind a legacy of autocratic rule and a preoccupation with defending national borders. The collapse of the Soviet regime required Russia to rebuild its political institutions, economic system, national identity, and relations with the outside world. During the Soviet period, state propaganda used the image of an international struggle between capitalism and socialism to justify its repressive control over society and its enormous military establishment. Now the country's leaders recognize that only through international integration can Russia hope to prosper. Under Putin the authorities aim to capture the benefits of economic integration with the developed capitalist world while at the same time building an authoritarian political order at home featuring direct state control of the strategically important sectors of the economy.

Gorbachev, Yeltsin, and Putin all believed that integration of Russia into the community of developed democracies was strategically important for Russia. Gorbachev was willing to allow communist regimes to fall throughout Eastern Europe for the sake of improved relations with the West. Yeltsin accepted the admission of East European states into the North Atlantic Treaty Organization (NATO) as a necessary condition for close relations with the United States and Europe. Putin has repeatedly emphasized that he regarded Russia's admission to the World Trade Organization (WTO) as critical for Russia's long-term economic success. Following the September 11, 2001, terrorist attacks on the United States, Putin immediately telephoned U.S. President George W. Bush to offer his support. Putin clearly saw an advantage for Russia in aligning itself with the United States against Islamic terrorism, which it identified as an immediate threat to its own security. Putin cited Russia's own war in Chechnya as part of the global struggle against Islamic terrorists.

Many elements of the political establishment criticized Gorbachev, Yeltsin, and Putin for making concessions to the United States and the West without receiving any benefits in return. Neither trade nor investment has blossomed as Russia had hoped, and Russia still depends on its raw materials exports to maintain a positive trade balance.

Russia has not fully embraced integration into the international community. It has expanded its military presence in several former Soviet republics, pressuring them to become satellites of Russia. In its brutal military campaigns in Chechnia, from 1994 to 1996, and then again from 1999 to the present, it has insisted that the war is a matter of domestic sovereignty and has refused to allow international human rights organizations to monitor Russian practices. The regime has forced the mass media to report a sanitized picture of the situation. Corruption and inefficiency in government, both at the central level and in many regions, deter foreign investors from making a serious commitment of resources. Russian leaders constantly urge foreign business to invest in Russia. But, as many foreign investors point out, why should they take a greater risk than Russia's own business community, which has sent some $300 billion to off-shore havens?

Russia thus has some distance to go before it is fully integrated politically or economically into the international community. Yet it is far more open than it was under Soviet rule, and its leaders recognize that they cannot retreat into isolation and autarky. Putin has made it clear, however, that Russia will accept international standards of democracy, human rights, and the rule of law only to the extent that they serve the state's strategic interests.

Russia's postcommunist transition has been difficult and incomplete. A framework of democratic institutions has been created, but increasingly, the informal rules governing the exercise of power are authoritarian. At the same time, the end of communism prompted the formation of tens of thousands of new social groups to organize for the protection of their interests. The spread of political and property rights has resulted in the emergence of a more pluralistic environment. Moreover, international factors—such as the dense network of international communications linking societies, the rapid expansion of cross-border trade and investment, and the global spread of norms and expectations centered on democracy, human rights, and the rule of law, together with the effects of domestic social changes such as rising educational levels—are likely to raise popular demands for democratic participation.

Russia's vast territory, weak government capacity, and tradition of state domination over society make it likely that the primary objective of its leaders for the foreseeable future will be to strengthen the state, both in its internal and international dimensions. The end of the communist regime and the dissolution of the Soviet Union damaged the state's capacity to enforce the laws, protect its citizens, and provide basic social services. Under Putin, the state has sought to rebuild its power by eliminating potentially independent sources of power in civil society and recentralizing executive power. At the same time, Putin seeks to knit Russia into the fabric of international trade and investment in order to promote economic development. In the long run, however, self-sustaining economic development will require the rule of law and effective institutions for articulating and aggregating social interests. The viability of Russia's postcommunist state will ultimately depend on how responsive and adaptive its institutions are to the demands of Russia's citizens in a globalized and interdependent world.

REVIEW QUESTIONS

- How did Yeltsin's "shock therapy" program contribute to the constitutional crisis of 1993?

- What effects did the constitutional struggles of 1992–1993 have on the features of the 1993 constitution?

- How has President Putin gone about strengthening the power of the central government at the expense of regional governments? What are his reasons for shifting the balance of power in this way?

- What are the main similarities and differences between the channels of elite recruitment under the Soviet system and today?

- Most Russians evaluate the pre-Gorbachev Soviet system favorably, yet would prefer not to bring it back. How would you explain this apparent contradiction?

- Why has United Russia been so successful as a "party of power"?

- What are the main obstacles to the rule of law in Russia? What changes in the political system would be required to overcome them?

KEY TERMS

bar
Chechnia
commercial courts
(*arbitrazhnye sudy*)
Communist Party of the
Russian Federation
(CPRF)
Constitutional Court
Federation Council
Federation of
Independent Trade

Unions of Russia
(FITUR)
glasnost
Gorbachev, Mikhail
governors
Komsomol (Communist
Youth League)
law-governed state
(*pravovoe gosudarstro*)
League of Committees of
Soldiers' Mothers

Lenin, Vladimir
Ilyich
loans for shares
nomenklatura
oligarchs
party of power
presidential decrees
privatization
procuracy
Public Chamber

Russian Union of
Industrialists and
Entrepreneurs (RUIE)
Security Council
shock therapy
Stalin, Joseph
State Council
State Duma
United Russia
Yukos

SUGGESTED READINGS

Aslund, Anders. *Building Capitalism: The Transformation of the Former Soviet Bloc.* Cambridge: Cambridge University Press, 2002.

Bahry, Donna. "Comrades Into Citizens? Russian Political Culture and Public Support for the Transition." *Slavic Review* 58, no. 4 (1999): 841–53.

Baker, Peter, and Susan Glasser. *Kremlin Rising: Vladimir Putin's Russia and the End of Revolution.* New York: Scribner, 2005.

Breslauer, George W. *Gorbachev and Yeltsin as Leaders.* Cambridge: Cambridge University Press, 2002.

Colton, Timothy J. and Stephen Holmes, eds. *The State After Communism: Governance in the New Russia.* Lanham, MD: Rowman & Littlefield, 2006.

Fish, M. Stephen. *Democracy Derailed in Russia: The Failure of Open Politics.* Cambridge: Cambridge University Press, 2005.

Hale, Henry. *Why Not Parties in Russia? Democracy, Federalism, and the State.* Cambridge: Cambridge University Press, 2006.

Hellman, Joel S. "Winners Take All: The Politics of Partial Reform in Postcommunist Transitions." *World Politics* 50, no. 1 (1998): 203–34.

Hill, Fiona, and Clifford Gaddy. *The Siberian Curse: How Communist Planners Left Russia Out in the Cold.* Washington, DC: Brookings Institution, 2003.

Huskey, Eugene. *Presidential Power in Russia.* Armonk, NY: M. E. Sharpe, 1999.

McFaul, Michael. *Russia's Unfinished Revolution: Political Change from Gorbachev to Putin.* Ithaca, NY: Cornell University Press, 2001.

Rose, Richard, and Neil Munro. *Elections Without Order: Russia's Challenge to Vladimir Putin.* Cambridge: Cambridge University Press, 2002.

Sakwa, Richard. *Putin: Russia's Choice.* London: Routledge, 2004.

Shleifer, Andrei, and Daniel Treisman. *Without a Map: Political Tactics and Economic Reform in Russia.* Cambridge: MIT Press, 2000.

White, Stephen, Richard Rose, and Ian McAllister. *How Russia Votes.* Chatham, NJ: Chatham House, 1997.

INTERNET RESOURCES

An invaluable source for daily news about Russia and neighboring countries is the Radio Free Europe-Radio Liberty Newsline: **www.rferl.org/newsline**

A useful daily e-mail newsletter containing news stories and commentary is Johnson's Russia list: **www.cdi.org/russia/johnson/**

A portal to a wide range of political resources on the Web is **www.politicalresources.net/russia.htm**

The University of Pittsburgh links to Web-based resources on Russia at: **www.ucis.pitt.edu/reesweb**

This is the home of "Friends and Partners," a joint Internet project by a team of Russians and Americans: **www.friends-partners.org**

The *Moscow Times* is an English-language daily newspaper published in Moscow, primarily for the expatriate community: **www.themoscowtimes.com**

The portal for the main institutions of the federal government—the president, the parliament, the government, and others—is **www.gov.ru/index.html.** Most of the content accessible through this site is in Russia, but some resources are in English.

The University of Strathclyde's Center for the Study of Public Policy provides a wealth of public opinion and electoral information from Russia: **www.RussiaVotes.org**

ENDNOTES

1. Richard Pipes, *Russia Under the Old Regime*, 2nd ed. (New York: Penguin Books, 1995).

2. Archie Brown, *The Gorbachev Factor* (New York: Oxford University Press, 1996).

3. For a comparison of the leadership styles of Gorbachev and Yeltsin, see George W. Breslauer, *Gorbachev and Yeltsin as Leaders* (Cambridge: Cambridge University Press, 2002); see also Archie Brown and Lilia Shevtsova, eds., *Gorbachev, Yeltsin, and Putin: Political Leadership in Russia's Transition* (Washington, DC: Carnegie Endowment for International Peace, 2001); Lilia Shevtsova, *Putin's Russia* (Washington, DC: Carnegie Endowment for International Peace, 2003); Richard Sakwa, *Putin: Russia's Choice* (London: Routledge, 2004).

4. Konstantin Smirnov, "Vse pravitel'stvo: ekonomicheskii blok," *Vlast,* 28 June 2004, pp. 63–78; World Bank, Russian Economic Report, June 2004. No. 8 (from website: www.worldbank.org.ru).

5. Many observers agreed that the point of the reform was to weaken the influence of local interests on Duma deputies, further centralizing power in the executive.

6. On nationality policy in the Soviet Union, see Terry Martin, *The Affirmative Action Empire: Nations and Nationalism in the Soviet Union, 1923–1939* (Ithaca, NY: Cornell University Press, 2001).

7. J. Paul Goode, "The Push for Regional Enlargement in Putin's Russia," *Post-Soviet Affairs* 20, no. 3 (July–September 2004): 219–57.

8. Guillermo O'Donnell, "Delegative Democracy," *Journal of Democracy* 5, no. 1 (1994): 55–69.

9. Quoted from text published on website Polit.ru, 26 May 2004.

10. From a survey conducted by the Levada Center in June 2005 and posted to its website: <http://www.levada.ru/press/2005070410.html>. The Levada Center is a widely respected independent public opinion survey firm.

11. From a survey in 2005 by the All-Russia Center for the Study of Public Opinion (VTsIOM) and reported by RFE/RL Newsline, 7 March 2005.

12. From a survey conducted by the Levada Center in January 2005 and posted to its website: <http://www.levada.ru/press/2005031100.html>.

13. Nationwide survey results conducted by the Public Opinion Foundation, reported by RFE/RL Newsline, 10 December 2001.

14. James L. Gibson, "The Resilience of Support for Democratic Institutions and Processes in the Nascent Russian and Ukrainian Democracies," in Vladimir Tismaneanu, ed., *Political Culture and Civil Society in Russia and the New States of Eurasia* (Armonk, NY: M. E. Sharpe, 1995), 57.

15. Yuri Levada, "Svoboda ot vybora? Postelektoral'nye razmyshleniia," published on website Polit.ru, 18 May 2004.

16. Levada Center, survey conducted October 2005; posted to website: <http://www.levada.ru/press/2005110901.html>.

17. L. Sedov, "Obshchestvenno-politicheskaia situatsiia v Rossii v iune 2004," from website of Levada Center <http://www.levada.ru/press/2004071402.print.html>.

18. Richard Rose, Neil Munro, and William Mishler, "Resigned Acceptance of an Incomplete Democracy: Russia's Political Equilibrium," *Post-Soviet Affairs* 20, no. 3 (2004): 195–218.

19. Richard Rose and Neil Munro, *Elections Without Order: Russia's Challenge to Vladimir Putin* (Cambridge: Cambridge University Press, 2002), 237.

20. Donna Bahry, "Society Transformed? Rethinking the Social Roots of Perestroika," *Slavic Review* 52, no. 3 (1993): 512–54.

21. Elena Lisovskaya and Vyacheslav Karpov, "New Ideologies in Postcommunist Russian Textbooks." *Comparative Education Review* 43, no. 4 (1999): 522–32.

22. RFE/RL Newsline, 1 December, 2003.

23. RFE/RL Newsline, 15 February 2006; 31 August 2006.

24. Daron Acemoglu and James A. Robinson, *Economic Origins of Dictatorship and Democracy* (Cambridge: Cambridge University Press, 2006); for studies of the effects of inequality on democracy in the United States, see Theda Skocpol and Lawrence R. Jacobs, *Inequality and American Democracy: What We Know and What We Need to Learn* (New York: Russell Sage, 2005).

25. Robert D. Putnam, *Making Democracy Work: Civic Traditions in Modern Italy* (Princeton, NJ: Princeton University Press, 1993).

26. Marc Morje Howard, *The Weakness of Civil Society in Post-Communist Europe* (Cambridge: Cambridge University Press, 2003).

27. Richard Rose and Neil Munro, *Elections Without Order: Russia's Challenge to Vladimir Putin* (Cambridge: Cambridge University Press, 2002), 224–25; Richard Rose, *Getting Things Done With Social Capital: New Russia Barometer VII* (Glasgow: Center for the Study of Public Policy, University of Strathclyde, 1998), 32–33.

28. Rose, *Getting Things Done.*

29. Turnout in the December 2003 parliamentary elections was reported to be 55.45 percent and for the presidential election in March 2004, 64.4 percent. In the United States, turnout of the voting-age population for the closely contested presidential election in 2000 was 51.3 percent.

30. VTsIOM survey findings, as reported on Polit.ru website, 10 January 2001.

31. A reform sponsored by President Putin and the United Russia party has moved to eliminate the "against all" option from future elections. Although the goal is to force voters to support one of the given parties, many observers—including the chairman of the Central Election Commission—warn that this change will reduce electoral turnout.

32. Eugene Huskey, "Nomenklatura Lite? The Cadres Reserve (*Kadrovyi reserv*) in Russian Public Administration" (NCEEER Working Paper, 24 October, 2003) (Washington, DC, National Council for Eurasian and East European Research).

33. Olga Kryshtanovskaya and Stephen White, "Putin's Militocracy," *Post-Soviet Affairs* 19, no. 4 (2003): 289–306.

34. Steven L. Solnick, *Stealing the State: Control and Collapse in Soviet Institutions* (Cambridge: Harvard University Press, 1998), 112–24.

35. Igor M. Bunin, ed., *Biznesmeny Rossii: 40 istorii uspekha* (Moscow: OKO, 1994), 366.

36. Jane I. Dawson, *Eco-Nationalism: Anti-Nuclear Activism and National Identity in Russia, Lithuania, and Ukraine* (Durham, NC: Duke University Press, 1996).

37. RFE/RL Newsline, 18 April 2006.

38. In a system where all prices were set by the state, there was no meaningful measure of profit in any case. Indeed, relative prices were profoundly distorted by the cumulative effect of decades of central planning. The absence of accurate measures of economic costs is one of the major reasons that Russia's economy continues to be so slow to restructure.

39. Article 59 of the constitution provides that young men of conscription age who are conscientious objectors to war may do alternative service rather than being called up to army service. Legislation specifying how this right may be exercised finally passed in 2002.

40. Several authors have examined the effect of Western aid on NGOs in Russia and other post-Communist countries. See Sarah L. Henderson, *Building Democracy in Contemporary Russia: Western Support for Grassroots Organizations* (Ithaca, NY: Cornell University Press, 2003); Thomas Carothers and Marina Ottaway, eds., *Funding Virtue: Civil Society Aid and Democracy* (Washington, DC: Carnegie Endowment for International Peace, 2000); Sarah E. Mendelson and John K. Glenn, eds., *The Power and Limits of NGOs: A Critical Look at Building Democracy in Eastern Europe and Eurasia* (New York: Columbia University Press, 2002).

41. The FITUR reached a Faustian bargain with the government over the terms of a new labor relations code, which was adopted in 2001. Under the new legislation, employers no longer have to obtain the consent of the unions to lay off workers. But collective bargaining will be between the largest union at each enterprise and the management unless the workers have agreed on which union will represent them. Thus the new labor code favors the FITUR at the expense of the smaller independent unions.

42. Richard Rose, *New Russia Barometer VI: After the Presidential Election* (Glasgow: Center for the Study of Public Policy, University of Strathclyde, Studies in Public Policy no. 272, 1996), 6; and Rose, *Getting Things Done*, 15. In 1996, the question was: At any point during the past 12 months, have you received your wages or pension late? In 1996, 78 percent responded yes, 21 percent no. In 1998, the question was: At any point during the past 12 months, have you received your wages late? 75 percent responded yes, 25 percent no.

43. RFE/RL Newsline, 13 January 1997; 17 January 1997; 18 February 1997; 25 November 1998; 14 January 1999; 27 January 1999; 15 September 1999; 26 June 2000.

44. Linda J. Cook, *Labor and Liberalization: Trade Unions in the New Russia* (New York: Twentieth Century Fund Press, 1997), 76–77.

45. Two recent books detailing the obstacles to the formation of a stable competitive party system are Henry Hale, *Why Not Parties in Russia?* (Cambridge: Cambridge University Press, 2006); Regina Smyth, *Candidate Strategies and Electoral Competition in the Russian Federation: Democracy Without Foundation* (Cambridge: Cambridge University Press, 2006).

46. Stephen White, Richard Rose, and Ian McAllister, *How Russia Votes* (Chatham, NJ: Chatham House, 1997), 254.

47. White, Rose, and McAllister, *How Russia Votes*, p. 241–70.

48. Quoted from a press release of the election observer mission of the Organization for Security and Cooperation in Europe, posted to its website immediately following the election, as reported by RFE/RL Newsline, 15 March 2004.

49. For an extensive overview of the tactics used by the authorities in Russia, Ukraine, and other post-Soviet countries to manipulate elections, see Andrew Wilson, *Virtual Politics: Faking Democracy in the Post-Soviet World* (New Haven, CT: Yale University Press, 2005).

50. Joel S. Hellman, "Winners Take All: The Politics of Partial Reform in Postcommunist Transitions," *World Politics* 50, no. 1 (1998): 203–34.

51. An excellent account of the "loans for shares" program, based on interviews with many of the participants, is Chrystia Freeland, *Sale of the Century: Russia's Wild Ride From Communism to Capitalism* (New York: Crown, 2000), 169–89.

52. Joseph R. Blasi, Maya Kroumova, and Douglas Kruse, *Kremlin Capitalism: Privatizing the Russian Economy* (Ithaca, NY: Cornell University Press, 1997), 50.

53. Blasi, Kroumova, and Kruse, *Kremlin Capitalism;* Michael McFaul, "State Power, Institutional Change, and the Politics of Privatization in Russia," *World Politics* 47 (1995): 210–43.

54. Thane Gustafson, *Capitalism Russian-Style* (Cambridge: Cambridge University Press, 1999), 2–3, 94–95.

55. "OECD Economic Survey of the Russian Federation, 2004: The Challenge of Sustaining Growth" (Paris: OECD, 2004). (from website: http://www.oecd.org/document/62/0,2340,en_2649_201185_32474302_1_1_1_1,00.html.

56. President's annual message to parliament, from Polit.ru, 26 May 2004.

57. The World Bank, *Transition: The First Ten Years—Analysis and Lessons for Eastern Europe and the Former Soviet Union* (Washington, DC: World Bank, 2002), 9.

58. REF/RL Newsline, 8 March 1999.

59. RFE/RL Newsline, 20 July 2006.

60. Russian military commanders reported that one-third of the men they had called up in the fall of 2004 were unfit to serve as a result of health problems. Polit.ru, 9 December 2004.

61. A vivid portrait of a recent jury trial in Moscow is presented by Peter Baker and Susan Glasser, *Kremlin Rising: Vladimir Putin's Russia and the End of Revolution* (New York: Scribner, 2005), 231–250.

62. G. A. Satarov, *Diagnostika rossiiskoi korruptsii: Sotsiologicheskii analiz* (Moscow: Fond INDEM, 2002), 16–17.

63. Ibid., 21.

64. Joel S. Hellman, Geraint Jones, and Daniel Kaufmann, "'Seize the State, Seize the Day': State Capture, Corruption, and Influence in Transition" (Policy Research Working Paper, no. 2444) (Washington, DC: World Bank Institute, September 2000).

65. Susan Rose-Ackerman, *Corruption and Government: Causes, Consequences and Reform* (Cambridge: Cambridge University Press, 1999), 159–74.

HEILONGJIANG
Qiqihar
Harbin
Changchun
JILIN
Sea
of
Japan

INNER
MONGOLIA
Shenyang
LIAONING

Ürümqi

XINJIANG

HEBEI
Hohhot   BEIJING ⭐
TIANJIN   Dalian

GANSU
Yumen

Yinchuan
NINGXIA
Taiyuan
SHANXI
Shijiazhuang
Jinan   Qingdao
SHANDONG

Yellow
Sea

Xining
QINGHAI
Lanzhou

Xi'an
SHAANXI
Zhengzhou
HENAN
JIANGSU
Hefei
Nanjing   SHANGHAI

TIBET
Lhasa

SICHUAN
Chengdu
Chang Jiang
HUBEI
Wuhan
ANHUI
Hangzhou
ZHEJIANG

East
China
Sea

CHONGQING

Changsha
Nanchang
JIANGXI
Fuzhou
FUJIAN

HUNAN

Guiyang
GUIZHOU

Kunming
YUNNAN

GUANGXI
Pearl River
GUANGDONG
Guangzhou
HONG KONG
MACAO

CHINA

0   200   400   600 Miles
0   200   400   600 Kilometers

Nanning
Zhanjiang

Haikou
HAINAN

South China
Sea

POLITICS IN CHINA

Melanie Manion

Country Bio

CHINA

Population
1,307.56 million

Territory
3,705,386 square miles

Year of PRC Inauguration
1949

Year of Current Constitution
1982

Head of Party and State
Hu Jintao

Head of Government
Wen Jiabao

Languages
Standard Chinese or Mandarin (Putonghua, based on the Beijing dialect), Yue (Cantonese), Wu (Shanghaiese), Minbei (Fuzhou), Minnan (Hokkien-Taiwanese), Xiang, Gan, Hakka dialects, minority languages

Religions
Daoism (Taoism); Buddhism; Muslim 2–3%; Christian 1% (est.). Note: officially atheist.

On October 1, 1949, Mao Zedong, the peasant revolutionary who had led the Chinese communists in war against the Japanese and in civil war, pronounced a basic communist victory, proclaimed a new regime, and promised a new era for China. From the centuries-old Gate of Heavenly Peace in Beijing, Mao formally inaugurated the People's Republic of China (PRC). For nearly three decades after, until his death in 1976, Mao was the chief architect and agitator for a comprehensive project of revolutionary transformation designed to lead a largely backward agrarian people to modernization, prosperity, and (ultimately) communist utopia. A few years after Mao's death, his successors officially and publicly rejected most of the premises, strategies, and outcomes of this revolutionary project, essentially declaring it a failure. They launched a new era of reform, ongoing today. Economic reform in post-Mao China is nearly as radical and dramatic as the revolutions that toppled most of the world's communist regimes in 1989 and 1990. The resulting transformation is awesome.

Without publicly abandoning the ultimate goal of communism, Mao's successors have defined their current quest mainly in pragmatic economic terms, rather than utopian ideological terms. They have identified economic growth as the nation's highest priority and the Communist Party's main assignment. To achieve this objective, the communist party-state has largely retreated from thirty years of direct administration of the economy. Openly acknowledging the superiority of the capitalist experience, Chinese reformers are promoting a **"socialist market economy,"** with a place for foreign investors, private entrepreneurs, and stock markets. More than anything else, Chinese leaders have staked their legitimacy on the performance of this new economy.

While embracing economic markets, Chinese leaders have repeatedly rejected political pluralism. The communist party-state was in clear evidence in Beijing on June 4, 1989, when the People's Liberation Army employed its tanks and machine guns to clear the streets and main public square of thousands of protesters. The regime tolerates no open challenge to the Communist Party's monopoly on political power.

For most of the 1.3 billion ordinary Chinese, political reform is mainly reflected in a new official acceptance of a private sphere and a new official toler-ance of political apathy. Compared with the Maoist years, when a taste for the music of Beethoven signi-fied dangerous "bourgeois decadence," much less in daily life today is considered political. Moreover, under the new regime, ordinary citizens need not necessarily demonstrate active support for official policies and the political system—so long as they do not engage in active opposition. Chinese leaders have not charted a road toward liberal democracy, at least not purpose-fully. Instead, the political system has become merely authoritarian in its limited reach, rather than perva-sively totalitarian.

Yet, post-Mao reform is more than the retreat of the state from the economy and the imposition of fewer demands on citizens politically. A project of institutionalization is underway in China, to cre-ate an infrastructure promoting more transparency, stability, and responsiveness. In large part, this is to encourage investment and innovation, to support the goal of economic growth. At the same time, Mao's successors are also committed to political institution-alization for political reasons: to safeguard against the arbitrary dictatorship and disruptive politics of the Maoist past. The effort has included better-crafted laws and a new legality, more assertive repre-sentative assemblies, and popularly elected grassroots leaders.

Much of China's transformation in the past quarter-century is only partly a direct result of the various policies that constitute reform. It is at least as much a by-product of these policies. Reform has set in motion processes of economic, political, and social change that appear now largely beyond the control of leaders at the political center. Consider a few examples. Eased restrictions on population movement have created a "floating population" of more than 100 million inter-nal migrants, most of them from the countryside and seeking work in towns and cities, many of them unreg-istered squatters, all of them reflecting a new relation-ship between state authority, social welfare, and market opportunity. Local governments, empowered by a new fiscal federalism, pursue local economic growth with less and less heed to central guidelines. Growth in individual wealth and a telecommunications revolu-tion have produced an astonishing 110 million Internet users in China, linking Chinese to one another and to the outside world in ways that are nearly impossible to control.

CURRENT POLICY CHALLENGES

Meeting with the president of the United States in late 2005, China's President Hu Jintao frankly acknowledged that problems of political corruption, rural unrest, a growing wealth gap, and severe pollu-tion consume nearly all his time.[1] Some of these problems represent new policy challenges for Chinese leaders; others are not new, but their magni-tude and impact have only recently been under-stood. The new and ongoing policy challenges arise very significantly from China's economic successes in the past quarter-century.

Since 1978, Chinese leaders have agreed to be judged mainly by their ability to foster economic growth and deliver a better material life for Chinese citizens. China's development has in fact been very impressive. Its economy has grown at a rate of nearly 10 percent per year since 1980, a record of sustained growth comparable only to Japan and Korea in the lat-ter half of the twentieth century. In terms of purchas-ing power parity, China is now the world's second largest economy (after the United States) and third largest recipient of foreign direct investment (largest among developing countries). In 2006, it overtook Japan as the world's biggest holder of foreign exchange reserves.

Economic success has not been costless. It has provided more opportunities to pursue private gain, legally and also illegally through the abuse of public office. Despite decades of anticorruption efforts, year after year, ordinary citizens tell pollsters that corrup-tion is one of China's most serious problems. In the cities, Chinese poke fun at the perceived insincerity of the anticorruption reforms: "not daring *not* to fight corruption, not daring to fight corruption seriously." In the countryside, villagers rise up to protest abuses of power by "local emperors" imposing illegal fees and excessive taxes.

In recent years, the requisition, rezoning, and sale of agricultural land by local governments has pro-voked rural riots, usually suppressed with great vio-lence. Land is not privately owned, but contracted for agricultural use by Chinese farmers. Local govern-ments have seized on more lucrative opportunities for land use provided by real estate and industrial devel-opment. Farmers tend to be poorly compensated in these instances of eminent domain for local economic development (and local government profit). Top

Chinese leaders have condemned these actions, not least of all because arable land is already scarce.

The growing wealth gap fuels the perceptions of official abuse. Chinese policymakers have promoted a policy that "some get rich first." One result is rapidly rising inequality. Rural incomes are about 30 percent of urban incomes, and coastal regions have been advantaged over the interior. Urban Chinese in modern Shanghai enjoy annual incomes exceeding $2,000, while rural Chinese in backward Guizhou province make do with $200. Poorer Chinese deeply resent the newly conspicuous economic inequalities of the socialist market economy. While some struggle for a basic livelihood, there are also Chinese entrepreneurs and venal officials who travel in luxury sedans, do business on cellular phones, and feast ostentatiously at expensive restaurants. In 2006, Chinese authorities admitted to a Gini coefficient of 0.46, mostly reflecting a gap between urban and rural residents.[2] As the wealth gap has exploded within a single generation, it has great potential to impact social stability.

According to the Ministry of Public Security, in 2005, China experienced 87,000 "public disturbances," both urban and rural—up 7 percent from the previous year. Land takings, economic distress, and political corruption certainly provoked much of this unrest. A nontrivial number of rural "disturbances" are directed against pollution, which has displaced tens of millions of farmers.

Although the Chinese have developed a significant legal and organizational infrastructure of environmental protection in the past decade, environmental pollution and degradation have increased at a rate that far outpaces the capacity of the state to protect the environment. This reflects developmental priorities: indeed, as late as the mid-1990s, Chinese leaders routinely articulated the principle of "first development, then environment." The World Bank estimates that annually 300,000 Chinese die prematurely from air pollution. Children breathe in the equivalent of smoking two packs of cigarettes per day. Sixteen of the world's twenty most polluted cities are Chinese cities—including Beijing, the site of the 2008 Olympic Games. The expanding ownership of private automobiles by the new middle class exacerbates the problem: Chinese domestically designed and manufactured automobiles emit ten to twenty times more pollutants than American or Japanese models.

As Chinese leaders confront their domestic challenges, they do so in a global context that they now actively engage. The U.S. government now uses the term "stakeholder" to describe the new role of China in the world. This has much to do with China's accession to the World Trade Organization (WTO) in 2001, which has further opened the economy, subjecting it to a new discipline of global competition and pushing development of the economic legal infrastructure. WTO accession agreements require China to fully open its banking sector to foreign investors in 2007—and this will accelerate an already rapid process of economic reform. China is not only an economic player, however. It has also shown its willingness to play a role in helping to resolve international crises, such as the production and testing of nuclear weapons by North Korea. As the only country with political influence over North Korea, China organized the six-party talks, bringing the United States to the negotiating table in a multilateral situation.

China has thoroughly abandoned the strictures of communist ideology, has experienced an awesome economic revolution, and is taking its place as an important world power. Yet, unlike most other communist regimes, which toppled in the face of popular uprisings, China has experienced no second political revolution. Today, it is still a communist party-state. Chinese policymakers have promoted limited liberalization, sometimes as an antidote to corruption at the grassroots. While they have opened up political processes to more diversified inputs, they have also firmly suppressed organized challenges to the Communist Party. A handful of leaders at the very top still monopolize the authority to choose what sorts of inputs from what sorts of groups are acceptable, and the decision rules are not always transparent.

Strikingly little remains of Mao's grand revolutionary schemes. Viewed from the perspective of the 1970s, the magnitude and pace of change in China in the past quarter-century are practically unimaginable. Chinese politics today is "post-Mao" politics in the sense that there is a new regime, not simply a change of leaders—and, given its dynamics, there appears to be no turning back. Of course, without a grasp of China's rich political history, it is not only impossible to appreciate what has (and has not) changed, but also impossible to understand the crucial context of post-Mao reform: what has been rejected.

HISTORICAL SETTING

When ordinary Chinese today are asked about what it is they, as Chinese, are most proud, many respond: "our long history." Chinese civilization emerged more than six thousand years ago. As a polity, imperial China was the longest-lived major system of governance in world history, enduring as a centralized state ruled with little change in political philosophy or bureaucratic organization for more than two millennia until the fall of the Qing, the last dynasty, in 1911.[3]

Traditional China was governed by an emperor and a unique bureaucracy of scholar-officials at the capital and in the localities, who gained their positions meritocratically through examinations that tested knowledge of the Confucian classics. Anyone was eligible to participate in the examinations, but successful performance required a classical education, usually through a private tutor, not available to most ordinary Chinese. **Confucianism** was basically a conservative philosophy. It conceived of society and the polity in terms of an ordered hierarchy of harmonious relationships. At the top of the hierarchy was the emperor, who maintained social order through his conduct as a moral exemplar. Confucianism blurred the distinction between state and society: it saw harmony (not conflict) as the natural social order; this harmony resulted because the virtuous emperor provided an example of correct conduct. Loyalty to the emperor was the highest principle in the hierarchy of relationships entailing mutual obligations throughout society.

Imperial Order to the Founding of the PRC

This remarkable imperial order began to crumble in the mid-nineteenth century, when Qing rulers proved unable to uphold their political authority and maintain territorial integrity in the presence of large-scale domestic rebellion and foreign economic and military encroachment. The republic founded in 1912 did not restore order or sovereignty to China, but effectively collapsed within a few years, as dozens of Chinese regional warlords ruling with personal armies competed for control of territory.[4] Nearly four decades of political upheaval and continuous warfare ensued, as the Chinese sought solutions to the problems of governance that had brought down the Qing.

The dominant problems were the struggle for national sovereignty and the struggle for peasant livelihood. The former involved two sorts of claims:

cession of Chinese territory in treaties imposed forcibly by Western powers beginning in the nineteenth century, and outright military invasion and occupation by the Japanese in the 1930s. As to the Chinese peasantry, poverty in the countryside due to socioeconomic conditions of exorbitant taxes, high rents, and usurious credit was aggravated by frequent floods and droughts, which usually brought ruin. An observer compared the condition of the Chinese peasant to a man standing up to his neck in water: one ripple would drown him.[5]

These two struggles were played out in the context of a competition to unify the country. By the 1920s, the **Nationalist Party** and army had emerged as the most prominent political and military force in the country. The Nationalists had their strongest social base in the urban areas; in the countryside, they were mainly dependent on the support of the landlord class. This largely explains Nationalist reluctance to implement land and social reforms to resolve the problems of Chinese peasants. Peasant poverty was exacerbated by absentee landlordism and the replacement of ties of mutual obligation with economic ties enforced by managing agents. Land distribution was not part of the Nationalist agenda; nor were tax controls or provision of cheap credit effectively implemented.

Between 1924 and 1927, the Nationalists allied with the communists in a battle to eliminate regional warlords and to unify China. By the late 1920s, the Nationalists had practically realized this aim. In 1927, they broke their alliance with the communists in a violent massacre that reduced the Communist Party from nearly 58,000 to 10,000 members. The break inaugurated a new civil war. In the end, the Nationalists were forced to retreat to the island of Taiwan in 1949.

By contrast with the Nationalists, the intellectual revolutionaries who founded the **Chinese Communist Party** in 1921 were unlikely contenders for power. The rise and eventual victory of the communists owe much to historic opportunities in the 1930s and 1940s. These opportunities were available for other forces to exploit too, but the communists exploited them best.[6] **Mao Zedong** emerged as leader of the communists in the mid-1930s, consolidating his leadership in the early 1940s.[7]

After the Nationalist attack in 1927, many communists retreated to the countryside. Mao had already reported on the spontaneous impulse for radical social change among the peasantry and had proposed a revolutionary strategy different from that suggested by communist theory or Russian experience. Mao rejected the idea that the Chinese communists could win power through a revolution of the small urban working class in China. Instead, he argued, a communist victory could be achieved only by providing leadership for a nascent rural revolution and building a guerrilla Red Army to surround the cities with the countryside. From a base in southeastern China, Mao and other communists implemented a program of political education and social change, including land redistribution. In 1934, a major Nationalist offensive forced them on a strategic retreat, the historic Long March, that ended at the caves of Yanan in China's northwest, where Mao and his communist forces, their numbers literally decimated, established their headquarters. From Yanan, they built on the strategy of rural revolution to further develop support in the countryside.

The second indispensable component in communist victory was the 1937 Japanese invasion of central China, beyond territory in the northeast that the Japanese had occupied since 1931.[8] Mao seized the strategic initiative to call for a truce in the civil war so that Chinese could unite to resist Japanese aggression. Nationalist leaders were initially wary. This combination of Nationalist reluctance and strong anti-Japanese sentiment in the cities and countryside earned the communists enormous popularity as the true nationalist resistance to foreign aggression. From 1937 to 1945, the communists grew in force from 40,000 to more than a million. Japanese defeat in World War II ended the alliance between Nationalists and communists. A new civil war began.[9] In four years, the communists won victory, as peasant revolutionaries and Chinese nationalists. Once in power, they turned their energies to the construction of socialism.

History of the PRC

The history of the People's Republic of China (PRC) can be divided into three major periods. In the first, between 1949 and 1957, the Chinese adopted a "lean to one side" strategy, emulating the experience of the first and most powerful communist state, the Soviet Union. The second period began in 1958, when the Chinese introduced their own model of revolutionary development. Except for a few years at the beginning of the 1960s, this Maoist model prevailed until Mao's death in 1976. A short transitional period ensued, during which immediate problems of policy orientation and leadership succession were resolved with the arrest and trial of key radical leaders. In December 1978, the third period, a new era of reform, ongoing today, was inaugurated with a Central Committee declaration favoring learning from practical experience and rejecting the ideological constraints of Maoism—or any theory.[10] **Deng Xiaoping,** China's new "paramount leader," charted and presided over the reforms. In the same sense that Chinese politics in the two decades ending in 1976 are appropriately characterized as the Maoist years, the last two decades of the twentieth century belong most to Deng—despite important differences in the power of these two leaders and how they wielded it.

"Lean to One Side" The Chinese communists had won power largely by ignoring Soviet advice. Once in power, however, they looked to the Soviet Union for a plan to build socialism. They concluded a treaty of friendship and alliance in 1950. Soviet financial aid to China in the 1950s was not large. Mainly, aid was given in a massive technology transfer: over 12,000 Soviet engineers and technicians were sent to work in China; over 6,000 Chinese studied in Soviet universities, tens of thousands more in Soviet factories on short-term training courses. With this Soviet assistance, the Chinese developed heavy industry, establishing a centralized bureaucracy of planning agencies and industrial ministries to manage the economy according to five-year plans. They nationalized private industry. In the early 1950s, they sent communists down to the grassroots to instigate and organize land reform, a violent "class struggle." Each peasant household was classified according to land holdings, and land seized from landlords was redistributed to poor peasants, the majority of the peasantry.[11] Agricultural collectivization followed. This process was also essentially coercive, especially in its later stages, but not as violent as land reform.

The "lean to one side" period did feature some Maoist strategies, especially in political participation and socialization. The Chinese implemented many policies by mobilizing the masses in intensive campaigns, with essentially compulsory participation. For the Chinese communists, potential regime opponents—such as intellectuals and capitalists—were capable of being politically transformed through practices such as "thought reform." Communist leaders were sufficiently confident about the results of political education and regime accomplishments to invite nonparty intellectuals to voice criticism in the Hundred Flowers Campaign in 1957. When criticism was harsh, revealing weak support for the communist system, the leaders quickly reversed themselves. They launched an Anti-Rightist Campaign, which discovered more "poisonous weeds" than "blooming flowers." About a half million people, many of them intellectuals, were persecuted as "rightists" in a campaign that effectively silenced political opposition for twenty years.[12] Mass campaigns, political education, and political labeling were all coercive measures that resulted in the persecution of millions. To some extent, this coercion had a characteristic Maoist (and Confucian) element: fundamentally, it rejected the Stalinist version of political purge as physical liquidation, because it viewed the individual as malleable and ultimately educable. Yet, "enemies of the people" were not spared: one million to three million landlords and "counterrevolutionaries" were persecuted to death in the early 1950s alone.

In 1956, frictions in relations with the Soviet Union began to develop. Tensions increased throughout the 1950s, resulting in the withdrawal of aid and advisers and a Sino-Soviet split that shocked the world in 1960. Major irritants included Soviet reluctance to support efforts to "liberate" Taiwan, Soviet unwillingness to aid China's nuclear development, and a relaxation of Soviet hostility toward the United States. At about the same time, Mao was reconsidering his view of the Soviet model of development and developing his own radical model of building communism.

Great Leap Forward The first five-year plan had invested in heavy industry, not agriculture. Following the Soviet model, central planners had not diverted resources from industry to promote agricultural growth. In 1958, Mao proposed a strategy of simultaneous development of industry and agriculture to be achieved in two ways: (1) the labor-intensive mass mobilization of peasants to increase agricultural output by building irrigation facilities, and (2) the organization of primitive production processes to give inputs to agriculture (such as small chemical fertilizer plants and primitive steel furnaces to make tools) without taking resources from industry. A crucial element of Mao's solution was an increase in size of the collective

farms. In order to build irrigation facilities, local communist officials needed to control a labor force of large numbers of peasants, larger than the current collectives that grouped together a few hundred households. By combining several collectives into one gigantic farm, Mao hoped to realize economies of scale. In 1958, with prodding from above, the people's communes were born, grouping together thousands of households in one unit of economic and political organization managed by Communist Party officials.

The Maoist model was not simply an economic development strategy. It was fundamentally a political campaign, a point exemplified in the main slogan of the **Great Leap Forward:** "politics in command."[13] The Great Leap Forward abandoned most material rewards for moral incentives. By 1958, in Mao's view, Chinese peasants had demonstrated tremendous enthusiasm and were ready to leap into communism, if properly mobilized by local leaders. In the politically charged climate, economic expertise was denigrated and caution criticized as lack of faith in the masses. Leaders in Beijing set output targets high, demanding that local leaders believe in the ability of the Chinese people to accomplish miracles. By implication, failure to achieve high targets could be due only to poor leadership. A dangerous vicious cycle was set in motion: local leaders competed to demonstrate their political correctness; when communes failed to meet targets set in Beijing, local leaders calculated output imaginatively to report targets had been met or exceeded; production results were increasingly exaggerated as reports went to higher and higher levels; the response from Beijing to the falsely reported leap in output was a further leap in targets.

In 1958, dislocation associated with forming the communes and peasant mobilization to help meet high steel output targets by making steel in primitive furnaces was so great that the autumn harvest was not all gathered. That year too, a false belief in excess production led to reduction in areas sown in grain. Even with reduced acreage, peasant contributions to agricultural labor were decreasing due to physical exhaustion, weak material rewards, and the abolition of private plots (and, in some cases, private property for complete communization). In 1959, when top Chinese leaders met to consider these problems, the Minister of National Defense criticized radicalism in policy implementation. In response, Mao accused the minister of factionalism, turned the meeting into a referendum on his leadership, and challenged others to dare to attack the Leap's radical principles.

The meeting was a terrible turning point. With political correctness reasserted, radicalism returned. Moreover, just as the 1957 antirightist campaign had silenced opposition outside the party, Mao's 1959 accusations and threats effectively silenced opposition in the top echelons of party leadership.[14] That same year, large parts of China suffered from severe drought, others from severe flooding, in one of the worst natural disasters experienced in decades.

Retreat from the Leap   Over the next three years, the famine cost an estimated 27 million lives.[15] China retreated from Maoist radicalism. Mao retreated from day-to-day management of public affairs, but continued in his position as Communist Party chairman. In the early 1960s, the communes ceased to be relevant to agricultural production. Instead, peasant households contracted with the state for production, selling the surplus in newly established free markets. In industry, there was a renewed reliance on material incentives, technical expertise, and profitability as the standard to judge performance. The education system emphasized the creation of a knowledgeable and highly skilled corps of managers and leaders. Policy processes took into account advice by experts, rather than reliance on mass miracles.

Cultural Revolution   By the mid-1960s, Mao had further developed his radical critique of the Soviet model and extended it to the Chinese experience. In China, Mao saw a "new class" of economic managers and political officials, privileged by elitist policies that increased social antagonisms. In 1966, Mao argued that many communist leaders (notably, China's head of state, Liu Shaoqi, but also others, including Deng Xiaoping) were corrupt "capitalist roaders" who opposed socialism and must be thrown out of power. He launched the Great Proletarian Cultural Revolution, yet another exercise in radical excess. The **Cultural Revolution** was simultaneously a power struggle, an ideological battle, and a mass campaign to transform culture. Compared with the Great Leap Forward, its impact on the Chinese economy was minor; its impact on society was devastating.

For Mao, the enemy of socialism was within the Communist Party. Unable to rely on the party to correct

Defense Minister Lin Biao sits beside Chairman Mao Zedong and Premier Zhou Enlai during the Cultural Revolution. PLA soldiers wave the Little Red Book of quotations from Chairman Mao, a reflection of the cult of Mao that Lin helped to build.

SV Bilderdienst/The Image Works

its mistakes, Mao instructed secondary school and university students to overturn "bourgeois culture" and "bombard the headquarters." The Communist Party became effectively powerless as an organization. For the first time since 1949, Chinese were free to organize politically. Unconstrained by the party, Chinese engaged in political action legitimated by their own interpretations of Mao Zedong Thought. Students formed radical Red Guard groups to criticize and persecute victims, often chosen quite arbitrarily or for reasons more personal than political. In schools, factories, and government agencies, those in power were criticized and persecuted. Persecution was frequently physical. It was not uncommon for victims to be held in makeshift prisons, forced to do harsh manual labor, and subjected to violent public "struggle sessions" to force them to confess their crimes. Many were "struggled" to death, and many others committed suicide. Factional fighting was inevitable, as rival Red Guard groups fought for power, each faction claiming true representation of Mao Zedong Thought.[16]

In 1967, the country was near anarchy. The schools had been shut down; most party and government offices no longer functioned; transportation and communications were severely disrupted; factional struggles were increasingly violent contests, some of them armed confrontations. Having unleashed social conflict, Mao had been able to manipulate it—but not to control it. Mao called on the army to restore order, a process that began in 1969.

The 1970s were years of more moderate conflict, mostly played out as a struggle at the apex of power rather than in society generally. Radical leaders (including Mao's wife) who had risen to power in the Cultural Revolution supported a continuation of radical policies. Other leaders, reinstated by Mao to balance the power of the radicals, supported policies of economic modernization. The conflict was ongoing at the time of Mao's death in 1976. Within two years, the economic modernizers had won. China embarked on a new course of reform, different from anything in the experience of any communist system.

SOCIAL CONDITIONS

Chinese society has changed in various ways since the communists came to power. These changes include social structural transformations engineered by the regime, especially in the early decades. This section focuses on basic features that make up the social environment for Chinese politics that have not undergone fundamental transformation but have changed only in degree, if at all.

First among these is China's huge population. When the communists came to power in 1949, China's population was 540 million. Today China remains the world's most populous country, with a population of 1.3 billion. As in the 1950s, most Chinese live in the countryside, although the proportion has been changing more rapidly in recent years. In the 1950s, about 85 percent of Chinese lived in the countryside; by 1980 that proportion had decreased only slightly, to 82 percent. More than two decades of economic reform produced significant transformation. De facto relaxation of rural to urban migration restrictions liberated the underemployed farming population to seek work in cities. Rural industrialization and the growth of towns also changed the situation. By 2005, only 57 percent of Chinese lived in the countryside. An increasing proportion of this rural population work at least part-time in industry. Before economic reforms in the 1980s, state-owned enterprises dominated industry in China. Today, rural collective industry, in the form of township and village enterprises under the direction of local governments, is the most dynamic industrial sector.

The second basic feature involves geography. Although China is the world's second largest country in area, the population is concentrated in the eastern third of the land. This is largely because only about a quarter of China's land is arable. Population growth and reduction in cultivated area have greatly exacerbated the land shortage. Despite efforts to preserve arable land for farming, China's leaders have been unable to reverse the reduction in cultivated area. In part, this is a result of agricultural decollectivization and a return to household farming: land is used for property borders, burial grounds, and bigger houses. In recent years, local government land requisitions for lucrative residential and industrial development have further reduced arable land and provoked much rural unrest. The basic problem of feeding China's large population can be expected to continue to loom large as more Chinese grow prosperous and change their diet: eating more, and eating more meat and less grain.

The third feature is that China is a multiethnic state. At least 92 percent of Chinese are ethnically Han, but there are fifty-five recognized **ethnic minorities,** ranging in number from a few thousand to more than 16 million. Although minorities make up only a fairly small proportion of China's population, areas in which minorities live comprise more than 60 percent of China's territory, and much of this is in strategically important border regions.[17] This includes Tibet (bordering India) and Xinjiang (bordering three new post-Soviet states), which have experienced fairly continuous minority unrest over the decades. The Chinese have maintained considerable armed forces in these areas to quell secessionist efforts.

Finally, Han Chinese share the same Chinese written language, a unifying force in China for more than two millennia, practically defining what it is to be Chinese. The same written language is spoken in many different dialects, however, often making communication difficult. Mandarin, based on the dialect of the Beijing locality, is the official language promoted by the communist regime through the education system and mass media.

STRUCTURE OF THE PARTY-STATE

From top to bottom, Chinese politics has changed noticeably since the Maoist period. Yet, the essential form of the Chinese political system retains an organizational design borrowed decades ago from the Soviet Union and developed nearly a century ago in Russia by Lenin—the design of the communist **party-state.**

Design Features

Lenin viewed political legitimacy in ways that justify a monopoly of power by a communist party elite that is not popularly elected. He believed that ordinary citizens do not understand their own real interests and that larger interests of society are not best advanced by aggregating interests that citizens articulate. According to Lenin, as ordinary citizens typically lack revolutionary consciousness and knowledge of communist theory, they are incapable of making the correct choices that will lead from capitalism to socialism and toward communism—a utopia characterized by a high level of economic prosperity, an absence of social conflict, and a minimal role for government. Lenin proposed a solution to this problem: a political party and political system built on the principles of guardianship and hierarchy.[18] To these two principles, Chinese leaders

added the idea of the mass line, formulated by Mao in the 1940s. Guardianship and hierarchy define the communist party-state. The mass line adds another dimension, which moderates guardianship.

Guardianship describes the main relationship between the Communist Party and society. The party bases its claim to legitimate rule not on representation of the expressed preferences of a majority but on representation of the "historical best interests" of all the people. In theory, as most ordinary citizens do not know their best interests, society is best led by an elite vanguard party with a superior understanding of the historical laws of development. The Communist Party is therefore an exclusive organization—in China, membership is about 5 percent of the population—not a mass political party with membership open to all. The notion of Communist Party leadership is explicitly set forth in each of the four Chinese constitutions promulgated since 1949, as is some version of the notion of dictatorship. Currently, the constitution describes the political system as a socialist state under the "people's democratic dictatorship." As the Communist Party is the only organization with the politically correct knowledge to lead society, it is the authoritative arbiter of the interests of the people. In effect, dictatorship in the name of the people is Communist Party dictatorship. Party leaders today are more informed of public opinion than in the past, but there is no place in the Chinese political system (or in Leninist theory) for organized opposition to Communist Party leadership.

Chinese Communist Party guardianship is, in theory, informed by the practice of the **mass line.** The party leads, but its leadership is not isolated from the opinions and preferences of the mass public. The degree to which mass preferences actually find expression in public policy depends on their fit with larger goals determined by party leaders. Party leaders at all levels (but especially at the grassroots) are supposed to maintain a close relationship with ordinary citizens so that the party organization can transform the "scattered and unsystematic ideas" of the masses into "correct ideas" and propagate them "until the masses embrace them as their own." In this way, policy is supposed to flow "from the masses to the masses."[19]

Party Organization The internal organization of the Communist Party is organized around a hierarchy of party congresses and committees extending from the top of the system down to the grassroots. Lower party organizations are subordinate to higher party organizations, and individual party members are subordinate to the party as an organization. Inner-party rules for decision making are based on the Leninist principle of **democratic centralism.**

In democratic centralism, democracy refers mainly to consultation. It requires that party leaders provide opportunities for discussion, criticism, and proposals in party organizations (often including lower party organizations) as part of the normal process of deciding important issues or making policy.

Centralism requires unified discipline throughout the party: top-level official party decisions are binding on party organizations and members. Centralism is never sacrificed to democracy. Party members are allowed to hold personal views contrary to party decisions and to voice them through proper party channels, but they are not free to act in ways that promote these views. According to the Communist Party constitution, the formation of "factions" or any sort of "small group activity" within the party is a punishable violation of organizational discipline. Communist Party hierarchy and the requirement that party members observe party discipline are designed as organizational guarantees that the party, in exercising leadership over society, acts as a unified force, responsive to the leadership of the highest level of party organization.

Ideology is today both less prominent and less coherent in Chinese politics than it was in the past. The principles of guardianship, hierarchy, and the mass line are not inconsequential abstractions, however. They have concrete practical implications, evident throughout the Chinese political system. Change in the system is evident too, of course, both as a product and by-product of policies of reform in the past two decades. Yet, while the political reforms of recent decades are not trivial, they do not add up to fundamental systemic change. For now, as in the past, the design of the communist party-state is a fair model of the organization of political power in China.

Two Hierarchies, with Party Leadership The design of the communist party-state is perhaps most evident in the organization of power in two hierarchies of political structures, illustrated in Figure 10.1. The focus in this section is politics at the national level, what the Chinese refer to as the political center of the system, but government structures are more or less duplicated at each level of the political system by Communist Party structures. In principle, there is a division of labor between party and government structures. In practice, the two often perform similar functions, with party structures and party officials exercising leadership over parallel government structures and government officials. This section on political structures distinguishes the party from the government, while elaborating on the variety of mechanisms the party uses to exercise control over officials in party and government structures. The following sections on policymaking and policy implementation emphasize that, because of the interconnectedness of party and government, distinctions between party and government are of only limited use in understanding decision making in China. Both party and government structures have changed since 1949. The description in the following section focuses on the system that emerged in the reform era.

Government Structures

At the political center in Beijing, the key government structures are the **National People's Congress (NPC),** which is China's legislature, and the **State Council,** which exercises executive functions. Under the State Council are government ministries and commissions, which have ranged in number from 32 to 100 since 1949. Below the political center, government structures extend downward in a five-tiered hierarchy consisting of 31 provinces, 333 large cities, 2,862 counties, 41,636 townships, and 629,000 villages. Local government structures (local people's congresses, local governments, and government departments) are found at the provincial, municipal, county, and township levels. The provincial level includes four megacities (Beijing, Shanghai, Tianjin, and Chongqing). As shown in Figure 10.1, Chinese voters elect delegates to township and county people's congresses only. Municipal, provincial, and national congress delegates are elected by congresses one level down. At all five levels, congress delegates elect their governments. Villages are popularly elected self-governing rural grassroots organizations, not part of the formal government hierarchy.

National People's Congress According to the constitution, the highest organization of state authority is the NPC.[20] The NPC and its permanent body, the NPC Standing Committee, exercise legislative functions.

CENTRAL STRUCTURES

| Legislature | Government | Judiciary | Party |

Premier WEN Jiabao

Standing Committee
10 members

State Council
30 members

Standing Committee
159 members

National People's
Congress
2,591 members

General Secretary
Hu Jintao

Standing Committee
9 members

Politburo
24 members

Central Committee
198 members

National Party
Congress
2,120 members

Supreme People's
Court

Supreme People's
Procuratorate

Government
ministries

Party
departments

LOCAL Governments and Legislatures   Party

Provincial governments

Provincial congresses

Municipal governments

Municipal congresses

County governments

County congresses

PUBLIC

Township governments

Township congresses

PUBLIC

KEY

Elects, appoints ⟶

Nominates ----►

Party exercises
nomenklatura authority

Chinese Political Structures

FIGURE 10.1

NPC delegates are elected for five-year terms by delegates in provincial-level congresses and the armed forces. Normally, NPC delegates assemble once annually for a plenary session of about two weeks (although they did not meet at all between 1965 and 1975). The number and composition of delegates are prescribed by law, but the NPC has always been huge. In 1986, the law set a ceiling of 3,000 delegates, which is about the number elected to each congress since 1983. By law, urban Chinese are overrepresented: a 1995 law set the ratio of rural to urban Chinese per NPC delegate at 4:1—already less unequal than in previous years, due to legal change as well as urbanization.

Formally, the NPC has extensive powers, including amendment of the constitution, passage and amendment of legislation, approval of economic plans and government work reports, and appointment of top state and government leaders. For most of the year, when the NPC is not in session, its Standing Committee of about 150 members, who reside in Beijing and meet regularly throughout the year, serves as the working legislative assembly. The 1982 constitution considerably strengthened the role of the NPC Standing Committee. It now exercises all but the most formal powers of the NPC and prepares the agenda for the annual NPC plenary sessions, when the full NPC typically ratifies its interim legislative actions.

Is the NPC (and its Standing Committee) a "rubber stamp" assembly? For the Maoist years, the answer is clearly "yes." In recent decades, however, the NPC has become more assertive, and its Standing Committee has assumed a greater role in law making. This is part of political reform undertaken in response to the extreme institutional nihilism of the Cultural Revolution. NPC assertiveness is evident in an increase in delegate motions (by an order of magnitude) and, more significantly, in dissenting votes. The practice of unanimous approval, once automatic, has ended, sometimes with embarrassing results. In 1998, 45 percent of NPC delegates demonstrated their disapproval of the government's failure to control corruption by abstaining or voting against the work report of the chief procurator. While this high level of dissent remains unusual for votes on work reports, economic plans, and official appointments, dissenting votes of 20 to 30 percent on draft laws are not uncommon. Actual failure to pass legislation submitted to the NPC has occurred twice: a draft of the controversial Enterprise Bankruptcy Law was voted down in 1986, and a very restrictive draft of the Law on Public Demonstrations was voted down not long after the crushing of the 1989 mass protests. Both laws were sent back for substantial revision before securing the requisite majority approval in the NPC. A dramatic example of the new view of NPC authority occurred in 1989, when Hu Jiwei circulated a petition among fellow NPC Standing Committee members to call an emergency meeting of the NPC to exercise its constitutional power to repeal martial law.

The full NPC cannot be expected to function routinely as a credible legislature because it is too large and meets too infrequently and briefly. More important is the lawmaking role of the less cumbersome NPC Standing Committee. In the early 1980s, many party and government elders retired from important positions in central and provincial administration to the NPC Standing Committee. Instead of retreating from political life, these elders used the Standing Committee as a channel for political influence. Their enhanced role was institutionalized with the establishment of a Legislative Affairs Committee (with significant staff) and eight permanent specialized legislative committees to consider draft legislation. With these changes, the NPC (and its Standing Committee) can no longer be dismissed as a rubber stamp. The legislature remains institutionally weak, however, for two main reasons (discussed later in this chapter): the practice of executive-led government (which does not distinguish the Chinese system from parliamentary systems in other countries) and the practice of Communist Party leadership (which is more fundamental).

State Council   In lawmaking, the State Council is the center of government activity, although this role too is newly enhanced.[21] The State Council is composed of the premier, who is head of government, and his cabinet of vice-premiers, state councillors, ministers, auditor general, and secretary general (currently thirty-six members, all formally nominated by the premier and appointed by the NPC). In 2003, Wen Jiabao became premier. The State Council has its own Standing Committee, which meets twice weekly, with members reporting on work in their assigned portfolios. As in parliamentary systems, the bulk of legislation is drafted by specialized ministries and commissions under the direction of the cabinet. Also, however, as most Chinese laws are drafted in general and imprecise language, they require detailed "implementing regulations" to have any effect. These regulations are typically drafted by State Council ministries (under the direction of the newly reestablished State Council Legislation Bureau) and promulgated by the ministries or State Council without consideration by the NPC or its Standing Committee.

Communist Party Leadership   The Communist Party exercises direct leadership over government and legislative functions in a variety of ways. Before the NPC assembles, party leaders convene a meeting of all delegates who are members of the Communist Party (73 percent of NPC delegates in 2006). At these meetings, leaders discuss the NPC agenda and offer "hopes" of the party leaders for the forthcoming session, including suggestions about the tone (how open or restrained

NPC debate should be, for example). Also, NPC powers of appointment are effectively nullified by party control over candidate nomination and the usual practice of an equal number of candidates and positions. For example, although the NPC formally appoints the president, vice president, premier, and cabinet members, there has never been more than one nominee for these positions and candidate nomination is decided at the party meeting convened before the NPC assembles. The only positions for which NPC elections have ever featured choice are the 1988 and 1998 elections to the NPC Standing Committee. Those elections featured no choice for positions of leadership, however, and only limited choice for regular NPC Standing Committee membership (about 6 percent more candidates than positions).

As to lawmaking, Communist Party leaders have veto power over all legislation of consequence. The system of party review of legislation that emerged in the early 1990s rejects party micromanagement of the State Council or NPC Standing Committee work. Nonetheless, all important laws, constitutional amendments, and political laws submitted to the NPC or its Standing Committee must have prior approval by the party center. In short, the Chinese system is executive-led government, but with an important difference having to do with the role of the Communist Party.

The president of the PRC is head of state. This is a purely ceremonial office, held by **Hu Jintao.** Hu is also head of the Communist Party organization and of the Central Military Commission, in which leadership of military forces is formally vested. The commission was established as a government structure only in 1982, but its Communist Party counterpart functioned long before then and remains in existence, with the same membership in party and government structures.

Judiciary Judicial authority rests with the Supreme People's Court at the center and with local people's courts below. Formally, the Supreme People's Court is responsible to the NPC. Courts at lower levels are responsible to the people's congresses at their respective levels and also take direction from courts above them.

The Supreme People's Procuratorate, restored in 1978 after decades of neglect, is the central prosecutorial agency. It sits at the top of a hierarchy of procuratorates extending down to the county level, each

formally responsible to a local people's congress and each also under the direction of the procuratorate above. The Supreme People's Procuratorate is responsible to the NPC.

Procuratorates act as a bridge between public security agencies and the courts. They supervise criminal investigations, approve arrests, and prosecute cases. Beginning in the mid-1980s, the most important role of the procuratorates has been investigation and prosecution of corruption. In each new congress session, the NPC appoints the chief justice of the Supreme People's Court and the chief procurator.

Party Structures

At the political center in Beijing, the key party structures are the National Party Congress and its Central Committee, the Politburo, and the Politburo Standing Committee. In addition, party departments are organized under a secretariat. Below the center, down to the township level, are local party congresses and local party committees.

National Party Congress As in the government hierarchy, while the formal power of Communist Party structures is directly proportional to size, actual impact on policy is inversely proportional to size. The Communist Party constitution vests supreme authority in the **National Party Congress,** but this structure is too big and meets too infrequently to play a significant role in political decision making. The Central Committee determines the number of congress delegates and the procedures for their election. Since 1949, National Party Congresses have ranged in size from one to two thousand delegates, with recent congresses at about two thousand delegates. In the past, the congresses met irregularly, but party constitutions since 1969 have stipulated that congresses are normally convened at five-year intervals. This has been more or less the practice since 1969 and has been strictly observed in the post-Mao years, as shown in Table 10.1. The seventeenth party congress met in October 2007.

National Party Congress sessions are short, about a week or two at most. A main function is to ratify important changes in broad policy orientation already decided by more important smaller party structures. Although party congresses yield no surprises, these changes receive their highest formal endorsement at

Chinese Communist Party Congresses and Growth of Party Membership, 1921–2005		TABLE 10.1
Congress	**Year**	**Party Members**
1st	1921	More than 50
2nd	1922	123
3rd	1923	432
4th	1925	950
5th	1927	57,900[a]
6th	1928	40,000
7th	1945	1.2 million
Founding of the PRC, 1949		
8th	1956	11 million
9th	1969	22 million
10th	1973	28 million
11th	1977	35 million
12th	1982	40 million
13th	1987	46 million
14th	1992	51 million
15th	1997	58 million
16th	2002	66 million
	2005	71 million

[a] Communist party membership dropped from 57,900 to 10,000 after April 1927, when the Nationalists broke the "united front" with the communists in a massacre that decimated communist forces and ignited civil war.

Source: *Beijing Review*, 41, no. 8 (1998): 22; *People's Daily*, 2 September 2002, and 19 June 2006.

the party congresses. Therefore, the sessions have the public appearance of major historic events. A second function of the National Party Congress is to elect the **Central Committee,** which exercises the powers of the congress between sessions. Official candidates for Central Committee membership are determined by the Politburo before the congress meets. According to the 1982 party constitution, elections to the Central Committee are by secret ballot, and wide deliberation and discussion of candidates precedes them. Of course, centralism prevails: elections rarely offer choice (or much choice) among candidates.

Central Committee The Central Committee is the Chinese political elite, broadly defined: it is a collection of the most powerful several hundred political leaders in the country. All Central Committee members hold some major substantive position of leadership, as ministers in the central state bureaucracy or provincial party leaders, for example. Membership on the Central Committee reflects this political power—it does not confer it. In this sense, the Central Committee is less important intrinsically as a political structure than extrinsically, for the different sorts of interests and constituencies represented by its members.

Although the Central Committee does not initiate policy, changes in policy or leaders at the political center must be approved by it. This is done fairly routinely at plenary sessions now convened at least annually. Party leaders at the top rely on the bureaucratic and regional elites on the Central Committee to ensure that the "party line" is realized in practice. Central Committee membership brings these elites into the process as participants and, in effect, guarantors: in endorsing party policy, members also take on responsibility for its realization.

Politburo The Central Committee elects the **Politburo,** the Politburo Standing Committee, and the party general secretary—all of whom are also Central Committee members. These leaders are at the very apex of the political system. The composition of these structures is determined by party leaders before the party congress, and elections are mainly ceremonial, featuring no candidate choice. The Politburo is the top political elite, usually no more than two dozen leaders, most of whom have responsibility for overseeing policymaking in some issue area. Its inner circle is the Politburo Standing Committee, typically no more than a half-dozen leaders, who meet about once weekly, in meetings convened and chaired by the party general secretary. Members of the Politburo and its Standing Committee are the core political decision makers in China, presiding over a process that concentrates great power at the top.

Top Leader and the Succession Problem Since the abolition of the position of party chairman in 1982, the top party leader is the general secretary, a position held by Hu Jintao since 2002 (see Box 10.1). The change in terminology reflects the effort to promote collective leadership, a reaction against norms of past years when Mao presided as nearly all-powerful chairman of the party until his death in 1976. Yet, if general secretaries in the 1980s and 1990s have been less powerful than Chairman Mao, this has mainly to do with the unusual elite politics of the post-Mao

BOX 10.1

Hu Jintao and the "Fourth Generation" of Leaders

In November 2002, Jiang Zemin relinquished to Hu Jintao the office of Communist Party general secretary. This event marked the first time in PRC history that the transfer of party leadership occurred as a regular matter at a party congress, rather than as a result of the death or political purge of the incumbent. Hu succeeded Jiang in his other offices in the years that followed: the presidency of the PRC in 2003, the chairmanship of the party Central Military Commission in 2004, and the chairmanship of the government Central Military Commission in 2005. Hu is a technocrat: he graduated in hydraulic engineering at the prestigious Qinghua University, which is known as China's MIT. He is typical of the "fourth generation" of Chinese leaders, the least dogmatic cohort to accede to top offices in Chinese politics. As president of the Central Party School in the 1990s, Hu supported bold studies of political reform, including reform of the party. However, as party leader, Hu has been less bold—promoting increased supervision of the mass media and strengthening control of Internet content, for example.

transition period and especially the role of Deng Xiaoping.[22]

In communist systems, the death of the top leader creates a succession crisis: there is no formal or generally acknowledged position of second-in-command and no regularized mechanism to choose a new top leader. Mao's death ushered in a power struggle at the top, won by Deng and his fellow modernizers. Deng, already in his seventies at the time of Mao's death, chose to eschew top formal leadership of party or government in the interest of resolving the problem of succession.

In the late 1970s, Communist Party elders who had formerly held important positions of power were reinstated after years of forced retirement during the Cultural Revolution. Within a few years, however, many of them retired (or semiretired) to the "second line," to serve as advisers and involve themselves only in major policy issues or broad strategy.

At the very top, a half-dozen elders, all senior communist revolutionaries in their eighties or nineties, continued to play key roles in decision making and occupy formal positions of leadership, although not the top party or government positions. The best example, of course, was "paramount leader" Deng himself. Deng never held the top formal position of leadership in party or government, although he was on the Politburo Standing Committee until 1987 and chaired the Central Military Commission until 1989. Just below this very small group at the top, elders retired to advisory positions on a Central Advisory Commission, set up in 1982. Other elders "retired" to formal positions on the NPC. Younger leaders were promoted to the top positions on the "first line," to allow them to develop their own bases of support and authority, with the support of their elder patrons.

This arrangement did not provide a solution to the succession problem, however. In principle, elders on the second line used their prestige and informal power to support younger leaders in top executive positions. In practice, younger leaders on the first line, in the effort to establish their own authority, sometimes adopted positions at odds with the views of elder patrons. Friction with party elders resulted in two purges of top party executives in the 1980s: Hu Yaobang was dismissed as party general secretary in 1987 and his successor Zhao Ziyang was dismissed in 1989 (see Figure 10.2). The situation today is different: by the mid-1990s, most of the elders at the very top, including Deng, had "gone to see Marx," and the Central Advisory Commission had been dismantled, having served its purpose of easing leaders into retirement. After a dozen years as party secretary and beneficiary of Deng's support until Deng's death in 1997, Jiang Zemin stepped down in 2002, lending his support to Hu Jintao.

Party Bureaucracy The party has its own set of bureaucratic structures, managed by the Secretariat. The Secretariat provides staff support for the Politburo, transforming Politburo decisions into instructions for subordinate party departments. Compared with their government counterparts, party departments are fewer in number and have more broadly defined areas of competence.

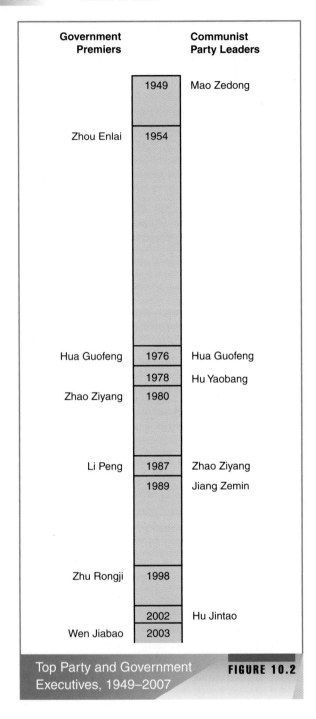

Government Premiers		Communist Party Leaders
	1949	Mao Zedong
Zhou Enlai	1954	
Hua Guofeng	1976	Hua Guofeng
	1978	Hu Yaobang
Zhao Ziyang	1980	
Li Peng	1987	Zhao Ziyang
	1989	Jiang Zemin
Zhu Rongji	1998	
	2002	Hu Jintao
Wen Jiabao	2003	

Top Party and Government Executives, 1949–2007   **FIGURE 10.2**

People's Liberation Army

The **People's Liberation Army (PLA),** which includes the navy, air force, and army, has played a major role in Chinese politics. Party and army were practically inseparable until 1949. After 1949, the PLA participated in important nonmilitary functions, such as economic construction. In the Cultural Revolution, the PLA was brought more directly into politics to resolve violent factional struggles in society, at a time when party and government structures had been shattered. In 1989, the PLA was instrumental in crushing the mass protests.

The PLA does not dictate policy to party leaders, but it is the self-appointed guardian of Chinese sovereignty and nationalism, with a particular interest in preventing Taiwan's independence.[23] This issue has the greatest potential to spark military confrontation, and it is a matter the Chinese claim is completely domestic. Since the mid-1980s, the PLA has engaged in a program of military modernization and professionalization, increasing defense expenditures, procuring new weapons systems and technologies, and streamlining forces to realize a "smaller but stronger" force of 2.5 million. Despite these efforts, the military gap between China and the West is not narrowing, but widening, as western military technological advances continue at an increasingly rapid pace. The PLA is at least a decade behind in almost all weapons systems and remains predominantly a land force.

Party Dominance

Party and government structures from top to bottom are staffed by more than 40 million officials on state salaries. One important mechanism of party leadership, described earlier in this chapter, is the structural arrangement: the duplication of political structures and the dominance of party structures and leaders over government structures and leaders. The Chinese Communist Party exercises leadership in political structures in other ways too. Among the most important are overlapping directorships, "party core groups," party membership penetration, and the *nomenklatura* system. Mechanisms of party leadership specific to policymaking are discussed in later in this chapter.

Nomenklatura *System*   The **nomenklatura** **system** is the most important mechanism by which the Communist Party exerts control over officials. In some sense, it is the linchpin of the political system. It refers to the management of all party and government officials in positions of even moderate importance by party committees. Party committees exercise authority over all major personnel decisions (such as appointment, promotion, transfer, and removal from office). Management authority is organized hierarchically and specified in lists of official positions. Any official at or above the rank of section chief is on such a list.[24] This amounted to about 8 million officials in the late 1980s, and the number must be considerably higher now.

Today, party committees, through their organization departments, directly manage all officials in positions one level down in the administrative hierarchy. At the top of the system, the Politburo exercises direct management authority over all officials at the provincial level in the territorial hierarchy and at the ministerial level in the bureaucratic hierarchy—about 7,000 officials in all (including the entire NPC Standing Committee, for example).

The extension of management authority downward in a hierarchy of dyadic relationships that are known to officials has important implications. Party leaders have a means of ensuring that the real constituency of every important official is the superior party committee—and ultimately the Central Committee and its Politburo. In looking ahead to career advancement, then, even officials who owe their positions formally to elections must look upward to "selectorates" of party committees rather than only (if at all) downward to electorates of congress deputies and ordinary citizens. Otherwise, they can be penalized. For example, for his effort in 1989 to assert NPC authority to repeal martial law, Hu Jiwei was expelled from the NPC Standing Committee.

Party Membership Another means by which the Communist Party exercises leadership over officials is in party membership penetration in political structures. The vast majority of officials in political structures (including government structures and positions filled by elections) are Communist Party members. At their places of work, officials are members of party committees, general branches, or branches located in a hierarchy of basic-level party organizations. They meet regularly to participate in party "organizational life," which is quite apart from their professional work. They are obliged to observe the inner-party discipline of democratic centralism. The routine activities of party branches in government offices are supervised by departments specially assigned to ensure that the Communist Party remains an active force in government structures. Because the party monopolizes

opportunities to get along and ahead in the Chinese political system, the organizational hierarchy and party discipline designed to guarantee unified party leadership over society also promote party leadership in political structures.

Party Core Groups Separate from the basic-level party organizations that bring party members in all workplaces under the Communist Party hierarchy are party core groups, formed in government structures only and composed of a handful of party members who hold the most senior positions.[25] The head of the party core group is normally also the head of the structure (for example, government ministers typically head party core groups of their respective ministries). Party core groups are appointed by the party committees one level up, and they answer to these party committees. While basic-level party organizations are mechanisms to promote unity and discipline under party leadership within political structures overall, party core groups are mechanisms to promote party leadership over leaders in their government host structures. Between 1987 and 1988, the system of party core groups was formally abolished (and many were actually dismantled) as part of a brief reform effort to separate party and government functions. Party core groups were quickly revived in 1989, however, after the purge of Zhao Ziyang, the leader most closely associated with the reform.

Overlapping Directorships Finally, the structural distinctions illustrated in Figure 10.1 mask some overlap of directorates in party and government structures. Hu Jintao is concurrently head of state, head of the party, and chairman of the Central Military Commission of both government and party. The practice of "wearing two hats" (party and government) has always been common. Premier Wen Jiabao is also at the apex of party power, as a member of the Politburo Standing Committee. Wu Bangguo, who chairs the NPC Standing Committee, is also a member of the Politburo Standing Committee. Overlapping directorships were much more extensive in the past than they are now. Membership of local party committees and their parallel governments used to be indistinguishable. In the 1980s, overlapping directorships were retained at the political center, but practically eliminated at lower levels. There is some evidence that they are returning.

Elite Recruitment Some key features of elite recruitment emerge from the discussion earlier in this chapter. First, membership in the Communist Party is a prerequisite for political elite status. Over the decades, the party has changed its focus of recruitment in society, reflecting larger changes in policy orientation. In the 1950s, for example, the party recruited most intensely among industrial workers, to build a more traditional Communist Party from a largely peasant base. In the Cultural Revolution of the 1960s and 1970s, radical leftist standards dominated—and recruitment was directed toward the less educated and less well connected. In the 1980s and 1990s, the party focused its recruitment effort on intellectuals, professionals, and (more ambivalently) private entrepreneurs—all social groups identified as important for China's development as a prosperous nation (see Box 10.2).

Second, the party controls not only accessibility to this fundamental prerequisite for elite status, but also possesses a powerful organizational mechanism to recruit and promote elites: the *nomenklatura* system. Both appointed and elected leaders are vetted for office, level by level, such that a party committee at some level is the real constituent for leaders below. Beijing has not relinquished this key power, despite significant economic decentralization in recent decades.

What determines who gets along and ahead in the Chinese political system? That is, what criteria have leaders at higher levels viewed as most important for promotion? While much is made of the role of informal politics in China, a systematic study of provincial leaders from 1949 to 1998 shows that economic performance is the most important determinant of elite promotion in the post-Mao era of reform.[26] Leaders in provinces with higher economic growth or revenue contributions to the center during their tenure are less likely to be demoted or retired from office. In short, to win the support of their real constituents in Beijing, provincial leaders have to "deliver the goods." This is not surprising, considering that leaders in Beijing have staked their claim to legitimacy on precisely this outcome.

Rule by Law

The principle of "rule of law" is traditionally associated with liberal democratic ideals. It implies a particular relationship between individuals and the state, the essence of which is protection of individual rights by limitations on arbitrary state power. Such limitations are enshrined in the law and in legal institutions. This notion makes no sense in traditional communist ideology: law is a weapon of the state to use in exercising dictatorship. In 1978, however, Chinese leaders began to revive and develop important ideas and institutions of legality that had flourished for a brief period in the

---

"Red Capitalists"

BOX 10.2

In the mid-1980s, many party and government officials plunged into the private sector economy, shedding their offices but not their Communist Party membership. With little fanfare, the party also began to recruit private entrepreneurs as new members—a practice that reflected the party's commitment to economic growth, but met strong opposition from many as an abandonment of basic communist tenets. How could millionaire exploiters represent Chinese workers and peasants? When private entrepreneurs lent their support to protesters in 1989, leaders imposed a ban on their recruitment into the party. More than a decade later, in 2000, party leader Jiang Zemin introduced a convoluted new formula to justify welcoming them back: the "three represents," added in 2004 to China's constitution. In this formula, the party does not simply represent workers and peasants, but represents the developmental needs of the advanced social productive forces, the promotion of advanced culture, and the fundamental interests of the greatest majority of the people. In 2001, on the party's eightieth anniversary, Jiang proposed lifting the ban on recruitment of private entrepreneurs into the party. His proposal was soon implemented. Today, one-third of private entrepreneurs are party members. Even though "red capitalists" still account for only a very small proportion of party members, their inclusion reflects a highly significant policy.

1950s. The new Chinese legality acknowledges **rule by law.**[27] Briefly, this means: there are laws, and all are equally subject to them. As the second principle is often violated, this may seem a trivial advance. It is not. The ongoing effort to establish rule by law in China has already changed the way Chinese act and think, in important ways.

Socialist Legality The initial Chinese experiment with "socialist legality" began with the promulgation of the first constitution in 1954 and ended in 1957 with the Anti-Rightist Movement. Legalistic perspectives were rejected as examples of "bourgeois rightist" thinking. Legal scholars and legal professionals were criticized and labeled as "rightists." Work on development of criminal law stopped. Legal training and legal scholarship practically ceased. Defense lawyers disappeared from the legal process. Party committees took direct control of legal proceedings. The abandonment of law reached a peak during the Cultural Revolution, when violent "class struggle" and "mass justice" substituted for any regularized procedures to resolve social conflicts. This degree of radical lawlessness was not characteristic of the entire Maoist period, but a general official hostility to law prevailed from the late 1950s.

Legal Reform Legal reform began in 1978. The legal system, barely functioning at the time, required urgent action for a number of reasons. First, there was an immediate need to establish legitimacy by righting past wrongs: investigating and reversing verdicts of dubious legality issued during the Cultural Revolution were a high priority. Second, Deng Xiaoping and other leaders wanted not only to restore public order and stability after years of chaos and uncertainty, but also to express their commitment to system building as a substitute for arbitrary political rule. Finally and not least of all, Chinese leaders hoped that the new legality would encourage economic investment and growth by promoting predictability—through transparent rules and impartial rule adjudication.

Rule by law requires laws. Nearly thirty years after the founding of the PRC, there was no criminal law. In 1978, Chinese leaders appointed committees of legal specialists to pick up work set aside for decades and to draft criminal codes for immediate promulgation. In 1979, the NPC passed the first criminal law and criminal procedure law. In the years that followed, as

government agencies issued interim regulations that amended and clarified the hastily drafted laws, the NPC Legislative Affairs Committee worked on legal revisions. In 1996 and 1997, the NPC passed substantially amended and more precise versions of the laws. The 1997 amended criminal law takes into account changes in the Chinese economy that have created opportunities for economic crimes almost unimaginable in 1979 (such as insider securities trading). It abolishes the vaguely defined crimes of "counterrevolution." The 1996 amended criminal procedure law grants the accused the right to seek counsel (a right rejected in the 1950s) at an early stage of legal proceedings.

Rule by law implies equality before the law. This idea stands in sharp contrast to both the politicized view of law in communist ideology and routine practices in the Maoist years. In 1978, the NPC restored the procuratorates, which had been abolished in the 1960s. A new important role of procuratorates in the 1980s and 1990s became the investigation and prosecution of official crimes, for which procuratorates have full independent responsibility, according to law. Chinese leaders have regularly and prominently voiced a commitment to equality before the law, stating that officials who abuse public office and violate laws must be punished. Equality before the law, labeled "bourgeois" in the 1950s, is featured in the 1982 constitution—which also, for the first time, subjects the Communist Party (not only party members) to the authority of the law. At the same time, as described later in this chapter, there has been an explosion of corruption in recent years. In practice, the Communist Party, through its political-legal committees and its system of discipline inspection committees, routinely protects officials from equality before the law in cases involving abuses of power.

At the end of the 1970s, most Chinese were ignorant of laws and mistrustful of legal channels, a reasonable position when politics routinely superceded law. In the 1980s, the authorities launched a number of campaigns to educate ordinary citizens about the content of important laws and about certain ideas, such as equality before the law. Developing legal norms when legality has been actively denounced (not merely neglected) for decades has been difficult. Yet, ordinary Chinese do use law to pursue their interests. One indicator of the effect of the legal education effort is the growth in lawsuits against government agencies and officials under the administrative litigation law. The

Cyber cafés are popular with urban Chinese youth. Even with some 50,000 cyber-police, it is impossible to fully monitor Internet activity.

AP Images

number of such lawsuits processed in the legal system has increased steadily since passage of the law in 1989. Even in cases not won outright in court, out-of-court settlements that favor plaintiffs have become sufficiently common to make lawsuits worthwhile.[28]

Criticism of Legal Practices Legal reform has provoked criticism of Chinese law and legal practices outside China.[29] Three examples illustrate. First, Chinese criminal law stipulates the death penalty in "serious circumstances" of smuggling, rape, theft, bribery, trafficking in women and children, and corruption. In periodic intensive efforts to "strike hard" at crime, the authorities have resorted widely to capital punishment. Critics argue that capital punishment is excessively harsh for these crimes. Second, by design, criminal proceedings are inquisitorial (not adversarial), focused on determination of punishment (not guilt). As cases are prosecuted only after sufficient evidence has been collected to demonstrate guilt, most prosecutions result in guilty verdicts. The right to seek counsel at an early stage of proceedings is recognized in the law, but the requirement is only that a public defender be assigned no later than ten days before trial. By that time, the case has been prepared for prosecution and usually a confession (for which the law promises leniency) has already been obtained. This practice of "verdict first, trial second" has been questioned and debated inside China and criticized outside China. Finally, despite abolition of specifically political crimes of counter-revolution, the Chinese authorities acknowledge "several thousand" political prisoners. While human rights groups estimate the number to be much larger, all critics view the situation as essentially inconsistent with the new law.

Nonetheless, the new legality has produced significant change. Today more than ever before, the Chinese state is more constrained by laws, while Chinese citizens are freer from political arbitrariness because of laws. Abuse of authority is acted on differently from before. The law is a weapon, because the regime has invested heavily in it. To the extent that, in practice, a double standard for citizens and officials persists, the law is a political weapon, which ordinary citizens can take up against perceived injustice. The official effort to build rule by law, by making law salient, has produced a basis for "rightful resistance" to hold the regime accountable to its own proclaimed standards.

POLITICAL SOCIALIZATION

One result of the economic policy of opening up to the outside is that Chinese leaders today cannot control information as in the Maoist years.[30]

Mass Media Ordinary Chinese are now routinely exposed to news and opinions about public affairs in their country through access to Hong Kong (which maintains relatively free and critical mass media) and the outside world in newspapers, books, radio and television broadcasts, and the Internet. Moreover, Chinese connect with one another to transmit information as never before: in blogs, bulletin boards, e-mail, telephone, and text messages. China imported its first mobile phone facilities in 1987; by mid-2006, the country had more than 420 million mobile phone subscribers, the largest number in the world. One result of the telecommunications explosion and the opening to the outside world is the dilution in importance of the state-dominated mass media. In 1978, there were fewer than 900 periodicals and 200 newspapers with a provincial circulation in China; today, there are nearly 9,500 periodicals and nearly 2,000 newspapers.

To be sure, not all messages in the media are acceptable. Yet, most of the new media outlets do not touch on politics, offering instead the latest perspectives on sports, fashion, music, and movie stars. New academic journals carry lively scholarly discussions about the economy, law, and politics, however. Moreover, Chinese journalists expose government wrongdoings and thwart official efforts to suppress news of disasters.

At the same time, Chinese leaders reserve the right to shut down publications that in their view go too far. A government watchdog department monitors the media, focusing especially on coverage of Taiwan, party leaders, major political events, and the interpretation of party history—all explicitly defined in regulations as politically sensitive topics "of importance to state security and social stability." Media content has been scrutinized more carefully in recent years. At the same time, the most effective censorship the authorities can exercise in the new context is self-censorship—which generally operates fairly well. This is especially the case with Internet chat rooms and bulletin boards, which are otherwise nearly impossible to monitor, despite a force of some 50,000 cyber-police.

Education System The new content and style of political socialization are clearly evident in the education system. Mao's successors inherited an educational system designed to build communist values—and fundamentally at odds with the priority of economic growth. During the Cultural Revolution, high school graduates were sent to factories or farms to acquire work experience and learn from the masses. University entrance examinations were replaced with recommendations by grassroots leaders, focusing on revolutionary political credentials. With the persecution of scholars and denigration of expert knowledge in the

China is no longer a bicycle nation. Chinese-designed and manufactured automobiles emit ten to twenty times more pollution than American or Japanese models.

Justin Guariglia/The Image Works

universities, the content of university education was redesigned to include more politics in every specialization. Graduates were more "red" than expert. An entire decade was lost. The generation that missed out on an education during this decade is known today as the "lost generation."

Today, with the return of the university entrance examinations and huge numbers of Chinese studying in foreign universities, the respect for expertise is thoroughly restored. Indeed, in fall 2006, on instructions from top party and government departments, colleges across the country reduced the seven compulsory courses on political ideology and party history to four, in the first major curricular change in twenty-five years.

POLITICAL CULTURE

Older and middle-aged Chinese have experienced not only the radicalism of the Maoist years, but also more than two decades of "reform and opening" to the outside world. Young Chinese have only the personal experience of the relatively open post-Mao years, including the decade of the 1990s that saw the "third wave" of democratization, with the triumph of democracy in nearly every communist country. When asked about the most memorable event in their lifetime, Chinese of all ages talk mainly about recent events, such as the post-Mao reforms.[31] Surely recent changes, both inside and outside China, have left their imprint on the way Chinese view their government and their relationship to political authorities.

Because Maoist-era leaders regarded social science with great suspicion, we have no good baseline of public opinion data by which to assess change over time in the beliefs of ordinary Chinese. We can say something about the Chinese political culture today, however, based on survey research in China, including surveys organized and conducted by political scientists based in the United States. What is the orientation toward politics of ordinary Chinese? In particular, to what extent do the beliefs of Chinese seem conducive to political change in the direction of further democratization?

Political Knowledge An important building block for democracy is a citizenry knowledgeable about politics and interested in public affairs, so as to be able to monitor the performance of representatives and leaders. Most ordinary Chinese follow public affairs at least weekly, mainly through radio or television programs and somewhat less through newspapers, but politics is not something that is a regular topic of discussion in China. A majority say they *never* talk about politics with others, a stark reflection of lack of active interest.

Political knowledge and interest are not uniformly distributed in China, of course. A more active knowledge and interest are seen among men, the more highly educated, and Chinese with higher incomes, which is not so different from what we observe in other countries. Not surprisingly, Chinese in Beijing are much more interested in politics than Chinese overall; in fact, they discuss politics very frequently. Yet, even if we consider the situation of Chinese overall, which includes the relatively less knowledgeable and less interested rural population, political knowledge in China today is higher than in Italy in the early 1960s and political discourse higher than in Italy or Mexico in the early 1960s.[32]

Political Values How do the Chinese view their communist government? With the increased availability of information on other countries, including liberal democracies, do the Chinese see their relationship with political authorities differently? Moreover, does the Chinese political culture reflect traditional values—the influence of Confucianism, which conceived of legitimacy to rule in moral terms?

Perhaps the most interesting perspective on contemporary Chinese political culture is a comparative one that considers its fate across three different Chinese political systems. An extraordinary survey of a representative sample of Chinese in mainland China, Hong Kong, and Taiwan, conducted in 1993 and 1994, provides this perspective and helps to sort out different influences of traditional culture, political system, and socioeconomic development.[33] Figure 10.3 compares responses of ordinary Chinese in the PRC, Hong Kong, and Taiwan to questions about political relationships. Two questions tap orientations to popular accountability and political liberty. Another frames relationships in traditional Confucian terms of virtuous leadership. Altogether, these questions probe Chinese support for values commonly associated with liberal democracy. The responses reveal a fairly consistent, easily interpretable, and striking pattern.

First, there seems to be a strong impact of political system. A majority of Chinese in the PRC reject every democratic value, and support for democratic values is generally lowest in the PRC. This is not surprising. By the early 1990s, when this survey was conducted, Taiwan's process of democratization was well underway. Hong Kong, while still under British colonial rule, had enjoyed very significant civil liberties for decades and was taking initial steps to increase electoral competition.

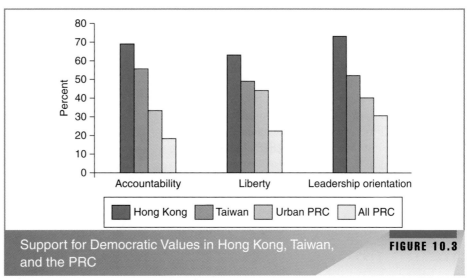

Support for Democratic Values in Hong Kong, Taiwan, and the PRC   **FIGURE 10.3**

Percent expressing *disagreement* with statements below.

Accountability: "Top government officials are like the heads of a big family. We should follow all their decisions on national issues."

Liberty: "The government should have the power to decide which opinions (perspectives) are to be circulated in a society and which are not."

Leadership orientation: "We can leave everything to morally upright leaders."

Source: Yun-han Chu and Yu-tzung Chang, "Culture Shift and Regime Legitimacy: Comparing Mainland China, Taiwan, and Hong Kong," in Shiping Hua, ed., *Chinese Political Culture, 1989–2000* (Armonk, NY: M. E. Sharpe, 2001), 332–33. Based on surveys conducted in 1993 and 1994.

Second, the influence of non-Chinese political socialization is evident. The traditional Confucian orientation to the moral state is least evident in Hong Kong: nearly three-fourths of Hong Kong Chinese reject the view that everything should be left up to virtuous leaders. By contrast, this view finds strong support in the PRC. Chinese in Taiwan are somewhere in the middle, perhaps reflecting rule by a Chinese government but a society long open to outside influences.

Third, and perhaps most interesting of all for speculation about support for democratization in the PRC, the responses show an impact of socioeconomic development. This is most evident in a comparison of responses in the PRC overall with those in urban China only. Urban Chinese are much more supportive of democratic values than are mainland Chinese generally.

In sum, traditional Chinese orientations to moral leadership appear to prevail in the PRC, and high proportions of the population have orientations unfavorable to democratization.[34] Barring the introduction of very major political change by the leaders themselves, popular disgruntlement about the performance of the government appears unlikely to transform itself into collective action for regime change. Overall, the responses suggest that mainland Chinese are "elitist

and authority-oriented," and this contributes to the stability of the communist regime.[35]

POLITICAL PARTICIPATION

In the communist party-state, political participation, interest articulation, and interest aggregation differ from the processes normally found in liberal democratic systems. The source of difference is, of course, different conceptions of the relationship between leaders and citizens: the notion of guardianship is fundamentally incompatible with liberal democratic notions of representation. The Communist Party organization claims to represent the interests of all society. It rejects, as unnecessary and unacceptable, political parties other than itself. While there has been change in political processes in recent decades, the "officially acceptable" forms of political participation, interest articulation, and interest aggregation in the Chinese political system continue to reflect the relationship of guardianship between party and society. This section discusses political participation; the next section explores interest articulation and aggregation.

Changes in the Rules An important aspect of political reform undertaken after Mao's death in 1976 has been the redefinition of what constitutes "officially acceptable" political participation in the Chinese system. Guidelines for the new political participation are evident in three categories of rule changes that have routinized participation and reduced its burden for ordinary Chinese. The changes reflect an official reaction against the disruption that characterized mass participation in the Maoist years (especially during the Cultural Revolution), an official assumption that economic growth is predicated on order and stability, and an official recognition that changes in economic relationships require adjustments in political relationships.

The first category of rule changes involves political participation, which has become essentially optional for ordinary Chinese since the early 1980s. In the first thirty years of communist rule, for a broad range of political activities, failure to participate was considered tantamount to opposition to the communist regime. Today, politics intrudes far less in the lives of ordinary Chinese. The scope and demands of politics have shrunk. The single most important measure signifying this change is the official removal, in 1979, of all class and political labels. After thirty years, the Chinese are no longer formally identified by class background or past "political mistakes." Not only does politics no longer dominate daily life, but in the diminished sphere of political activities, political apathy is no longer risky for ordinary Chinese.

The second category has been the assiduous avoidance by the regime to rouse the mass public to realize policy objectives. In the Maoist years, by contrast, the quintessential form of political participation was the **mass mobilization campaign**—intensive, large-scale, disruptive group action, implemented by grassroots leaders. The Great Leap Forward launched in 1958 and the Cultural Revolution launched in 1966 were essentially mass campaigns, on a gargantuan scale. Typically in mass campaigns, grassroots party leaders, responding to signals from the political center, roused ordinary Chinese to achieve regime goals of various sorts, often aimed at identified categories of enemies—such as "counterrevolutionaries" in 1950–1951; the "landlord class" in 1950–1952; the "rightists" in 1957; and the "unclean cadres" in 1962–1963. Mass-campaign

methods were adopted for nonpolitical objectives too, such as the ill-conceived and ecologically harmful effort to eradicate "four pests" (sparrows, rats, flies, and mosquitoes) in 1956. Participation in campaigns was virtually compulsory. Only three years after Mao's death, Chinese leaders issued an official rejection of mass campaigns as a mode of political participation. Many leaders who emerged at the top echelons of power in the late 1970s had themselves been victims of persecution in the Cultural Revolution. The social disorder of campaigns was rejected as antithetical to the new priority of economic growth.

The third category is the rejection of mass mobilization as the dominant mode of political participation. Chinese leaders have instead encouraged ordinary citizens to express their opinions and participate in politics through a variety of regular official channels, some new, others newly revived: offices to receive complaints, centers and telephone hotlines to report abuses of power, and letters to newspaper editors, for example.[36] Not least of all, the authorities have introduced important reforms in elections. As a consequence, political participation in China is varied and extensive in scope. Table 10.2 shows findings from a survey conducted in Beijing in the 1980s and 1990s. The extent of citizen participation in a wide range of activities is quite remarkable, not at all the picture of Maoist mobilization.

Elections and an electoral connection between citizens and leaders are integral to liberal democratic conceptions of representation. For this reason, governments and nongovernmental organizations in liberal democracies have paid close attention to electoral reforms in China.

Local Congress Elections Elections to local people's congresses in the Maoist years were political rituals, featuring no candidate choice and no secret ballot. Voters directly elected deputies to township-level congresses only; at higher levels, deputies were elected by congresses at the level immediately below. Such elections served as vehicles of regime legitimation, popular education, and political socialization, but they did not really allow ordinary citizens to choose representatives.

In 1979, a new election law introduced direct election of deputies to county-level congresses, mandated secret ballots rather than public displays of support,

Political Participation in Beijing (percent reporting having participated in political act)		TABLE 10.2
Political Act	**1988**	**1996**
Voting for deputies in 1988 local congress elections	71.5	81.0
Contacting leaders of workplace	51.2	54.2
Complaining through bureaucratic hierarchy	43.0	47.5
Voting for leaders in workplace	34.8	16.1
Complaining through trade unions	18.9	24.4
Using connections (*guanxi*)	15.5	16.6
Complaining through political organizations	15.0	17.7
Slowing down on the job	12.6	9.3
Writing letters to government officials	12.5	15.3
Persuading others to attend campaign meetings for congress deputies	8.9	13.0
Complaining through congress deputies	8.6	14.1
Persuading others to attend campaign or briefing meetings at workplace	7.7	5.4
Organizing others to fight against leaders	7.6	3.0
Writing letters to newspaper editors	6.8	8.3
Persuading others to vote for certain leaders in workplace elections	5.7	3.5
Whipping up public opinion against workplace leaders	5.1	1.7
Persuading others to vote for certain deputies in congress elections	4.7	8.0
Giving gifts in exchange for help	4.6	8.0
Persuading others to boycott unfair workplace elections	4.6	2.9
Reporting to complaint bureaus	4.0	8.1
Persuading others to boycott unfair congress elections	3.7	6.8
Bringing cases to court	1.2	4.5
Participating in strikes	0.9	2.6
Participating in demonstrations	0.4	1.4

Source: Tianjian Shi, "Mass Political Behavior in Beijing," in Merle Goldman and Roderick MacFarquhar, eds., *The Paradox of China's Post-Mao Reforms* (Cambridge: Harvard University Press, 1999), 155.

and required the number of candidates to be one and a half times the number of deputies to be elected.

Although local Communist Party organizations continue to play a key leadership role in election committees, essentially vetting candidates, not all candidates can win under current rules. Some officially nominated candidates lose elections. Indeed, some candidates officially designated for government office lose elections. A growing number of candidates who are not Communist Party members have competed and won in elections. A smaller number of government executives nominated by deputies are not official candidates and win without official endorsement.[37] An electoral victory signifies some degree of popular support, while losing signifies a problematic relationship with the mass public. At a minimum, the new rules are a means for the Communist Party organization to gauge popular views about local officials, diversify the pool from which leaders are recruited, and monitor local leaders. To be sure, the new rules have not produced radical change. Nor can such an outcome be expected without further change in rules: no platform of opposition to the Communist Party is permissible.

Village Committees China also now has nearly two decades of experience with rural grassroots democratization, formally approved in November 1987 when the NPC, after over a year of debate, passed a provisional version of the Organic Law on Village Committees. A final revised version was passed in November 1998.

The law defines **village committees** as "autonomous mass organizations of self-government," popularly elected in elections featuring choice among candidates for three-year terms and accountable to a village council comprised of all adult villagers.

The introduction of popularly elected village committees in 1987 was designed to strengthen state capacity to govern in the aftermath of agricultural decollectivization. In the early 1980s, the people's communes had been dismantled and replaced with township governments. Land and other production inputs were divided among peasant households to manage on their own, free markets were opened, most obligatory sales to the state were abolished, and private entrepreneurship was promoted.[38] The results of these reforms were successful by most economic standards, but disastrous in their consequences for rural leadership. As villagers gained greater economic initiative and autonomy, the power of the Chinese party-state to exact compliance was enormously weakened. By the mid-1980s, village leadership had seriously atrophied. Leaders were enriching themselves at the expense of the community, and villagers were resisting their efforts to implement unpopular policies. Violent conflicts between villagers and village leaders had become common. The revitalization of village committees in 1987 was designed to make the countryside more governable by increasing accountability. Presumably, villagers would be more responsive to leaders elected from below rather than those imposed from above as before.

In 1998, when the NPC affirmed the experience of village elections, most villages had undergone at least three rounds of elections, with enormous local variation in implementation. In many villages, the village Communist Party branch controlled candidate nomination, there was no candidate choice for the key position of village committee director, and voting irregularities were common. Even in villages that made serious progress—with genuinely competitive elections, widespread popular participation in candidate nomination, and scrupulous attention to voting procedure—real managerial authority often resided not with the popularly elected village committee but with the village Communist Party branch. Even today, too little is known to generalize about overall progress in village elections, its determinants, or its consequences.[39] Certainly, to the degree that the practices of grassroots democracy acquire the force of routine and expectations accumulate, however slowly, among nearly 750 million Chinese in more than 600,000 villages, political participation in the countryside will change profoundly.

"Unacceptable" Political Participation More dramatic than the reforms that have redefined officially acceptable political participation has been the political action of ordinary Chinese in city streets and squares beginning in the late 1970s. With strikes, marches, posters, petitions, and occupation of public spaces, ordinary citizens have acted as if political reform comprehended or condoned mass political action and public disorder. The official record suggests the contrary, however.

In 1980, the right to post "big-character posters" (usually criticisms of leaders, written by individuals or groups and posted on walls), introduced during the Cultural Revolution, was removed from the Chinese constitution. In 1982, the constitutional right to strike was rescinded. As for mass protests, the official view was made clear in 1979 with the introduction of the "four fundamental principles" that political participation must uphold: (1) the socialist road, (2) Marxism-Leninism-Mao Zedong Thought, (3) the people's democratic dictatorship, and (4) the leadership of the Communist Party. Of these principles, only the last is necessary to restrict political participation effectively, as the content of the first three has become what party leaders make of it. Participants (especially organizers) face real risks of physical harm and criminal punishment. Why then did ordinary citizens engage in mass protests with increasing frequency in the 1970s and 1980s? Why did urban worker and peasant unrest increase in the 1980s and 1990s?

Different sorts of "officially unacceptable" political participation have different explanations, but none can be explained without reference to the post-Mao reforms. On the one hand, economic reforms have produced some socially unacceptable outcomes: more (and more visible) inflation, unemployment, crime, and corruption, for example. Rural unrest has typically been triggered by local corruption and exaction of excessive (often illegal) taxes and fees. Urban unrest—strikes, slowdowns, and demonstrations—has increased too, as state enterprises struggle to survive in the socialist market economy. A number of enterprises have been closed down; many have engaged in massive layoffs; others have been unable to pay bonuses and pensions. For the first time since

1949, many urban Chinese have been living on fixed incomes, no incomes, or unpredictable incomes as the cost of living increases.

Protesters and Reformers In 1989, a different sort of urban unrest captured the attention of the world news media and, consequently, of the world. The demonstration that brought a million people to Tiananmen Square was the third major political protest movement since Mao's death. The first was in 1978–1979, and the second in 1986–1987. All three were officially unacceptable, all were linked in some important way to official reforms and reformers, and all ended in failure for mass protesters (and resulted in setbacks to official reforms too).[40]

Despite links between protesters and official reformers, the post-Mao movements were not mass mobilization campaigns. As they were not explicitly initiated by the regime, once underway they could not be easily stopped with an official pronouncement from the political center. Instead, the authorities turned to coercive force wielded by the police, the armed police, and ultimately the army to terminate the protests with violence.

Protests are officially unacceptable mainly because of their form of expression. The official consensus since December 1978 has been that the most important priority for China is economic growth, with social order and stability are prerequisites for growth. Mass protests are distinctly disorderly. Further, as a form of political participation, mass protests are a symptom of regime failure in two senses. By turning to the streets to articulate their demands, protesters demonstrate that official channels for expressing critical views are not working and that they do not believe the Communist Party's claim that it can correct its own mistakes. Further, protesters are clearly not alienated from politics: while they reject official channels of participation, they are not politically apathetic; indeed, they articulate explicitly political demands despite serious risks and the difficulty associated with organizing outside the system. In short, political protests signify that mass political participation can neither be contained within official channels nor deterred with a better material life.

For the most part, despite some radical elements, the protests have not been blatantly antisystem in their demands. This does not appear to be merely strategic. Rather, the protests are something of a rowdy mass counterpart to the official socialist reform movement, exerting more pressure for more reform, and (while officially unacceptable) often linked with elite reformers.

In the **Democracy Movement** of 1978–1979, Deng Xiaoping publicly approved many of the demands posted on Democracy Wall and published in unofficial journals, which called for a "reversal of verdicts" on individuals and political events. The demands were an integral part of the pressure for reform that surrounded the meetings of top leaders in

In 1989, ordinary Chinese participated in the largest spontaneous protest movement the communists had ever faced. A lone protester shows defiance of regime violence in his intransigent confrontation with a Chinese tank.

AP Images

BOX 10.3

Wei Jingsheng and the "Fifth Modernization"

In late 1978, in an atmosphere of great change that included official "reversals of verdicts" of the Cultural Revolution, many Chinese began to gather regularly at a large wall close to Beijing's Tiananmen Square to post, read, and discuss political posters. One of the boldest posters to appear on Democracy Wall was an essay by Wei Jingsheng. It argued that the ambitious new program to modernize agriculture, industry, national defense, and science and technology could not succeed without a "fifth modernization"—democracy. Wei wrote: "The hated old political system has not changed. Are not the people justified in seizing power from the overlords?" Wei published even more critical essays in his unofficial journal *Explorations,* one of more than fifty such journals circulating at the time. In March 1979, he posted an attack on Deng Xiaoping, asking: "Do we want democracy or new dictatorship?" Wei was tried and convicted of "counterrevolutionary crimes" and "leaking state secrets" to foreigners. Some fifteen years later, Wei was released from prison, only to be rearrested for dissident activities. In 1997, after years of pressure from human rights groups and governments outside China, China's most famous political dissident was released and exiled to the United States, where he continues to criticize the Chinese authorities.

late 1978, allowing elite reformers to argue for major changes in policy and political orientation. The poster campaign and unofficial journals were tolerated. To be sure, when a bold dissidenter named Wei Jingsheng demanded a "fifth modernization," by which he meant democracy of a sort never envisaged by the communists, the Chinese authorities promptly sentenced him to a fifteen-year prison term (ostensibly for revealing state secrets) and introduced the "four fundamental principles" to establish the parameters of acceptable debate[41] (see Box 10.3).

When the Communist Party congress convened in late 1987, party leader Zhao Ziyang acknowledged conflicts of interest in society at the current time. The years 1988 and 1989 were high points for political liberalization. The political criticism expressed in Tiananmen Square in 1989 largely echoed public views of elite reformers in the party and government. From the perspective of communist authorities, the real danger in 1989 was not the content of mass demands but the organizational challenge: students and workers organized their own unions, independent of the party, to represent their interests.

The challenge was exacerbated by an open break in elite ranks when Zhao Ziyang voiced his support for the protesters and declared his opposition to martial law. Other party and government leaders and retired elders, including Deng Xiaoping—many of whom had been victims of power seizures by youths in the Cultural Revolution—viewed the problem as a basic struggle for the survival of the system and their own positions. The movement was violently and decisively crushed with tanks and machine guns in the **Tiananmen massacre** of June 4, 1989.[42]

All three protests ended in defeat for the participants: prison for the main protest organizers in 1979, expulsion from the Communist Party for intellectual leaders in 1987, and prison or violent death for hundreds in 1989. The defeats extended beyond the mass protest movement to encompass setbacks to the official reform movement too. When demands for reform moved to the city streets, more conservative leaders attributed the social disorder to an excessively rapid pace of reform. The result was a slower pace or postponement of reforms. Twice, the highest party leader was dismissed from office as a result of the mass protests (Hu Yaobang in 1987 and Zhao Ziyang in 1989), and the official reform movement lost its strongest proponent.

INTEREST ARTICULATION AND AGGREGATION

Most ordinary citizens engage in interest articulation without interest aggregation. This takes the form of personal contacts to articulate individual concerns about the effects of policies on their lives. Much of this interest articulation takes place at the workplace. As shown earlier in Table 10.2, more than 50 percent of those surveyed in Beijing in the 1980s and 1990s had engaged in precisely this sort of low-level politics. And more than 15 percent of those surveyed had made use of personal connections. For the most part, the function of interest aggregation is monopolized by the Communist Party, although the party's role in interest aggregation is being diluted and the methods it employs have also evolved.

Organizations under Party Leadership   Under the formal leadership of the Communist Party are eight "satellite parties," a legacy of the communist pre-1949 strategy of provisional cooperation with noncommunist democratic parties.[43] These parties have no real role in policymaking, but they are represented (with prominent nonparty individuals) in the Chinese People's Political Consultative Conference. In 1989 the Central Committee proposed greater cooperation with the noncommunist parties by regular consultation with their leaders on major policies—or at least a stronger effort to inform the parties of Communist Party policies. Of course, this proposal referred only to the eight officially tolerated parties. In 1998, the authorities arrested, tried, and imprisoned a veteran of the 1978–1979 Democracy Movement who attempted to register a fledgling China Democracy Party.

The other older formal organizations that aggregate like interests in the Chinese political system are the "mass organizations," extensions of the Communist Party into society, nationwide in scope and organized hierarchically. The All-China Federation of Trade Unions and the Women's Federation remain active and important mass organizations today. Mass organizations are led by Communist Party officials, who are specially assigned to these positions and who take direction from party committees. The main function of these organizations is not to aggregate and represent group interests for consideration in the policymaking process, but to facilitate propagation of party policy to the relevant groups. Essentially, mass organizations represent the interests of the Communist Party to the organized "interest groups" it dominates, not vice versa. The classic description of this relationship refers to mass organizations as "transmission belts" for the Communist Party.

NGOs and GONGOs   A very different set of associations emerged in the late 1980s with official encouragement. These "social organizations," over 170,000 in number, range widely in form and focus. In form, they include genuine nongovernmental organizations (NGOs) and government-organized nongovernmental organizations (**GONGO**s). Some GONGOs are essentially front organizations for government agencies, set up to take advantage of the interest of foreign governments and international NGOs to support the emergence of Chinese civil society. Other GONGOs have strong and mutually beneficial relationships with NGOs, acting as a bridge to government agencies. In focus, GONGOs and especially NGOs cover a wide range of interests and activities.

Among the most interesting GONGOs are the business associations set up to organize firms: the Self-Employed Laborers Association, the Private Enterprises Association, and the Federation of Industry and Commerce. The Federation of Industry and Commerce, which organizes the largest Chinese firms, has independent resources that have permitted it to create a separate organizational network (chambers of commerce), a national newspaper, and a financial institution to provide credit to members.

Among NGOs, the 250 organizations that focus on environmental issues are at the vanguard of NGO activity.[44] The largest, best funded, and best organized environmental NGOs focus primarily on species and nature conservation and environmental education. With strong support from the media, these NGOs often work with central authorities to expose and counter local government failure to implement environmental laws and policies. One environmental NGO trains lawyers to engage in enforcement of laws, educates judges about the issues, and litigates environmental cases.

Individual environmental activists have also organized to influence political decisions. A good example is the independent publication of *Yangtze! Yangtze!*, a collection of papers by scientists and environmentalists critical of the world's biggest and most controversial hydroelectric project, the Three Gorges Dam. The study was released in early 1989 with the aim of influencing the widely publicized NPC vote to approve dam construction. Although it failed to halt approval, nearly a third of NPC delegates voted against the project or abstained—prompting the government to postpone dam construction until the mid-1990s (see Box 10.4).

Considering the "Leninist organizational predisposition" to thwart organizational plurality, the

BOX 10.4

The Three Gorges Dam

The Three Gorges Dam, essentially completed in May 2006, is the biggest, most costly, and most controversial hydropower station ever built. It was conceived to regulate the flow of the Yangtze, the third most powerful river in the world. Three times in the past century, the river has flooded, killing hundreds of thousands of people. The new dam will supply an estimated 10 percent of China's electric power, for industrial production and "basic electrification" of the countryside. Building it displaced more than a million people. Environmentalist opponents of the dam are concerned about damage to the ecosystem and endangerment of some species of fish and birds. Other critics are concerned about flooding more than 100 significant archeological sites. Opposition to the dam also focuses on safety issues: problems of sedimentation may cause floods upstream and weaken foundations of cities built on silt downstream. Most opponents suggested building several smaller dams, rather than one mega-dam. Central to these concerns are doubts that the government sufficiently considered expert advice in designing the project—which was a dream of Chinese leaders since 1919 and took on meaning as a political accomplishment.

encouragement of NGO emergence and activity in the Chinese context seems puzzling.[45] It is explained by the closure of many state enterprises and the downsizing of government at all levels, in the 1980s and 1990s, creating a need for the growth of social organizations to take on some former government functions, especially social welfare functions. Essentially, this change shifts the burden from government to society. The 1998 plan to downsize the central government bureaucracy explicitly noted that many functions "appropriated by government" must be "given back" to society and managed by new social associations. This plan opened the political space for the emergence of NGOs. The authorities also recognize that NGOs can help the center monitor local government policy implementation; this is the role that environmental NGOs have played most prominently, for example.

For the most part, NGO activity is in fact well within the parameters of officially acceptable political participation. Most groups do not seek autonomy from the state, but rather seek "embeddedness" within the state. To be autonomous is to be outside the system and relatively powerless, unable to exercise influence. In sum, for the most part, the emerging Chinese civil society aggregates and articulates its interests without challenging the state.

To be sure, the authorities have taken measures to guarantee that NGOs work with (not against) them. An elaborate set of regulations requires social organizations to affiliate with a sponsor that is responsible for their activity, to register with the government, and to have sufficient funding and membership. The regulations also prohibit the coexistence of more than one organization with the same substantive focus at the national level or in any particular locality. This preserves the monopoly of the official mass organizations to represent the interests of women and workers, for example.

In practice, however, it is simply impossible really to control NGO activity: some NGOs register as businesses, others thrive as Internet-based virtual organizations, and government sponsors cannot monitor the organizations registered as their affiliates. For example, the All-China Women's Federation is responsible for more than 3,000 social organizations dealing with women's issues. In this context, Chinese NGOs can be expected to continue to grow.

It is important to note that one significant social group lacks a legitimate organizational channel (even a mass organization) that aggregates its interests: farmers. To the extent that Chinese farmers engage in collective action to articulate their interests, it is largely through petitions and protests.

POLICYMAKING AND IMPLEMENTATION

Today, it is inconceivable that a scheme such as the Great Leap Forward could be launched and implemented as it was in the 1950s. Controversial policies are no longer adopted at the whim of a single leader;

experts play a significant role in policy formulation; experimentation in selected localities precedes widespread implementation; and local authorities no longer slavishly sacrifice local development goals to meet unrealistic campaign targets dictated by the center.

The single most important difference distinguishing policy processes of the 1950s from those of the 1990s and after, however, is the recent greater reliance on consultation and consensus building among a wider range of bureaucratic, local, and economic players. This change is partly due to economic reforms that provide increased opportunities and incentives for players to devote resources to projects outside the state plan rather than to state-mandated projects. In discussing policy processes, the Chinese often refer to the following expression: "The top has its policy measures; the bottom has its countermeasures." Having renounced campaigns and purges, policymakers at the top have instead worked to forge agreements with a variety of players at the political center and in the localities so that policies adopted are implemented, not ignored or radically reshaped in the course of implementation. At the apex of the system, consultation has become even more important, because no leader possesses either the experience or the personal prestige of a Mao Zedong or a Deng Xiaoping.

The political structures described at the beginning of this chapter are essential points of reference for the description of policymaking and policy implementation here. However, key features of policy processes are not well illustrated by consideration of these formal structures alone. As elaborated below, the formal distinction between party and government structures is less relevant than it appears; at least one key structure does not appear on formal organizational charts; and authority is more fragmented and less well bounded than formal structure suggests.

Policymaking

Policymaking in China today is less concentrated and more institutionalized than ever before. It involves three sets of institutional players: the party, the government, and the legislature, as shown in Figure 10.4. It is also useful to distinguish three tiers in the policymaking process. Different party, government, and legislative structures at different tiers interact at different stages of the process. Moreover, a number of

individual players overlap, appearing in more than one set of institutions. This section traces the process by which major policies emerge and are eventually formalized as laws. It is worth noting, however, that many important policy decisions do not go through the legislature at all. For example, the State Council has the power to issue administrative regulations, decisions, instructions, orders, and measures to local governments; central government ministries issue their own departmental regulations, clarifications, and responses to respective local government departments; the Communist Party Politburo and individual party departments have their own separate systems of regulations, decisions, instructions, orders, and measures issued to counterparts in the localities and lower levels of the party bureaucracy.

Three Tiers in Policymaking At the very top tier are the leaders at the apex of the party: in the Politburo and its Standing Committee. The party generalists at this tier are each typically responsible for at least one broad policy area. As a group, they make all major policy decisions. Formally, the Politburo has the ultimate authority to determine major policies, but it probably meets in plenary session only about once monthly for a morning to ratify policies already approved by the Politburo Standing Committee. It is useful to recall here that the leaders at the top of the party hierarchy include not only party leaders but also the prime minister and the NPC chairman. Overlapping directorships help coordinate major decision making across the three sets of institutions.

The most thorough consideration of policy options and shaping of policy decisions occur at the second tier—within **leading small groups (LSGs),** which are defined by broad policy areas.[46] LSGs are headed by leaders at the top tier of the party, although deputy heads are likely to be outside the top tier. LSGs have sweeping mandates to preside over policy research, formulation of policy proposals, sponsorship of policy experiments in the localities, and drafting of policy documents. LSGs bring together all the senior officials with responsibility for different aspects of a policy area.[47] They exercise leadership as policies emerge onto an initial agenda, and they make specific recommendations to the Politburo Standing Committee once policies are ready to move onto the legislative agenda. They are a crucial coordinating mechanism in the policymaking process, linking top

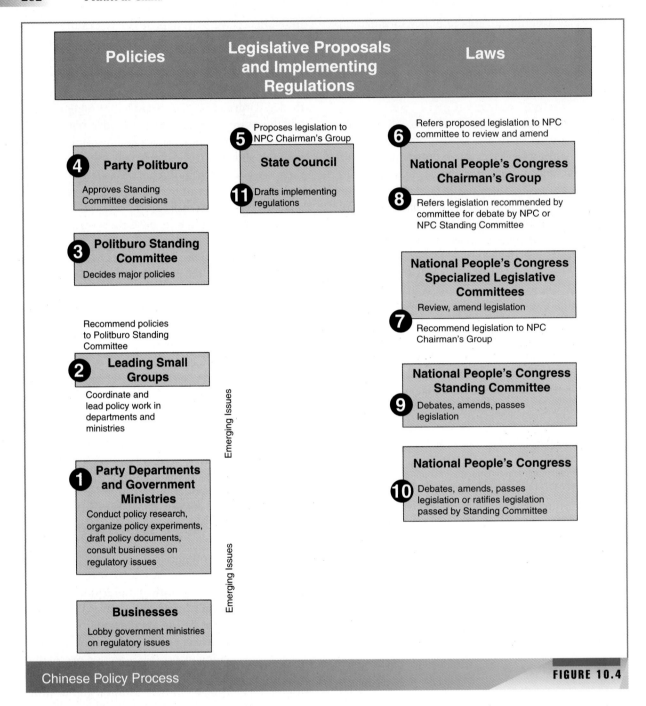

FIGURE 10.4

Chinese Policy Process

decision makers to bureaucracies and bridging institutional systems.

Coordinating mechanisms are particularly important to policymaking in the Chinese system because authority is formally structured so as to require the cooperation of many bureaucratic units,

nested in separate chains of authority. The fragmentation of formal authority and its resolution by formal and informal coordinating mechanisms at the top of the system have led some scholars to characterize the Chinese system as one of **fragmented authoritarianism**.[48]

In what ways is formal authority fragmented? The best example is the system of dual subordination. On the one hand, authority is organized in systems of vertical bureaucracies in hierarchies that extend from ministries at the center to lower-level departments in the localities. Each ministry under the State Council is at the top of a hierarchy of subordinate departments that exist at the provincial, county, and township levels of government. On the other hand, the central ministry and subordinate departments are all government departments and, as such, are subordinate to their respective governments too. The Chinese refer to the two structural arrangements as "lines" and "pieces." Authoritative communications are channeled from top to bottom (vertically, in lines) and also from governments to their departments (horizontally, in pieces). The two sorts of authority come together only at the center, at the level of the State Council. Simply put, then, all local government departments have two bosses in their formal authority relationships—not to mention their relationships with party departments in the same issue area and party committees with *nomenklatura* authority over them. In Chinese terminology, there are "too many mothers-in-law." This structure of formal authority routinely creates blockages in policy processes. Many policy issues cannot be resolved at lower levels but must be pushed up to a sufficiently high level, such as an LSG, that spans many authority structures and can overcome bureaucratic impasses below.

Below leading small groups, at the third tier, are the relevant party departments and government ministries. As LSGs have little staff of their own, the research centers and staff in departments and ministries at the third tier do the actual work of gathering information and drafting policy documents. Increasingly, with a high proportion of policy related to economic matters, government ministries play a key role—but at this tier it is the specific policy area that determines which bureaucratic players are most involved.

From Agenda Setting to Implementing Regulations There are five main stages in policymaking and lawmaking: agenda setting; interagency review; Politburo approval; NPC review, debate, and passage; and the drafting of implementing regulations.[49] The two stages that have the most impact on substance are interagency review and drafting of implementing regulations. The State Council dominates both these stages.

LSGs provide leadership and coordination among party departments and government ministries, from which draft proposals emerge. Leaders of departments and ministries are continuously considering relevant policy issues and waiting for (or creating) opportunities to push proposals onto the agenda. A draft proposal is on the agenda when it is assigned to interagency review.

Interagency review is usually a very prolonged process, still at the third tier, initially involving only the most relevant ministries but gradually incorporating a wider group of departments, localities, and other players. At some point, either the State Council Legislation Bureau or the Legislative Affairs Work Committee approves a drafting group for the law. The last phase of interagency review is opinion solicitation. By then, most of the law's content has already been decided. This does not imply that relevant nonbureaucratic players are shut out of the policy process, however—at least in economic policymaking.

New case studies of the government–business relationship in China show that marketization has prompted Chinese firms to take an active interest in the many industrial policies and regulations that impact their competitiveness.[50] Businesses interact regularly with government departments on midrange policies, such as industry standards, tax rates, prices, and international competition—mostly regulatory issues that do not go through the legislative process. Interacting takes two forms: consultation and lobbying. On the one hand, government departments now routinely take the initiative to consult with relevant businesses before drafting industrial policies and regulations, calling meetings of key players or inviting them to formal hearings, for example. Similarly, business executives, including foreign business executives, now routinely lobby government officials to influence policy in favor of the firm or industry. Larger firms have the most direct and regular access to government officials, although large state-owned enterprises (SOEs) appear to have more access than large foreign firms, perhaps a legacy of interaction under central planning or the enormous importance of these players to social stability. Businesses lobby all departments relevant to policies that impact them, with one unsurprising exception: despite the influence of environmental regulations on industry competitiveness, businesses typically ignore the State Environment Protection Agency (SEPA)—reflecting an assumption that environmental protection is at odds with economic profits.

For policies that will involve passage of legislation, after interagency review, a draft proposal is included on the Legislation Bureau's or Legislative Affairs Work Committee's annual legislative plan. Politburo approval precedes NPC passage of any major piece of political, economic, or administrative legislation, although this practice is not formally required in any legal document.

Officially, legislation may be proposed by the State Council, its ministries, or groups of NPC delegates. Not surprisingly in this quasi-parliamentary system, the overwhelming majority of legislation is proposed by the State Council and its ministries at the third tier. Although it is unusual for laws to pass through NPC review without amendment, a bill approved in principle by the Politburo is not normally opposed in the NPC.

The NPC review stage begins with referral (by the NPC Chairmen's Group) of the draft legislation to a specialized legislative NPC standing committee for review and amendment. The structure that links party and legislative institutions at this stage is the NPC Standing Committee party group. After draft legislation is recommended by an NPC legislative committee, the party group (acting officially through the NPC Chairmen's Group) decides whether the draft will be debated in the NPC Standing Committee or the full NPC. It is common for the NPC Standing Committee to debate and revise draft legislation many times before voting on passage. When draft legislation encounters significant opposition in the NPC, a vote is usually postponed to avoid a public show of opposition.

After a law is passed, implementing regulations are drawn up, usually by the State Council Legislation Bureau. Implementing regulations transform laws into language that can be applied by local governments and subordinate departments throughout the country. Through implementing regulations, the State Council regains design control over policy before releasing it for implementation.

Policy Implementation

Although the state has partially retreated from direct control over many aspects of the economy, politics, and society in recent decades, the proportion of decisions affecting all three spheres that is made at the political center in China remains higher than that in liberal democracies. Considering this scope, the fragmented structure of authority, and the size and regional diversity of the country, policymakers are seriously constrained in their efforts to elicit effective policy implementation, despite the recent trend toward greater consultation and consensus building to bring relevant departments and localities into the policy process at an earlier stage.

This section discusses problems of policy implementation in China. It is worth pointing out here, however, that despite problems and their consequences for unsuccessful policy implementation, the Chinese authorities have achieved impressive policy success in two areas designated as vitally important for the country's development: promoting economic growth and controlling population growth. They have been less successful in another policy area: environmental protection. These examples of policy performance are discussed at length later in this chapter. Here, the focus is on general issues in policy implementation.

Monitoring The major issue of policy implementation is the monitoring problem, especially serious in China because of the constraints noted earlier.[51] How do China's policymakers ensure that central-level decisions are translated into actions at lower levels? Central authorities have a very limited capacity to monitor the many aspects of the economy, politics, and society affected by their policies. To cope, they adopt fairly simplistic performance indicators. Not only are these problematic as accurate measures of compliance, but also they can produce unanticipated results. Additionally, policymakers rely mainly on departments and localities, which have their own particular interests to pursue, for much of the information on which to base evaluations of performance. Leaders at the political center have attempted in recent years to develop channels of information independent of ministries and local governments. The National Bureau of Statistics has been given more resources and responsibilities to gather and compile information relevant to policymaking and assessment of policy performance. Research institutes and public opinion polls have also played a greater role in channeling different sorts of information to leaders at the political center. The State Auditing Administration and the Ministry of Supervision, both newly established in recent years, are designed to improve central capacity to measure and monitor implementation. Nonetheless, central authorities are unable to verify most reports independently. As a result, information is routinely distorted to make policy implementers appear compliant. Policymakers appear to take this bias into consideration when assessing implementation.

Policy Priorities As policymakers routinely communicate multiple (and conflicting) policy objectives downward through several channels, local authorities must arrive at a reasonable ordering of policy priorities. In deciding priorities, local objectives as well as the apparent priorities of the political center are considered. Local governments and parallel party committees are multitask agencies. Policy priorities communicated in documents channeled down from Beijing in the functionally specialized line hierarchies of government may not be treated as policy priorities by local governments. Policies appear more likely to be implemented in conformity with central directives when signals from the center indicate that top leaders have reached a consensus among themselves and are paying attention. This sort of signal is generally communicated through documents issued by executive organizations (not simply central ministries) of the Communist Party (not simply the government). Party executives may also signal their attention to the implementation of policy issues by speaking at work conferences convened to assess progress in particular areas or establishing an ad hoc leading small group to manage a particular policy problem.

Adapting Policy to Local Conditions Chinese politics presents no electoral incentives for top leaders to line up public policy with the expressed preferences of special interest groups or ordinary voters. To be sure, policymakers consult the players they view as relevant to policy outcomes. Yet, with restrictions on investigation or criticism by the mass media and the prohibition on organized opposition groups, policymakers face relatively little routine outside pressure in formulating policies. Despite increased consultation of players below the top tiers, the policymaking process is relatively closed compared with liberal democracies. In a structural context that limits widespread input and provides no electoral connection to policymakers at the top, reshaping policy in the course of policy implementation is often the most effective way for officials

to influence policy outcomes. Leaders at the political center accept a certain amount of "adaptation of central policy to local conditions"—indeed, this is a stock phrase of Chinese politics.

Corruption

Economic reform has produced unprecedented growth and prosperity, but also the conditions for new forms of **corruption.** Since the early 1980s, the economy, no longer centrally planned but not fully marketized, has provided opportunities for officials to gain privately from abuse of their control over resources, contracts, and permissions. On the one hand, the new opportunities for corruption may have eased resistance by officials with the most to lose from economic reform. On the other, abuse of public office to pursue private gain has grown in scope, scale, volume, and severity to become one of the gravest challenges facing the regime, even threatening the Chinese armed forces.[52] In public opinion polls conducted over the years, Chinese citizens consistently view corruption as a serious social problem, often the most serious problem. The huge 1989 mass protests, as much about corruption as about democracy, reflected and aired this view.

Chinese leaders are alarmed about corruption, recognizing the threat to regime legitimacy and political stability. Since 1982, they have waged a nearly continuous corruption control effort. While corrupt officials have been prosecuted and punished, the battle against corruption suffers from a basic contradiction between Communist Party leadership and rule by law in China. In principle, as described earlier, equality before the law is a core component of the new legality. In practice, the Chinese legal system has not been used to full effect to control corruption. An important obstacle is a structural one, reflecting a more basic political obstacle. In 1978, party leaders reinstated discipline inspection committees, specialized departments subordinate to party committees at each level of the party hierarchy. Discipline inspection committees investigate misconduct and enforce ethical and political standards for party members. As the preponderance of officials are party members, discipline inspection committees investigate corruption. Regulations require the transfer of criminal cases to procuratorates, but party investigations and party punishments generally precede criminal investigations. Procuratorates routinely encounter obstacles in their efforts to prosecute such cases, not only because officials call up networks of cronies for support but also because successful prosecution is botched when officials have sufficient time to destroy evidence. In principle, the system holds Communist Party members to a higher standard of conduct than ordinary citizens. In practice, exemption from prosecution and substitution of disciplinary action for criminal punishment are very common for officials (but not for ordinary citizens). Public cynicism about corruption control is understandable. In the instances that high-ranking officials are removed from office and sentenced through the legal system, many interpret it as the outcome of a political power struggle.

The problem of corruption and corruption control reflects a basic contradiction between the principles of Communist Party leadership and rule by law. If law is supreme, then the party is subordinate to law and under supervision by procuratorates and courts, not vice versa. So long as party leaders cannot commit to supervision by an impartial legal system, the building of a legal infrastructure will not amount to rule by law. Yet, to commit to such supervision calls into question party leadership and the foundations of the communist party-state.

POLICY PERFORMANCE

In late 1978, China's leaders defined economic growth as the most important policy priority for decades to come. Despite disagreement about the appropriate pace and scope of economic reform, there has been consensus on a broad strategy of retreat from direct state intervention. The Chinese state has been achieving more by directly controlling less. This strategy has applied not only to economic goals but also to most other policy goals in the reform era. This includes environmental protection, which is less well suited to such a strategy. The important exception has been population control, which Chinese leaders identified as a major policy priority in the late 1970s. The one-child family policy introduced in 1978 features the Chinese state in a more directly interventionist role in population control than ever before.

This section examines the performance of policies of economic reform, environmental protection, and compulsory family planning, focusing on the role of the state in achieving policy goals.

Economic Growth

Although the Chinese have moved only slowly on political reforms, they have been bold in economic reforms. Since 1978, Chinese leaders have staked their political legitimacy on economic growth, more than anything else. For the most part, the gamble has succeeded. Chinese economic growth, illustrated in Table 10.3, has averaged just under 10 percent per year since 1980.[53] Real per capita income has grown rapidly, to more than $1,700 in 2005 or nearly $6,000 in purchasing power parity (PPP). Although China is still very much a developing country, it is the world's second largest economy in PPP terms. Economic reform has been a remarkable success story. It has been achieved through three major strategies: opening up the economy to the world outside; marketizing the economy; and devolving authority downward to create incentives for local governments, enterprises, households, and individuals to pursue their own economic advancement.

In the late 1970s, Chinese leaders rejected the economic autarky of Maoist "self-reliance," instead opening up the country to foreign trade and investment. As shown in Table 10.4, China had become a major trading economy, moving toward a trade surplus in 1990. The favorable trade balance has allowed China to amass one of the world's largest foreign exchange reserves. It has also created frictions with the United States and some other trading partners. Foreign-invested firms are responsible for much of China's

TABLE 10.3

Economic Performance, 1980–2005 (in constant yuan)

	GDP (billion yuan)	GDP per Capita (yuan)
1980	452	460
1985	898.9	853
1990	1,859.8	1,634
1995	5,749.5	4,854
2000	8,825.4	7,086
2005	18,232.1	14,025
	U.S. $2,279 billion	U.S. $1,753 ($6,800 PPP)

Sources: State Council Information Office, China Internet Information Center at http://www.china.org.cn; National Bureau of Statistics of China, Statistical Communique, 28 February 2006 at http://www.stats.gov.cn; 2005 PPP figure is from Central Intelligence Agency, *World Factbook* at http://www.cia.gov/cia/publications/factbook/.

	TABLE 10.4

Foreign Trade, 1978–2005 (in U.S. billion constant dollars)

Year	Trade Volume	Imports	Exports
1978	20.64	10.89	9.75
1979	29.33	15.67	13.66
1980	38.14	20.02	18.12
1981	44.03	22.02	22.01
1982	41.61	19.29	22.32
1983	43.62	21.39	22.23
1984	53.55	27.41	26.14
1985	69.60	42.25	27.35
1986	73.85	42.91	30.94
1987	82.65	43.21	39.44
1988	102.79	55.27	47.52
1989	111.68	59.14	52.54
1990	115.44	53.35	62.09
1991	135.70	63.79	71.91
1992	165.53	80.59	84.94
1993	195.70	103.96	91.74
1994	236.62	115.61	121.01
1995	280.86	132.08	148.78
1996	289.88	138.83	151.05
1997	325.16	142.37	182.79
1998	323.95	140.24	183.71
1999	360.63	165.70	194.93
2000	474.29	225.09	249.20
2001	509.65	243.55	266.10
2002	620.77	295.17	325.60
2003	850.99	412.76	438.23
2004	1,154.55	561.23	593.32
2005	1,421.90	659.95	761.95

Source: National Bureau of Statistics of China, *2006 China Statistical Abstract* (Beijing: China Statistics Press, 2006), 169.

did not initially set out with a stated goal or program to create a socialist market economy. Indeed, the goal to create a market system was not officially affirmed until 1993. Rather, economic reform proceeded incrementally, in a process often described as "crossing the river by groping for stones." Initially, some top party leaders envisaged only a small secondary role for the market economy, as a "bird in a cage" of the planned economy. By the mid-1990s, however, the Chinese economy had basically "grown out" of the plan.[54] In 1998, the Chinese approved a "shareholding system" that is essentially privatization, thinly disguised to maintain ideological orthodoxy.

The emergence of scarcity prices, reflecting market supply and demand, to replace prices determined bureaucratically by central authorities is a good example of this incrementalism. Initially, the government pursued a "two-track" pricing system: it maintained bureaucratic prices for some key industrial inputs, but allowed scarcity to determine prices of other commodities. Some scarcity prices were determined fully by market forces; others were allowed to rise and fall within a range. Over time, the number of commodities with bureaucratic prices was steadily decreased. By the mid-1990s, two-track prices were a thing of the past.

Finally, a key economic reform strategy has been decentralization. Leaders in Beijing have devolved authority to empower local governments, enterprises, households, and individuals. Agricultural decollectivization in the early 1980s was the first such reform, replacing collective farming with household farming. Individual entrepreneurs emerged at about the same time, engaging in small-scale production or providing services (such as transportation of commodities to markets) long ignored under central planning. Existing rural enterprises were allowed to expand into practically any product line, rather than being restricted to "serving agriculture," as before. Most of these industries were organized as "collective enterprises," with formal ownership by the township or village community and with strong direct involvement of local government in management. These small-scale township and village enterprises (TVEs) proved themselves adaptable to the demands of the new market environment. They drove much of China's rapid growth in the 1980s and into the 1990s. Fiscal arrangements negotiated in the mid-1980s also favored local governments, at the expense of the center; in a renegotiation in the mid-1990s, the central government

exports, reflecting the country's appeal—through preferential policies, cheap labor, and a potentially huge market—as a destination for foreign direct investment (FDI). China attracts more FDI than any other developing nation; overall, it is the world's third largest recipient of FDI. The role of FDI in promoting economic growth through exports has compensated for the weakness of Chinese private capital as the country emerged from its socialist economic past.

Post-Mao leaders inherited a centrally planned economy, organized according to a Stalinist model borrowed from the Soviet Union in the 1950s. They gained back some revenues, but without removing incentives for local economic initiative.

The reform of the state-owned enterprise (SOE) system began in the mid-1980s. Initial reforms created incentives to boost production by replacing government appropriation of all SOE profits with a system of taxing profits—allowing SOEs to retain a portion of profits. Of course, until prices reflected scarcity, the incentives remained weak. More important, SOEs employed (and employ) a very high proportion of urban workers. This effectively put SOEs on a "soft budget constraint": as local governments feared worker unrest, unprofitable SOEs did not fear bankruptcy; they could count on state banks to bail them out. In 1993, the Chinese authorities announced that one-third of SOEs were loss-making and one-third barely breaking even. In 1994, the Company Law was passed to provide a legal framework for corporatization. A strategy of "targeting the large, releasing the small" emerged: Beijing continued to nurture about 1,000 large SOEs, encouraging them to form giant conglomerates, assisting them with loans but imposing greater financial discipline; the smaller SOEs were left to confront market forces and reorganize themselves through mergers, takeovers, conversion into shareholding companies, or outright closure. This dual process of corporatization and reorganization continues today, with increasing privatization through conversion to shareholding and greater political toleration of SOE closures and sales, including sales to foreign partners.

Environmental Degradation

China's rapid economic growth has resulted in serious environmental damage. Environmental pollution and degradation have increased at a rate that outpaces the capacity of the Chinese state to protect the environment.[55] Township and village enterprises contribute more than half of pollutants of all kinds, dumping their untreated waste directly into rivers and streams and relying heavily on coal for energy. Use of coal, a major source of air pollution but a vital contributor to energy supply (see Box 10.5), has doubled since the economic reforms. Water scarcity poses a major challenge: prices do not reflect scarcity because most water is directed toward agriculture for irrigation, and local governments fear rural unrest will erupt with meaningful water price increases. Integration into the global economy

has made China a global market for resource-intensive goods, such as paper and furniture—producing a massive drop in forest coverage with increases in logging by Chinese and multinational businesses. China has also become a destination of choice for some of the world's most environmentally damaging industries.

Environmental economists at the World Bank and other organizations estimate the cost to the Chinese economy of environmental degradation and resource scarcity at 8 to 12 percent of GDP annually. This includes health and productivity losses associated with air pollution and water scarcity costs in lost industrial output. Even so, through the mid-1990s, leaders and the Chinese media continued to articulate the principle of "first development, then environment." The ideal of sustainable development, prominent in official

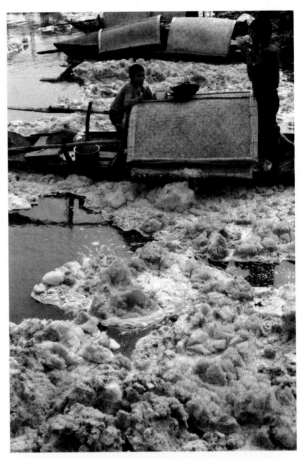

The policy of "first development, then environment" has taken a heavy toll. Pollution far outpaces the government's capacity for environmental protection.

Topham/The Image Works

Shutting Down 5,000 Coal Mines

BOX 10.5

China depends on coal for more than 65 percent of its growing energy needs, but in 2005 the central government ordered more than 5,000 coal mines shut down. China's mines are the most dangerous in the world: in that year alone, nearly 6,000 Chinese coal miners died in mining accidents, almost 80 percent of the world's total mining fatalities. The mines ordered closed were both unsafe and illegal. Many were lucrative small-scale mines, managed as township or village enterprises. Others were privately owned, often with local officials holding private (strictly illegal) shares. Mine managers routinely flout safety standards, taking local government acquiescence for granted. The miners generally resign themselves to the high risks, because mining pays better than alternative employment in agriculture. In such conditions, despite laws, orders, and rhetoric on industrial safety, dangerous mines will continue to operate. Undoubtedly, they include many mines shut down in 2005.

---

rhetoric today, was incorporated into the economic planning process only in 1992.

Over the past decade, China has erected a legal and bureaucratic infrastructure of environmental protection. In 1984, the State Council established a central government department responsible for environmental matters; in 1989, the NPC adopted an environmental protection law; and in 1993, a specialized legislative environmental protection and natural resources committee was established in the NPC.

Nonetheless, in the policymaking process, the environmental bureaucracy is weak in negotiations with the many ministries with developmental priorities. The problem is even more serious at the local level. The laws that emerge tend to be too diluted and general to provide useful guidelines for enforcement.

The Chinese tally a great number of enforcement successes over the past decade: the resolution of more than 75,000 environmental law violation cases, the closure of more than 16,000 enterprises for illegal discharge of pollutants, and the issuance of more than 10,000 warnings to environment polluters.[56] Yet, the devolution of authority to local governments, a strategy that unlocked economic growth, constitutes a fundamental obstacle to enforcement.

Although local environmental protection bureaus (EPBs) are nominally accountable to both the State Environmental Protection Agency (SEPA) in Beijing and their local governments, they depend on local governments for their growth and survival—budgets, career advancement, staff size, and allocation of resources, such as vehicles and office buildings. Local government developmental priorities practically always dominate efforts to enforce environmental standards, especially when enterprises are collective enterprises or firms with a large number of workers. Pollution discharge fees are routinely not collected (or not fully collected), and legal requirements to improve pollution control capacity are routinely waived. The 2006 policy decision to consider environmental protection performance, including energy use, in evaluating local governments may have some impact, but its importance is unlikely to trump economic growth in the near future.

Environmental protection is also underfunded. The five-year plan adopted in March 2006 budgeted 1.6 percent of GDP for environmental protection—an increase over past years but nonetheless an amount that Chinese scientists believe is well below what is needed to produce notable improvements. At the same time, the Chinese set an ambitious policy goal: 10 percent of its energy needs to be supplied by environmentally friendly renewable sources by 2010.

Population Control

While reducing state intervention to promote economic growth, policymakers have increased their intervention involving a new policy priority: population control. For most of the Maoist years, population planning was not actively promoted. In 1978, with the population close to a billion and amid rising concern about meeting economic goals and ensuring basic livelihood, employment opportunities, and social security support at the current rate of population growth, China's leaders declared population control a major policy priority. State-sponsored family planning was added to the constitution, and an ideal family size of one child was endorsed as national policy. According to this policy, most couples are required to stop childbearing after one or two births. Married couples in urban areas, with few exceptions, are restricted to one child. In rural areas, married couples are subject to rules that differ across provinces. In some provinces, two children are normally permitted; in others, only one child is permitted; in most provinces, a second child is permitted only if the first is a girl.

One-Child Family Policy   The **one-child family policy** is inherently difficult to implement in China, particularly in the countryside, where nearly 60 percent of Chinese live.[57] There, the population is relatively poorly educated and has poor access to public health facilities—circumstances that do not facilitate an effective family planning program. Traditional views about the family prevail: as in most agrarian societies, big families and many sons are viewed as ideal. Moreover, in China, a married daughter joins the household of her husband, while a married son

remains in the household to support aging parents. Decollectivization and the return to household farming in the early 1980s enhanced the value of sons compared to daughters, for their labor power. The dismantling of the commune system has also left the state less able to monitor compliance, just as the new economic independence of peasants has left the state less able to enforce compliance. Finally, population control involves the state as the dominant decision maker in choices that are traditionally viewed, in China as elsewhere, as private family matters.

Despite the inherent difficulties, the Chinese have succeeded in curbing population growth dramatically, as is illustrated in Figure 10.5. A population structure normally resembles a pyramid: with relatively unchanged rates of births and deaths, the proportion of population from top to bottom is progressively bigger. The population pyramid in Figure 10.5 deviates from this form in a few places. The first, located at about the middle of the pyramid, reflects fewer births as well as differentially more deaths among the young in the disaster following the Great Leap Forward, in the cohort aged 45–49 in 2005. The second, evident beginning with the cohort aged 25–29 in 2005, reflects the impact of

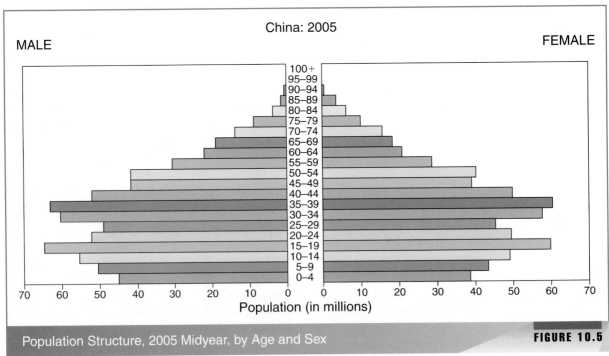

Population Structure, 2005 Midyear, by Age and Sex

FIGURE 10.5

family planning policies introduced in the 1970s. Variation in policy emphasis by leaders at the political center is reflected in variation in number of births, beginning in the mid-1970s. Implementation of the one-child family policy began in 1979. In 1983, responding to concerns at the political center, implementation became more coercive. From 1984 through the late 1980s, the policy was relaxed and implementation in the countryside faltered due to difficulties associated with decollectivization. Births rose immediately. From 1989 to the present, policy implementation has been stringent. Urban-rural outcomes differ significantly, however. In the cities, the one-child family appears to be the accepted norm. In the countryside, however, any relaxation of policy has been reflected in immediate big increases in births.[58]

Policy Implementation Policy implementation has taken a number of forms: a legal requirement of late marriage, a requirement of insertion of an intrauterine device after a first birth, and a requirement of sterilization of one partner after a second birth. There are incentives to sign a one-child family certificate after the first birth, including priority in entrance to schools and funding for health fees for the child. Fines are imposed on the family for policy violations. Birth planning workers at the grassroots are given birth quotas from higher levels, which they allocate on the basis of family circumstances. From the perspective of leaders at the political center, abortion is a sign of failure, not success, in policy implementation. At the grassroots, from the perspective of birth planning workers, however, the obvious fact is that abortions do not add above-plan births. Undeniably, birth planning workers have incentives to encourage abortions and face few disincentives for doing so.

Perverse Outcomes In recent years, policymakers have expressed concern about a perverse result of compulsory family planning: the shortage of young girls, compared with boys. Recent figures show atypical birth disparities: a national average of 118 newborn boys to 100 newborn girls in 2005. These figures compare with an international average of about 106 boys to 100 girls.

The shortage of girls reflects the traditional Chinese preference for male children in the context of compulsory family planning. Traditional practices of female infanticide as well as abandonment and severe neglect of girls beyond infancy have led to excess female infant mortality. Not least of all, missing girls are increasingly the result of sex-selective abortion, made possible with the widespread use of ultrasound technology in the early 1980s. These practices prompted top legislators to consider criminalizing such abortions, although ultimately they decided against it.

China's success in reducing population growth has strong supporters and detractors outside the country. The official Chinese response to criticism from human rights advocates has focused on "economic rights" that the government argues would be denied to all Chinese in the decades to come if population growth is not brought under control.

HONG KONG

In 1842 and 1860, the island of **Hong Kong** and adjacent territory on the Chinese mainland were ceded by treaty to Britain in perpetuity. In 1898, more adjacent territory was ceded in a ninety-nine-year lease. These cessions were largely the outcome of British victory in wars fought to impose trade on China. For nearly a century, Hong Kong (including the adjacent territories) was a British colony, ruled by a governor appointed in London. Hong Kong flourished economically, with a disciplined labor force of Chinese immigrants, a free-market economy, and a government commitment to rule of law and civil liberties but not elected government.

In 1984, the Chinese communist authorities elaborated the principle of **"one country, two systems,"** applicable to Hong Kong after 1997. China and Britain signed a joint declaration: Hong Kong would revert to Chinese sovereignty in 1997, but would continue to enjoy "a high degree of autonomy." The Chinese agreed that Hong Kong would enjoy economic, financial, and monetary autonomy, maintaining its capitalist system, legal system, and way of life for fifty years. At midnight on June 30, 1997, Hong Kong became a special administrative region of communist-ruled China.

The British had made little effort to democratize politics in Hong Kong through the 1980s. The governor had consulted business elites and other key constituencies on policy affairs, but there had been no elected legislature or government. Nor had political parties really developed in such an environment. All this changed in 1989.

The Tiananmen massacre galvanized Hong Kong Chinese and British expatriates into efforts to accelerate the pace of political democratization before 1997. In 1991, in the first direct elections to the Legislative Council, only a third of the legislative deputies were directly elected. In 1995, a controversial electoral reform bill introduced by Governor Christopher Patten guided elections: for the first time, ordinary Hong Kong citizens elected all deputies in the Legislative Council. Hong Kong's most liberal democratic parties won overwhelmingly in geographic voting districts. Openly pro-Beijing forces did poorly.

Communist authorities rejected the elections and the legislature as violations of the Basic Law, Hong Kong's miniconstitution passed in China's National People's Congress in 1990. They supervised selection of a chief executive and provisional legislature in 1996. At the moment of the historic handover, this chief executive and provisional legislature officially replaced the governor and the legislature elected in 1995.

Since the handover, Beijing authorities have been less heavy-handed than feared. Hong Kong today enjoys most of the same civil liberties as under British rule. Human rights organizations and pro-democracy organizations that monitor and support progress in the PRC have bases in Hong Kong. Hong Kong newspapers provide information about politics in the PRC and are critical in ways not permitted on the mainland. Chinese communist authorities hope that success in implementing "one country, two systems" in Hong Kong will woo Taiwan back to the PRC too.

TAIWAN

Taiwan, governed by the Nationalists as the **Republic of China** since 1945, lies a mere 100 miles off the east coast of the Chinese mainland. Communist "liberation" of Taiwan became moot when the United States sent its Seventh Fleet to the Taiwan Strait, declaring an American interest in the security of Taiwan after the outbreak of the Korean War in the 1950s. For the next three decades, the Chinese routinely bombarded

offshore islands of Taiwan and continued to threaten liberation by military force. For the most part, however, it was a cold war—and until the 1970s, Taiwan was the clear winner, enjoying international recognition as the sole legitimate representative of China.

In the 1970s, two major events affected Taiwan's status. In 1971, Taiwan lost its membership in the United Nations and its seat on the Security Council to China. In 1979, the United States recognized China diplomatically, downgrading the relationship with Taiwan to one of unofficial liaison. Today, fewer than thirty countries recognize Taiwan. These events have put China in a position of relative strength.

The two sides have engaged in negotiations on and off over the years. Since democratization in the late 1980s, Taiwan's leaders are more constrained than ever to represent majority public opinion, which does not support unification with the mainland. The election of a pro-independence party candidate to the presidency in 2000 exacerbated friction across the Taiwan Strait.

CHINA'S POLITICAL FUTURE

Two main themes have run through this study of Chinese politics today. First, despite very significant economic liberalization and a nascent political institutionalization, Chinese politics takes place within the boundaries of what is still essentially a communist party-state. Second, the dramatic changes sweeping the Chinese economy, polity, and society, many of which now seem beyond the control of political leaders, are as much a by-product of reform as a direct product of reform policies. The first theme cautions against liberal democratic optimism when considering China's political future. The second reminds us that the script of the political future will not be written by Chinese communist leaders alone.

In this new century, China must confront a number of key issues that will significantly determine its development. Can structures and processes that bolster and foster economic growth safeguard against the threat of more significant political liberalization and eventual democratization—which remain unacceptable to the Chinese authorities?

Around the world, political change in recent decades has created an age of democratization—the result, in many countries, of revolutions that toppled communist regimes older than the Chinese regime. Will the "third wave" of world democratization reach China early in the twenty-first century?

Certainly, liberal democratic ideals and practices are quite alien to Chinese culture. Chinese history provides no examples of democratic rule, and the Chinese cultural tradition expresses no concerns to protect individuals by checking state power. Past experience and cultural tradition, then, offer little encouragement to those looking for the seeds of democratization in China.

Yet, authoritarianism has not survived intact with economic modernization in many East Asian countries that have a similar lack of historical and cultural foundations for democracy. To be sure, even with continued economic growth, China will differ

from these countries for many years to come. It will be bifurcated in its development: middle-class prosperity is emerging in the big cities and coastal regions, but Chinese in the countryside will remain relatively poor for some time.

With reform, for most ordinary Chinese, the party has demanded less and delivered more in recent decades. Unlike communist parties that gained (and held) power with the aid of Soviet troops and tanks, the Chinese Communist Party has indigenous and nationalist roots. Barring a major economic crisis, it is less likely to collapse in the face of the sort of mass discontent that toppled communist regimes in Eastern Europe. More likely, in the medium term at least, the party will continue to transform China in the years to come and to transform itself in order to continue to rule.

KEY TERMS

Central Committee
Chinese Communist Party
Confucianism
corruption
Cultural Revolution
Democracy Movement
democratic centralism
Deng Xiaoping
ethnic minorities
fragmented authoritarianism

GONGOs
Great Leap Forward
guardianship
Hong Kong
Hu Jintao
leading small groups (LSGs)
Mao Zedong
mass line
mass mobilization campaign

Nationalist Party
National Party Congress
National People's Congress (NPC)
nomenklatura system
one-child family policy
one country, two systems
party-state
People's Liberation Army (PLA)
Politburo

Republic of China
rule by law
socialist market economy
State Council
Taiwan (Republic of China)
Tiananmen massacre
village committees

SUGGESTED READINGS

Bianco, Lucien. *Origins of the Chinese Revolution, 1915–1949.* Stanford, CA: Stanford University Press, 1971.

Chang, Jung. *Wild Swans: Three Daughters of China.* New York: Anchor, 1991.

Economy, Elizabeth C. *The River Runs Black: The Environmental Challenge to China's Future.* Ithaca, NY: Cornell University Press, 2004.

Goldman, Merle, and Roderick MacFarquhar, eds. *The Paradox of China's Post-Mao Reforms.* Cambridge: Harvard University Press, 1999.

Gries, Peter Hays, and Stanley Rosen, eds. *State and Society in 21st-century China: Crisis, Contention, and Legitimacy.* New York: RoutledgeCurzon, 2004.

Lieberthal, Kenneth. *Governing China: From Revolution Through Reform.* 2nd ed. New York: Norton, 2004.

Nathan, Andrew J. *Chinese Democracy.* Berkeley: University of California Press, 1986.

Spence, Jonathan D. *The Search for Modern China.* New York: Norton, 1990.

Weston, Timothy B., and Lionel Jensen, eds. *China Beyond the Headlines.* Lanham, MD: Rowman & Littlefield, 2000.

Wong, Jan. *Red China Blues.* Sydney, Australia: Doubleday, 1996.

INTERNET RESOURCES

www.china.org.cn/english. China Internet Information Center, State Council Information Office. Authorized website of Chinese government, link to National People's Congress. Access to government White Papers, news, statistical data.

www.stats.gov.cn/english/. National Bureau of Statistics. Official monthly and yearly statistics, including downloadable Excel files.

www.chinadaily.com.cn. *China Daily.* News from China directed toward external readership.

http://english.peopledaily.com.cn/. *People's Daily.* Official newspaper of Communist Party of China.

www.scmp.com. *South China Morning Post.* News about Hong Kong and mainland China, from Hong Kong.

www.wws.princeton.edu/~lynn/chinabib.pdf. Contemporary China bibliography, Professor Lynn White, Princeton University.

www.uschina.org/. United States–China Business Council. Analysis and advocacy of policy issues of interest to U.S. corporations engaged in business relations with China.

ENDNOTES

1. *New York Times*, 17 April 2006.

2. Lou Jiwei, Deputy Minister of Finance, *People's Daily* online, 22 June 2006. Bai Jinfu, a former deputy director of a research center under the State Council, estimates the Gini coefficient to be 0.50. See *South China Morning Post* online, 11 July 2006.

3. For a good, very readable discussion of Chinese history beginning with the late Ming (seventeenth century) and extending into the 1980s, see Jonathan D. Spence, *The Search for Modern China* (New York: Norton, 1990). Other good historical overviews include Charles O. Hucker, *China's Imperial Past: An Introduction to Chinese History Culture* (Stanford, CA: Stanford University Press, 1975); Immanuel C. Y. Hsu, *The Rise of Modern China*, 5th ed. (New York: Oxford University Press, 1995).

4. See Hsi-sheng Chi, *Warlord Politics in China, 1916–1928* (Stanford, CA: Stanford University Press, 1976); Edward A. McCord, *The Power of the Gun: The Emergence of Modern Chinese Warlordism* (Berkeley: University of California Press, 1993).

5. R. H. Tawney, *Land and Labour in China* (London: Allen & Unwin, 1932).

6. See especially Lucien Bianco, *Origins of the Chinese Revolution, 1915–1949* (Stanford, CA: Stanford University Press, 1971). See also Benjamin Schwartz, *Chinese Communism and the Rise of Mao* (Cambridge: Harvard University Press, 1951).

7. The classic political biography of Mao is Edgar Snow, *Red Star Over China* (New York: Grove Press, 1968). Of the many excellent studies by Stuart R. Schram, see especially *The Political Thought of Mao Tse-tung*, rev. ed. (New York: Praeger, 1969); *The Thought of Mao Tse-tung* (Cambridge: Cambridge University Press, 1989), and his biography of Mao, *Mao Tse-tung*, rev. ed. (Harmondsworth: Penguin, 1967). After Mao's death, scholars appraised Mao and his legacy from a variety of perspectives in Dick Wilson, ed., *Mao Tse-tung in the Scales of History: A Preliminary Assessment* (Cambridge: Cambridge University Press, 1977).

8. See Chalmers A. Johnson, *Peasant Nationalism and Communist Power: The Emergence of Revolutionary China* (Stanford, CA: Stanford University Press, 1962).

9. See Suzanne Pepper, *Civil War in China: The Political Struggle, 1945–1949* (Berkeley: University of California Press, 1978).

10. For a good selection of essays offering a comprehensive overview of PRC history, see Roderick MacFarquhar, ed., *The Politics of China: The Eras of Mao and Deng*, 2nd ed. (Cambridge: Cambridge University Press, 1997). Other good discussions of post-Mao history are found in Richard Baum, *Burying Mao: Chinese Politics in the Age of Deng Xiaoping* (Princeton, NJ: Princeton University Press, 1994); Harry Harding, *China's Second Revolution: Reform After Mao* (Washington, DC: Brookings Institution, 1987). Good discussions of particular topics of reform are found in Merle Goldman and Roderick MacFarquhar, eds., *The Paradox of China's Post-Mao Reforms* (Cambridge: Harvard University Press, 1999).

11. The classic account is by William Hinton, who observed land reform before 1949 in *Fanshen: A Documentary of Revolution in a Chinese Village* (New York: Viking, 1966).

12. Roderick MacFarquhar, ed., *The Hundred Flowers Campaign and the Chinese Intellectuals* (New York: Praeger, 1960); Fu-sheng Mu, *The Wilting of the Hundred Flowers Movement: Free Thought in China Today* (London: Heinemann, 1962).

13. See Dali L. Yang, *Calamity and Reform in China: State, Rural Society, and Institutional Change Since the Great Leap Famine* (Stanford, CA: Stanford University Press, 1996).

14. See Frederick C. Teiwes, *Politics and Purges in China: Rectification and the Decline of Party Norms, 1950–1965* (Armonk, NY: M. E. Sharpe, 1979); Frederick C. Teiwes, *Leadership, Legitimacy, and Conflict in China: From a Charismatic Mao to the Politics of Succession* (Armonk, NY: M. E. Sharpe, 1984).

15. See Jasper Becker, *Hungry Ghosts: Mao's Secret Famine* (New York: Free Press, 1996).

16. Some of the best accounts of the Cultural Revolution are biographical or autobiographical. See, for example, Gordon A. Bennett and Ronald N. Montaperto, *Red Guard: The Political Biography of Dai Hsiao-ai* (Garden City, NY: Doubleday, 1971); Jung Chang, *Wild Swans: Three Daughters of China* (New York: Anchor, 1991); Yuan Gao, *Born Red: Chronicle of the Cultural Revolution* (Stanford, CA: Stanford University Press, 1987); Liang Heng and Judith Shapiro, *Son of the Revolution* (New York: Knopf, 1983); Anne F. Thurston, *Enemies of the People: The Ordeal of the Intellectuals in China's Great Cultural Revolution* (Cambridge: Harvard University

Press, 1988); Daiyun Yue and Carolyn Wakeman, *To the Storm: The Odyssey of a Revolutionary Chinese Woman* (Berkeley: University of California Press, 1985); Nien Cheng, *Life and Death in Shanghai* (New York: Grove Press, 1986).

17. See Dru C. Gladney, *Muslim Chinese: Ethnic Nationalism in the People's Republic* (Cambridge: Council on East Asian Studies, Harvard University, 1991); Stevan Harrell, ed., *Cultural Encounters on China's Ethnic Frontiers* (Seattle: University of Washington Press, 1995).

18. An excellent discussion of guardianship is found in Robert A. Dahl, *Democracy and Its Critics* (New Haven, CT: Yale University Press, 1989), ch. 4. On Leninism in general, see especially Alfred G. Meyer, *Leninism* (Cambridge: Harvard University Press, 1957).

19. Mao Zedong, "Some Questions Concerning Methods of Leadership," in *Selected Works of Mao Tse-tung,* vol. 3 (Peking: Foreign Languages Press, 1965), 117–22.

20. On the changing role of the NPC, see Murray Scot Tanner, *The Politics of Lawmaking in Post-Mao China: Institutions, Processes, and Democratic Prospects* (New York: Oxford University Press, 1999); "Breaking the Vicious Cycles: The Emergence of China's National People's Congress," *Problems of Post-Communism* 45, no. 3 (1998): 29–47. For an historical perspective, see Kevin J. O'Brien, *Reform Without Liberalization: China's National People's Congress and the Politics of Institutional Change* (Cambridge: Cambridge University Press, 1990).

21. See Murray Scot Tanner, "How a Bill Becomes a Law in China: Stages and Processes of Lawmaking," *China Quarterly*, no. 141 (1995): 39–64.

22. See the selection of essays in David Shambaugh, ed., *Deng Xiaoping: Portrait of a Chinese Statesman* (New York: Oxford University Press, 1995).

23. Tai Ming Cheung, "The Influence of the Gun: China's Central Military Commission and Its Relationship With the Military, Party, and State Decision-Making Systems," in David M. Lampton, ed., *The Making of Chinese Foreign and Security Policy in the Era of Reform* (Stanford, CA: Stanford University Press, 2001), 61–90; Michael D. Swaine, "Chinese Decision-Making Regarding Taiwan, 1979–2000," in *The Making of Chinese Foreign and Security Policy in the Era of Reform*, 289–336. On military modernization, see David Shambaugh and Richard H. Yang, eds., *China's Military in Transition* (Oxford: Clarendon Press, 1997); David Shambaugh, "The People's Liberation Army and the People's Republic at 50: Reform at Last," *China Quarterly*, 159 (1999): 660–72.

24. See Melanie Manion, "The Cadre Management System, Post-Mao: The Appointment, Promotion, Transfer, and Removal of Party and State Leaders," *China Quarterly*, 102 (1985): 203–33; John P. Burns, *The Chinese Communist Party's Nomenklatura System* (Armonk, NY: M. E. Sharpe, 1989); "Strengthening Central CCP Control of Leadership Selection: The 1990 *Nomenklatura,*" *China Quarterly*, 138 (1994): 458–91.

25. See Hsiao Pen, "Separating the Party From the Government," in Carol Lee Hamrin and Suisheng Zhao, eds., *Decision-Making in Deng's China: Perspectives From Insiders* (Armonk, NY: M. E. Sharpe, 1995), 153–68.

26. See Zhiyue Bo, *Chinese Provincial Leaders: Economic Performance and Political Mobility Since 1949* (Armonk, NY: M. E. Sharpe,

2002). For an earlier discussion of elite recruitment and mobility, based on case studies, see David M. Lampton, *Paths to Power: Elite Mobility in Contemporary China* (Ann Arbor: Center for Chinese Studies, University of Michigan, 1986).

27. For an overview of the change, see Richard Baum, "Modernization and Legal Reform in Post-Mao China: The Rebirth of Socialist Legality," *Studies in Comparative Communism* 19, no. 2 (1986): 69–103. For notions underlying the change, see Carlos W. H. Lo, "Deng Xiaoping's Ideas on Law: China on the Threshold of a Legal Order," *Asian Survey* 32, no. 7 (1992): 649–65. For a description of the law in practice in post-Mao China, see James V. Feinerman, "Economic and Legal Reform in China, 1978–91," *Problems of Communism* 40, no. 5 (1991): 62–75; Pitman B. Potter, ed., *Domestic Law Reforms in Post-Mao China* (Armonk, NY: M. E. Sharpe, 1994); "The Chinese Legal System: Continuing Commitment to the Primacy of State Power," *China Quarterly*, no. 159 (1999): 673–83; Stanley B. Lubman, *Bird in a Cage: Legal Reform in China After Mao* (Stanford, CA: Stanford University Press, 1999).

28. See Minxin Pei, "Citizens v. Mandarins: Administrative Litigation in China," *China Quarterly,* 152 (December 1997): 832–62.

29. See, for example, Donald C. Clarke and James V. Feinerman, "Antagonistic Contradictions: Criminal Law and Human Rights in China," *China Quarterly*, 141 (1995): 135–54.

30. See the account of "thought work" in Daniel Lynch, *After the Propaganda State: Media, Politics, and "Thought Work" in Reformed China* (Stanford, CA: Stanford University Press, 1999).

31. M. Kent Jennings and Ning Zhang, "Collective Memories in the Chinese Countryside" (paper presented at the Annual Meeting of the International Society of Political Psychology, July 2002, Berlin). Chinese who were adolescents during the Cultural Revolution also recall that event as memorable, more so than do Chinese in other age groups.

32. See Tianjian Shi, "Cultural Values and Democracy in the People's Republic of China," *China Quarterly*, 162 (2000): 540–59; Yang Zhong, Jie Chen, and John Scheb, "Mass Political Culture in Beijing: Findings From Two Public Opinion Surveys," *Asian Survey* 38, no. 8 (1998): 763–83. For a comparative perspective, see Gabriel A. Almond and Sidney Verba, *Civic Culture: Political Attitudes and Democracy in Five Nations* (Princeton, NJ: Princeton University Press, 1963).

33. Yun-han Chu and Yu-tzung Chang, "Culture Shift and Regime Legitimacy: Comparing Mainland China, Taiwan, and Hong Kong," in Shiping Hua, ed., *Chinese Political Culture, 1989–2000* (Armonk, NY: M. E. Sharpe, 2001), 320–47. See also Tianjian Shi, "Cultural Values and Political Trust: A Comparison of the People's Republic of China and Taiwan," *Comparative Politics* 33, no. 4 (2001): 401–19.

34. This is the conclusion of Tianjian Shi, based on analysis of the same survey data. See "Cultural Values and Democracy in the People's Republic of China." See also Andrew J. Nathan and Tianjian Shi, "Cultural Requisites for Democracy in China: Findings From a Survey," *Daedalus* 122, no. 2 (1993): 95–123.

35. Two independent sets of surveys, including surveys of the more politically knowledgeable and interested Beijing population, conclude this in almost exactly the same words. See Shi, "Cultural Values and Democracy in the People's Republic of China"; Zhong, Chen, and Scheb, "Mass Political Culture in Beijing."

36. See the excellent discussion of forms of political participation in Tianjian Shi, *Political Participation in Beijing* (Cambridge: Harvard University Press, 1997), ch. 2.

37. On the Maoist period, see James R. Townsend, *Political Participation in Communist China* (Berkeley: University of California Press, 1967). On post-Mao elections, see Andrew Nathan, *Chinese Democracy* (Berkeley: University of California Press, 1985); Robert E. Bedeski, "China's 1979 Election Law and Its Implementation," *Electoral Studies* 5, no. 2 (1986): 153–65; Barrett L. McCormick, *Political Reform in Post-Mao China* (Berkeley: University of California Press, 1990); J. Bruce Jacobs, "Elections in China," *Australian Journal of Chinese Affairs*, 25 (1991): 171–200; Melanie Manion, "Chinese Democratization in Perspective: Electorates and Selectorates at the Township Level. Report from the Field," *China Quarterly*, 163 (2000): 133–51.

38. On rural decollectivization, see especially Daniel Kelliher, *Peasant Power in China: The Era of Rural Reform, 1979–1989* (New Haven, CT: Yale University Press, 1992); Kate Xiao Zhou, *How the Farmers Changed China: Power of the People* (Boulder, CO: Westview Press, 1996).

39. See Melanie Manion, "The Electoral Connection in the Chinese Countryside," *American Political Science Review* 90, no. 4 (1996): 736–48; Tianjian Shi, "Economic Development and Village Elections in Rural China," *Journal of Contemporary China* 8, no. 22 (1999): 433–35; Anne F. Thurston, *Muddling Toward Democracy: Political Change in Grassroots China* (Washington, DC: United States Institute of Peace, 1999); Lianjiang Li, "Elections and Popular Resistance in Rural China," *China Information* 16, no. 1 (2002): 89–107.

40. On protest movements in the 1970s and 1980s, see especially Andrew J. Nathan, *Chinese Democracy* (Berkeley: University of California Press, 1985); Jeffrey N. Wasserstrom and Elizabeth J. Perry, eds., *Popular Protest and Political Culture in Modern China: Learning From 1989* (Boulder, CO: Westview, 1992); Gregor Benton and Alan Hunter, *Wild Lily, Prairie Fire: China's Road to Democracy, 1942–1989* (Princeton, NJ: Princeton University Press, 1995).

41. James D. Seymour, ed., *The Fifth Modernization* (Stanfordville, NY: Human Rights Publishing Group, 1980).

42. On the 1989 protests, see Michel Oksenberg, Lawrence R. Sullivan, and Marc Lambert, eds., *Beijing Spring, 1989: Confrontation and Conflict, The Basic Documents,* (Armonk, NY: M. E. Sharpe, 1990); Han Minzhu and Hua Sheng, eds., *Cries for Democracy: Writings and Speeches From the 1989 Chinese Democracy Movement* (Princeton, NJ: Princeton University Press, 1990); Tony Saich, ed., *The Chinese People's Movement: Perspectives on Spring 1989* (Armonk, NY: M. E. Sharpe, 1990); Jonathan Unger, ed., *The Pro-Democracy Protest in China: Reports From the Provinces* (Sydney: Allen & Unwin, 1991); Craig Calhoun, *Neither Gods Nor Emperors: Students and the Struggle for Democracy in China* (Berkeley: University of California Press, 1995).

43. See James D. Seymour, *China's Satellite Parties* (Armonk, NY: M. E. Sharpe, 1987).

44. See Fengshi Wu, *New Partners or Old Brothers? GONGOs in Transnational Environmental Advocacy in China*, China Environmental Series, no. 5 (Washington, DC: Woodrow Wilson Center Press, 2002); Elizabeth C. Economy, *The River Runs Black: The Environmental Challenge to China's Future* (Ithaca, NY: Cornell University Press, 2004), 129–76.

45. For good discussions of NGOs and their relationship to the state, see especially Tony Saich, "Negotiating the State: The Development of Social Organizations in China," *China Quarterly*, 161 (2000): 124–41; Bruce Dickson, *Red Capitalists in China: The Party, Private Entrepreneurs, and Prospects for Political Change* (Cambridge: Cambridge University Press, 2003), 1–28.

46. The most thorough description and thoughtful analysis of leading small groups is by Carol Lee Hamrin, "The Party Leadership System," in Kenneth G. Lieberthal and David M. Lampton, eds., *Bureaucracy, Politics, and Decision Making in Post-Mao China* (Berkeley: University of California Press, 1992), 95–124. See also David M. Lampton, ed., *The Making of Chinese Foreign and Security Policy in the Era of Reform* (Stanford, CA: Stanford University Press, 2001), especially the contribution by Lu Ning, "The Central Leadership, Supraministry Coordinating Bodies, State Council Ministries, and Party Departments," 39–60.

47. These areas are defined in very comprehensive terms, such as party affairs, national security and military issues, foreign affairs, legal issues, personnel, finance and the economy.

48. See Kenneth Lieberthal and Michel Oksenberg, *Policy Making in China: Leaders, Structures, and Processes* (Princeton, NJ: Princeton University Press, 1988).

49. See Murray Scot Tanner, "How a Bill Becomes a Law in China: Stages and Processes in Lawmaking," *China Quarterly*, 141 (1995): 39–64; *The Politics of Lawmaking in China: Institutions, Processes, and Democratic Prospects* (Oxford: Oxford University Press, 1999).

50. Scott Kennedy, *The Business of Lobbying in China* (Cambridge: Harvard University Press, 2005).

51. See David M. Lampton, ed., *Policy Implementation in Post-Mao China* (Berkeley: University of California Press, 1987); Yasheng Huang, "Administrative Monitoring in China," *China Quarterly*, 143 (1995): 828–43.

52. See especially Ting Gong, "Forms and Characteristics of China's Corruption in the 1990s: Change With Continuity," *Communist and Post-Communist Studies* 30, no. 3 (1997): 277–88; Xiaobo Lu, "Booty Socialism, Bureau-preneurs, and the State in Transition," *Comparative Politics* 32, no. 3 (2000): 273–94; Yan Sun, "Reform, State, and Corruption: Is Corruption Less Destructive in China Than in Russia?" *Comparative Politics* 32, no. 1 (1999): 1–20; James Mulvenon, *Soldiers of Fortune: The Rise and Fall of the Chinese Military-Business Complex, 1978–1998* (Armonk, NY: M. E. Sharpe, 2001).

53. This (economic growth rate) is based on official Chinese statistics, which probably overstate real growth rates. One estimate suggests average annual rate of gross domestic product (GDP) growth in the 1980s and 1990s may have been as low as 7.9 percent rather than the official figure of 9.9 percent. Of course, this estimate would still have made China one of the five most rapidly growing economies in the world. See Nicholas R. Lardy, *China's Unfinished Economic Revolution* (Washington, DC: Brookings Institution, 1998). More recently, Thomas G. Rawski has ignited controversy with his significantly lower estimates of growth for 1998–2001 (i.e., annual growth rates ranging from 2.5 to 4.0 percent), based on low energy consumption. See "How Fast Is China's Economy Really Growing?" *China Business Review* 29, no. 2 (2002): 40–43.

54. See Barry Naughton, *Growing Out of the Plan: Chinese Economic Reform, 1978–1993* (Cambridge: Cambridge University Press, 1996).

55. Two excellent recent sources on the environment are Elizabeth C. Economy, *The River Runs Black: The Environmental Challenge to China's Future* (Ithaca, NY: Cornell University Press, 2004); Kristen A. Day, ed., *China's Environment and the Challenge of Sustainable Development* (Armonk, NY: M. E. Sharpe, 2005).

56. State Council Information Office, 2006 White Paper on the Environment, "Environmental Protection in China (1996–2005)."

57. See Susan Greenhalgh, Zhu Chuzhu, and Li Nan, "Restraining Population Growth in Three Chinese Villages, 1988–93,"

Population and Development Review 20, no. 2 (1994): 365–95.

58. See the excellent study by Judith Banister, "China: Population Dynamics and Economic Implications," in Joint Economic Committee, U.S. Congress, *China's Economic Future: Challenges to U.S. Policy* (Armonk, NY: M. E. Sharpe, 1997), 339–60. On coercion in implementation, see John Aird, *Slaughter of the Innocents: Coercive Birth Control in China* (Washington, DC: AEI Press, 1990).

PACIFIC
OCEAN

MEXICO

Tijuana

BAJA CALIFORNIA

Gulf of California

BAJA CALIFORNIA SUR

Ciudad
Juárez

SONORA

CHIHUAHUA

Chihuahua

Rio Grande

Conchos R.

Rio Bravo del Norte

Yaqui R.

SINALOA

DURANGO

COAHUILA

Monterrey
**NUEVO
LEÓN**

ZACATECAS

TAMAULIPAS

Gulf of Mexico

NAYARIT

AGUAS-
CALIENTES

SAN LUIS
POTOSÍ

Tampico

Lerma R.

Pánuco R.

GUANAJUATO
León

Guadalajara

QUERÉTARO
Querétaro

HIDALGO

Mérida
YUCATÁN

JALISCO

MEXICO
CITY

TLAXCALA
Veracruz

Bay of
Campeche

QUINTANA
ROO

COLIMA

MICHOACÁN

MORELOS
Puebla
PUEBLA

VERACRUZ

CAMPECHE

TABASCO

Balsas R.

GUERRERO

OAXACA

CHIAPAS

Gulf of
Tehuantepec

0   100   200   300 Miles
0   100   200   300 Kilometers

POLITICS IN MEXICO

Wayne A. Cornelius and Jeffrey A. Weldon

Country Bio

Population
106 million

Territory
761,602 square miles

Year of Independence
1810

Year of Current Constitution
1917

MEXICO

Head of State
President Felipe Calderón Hinojosa

Head of Government
President Felipe Calderón Hinojosa

Languages
Spanish, various Mayan, Nahuatl, Zapotec, and other regional indigenous languages

Religions
nominally Roman Catholic 89%; Protestant 6%

It is election night. Friends and family gather around televisions to watch the returns, as computer-generated graphics showing vote trends flash on and off the screen. Mirroring the final preelection surveys, exit poll results show a presidential race that is too close to call. A few hours after the polls close, both major candidates appear on television to claim victory. More than a month passes, but the election outcome remains in doubt. Millions of votes are recounted. Election officials are accused of incompetence and bias in the vote-counting. It would be up to the lawyers and the courts to determine who will be the country's next president. More than two months after the election, the court finally declares a winner.

What is striking about this picture is that it occurred not in the United States (2000, Bush v. Gore), but in Mexico (2006, Calderón v. López Obrador). For more than six decades, the outcomes of Mexican presidential elections had been known the moment that the ruling **Partido Revolucionario Institucional (PRI)** announced its nominee. Since the hotly contested but fraud-ridden presidential election of 1988, however, Mexico has experienced a remarkable passage from a political system in which systematic manipulation of elections by the ruling party was condoned by senior

political leaders and cynically accepted by the general public to one in which government respect for voters' preferences is expected—indeed, demanded. This and other key elements of modern democratic politics have become routinized in Mexico.

Recurrent economic crises (1976–1977, 1982–1989, 1994–1996) were among the most powerful catalysts for this revolution in citizen expectations. The vast majority of Mexicans suffered severe economic pain during these two decades, directly attributable to government mismanagement of the national economy. Millions of jobs were lost, real wages were stagnant or declining in all but a few years of the period, savings and businesses were decimated by inflation and currency devaluations, and government benefits for the middle and lower classes were slashed in the austerity budgets necessitated by the economic crises.

The 1988 presidential election brought a tidal wave of antigovernment protest voting, with the PRI's candidate eking out a bare majority victory.[1] The government could contain the discontent and keep the PRI in power because it completely dominated the machinery of elections as well as the mass media. In the 1994 election, the PRI rode the coattails of the still highly popular

President Carlos Salinas, and took advantage of public anxieties created by the Zapatista rebellion in Chiapas.

In the 2000 election, however, voters were furious at having been deceived twice by their government, first during the oil boom era of 1977–1981 and then during the Salinas presidency (1988–1994), periods when the government created an illusion of prosperity and boundless future economic gains. Salinas was almost universally blamed for the economic crisis that engulfed Mexico within weeks after he left office. For the first time in 71 years, the voters soundly rejected the presidential candidate of the PRI, turning to Vicente Fox, a maverick former Coca Cola executive-turned-politician who ran under the banner of **Partido Acción Nacional (PAN).**

Public confidence that a vote for some alternative to the PRI would actually be respected by the authorities had been boosted significantly by several rounds of reforms in the federal electoral law in the 1990s—changes that the government proposed and the PRI endorsed, under strong pressure from citizens and the opposition parties. These procedures added so many procedural safeguards into the conduct of elections that the worst, old-style forms of vote fraud (stuffing ballot boxes or stealing them, falsifying vote tallies, etc.) became virtually impossible. Most importantly, the law created a new federal elections agency independent of government and PRI

President Vicente Fox on his inauguration day in 2000, flashing his trademark "YA!" ("NOW!") sign.

AFP/Corbis

authority and made it responsible for organizing all phases of the electoral process, giving all parties access to the media, allocating public funds for campaigns, recruiting and training citizens to run the polling places, counting votes, and certifying the results.

The results of the 1997 elections for Congress had been a stunning setback for the PRI, which lost 112 of 300 single-member districts. For the first time since 1929, the PRI had to surrender control of the Chamber of Deputies (the lower house of Congress) to a coalition of four opposition parties. The PRI also lost its two-thirds majority in the Senate, which is needed to approve constitutional amendments. In the 2000 elections, the PRI lost the presidency for the first time and continued to lose ground in Congress. In 2006, the PRI finished in a distant third in the race for president, and its delegation in Congress was reduced to about a fifth of the lower chamber.

While its 2006 presidential candidate was trounced, the PRI retained control of over half of the state governorships (see Figure 11.1). All of these factors exemplify Mexico's shift toward a much more competitive, pluralistic political system, in which no single party is dominant throughout the country but each of the three major parties has regional strongholds.

Beyond the division of power that has prevailed at the federal level since 1997, divided governments at the state level have become commonplace. During the 1989–1997 period, for example, seven states had legislatures controlled by a party different from that of the state's governor. Mexicans elected non-PRI candidates as governors in ten (out of thirty-two) states during this period; prior to 1989 no opposition party victory at the state level had been recognized by the government.

The presidential election of 2006 featured three strong candidates and a highly divided electorate. Late polling showed a very close race, with the two leading candidates within the margin of statistical error.

The PRD's candidate, Andrés Manuel López Obrador—the mayor of Mexico City from 2000 to 2005—had been leading in the polls for most of the preceding two years. In 2004, the federal attorney general's office began investigating López Obrador, who was accused of violating a court order arising from a land-use dispute in Mexico City. Because he was an elected official, he had the benefit of immunity from prosecution, and a ruling by the federal Chamber of Deputies was required to remove that immunity. After the attorney general formally sought an indictment

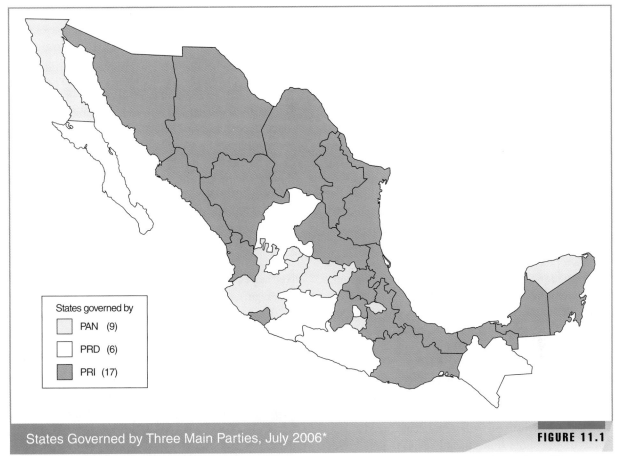

States Governed by Three Main Parties, July 2006*

FIGURE 11.1

*PAN-governed states were Aguascalientes, Baja California, Guanajuato, Jalisco, Morelos, Queretaro, San Luis Potosí, Tlaxcala, and Yucatan.
PRD-governed states were Baja California Sur, Chiapas, Distrito Federal, Guerrero, Michoacan, and Zacatecas.
PRI-governed states were Campeche, Chihuahua, Coahuila, Colima, Durango, Hidalgo, Mexico, Nayarit, Nuevo León, Oaxaca, Puebla.
Quintana Roo, Sinaloa, Sonora, Tabasco, Tamaulipas, and Veracruz.*

against López Obrador, in April 2005, the chamber voted to remove his immunity (the PRI and the PAN voted in favor and the **Partido de la Revolución Democrática (PRD)** against). People who are under indictment or are serving sentences after convictions are ineligible to run for federal office, so the removal of his immunity made López Obrador ineligible to run for president. His supporters claimed that the true rationale for the indictment was to remove the leading candidate from the presidential race. His opponents claimed that the charges were genuine and demonstrated his lack of respect for the separation of powers.

Responding to mounting domestic and international criticism of the López Obrador indictment, President Fox fired the attorney general and dismissed the charges against the mayor. This episode increased the popularity of López Obrador, who portrayed himself as the victim of a conspiracy organized by the Fox

government, the PAN, the PRI, and the private sector. He returned to his job as Mexico City mayor, resigning a few months later to run for president.

When the PRI lost power in 2000, its president, Roberto Madrazo, became the leading candidate for that party's 2006 presidential nomination. However, not all PRIistas favored Madrazo. Four candidates ran against him in an August 2005 first-round "primary," which consisted of a series of public opinion polls. The former governor of the State of Mexico emerged as the winner, but he was forced to withdraw after media reports revealed that he had acquired a suspiciously large fortune in real estate. Madrazo quickly gained the PRI nomination in a virtually uncontested primary election.

Felipe Calderón was an underdog to become the PAN's 2006 candidate. Santiago Creel, the Interior Minister in the Fox administration, had been the front-runner since 2001. The PAN scheduled three regional primaries, with the rule that the candidate who won the most votes, summing across the three primaries, would win the nomination. The primary was limited to PAN members and "adherents" (a category invented by the party to allow sympathizers to vote in some internal primaries). The race turned out to be more competitive than expected. Calderón surprised nearly everyone by winning the first primary by ten points. He won the second and third primaries by a sufficient margin to win an absolute majority of votes. Because he was the only candidate nominated in a competitive primary, Calderón received a healthy bounce in the polls.

López Obrador began campaigning in fall 2005 with a healthy lead; Calderón started out in third place in most polls, but within striking distance of the PRI candidate. After lengthy negotiations, the candidates agreed on two nationally televised debates, in April and June. López Obrador hoped to sit on his lead and declined to participate in the first debate. He also began to ridicule the still highly popular President Fox, calling him a "*chachalaca*" (a large, wild bird that screeches loudly) and telling him to "shut up." Many Mexicans took this as an insult to the presidency and were offended.

At this point, the Calderón campaign "went negative," running a series of ads comparing López Obrador with leftist/populist Venezuelan President Hugo Chávez. Some of the spots showed both Chávez and López Obrador ridiculing President Fox. Their message: López Obrador, like Chávez, was a dangerous authoritarian. The ads also claimed that López Obrador would increase public debt to finance his expensive social welfare and public works projects, which would push Mexico toward another economic crisis. At the end of each spot, the PAN claimed that López Obrador was a "Menace to Mexico."

By early April, Calderón, who had beaten Madrazo in the first televised debate, had overtaken López Obrador in most polls, with the PRI's Madrazo in third place. López Obrador complained to the Federal Electoral Institute (IFE) about the PAN's negative advertising campaign and persuaded it to ban many of the offending spots. López Obrador regained some ground by participating in the second debate, and by launching his own highly negative ads against the PAN candidate. By the end of June, most polls showed the race tied between Calderón and López Obrador, or with small advantages for either candidate.

On election day, July 2, 2006, the race was so close that the IFE declined to release the results of its quick count (essentially an exit poll, except that it sums results from a sample of precincts rather than a sample of individual voters). The computerized preliminary results showed Calderón with a small lead (about 1 percent). Both López Obrador and Calderón claimed victory. On July 5, the formal count of the votes began in each of the 300 electoral districts. The next day, the IFE announced that Calderón had won by 0.58 percent, or about 244,000 votes out of nearly 42 million cast (see Table 11.1).

The election results divided Mexico in two, with the PAN winning most of the northern states (except Zacatecas and Baja California Sur, both governed by the PRD). The PRD won every state to the south, except Yucatán (governed by the PAN) and Puebla (where the PRI governor was under the clouds of scandal). Calderón and López Obrador each won sixteen states. Madrazo, incredibly, won not a single state (see Figure 11.2).

Felipe Calderón, presidential candidate of the PAN, celebrates his razor-thin election victory on July 5, 2006.

Wesley Bocxe/The Image Works

TABLE 11.1

Votes for President of Mexico in 2006   (official district counts, including voters abroad)

Candidate	Votes	% of Valid Votes
Felipe Calderón (PAN)	15,019,300	36.70
Andres Manuel López Obrador (PRD-PT-Convergencia)	14,767,438	36.09
Roberto Madrazo (PRI-PVEM)	9,302,801	22.73
Patricia Mercado (PASC)	1,129,737	2.76
Roberto Campa (Nueva Alianza)	401,932	0.98
Nonregistered candidates	298,018	0.73
Invalid votes	937,735	
Total votes	**41,856,961**	**100.00**

Source: Instituto Federal Electoral (http://www.ife.org.mx), 2006.

Number of States
- PAN (16)
- Allianza por el Bien de Todos (PRD, PT, Convergencia) (16)
- Allianza por México (PRI, PVEM) (0)

States Won by Presidential Candidates in 2006 Election

FIGURE 11.2

López Obrador and the PRD immediately claimed that there had been electoral fraud, orchestrated by the PAN, the PRI, the Federal Electoral Institute, and the business community. They initially claimed that the fraud was achieved through lines of code in the computer program that added up the votes on election night (although the votes were counted by hand in the precincts and with calculators and standard spreadsheets in the electoral districts). Eventually, the PRD dropped the computer-fraud argument and charged instead that there had been "old-fashioned" fraud in the precincts, with poll workers adding votes for Calderón and invalidating votes for López Obrador. The PAN and the IFE pointed out that the PRD's polling place representatives had not complained of fraud on election day. López Obrador responded that his party's representatives must have been bribed.

The PRD asked the Federal Electoral Tribunal to order a nationwide recount of votes. The court refused this request and instead ordered recounts in about 9 percent of the 130,000 precincts—those where there had been arithmetical inconsistencies in the reported vote. The PRD then argued that if the recount did not turn the outcome in López Obrador's favor, the entire election should be annulled. The PRD's case for annulment was based on the claim that government had intervened improperly in the electoral process, through President Fox's criticism of López Obrador during the campaign and his open support of Calderón's candidacy.

To pressure the electoral tribunal to order a complete recount, the PRD launched a civil disobedience campaign in Mexico City. Hundreds of thousands of López Obrador's followers demonstrated in the Zócalo (the central plaza). Then thousands of protesters set up tents on Paseo de la Reforma (the principal boulevard) and the Zócalo, blocking all traffic in the heart of Mexico City. The partial recount and the subsequent nullification of some disputed precincts shifted about 14,000 votes to López Obrador—not enough to extrapolate a change in the outcome had all votes been recounted. Calderón's victory was certified by the electoral tribunal in early September. But López Obrador refused to recognize the "spurious president," and in November 2006 inaugurated himself as "the legitimate president of Mexico" before 100,000 of his supporters in the Zócalo. He vowed to lead "years of resistance" throughout the country and to pressure the Calderón government into adopting his legislative proposals, including measures for breaking up business monopolies and creating a

Andrés Manuel López Obrador, presidential candidate of the PRD, refuses to concede electoral defeat in July 2006.

AP Images

universal health care system. Undoubtedly policymaking in the Calderón administration will be shaped by the divisive 2006 election.

CURRENT POLICY CHALLENGES

Mexico had entered the twenty-first century with huge social and economic problems: an economy that produces far too few jobs to accommodate the young people entering the labor market each year; an educational system sorely in need of modernization; a growing impoverished population, with at least half of all Mexicans living below the official poverty line; a highly unequal distribution of income; a huge developmental gap between the affluent, urbanized, economically modern northern states and the poor, rural, heavily indigenous south; acute environmental problems that damage the health of both rural and urban dwellers; and a criminal justice system that barely functions, routinely violates the human rights of citizens, and is heavily corrupted by drug trafficking. The PRI lost its grip on the Mexican political system in

López Obrador's supporters demonstrate in Mexico City's Zócalo (central plaza), August 2006.

Corbis

large part because it had failed to deal effectively with these problems. It remains to be seen whether the democratic "opposition," now in power, can manage them with conspicuously greater success.

Several emerging policy challenges will be no less daunting. As a developing country, Mexico has to play catch-up with its international trade partners and competitors. It must modernize its agricultural sector to allow it to survive competition from the United States and Canada, where subsidies and more efficient methods make agricultural goods cheaper. This vulnerable sector will be further challenged when trade barriers are eliminated completely in 2008. Mexico needs to replace its antiquated and inefficient labor law with new statutes that both protect workers and encourage job creation. It must renovate the energy sector—oil, electricity, and natural gas—either by increasing government spending or by allowing more private or foreign investment, which would require controversial constitutional amendments. An unfamiliar demographic problem is beginning to emerge—an aging population—and the Mexican people must soon bolster the funding of private and government-sponsored pension plans. Finally, the government must expand the tax base to provide the resources needed to address all of these challenges.

On the political front, additional changes in electoral rules are needed to close loopholes concerning the financing of campaigns, to make it more difficult for elected officials to use government resources to promote their party's candidates, and to allow the immediate reelection of legislators, which would make them more responsive and accountable to their constituents. But in terms of consolidating a fully democratic system, these refinements may be less important than the rapidly spreading belief that alternation in power among Mexico's main parties, at all levels of governance, is both desirable and achievable. In short, most Mexicans seem to have concluded that it is time to get on with the business of modern democracy.

HISTORICAL PERSPECTIVES

Colonialism and Church-State Relations

Long before Hernán Cortés landed in 1519 and began the Spanish conquest of Mexico, its territory was inhabited by numerous Indian civilizations. Of these, the Maya in the Yucatán peninsula and the Toltec on the central plateau had developed the most complex political and economic organizations. Both of these civilizations had disintegrated, however, before the Spaniards arrived. Smaller Indian societies were decimated by diseases introduced by the invaders or were vanquished by the sword. Subsequent grants of land and Indian labor by the Spanish Crown to the colonists further isolated the rural Indian population and deepened their exploitation.

The combined effects of attrition, intermarriage, and cultural penetration of Indian regions have

BOX 11.1

Key Political Events in Mexico

1810–1821	War of Independence against Spain
1846–1848	War between Mexico and the United States
1910–1920	Mexican Revolution
1917	New constitution issued, incorporating Revolutionary goals and ideals
1924–1928	Presidency of Plutarco Elías Calles
1927–1929	Cristero Rebellion (Catholic Church vs. State)
1928	Alvaro Obregón elected president, assassinated a few months later
1928–1934	"Jefe Máximo" Plutarco Elías Calles rules from behind the scenes, under several provisional presidents (the "Maximato" period)
1929	Plutarco Elías Calles establishes Partido Nacional Revolucionario (PNR)
1934–1940	Presidency of Lázaro Cárdenas
1938	President Cárdenas reorganizes PNR, which becomes the Partido de la Revolución Mexicana (PRM); Cárdenas nationalizes oil industry
1939	Partido Acción Nacional (PAN) founded
1940–1946	Presidency of Manuel Avila Camacho
1946–1952	Presidency of Miguel Alemán
1946	PRM is restructured, renamed the Partido Revolucionario Institucional (PRI)
1952–1958	Presidency of Adolfo Ruiz Cortines
1958–1964	Presidency of Adolfo López Mateos
1964–1970	Presidency of Gustavo Díaz Ordaz
1968	Student protest movement challenges the government and is violently repressed (the "Tlatelolco massacre")
1970–1976	Presidency of Luis Echeverría
1976–1982	Presidency of José López Portillo; period of the oil export boom
1981–1982	Drop in world oil prices and rising interest rates cause economic collapse; Mexico unable to service its external debt
1982–1988	Presidency of Miguel de la Madrid
1988–1994	Presidency of Carlos Salinas de Gortari
1994	North American Free Trade Agreement (NAFTA) goes into effect; peasant rebellion erupts in the state of Chiapas; PRI presidential candidate Luis Donaldo Colosio assassinated and replaced by Ernesto Zedillo; peso sharply devalued, provoking a deep economic crisis
1994–2000	Presidency of Ernesto Zedillo
1997–2000	PRI loses majority control in the Chamber of Deputies
2000	PRI loses the presidency for the first time in 71 years
2000–2006	Presidency of Vicente Fox
2006	PAN wins the presidency again and a plurality in both houses of Congress; closeness of the presidential result provokes large-scale protests and a partial recount
2006–2012	Presidency of Felipe Calderón

drastically reduced the proportion of Mexico's population culturally identified as Indian. By the 1990 census figures, 7.9 percent of the nation's population spoke an Indian language.[2] The Indian minority has been persistently marginal to the national economy and political system. Today, the indigenous population is heavily concentrated in rural communities that the government classifies as the country's most economically depressed and service-deprived, located primarily in the southeast and the center of the country. They engage in rainfall-dependent subsistence agriculture, using traditional methods of cultivation, are seasonally employed as migrant laborers in commercial agriculture, or produce crafts for sale in regional and national markets. The Indian population is an especially troubling reminder of the millions of people who have been left behind by uneven development in twentieth-century Mexico.

The importance of Spain's colonies in the New World lay in their ability to provide the Crown with vital resources to fuel the Spanish economy. Mexico's mines provided gold and silver in abundance until the wars of independence began in 1810. After independence, Mexico continued to export these ores, supplemented in subsequent eras by hemp, cotton, textiles, oil, and winter vegetables.

Since the Spanish conquest, the Roman Catholic Church has been an institution of enduring power in Mexico. Priests joined the Spanish invaders in an evangelical mission to convert the Indians to Catholicism, and individual priests have continued to play important roles in national history. Father Miguel Hidalgo y Costilla helped launch Mexico's war of independence in 1810, and Father José María Morelos y Pavón replaced Hidalgo as spiritual and military leader of the independence movement when the Crown executed Hidalgo in 1811.

During Mexico's postindependence period, institutional antagonisms between the church and the central government have occasionally flared into open confrontations on such issues as church wealth, educational policy, the content of public school textbooks, and political activism by the church. The Constitutions of 1857 and 1917 formally established the separation of church and state and defined their respective domains. Constitutional provisions dramatically reduced the church's power and wealth by nationalizing its property, including large agricultural landholdings. The 1917 Constitution also made church-affiliated schools subject to the authority of the federal government, denied priests the right to vote or speak publicly on political issues, and gave the government the right to limit the number of priests who can serve in Mexico. Government efforts during the 1920s to enforce these constitutional provisions led to a civil insurrection that caused 100,000 combatant deaths, uncounted civilian casualties, and economic devastation in a large part of central Mexico. The settlement of this "Cristero rebellion" established, once and for all, the church's subordination to the state, in return for which the government relaxed its restrictions on church activities in nonpolitical arenas.

This accord inaugurated a long period of relative tranquility in church-state relations, during which the government and the church ignored many of the anticlerical provisions of the 1917 Constitution (such as the prohibition on church involvement in education). The central church hierarchy—among the most conservative in Latin America—cooperated with the government on a variety of issues, and the church posed no threat to the ruling party's hegemony.

Revolution and Its Aftermath

The nationwide civil conflict that erupted in Mexico in 1910 is often referred to as the first of the great "social revolutions" that shook the world early in the twentieth century. Mexico's upheaval, however, originated within the country's ruling class. The revolution did not begin as a spontaneous uprising of the common people against an entrenched dictator, Porfirio Díaz, and against the local bosses and landowners who exploited them. Even though hundreds of thousands of workers and peasants ultimately participated in the civil strife, most of the revolutionary leadership came from the younger generation of middle- and upper-class Mexicans who had become disenchanted with three and a half decades of increasingly heavy-handed rule by the aging dictator and his clique. These disgruntled members of the elite saw their future opportunities for economic and political mobility blocked by the closed group surrounding Díaz. Their battle cry was "effective suffrage, no reelection"—the end of self-perpetuating dictatorship made possible by sham elections.

Led by Francisco I. Madero, whose family had close ties with the ruling group, these liberal middle-class reformers were committed to opening up the political system and creating new opportunities for themselves within a capitalist economy whose basic features they did not challenge. They did not seek to destroy the established order. Instead, they sought to make it work more in their own interest, rather than that of the foreign capitalists who dominated key sectors of Mexico's economy during the Porfirian dictatorship.

Of course, some serious grievances had accumulated among workers and peasants. Once the rebellion against Díaz got underway, leaders who appealed to the disadvantaged masses pressed their claims against the central government. Emiliano Zapata led a movement of peasants in the state of Morelos; they were bent on regaining the land they had lost to the rural aristocracy by subterfuge during the Porfiriato. In the north, Pancho Villa led an army of jobless workers, small landowners, and cattle hands, whose main interest was steady employment. As various revolutionary leaders contended for control of the central government, the political order that had been created and enforced by Díaz disintegrated into warlordism—powerful regional gangs led by revolutionary *caudillos* (political-military strongmen) who aspired more to increasing their personal wealth and social status than to leading a genuine social revolution.

The first decade of the revolution produced a new, remarkably progressive constitution, replacing the Constitution of 1857. The young, middle-class elite that dominated the constitutional convention of 1916–1917 "had little if any direct interest in labor unions or land distribution. But it was an elite that recognized the need for social change. . . . By 1916, popular demands for land and labor reform were too great to ignore."[3] The Constitution of 1917 established the principle of state control over all natural resources, subordination of the church to the state, the government's right to redistribute land, and rights for labor that had not yet been secured even by the labor movement in the United States. Even so, nearly two decades passed before most of these constitutional provisions began to be implemented.

Many historians today stress the continuities between prerevolutionary and postrevolutionary Mexico. The processes of economic modernization, capital accumulation, state building, and political centralization that gained considerable momentum during the Porfiriato were interrupted by civil strife from 1910 to 1920. They resumed once a semblance of order had been restored. During the 1920s, the central government set out to eliminate or undermine the most powerful and independent-minded regional *caudillos* by co-opting the local power brokers, known as *caciques.* These local political bosses became, in effect, appendages of the central government, supporting its policies and maintaining control over the population in their communities. By the end of this period, leaders with genuine popular followings (like Zapata and Villa) had been assassinated and control had been seized by a new postrevolutionary elite bent on demobilizing the masses and establishing the hegemony of the central government.

The rural aristocracy of the Porfiriato had been weakened but not eliminated; its heirs still controlled large concentrations of property and other forms of wealth in many parts of the country. Most of the large urban firms that operated during the Porfiriato also survived, further demonstrating that the revolution was not an attack on private capital per se. Except during the years of most intense violence (1914–1917), the revolution had surprisingly minor effects on private investment and economic growth.

The Cárdenas Upheaval

Elite control was maintained during the 1930s, but this was nevertheless an era of massive social and political upheaval in Mexico. During the presidency of Lázaro Cárdenas (1934–1940), peasants and urban workers succeeded for the first time in pressing their claims for land and higher wages; in fact, Cárdenas actively encouraged them to do so. The result was an unprecedented wave of strikes, protest demonstrations, and petitions for breaking up large rural estates.

Most disputes between labor and management during this period were settled, under government pressure, in favor of the workers. The Cárdenas administration also redistributed more than twice as much land as that expropriated by all of Cárdenas's predecessors since 1915, when Mexico's land reform program was formally initiated. By 1940, the country's land tenure system had been fundamentally altered, breaking the traditional domination of the large haciendas and creating a large sector of small peasant farmers (*ejidatarios*)—more than 1.5 million of them—who had received plots of land under the agrarian reform program. The Cárdenas government actively encouraged the formation of new organizations of peasants and urban workers, grouped the new organizations into nationwide confederations, and provided arms to rural militias formed by the *ejidatarios.* Even Mexico's foreign relations were disrupted in 1938 when the Cárdenas government nationalized oil companies that had been operating in Mexico under U.S. and British ownership.

Mexican intellectuals frequently refer to 1938 as the highwater mark of the Mexican revolution as measured by social progress; they characterize the period since then as a retrogression. Certainly, the distributive and especially the redistributive performance of the Mexican government declined sharply in the decades that followed, and the worker and peasant organizations formed during the Cárdenas era atrophied and became less and less likely to contest either the will of the government or the interests of Mexico's private economic elites. De facto reconcentration of landholdings and other forms of wealth occurred as the state provided increasingly generous support to the country's new commercial, industrial, and financial elites during a period of rapid industrialization.

The Cárdenas era fundamentally reshaped Mexico's political institutions. The presidency became the primary institution of the political system, with sweeping powers exercised during a constitutionally limited six-year term with no possibility of reelection; the military was removed from overt political competition and transformed into one of several institutional pillars of the regime; and an elaborate network of government-sponsored peasant and labor organizations provided a mass base for the official political party and performed a variety of political and economic control functions, utilizing a multilayered system of patronage and clientelism.

By 1940, a much larger proportion of the Mexican population was nominally included in the national political system, mostly by their membership in peasant and labor organizations created by Cárdenas. No real democratization of the system resulted from this vast expansion of "political participation," however. Although working-class groups did have more control over their representatives in the government-sponsored organizations than over their former masters on the haciendas and in the factories, their influence over public policy and government priorities after Cárdenas was minimal and highly indirect. Policy recommendations, official actions, and nominations for elective and appointive positions at all levels still emanated from the central government and official party headquarters in Mexico City, filtering down the hierarchy to the rank and file for ratification and legitimation.

The Era of Hegemonic Party Rule

The political system shaped by Lázaro Cárdenas proved remarkably durable. From 1940 until the late 1980s, Mexico's official party-government apparatus was the most stable regime in Latin America. It had a well-earned reputation for resilience, adaptability to new circumstances, a high level of agreement within the ruling elite on basic rules of political competition, and a seemingly unlimited capacity to co-opt dissidents, both within and outside of the ruling party. As late as 1990, the celebrated Peruvian novelist Mario Vargas Llosa could plausibly describe Mexico's regime as "the perfect dictatorship," combining stability, legitimacy, and durability in a way that even the former Soviet Union and Castro's Cuba had never achieved.[4]

With the fall of the Communist Party of the Soviet Union in 1991, the PRI became the world's longest continuously ruling political party. Since 1929, when the "official" party was founded, both political assassination and armed rebellion had been rejected as routes to the presidency by all contenders for power. A handful of disappointed aspirants to the ruling party's presidential nomination mounted candidacies outside the party (in the elections of 1929, 1940, 1946, 1952, and 1988), but even the most broadly supported of these breakaway movements were successfully contained through government-engineered vote fraud and intimidation.

In the early 1970s concerns had been raised about the stability of the system, after the bloody repression of a student protest movement in Mexico City by President Gustavo Díaz Ordaz on the eve of the 1968 Olympic Games. The student massacre marked the opening of a "dirty war" in which the army and police forces are believed to have executed, without trial, more than 700 alleged enemies of the state. Many analysts at that time suggested that Mexico was entering a period of institutional crisis, requiring fundamental reforms in both political arrangements and strategy of economic development.

But the discovery of massive oil and natural gas resources during the late 1970s gave the incumbent regime a new lease on life. Continued support of the masses and the elites was purchased with an apparently limitless supply of petro-pesos, even without major structural reforms. The government's room for maneuver was abruptly erased by the collapse of the oil boom in August 1982, owing to a combination of adverse international economic circumstances (falling oil prices, rising interest rates, recession in the United States) and fiscally irresponsible domestic policies. Real wages and living standards for the vast majority of Mexicans plummeted, and the government committed itself to a socially painful restructuring of the economy, including a drastic shrinkage of the sector owned and managed by the government itself.

The economic crisis of the 1980s placed enormous stress on Mexico's political system. In the July 6, 1988, national elections, the PRI suffered unprecedented reverses in both the presidential and congressional races. The vote share officially attributed to Carlos Salinas was more than 20 percentage points below that of PRI presidential candidate Miguel de la Madrid in the 1982 election. Ex-PRIista Cuauhtémoc Cárdenas, son of the much-revered former President Lázaro Cárdenas, heading a hastily assembled coalition of minor leftist and nationalist parties, was officially credited with 31.1 percent of the presidential vote—far more than any previous opposition candidate but probably much less than he actually received if the vote count had been honest.[5] A diminished PRI delegation still controlled the Congress, but the president's party had lost the two-thirds majority needed to approve constitutional amendments.

Carlos Salinas breathed new life into the creaking PRI apparatus. His brand of strong presidential leadership and his accomplishments—especially the toppling of corrupt labor union bosses, a sharp reduction in inflation, and the National Solidarity Program, a new-style antipoverty and public works program that increased government responsiveness to lower-class needs—sufficed to rebuild electoral support for the PRI and to paper over the cracks within the ruling political elite. Salinas opened the Mexican economy to foreign trade and investment, and privatized hundreds of inefficient state-owned companies. Mexico at last seemed poised to make a giant leap from Third World to First World status. While political liberalization had proceeded slowly and unevenly under Salinas, far behind the pace of his sweeping free-market economic reforms, Mexico appeared to be coasting inexorably toward a transfer of power to yet another PRI national government in 1994.

The illusion of proximate economic modernity and political inevitability was shattered on New Year's Day 1994, by a "postmodern" peasant revolt in Chiapas, Mexico's most underdeveloped and politically backward state. An estimated 2,000 primitively armed but well-disciplined Indian rebels seized control of four isolated municipalities and declared war on the central government—something that had not happened since 1938. Their demands for social justice and democracy resonated throughout Mexico, long after the initial skirmishes with the Mexican army had claimed at least 145 lives and a cease-fire had been negotiated. Suddenly, middle- and upper-class Mexicans, as well as foreign governments and investors, were reminded of the persistence of political repression, human rights violations, extreme poverty, and inequality in Mexico. The impoverished Indians who took up arms against the state in Chiapas symbolized the many millions of Mexicans who had been left behind in the drive for economic modernity and internationalism.

Less than three months after the Chiapas rebellion erupted, President Salinas's hand-picked successor, Luis Donaldo Colosio, was assassinated while campaigning in Tijuana. The crime has never been solved. With a last great exertion of presidential will, Carlos Salinas imposed on the PRI another hand-picked successor, economist-technocrat Ernesto Zedillo, to replace the slain Colosio. In August 1994, in a high-turnout election that was judged by most independent observers at the time to be the cleanest in Mexico's postrevolutionary history, the opposition parties were soundly defeated. Not only did the PRI retain control of the presidency (albeit with just a plurality of 48.8 percent of the total votes cast), it also maintained an ample majority in the federal Congress.[6]

The End of PRI Dominance

The appearance of restored stability created by the ruling party's impressive performance in the August 1994 elections was short-lived. In December 1994, a militarily insignificant renewal of the Zapatista rebels' activities in Chiapas, followed immediately by a sustained speculative attack on the overvalued peso by short-term foreign and domestic investors, opened a Pandora's box of economic and political troubles. What began as a currency and financial liquidity crisis quickly evolved into a massive capital flight and a deep recession. After publicly criticizing Zedillo and his cabinet ministers for provoking the economic crisis by mishandling the devaluation of the peso, ex-President Salinas went into de facto exile in Ireland. The Zedillo administration in turn made Salinas the scapegoat for the financial collapse.

By the late 1990s, the PRI once again appeared to be in a state of accelerated decomposition. Divisions within the party were deeper than at any time since the mid-1930s. With the defeat of its presidential candidate in 2000, the PRI lost control of the vast patronage resources of the central government, which were crucial to keeping it in power for more than seven decades. After its disastrous, third-place finish in the 2006 presidential election, the PRI seemed to be retreating into its regional strongholds, with its status as a national party in jeopardy.

International Environment

Since independence, Mexico's politics and public policies have always been influenced by proximity to the United States. Porfirio Díaz is widely reputed to have exclaimed, "Poor Mexico! So far from God and so close to the United States." Indeed, this proximity has made the United States a powerful presence in Mexico. A wide array of factors—the 2,000-mile land border between the two countries; Mexico's rich supplies of minerals, labor, and other resources needed by U.S. industry; and Mexico's attractiveness as a site for U.S. private investment—has made such influence inevitable.

Midway through the nineteenth century, Mexico's sovereignty as a nation was directly threatened when the U.S. push for territorial and economic expansion met little resistance in northern Mexico. Emerging from a war for independence from Spain and plagued by chronic political instability, Mexico was highly vulnerable to aggression from the north. By annexing Texas in 1845 and instigating the Mexican-American War of 1846 to 1848 (Ulysses S. Grant later called it "America's great unjust war"), the United States seized half of Mexico's national territory: disputed land in Texas; all of the land that is now California, Nevada, and Utah; most of New Mexico and Arizona; and part of Colorado and Wyoming. This massive seizure of territory, along with several later military interventions and meddling in the politics of "revolutionary" Mexico that extended throughout the 1920s, left scars that have not healed. Even today, the average Mexican suspects that the United States has designs on Mexico's remaining territory, its oil, even its human resources.

The lost territory includes the U.S. regions that have been the principal recipients of Mexican immigrant workers in this century. This labor migration, too, was instigated mainly by the United States. Beginning in the 1880s, U.S. farmers, railroads, and mining companies, with U.S. government encouragement, obtained many of the workers needed to expand the economy and transport systems of the Southwest and Midwest by sending labor recruiters into northern and central Mexico.

By the end of the 1920s, the economies of Mexico and the United States were sufficiently intertwined that the effects of the Great Depression were swiftly transmitted to Mexico, causing unemployment to rise and export earnings and gross national product (GNP) to plummet. In response to these economic shocks, Mexico tried during the 1930s to reduce its dependence on the United States as a market for silver and other exports. The effort failed. By 1940, Mexico was more dependent than before on the flow of goods, capital, and labor to and from the United States.

After 1940, Mexico relied even more heavily on U.S. private capital to help finance its drive for industrialization. The United States also experienced severe shortages of labor in World War II, and Mexico's dependence on the United States as a market for its surplus labor became institutionalized through the so-called *bracero* program of importing contract labor. Operating from 1942 to 1964, this program brought more than 4 million Mexicans to the United States to work in seasonal agriculture. After the demise of the *bracero* program, migration to the United States continued, with most new arrivals entering illegally. By 2005, 6.2 million Mexicans had taken up residence in the United States illegally, and as many as 400,000 new unauthorized migrants continued to arrive each year.[7]

The U.S. stake in Mexico's continued political stability and economic development has increased dramatically since World War II. In recent years, Mexico has been one of the three largest trading partners of the United States (with Canada and Japan). Employment for hundreds of thousands of people in both Mexico and the United States depends on this trade. In 1982, when U.S. trade with Mexico fell by 32 percent because of Mexico's economic crisis, an estimated 250,000 U.S. jobs were lost. Largely because of the 1994 peso devaluation, which made Mexico's exports cheaper in the United States and U.S. products unaffordable to most Mexican consumers, the overall U.S. trade deficit soared to record levels in the first quarter of 1995.

Despite the sharp fluctuations in its economy since the early 1980s, Mexico is one of the preferred sites for investments by U.S.-based multinational corporations, especially for investments in modern industries (such as petrochemicals, pharmaceuticals, food processing, machinery, transportation, and athletic footwear). In recent years, 55 percent of total foreign direct investment in Mexico has come from the United States. Subsidiaries of U.S. companies produce half of the manufactured goods exported by Mexico. Firms in Mexico's own private sector have actively sought foreign capital to finance new joint ventures and expand plant facilities.

Mexico's external economic dependence is often cited by both critics and defenders of the Mexican system as an all-encompassing explanation for the country's problems. In fact, economic ties between Mexico and the United States usually explain only part of the picture. And these linkages do not necessarily predetermine the choices of policy and development priorities that are set by Mexico's rulers. But Mexico's increasingly tight linkage to the U.S. economy limits the range of choices that can be made by Mexican officials; and economic fluctuations in the United States are a large source of uncertainty in Mexico's planning and policymaking.

The international environment of Mexico's political system was transformed fundamentally by the signing of the North American Free Trade Agreement (NAFTA) in 1993. NAFTA made Mexico a much more attractive investment site for U.S. firms seeking low-cost labor and for Asian and European firms seeking privileged access to the U.S. market. While Carlos Salinas opposed such an agreement during his 1988 presidential campaign (because "there is such a different economic level between the U.S. and Mexico"), he soon found himself with no alternative to pursuing increased economic integration with the United States. With about one million new job seekers entering its labor force each year, Mexico desperately needed to increase its rate of economic growth. The only way to do that while containing inflation was to stimulate a massive new infusion of investment capital from abroad. By 1998, thanks to NAFTA, Mexico had surpassed Japan to become the United States' second most important trading partner (after Canada).

Less than a year after NAFTA was implemented, the implications of the much closer linkage between the U.S. and Mexican economies became painfully clear, when a new financial crisis erupted in Mexico. While there was virtually no political constituency within the United States for a U.S. government "bailout" of Mexico, and no enthusiasm among Mexicans for taking on more foreign loans and using the country's oil revenues to collateralize them (just one of the stringent conditions imposed by the United States), neither government had any realistic alternative to such a rescue. A Mexican default on repayment of nearly $30 billion in *tesobonos* (short-term bonds issued by the Mexican treasury) held mostly by U.S. pension funds, mutual funds, and other institutional investors would have threatened the assets of many millions of American households whose money had been invested in the high-yielding Mexican government bonds. Moreover, a meltdown of the Mexican economy could have caused a dramatic surge in illegal immigration to the United States. Consequently, a nearly $50 billion multilateral package of loan guarantees and credit line swaps—including $20 billion from a U.S. government currency stabilization fund—was made available to Mexico in January 1995.

The net macroeconomic impact of NAFTA has been positive for Mexico, as well as for the United States and Canada. However, NAFTA has not reduced the U.S.-Mexico income gap. GDP has risen in Mexico, but it has risen much faster in the United States (see Figure 11.3). Today, annual U.S. gross domestic product

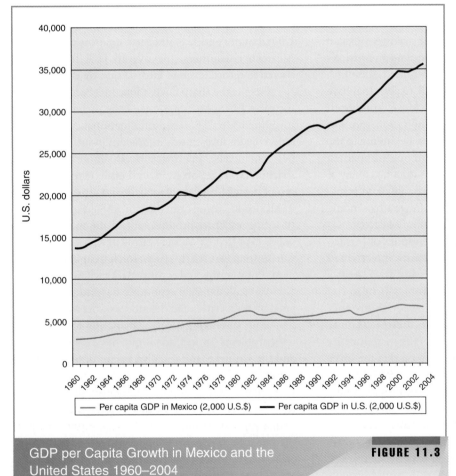

FIGURE 11.3

GDP per Capita Growth in Mexico and the United States 1960–2004

Source: Instituto Nacional de Estadística, Geografía e Informática, www.inegi.gob.mx, 2006.

(GDP) per capita is more than six times that of Mexico. If anything, NAFTA has increased illegal migration to the United States and made Mexico's economy more dependent on money remitted by its citizens working in the United States, who sent an estimated $24 billion home in 2006. NAFTA created jobs in Mexico's manufactured-export sector, but competition from cheaper U.S. imports has put millions of small farmers out of work, and the nonagricultural jobs that have been created under NAFTA do not pay enough to lift most Mexican families out of poverty.

POLITICAL CULTURE AND SOCIALIZATION

Most of what we know empirically about Mexican political culture is based on research completed during the period of sustained economic growth and virtually unchallenged one-party rule in Mexico, from 1940 through the mid-1970s. The portrait of Mexican political culture that emerges from these studies can be summarized as follows: Mexicans are highly supportive of the political institutions that evolved from the Mexican Revolution, and they endorse the democratic principles embodied in the Constitution of 1917. However, they are critical of government performance, especially in creating jobs, reducing social and economic inequality, fighting crime, and delivering basic public services. Most government bureaucrats and politicians are viewed as distant, elitist, and self-serving, if not corrupt. Mexicans traditionally have been pessimistic about their ability to affect election outcomes, anticipating fraud and regarding attendance at campaign rallies and voting as ritualistic activities.

On the surface, this combination of attitudes and beliefs seems internally contradictory. How could Mexicans support a political system that they see as unresponsive or capricious at best, in which they are mere "subjects" rather than true participants? Historically, popular support for the Mexican political system derived from three sources: the revolutionary origins of the regime, the government's role in promoting economic growth, and its performance in distributing concrete, material benefits to a substantial proportion of the Mexican population since the Cárdenas era. Each of these traditional sources of support has been undermined to some extent since 1976.

The official interpretation of the 1910 revolution stressed symbols (or myths), such as social justice, democracy, the need for national unity, and the popular origins of the current regime. The government's identification with these symbols was constantly reinforced by the mass media, public schools, and the mass organizations affiliated with the official party. Over the years, the party's electoral appeals were explicitly designed to link its candidates with agrarian reform and other revered ideals of the revolution, with national heroes like Emiliano Zapata and Lázaro Cárdenas, and with the national flag. (The PRI emblem conveniently has the same colors, in the same arrangement.) However, President Salinas broke decisively with so many tenets of "revolutionary ideology" (strict church-state separation, land reform, economic nationalism, etc.) that the PRI's claim to the revolutionary mantle became tenuous. Indeed, since the late 1980s, that mantle has been claimed by the PRD.

Relatively few Mexicans based their support for the system primarily on its revolutionary origins or symbolic outputs, however. For most sectors of the population, symbols were supplemented with particularistic material rewards: plots of land or titles to land that had been occupied illegally, schools, low-cost medical care, agricultural crop price supports, government-subsidized food and other consumer goods, and public sector jobs. For more than forty years, the personal receipt of some material "favor" from the official party-government apparatus, or the hope that such benefits might be received in the future, ensured fairly high levels of mass support for the system. Even now, Mexicans' concept of democracy emphasizes economic and social outputs rather than procedural liberties.[8]

In the 2006 election, many voters were attracted to PRD candidate López Obrador by his performance as Mexico City mayor, delivering high-visibility public works and monthly payments to senior citizens. PAN candidate Felipe Calderón promised to reduce social inequality through a major expansion of Oportunidades, a federal welfare program already benefiting 5 million low-income families. While not on a par with traditional vote-buying by the PRI—trading specific material payoffs for votes at the individual level—such campaign strategies clearly resonate with an electorate whose concept of democracy is still largely distributive.

Despite their growing distrust of key political institutions (especially Congress and the political parties), a plurality of Mexicans have remained "system loyalists." Indeed, Mexicans' pride in their country still seems rooted largely in their nation's political institutions. Survey data collected during the 1980s and 1990s consistently revealed the Mexican people's fundamental aversion to notions of radical transformation, especially if violence might result.[9] Nevertheless, most Mexicans today do not hesitate to criticize the way in which their government functions, and many more feel free to demonstrate their dissatisfaction by voting to throw the rascals out. In 1998, for example, the PAN lost control of the governorship of Chihuahua, partly because of the previous PANista governor's lackluster record in crime-fighting.

Historically, most Mexicans tolerated corruption in government as a price to be paid in order to extract benefits from the system or to deal with police harassment. But the unbridled corruption of the López Portillo and the Salinas administrations drastically reduced such tolerance, and an upsurge in drug-related corruption in the 1990s—reaching into the highest levels of the government bureaucracy and the national security apparatus—angered many Mexicans. They feared that their government had been taken over by "*narco-políticos*"—public officials in league with corrupt police and drug lords. The slowness of the Vicente Fox administration to root out government and police corruption, despite its independence from the structure of corruption created under PRI rule, was a source of public anger by the end of Fox's term.

Despite much more competition in the electoral system since the 1980s, the average Mexican remains relatively uninterested in politics. At the beginning of the bitterly fought presidential election campaign of 2006, two-thirds of the interviewees in a national survey expressed little or no interest in politics, and 55 percent said they rarely or never discussed politics with other people. These percentages are essentially unchanged since the 2000 presidential campaign.[10]

In the last two national elections, however, Mexicans have shown themselves to be sensitive to short-term campaign stimuli, such as presidential candidates' debates, negative television ads, and "straight news" media coverage. In fact, Mexicans appear more susceptible to persuasive campaign appeals than voters in the United States and other established democracies. Relatively more Mexicans change their party identification during the course of a campaign.[11] While such findings may indicate the absence of a core set of stable political beliefs, they reveal that Mexicans are paying close attention to the options provided by political competitors, at least during hard-fought national election campaigns.

Mass Political Socialization

How do Mexicans form their attitudes toward the political system? In addition to the family, the schools and the Catholic Church are important sources of preadult political learning. All schools, including church-affiliated and lay private schools, must follow a government-approved curriculum and use the same set of free textbooks, written by the federal Ministry of Education. Although the private schools' compliance with the official curriculum is often nominal, control over the content of textbooks gives the government an instrument for socializing children to a formal set of political values.

Under PRI rule, school-based political learning stressed the social and economic progress accomplished under postrevolutionary governments. The president was depicted as an omnipotent authority figure whose principal function is to maintain order in the country. Thus, despite the many egregious failures of presidential leadership that Mexicans have witnessed since the mid-1970s, many continue to express a preference for strong presidentialist government. However, mass public education has increased criticism of partisan politics and poor government performance. Higher levels of education are also associated with stronger support for the right to dissent and other democratic liberties.

The Catholic Church has been another key source of values affecting political behavior in Mexico. Church-run private schools have proliferated in recent decades. Along with secular private schools, they provide education for a large portion of children from middle- and upper-class families. Religious schools and priests have criticized anticlerical laws and policies, promoted individual initiative (as opposed to governmental action), and preached against abortion and gay marriage. They have also stressed the need for moral Christian behavior in public life.

As adults, Mexicans learn about politics from their personal encounters with government functionaries and the police. They also learn from participating in local community-based organizations and popular movements that seek collective benefits or redress of grievances from the government. There has been an impressive proliferation of popular movements in Mexico since 1968, when the student protest movement was violently repressed. The catalysts for this new wave of popular movements included gangsterism in government-affiliated labor unions, increasingly blatant PRI vote fraud in state and local elections during the 1980s, environmental disasters, and the implementation of neoliberal economic policies that adversely affected low- and middle-class segments of the society.

While most of these popular movements are quite localized in scope and concerns, a few have grown to embrace thousands of Mexicans in many different states. For example, the Civic Alliance—a coalition of hundreds of nongovernmental organizations, independent labor unions, and popular movements—has mobilized tens of thousands of Mexican citizens and hundreds of foreign observers to scrutinize the conduct of every national election since 1994 and publish reports on election irregularities. Nevertheless, nongovernmental organizations remain heavily concentrated in the Mexico City metropolitan area, where nearly 30 percent of the country's NGOs are registered. By contrast, the state of Chiapas hosts only 0.3 percent.

For seven decades, the PRI-government apparatus systematically used the mass media as an agent of political socialization. Although the government did not often directly censor the media, there were significant economic penalties for engaging in criticism or investigative reporting that seriously embarrassed the president. For example, government advertising—a major source of revenue for most newspapers and magazines—could be withheld from offending publications. The Salinas administration ended the longstanding practices of bribing reporters to get favorable treatment and threatening to cut off newsprint to troublesome periodicals.

Since the PRI lost control of the presidency in 2000, the mass media have been much more openly critical of government performance. Many newspapers and news magazines retain their PRI partisan bias and energetically criticize the president and other PANista officials. The independent media have kept up

their intense scrutiny of the executive branch and are also highly critical of what they see as incompetence and inefficiency in Congress.

The print media reach only a tiny fraction of the Mexican population (even the largest Mexico City newspapers have circulations under 100,000). Until recently, television was virtually monopolized by a huge private firm, Televisa, which had a notoriously close working relationship with the PRI-government apparatus and invariably defended the incumbent president's performance. One consequence of the Salinas administration's privatization program was the breakup of Televisa's virtual monopoly. A formerly government-owned television channel in Mexico City has grown quickly into a rival network, TV Azteca, and Televisa itself has adjusted to the competition by giving much more coverage to opposition voices. In 2006, Congress approved a bill that would end government discretion in the awarding of specific parts of the television broadcasting spectrum. The Interior Ministry had in the past used its control of these concessions to guarantee positive media treatment of the government. The television spectrum will now be auctioned off to the highest bidders. Opponents criticized this reform, claiming that it would exacerbate Televisa's monopoly because the corporation could often end up being the highest bidder. It has become a question of weighing pluralism in the government against pluralism in the market.

Moreover, electoral system reforms enacted in 1996 require the Federal Electoral Institute to systematically monitor campaign coverage by the national and local electronic media in order to determine whether they favor one party over another. These efforts have forced the media to act in a more balanced fashion. Consequently, exposure to the mass media no longer socializes the Mexican public to a particular set of political orientations sanctioned by incumbent authorities.

Political Participation

Traditionally, most political participation in Mexico has been of two broad types: (1) ritualistic, regime-supportive activities (for example, voting, attending campaign rallies); and (2) petitioning or contacting of public officials to influence the allocation of some public good or service. By law, voting is obligatory in

Mexico, though there are no civil penalties for not voting. Evidence of having voted in the most recent election has sometimes been required to receive public services. People participate in campaign rallies mostly because attending might have a specific material payoff (a free meal, a raffle ticket, a T-shirt), or because failure to do so could have personal economic costs. In the past, as they went to the polls, Mexicans knew that they were not selecting those who would govern but merely ratifying the choice of candidates made earlier by the PRI-government hierarchy. Some voted because they regarded it as their civic duty, others because they wished to avoid difficulty in future dealings with government agencies. Some voted in response to pressures from local *caciques* and PRI sector representatives. And some, especially in rural areas, freely sold their votes in return for handouts from local officials.

As elections have become moments of genuine political confrontation in most parts of Mexico, the ritualistic quality of voting and participating in campaign activities has diminished. Since 1994 Mexico has experienced an explosion in political participation,

evidenced not only by the virtually nonstop protests of citizens' movements of all types, but also by a sharp rise in turnout in federal elections. The turnout of registered voters rose from 49 percent in the 1988 presidential election, to 61 percent in the midterm 1991 elections, to 78 percent in the 1994 presidential election (see Figure 11.4). In the highly competitive 2006 presidential election, over 41,800,000 Mexicans cast their votes, a turnout rate of 59 percent. The total included 33,131 Mexicans abroad who were permitted to vote absentee in the presidential election for the first time.

Unfortunately, valid comparisons with electoral participation rates in the pre-1988 period are impossible, since the 1988 presidential election was the first for which reasonably accurate turnout figures were made public. In all previous national elections, the government inflated turnout statistics in an effort to convince Mexicans and the outside world that it had succeeded in relegitimating itself in impressive fashion.

The closeness of the 2006 presidential vote and the PRD's accusations of bias and manipulation temporarily damaged the credibility of the Federal

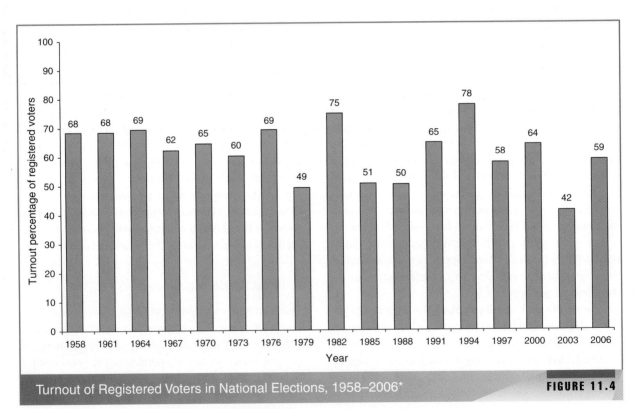

Turnout of Registered Voters in National Elections, 1958–2006*   **FIGURE 11.4**

*Beginning in 1970, the legal voting age was lowered from 21 to 18.

Sources: Data from Comisión Federal Electoral for 1958–1991; from Instituto Federal Electoral for 1994–2006.

Electoral Institute, but over half of the public interviewed in postelection surveys thought the vote count had been clean. As long as electoral politics remain as competitive as in the period since 1988, and potential voters continue to believe in the security of the electoral system, we can expect further, gradual movement toward a genuinely participant political culture in Mexico.

POLITICAL STRUCTURE AND INSTITUTIONS

Mexican politics has long defied easy classification. In the 1950s and 1960s some U.S. political scientists depicted the regime as a one-party democracy that was evolving toward "true" (North Atlantic–style) democracy. They recognized certain imperfections, but in the view of these analysts, political development in Mexico was simply incomplete. After the government's massacre of student protesters in 1968 and 1971, most analysts described the system as authoritarian, but even this characterization was subject to qualification.

By the 1990s, Mexico seemed to belong to a rapidly expanding category of hybrid, part-free, part-authoritarian systems that did not conform to classical typologies. Such labels as "selective democracy," "hard-line democracy," *democradura* (a Spanish contraction of "democracy" and "dictatorship"), and "modernizing authoritarian regime" have been applied to such systems. These are characterized by partly competitive (though not necessarily fair and honest) elections that install governments more committed to maintaining political stability and labor discipline than to expanding democratic freedoms, protecting human rights, or mediating class conflict.

Since the democratic breakthrough election of 2000, tolerance of undemocratic practices (for example, electoral fraud, selective repression of dissidents, and heavy-handed control of mass media) has declined dramatically. The functioning of all political institutions is scrutinized intensely, and they are held to much higher standards than ever before. The political design issue is no longer regime transition but how to improve democratic institutions already in place, especially to eliminate the structure of corruption that still supports abuses of authority and the electoral process at the local level in some parts of the country.

On paper, the Mexican government is structured much like the U.S. government: a presidential system, three autonomous branches of government (legislative, executive, and judicial) with checks and balances, and federalism with considerable autonomy at the local (municipal) level (see Figure 11.5). Until the late 1990s, however, Mexico's system of government was in practice far removed from the U.S. model. Decision making was highly centralized. The president, operating with relatively few restraints on his authority, completely dominated the legislative and judicial branches. Supreme Court justices were presidentially appointed and confirmed by a simple majority of the PRI-dominated Senate. Each incoming president replaced most justices, which made the judges agents of the executive branch. Until 1997, the ruling PRI continuously controlled both houses of the federal legislature. Opposition party members could criticize the government and its policies vociferously; but their objections to proposals initiated by the president and backed by his party in Congress rarely affected the final shape of legislation. Courts and legislatures at the state level normally mirrored the preferences of the state governors, many of whom themselves were handpicked by the incumbent president.

Until the late 1990s, the overwhelming majority of those elected to public office in Mexico were, in effect, political appointees—named to their positions by higher-ups within the PRI-government apparatus. Selection as a candidate of the PRI was tantamount to election, except in a handful of municipalities and congressional districts where opposition parties were so strong that they could not be ignored. Since reelection to office is prohibited at all levels of government, those elected on the PRI ticket were accountable and responsible not primarily to the people who elected them, but also to their political patrons within the regime. Nominating conventions—if held at all—were attended only by party activists, whose role was to ratify the choices made in private by officials at higher levels.

In 1988 the ruling party's control of the Congress was weakened significantly, setting the stage for a new era in executive-legislative relations. In that year's national elections, 66 PRI district-level candidates for seats in the lower house of Congress were defeated—nearly as many as the total of ruling party candidates defeated in all elections between 1946 and 1985. Between 1988 and 1991, the PRI was reduced to a bare

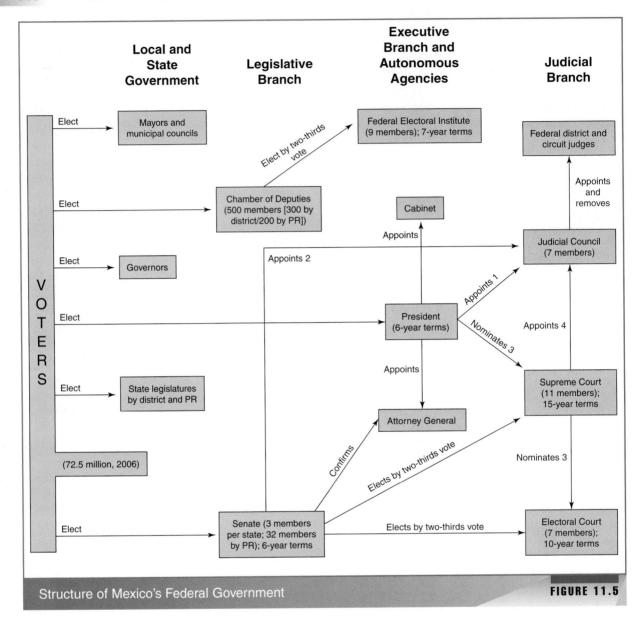

Structure of Mexico's Federal Government

FIGURE 11.5

working majority in the Chamber of Deputies (260 out of 500 seats), and for the first time since the ruling party was founded in 1929, opposition party candidates were elected to the Senate (four out of sixty-four seats). Because the PRI no longer commanded a two-thirds majority in the lower house, President Salinas had to negotiate with the opposition party delegations (he chose to deal mostly with the PAN) to secure passage of key legislation amending the Constitution.[12] Moreover, the Congress had ceased to function as a reliable instrument for internal distribution of power and its perks with the ruling

party. With the recognition of so many opposition victories for congressional seats in 1988, aspiring PRIistas had to face the reality that nomination by their party was no longer equivalent to election. The tradition of the *carro completo* (clean sweep) by PRI candidates had ended.

The electoral law reform of 1993 further transformed the Congress by greatly increasing the representation of opposition parties in the Senate. The Senate was doubled in size (the current rules call for three senators per state, plus thirty-two senators elected by proportional representation in a closed national list). The reforms guaranteed that the opposition parties, combined, would control at least one-third of the Senate seats, compared with less than 5 percent during the 1988–1993 period. The 1993 reforms also expanded the opposition parties' presence in the Chamber of Deputies, guaranteeing that no party could have more than 300 out of 500 seats.

As part of an overall strategy to broaden the base of support for his administration, President Zedillo offered to share power with the Congress in several key areas. He proposed congressional approval of all major judicial appointments as well as oversight of all federal spending by a new auditing agency under congressional control.

The Congress, including the PRI's delegation, responded to Zedillo's challenge. In March 1995, after some fifty PRI deputies threatened to vote against a key element of the government's postdevaluation austerity plan—an increase in the value-added tax, which is levied on virtually all goods and services, from 10 percent to 15 percent—Zedillo found it necessary to aggressively lobby the congressional leaders of his own party to secure approval of the much-despised tax increase. Only Zedillo's arm twisting, combined with PRIistas' fears that the president would begin working directly with the opposition party members if his own party split on this crucial vote, prevented a wholesale breakdown of party discipline. The tax increase, combined with voter resentment over the 1995–1996 recession, led to the PRI's "defeat" in the 1997 midterms, when the party won only 239 seats in the Chamber of Deputies—twelve short of a majority.

Since 1997, the government has lacked a majority in either or both chambers of Congress. President Vicente Fox had to lobby and negotiate with Congress on a routine basis to pass legislation, as will President Felipe Calderón. The era when Congress's sole functions were to serve as a debating arena for the opposition parties (and for factions within the ruling party until the whips were applied) and as a rubber stamp for decisions already taken by the president has clearly ended.

Federalism

Despite the federalist structure of government that is enshrined in the 1917 Constitution and legal codes, with their emphasis on the *municipio libre* (the concept of the free municipality, able to control its own

affairs), in practice the Mexican political system has usually functioned in a manner classified as **political centralism.**

From the 1920s through the Salinas presidency, the concentration of decision-making power at the federal level in most policy areas was continuous. Control over the preparation, conduct, and validation of elections—placed entirely at the municipal and state levels by the initial postrevolutionary electoral code, enacted in 1918—also passed to agencies that were part of the federal government apparatus or state-level entities controlled by federal authorities. A high degree of political centralism has been considered one of the main factors underlying Mexico's long-term political stability, although research at the state and local levels has demonstrated that political control by the center has been far less complete than is commonly assumed.[13]

Mexico is divided into thirty-one states and the Federal District, each one divided into *municipios*—politico-administrative units roughly equivalent in size and governmental functions to county governments in the United States. The *municipio* is governed by an *ayuntamiento*, or council, headed by a *presidente municipal* (mayor). Municipal officials are elected every three years. Each successive layer of government in Mexico is significantly weaker, less autonomous, and more impoverished than the levels above it. The federal government now controls about 90 percent of total public revenues—one of the highest degrees of fiscal centralization in Latin America.[14]

All of Mexico's seven most recent presidents entered office pledging to renew the "struggle against centralism," but serious efforts to decentralize have been made only since 1984. Under de la Madrid and Salinas, a limited form of revenue sharing was implemented, and the federal Constitution was amended to enhance the capacity of local governments to raise their own revenues. Partially successful efforts were also made to shift decision-making authority over public education and health care from the federal government to the states.[15] At the same time, the Salinas administration's National Solidarity Program (PRONASOL)—its principal social program, reaching into more than 95 percent of the country's 2,378 municipalities—was structured and administered to reinforce highly centralized presidential rule.

More assertively than any of his predecessors, President Zedillo vowed to reduce centralism. He went so far as to sign an agreement with the country's state governors and mayors calling for constitutional amendments that would provide the legal framework for "a new Mexican federalism." Zedillo promised a more equitable distribution of federal funds to the states and devolution of some functions that had been usurped by the federal government. But some federal ministries, especially the Treasury Department, have resisted further revenue sharing with municipal governments on the grounds that they lack the administrative capacity to make effective use of additional resources.

The state governors represent another potential obstacle to the "new federalism." The governors retain control over all resources transferred from the federal government, and effective administrative decentralization down to the municipio level would require them to relinquish a major portion of their political power—something that they have successfully resisted. It is clear that, even under a president strongly committed to redistributing resources and sharing power with subnational units of government, movement toward U.S.-style federalism in Mexico will meet with opposition from many different quarters, including federal government agencies and the states themselves.

The Legislative Branch

Mexico's political system has been commonly described as presidentialist or presidentially centered. Nonetheless, these characterizations were based on observed practices in a dominant-party regime, in which the institutional rules of the party had overwhelmed the formal constitutional rules. A careful examination of the Mexican Constitution reveals a president who is among the more constitutionally constrained in Latin America and a Congress with strong, sometimes dominant powers over the other branches of government. The difference between the informal and formal institutions is the history of the PRI government.

The federal Congress has two houses: a 128-member upper chamber, the Senate; and a 500-member lower house, the Chamber of Deputies. Both chambers employ a so-called mixed-member system in which some of the members are elected by plurality vote in single-member districts, while others are elected by a system of compensatory proportional representation on closed-party lists.[16] The current electoral rules for the Senate, dating to 1996, call for plurality elections in each of the thirty-two states whereby each party

nominates a slate of two Senate candidates. The party that wins a plurality elects both candidates from the slate to the Senate. The party that places second sends the first candidate on the list to the upper chamber. Furthermore, thirty-two senators are elected by proportional representation on closed national lists, so that each party that wins at least 2 percent of the national vote elects its proportional share of the thirty-two list senators. The rules prevent any party from winning more than two-thirds of the seats in the Senate except under extraordinary circumstances (a party would have to place first in every state and win more than two-thirds of the national vote).

For the Chamber of Deputies, 300 members are elected by plurality in single-member districts, and an additional 200 deputies are elected by proportional representation in five regional closed lists. Each party that wins at least 2 percent of the national vote is entitled to its proportional share of the list deputies with a few restrictions. First, no party can ever have more than 300 total seats, which restricts the largest party to less than the two-thirds majority required for constitutional reforms. Second, no party's share of the total number of seats can exceed by more than 8 percent its share of the national vote. This means that in order to win a majority in the lower chamber, a party must win more than 42 percent of the vote and a sufficient margin of victory over the second-place party (usually around four percentage points) to win enough districts.

The mixed-member system directly affects the party system. Usually, plurality systems lead to two-party systems, as the voters find that it is better to coordinate their votes toward one of the two leading parties rather than waste them on third-party candidates. Proportional representation systems tend to create multiparty systems, because votes for the larger minority parties are not wasted. In Mexico, the mixed-member system has yielded a three-party system, in which most regions now have two-party systems (respecting the tendencies of the plurality system) but nationally the vote is split into three main blocs. The three parties with significant representation in the Mexican Congress in the 60th Legislature (2006–2009) are the PAN (with 41 percent of the seats), the PRD (with 25 percent), and the PRI (with 21 percent). The low threshold allows small parties to attain representation in the Chamber of Deputies, as well: five small parties won seats in the 60th Legislature (see Table 11.2).

	Seats Won by Plurality Vote	Seats Won by P. R. System	Total	Percentage
Chamber of Deputies				
Partido Acción Nacional (PAN)	137	69	206	41.2
Partido de la Revolución Democrática (PRD)[1]	90	36	126	25.2
Partido Revolucionario Institucional (PRI)[2]	63	41	104	20.8
Partido Verde Ecologista de México (PVEM)[2]	2	17	19	3.8
Convergencia[1]	5	11	16	3.2
Partido del Trabajo (PT)[1]	3	13	16	3.2
Nueva Alianza	0	9	9	1.8
PASC	0	4	4	0.8
Total	300	200	500	100
Senate				
Partido Acción Nacional (PAN)	41	11	52	40.6
Partido Revolucionario Institucional (PRI)[2]	27	6	33	25.8
Partido de la Revolución Democrática (PRD)[1]	23	6	29	22.7
Partido Verde Ecologista de México (PVEM)[2]	2	4	6	4.7
Convergencia[1]	3	2	5	3.9
Partido del Trabajo (PT)[1]	0	2	2	1.6
Nueva Alianza	0	1	1	0.8
Total	96	32	128	100

Composition of the Mexican Congress, 2006–2009 — TABLE 11.2

[1]Alianza por el Bien de Todos
[2]Alianza por México

Source: Instituto Federal Electoral (http://www.ife.org.mx), 2006.

The mixed-member system complicates creating majorities in either chamber. Since the 8-percent rule on maximum overrepresentation was established in the lower house, no party has been able to achieve a majority. The Senate rules went into effect fully for the first time in the 2000 elections. Now, when the race is close between the first- and second-place parties, it is also unlikely that a majority party will emerge in the Senate. This means that the party of the president will rarely have a majority in Congress, thus creating a situation of divided government.

Like the U.S. Constitution, the 1917 Mexican Constitution lists the legislative branch first. The Congress is primarily responsible for enacting nearly all public policy, with only a few exceptions. The president has constitutional decree powers only over questions of land reform (expropriation decrees) and tariffs and quotas in international trade (in which he can unilaterally adjust tariffs and quotas if the circumstances call for modifications). All regular legislation must be approved by both chambers in the same form, and then submitted to the president for publication. The president must publish the bill within ten days or return the bill to the chamber of origin (see Box 11.2).

A presidential veto can take two forms: one is a regular veto, in which the president expresses his rejection of a bill; the second is a corrective veto, in which the president requests that Congress amend the bill, usually because of technical errors in the text. In either case, Congress can insist on the original text of the bill by a two-thirds vote, after which the president must publish the legislation. In case of corrective vetoes, Congress often modifies the bill as requested and sends it back to the president for promulgation.

Each of the two chambers has exclusive powers and areas of specialization. The Chamber of Deputies specializes in fiscal legislation. All revenue bills must originate in the lower chamber. The Chamber of Deputies first approves the revenue and tax legislation, sending it to the upper chamber for Senate approval.

BOX 11.2

How a Bill Becomes a Law in Mexico

- Bills can be introduced by federal deputies, senators, the president, or the state legislatures. All revenue bills, regardless of the sponsor, must be introduced in the Chamber of Deputies. Therefore, the president's annual economic package is sent to the Chamber of Deputies. However, senators can introduce revenue legislation directly in the Chamber of Deputies. All other legislation can begin in either the Chamber of Deputies or the Senate. The federal bureaucracy assists the president in preparing executive bills for introduction.

- All bills are sent to committees. There are twenty-nine committees in the Chamber of Deputies and thirty in the Senate. Committees amend most legislation before reporting it to the floor (87 percent in the Chamber of Deputies, and 75 percent in the Senate). The federal bureaucracy often sends commentary on pending legislation to the relevant committees. The legislators are not required to heed these opinions.

- All legislation reported by committee is voted on the floor. The chamber can amend legislation from committees, but only 34 percent of the legislation is amended on the floor in the Chamber of Deputies, and only 24 percent on the floor of the Senate. If a bill is approved by the first chamber, it is sent to the other chamber for approval.

- In the second chamber, bills are sent to committee. Routine legislation is usually reported to the floor without amendment. Important bills are usually amended in committee. If the second chamber approves the bill on the floor without amendment, it is sent to the president; if the bill is amended, it is sent back to the first chamber for approval. Bills can be considered twice by each chamber before a final version is settled on.

- The president must sign or veto a bill within ten days, unless Congress has ended its session. In those cases, the president must dispatch the bills before the next session begins. The federal bureaucracy usually makes recommendations to the president on whether to sign or veto a bill. If the president vetoes a bill, it is sent to the first chamber for reconsideration. If the first chamber rejects the veto by a two-thirds vote, it is sent to the other chamber. If the second chamber also rejects the veto by a two-thirds vote, the president must publish the law. The president also has a corrective veto, in which he can return a bill to the first chamber, suggesting amendments. Each chamber may accept these amendments by a majority vote, or reject the amendments by a two-thirds vote.

- The annual appropriations bill is considered by only the Chamber of Deputies. The president sends the appropriations bill to the chamber by September 8. The chamber must approve the bill, with or without amendments, by November 15, sending the bill back to the president. If the president vetoes the bill, the Chamber of Deputies can accept his suggestions by a majority vote or reject them by a two-thirds vote. The Senate never considers appropriations.

However, only the Chamber of Deputies approves the appropriations legislation. This gives the Chamber of Deputies extraordinary influence over the federal public administration. Likewise, the lower chamber has exclusive powers over budgetary oversight and approves the public accounts.

The Senate has exclusive power to oversee foreign affairs. The Mexican president is supposed to conduct foreign relations under seven constitutionally specified doctrines: self-determination, nonintervention, the peaceful solution of conflicts, the prohibition on the international use of force, legal equality among countries, international cooperation toward development,

and the pursuit of peace and international security. The upper chamber has the power to monitor foreign affairs, and it approves treaties submitted by the president by a majority vote. Jointly with the Chamber of Deputies, the Senate must approve all foreign travel by the president. If the Congress does not approve of the executive's foreign policy, the president would be unable to conduct foreign affairs outside of Mexico's borders.

The Senate also has the power to remove state governors and depose state legislatures. The Constitution allows the Senate to topple state governments when it recognizes that the state can no longer provide for domestic security. This requires a vote of the upper chamber; afterwards, the president proposes a list of three candidates from which the Senate elects the interim governor by a two-thirds vote. Prompted by PRI presidents, the Senate deposed many governors during the twentieth century, though usually for political reasons rather than for security motives. The Senate also regulates pacts between the federal and state governments concerning revenue-sharing and program administration.

Federal deputies and senators have shown extraordinary levels of party discipline in recent years. For example, during the last two years of the 57th Legislature (1997–2000), on average 99.6 percent of the PRIista deputies voted together on party bills. Party cohesion for the PANista deputies in the 57th Legislature was about 92 percent, and for PRDista deputies, 93 percent. During the 58th Legislature (2000–2003), cohesion among PAN deputies increased to 94 percent, and hit 98.4 percent during the 59th (2003–2006), nearly equaling the levels of PRI discipline when it held the presidency. Meanwhile, PRI discipline declined to 90 percent during the first two terms in which it did not control the executive branch (see Table 11.3).

High party discipline in Mexico has two main sources.[17] First, consecutive reelection for deputies and senators is prohibited. This nearly eliminates accountability of the representatives to their constituents. Voters can neither reward their legislators for good performance nor punish them for bad representation. Since federal legislators are not required to seek cues from their electorate, they look elsewhere for guidance, and the party leadership is more than willing to provide it. Second, nomination procedures in each of the parties are relatively closed. The leadership traditionally has selected candidates directly in the PRI and the PRD, while PANista candidates are nominated in closed (but often competitive) conventions of party activists. This further focuses the legislators on party leadership, because without the support of the party elite their political futures would be dismal.

Each party generally votes as a bloc in Congress, which creates incentives for the leaders of each of the parties to negotiate bills among themselves rather than allow the rank-and-file members to work out compromises in committee. Other rules of Congress grant extensive authority to the coordinators of the parties (such as the power to assign members to committees and dole out office space and expense accounts to the deputies). Together, these institutions create a highly centralized legislative branch. When the president was recognized as the natural leader of the majority party in the Congress, the centralized tendencies in that branch allowed him to rule as a near dictator without changing any constitutional norms.

The Executive Branch

Despite the constitutionally limited powers of the executive branch, no one would dispute that the president was the dominant political actor in Mexico for the greater part of the twentieth century. In addition to his rather modest constitutional powers, the

		PRI	PAN	PRD	PVEM	PT
57th Legislature	Mean	99.6	92.2	92.8	97.5	88.9
(1997–2000)	s.d.	1.3	12.6	13.9	8.0	16.4
58th Legislature	Mean	90.0	94.3	91.5	95.8	97.3
(2000–2003)	s.d.	13.3	12.6	15.5	9.3	9.7
59th Legislature	Mean	90.5	98.4	95.2	96.4	96.7
(2003–2006)	s.d.	11.9	6.1	9.2	9.8	11.2

TABLE 11.3

Party Cohesion in the Chamber of Deputies: Party Votes, 1998–2006 (percentages)

Note: Data for the 57th Legislature begins October 8, 1998. Party votes are roll calls in which at least one party dissented from the rest. Party cohesion is the percentage of the party voting with the majority of that party; "s.d." is the standard deviation.

Source: For the 57th Legislature, Jeffrey A. Weldon, "Institutional and Political Factors in Party Discipline in the Chamber of Deputies, 1998–2002," presented at the First Latin American Political Science Congress, Salamanca, Spain, July 2002. Data for the last two legislatures calculated by Weldon. From the *Diario de los Debates* and *Gaceta Parlamentaria* of both Chambers.

Mexican president possessed a broad range of unwritten but generally recognized "metaconstitutional" powers that traditionally ensured his dominance over all of the country's other political institutions.[18] Mexicans use the term *presidencialismo* to connote this extraordinary concentration of powers, formal and informal, in the hands of the president, and the implication that incumbents frequently abuse these powers in pursuit of personal and political ends.

On any issue of national political significance, the federal judiciary would take its cue from the incumbent president. Until very recently, the Supreme Court never found presidential decisions or legislation enacted at the behest of the president to be unconstitutional, and Congress never challenged presidential appointments to the federal judiciary. The president had the informal power to seat and unseat state governors, mayors, and members of Congress. For example, during President Salinas's term, seventeen state governors resigned, most under pressure from Los Pinos (the residence of the Mexican president). From 1929 through 1994, the president also functioned as the "supreme head" of the official party, choosing its leaders, dictating his legislative proposals to the PRI delegation in Congress, shaping the party's internal governance, imposing his personal choices for the PRI's gubernatorial and congressional candidates, and—most importantly—controlling the selection of the party's next presidential nominee.

The absence of a rigid, fully elaborated political ideology made it possible for a Mexican president to have a pragmatic, flexible program and style of governance. The so-called ideology of the Mexican Revolution was never more than a loosely connected set of goals or symbols. The only "revolutionary" ideology that has been scrupulously observed is the constitutionally mandated no-reelection principle for the presidency: the president is limited to a single six-year term.[19]

During the PRI's seven decades of rule at the national level, three factors were required to create strong presidentialism.[20] First, the president's party had to have a majority in both chambers of Congress. Under **divided government,** the opposition majorities in Congress are unlikely to follow the dictates of the president. Second, there must be high levels of discipline in the majority party of Congress. This was achieved by the mechanisms described earlier. If there is insufficient discipline, the Mexican president would look more like most U.S. presidents, because the members of Congress act as free agents. Third, the president must be considered the leader of his party. In the 1930s, the first two factors were in place, but the leader of the party, Plutarco Elías Calles, received all of the benefits of the disciplined party, not the president. After Cárdenas reorganized the official party along lines of authority that led directly to himself, strong *presidencialismo* was finally achieved.

All three key ingredients of strong presidentialism were generally in place from 1946 to 1994. Even a bare 52-percent PRI majority in the 54th Legislature (1988–1991) was sufficient to maintain a strong presidency for Salinas. His successor, Ernesto Zedillo, adhered to a very different model of presidential leadership. Most importantly, Zedillo refused to assume the president's traditional role as leader of the PRI. He publicly pledged to refrain from interfering in internal party matters, including candidate selection. He also assured that, unlike his predecessors, he would not involve himself in adjudicating disputed elections, thereby serving notice to the PRI that the president could no longer be relied on to be the ultimate guarantor of the party's electoral victories.

The most important test of Zedillo's resolve to recast the institution of the presidency came as his term was ending. Tradition dictated that, at that point, he would exercise his metaconstitutional power as incumbent president to select his own successor, with minimal input from other key actors in the ruling coalition. (In September 1990, Luis Echeverría became the first former president to publicly acknowledge this crucially important, unwritten rule of the Mexican political system.) In the presidential succession of 2000, PRI leaders—with President Zedillo's blessing—opted to hold a nationwide primary election in November 1999 to determine the party's 2000 presidential candidate. Four veteran PRI politicians entered the race, campaigned actively for the nomination, and debated each other on national television. The winning candidate, Francisco Labastida, was widely considered to be Zedillo's favorite. The primary was considered a great success by the media and the party, and after some counseling from the president, the losers accepted defeat. However, seven months after the first open PRI primary for the presidency, the PRI candidate himself had to accept defeat in the general election.

In the 2006 succession, the outgoing president had even less influence. The PAN maintained some distance between itself and the presidency during the entire Fox administration, and the president had no influence in the selection of PANista candidates for state or congressional offices. Vicente Fox's preferred candidate for the PAN's 2006 presidential nomination was soundly defeated in the party's primary elections by Felipe Calderón, who during his campaign criticized errors of political management by the Fox team.

Executive-Legislative Relations

The dynamics of executive-legislative relations in Mexico used to be determined by the metaconstitutional powers of the president. The operation of the three key factors outlined earlier—unified government, high party discipline in the ruling party, and the recognition of the president as the de facto head of the party—explained a compliant Congress. Today, now that the first and third factors no longer hold, executive-legislative relations follow constitutional rather than partisan norms, and Mexico either enjoys or suffers from the everyday republican conflicts of separation of powers.

Comparing the levels of productivity of the last six legislatures allows us to evaluate the executive's influence over the legislative branch under varying conditions of the metaconstitutional conditions listed earlier, as well as the relative strength of the president's party in the lower chamber (see Table 11.4). During the 54th Legislature (1988–1991), the first half of the Salinas presidency, the PRI held a small majority of 52 percent of the lower chamber. Despite the marginal majority, 98.6 percent of the executive's public bills were approved. Of the 110 bills approved during the 54th Legislature, nearly two-thirds had originated in the executive branch. The 55th Legislature (1991–1994) gave the PRI and Salinas a large majority in the Chamber of Deputies, around 63 percent. Again, 98.5 percent of the president's public bills were approved. More than three out of every five bills that were eventually approved in the lower chamber had been introduced by the executive. During both legislatures, the three conditions for metaconstitutional power were strongly in place.

During the 56th Legislature (1994–1997), the first half of President Zedillo's term, the president was no longer functioning as de facto leader of his party: Zedillo had promised to keep a healthy distance between himself and the PRI. Nevertheless, the lower chamber approved 98.9 percent of his bills, thanks to the three-fifths majority held by the ruling party. Nearly three-quarters of all of the bills approved by the chamber had originated in the executive branch. Although the president had claimed that he was no longer interested in being the head of the PRI, it appears that the party was not yet listening.

In the 57th Legislature (1997–2000), divided government prevailed for the first time since 1928. The PRI held just under 48 percent of the seats in the lower chamber, while the PAN and the PRD each had about a quarter of the seats. Thus, the first of the conditions for metaconstitutional power—unified government—was eliminated. Under divided government, 90 percent of the president's bills were approved—a decline of nine percentage points from the previous legislature. In fact, two executive-introduced bills were defeated: the revenue law for 1998 (a substitute bill was subsequently approved) and a bank bailout bill. Since 1928, a majority of the bills that the Chamber of Deputies approved had originated in the executive branch. In the 57th Legislature, this trend was abruptly reversed: only 31 percent of the bills approved in the term had been introduced by the executive, while nearly 60 percent had been sponsored by deputies.

By the time that the 58th Legislature had convened in 2000, metaconstitutional presidentialism had ended. The first condition—unified government—remained unfulfilled. President Fox's PAN held only 41 percent of the seats in the lower chamber. Nor was Fox treated as the head of his party. The PAN delegation occasionally voted against the preferences of the president, as they did in 2001 when they opposed allowing representatives of the Zapatista rebels to speak from the podium of the Chamber of Deputies. Nearly 90 percent of Fox's bills were approved during the 2000–2003 term, an achievement no different from Zedillo's under divided government. However, nearly every bill that Fox had sent to Congress had been extensively amended in at least one of the chambers. Never before has a higher percentage of executive bills been amended, either in committee or on the floor.

In the 2003 midterm election, the PRI ended up with nearly 45 percent of the seats, while the PAN won only 30 percent. The PRD also increased its size in the lower chamber, winning nearly one-fifth of the seats, mostly due to district victories in the Federal District.

| Sponsorship and Approval of Public Bills in the Chamber of Deputies, 1988–2006 | | | | | TABLE 11.4 |

Legislature	% of Deputies from President's Party	Sponsor*	% of Total New Bills Introduced	% of Total Bills Approved	% of Sponsor's Bills Approved
54th (1988–1991)	52	Executive	22.8	65.1	98.6
		Deputies	77.2	34.9	15.6
		Other	0.0	0.0	—
		Total	100.0	100.0	34.5
55th (1991–1994)	63	Executive	42.4	62.6	98.5
		Deputies	56.3	36.5	38.5
		Other	1.3	0.9	50.0
		Total	100.0	100.0	50.0
56th (1994–1997)	60	Executive	33.8	74.2	98.9
		Deputies	61.7	24.2	16.2
		Other	4.5	1.7	16.7
		Total	100.0	100.0	42.7
57th (1997–2000)	48	Executive	10.1	31.0	90.0
		Deputies	81.9	59.6	20.8
		Other	7.9	9.4	32.2
		Total	100.0	100.0	28.6
58th (2000–2003)	41	Executive	6.8	23.7	89.9
		Deputies	77.3	57.7	18.4
		Other	15.8	18.6	30.0
		Total	100.0	100.0	24.9
59th (2003–2006)	30	Executive	2.8	8.6	73.2
		Deputies	85.8	72.0	19.6
		Other	11.4	19.4	38.0
		Total	100.0	100.0	23.3

*"Other" includes bills introduced by state legislatures, revenue bills presented in the lower chamber by senators, and bills that originated in the Senate that had been introduced there by senators. Executive bills that originated in the Senate are classified under the "Executive" category.

Source: *Diario de los Debates* and the *Gaceta Parlamentaria* of the Chamber of Deputies. Data compiled at ITAM under the direction of Jeffrey Weldon.

During the 59th Legislature (2003–2006), only 73.2 percent of the president's bills were approved, and a mere 8.6 percent of the bills approved by the Chamber of Deputies originated in the executive branch. However, overall productivity in the lower chamber reached an all-time high. The deputies approved more bills than any previous legislature, more than doubling the record set in 1937–1940 during the Cárdenas reform era.

Mexico's first "opposition" president had difficult relations with a Congress in which the opposition parties—when united—had majority control. In March 2001, Fox introduced a major tax reform that would have placed a 15-percent value-added tax (VAT) on food, medicines, books, and private school tuition. Opposition legislators in the Chamber of Deputies, led by the PRI and the PRD, strongly opposed this provision, and the PAN deputies were reluctant to join what appeared to be a lost cause in support of their president. After several months of intense debate, the VAT proposal was killed and replaced by a 5-percent excise tax on certain "luxury" goods, which failed to raise much revenue and was later abandoned. In April 2002, with the PRI and PRD members again leading the pack, the Senate denied Fox permission to make a trip to several U.S. and Canadian cities, to demonstrate its opposition to various elements of his foreign policy. The trip was cancelled.

Executive-legislative relations worsened during the second half of Fox's term. The proposal to raise the VAT was reintroduced in the fall of 2003, but the Chamber of Deputies narrowly defeated the bill on the floor. Later, the lower chamber rejected Fox's request to receive a medal from the United Nations Food and Agriculture Organization, demonstrating opposition to his agricultural policies. This was the first time that congressional authorization for an international or foreign medal had been denied to the president.

In the fall 2004 term, the opposition coalition in the Chamber of Deputies amended Fox's revenue bill, increasing dependence on oil sources as a part of expected federal revenue and raising the deficit target. The opposition also modified considerably the federal appropriations bill, decreasing or eliminating a number of federal programs and increasing pork-barrel expenditures for PRI and PRD states. Fox vetoed the appropriations bill; this was the first budget veto cast by a president since 1933. The Chamber of Deputies disputed the veto by filing a suit in the Supreme Court, claiming that the president did not have the constitutional power to veto the budget (despite the fact that there had been forty-five vetoes of the budget between 1917 and 1933, none of which had been challenged on constitutional grounds by Congress). The Supreme Court suspended the expenditures to which the president had objected, and later ruled that the budget veto was indeed constitutional. Such tests of will between the executive and legislative branches are increasingly common in Mexico's era of divided government, with the judicial branch assuming an increasingly important role as arbiter between the two branches.

In the 2006–2009 term, Congress will again lack a majority for any party. In his campaign, Felipe Calderón pledged to form a coalition government in which positions in the president's cabinet would be awarded to opposition parties in return for legislative support in the Congress. With his party holding only a plurality of seats in each house (41 percent in the Chamber of Deputies and 40.6 percent in the Senate), Calderón will need the support of other parties to pass legislation. After the election, Calderón promoted the idea of a coalition government, with the intention of including members of other parties in his cabinet to commit their parliamentary groups to support his legislative agenda. However, the opposition parties declined to participate in his administration.

RECRUITING THE POLITICAL ELITE

What kinds of people gain entry into Mexico's national political elite, and who makes it to the top? At least since the days of the Porfiriato, the Mexican political elite has been recruited predominantly from the middle class. The 1910 revolution did not open up the political elite to large numbers of people from peasant or urban laborer backgrounds. That opening occurred only in the 1930s, during the Cárdenas **sexenio (six-year term),** and then mainly at the local and state levels rather than the national elite level. By 1989, only 8.3 percent of all state governors, senators, cabinet, and subcabinet members had peasant or working-class origins; in a sample of 1,113 federal government bureaucrats, only 0.7 percent said that their fathers were peasants while 0.9 percent described them as workers.[21]

In the last three PRI-dominated administrations (1982–2000), the national political elite was drawn heavily from the ranks of *capitalinos*—people born or raised in Mexico City. By the 1980s more than half of the presidential cabinet had been born in Mexico City and an even higher percentage had been raised there.[22] Postgraduate education, especially at elite foreign universities and in disciplines like economics and public administration, became much more important as a ticket of entry into the national political elite. Over half of the cabinet members appointed by Presidents de la Madrid, Salinas, and Zedillo had studied economics or public administration, and over half of those who received training in these subjects at the graduate level did so in the United States. The economic cabinets of these three presidents were filled with recipients of Ph.D.s from universities such as Harvard, MIT, Stanford, Yale, and the University of Chicago. Typically, the PRIista *técnicos* (technocrats) spent their entire career within the government bureaucracy, especially the financial and planning agencies, never engaging in partisan politics. The economic policy debacles presided over by technocrat presidents and cabinet ministers in the 1990s discredited this breed of

Mexican officials in the eyes of the public as well as the party leaderships. Significantly, a national PRI assembly in 1996 removed most technocrats from the line of presidential succession by requiring the party's future presidential nominees to have previously held elective office.

Relatively few card-carrying technocrats found their way into the cabinet of Vicente Fox, who favored persons with nongovernmental experience, a bachelor's or master's degree in business administration, educated in Mexico—like himself. Nearly half (45 percent) of Fox's top fifty-two appointees—many of them recruited through professional head-hunting firms—had no previous public-sector experience. The involvement of persons with private-sector experience in the Fox administration (46 percent) was far greater than in any of the PRI governments since 1929. Fox also broke with his PRI predecessors in recruiting more top officials from outside of Mexico City (60 percent of his top officials were from the provinces), and more who had received their undergraduate education in private rather than public universities (54 percent).

Most strikingly, 75 percent of Fox's original top fifty-two appointees had no known political party affiliation. Fewer than one-fifth were recruited from the PAN.[23] Only four members of Fox's original cabinet had a history of militancy in the PAN, and the dearth of card-carrying PANistas was even more conspicuous at the subcabinet level. Some ministries were nearly devoid of PANistas.

Fox's reluctance to call on experienced PAN partisans until late in his term was consistent with his "independent" campaign for the presidency—not dependent on the PAN apparatus and even opposed by significant segments of it—and with his professed insistence on building a team of the "best and brightest" managers, regardless of partisanship. But Fox's extreme distancing from his own party in staffing his administration contributed to tense relations with the PAN's congressional delegation and made it more difficult for him to achieve some policy goals. During the second half of the Fox *sexenio,* the president increased substantially the number of PANistas in his cabinet, and party loyalty to the president in Congress consequently improved.

In terms of professional background, Fox's successor, Felipe Calderón, is something of a throwback to the late technocratic PRI presidents. Calderón earned Master's degrees in economics and public administration (the latter from Harvard University's Kennedy School of Government). However, in contrast to the last five PRI presidents, Calderón also had extensive experience in party politics and elective office. He was twice elected to a seat in Congress and once to the legislative body of Mexico City, and like the other two major presidential candidates in 2006, Calderón also served as his party's national chairman. He later served as director of BANOBRAS, a federal development bank, and as Secretary of Energy in Fox's cabinet. Calderón's own economic cabinet is dominated by technocrats holding doctoral degrees from U.S. universities, including Chicago, Columbia, MIT, and the University of Pennsylvania.

Since the 1970s, kinship ties have become more important as a common denominator of those who attain top positions of political power. Increasingly, such people are born into politically prominent families that have already produced state governors, cabinet ministers, federal legislators, and even presidents. Two of the three major presidential candidates in 2006 exemplify this pattern. Felipe Calderón's father was one of the founders of the PAN; Roberto Madrazo's father had been national chairman of the PRI. Only López Obrador was not born into a politically influential family.

These political families are increasingly interconnected: At least one-third of the government officials and politicians interviewed by one researcher for several books on the Mexican political elite were related to other officials, not counting those related through marriage and the traditional rite of *compadrazgo* (becoming a godparent to a friend's child).[24] Family connections can give an aspiring political leader a powerful advantage over rivals.

The growing importance of kinship ties and other indicators of increasing homogeneity in personal backgrounds causes some observers to worry that Mexico's political elite is becoming more closed and inbred. While its social base may indeed be narrowing, the modern Mexican political elite still shows considerable fluidity; the massive turnover of officeholders every six years is proof of that. This factor helps to explain why in Mexico—unlike other postrevolutionary countries, such as China and (until recently) the Soviet Union—the regime did not become a gerontocracy. In fact, the median age of cabinet members and presidential aspirants in Mexico has been dropping; in recent *sexenios,* most have been in their late 30s or early 40s. Exemplifying this trend, Felipe Calderón was 44 years old when elected to the presidency.

INTEREST REPRESENTATION
AND POLITICAL CONTROL

In Mexico's presidentialist system, important public policies used to be initiated and shaped by the inner circle of presidential advisers before they were even presented for public discussion. Thus, most effective interest representation took place within the upper levels of the federal bureaucracy. The structures that aggregate and articulate interests in Western democracies (the ruling political party, labor unions, and so on) actually served other purposes in the Mexican system: limiting the scope of citizens' demands on the government, mobilizing electoral support for the regime, helping to legitimate it in the eyes of other countries, distributing jobs and other material rewards to select individuals and groups. For example, the PRI typically had no independent influence on public policymaking; nor did the opposition parties, except where they controlled state or local governments.

From the late 1930s until the PRI's defeat in 2000, Mexico had a **corporatist** system of interest representation in which each citizen and societal segment was expected to relate to the state through a single structure "licensed" by the state to organize and represent that sector of society (peasants, urban unionized workers, businesspeople, teachers, and so on). The official party itself was divided into three **sectors**: (1) the Labor Sector, (2) the Peasant Sector, and (3) the Popular Sector, a catch-all category representing various segments of the middle class (government employees, other white-collar workers, small merchants, private landowners) and residents of low-income urban neighborhoods. Each sector in the PRI is dominated by one mass organization; other organizations are affiliated with each party sector, but their influence is dwarfed by that of the "peak" organization. Thus, the **Confederación de Trabajadores de México (CTM)** has dominated the Labor Sector; the **Confederación Nacional Campesina (CNC)** the Peasant Sector; and the **Confederación Nacional de Organizaciones Populares (CNOP)** the Popular Sector.

A number of powerful organized interest groups—foreign and domestic entrepreneurs, the military, the Catholic Church—were not formally represented in the PRI. These groups often dealt directly with the government elite, often at the presidential or cabinet level. They did not need the PRI to make their preferences known. They also had well-placed representatives within the

executive branch who could be counted on to articulate their interests. In addition, the business community was organized into several government-chartered confederations. Since the Cárdenas administration, all but a small minority of the country's industrialists were required by law to join one of these employers' organizations, which channeled business interests into a few, well-controlled outlets. These confederations still exist, but the Supreme Court ruled in 1999 that compulsory membership was an unconstitutional restriction on the freedom of association.

Because the ruling party and the national legislature did not effectively aggregate interests in the Mexican system, individuals and groups seeking something from the government often circumvented their nominal representatives in the PRI sectoral organizations and the Congress, and sought satisfaction of their needs through personal contacts within the government bureaucracy. These **patron-client relationships** compartmentalized the society into discrete, noninteracting, vertical segments that served as pillars of the regime. Within the lower class, for example, unionized urban workers were separated from nonunion urban workers; *ejidatarios* from small private landholders and landless agricultural workers. The middle class was compartmentalized into government bureaucrats, educators, health care professionals, lawyers, economists, and so forth. Thus competition among social classes was replaced by highly fragmented competition within classes.

The articulation of interests through patron-client networks assisted the PRI regime by fragmenting popular demands into small-scale, highly individualized or localized requests that could be granted or denied case by case. Officials were rarely confronted with collective demands from broad social groupings. Rather than having to act on a request from a whole category of people (slum dwellers, *ejidatarios,* teachers), they had easier, less costly choices to make (as between competing petitions from several neighborhoods for a paved street or a piped water system). The clientelistic structure thus provided a mechanism for distributing public services and other benefits in a highly selective, discretionary if not always arbitrary manner. This system put the onus on potential beneficiaries to identify and cultivate the "right" patrons within the government bureaucracy. The prohibition on consecutive reelection prevented local elected officials from taking on the role of patron. As they could be neither punished nor rewarded for their performance, elected politicians abdicated this responsibility, and it was only natural that the bureaucracy would replace them in the role of patron.

After the dismal performance of the sectoral organizations in delivering votes to Carlos Salinas in the 1988 presidential election, the dysfunctional nature of the corporatist system of interest representation became a matter of urgent concern for the government elite. Salinas and PRI leaders chose to deemphasize, if not eliminate, the role of the discredited sectors in interest articulation and aggregation. They decided that ossified corporatist structures should be supplemented with territorially based "movements" and committees, led by new cadres who could distance themselves (and, implicitly, the PRI itself) from the detested bosses who ran the sectoral organizations and foster a more direct relationship between the PRI and individual citizens.

Unquestionably, the PRI's vaunted political control capabilities were weakened by the economic and political crises of recent *sexenios*. Nevertheless, the traditional instruments of control—patron-client relationships, *caciquismo* (local-level boss rule), the captive labor movement, selective repression of dissidents by government security forces—are still effective in some PRI-controlled states.

In many of the states and localities where the PAN has come to power since the 1980s, officials have attempted to implement very different models of state-society relations, aimed at increasing civic participation in public administration and placing greater reliance on public-private partnerships. For example, the Citizen Wednesday program, pioneered by the PANista mayor of León, Guanajuato, "encouraged citizens to make their particular needs and concerns known to the local government through weekly, one-on-one sessions with the heads of municipal departments for public lighting, paving, sewerage, water, public safety, and social welfare. . . . The program soon became the principal point of access between citizens and the government in León. It was quickly adopted by other PAN governments throughout Mexico."[25]

In other places, however, the limited success of PAN administrations in solving high-salience public security and urban development problems has undermined attempts to build new, enduring state-society relationships. For example, in 2004, disillusioned voters in the key northern border city of Tijuana turned out

the PAN after three terms, installing as mayor a traditional PRI politician with a reputation for corruption and authoritarianism. He quickly set about restoring the corporatist networks that his PANista predecessors had labored to dismantle.

POLITICAL PARTIES

The Partido Revolucionario Institucional

The Partido Revolucionario Institucional (PRI) was founded in 1929 by President Plutarco Elías Calles to serve as a mechanism for reducing violent conflict among contenders for public office and for consolidating the power of the central government, at the expense of the personalistic, local, and state-level political machines of the decade following the 1910–1920 revolution. Between 1920 and 1929, there had been four major rebellions against the national executive by these subnational political machines. As historian Lorenzo Meyer has observed, the PRI was a party born not to fight for power, nor to share it with the opposition, "but rather to administer it."[26]

For more than half a century, the ruling party served with impressive efficiency, as a mechanism for resolving conflicts, for co-opting newly emerging interest groups into the system, and for legitimating the regime through the electoral process. Potential defectors from the official party were deterred by the government's manipulation of electoral rules, which made it virtually impossible for any dissident faction to bolt from the party and win the election. Dissident movements did emerge occasionally, but before the neo-Cardenista coalition contested the 1988 election, no breakaway presidential candidacy had been able to garner more than 16 percent of the vote (by official count).

In 1938 President Lázaro Cárdenas transformed the official party from a mechanism for elite conflict resolution and co-optation into a mass-based political party that could be used explicitly to build popular support for government policies and mobilize participation in elections. Cárdenas accomplished this by merging into the official party the local-, state-, and national-level organizations of peasants and urban workers that had been created during his presidency. This reorganization established the party's claim to be an inclusionary party—one that would absorb the diverse economic interests and political tendencies represented in Mexican society. By including lower income sectors, it reinforced the revolutionary credentials of the party, as well. The official party and its affiliated mass organizations occupied so much political space that opposition parties found it difficult to recruit supporters.

From the beginning, the official party was an appendage of the government itself, especially of the presidency. It was never a truly independent arena of political competition. A handful of nationally powerful party leaders, such as Fidel Velázquez, the patriarch of the PRI-affiliated labor movement until his death in 1997, occasionally constrained government actions, but the official party itself never determined the basic directions of government economic and social policies. Indeed, one of the key factors underlying the erosion of party unity and discipline since the late 1980s and the PRI's overwhelming defeats in state-level elections beginning in 1995, leading to its loss of the presidency in 2000, was the party's inability to distance itself from the unpopular austerity policies made by the technocrats in the federal government.

The official party traditionally enjoyed virtually unlimited access to government funds to finance its campaigns. No one knew how much was actually being siphoned from government coffers to the PRI, because Mexico had no laws requiring the reporting of campaign income and expenditures. When a PANista government took power in the state of Baja California in 1989, it found bank and legal records showing that more than $10 million in government funds had been channeled to the PRI for its 1989 gubernatorial campaign in that state. Reforms to the federal electoral code between 1993 and 1994 established minimal public reporting requirements for campaign income and expenditures, as well as Mexico's first-ever limits on individual and corporate contributions to electoral campaigns.

In the 1993–1994 electoral code reforms, ceilings on private contributions were set very high—the equivalent of $650,000 for an individual contribution. With its privileged access to financing from big business, the PRI continued to outspend its opponents by a huge margin, even without cash from government sources. In 1994, the PRI legally spent $44 million on its presidential campaign. It had even more money to spend on its campaigns, at all levels, than ever before, despite the contribution limits included in the electoral code reforms. In the same year, Roberto Madrazo, the PRI candidate for governor in the state of Tabasco (and 2006 presidential candidate), spent in excess of $50 million on his campaign—many times the limit for a gubernatorial race.

Yet another round of electoral reforms, passed by Congress in 1996, limited total private contributions to any party to 10 percent of the total amount of regular public financing to all parties, and no individual can contribute more than 0.05 percent of the total regular public financing. Also, the reforms greatly increased public funding for all parties. (In the 2006 presidential campaign, the three main candidates received and spent more than $200 million in public funds.) The law also added a new prohibition on "the use of public resources and programs to benefit any political party or electoral campaign."

Campaign finance abuses did not disappear, however. After the 2000 presidential election, the federal internal auditor discovered that the government-owned oil company, PEMEX, had made a $140 million loan to the oil-workers' union, one of the two most important PRI-affiliated labor unions. These funds were subsequently donated to the campaign of PRI candidate Francisco Labastida.

As the party in power, the PRI profited from a vast network of government patronage through which small-scale material benefits could be delivered to large segments of the population. The president himself controlled a large slush fund ("*la partida secreta*"), authorized each year by Congress as part of the federal government budget, that could aid PRI officials and finance the party's campaigns as needed. By the late 1990s, in the context of an increasingly competitive electoral system, such "incumbency advantages" were being intensely criticized by the opposition parties and the media. Responding to this pressure, Ernesto Zedillo virtually eliminated the presidential "secret budget."

Historically, the official party's most potent advantage over the competition was its ability to commit electoral fraud with relative impunity. A wide variety of techniques were used: stuffing the ballot boxes; disqualifying opposition party poll watchers; relocating polling places at the last minute to sites known only to PRI supporters; manipulating voter registration lists, padding them with nonexistent or nonresident PRIistas, and/or *rasurando* (shaving off) those who are expected to vote for opposition parties; issuing multiple voting credentials to PRI supporters; buying, "renting," or confiscating opposition voters' credentials, often in return for material benefits; organizing *carruseles* (flying brigades) of PRI supporters transported by truck or van to vote at several different polling places; and so forth.

Moreover, until 1996, the PRI held majority representation in all of the state and federal government entities that controlled vote counting and certification. The PRI could count on these bodies to manipulate the tallies to favor its candidates or, in cases where the opposition vote got out of control, nullify the unfavorable election outcomes. Adding votes to the PRI column, rather than taking them away from opposition parties, was the most common form of electoral fraud. In some predominantly rural districts, this practice led to election results in which the number of votes credited to the PRI candidate exceeded the total number of registered voters, or even the total number of adults estimated from the most recent population census.

In a successful effort to build up domestic and international credibility for the 1994 national elections, the Salinas government introduced a number of important safeguards against fraud. New, high-tech, photo-identification voter credentials were issued to the entire electorate. The Federal Electoral Institute (IFE) was greatly strengthened and given greater autonomy. The PRI and its government representatives were denied a majority on the IFE's decision-making board. A new system of independent electoral tribunals was established to adjudicate election disputes, and a special prosecutor's office was established to investigate alleged violations of the electoral laws. The law defined a broad range of electoral offenses—not previously subject to prosecution—as electoral crimes (though the special prosecutor was appointed by the president and reported to the federal attorney general, who was unlikely to bring charges against important PRI leaders or government officials). The role of independent, Mexican citizen observers in monitoring the casting and tallying of votes was formally recognized, and the presence of foreign electoral observers (euphemistically termed "international visitors") was legalized. Exit polls of voters and "quick counts" of the actual vote in sample precincts by the IFE as well as private organizations were authorized and publicly announced on election night.

Taken together, these innovations, which cost the Mexican taxpayers more than $1 billion, represented a major advance toward improving the security, professionalism, and fairness of the Mexican electoral system. However, various types of irregularities—especially

violations of ballot secrecy and efforts by local bosses to induce voters to support the PRI—were still widespread in the more isolated, rural areas. Subsequent state and local elections in various parts of the country have demonstrated that subnational PRI leaders continue to use direct threats and other forms of intimidation, particularly against peasant voters.

The 1996 electoral reform greatly increased the institutional autonomy of the IFE. The Interior Minister was removed as president of the IFE and replaced by a nonpartisan president and eight nonpartisan commissioners. These nine electoral commissioners were elected for a seven-year term by a two-thirds vote of the Chamber of Deputies. Since no party can control more than 60 percent of the seats in the lower chamber, the IFE commissioners are elected by consensus of all of the parties. In the national elections from 1997 through 2006 there was very little evidence of systematic fraud. Since the IFE controls most of the process in a nonpartisan manner (for example, all poll workers are chosen at random from voter registration lists, as jurors are selected in the United States), the remaining sources of electoral fraud are vote-buying (still common in some states, especially in the Southeast) and the buying or renting of voter credentials. Both practices are illegal, but neither is easy for federal electoral authorities to police.

The share of the vote claimed by the PRI had been declining for three decades, but until recently the erosion was gradual and did not threaten the party's grasp on the presidency and state governorships (see Figure 11.6). In the 1980s and 1990s, however, Mexican elections became much more competitive. The proportion of electoral districts dominated to varying degrees by the PRI dropped dramatically, from 70 percent in 1979 to 1 percent in 2000. The "Soviet-style" precincts that regularly delivered 98 to 100 percent of their votes to PRI candidates have disappeared.

In the four elections prior to 2006, the PRI did best among older voters, the less educated, and low-income people. It has also held the loyalty of a plurality of union members. However, the corporatist vote in general is no longer a dependable source of support for the PRI, and the low mobilization of these voters was one of the major reasons for its defeat in the 2000 elections.

Another key factor accounting for the long-term decline in the PRI's effectiveness as a vote-getting machine is the massive shift of population from rural

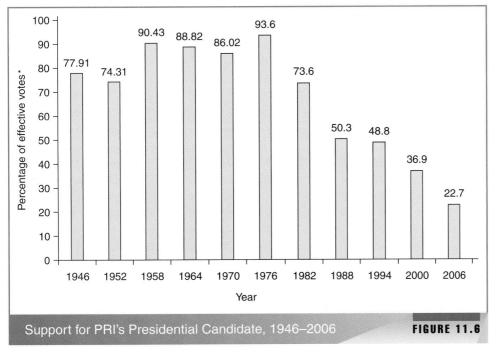

Support for PRI's Presidential Candidate, 1946–2006   **FIGURE 11.6**

*Percentage base includes annulled votes and those cast for independent candidates.

Note: The 1976 PRI candidate, José López Portillo, ran virtually unopposed because the PAN failed to nominate a candidate. The only other significant candidate was Valentín Campa, representing the Communist Party, which was not legally registered to participate in the 1976 election. More than 5 percent of the votes were annulled.

Sources: Data from Comisión Federal Electoral, 1946–1988; and Instituto Federal Electoral, 1994–2006.

to urban areas that has occurred in Mexico since 1950. In that year, 57 percent of the population lived in isolated rural communities of fewer than 2,500 inhabitants. By 1990 less than 29 percent lived in such localities. This massive rural-to-urban migration is reflected in occupational statistics: In urban Mexico, authoritarian control mechanisms are less efficacious. Education and income levels are higher, and the middle classes—which provide a considerable share of the opposition vote—are larger. A smaller proportion of the population is subject to pressures from local-level bosses.

The PRI is significantly weaker in cities with 100,000 or more inhabitants, where more than half of the Mexican population now lives. Mexico City has been a particular disaster area for the PRI in recent elections. The PRI lost the mayoral races in Mexico City by large margins in 1997, 2000, and 2006. Including elections for mayor, congressional seats, ward presidents, and local assembly seats, the PRI has won only one out of 330 majority races in the last four electoral cycles in Mexico City. Even in rural areas, however, the PRI's formerly safe vote continues

to erode. While the PRI still gets a higher share of the vote in rural areas than any other party, the average vote for PRI candidates in rural precincts fell markedly from 1982 through 2006.[27]

The PRI has had to adjust from being an official party—a political machine based on incumbency advantages—to being a party out of power. PRI legislators for the first time have had to figure out how to vote without presidential leadership. The whole party has had to define its ideology as a political party, not as an instrument of power. During the Fox *sexenio*, the main issues that distinguished the PRI from the government were taxes (the PRI wanted less), spending (the PRI wanted more), and reform of the government-owned electrical energy industry. Regarding the last issue: the Fox administration sought increased private investment in this sector and advocated changing the Constitution to attract it; the PRI was torn between allowing more private investment without constitutional changes and maintaining a state monopoly in the utility.

The Partido Acción Nacional

The Partido Acción Nacional (PAN) was established in 1939, largely in reaction to the leftward drift of public policy under President Lázaro Cárdenas, particularly his policies in support of socialist public education. Its founders included prominent Catholic intellectuals who espoused an early Christian democratic ideology, and the party has traditionally opposed government restrictions on church activities. The party attacked political centralism and advocated expanded states' rights long before it was fashionable to do so. The PAN's principal constituency has always been the urban middle class, but is has also attracted votes among the socially conservative peasants and the urban working class.

Between 1964, when a primitive form of proportional representation increased opposition presence in the Chamber of Deputies, and the mid-1990s, when the PAN was governing many municipal and state governments, the focus of PANista representation was in the federal Congress, especially the lower chamber (the first PANista was elected to the Senate only in 1991). In these years, PAN deputies would typically begin their congressional terms fighting electoral fraud from the previous election, in an attempt to increase the number of PANista deputies. Then they would settle in and begin to propose legislation. Until the Salinas years, these bills would almost always be ignored in the chamber at the time of introduction; but eventually most of the PAN's legislative proposals were adopted by the federal executive and reintroduced and approved by Congress.

Among the PANista ideas later embraced by PRI governments were increased proportional representation in both chambers of Congress, autonomous electoral courts and electoral agencies, the permanent voting credential, increased municipal autonomy, increased autonomy and authority for the Supreme Court, increased self-governance for the Federal District (Mexico City), federal revenue-sharing with the states, liberalization of the social security systems, a national consumer protection agency, and profit-sharing with employees.

The PAN's regional strongholds include the North, the Center-West, and some of the large municipalities of the states of México and Veracruz. Between 1989 and 2001, the PAN won gubernatorial elections in nine states (Baja California, Chihuahua, Guanajuato, Jalisco, Nuevo León, Querétaro, Aguascalientes, Morelos, and Yucatán), and it managed to create a de facto two-party system with the PRI in most of these states.

In 1995, the PAN retained control of the governorship of Baja California, thereby accomplishing something that no opposition party had previously done: the transfer of power from one elected opposition governor to another. The PAN failed to retain the governorship of Chihuahua in 1998, Nuevo León in 2003, and Nayarit in 2004, losing in each instance to the PRI. However, by 2006, PAN candidates had won three consecutive races for governor in Guanajuato, Baja California, and Jalisco, and the party had won two consecutive governorships in Aguascalientes, Querétaro, and Morelos. The PAN picked up the governorships of San Luis Potosí in 2003, and took Tlaxcala from the PRD in 2004. In 2003 and 2004, the party also lost very close races to the PRI in Campeche, Sonora, Veracruz, and Oaxaca—all previously PRI strongholds. Over the last decade, the PAN has governed nearly all of the twenty largest cities in Mexico, with the conspicuous exception of Mexico City, and it has also governed most of the capital cities of the country.

The ideological position of the PAN has been relatively constant over the last six decades. It could be classified as the center-right, with strong elements of Christian socialism (which covers a wide range of policies, from center-left on labor issues to right-of-center on abortion), combined with traditional liberal attitudes on trade, municipal decentralization, and general democratization. The party is affiliated with international Christian Democratic organizations. The PAN's relative position on the ideological spectrum has depended mostly on the positioning of the PRI, whose pendulum has shifted to positions clearly to the left of the PAN (as in the 1970s) or to the right of the PAN (as was the case from 1988 to 2000).

Statistical analysis of roll-call votes in the 57th Legislature (1997–2000) places the PAN at the center of the political spectrum, to the left of the PRI. Although roll calls are not available for earlier years, congressional debates suggest that the PAN held a similar position for most of the Salinas and Zedillo years. Despite the nationalist and populist background of their party, PRI deputies found themselves voting to the right of the PAN because they had to support the neoliberal economic policies and austerity measures of PRI presidents. However, since 2001, under a PANista president, PAN members generally voted to the right of the PRI. Now it is the PAN deputies who must support the austerity programs of their president, while PRI deputies are liberated to vote their conscience and constituencies rather than take cues from the president.

The PAN has worked long and hard to develop a strong network of grassroots militants. While clearly the leader today among Mexico's parties in terms of organizational strength, the PAN is a party with several major weaknesses. Since the mid-1970s it has been divided into moderate-progressive and militant-conservative ("neo-PANista") factions, which have jockeyed for control of the party machinery and carried out purges of opposing faction members when they were in power.

Vicente Fox's ideology was closer to the moderate-progressives than to the neo-PANistas. This helped the PAN gain control of the presidency in 2000, by attracting an ideologically diverse group of voters, united mainly by their desire to remove the PRI from power.[28] In recent years, the PAN has continued its evolution toward a catch-all party, while still embracing with greater enthusiasm than its rivals the free-market, pro-foreign investment policies favored by the country's business community.[29]

The Partido de la Revolución Democrática

Before 1988, the Mexican left had spawned political parties like the Partido Popular Socialista (PPS), which for decades served as a home for socialists and other left-of-center politicians willing to collaborate with the government and even to endorse the PRI's presidential candidates, in exchange for a seat in Congress. The more independent left—that is, those who did not cooperate openly with the ruling party—was traditionally represented by the Partido Comunista Mexicano (PCM). The Communists were allowed to compete legally in elections during the presidency of Lázaro Cárdenas, but their party was subsequently outlawed and did not regain legal representation until 1979, when its congressional candidates won 5 percent of the vote.

During most of the 1980s, even in the face of Mexico's gravest economic crisis since the 1910 Revolution, and despite a series of party mergers intended to reduce the fractionalization of the leftist vote, the parties on the left lost ground electorally. They were hampered by constant internal squabbling (motivated mostly by personalistic rivalries, and to a lesser extent to ideological cleavages), an inability to do effective grassroots organizing, and an identification with discredited, statist economic policies.

The key to the left's rejuvenation in 1988 was a split within the PRI leadership—the most serious since the early 1950s. In August 1986 a number of nationally prominent PRI figures, all members of the party's center-left wing, formed a dissident movement within the PRI known as the Corriente Democrática (CD). They were led by Porfirio Muñoz Ledo (former head of the PRI, runner-up candidate for the party's

presidential nomination in 1976, former secretary of labor and secretary of education), and Cuauhtémoc Cárdenas, who was just finishing his term as governor of the state of Michoacán. The CD criticized the de la Madrid administration's economic restructuring program and sought a renewed commitment by the PRI to traditional principles of economic nationalism and social justice. Most urgently, CD adherents called for a top-to-bottom democratization of the PRI, beginning with the elimination of the *dedazo* (the unilateral selection by the outgoing president) as the mechanism for determining the party's presidential candidate. The CD's proposals were widely interpreted as a last-ditch attempt by the PRI's traditional politicos to recover leadership of the party by influencing the outcome of the 1987–1988 presidential succession. The CD's demands for reform were resoundingly rejected by the PRI hierarchy, and its leaders formally split from the party in October 1987.

Confronted with the defeat within the PRI, Cárdenas accepted the presidential nomination of the Partido Auténtico de la Revolución Mexicana (PARM), a conservative, nationalist party established by another group of dissident PRIistas in 1954. Later, four other parties—all on the left and including the remnants of the old Mexican Communist Party—joined the PARM to form a coalition, the Frente Democrático Nacional (FDN), to contest the 1988 presidential election, with Cárdenas as their candidate. Soon after the 1988 elections, however, the left's long-standing ideological and personalistic cleavages reasserted themselves, and by 1991, when midterm elections were held, most of Cárdenas's 1988 coalition partners had gone their separate ways, leaving the newly constituted PRD as the principal standard-bearer of the left. Even within the PRD, serious disagreements emerged over such issues as the degree of democracy in internal party governance and strategies for dealing with the government (dialogue and collaboration on certain issues versus permanent confrontation).

The left's problems in the early 1990s were not all self-inflicted. Under Salinas, the government showed no inclination to negotiate seriously with the Cardenista left. Salinas showed much greater willingness to recognize electoral victories of the PAN than those claimed by the PRD. And when the PRD's victories (all at the municipal level) were recognized, the city governments under its control were punished and starved for resources by PRI state governors. Conflicts between PRD militants and local PRI *caciques* were bitter, with hundreds of PRD activists murdered during the first five years of the party's existence.

President Zedillo opened a new chapter in PRD-government relations, recognizing Cuauhtémoc Cárdenas's overwhelming victory in the 1997 mayoral race in Mexico City. In 1998–1999, the PRD won gubernatorial elections in the states of Zacatecas, Tlaxcala, and Baja California Sur. In 2000, it picked up the state of Chiapas, and again won the Mexico City mayoralty. In 2001, the PRD finally won Cárdenas's home state of Michoacán, after nominating his son, Lázaro, for governor. In all of these early victories, except for Mexico City and Michoacán, the PRD candidates were defectors from the PRI who had been passed over for the party's gubernatorial nomination.

These outcomes illustrate a key advantage for the PRD in Mexico's current three-party competition: in places where the PRI organization is fractured by internal rivalries, where the local factions are unable to reach consensus on a candidate, the PRD is usually the main beneficiary. For PRIistas whose political aspirations are thwarted by their own party, the PRD—the party run by ex-PRIistas—is a natural new home.

During the Fox administration, the PRD lost the governorship of Tlaxcala to the PAN but picked up the state of Guerrero (where Acapulco is located); retained the governorships of Baja California Sur, and Zacatecas; and won the Federal District (the Mexico City mayoralty) for the third consecutive time.

Until 2000, the PRD continued to take policy positions to the left of the ruling party on some issues (for example, arguing against the use of any taxpayer money to bail out bankers who made bad loans during the Salinas *sexenio*). Its differences with most recent government policies were matters of degree, pacing, and how much was being done to ameliorate the social costs of these policies, rather than their basic direction. During the 57th Legislature (1997–2000), when for the first time the PRI lost majority control of the lower chamber, the PRD tended to vote with the PAN and against the PRI on issues of political reform and to enhance the oversight of the legislative branch over the federal executive. On most economic issues, the PAN and the PRI voted together, with the PRD often voting against.

In the 58th Legislature (2000–2003), the PRD took a more radical stance on policy issues and was more intransigent in its relations with the other parties. In part this is due to the diminished presence of the party in the Congress—about 60 percent smaller than the PRD delegation in the 1997–2000 period. It introduced bills that, taken together, amounted to a sweeping restructuring of the Mexican political system, designed to weaken the federal executive. One bill would have introduced a parliamentary system with an elected president, akin to the presidential-premier system in France. In the 59th Legislature (2003–2006), the much larger PRD delegation increased its opposition to the federal government's economic policies. Once the party realized that it could win the presidency in 2006, it backed off pressing its bills to weaken the executive branch and to foment a parliamentary system.

In its early years, the PRD did a poor job of mobilizing previously uncommitted voters. It had retained many of the urban working-class voters who traditionally supported the parties of the independent left, but it was not very successful in establishing ties with the popular movements that had developed outside of the PRI-affiliated corporatist structures. However, its ties to the rural areas were underdeveloped, and the PRD had been dominated by Mexico City–based politicians and intellectuals for whom the provinces hardly existed. Central party leaders often shortchanged local organizers in their allocation of party funds. This trend was reversed in the 2006 election, when the PRD under López Obrador proved much more effective at mobilizing rural voters.

The Shifting Social Bases of Mexico's Parties

The social bases of political support for the parties shifted dramatically in the 2006 election (see Table 11.5). Before 2006, the PRI's most dependable base was the rural voter. It also did relatively well with women and older voters. In 2006, the PRD's López Obrador did best among rural voters, and Madrazo of the PRI finished third among such voters, even behind Calderón (PAN). As in 2000, the PAN did best among urban voters, but the PRD finished ahead of the PRI for the urban vote in 2006.

There was a sizable gender gap in the 2000 election, with the PAN doing particularly well among male voters and the PRI relatively better among women. In 2006, the PRD took the male vote by a small margin, but Calderón did much better among women. In both cases, women tended to support the candidate who appeared to pose less of a threat to economic stability.

TABLE 11.5

Party Choice in 2006 Presidential Election, by Demographic Attribute (percentages)

	PAN	PRI	PRD	Others
Type of Locality				
Urban	40	20	35	5
Rural	31	28	36	3
Region				
North	43	27	24	6
Center-West	46	20	27	4
Center	34	15	44	7
South	27	29	40	4
Gender				
Male	36	22	37	2
Female	38	23	32	4
Age				
18–29	38	21	34	6
30–49	38	21	35	4
50	34	26	37	2
Education				
None and Primary	34	29	33	3
Secondary	37	21	35	5
University	42	14	38	5
Annual Income (dollars)				
Under $2,161	31	30	34	4
$2,162–$4,321	32	24	39	4
$4,322–$7,021	36	21	37	5
$7,022–$9,938	43	16	36	4
Above $9,939	50	14	30	5

Source: Nationwide exit poll conducted by *Reforma* newspaper (Mexico City), 3 July 2006.

In 2000, the PAN did best among voters below age 50, while the PRI was preferred by older voters. This was probably because this segment of the electorate remembered the social benefits and economic growth achieved in the better years of PRI rule. In 2006, the PAN again carried younger voters, but now voters over age 50 chose the PRD, possibly because, as mayor of Mexico City, López Obrador had introduced a pension plan for senior citizens.

In 2000, the PRI did better among voters with lower education, taking the vote among those with less than a secondary education. The PAN did best, by a large margin, among voters with higher levels of education. In 2006, education mattered less in determining the vote. Calderón attracted the most votes at all levels of education, and López Obrador placed second. López Obrador did relatively well among higher educated voters because of the strong support that he received from public university students.

In 2006, the PRD did best among the poor and the lower middle class. Both López Obrador and Madrazo promised reforms that would increase the spending power of voters with incomes below about U.S. $10,000 per year (the PRD through subsidies, and the PRI through income tax cuts). The PAN did much better among higher income voters, who were attracted by its pro-business platform and frightened by the populism of López Obrador.

In general, however, social class was not nearly as important to voters' choices in 2006 as was the region in which they live. The PRD was weak in most of the northern and central states but had strong support in the Mexico City metropolitan area and the South, while the PAN's support was concentrated in the North and center of the country. In 2006, region was as powerful a predictor of party preference as all other demographic variables combined (age, gender, income, education, skin color, urban vs. rural residence). Thus, the dominant cleavage in Mexico's electorate today is not social class but region—especially, the North-South split.[30]

GOVERNMENT PERFORMANCE

Promoting Economic Growth and Reducing Poverty

There is little debate about the importance of the state's contribution to the economic development of Mexico since 1940. Massive public investments in infrastructure (roads, dams, telecommunications, electrification) and generous, cheap credit provided to the private sector by Nacional Financiera and other government development banks made possible a higher rate of capital accumulation, stimulated higher levels of investment by domestic entrepreneurs and foreign corporations, and enabled Mexico to develop a diversified production capacity second only within Latin America to that of Brazil.

From 1940 until well into the 1970s, a strong elite consensus prevailed on the state's role in the economy. The state facilitated private capital accumulation and protected the capitalist system by limiting popular demands for consumption and redistribution of wealth; it established the rules for development; and it participated in the development process as the nation's largest single entrepreneur, employer, and source of investment capital. The state served as the "rector" (guiding force) of this mixed economy, setting broad priorities and channeling investment (both public and private) into strategic sectors. Acting through joint ventures between private firms and state-owned enterprises, the government provided resources for development projects so large that they would have been difficult or impossible to finance from internal (within-the-firm) sources or through borrowing from private banks.

The result, from the mid-1950s to the mid-1970s, was the much-touted "Mexican miracle" of sustained economic growth at annual rates of 6 to 7 percent, coupled with low inflation (5 percent per annum

between 1955 and 1972). By 1980, the gross national product had reached $2,130 per capita, placing Mexico toward the upper end of the World Bank's list of semi-industrialized or "middle-developed" countries. As sole proprietor of PEMEX, the state oil monopoly, the government was responsible for developing the crucial oil and natural gas sector of the economy. By the end of the oil boom (1978–1981), oil was generating more than $15 billion a year in export revenues and fueling economic growth of more than 8 percent per year— one of the world's highest growth rates.

It is the distributive consequences of this impressive performance in economic development and the manner in which it was financed by the PRI governments of the 1970s and 1980s that have been harshly criticized in retrospect. From Miguel Alemán (1946–1952) to the present, all but one or two of Mexico's presidents and their administrations reflected the private sector's contention that Mexico must first create wealth and then worry about redistributing it—the belief being that the state would quickly be overwhelmed by popular demands that it could not satisfy. By the early 1970s, however, there was convincing evidence that an excessively large portion of Mexico's population was being left behind in the drive to become a modern, industrialized nation.

This is not to say that some benefits of the development process did not trickle down to the poor. From 1950 to 1980, poverty in absolute terms declined. The middle class expanded to an estimated 29 percent of the population by 1970. From 1960 to 1980, illiteracy dropped from 35 to 15 percent of the population, infant mortality was reduced from 78 to 70 per 1,000 live births, and average life expectancy rose from 55 to 64 years. Clearly, the quality of life for many Mexicans— even in isolated rural areas—did improve during this period, although several other Latin American countries (Chile, Colombia, Costa Rica, Cuba, Ecuador, El Salvador, and Venezuela) achieved higher rates of improvement on indicators of social well-being than did Mexico during the same period.

There was, however, a dark side to Mexico's economic miracle. From 1950 to the mid-1970s, ownership of land and capital (stocks, bonds, time deposits) became increasingly concentrated. Personal income inequality also increased, at a time when, given Mexico's middle level of development, the national income distribution should have been shifting toward greater equality, according to classical economic development theory. Indeed, Mexico apparently had a higher overall concentration of income in the mid-1970s than in 1910, before the outbreak of the revolution. By 1977, the poorest 70 percent of Mexican families received only 24 percent of all disposable income, while the richest 30 percent of families received 76 percent of income. With only brief interruptions, the trend toward greater income inequality continued in the 1980s and 1990s.

Other social indicators mirrored the pattern of personal income distribution. By 1989, more than one-quarter of Mexican children under age 5 in rural areas were malnourished; the incidence of severe malnutrition among such children had risen by 100 percent during the preceding ten years. While 78 percent of Mexico's elementary school-age children were enrolled in 1990, only 54 percent of those starting primary school finished it. Among the dwellings included in the 1990 census, 57 percent had no sewerage connections, 50 percent had no piped water inside the dwelling, and 13 percent had no electricity.

By every indicator of economic opportunity and social well-being, there are vast disparities among Mexico's regions and between rural and urban areas. Unemployment and underemployment are concentrated overwhelmingly in the rural sector, which contains at least 70 percent of the population classified as living in extreme poverty. The rate of infant mortality in rural areas is nearly 50 percent higher than the national average. Interregional disparities in social well-being are equally extreme. In 2000, the percentage of persons with incomes lower than two minimum salaries (a bare subsistence level) ranged from 22 percent in Baja California to 76 percent in Chiapas. A composite index of social well-being in 2000 shows the Federal District (Mexico City) and the northern border states as being the most privileged, and the southern states (especially Chiapas, Oaxaca, and Guerrero) as the most marginalized (see Figure 11.7). This pattern of extreme spatial inequalities has remained essentially unchanged for several decades.

The policies and investment preferences of Mexico's postrevolutionary governments contributed much to the country's highly inegalitarian development. At minimum, the public policies pursued since 1940 failed to counteract the wealth-concentrating effects of private market forces. Evidence is strong that some government investments and policies actually reinforced these effects. For example, during most of the post-1940 period, government tax and credit policies worked primarily to the advantage of the country's wealthiest agribusiness and industrial entrepreneurs. Government expenditures for social security, public health, and education remained relatively low by international standards. By the late 1970s, Mexico was still allocating a smaller share of its central government budget to social services than some countries, such as Bolivia, Brazil, Chile, and Panama. The slowness with which basic social services were extended to the bulk of the population in Mexico was a direct consequence of the government's policy of keeping inflation low by concentrating public expenditures on subsidies and infrastructure for private industry, rather than on social programs and subsidies to consumers.

Even during the period between 1970 and 1982, when populist policies were allegedly in vogue and government revenues were expanding rapidly because of the oil export boom, public spending for programs like health and social security remained roughly constant, in real per capita terms. The economic crisis that erupted in 1982, after an unprecedented run-up in Mexico's domestic and externally held debt, made it impossible to maintain even that level of government commitment to social well-being. By 1986, debt service was consuming over half of the total federal government budget, necessitating deep cuts in spending for health, education, consumer subsidies, and job-creating public investments. Social welfare expenditures per capita fell to 1974 levels.

Mexico's macroeconomic adjustment program was considerably more severe than those in other major Latin American countries that also experienced debt crises during the 1980s. The severity of the adjustment is reflected particularly in minimum real wages, which fell by two-thirds between 1980 and 1989. Despite a modest resurgence of economic growth in the early 1990s, by the end of the Salinas *sexenio* real wages for most Mexicans had still not recovered their levels of 1981. The economic crisis of the mid-1990s caused most Mexicans to lose whatever ground they had gained during the Salinas years. By 2002, half of Mexico's population was living at or below the World Bank's official poverty level, and one-fifth were living in extreme poverty.

Under Mexico's four most recent presidents, the government has implemented a **neoliberal economic development model** stressing the need to give much freer rein to market forces. The primary objective of this

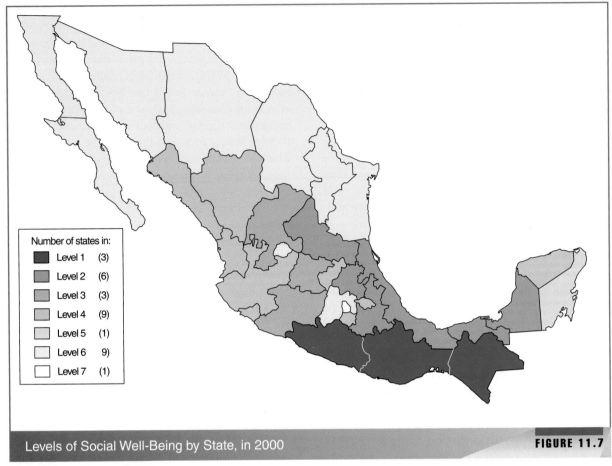

Levels of Social Well-Being by State, in 2000

FIGURE 11.7

Number of states in:
- Level 1 (3)
- Level 2 (6)
- Level 3 (3)
- Level 4 (9)
- Level 5 (1)
- Level 6 9)
- Level 7 (1)

Level 1: Chiapas, Guerrero, Oaxaca
Level 2: Campeche, Hidalgo, Puebla, San Luis Potosí, Tabasco, Veracruz
Level 3: Guanajuato, Michoacán, Zacatecas
Level 4: Colima, Durango, Jalisco, Morelos, Nayarit, Querétaro, Sinaloa, Tlaxcala, Yucatán
Level 5: Quintana Roo
Level 6: Aguascalientes, Baja California, Baja California Sur, Coahuila, Chihuahua, México, Nuevo León, Sonora, Tamaulipas.
Level 7: Distrito Federal

Note: Level of social well-being is measured by characteristics of dwellings (have electricity, refrigerator, television, concrete vs. dirt floors, sewerage connection, private bathroom; number of rooms; use something other than firewood or coal for cooking) and population characteristics (percentage economically active; literate; 6–19-year-olds who attend school; receive health care; live in urban area; average number of children born to women over age 12).

Source: Instituto Nacional de Estadística, Geografía e Informática, www.inegi.gob.mx.

"technocratic free-market revolution" has been to attract more private investment (especially foreign capital) and thereby push up Mexico's rate of economic growth. While drastically shrinking the public sector of the economy through a sweeping privatization program and opening up nearly all sectors of the economy to private investment (including those formerly reserved to the state), the technocrats were unwilling to completely surrender the government's traditional "rectorship" role in the economy. "The new [government] elite did not

believe that the market, left to its own devices, would resolve all problems through invisible hands."[31]

This concern is reflected in the considerable spending by the last three administrations on social welfare initiatives, like Salinas's National Solidarity Program, Zedillo's PROGRESA program, and Fox's Oportunidades program—all efforts to construct a minimal safety net for the millions of low-income Mexicans who were the short-term "losers" from neoliberal economic policies and trade liberalization under the

North American Free Trade Agreement (NAFTA). But these carefully targeted social programs were not sufficient to offset the structural impoverishment caused by falling real wages, the elimination of millions of jobs, and the slashing of most consumer subsidies.

During the Fox administration, the government implemented a new health care program known as the **Seguro Popular** (Popular Health Insurance), designed to provide health services to people who were not covered by the Social Security Institute's health programs. Social security in Mexico provides health coverage for salaried persons, but the unemployed, the self-employed, and many rural workers are excluded from the system. The Seguro Popular program requires beneficiaries to enroll in the program and pay relatively affordable premiums. The poorest Mexicans (the bottom 20 percent) do not have to pay premiums. The goal of the Seguro Popular is to achieve universal health insurance coverage by 2010.

It is clear that the market-oriented development model of the past two decades has exacerbated—not alleviated—Mexico's poverty and inequality problems, even when the model was apparently working well in macroeconomic terms (that is, from 1989 through 1992).[32] Moreover, Mexico's experience with rapid economic growth during the "miracle" years of the 1950s and 1960s and the oil boom of the late 1970s and early 1980s suggests that without strong, sustained government action to correct for market failures and improve human capital endowments through education and job training, income concentration, and related social problems will continue unabated.

Net job creation in Mexico under neoliberal economic policies since the late 1980s has been anemic, despite a huge influx of foreign capital. This dismal performance can be explained in part by the fact that well over half of the foreign funds received by Mexico during this period were invested in stocks, short-term government-issued bonds, and other financial instruments, rather than in job-creating, direct investment projects. Equally important, the government's strategy of promoting export-led development has induced many private firms to become more competitive in the global marketplace by shedding labor and becoming more capital-intensive.

Thus it has yet to be proved that economic liberalization and free trade can yield significantly higher rates of job creation, especially jobs that pay enough to lift Mexican families above the poverty line. There is a growing consensus that the government will have to do much more to upgrade workers' skills through vocational education and subsidized, on-the-job training if Mexico is to realize a greater return from its painful shift to an open, market-oriented development strategy. A fundamental reform of the country's public education system will be necessary to achieve a better distribution of the gains from NAFTA.

Financing Development and Controlling Inflation

From 1940 to 1970, Mexico's public sector acquired an international reputation for sound, conservative monetary and fiscal policies. This conservative style of economic management, coupled with Mexico's long record of political stability, gave the country an attractive investment climate. By 1982, this image had been shattered; the public sector (and much of the private sector) was suffering from a deep liquidity crisis, and inflation had reached levels unheard of since the first decade of the Mexican Revolution, when paper currencies lost most of their value. What happened?

The basic difficulty was that the government had attempted to spend its way out of the social and economic problems that had accumulated since 1940, without paying the political cost that sweeping redistributive policies would have entailed. Instead, it attempted to expand the entire economic pie by enlarging the state's role as banker, entrepreneur, and employer. Since 1940, and especially after 1970, Mexico's public sector expanded steadily while its revenue-raising capability lagged. The result was ever-larger government deficits, financed increasingly by borrowing abroad.

For most of the post–World War II period, Mexico's tax effort—its rate of taxation and its actual performance in collecting taxes—was among the lowest in the world. Officials feared that any major alteration in the tax structure would drive domestic and foreign capital out of the country. Two modest attempts at tax reform, in 1964 and 1972, failed because of determined opposition from the business community. When the private sector refused to accede to higher taxes, the Echeverría administration opted for large-scale deficit financing, external indebtedness, and a huge increase in the money supply. The public sector itself was vastly enlarged, increasing the number of state-owned enterprises from eighty-four in 1970 to 845 in 1976. Fiscal restraint was finally forced on the government by depletion of its currency reserves in 1976.

Echeverría's successor, José López Portillo, at first attempted to reverse the trend toward larger government deficits, but the effort was abandoned when the treasury began to swell with oil export revenues. Again, the temptation was to address basic structural problems by further expanding the state sector, and López Portillo found it impossible to resist. Oil revenues seemed to be a guaranteed, limitless source of income for the government. Mexico borrowed heavily from abroad, anticipating a steady rise in oil prices. When world oil prices declined in 1981 and 1982, the government was forced to suspend repayment of the foreign debt and negotiate a long-term reduction in interest rates—the first of several debt "restructurings," the most recent of which was completed in 1990.

Deficit financing, especially in the context of the overheated economy of the oil boom years, also touched off a burst of inflation. The average annual inflation rate rose from 15 percent during Echeverría's presidency (nearly triple the average rate between 1940 and 1970), to 36 percent under López Portillo and 91 percent during the de la Madrid *sexenio* (159 percent in 1987; see Figure 11.8). Both the de la Madrid and Salinas

administrations made reducing the inflation rate their top economic priority, but Salinas was much more effective in bringing inflation under control than his predecessor. His principal instrument was price and wage controls, enforced by a formal, trilateral government-business–organized labor "pact" that was renewed six times, with some adjustments, at twelve- to eighteen-month intervals. This form of shock therapy brought the inflation rate down to single digits by 1994.

The other key to Salinas's success in fighting inflation was deep cuts in spending to reduce and eventually eliminate the public deficit, coupled with unprecedented steps to boost federal government revenues. These measures included the sale or closure of hundreds of state-owned enterprises, vigorous enforcement of the tax laws (only two individual tax evaders had been caught and imprisoned between 1921 and 1988), and the introduction of a 2 percent annual tax on total business assets, intended to reduce manipulations that had previously enabled 70 percent of Mexico's businesses to evade paying any taxes.

Even after the Salinas administration's "successful" tax reform, however, the federal government still obtained most of its revenues (over 60 percent) from socially regressive indirect taxes, primarily the value-added tax levied on about 70 percent of all goods and

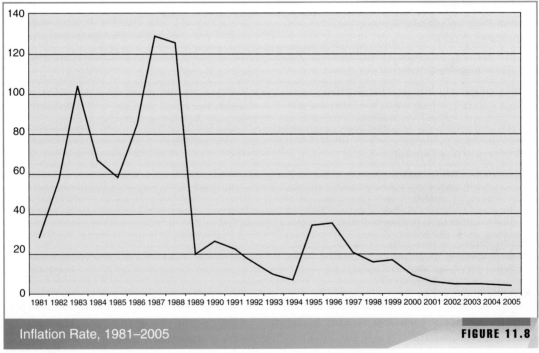

Inflation Rate, 1981–2005

FIGURE 11.8

Source: Instituto Nacional de Estadística, Geografía e Informática, www.inegi.gob.mx, 2006.

services. Personal income tax rates for the wealthiest Mexicans were actually reduced from 50 percent in 1988 to 35 percent in 1990, and a proposed tax on capital gains by individual investors in the stock market was shelved. "As on previous occasions, the government decided it was too risky to tax the savings of the richest Mexicans. The threat of capital flight . . . remained a powerful constraint on the government's taxing powers."[33]

The deep financial crisis that erupted in the first month of Ernesto Zedillo's presidency raised serious questions about the wisdom of the Salinas administration's obsessive pursuit of one-digit inflation, as well as its decision to "live with" a seriously overvalued peso until after the August 1994 national elections—indeed, until after President Salinas had left office. An earlier, staged devaluation would have boosted inflation and interest rates at a politically inopportune moment, but it could have prevented the financial panic and massive capital flight that followed the sudden, mega-devaluation of December 20, 1994. More than $10 billion in investment capital fled Mexico within a week; the peso had to be sharply devalued, eventually losing more than half of its value against the U.S. dollar; and the government came within a few days of insolvency as its foreign currency reserves were depleted.

Salinas and his financial ministers were also justly criticized for creating illusions of prosperity by financing a huge current accounts deficit (resulting mostly from a flood of consumer imports) with short-term, highly speculative capital. That "hot money"—mostly from large, U.S. institutional investors—flowed into *tesobonos,* the high-yielding, U.S. dollar-denominated bonds with maturities ranging from twenty-eight to 180 days that were issued by the Mexican Treasury in prodigious quantities beginning in 1989. By the end of 1994, Mexico's debt in *tesobonos* had grown to almost $30 billion, and with the central bank's reserves virtually depleted by its efforts to fend off six speculative attacks on the peso during 1994, there was no way to pay off these bonds as they matured. Only massive financial assistance from the United States prevented a default and a general collapse of the Mexican economy.

How could a technocratic government that had earned worldwide respect for its skillful management of the economy, even in the midst of the political shocks of 1994, have erred so grievously? Most likely, a combination of political and personal factors led to the debacle: the government's need to paper over the financial cracks that were developing in order to achieve a decisive PRI

victory in the 1994 elections; Carlos Salinas's desire to protect his image in the midst of a difficult and ultimately unsuccessful campaign to become head of the World Trade Organization after he left the presidency; and the ineptitude and inexperience of President Zedillo's newly installed economic team in dealing with skittish private investors. In any case, the Mexican government suffered a severe loss in credibility abroad, and the average Mexican has paid—and will continue to pay—a high price for the politically motivated manipulation of macroeconomic policy.

Under President Fox, macroeconomic stability was maintained through a combination of fiscal restraint and good fortune; government revenues were boosted by rising oil prices in global markets, and the U.S. market for Mexico's exports was strong after the U.S. economy recovered from the 2001–2002 recession. The absence of a major, end-of-*sexenio* economic crisis—for the first time since 1970—was a key factor in Felipe Calderón's victory in 2006. Calderón could plausibly claim that he was better equipped than his opponents to continue the economic policies that had averted such crises under Fox.

Establishing the Rule of Law

The one area of performance in which the Mexican government has been failing most conspicuously, especially since the mid-1990s, is the administration of justice. From the poorest urban workers to middle-class professionals to the richest business tycoons, Mexicans are appalled and incensed that the government seems totally incapable of dealing effectively with street crime—armed robberies, muggings, kidnappings, rapes, and homicides. Surveys in the late 1990s found that virtually every resident of Mexico City had either been a crime victim or had a close relative or friend who had suffered the same fate in recent years.

Nationally, homicide rates rose by nearly 20 percent in the 1990s, and by far more in many of the states (for example, 230 percent in Guerrero; 211 percent in Chihuahua). Statistics on street crime (robberies, assaults, muggings) showed an even steeper increase in the mid-1990s. In Mexico City, the total number of crimes reported to police doubled from 1993 to 1997. And official crime statistics have understated the magnitude of the problem because of widespread underreporting. Three-quarters of crimes go unreported due to citizens' low expectation that the perpetrators will be caught and punished, and to fears of reprisals by either criminals or the police.[34]

The swelling public clamor to establish the rule of law in Mexico encompasses a broad range of demands: make the system of justice work more efficiently (that is, actually solve crimes, try and jail the perpetrators); reduce police corruption and brutality; ensure that people accused of crimes are treated fairly, respecting their constitutionally guaranteed rights and liberties, regardless of social class or political connections; make the system of justice equally accessible to citizens seeking redress of grievances; make elected officials accountable, legally, for their actions ("end impunity"); and increase the independence of the judiciary, especially vis-à-vis the executive branch.

President Zedillo began tackling the rule of law problem by addressing the last of these demands. In his first significant official act upon taking office in December 1994, he replaced all but two of the incumbent Supreme Court justices and reduced the size of the Supreme Court from twenty-four to eleven justices. He changed the terms of the justices from six-year periods, coinciding with the six-year presidential term, to fixed, fifteen-year terms. He also changed the requirement for confirmation of Supreme Court justices by the Senate, from a simple majority to two-thirds of the Senate. This means that the president's nominees must attract at least some votes from the opposition parties; they cannot be rubber-stamped by a PRI majority. Finally, Zedillo expanded the judicial review powers of the Supreme Court by explicitly granting the Court the ability to declare acts of Congress and other federal government actions unconstitutional.

The 1994 reforms made it possible for the opposition parties to bring various laws and government actions forward to the Supreme Court for constitutional review. For example, the cases brought in 1995 and 1996 included challenges to an increase in the federal sales tax that the Congress (then under PRI control) had approved in 1995. Demands for investigations of human rights violations, such as a massacre of unarmed peasant political activists by state police in Guerrero, also came before the Court. Another case challenged the president's use of the military to deal with the Zapatista rebellion in Chiapas, without first declaring an official state of emergency. Several of these cases were dismissed on legal technicalities. In other cases, a 6-to-5 majority of the justices ruled against the federal government's position, but under the 1994

judicial reforms it would have taken a *supermajority* of eight out of eleven justices to strike down a law or official action as unconstitutional, so the Court's decision had no practical impact in these cases.

These outcomes illustrate a major limitation of Zedillo's 1994 judicial reforms: The requirement that laws can be declared unconstitutional only with a supermajority ruling of Supreme Court justices is a very high threshold, one that can stymie the Court in dealing with the most sensitive political issues rulings.[35] In short, while Zedillo was willing to expand the Supreme Court's powers of judicial review and thereby reduce its subordination to the executive, he wanted to keep the Court on a fairly short leash.

Another major limitation of the 1994 reforms is that they apply only to the top level of the federal judiciary: state-level courts continue to function as before, and the federal Supreme Court must still rely on state-level officials to implement its rulings. In the campaign spending and human rights violation cases mentioned earlier, PRI-dominated state legislatures simply ignored or overturned the Supreme Court's rulings. Until Court decisions based on abstract principles of law cannot be undermined by political actors whose interests could be damaged by those rulings, the goal of a "government of laws, not men" will remain elusive in Mexico.

To the average citizen, what matters most is being liberated from the constant preoccupation with matters of personal security: how to avoid becoming a victim of violent crime. The causes of rising crime rates in Mexico are not difficult to identify. In the 1990s, Mexico became an increasingly important conduit for illegal drugs destined for the U.S. market. In states where drug trafficking is concentrated (Baja California, Chihuahua, Sinaloa, Jalisco), a high percentage of violent crime is related to the operations of drug cartels. Drug trafficking has also contributed mightily to the corruption of police, prosecutors, judges, and military personnel.

The police forces—federal, state, and local—themselves are a major source of Mexico's crime problem. Not only are they corruptible (because of low pay and low professionalization), they actually commit a sizable portion of crimes, especially in large cities. In recent years, most of the kidnappings of urban residents, carried out to extort money from them and their relatives, have involved former or active-duty police officers. A remarkably large number of Mexican

Former New York City Mayor Rudolph Giuliani (center) and Mexico City Mayor Marcelo Ebrard (left) tour the main plaza of Mexico City.

Famed for reducing crime in New York in the 1990s with his "zero tolerance" policy, Giuliani was hired in 2001 as a $4.3 million consultant by a group of prominent Mexican businessmen to produce a plan for reducing the capital's crime rate.

Daniel Aguilar/Reuters/Corbis

police officers are actually wanted for crimes, but the warrants for their arrest never get served because the offenders are protected by corrupt superior officers. Simply firing criminal elements in the police forces is not the solution, since they only return to the street as civilians, committing crimes with impunity.

Social and economic factors have also contributed powerfully to the recent epidemic of crime in Mexico. The rise in violent crime in the mid-1990s coincided with a sharp increase in the number of people living in poverty, the number of unemployed and severely underemployed people—all consequences of the deep economic crisis that erupted in 1994. In a quantitative analysis of homicide rates in a national sample of 1,750 *municipios* in Mexico, a general index of poverty was, by far, the single most important predictor of homicide rates at the local level. Other indicators of economic distress—the unemployment rate and the degree of income inequality in a *municipio*—were also significant predictors. So were certain demographic variables, like the percentage of single mothers.[36] The frequency of female-headed households is an indicator of the breakdown of the Mexican family structure, which is strongly related to adverse economic conditions and the necessity for household heads to migrate to the United States for long periods to supplement the family's income.

Finally, the inefficiency or malfunctioning of the criminal justice system is a major contributor to crime in Mexico. The actual probability of being caught, convicted, and serving substantial prison time is far too low to serve as a significant deterrent to crime. For example, out of every 100 crimes committed in Mexico in 2001, only twenty-five were reported to police, only 1.2 went to trial, and only 0.4 cases resulted in a jail sentence of more than two years.[37]

Potential remedies for Mexico's dysfunctional criminal justice system include implementing tighter screening, testing, and monitoring of law enforcement personnel; increasing the pay and improving the training for police; making criminal proceedings more transparent and efficient by introducing oral argument; giving public prosecutors greater autonomy to prevent undue interference from politicians; standardizing sentencing guidelines nationwide; making the corrections system more humane and effective in rehabilitation; and funding more ambitious crime prevention programs aimed at young people. None of these possible remedies is a panacea, and most experts believe that real progress in reducing public insecurity will depend on addressing the root causes, including joblessness and extreme income inequality.

MEXICO'S POLITICAL FUTURE

In the months following Vicente Fox's victory in the 2000 presidential elections there was a major debate among Mexican intellectuals and the political elite over whether the country had successfully completed its transition to democracy, with the alternation of power in the presidency, or whether further and deeper structural reforms would be necessary before Mexico should be classified as a democratic republic. In the aftermath of the 2006 election, particularly because of the disputed presidential result, precisely the same debates are being rehashed.

It is certain that elections in Mexico at the federal level are now as democratic and transparent as nearly any other country in the Americas. Electoral law reforms have ended most forms of fraud that were typical in the past. The Federal Electoral Institute has a strong record as a guardian of democracy. Campaign finance regulation is still deficient (disclosure rules for private contributions are very weak; the IFE can impose fines for violations only after the election), but with generous public financing of all parties' campaigns, the playing field has been leveled. Considering that the PRI-government apparatus functioned as a political machine—in which maintaining power in the executive branch was absolutely necessary to maintain the incentive structure for the rest of the political elite—the end of PRI domination of the presidency arguably has concluded the authoritarian era of Mexican politics. At the same time, many argue that a mere alternation in power is insufficient to consolidate a democratic transition. They claim that structural reforms, especially a comprehensive state reform, are required before the transition to democracy can be completed. In the first months after Mexico's 2000 election, there was a major movement to replace the 1917 Constitution, creating a system with a weaker president and stronger Congress, courts, and state governments. There was talk of changing the electoral formulas once again (though, of course, each party proposed formulas that were either more or less proportional, according to their relative electoral strengths).

The political strategies that follow from these two concepts of Mexico's transition are very different. The notion that the political transition was completed with the alternation in power in 2000 leads to political actors facing up to the problem of divided government, accepting that the electorate gave mixed signals on election day, and allowing each branch of government to make the best of the situation considering the constitutional powers that it holds. Therefore, the Congress should not consider executive bills to be untouchable (and considering the frequency with which they are amended in the chambers, this certainly seems to be the case). The president should use his constitutional decree powers and his veto as he sees fit, and not worry that their use be considered an affront to the legislative branch. The Supreme Court should arbitrate. Both the president and the parties in Congress should use publicity in the press to get their message out and pressure the other branch to give in.

The opposing camp calls for national political accords and consensus on all basic matters of governance. They believe that the constitutional boundaries between the branches must be redefined, again by consensus. Proponents of this plan in the executive branch want to create a strong, flexible presidency, while those in the opposition parties want congressional dominance or even parliamentary government.

There is little doubt that Mexico should now be classified as a democracy in terms of electoral transparency and even personal freedoms. Despite all of the sound and fury between the executive and legislative branches under divided government, there is little doubt that Mexico now has one of the best-functioning democratic political systems in Latin America—certainly closer to Chile and Costa Rica than to Brazil, Argentina, or Venezuela. While the PRI's abysmal performance in the 2006 election moved Mexico closer to a two-party system, the overall results of the election suggest that the three-party system that took shape in the late 1980s will endure for at least another *sexenio*.

Electoral shenanigans still take place in some states, but at the national level, when the attention of all of the major parties is closely focused on the process, recent elections have been remarkably clean. International election observers, hundreds of whom have been present for each of these elections, and academic analysts have found no evidence of systematic fraud.[38]

The large-scale civil disobedience campaign carried out by losing candidate López Obrador in an attempt to overturn the 2006 election result severely tested Mexico's new democratic institutions. López Obrador's party now faces a fundamental choice: admit electoral defeat and work within the Congress to push legislative remedies to the social problems that the PRD has highlighted, or engage in a sustained resistance campaign aimed at destabilizing the government and blocking its policy initiatives. The latter choice could end up weakening Mexico's fragile democracy, and it would make the PRD an antisystem party, working outside of the institutional framework. Such parties often receive considerable media attention, but they are less likely to be able to influence public policy.

REVIEW QUESTIONS

- How does political recruitment in the PAN differ from traditional forms of recruitment in the PRI? What explains these differences?

- What is metaconstitutional presidentialism? What are the conditions that bring it about? Was Vicente Fox able to govern without the benefit of metaconstitutional powers?

- What explains the shift in party preferences between 2000 and 2006? Which parties benefit and which lose out in this change in public preferences?

- How much of the political and public policy legacy of Lázaro Cárdenas survives intact today?

- Have the judicial reforms of recent years achieved the desired effect in terms of division of powers, corruption, and public security? What are the main obstacles to progress in this issue area?

- Have the 1996 electoral reforms been successful in stemming electoral fraud? Have they achieved general public acceptance of electoral returns? What further reforms could improve the results in either case?

- What are the effects of the prohibition of immediate reelection of federal legislators? What are the effects of the absolute prohibition of reelection of the president?

KEY TERMS

caciques

Cardenismo

Confederación de Trabajadores de México (CTM)

Confederación Nacional Campesina (CNC)

Confederación Nacional de Organizaciones Populares (CNOP)

corporatism/corporatist

divided government

municipios

neoliberal economic development model

Partido Acción Nacional (PAN)

Partido de la Revolución Democrática (PRD)

Partido Revolucionario Institucional (PRI)

patron–client relationships

political centralism

presidencialismo

sectoral organizations sectors (of the PRI)

sectors

Seguro Popular

sexenios

técnicos

SUGGESTED READINGS

Babb, Sarah. *Managing Mexico: Economists From Nationalism to Neoliberalism.* Princeton, NJ: Princeton University Press, 2001.

Bruhn, Kathleen. *Taking on Goliath: Mexico's Party of the Democratic Revolution.* University Park, PA: Pennsylvania State University Press, 1997.

Camp, Roderic A. *Generals in the Palacio: The Military in Modern Mexico.* New York: Oxford University Press, 1992.

———. *Crossing Swords: Politics and Religion in Mexico.* New York: Oxford University Press, 1997.

———. *Mexico's Mandarins: Crafting a Power Elite for the Twenty-First Century.* Berkeley: University of California Press, 2002.

Centeno, Miguel Angel. *Democracy Within Reason: Technocratic Revolution in Mexico,* 2nd ed. University Park: Pennsylvania State University Press, 1997.

Chambers, Edward J., and Peter H. Smith, eds. *NAFTA in the New Millennium.* La Jolla and Edmonton: Center for U.S.-Mexican Studies, University of California-San Diego and University of Alberta Press, 2002.

Chand, Vikram K. *Mexico's Political Awakening.* Notre Dame, IN: University of Notre Dame Press, 2001.

Cornelius, Wayne A. et al., eds. *Subnational Politics and Democratization in Mexico.* La Jolla: Center for U.S.-Mexican Studies, University of California-San Diego, 1999.

Cornelius, Wayne A., and Jessa M. Lewis, eds. *Impacts of Border Enforcement on Mexican Migration: The View From Sending Communities.* Boulder, CO: Lynne Rienner Publishers, 2006.

Cornelius, Wayne A., and David A. Shirk, eds., *Reforming the Administration of Justice in Mexico.* Notre Dame, IN: University of Notre Dame Press, 2007.

Díaz-Cayeros, Alberto. *Federalism, Fiscal Authority, and Centralization in Latin America.* Cambridge: Cambridge University Press, 2006.

Domínguez, Jorge I., and James A. McCann. *Democratizing Mexico: Public Opinion and Elections.* Baltimore, MD: Johns Hopkins University Press, 1995.

Domínguez, Jorge I., and Chappell Lawson, eds. *Mexico's Pivotal Democratic Election.* Stanford, CA and La Jolla: Stanford

University Press and Center for U.S.-Mexican Studies, University of California–San Diego, 2003.

Domínguez, Jorge I., James A. McCann, and Alejandro Poiré, eds. *Toward Mexico's Democratization: Parties, Campaigns, Elections, and Public Opinion.* New York: Routledge, 1999.

Eisenstadt, Todd A. *Courting Democracy in Mexico: Party Strategies and Electoral Institutions.* Cambridge: Cambridge University Press, 2004.

Knight, Alan. *The Mexican Revolution,* 2 vols. Lincoln: University of Nebraska Press, 1990.

Krauze, Enrique. *Mexico—Biography of Power: A History of Modern Mexico, 1810–1996.* New York: HarperCollins, 1997.

Lawson, Chappell. *Building the Fourth Estate: Democratization and the Rise of a Free Press in Mexico.* Berkeley: University of California Press, 2002.

Levy, Daniel C., Kathleen Bruhn, and Emilio Zebadúa. *Mexico: The Struggle for Democratic Development.* Berkeley: University of California Press, 2001.

MacLeod, Dag. *Downsizing the State: Privatization and the Limits of Neoliberal Reform in Mexico.* University Park: Pennsylvania State University Press, 2004.

Magaloni, Beatriz, *Voting for Autocracy: Hegemonic Party Survival and Its Demise in Mexico.* Cambridge: Cambridge University Press, 2006.

Peschard-Sverdrup, Armand B., and Sara R. Rioff, eds. *Mexican Governance: From Single-Party Rule to Divided Government.* Washington, DC: Center for Strategic and International Studies, 2005.

Rodríguez, Victoria E., ed. *Women's Participation in Mexican Political Life.* Boulder, CO: Westview, 1998.

Rubin, Jeffrey. *Decentering the Regime: Ethnicity, Radicalism, and Democracy in Juchitán, Mexico.* Durham, NC: Duke University Press, 1997.

Shirk, David A. *Mexico's New Politics: The PAN and Democratic Change.* Boulder, CO: Lynne Rienner Publishers, 2005.

Smith, Peter H. *Labyrinths of Power: Political Recruitment in Twentieth-Century Mexico.* Princeton, NJ: Princeton University Press, 1979.

Snyder, Richard. *Politics After Neoliberalism: Reregulation in Mexico.* Cambridge: Cambridge University Press, 2001.

Ward, Peter M. *Mexico City,* 2nd ed. New York: Wiley, 1998.

Ward, Peter M., and Victoria E. Rodríguez. *Bringing the States Back In: New Federalism and State Government in Mexico.* Austin: Lyndon B. Johnson School of Public Affairs, University of Texas–Austin, 1999.

INTERNET RESOURCES

President's Office: **www.presidencia.gob.mx**

Chamber of Deputies: **www.diputados.gob.mx**

Senate: **www.senado.gob.mx/ingles**

National Statistical Institute: **www.inegi.gob.mx**

National Population Council: **www.conapo.gob.mx**

Federal Electoral Institute: **www.ife.org.mx**

ENDNOTES

1. PRI candidate Carlos Salinas de Gortari was credited with 50.74 percent of the valid votes cast. However, if the 695,042 "spoiled" ballots and 14,333 votes cast for nonregistered presidential candidates are included in the calculation, Salinas won by a plurality of only 48.7 percent.

2. This percentage represents an undercount, since the census identifies as Indians only people over age 50. Indians of all ages constitute an estimated 15 percent of the total population.

3. Peter H. Smith, "The Making of the Mexican Constitution," in William O. Aydelotte, ed., *The History of Parliamentary Behavior* (Princeton, NJ: Princeton University Press, 1977), 219.

4. Quoted in Denise Dresser, "Five Scenarios for Mexico," *Journal of Democracy* 5, no. 3 (July 1994): 57.

5. The actual extent of irregularities in the 1988 presidential vote will never be determined. Within a few hours after the polls closed, with early returns showing Cárdenas ahead by a significant margin, top authorities ordered the computerized count to be suspended. When results for a majority of the country's polling places were announced six days later, Salinas had won. There is no corroborating evidence from exit surveys of voters,

because the government denied permission for such surveys in 1988. The PRI-controlled Congress later ordered the ballots stored in its basement to be burned, thereby eliminating any possibility of challenging the election outcome. Study of the partial, publicly released results and preelection polling data has led most analysts to conclude that Salinas probably did win but that his margin of victory over Cárdenas was much smaller than the 19-point spread indicated by the official results.

6. According to statistics of the IFE, Zedillo won 50.18 percent of the valid votes (i.e., excluding "spoiled" ballots and write-in votes cast for unregistered candidates). However, if the calculation is based on total votes cast (including those annulled by electoral authorities), his share of the vote declines to 48.77 percent.

7. Jeffrey S. Passel, "The Size and Characteristics of the Unauthorized Migrant Population in the U.S." (Research Report, Pew Hispanic Center, Washington, DC, 7 March, 2006).

8. See Roderic A. Camp, *Citizen Views of Democracy in Latin America* (Pittsburgh, PA.: University of Pittsburgh Press, 2001).

9. For illustrative survey data from the early 1990s, see Jorge I. Domínguez and James A. McCann, *Democratizing Mexico:*

Public Opinion and Electoral Choices (Baltimore, MD: Johns Hopkins University Press, 1996), 29–47.

10. James A. McCann and Chappell Lawson, "An Electorate Adrift?—Public Opinion and the Quality of Democracy in Mexico," *Latin American Research Review*, 38 no. 3 (2003): 60–81; Francisco Flores-Macías and Chappell Lawson, "Mexican Democracy and Its Discontents," *Review of Policy Research*, forthcoming, 2006.

11. McCann and Lawson, "An Electorate Adrift?"; Jorge I. Domínguez and Chappell Lawson, eds., *Mexico's Pivotal Democratic Election* (Stanford and La Jolla: Stanford University Press/Center for U.S.-Mexican Studies, University of California–San Diego, 2003).

12. Constitutional reforms are very common in Mexican law because regular statutory reforms or new policy programs frequently require constitutional sanction before they can be enacted. Therefore, constitutional reforms in Mexico are not only questions of basic structural or political reform, but also matters of public policy.

13. See Alan Knight, "Historical Continuities in Social Movements," in Joe Foweraker and Ann L. Craig, eds., *Popular Movements and Political Change in Mexico* (Boulder, CO: Lynne Rienner, 1990), 78–102; Jeffrey W. Rubin, *Decentering the Regime: Ethnicity, Radicalism, and Democracy in Juchitán, Mexico* (Durham, NC: Duke University Press, 1997); Wayne A. Cornelius, Todd Eisenstadt, and Jane Hindley, eds., *Subnational Politics and Democratization in Mexico* (La Jolla: Center for U.S.-Mexican Studies, University of California–San Diego, 1999).

14. Alberto Díaz-Cayeros, *Federalism, Fiscal Authority, and Centralization in Latin America* (Cambridge: Cambridge University Press, 2006), 8, 143–47.

15. See Victoria E. Rodríguez, *Decentralization in Mexico: From Reforma Municipal to Solidaridad to Nuevo Federalismo* (Boulder, CO: Westview, 1997); Peter M. Ward and Victoria E. Rodríguez, *Bringing the States Back In: New Federalism and State Government in Mexico* (Austin: Lyndon Baines Johnson School of Public Affairs, University of Texas–Austin, 1999).

16. For a recent discussion of mixed-member electoral systems in general, and comparisons between Mexico's electoral regime with similar systems, see *Mixed-Member Electoral Systems: The Best of Both Worlds?* Matthew Soberg Shugart and Martin P. Wattenberg, eds. (Oxford: Oxford University Press, 2001).

17. See Jeffrey A. Weldon, "Political Sources of *Presidencialismo* in Mexico," in Scott Mainwaring and Matthew Soberg Shugart, eds., *Presidentialism and Democracy in Latin America* (New York: Cambridge University Press, 1997), 225–58.

18. For a conventional interpretation of the powers of the Mexican president, see Luis Javier Garrido, "The Crisis of *Presidencialismo*," in Wayne A. Cornelius, Judith Gentleman, and Peter H. Smith, eds., *Mexico's Alternative Political Futures* (La Jolla: Center for U.S.-Mexican Studies, University of California–San Diego, 1989), 417–34.

19. The purported rationale for this principle, applied to the president in the 1917 Constitution and extended to members of Congress in 1933, was to ensure freedom from self-perpetuating, dictatorial rule in the Porfirio Díaz style. However, the real reason for prohibiting the consecutive reelection of deputies and senators was probably to cut the ties between local political bosses and their federal legislators, at a time that the ruling party was seeking greater centralization of authority.

20. See Weldon, "The Political Sources of *Presidencialismo* in Mexico."

21. Miguel Angel Centeno, *Democracy Within Reason: Technocratic Revolution in Mexico*, 2nd ed. (University Park: Pennsylvania State University Press, 1997), 112.

22. Centeno, *Democracy Within Reason*.

23. David A. Shirk, *Mexico's New Politics: The PAN and Democratic Change* (Boulder, CO: Lynne Rienner Publishers, 2005), 191–94.

24. Unpublished data from Roderic A. Camp. See also Roderic A. Camp, "Family Relationships in Mexican Politics," *Journal of Politics* 44 (August 1982): 848–62; Peter H. Smith, *Labyrinths of Power: Political Recruitment in Twentieth-Century Mexico* (Princeton, NJ: Princeton University Press, 1979), 307–10.

25. Shirk, *Mexico's New Politics*, 181.

26. Lorenzo Meyer, "La Democracia Política: Esperando a Godot," *Nexos* 100 (April 1986): 42.

27. Joseph L. Klesner, "Electoral Competition and the New Party System in Mexico," *Latin American Politics and Society*, 47, no. 2 (2005): 103–42; Klesner, "Social and Regional Factors in the 2006 Presidential Election" (unpublished paper, Dept. of Political Science, Kenyon College, August 2006).

28. Alejandro Moreno, *El votante mexicano* (México, DF: Fondo de Cultura Económica, 2003).

29. As Joseph Klesner has shown, both the PAN and the PRD now exhibit catch-all characteristics, driven by the dealignment of the electorate from the PRI and the desire of its rivals to broaden their constituencies by capturing these "delinked" voters. Klesner, "Electoral Competition and the New Party System."

30. Chappell Lawson, "Blue States and Yellow States: Preliminary Findings From the Mexico 2006 Panel Study" (unpublished paper, Dept. of Political Science, Massachusetts Institute of Technology, 27 July, 2006).

31. Centeno, *Democracy Within Reason*, 194.

32. A wealth of statistical data demonstrating these trends can be found in Enrique Dussel Peters, *Polarizing Development: The Impact of Liberalization Strategy* (Boulder, CO: Lynne Rienner, 2000).

33. Carlos Elizondo, "In Search of Revenue: Tax Reform in Mexico Under the Administrations of Echeverría and Salinas," *Journal of Latin American Studies* 26, no. 1 (February 1994): 159–90.

34. Guillermo Zepeda Lecuona, "Criminal Investigation and the Subversion of the Principles of the Justice System in Mexico," in Wayne A. Cornelius and David A. Shirk, eds., *Reforming the Administration of Justice in Mexico* (Notre Dame, IN: University of Notre Dame Press, 1997).

35. Sara Schatz, "A Neo-Weberian Approach to Constitutional Courts in the Transition From Authoritarian Rule: The Mexican Case, 1994–1997," *International Journal of the Sociology of Law* 26 (1998): 217–44.

36. Andrés Villarreal, "Structural Determinants of Homicide in Mexico" (paper presented at the annual meeting of the American Sociological Association, 5 January, 1999).

37. Zepeda Lecuona, "Criminal Investigation."

38. Regarding the 2006 election, see Luis Estrada and Alejandro Poiré, "La Evidencia del Fraude," *Reforma*, 13 August, 2006 (Enfoque supplement), 12–13.

POLITICS IN IRAN

H. E. Chehabi and Arang Keshavarzian

Country Bio

Population
66.3 million

Territory
636,296 square miles

Year of Independence
550 B.C.

Year of Current Constitution
1979, amended in 1989

IRAN

Head of State
Ali Khamenei

Head of Government
Mahmud Ahmadinejad

Languages
Persian, regional languages

Religions
Twelver Shiite Muslim 90%; Sunni Muslim 10%;
non-Muslims less than 1%

The Islamic Republic of Iran is the world's only **theocracy,** a form of government in which ideally all laws are grounded in religion and express the will of God, and a clergy exercises supreme power. While Islamic law has always been applied to varying degrees in Muslim states, it has almost always been complemented by some sort of nonreligious customary law. Moreover, various sultans, shahs, sheikhs, and, since the twentieth century, presidents or prime ministers have traditionally exercised political power in the Muslim world. Genuine theocracies have been very rare. Although the **ulema,** as religious scholars are called in the Muslim world, have been critical of rulers who strayed from the path of Islam, they almost never aspired to exercise power directly as they do in Iran today. Therefore, far from being a manifestation of Islamic conservatism, Iran's current theocratic regime constitutes a break with Muslim tradition. The only other Muslim theocracy of the twentieth century was that of the Taliban in Afghanistan (1996–2001), who, unlike the ulema of Iran, never gained control over the entire country and whose regime was generally not recognized by the international community.

The Islamic Republic of Iran was established in 1979, a few months after a popular revolution uniting poor and middle-class, religious and secular people overthrew **Mohammad-Reza Shah Pahlavi** (r. 1941–1979), the last ruler of the country's ancient monarchy. **Ruhollah Khomeini,** a charismatic clerical leader who had authored a blueprint for theocratic government in the early 1970s, led the 1979 revolution. In this blueprint, Khomeini opposed democracy on religious grounds. Sovereignty, he argued, belongs to God alone. Divine law, known as the *shari'a,* as interpreted and applied by the ulema, takes precedence over laws made by human legislators. In spite of its beginnings as a clerical dictatorship, Iran developed a very lively political system after Khomeini's death in 1989. Presidential, parliamentary, and local elections offer the citizens a choice of candidates advocating differing policies. The emergence of limited democratic practices and institutions under a regime founded on the negation of democracy is only one of many paradoxes to be found in Iran. Most Third World dictatorships pay lip service to democracy while routinely violating its spirit and undermining its practice.

CURRENT POLICY CHALLENGES

As long as **Islamists**—by which we mean people who consider the religion of Islam a political ideology that addresses issues of private and public life—are in political opposition, it is easy for them to blame the shortcomings of the society on inadequate attention to the teachings of Islam and the "blind following of Western models." Islamists promise a society characterized by social justice and moral propriety in which an "authentic" Muslim culture can flourish uncontaminated by Western "decadence." Iran is the first country in which Islamists have had to deliver on these promises.

During the first decade of the Islamic Republic some redistribution of wealth did indeed take place, as the government expropriated much of the property of the old prerevolutionary elite. The new leadership came mostly from humble or middle-class backgrounds and adopted populist policies that somewhat bettered the lot of the poorest. For instance, the new regime invested heavily in rural development, including in health, women's education, and roads. However, the postrevolutionary reality is far from ideal, and poverty, inequality, and underemployment continue to be major public grievances. Possessing the world's second largest oil and gas reserves, the public expects its government to improve the lot of ordinary Iranians and establish the basis for long-term and sustainable development. However, transforming natural wealth into income and long-term investment has proven difficult. In the ideological climate of the Islamic Republic, industrial entrepreneurs are seen as exploiters, and so private investment tends to go into speculation and rent seeking rather than long-term industrial investment aimed at enhancing exports and creating sustainable development. Consequently, job creation has been very inadequate.

The need to increase economic output in order to provide employment for a rapidly growing labor force is perhaps the greatest challenge facing the government. Iran's population grows by about one million every year (see Figure 12.1). Although the government has been quite successful in bringing down the birth rate, the effects of the lower population growth rate will not be felt for many years. In 2002, 59 percent of the total population was under age 25.[1] Even under the best circumstances it would be difficult to provide employment for the 800,000 men and women who enter the labor market every year, but Iran's antientrepreneurial outlook as well as its unattractiveness to foreign investment mean that the situation is even worse. Regional conflicts and the continuing tension between Iran and the United States discourage both foreign and domestic investment. At the same time, a vastly expanded educational system means that many of the young unemployed hold an academic degree, which adds to their frustration and discontent. This discontent has produced massive migration. In recent years 200,000 Iranians have been leaving per year, causing one of the most massive brain-drains in the world. One in four Iranians with a higher education degree lives abroad.[2] The Islamists'

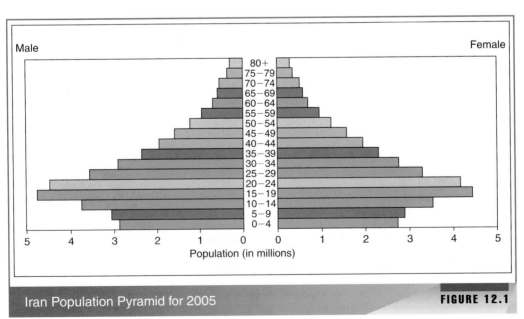

Iran Population Pyramid for 2005

FIGURE 12.1

Source: U.S. Census Bureau, International Data Base.

anti-Western stance notwithstanding, millions of young Iranians dream of moving to the West.

The presence of a large Iranian diaspora in the United States, Canada, and Europe has made life in the West familiar for Iranians. Even poorer Iranians often have a friend or relative in Los Angeles ("Tehrangeles") or Toronto ("Tehranto"). Thanks to cheap telephone cards and the Internet they can stay in touch with their relatives and friends abroad. When they compare the opportunities Iran offers them with those their cousins enjoy "on the other side," they find them terribly wanting.

Corruption makes matters even worse. The print media increasingly report about corruption, and it is debated in Parliament and by politicians. As many Iranians struggle to find gainful employment and make ends meet, a new elite has made fortunes by exploiting personal connections to the officials who control access to hard currency, import licenses, and tax shelters. The relatives of former president **Ali-Akbar Hashemi Rafsanjani** are often cited as examples of the wealth nourished by privileged access and information.

For all these reasons, the promises of the Islamic revolutionaries concerning a more just and more moral society ring hollow with many Iranians, half of whom are too young to recall the corruption, political repression, and inequality under the Shah. As a result, the theocratic model of government has suffered a massive loss of legitimacy. While the people may still be religious, the ulema no longer command their deference and respect. In addition, Islam itself is developing in new directions that question the right of the ulema to rule.

A new challenge concerns dissatisfaction with the status quo among some of Iran's ethnic minorities, who live mostly in the country's peripheral areas. Azeris live in the northwest, Kurds in the west, Arabs in the southwest, Turkomans in the northeast, and Baluchis in the southeast.[3] All these minorities have ethnic kin on the other side of the border. Until recently, this did not matter much, since they constituted minorities on the other side as well. With the breakup of the Soviet Union, however, independent Azerbaijan exerts a certain attraction for Azeris in Iran. The consolidation of a semi-independent Kurdish state in Iraq plays a similar role for Kurds in Iran (and Turkey). Iran's Arabs, until now loyal to the Iranian state because they are mostly Shiites, may

become less certain of their national affiliation if Shiites gain the upper hand in neighboring Iraq. For the time being, such challenges to Iran's territorial integrity are relatively weak compared with neighboring states, such as Iraq and Turkey. But these challenges are growing, partly because the government is seen as favoring the Persian-speaking majority and partly because they are subtly encouraged by outside powers.

Like other Third World countries, Iran faces general challenges of community and development. Iran's leaders are confronted with the daunting tasks of integrating large groups of disaffected citizens (the young, the unemployed, and ethnic minorities) and producing enough economic development to improve living conditions for these groups. The Islamic regime's failure to address these issues has dented its legitimacy considerably.

Historical Legacy

Iran, like China and Japan, is one of a handful of non-Western states that were never formally colonized by Europeans. Iran's borders were not drawn artificially by colonial powers but result from the historical balance of power between its shahs and their neighboring rulers. The Iranian state tradition is over twenty-five centuries old, but the current Iranian state was set up in the early sixteenth century by the Safavid dynasty. The dynasty's most lasting impact was the establishment of **Twelver Shiism** as the official state religion and the conversion of most Iranians who had been **Sunnis** to Shiism. Historically, the shrine cities of Iraq had been the cradle of this branch of Islam, but with the establishment of a powerful Shiite state in Iran, Iran became the political center of the Shiite world.

Twelver Shiism

The split between Sunnis (who constitute about 90 percent of all Muslims) and the Shiites came about after the death of the founder of Islam, the Prophet Muhammad. Muhammad was not only the founder of a new religion but also a political leader. Therefore, after he died in 628 C.E. the nascent Muslim community had to find a leader to succeed him. A minority of believers, who later came to be known as Shiites, deemed the descendants of the Prophet to be his only rightful successors. Shiites call these hereditary successors to the Prophet *Imams*. Of particular importance is the Third Imam, Husayn, whose martyrdom in 680 C.E. symbolizes for Shiites the struggle of the just against the unjust. This event is still commemorated yearly in emotional processions that acquire a political dimension in times of political crisis.

While some small Shiite sects believe in an unbroken line of Imams all the way to the present, the vast majority believe that the twelfth was the last of the Imams, hence their name. According to these Shiites, the twelfth Imam disappeared from view as a child in 874 C.E., but did not die. He is alive (rather like Elijah in the Jewish tradition) and will come forth and show himself to establish a just rule at the end of time. In other words, he is a messiah-like figure. From the moment the Twelfth Imam disappeared from public view, therefore, Twelver Shiite political thought faced a dilemma. The only figure who could exercise legitimate rule over the community of believers was not physically present, and no one knew when he would reveal himself. Most of the time this dilemma did not matter in practice, because Shiites were a minority lacking political power, making their political theology inconsequential.

With the establishment of a Twelver Shiite state by the Safavid dynasty in sixteenth century, the unavailability of the one truly legitimate ruler became an existential problem. In the absence of the Twelfth Imam, who had the right to rule in practice? Most ulema were willing to accord this right to the secular rulers, the shahs, so long as they ruled justly and in accordance with Islam. By the end of the seventeenth century, however, a minority of ulema argued that for the rule of a shah to be legitimate, he had to have the ulema's explicit endorsement. After the fall of the Safavids in 1722 Iran was in the grip of civil wars as various short-lived dynasties succeeded each other. The Qajar dynasty finally emerged victorious in 1796.

During this troubled century the ulema established themselves as an institution independent of the state. Since the state was in disarray much of the time, believers' tithes were increasingly paid to the ulema directly, assuring them of financial independence. Moreover, the center of Twelver Shiism, the city of Najaf, lay in Ottoman Iraq, outside the control of Iran's worldly authorities. Beginning in the nineteenth century, therefore, the ulema had greater social, political, and religious prominence in Iran than in the Sunni world. They had their own sources of income and were beyond the control of the state. Without this legacy the

establishment of a theocracy would not even have been conceivable in the 1970s.

In some ways the role and function of the ulema resemble that of a clergy in Christian countries. However, while the Shiite ulema form a loose hierarchy, they are not organized in a pyramidal structure like the Roman Catholic Church. There is no equivalent of the pope, and no one leader can define dogma in a way that is binding for everyone else. Consequently, the ulema have often disagreed among each other on political and even minor religious matters, a state of affairs that, as we will see, has not ended with the creation of an Islamic state.

Constitutionalism in Iran

Iran's geographic location between the Russian empire in the north and the British empire in the south allowed it to survive the heyday of European imperialism as an independent state. Both empires allowed it to remain a neutral buffer between their respective domains. Nevertheless educated Iranians recognized the fragility of their country's sovereignty. As they became more familiar with Europe in the nineteenth century, they became more aware of their own backwardness. As long as Iran was less developed than Europe, it would forever remain vulnerable to imperialist encroachment. Consequently, "catching up with the West" became the major goal of Iran's intellectual and political elite. They believed that the rule of law was the secret of European superiority, whereas arbitrary rule prevailed in Iran. They concluded that constitutional government had to be introduced to strengthen the nation. Japan's victory over Russia in the war of 1905 confirmed Iranian constitutionalists in their view. For the first time an Asian power had vanquished a European one, and Iranians argued that this reversal of fortunes occurred because Japan was the only constitutional power in Asia and Russia was the only autocracy among the major European powers.

In 1905 widespread dissatisfaction with the way the country was governed led to a popular movement that eventually wrested a constitution from the shah in December 1906. Shiite ulema played a major role in the constitutionalist movement. Until a few years earlier the Iranian state had been characterized by an implicit contract between worldly and spiritual authorities. The shah upheld the official religion, and the ulema legitimated the shah's rule. But by the early twentieth century many politically active ulema shared the views of merchants and Western-educated intellectuals: that the powers of the monarchy needed to be curtailed. They believed that the citizenry had the right to elect a representative parliament; that the shah could name a prime minister only in agreement with parliament; and that parliament could hold the government accountable. These very European ideas were criticized by conservative ulema for being alien to Islam, but constitutionalist ulema found ways to justify them in Islamic terms. Most famously, Ayatollah Muhammad-Husayn Na'ini argued that a despotic shah violated the rights of the Twelfth Imam and those of the people, whereas rule by the people violated only the rights of the Twelfth Imam. He concluded that while neither form of government was ideal, the latter was the lesser evil and thus preferable to the former.[4] This argument implied the novel idea that as long as the Twelfth Imam chose to remain in hiding, the believers themselves were his deputies. This elegant formulation reconciled Shiism's core beliefs with modern notions of constitutionalism and is a legacy that the revolutionaries of 1979 could not ignore as they set out to create an Islamic state.

The Pahlavi Monarchy

The Constitution of 1906 did not bring the hoped-for progress, however. In a 1907 secret agreement Britain and Russia divided Iran into two spheres of influence. During World War I, belligerents repeatedly violated Iran's neutrality and fought each other on Iranian territory, causing much hardship to the population. By the end of the war, local warlords were challenging the authority of the central government in peripheral regions.

In 1921, a *coup d'état* put an end to the rule of the old establishment. The commander of the troops, Reza Khan, lost no time in extending government control over rebellious provinces and began an ambitious modernization program to develop and centralize state authority. By 1925, he ousted the ruling Qajar dynasty and had Parliament proclaim him new ruler as Reza Shah Pahlavi. From his coronation in 1926 until his ouster by the British in the wake of the Allied occupation of Iran in 1941, he ruled as dictator, although he left the Constitution formally in place. Reza Khan initially enjoyed the support of most of the clergy. But in the 1930s his relations with the ulema deteriorated after he implemented reforms that reduced their social functions and aimed at westernizing the daily culture of Iranians, such as prohibiting women's veiling. With his departure into exile politics opened up again. His 21-year-old son and successor, Mohammad-Reza Shah Pahlavi, did not have the authority yet to continue his father's ways (see Figure 12.2).

Between 1941 and 1953 Iran's political system included three main camps. First, the pro-Western conservative establishment, including the Shah and the landlords, was supported tacitly by most of the ulema. Second was the pro-Soviet communist **Tudeh**

Year	Head of State	President	Prime Minister
1941	Shah: Mohammad-Reza Pahlavi	—	—Various cabinets
1951	—	—	Mohammad Mossadegh (51–53)
—	—	—	—Various cabinets
1965	—	—	Amir-Abbas Hoveyda
1977	—	—	Jamshid Amuzegar
1979	Leader: Ruhollah Khomeini	—	Mehdi Bazargan
1980	—	Abolhasan Banisadr	—
1981	—	Ali Rajai, Ali Khamenei	Mir-Hosein Musavi
1989	Ali Khamenei	Ali-Akbar Hashemi Rafsanjani	Position abolished
1997	—	Mohammad Khatami	—
2005	—	Mahmud Ahmadinejad	—

Iranian Regimes   **FIGURE 12.2**

Party. Third, was the neutralist National Front, which aimed at establishing the full rule of law within the country and consolidating its standing among nations. As the National Front saw it, the nation's sovereignty was compromised by British control over Iran's oil resources through the British-owned Anglo-Iranian Oil Company(AIOC). The Iranian government had no say in the company, not even the right to see its books. From 1945 to 1950, the total net profits of the AIOC were £ 250 million after deducting high British taxes, royalties, and exaggerated depreciation figures; At the same time, royalties paid to Iran for its oil amounted to merely £ 90 million.[5]

The leader of the National Front was **Mohammad Mossadegh,** who advocated nationalizing the Iranian oil industry. This was accomplished in March 1951, and soon thereafter Mossadegh was elected prime minister by Parliament. Subsequent negotiations between the Iranian and British governments to resolve the oil dispute failed. Consequently, the British began plotting Mossadegh's overthrow, which was accomplished with the help of the U.S. Central Intelligence Agency (CIA) in August 1953.[6]

Iran's political system reverted to royal autocracy as the second ruler of the Pahlavi dynasty increasingly asserted himself, taking full command of the country in January 1963. He launched a reform program that became known as the "White Revolution," which included land reform and the granting of the suffrage to women. In the 1950s the Shah had enjoyed the support of the clerical hierarchy, but by the early 1960s his dictatorial methods and westernizing policies elicited the anger of religious traditionalists. These traditionalists rioted in June 1963 in support of a new oppositional member of the ulema, Ruhollah Khomeini. The riots were suppressed with bloodshed, and Khomeini was arrested and exiled. He finally settled in the Shiite shrine city of Najaf in Iraq; he remained there until October 1978, when he was expelled by Saddam Hussein and sought refuge in Paris until his triumphant return to Iran on February 1, 1979.

Until 1963, opposition to royal autocracy was carried out in the name of the Constitution of 1906, which the two Pahlavi shahs were criticized for not respecting. Free elections were the opposition's main demand. After 1963, however, opponents of the Shah, increasingly driven underground or abroad, despaired of ever attaining constitutional rule by peaceful means and became radicalized. Gradually the Constitution

itself suffered a loss of legitimacy. Opponents of the Shah demanded the abolition of the monarchy and its replacement by a new regime. Given the Shah's suppression of civil society and of the secular opposition, mosques and religious circles became the only places where one could speak one's mind. Thus, religion became a more prominent political force, despite the secularist policies of the state. By the 1970s Shiite activists, many of them students or followers of Khomeini, were arguing about the shape of the ideal Islamic state.

While the Shah's regime was increasingly contested at home, it continued to receive support from the West in general and the United States in particular. Since the Shah's rule had been made possible through the direct intervention of the CIA, his opponents thought of him as an American puppet whose policies were designed to benefit the United States rather than Iran. Opposition to the Shah thus logically entailed opposition to the United States and Israel, with which the Shah had contracted a strategic alliance directed against radical Arab states, such as Egypt, Iraq, and Syria. In recent years, evidence has appeared suggesting that at the height of his power in the early 1970s the Shah, far from being manipulated by the United States, was actually successful in manipulating U.S. policymakers to achieve his ends.[7]

Although Iran's first revolution failed to produce a constitutional state based on the rule of law, during the seven decades of its life Iran acquired the trappings of a modern nation-state. The government acquired a monopoly on the use of force; introduced unified legal codes; developed a functioning civil service, including a territorial administration that extended the writ of the state into distant provinces; and secured the country's international borders. These accomplishments gave the new theocracy the form of an Islamic *republic* in the aftermath of the revolution of 1978–1979.

The Islamic Revolution

In 1977 Jimmy Carter became president of the United States and U.S. foreign policy began emphasizing respect for human rights by American allies.[8] Unbeknownst to the public, the Shah had terminal cancer. To ensure a smooth transition to his heir at a time when U.S. support could no longer be taken for granted, he began liberalizing Iran's political system in 1977. Amir-Abbas Hoveyda, who had been prime minister since 1965 and embodied the cabinet's subservience to the Shah, was replaced with former finance minister Jamshid Amuzegar. But various dissident and social groups with grievances took advantage of this liberalization to push for greater reforms. From late 1977 to early 1979 the calls for greater liberalization snowballed into a call for the abolition of the monarchy by a largely urban coalition. This coalition consisted of intellectuals, university and high school students and teachers, bazaar merchants, politically active clerics and seminarians, industrial workers, and, in the final stage, state employees and white-collar workers.[9] The popular movement against the regime's despotism, corruption, and alliances with the United States and Israel united such diverse ideological factions as liberal adherents of the 1906 Constitution, Marxist-Leninist leftists, and Islamists. The latter comprised democrats whose reading of Islam was decidedly liberal and noncoercive, leftists who stressed the egalitarian aspects of Islam, and direct followers of Khomeini who championed an Islamic state supervised by clerics. These activists organized massive meetings, demonstrations, and strikes, and they distributed antiregime pamphlets in a largely peaceful manner.[10] In his reaction, the Shah vacillated between repressing the movement with force and making belated concessions to it. The result was that the activists became ever more radicalized during 1978, finally driving him and his family into exile in January 1979.[11]

In the course of the revolutionary uprising and immediately after the departure of the Shah's family,

Khomeini's followers were the best-organized and most united force, and they rapidly sidelined the nonclerical currents in their coalition. The organizational power of Khomeini and his followers was enhanced by their access to independent sources of revenue, as traditionally observant Shiites pay their tithes directly to the ulema. In 1970 Khomeini had revived the strain in Twelver Shiite thought that called for clerical oversight of government and carried it to its logical conclusion. In a treatise titled "Islamic Government" he argued that God had revealed his laws to humankind, not so that they would be ignored until the moment the Twelfth Imam revealed himself, but in order to apply them here and now. Khomeini further observed that the people most suited to rule in accordance with divine law are those who know it best, namely the ulema themselves. This principle came to be known as **velayat-e faqih,** which is best translated as "guardianship of the jurisprudent"[12] (see Box 12.1).

Given Khomeini's charismatic leadership of the revolution, his followers succeeded in late 1979 to enshrine this principle in the new Iranian Constitution. However, in deference to the preexisting constitutional tradition and to placate the many non-Islamists and moderate Islamists who had participated in the revolution, the Constitution maintained a Parliament elected by universal suffrage. The shah was replaced with an elected president. The Islamic Republic was thus born with a mixed political system that is informed by both a version of Twelver Shiite political doctrine and Western notions of popular sovereignty and division of powers.[13]

Velayat-e Faqih

BOX 12.1

Velayat-e faqih—the lynchpin of Iran's theocratic Constitution—is best translated as "guardianship of the jurisprudent." Ayatollah Ruhollah Khomeini described this while he was in exile in 1970 in Iraq. Khomeini argued that since God revealed the laws according to which Muslims should live and organize their community, Muslims should apply these laws in practice rather than just debate them theoretically. The most qualified people to supervise the application of these laws in the state, he wrote, are those who know them best (that is, the clerics who specialize in jurisprudence). He

concluded that such a cleric must therefore be the head of state. In 1979 this principle was enshrined in the Constitution of the Islamic Republic of Iran, and Khomeini himself became the ruling jurisprudent, referred to henceforth as "Leader." For the first time in Iranian history, religious and worldly authorities were fused. *Velayat-e faqih* is not strongly grounded in scripture, and most Twelver Shiite clerics disagree with the principle. They see the task of the Shiite clergy as being that of guiding the believers and advising rulers, as can be seen in post-Saddam Iraq.

From 1979 to June 1981 secular moderates, leftists, leftists, moderate Islamists, and radical Islamists inspired directly by Khomeini competed for power. As time went on, the confrontation between adherents of *velayat-e faqih* and their opponents became ever more implacable and violent. In fact, far more people were killed in confrontations among the revolutionaries than had died as a result of the Shah's half-hearted efforts to suppress the revolutionary mass movement. By the summer of 1981 the supporters of Khomeini gained the upper hand and began instituting Islamic law in all spheres of public life. Their suppression of all who opposed them was facilitated by the war that was now raging with neighboring Iraq.

Iran–Iraq War

Soon after the revolution, Khomeini began calling for the overthrow of the Iraqi president, Saddam Hussein. This provoked Saddam Hussein to attack Iran in September 1980. The war that ensued lasted until 1988 and ended in a stalemate.

Officially termed the "imposed war" or the "sacred defense" in Iran, the war was a major watershed. Over two million Iranians were mobilized, with over one million killed and injured, many due to Iraq's use of chemical weapons.[14] The war enabled the revolutionary regime to consolidate its hold on power by calling for national unity in the face of a foreign invasion. The war became a means to suppress dissent and public debate. At the level of society, the conflict created a "war generation" of young men who were shaped as much by their experiences at the front as by the revolution. Now many of these soldiers and officers are in their forties and fifties, and some are demanding a bigger say in national and local politics. These veterans have tended to call for more "social order" and a greater state role in providing for the lower classes, who volunteered and perished in the war in disproportionately large numbers.

The Legacy of Oil Wealth: A Rentier State

Like other nations enriched by large amounts of natural resources such as oil or diamonds, the Iranian state has particular characteristics that shape its relations with society. The export of petroleum products has made the Iranian state dependent on the world economy for the bulk of its budget. This revenue is rent, which is a windfall accruing directly to the treasury.

Since the 1960s, Iran's budget has not depended on domestic revenues (taxes or borrowing), which has made the state largely autonomous from society.[15] Unlike most states that must bargain with social groups to generate revenue for public projects, to pay public employees, and to fight wars, **rentier states** like Iran can sustain themselves independently of social pressures and powerful interest groups. At the same time, the state is particularly susceptible to fluctuations in the world oil market, making long-term planning more difficult. The massive revenue from petroleum exports has often been cited as a major reason for the Iranian state's unresponsiveness to social demands, and even its authoritarianism.[16] Thus, what was initially thought of as a blessing is now often seen as a curse (we will discuss interest aggregation later in this chapter).

INSTITUTIONS OF THE ISLAMIC REPUBLIC

Two types of institutions coexist in the political system of the Islamic Republic of Iran: appointed and elected offices. This dualism reflects the attempted synthesis between divine and popular sovereignty enshrined in the Constitution. The institutional structure of Iran is further complicated by the existence of what is known as **multiple power centers,** institutions created by the revolutionaries to supplement the activities of the traditional state institutions, with which they share overlapping responsibilities.

Leader

The highest authority in the Islamic Republic is the **Leader,** who combines religious and temporal authority in accordance with the theocratic principle of *velayat-e faqih*. The position was tailor-made for Khomeini himself, who was both a high-level member of the ulema and a charismatic political leader. For his succession, the Constitution provided for a popularly elected **Assembly of Experts,** consisting of ulema who would chose the Leader from among the most learned ulema. By 1989, however, none of the ulema who had the requisite learning shared his notions of theocratic rule. Consequently, in April 1989 Khomeini appointed an assembly to revise the Constitution to relax the religious requirements of the office. Khomeini died on June 3, 1989. The Assembly of Experts chose **Ali Khamenei,** who had been president for eight years but was a low-level cleric, to be the new Leader. From the outset, much of the clerical hierarchy contested Khamenei's religious authority, reopening the split between state and "church" that the Islamic Republic had supposedly closed with its fusion of worldly and spiritual authorities.

The Leader sets the overall policies of the state and appoints some of its key figures, such as the head of the Judiciary, half the members of the **Council of Guardians,** the members of the **Expediency Council,** the director of the state radio and television broadcasting monopoly, and the commanders of the various military forces. He also oversees the numerous parastatal economic foundations and organizations that were formed after the revolution out of the expropriated companies belonging to the previous economic elite. These organizations are ostensibly oriented toward charity and bear such names as the Foundation of the Disinherited and War Injured and the Martyr's Foundation. In fact, they are major holding companies that benefit from state resources and subsidies without being accountable to and regulated by the elected government. Khamenei has used these "nonprofit" organizations as a means to distribute patronage[17](see Box 12.2).

In theory, the Assembly of Experts, which is elected every ten years by universal suffrage, is more powerful than the Leader. It elects him and can dismiss him if he can no longer assume the responsibilities of his office or proves unworthy of it. However, candidacies to the Assembly of Experts are subject to the approval of the Council of Guardians, whose members are chosen by the Leader, who thus maintains his supremacy in practice.

President

The president is elected by universal suffrage every four years. He must be a Twelver Shiite and a male. However, a number of women have tried, always unsuccessfully, to become presidential candidates. Until 1989 the office was largely ceremonial and the

---

BOX 12.2

The Martyr's Foundation

Among the most powerful **parastatal foundations** is the Martyr's Foundation (Bonyad-e Shahid) established in 1979. Its original mandate was to provide for the needs of families of those who were martyred and the disabled in the Islamic Revolution and the Iran–Iraq war. The foundation provides support to 188,000 people by giving aid, priority admission for education, in-kind transfers, housing services to relatives of martyrs and disabled veterans, and other benefits. These services are funded by assets formerly belonging to supporters of the shah that were expropriated, allocations from the state budget and the office of the Leader, and profits from the operation of the foundation's various firms. In the mid-1980s it was reported that the Martyr's Foundation owned $3.3 billion in capital reserves, including sixty-eight industrial factories, seventy-five commercial firms, twenty-one construction companies, and many farms and pieces of urban property.

To administer this large and diverse economic conglomerate, the Martyr's Foundation employs 30,000 people and has a whole host of subdivisions, such as the International Relations Office and the Marriage Bureau for Widows of Wartime Martyrs. The foundation also puts out a magazine that spreads the early revolutionary ideology. In 1993, the foundation established the Shahid Investment Company in order to pool the savings of surviving relatives of the martyrs and invest them. By 2000 shareholders were complaining that the investment company never disclosed its accounts to the shareholders. Mehdi Karrubi was the president of the foundation from 1980 to 1992. Karrubi became speaker of the Sixth Parliament (2000–2004). He ran for president in 2005 on a pro-welfare and distribution platform and came in third only narrowly behind Hashemi-Rafsanjani and Ahmadinejad in the first round.

Sources: Ali A. Saeidi, "The Accountability of Para-governmental Organizations (*bonyad*s): The Case of Iranian Foundation," *Iranian Studies* 37, no. 3 (September 2004), 488; Wilfried Buchta, *Who Rules Iran? The Structure of Power in the Islamic Republic* (Washington, DC: Washington Institute, 2000),75.

executive branch of government was headed by a prime minister chosen by Parliament. In the course of the 1989 constitutional revision the office of prime minister was abolished and the presidency became an executive one. The president heads the Executive except in matters reserved for the Leader, signs bills into law once they have been approved by the legislature, and appoints the members of the cabinet and provincial governors, subject to parliamentary approval. He can be impeached by Parliament, at which point the Leader can dismiss him. The president does not have to be a cleric, but between 1981 and 2005 three different members of the ulema held the office for two consecutive terms each, reflecting the hegemony of that group in the Islamic Republic. The June 2005 election of Mahmud Ahmadinejad, a lay (that is, a nonulema) Islamist and a veteran of the Iran–Iraq war, may herald the partial replacement of the clergy by the "war generation," men who risked their lives in the revolution and the war and feel that it is time that they reap the benefits of their sacrifices.

Parliament

Iran's unicameral Parliament, the **Majles,** comprises about 290 members elected by universal suffrage for four-year terms. Members have to be Muslims, but the Constitution provides for five members of Parliament (MPs) to represent Christians (three), Jews (one), and Zoroastrians (one).

The Majles has law-making powers, but its legislative output must not contravene the Constitution or Islam, as determined by the Council of Guardians (as we will discuss shortly). It has the right to investigate affairs of state, to approve or reject the presidents'

cabinet appointments, and to call ministers to account and subject them to votes of no-confidence.

In his treatise on Islamic government, Khomeini assigned little importance to Parliament, arguing that Islam had already laid down laws for most matters. A legislative assembly's task was to draw up rules and regulations for minor issues not dealt with in Islamic jurisprudence. Since 1979, however, the Majles has shown remarkable dynamism and initiative. For one, the traditional corpus of Islamic law proved to be woefully inadequate for the purpose of governing a modern state, requiring Parliament to fill some of the gaps. Furthermore, the legislative deputies have vigorously debated state business and held government officials accountable, the office of the Leader excepted.

In the first Parliament of the Islamic Republic almost half of all deputies were clerics. Under the Shah no free elections had taken place, so few people had enough name recognition at the local level to get themselves elected to Parliament. Consequently, in many places voters chose the local cleric. But over time, the percentage of clerics in the Majles has declined, as can be seen in Table 12.1. Although the ulema had generally opposed female suffrage in 1963, the founders of the Islamic Republic maintained women's active and passive suffrage in spite of their patriarchal disposition. Since 1980 every legislature has included female deputies, who have often spoken out on women's rights. Table 12.1 shows the evolution of the number of women who have held seats in the Parliament of the Islamic Republic.

Nonetheless, two features of the political system seriously limit the Majles's legislative role. First, many policies, rules, and regulations are set by unelected specialized bodies; second, all its bills are subject to the

Women in Parliament

TABLE 12.1

	Female MPs	Clerical MPs	Total MPs
First Majles (1980–1984)	4	131	263
Second Majles (1984–1988)	4	122	269
Third Majles (1988–1992)	4	77	267
Fourth Majles (1992–1996)	9	65	270
Fifth Majles (1996–2000)	10	53	274
Sixth Majles (2000–2004)	13	35	278
Seventh Majles (2004–2008)	12	42	281

veto of the Council of Guardians. Under the Islamic Republic, the Majles has been a forum where policies are discussed and proposals aired, and where some state officials are taken to account.[18]

Council of Guardians

The Constitution of 1906 provided for a committee of five Majles deputies who were members of the ulema to examine legislation for its compatibility with Islam. This committee was never constituted, however. In order to forestall any possibility for compromising the Islamic character of the state, the 1979 Constitution instituted an altogether separate body for ensuring the conformity of legislation with Islam: the Council of Guardians.

The body consists of six members of the ulema and six lay Muslim lawyers. The ulema are appointed by the Leader, the lawyers are nominated by the head of the Judiciary (who is himself appointed by the Leader) but approved by Parliament. The compatibility of laws with Islam is determined by the six ulema members only; their compatibility with the Constitution by the entire council. Through the years the Council of Guardians has rejected numerous bills because it interpreted them as violating the Constitution and/or Islamic law.

The Council of Guardians also "supervises" the elections to the Assembly of Experts, the presidency, and Parliament. It has interpreted this provision of the Constitution to signify that it can vet candidacies. It uses this self-ascribed power to limit citizens' choice at elections by not allowing candidates of whose views it disapproves to run. When in 1991 the Majles passed a law stripping the council of these powers, the latter, unsurprisingly, declared the law to be contrary to the Constitution.

Expediency Council

Disagreement between Parliament and the Council of Guardians has been endemic in the Islamic Republic, resulting in legislative gridlock. As long as Khomeini was alive, he acted as the ultimate arbiter when a protracted stalemate arose, as all involved deferred to him. In early 1988 Khomeini set up a new collective body to arbitrate in such cases, and it was aptly called the "Council for the determination of what is in the interest of the regime," an unwitting admission that conformity to the teachings of Islam now took a back seat to political expedience. Indeed, official Iranian

documents render the name of this body in English as "Expediency Council." Its existence was anchored in the constitutional revision of 1989.

The Leader directly appoints over thirty members of this body, who are chosen mainly from among top government officials, key cabinet members and military leaders, the ulema members of the Council of Guardians, as well as ulema chosen for their personal prestige. In addition to arbitrating conflicts between the Majles and the Council of Guardians, the Expediency Council has the constitutional mandate of advising the Leader in formulating overall state policy.

An Honestly Undemocratic Constitution

As our discussion shows, the authority of the elective offices of the Islamic Republic, essentially the presidency and Parliament, is systematically circumscribed by unelected bodies. To be sure, the Leader is chosen by an elected body, the Assembly of Experts, but there is no limit on his term, making him for all intents and purposes an unremovable leader with vast powers. By appointing the head of the judiciary and the commanders of the police, army, and **Islamic Revolutionary Guard Corps (Pasdaran),** he, rather than the president and Parliament, controls the coercive apparatus of the state.

The limited authority of the president and Parliament became startlingly blatant when reformists, bent on liberalizing Iranian politics and society, won a string of elections in the late 1990s. They gained control of the presidency in 1997 and 2001 with the election of **Mohammad Khatami,** and of Parliament in 2000. However, Leader Ali Khamenei openly sided with antireformist conservatives, whom he chose as the head of the Judiciary and as the members of the Council of Guardians. When the lawyers proposed by the Judiciary to fill vacant seats on the Council of Guardians failed to gain the endorsement of the reformist Parliament in 2001, the Leader simply refused to schedule the swearing-in ceremony of the reformist president, who had just been reelected with 77.9 percent of the popular vote. In the end, the lawyers took their seats without gaining majority support in Parliament, after which the Leader consented to swear in the president.

Although the reformists tried to bring about change by legal and constitutional means, the fact that they were ultimately stymied by the leader, the Council of Guardians, and the Judiciary, using powers granted to them by the Constitution, shows that this Constitution is, if not liberal and democratic, at least honest: its provisions need not be violated to prevent democratic governance.

The same can be said for citizens' rights. Although freedom of speech and association and the safety of the person are guaranteed, these are usually qualified by the clause "within the criteria of Islam," leaving the authorities considerable leeway to abridge them. The same is true for the equality of citizens. Christian, Jewish, and Zoroastrian Iranians are accorded some legal recognition and can practice their religion freely. However, Iran's largest non-Muslim minority, the adherents of the Baha'i faith, are considered heretics and systematically discriminated against; to this day they may not attend university, for instance. Even Sunni Muslims, representing about 10 percent of the total population, are systematically discriminated against in the civil service and are not allowed to maintain a mosque of their own in Tehran. In the words of a prominent exiled Iranian human rights lawyer, in the Islamic Republic "the rights of the clerics do not equal those of nonclerics, the rights of Twelver Shiites do not equal those of non-Twelver Shiites, the rights of Shiites do not equal those of Sunnis, the rights of Muslims do not equal those of non-Muslims, the rights of 'recognized religious minorities' do not equal those of other 'minorities,' and the rights of men do not equal the rights of women."[19] The explicit denial of legal equality to citizens found throughout Iran's Constitution and legal system stands in sharp contrast to the universalist language of many other Third World regimes.

Multiple Power Centers

When the revolutionaries took over the state in 1979, they inherited an administrative bureaucracy whose commitment to the new ideology they did not trust. Not content with purging state institutions of individuals they deemed counterrevolutionary, they built new ones whose competency overlapped with the old established ones. The idea was that the old institutions would more or less carry on with business as usual, while the new institutions would actively pursue the realization and defense of the new Islamic order (see Figure 12.3). Examples include the Construction Jihad, which sent young people to the rural areas to help develop them in parallel to the ministry of agriculture, the office of the revolutionary prosecutor (paralleling the ministry of justice), and the *komitehs* (paralleling the police). The most important example is the Islamic Revolutionary Guard Corps, known in Persian as *Pasdaran*, whose original function was to safeguard the revolution but which in time developed into a parallel army and even acquired an air force and a navy. These revolutionary institutions prevented the provisional government, which had taken over the Shah's administrative apparatus, from gaining control of the country.[20]

As hardliners consolidated their rule in the mid-1980s, they attempted to merge state and revolutionary organizations. However, these attempts were mostly unsuccessful and the revolutionary organizations are still active. In the late 1990s, as some state institutions came under the control of the reformists, conservatives created new parallel institutions under the aegis of the office of the Leader. Thus, when the ministry of information, as the secret police is called, came to be staffed mainly by reformists, the Judiciary, whose head is named by the Leader, proceeded to set up a parallel secret police (which even maintains a prison system for political prisoners). These multiple power centers complicate policymaking considerably, as we shall see.

With these caveats about the relative importance of Iran's republican institutions in mind, let us now turn to elections and parties.

ELECTIONS AND PARTIES

The Prerevolutionary Legacy

With the brief exception of the 1940s, between 1906 and 1979 competitive elections were rarely held in Iran. In 1963 the Shah gave women the active and passive suffrage. This action did not mean much in practice because there were no free elections for the remainder of his reign, but it did establish standards that could not be undone. Although much of the ulema had vehemently opposed the extension of the suffrage to women in 1963, the mobilization of women in the course of the revolution was so important that it was simply not possible to deprive them of the right to vote again. In fact, the electorate was enlarged by fixing the minimum voting age at 15.

Under the monarchy political parties were mostly weak and ephemeral. After World War II,

Nation

President
Mahmud Ahmadinejad
(elected for four years;
max. 2 terms in office)

Assembly of Experts
(majles-e khobregan)*
86 clerical members
(elected for eight years)

Parliament
(majles-e shura-ye eslami)
290 representatives
(elected for four years)

Council of Ministers
22 ministers
(confirmed by Parliament)

Supreme Leader*
Ali Khamenei
(lifetime appointment)

Council of Guardians
(shura-ye negahban)
12 members

Head of the Judiciary*

Head of the Supreme Court*
(five-year term)

6 Clerical Members of the
Council of Guardians

Chief Public Prosecutor*
(five-year term)

Expediency Council
(31 members)

6 Lay Jurists in the
Council of Guardians
(appointed on advice of
Parliament)

Voice and Vision (Radio and
Television) *(seda va sima)**

Commander of the Islamic
Revolutionary Guard Corps*

Commander of the Regular
Military *(artesh)*

Chief of the General Staff of
the Armed Forces*

Commander of the Law
Enforcement Forces
(niruha-ye entezami)*

Function of Council of Guardians:

1. Determine compatibility with
   Islam of laws approved by
   Parliament
2. Monitor all elections
   (preselects candidates)
3. Interpret the constitution

········▶ Confirmation

──────▶ Election

‐ ‐ ‐ ▶ Appointment

*As of April 2000, these power
centers are dominated by the
traditionalist right

Formal Constitutional Power Structure in Iran   **FIGURE 12.3**

Source: Adapted from Wilfried Buchta, *Who Rules Iran?* (Washington, DC: Washington Institute for Near East Policy, 2000). © Wilfried Buchta, Rabat 2000.

two groupings succeeded in establishing a lasting societal presence: the Communist Tudeh Party and the nationalist National Front of Mohammad Mossadegh. These two were revived in the course of the revolution of 1978. However, they were overshadowed by more radical leftist or Islamist groups that had emerged from the armed struggle against the Shah, such as the Marxist-Leninist Fada'iyan-e Khalq and the leftist Islamist Mojahedin-e Khalq. Initially, the Liberation Movement of Iran (LMI), a moderate Islamist offshoot of the National Front founded in 1961, fared somewhat better. Its leaders largely staffed the provisional government of Prime Minister Mehdi Bazargan that administered the country from February to November 1979, when they resigned in protest over radical students' seizure of American diplomats as hostages. In 1981 the National Front, the Fada'iyan-e Khalq, and the Mojahedin-e Khalq were banned for advocating policies that contradicted the basic premise of the Islamic Republic. In 1983 the Tudeh Party was disbanded and its leaders jailed for having spied for the Soviet Union. The LMI, for its part, has managed to maintain a low-level activity within the country.

Postrevolutionary Parties

In early 1979 a group of loyal followers of Khomeini, including later President Rafsanjani and Leader Khamenei, founded a new party to work toward the realization of their version of an Islamic state: the Islamic Republican Party (IRP). Soon, however, different factions crystallized within the IRP around different economic, social, and foreign policy agendas. Factionalism having rendered the party dysfunctional, Rafsanjani and Khamenei announced the dissolution of the IRP in a letter to Khomeini in June 1987. They said that the party had achieved its goal, the establishment of *velayat-e faqih*, and had thus ceased to have a *raison d'être*.

But the underlying reasons for the factionalism did not go away. Some regime figures advocated more state intervention in the economy on the grounds that Islam is the religion of social justice and that therefore an Islamic government must look after the interests of the poor. Others argued that Islam protects the sanctity of private property, and that therefore more laissez-faire policies were in order as long as everybody adhered to the rules that Islamic jurisprudence established for the conduct of economic activity. As the leaders of the Islamic Republic grappled with the problem of translating Islam into a political ideology that provides guidance for the solution to all problems, it became clear that divergent policy options could be derived from Islamic principles. In 1987 the Speaker of Parliament Rafsanjani admitted that there were "two powerful wings" within the Islamic Republic, adding that "basically they represent two unorganized parties. Indeed when they describe the positions they hold, they are two parties, not two wings."[21] The tensions came out into the open in 1988 when the Society of Militant Clergy, a pro-*velayat-e faqih* group, split in two as some less conservative members, including future President Mohammad Khatami, left to form the Association of Militant Clerics.

As long as Khomeini was alive, he acted as the ultimate arbiter among the factions, as all deferred to him. When government figures turned to him to break a factional deadlock over a policy, he would normally urge all to cooperate. But when pressed, more often than not Khomeini came out against the conservatives. After Khomeini's death in 1989, the fact that the leadership of the Islamic Republic included no high-ranking ulema combined with the rivalry of opinions among the ulema allowed many policy disagreements to remain unresolved. These disagreements were channeled into the political system and became the basis of electoral competition, as different candidates espoused opposing views for which they sought people's votes. This factor has given Iranian elections a poignancy they lack in other nondemocratic states.

Ideological differences became the basis of factional politics among three broad clusters in the political elite: conservatives, pragmatists, and radicals. The conservatives were clerics and lay politicians who favored stricter social rules (such as gender segregation in public places), and called for greater authority to be given to the Leader at the expense of elected bodies, while simultaneously (and confusingly) supporting freer, market-oriented economic policies. Pragmatists, including Rafsanjani and many technocrats who staffed the ministries in the 1990s, were more accommodating on social issues and supported economic liberalization and the privatization of state-owned and parastatal companies. Moreover, they toned down support for exporting the revolution and were somewhat more conciliatory regarding U.S.–Iranian relations. Finally, the radicals were the younger Islamist revolutionaries and clerics who were influenced by leftist and anti-imperialist politics. In the 1980s and the early 1990s they called for increased state control of the economy to ensure greater social justice and were active in supporting Islamist struggles in the Middle East. Beginning in the mid-1990s, these radicals modified their positions and became more liberal (as we will discuss later).[22]

As a result of the political liberalization linked to the election of Mohammad Khatami, a number of political parties appeared on the scene. With the possible exception of the Islamic Iran Participation Front, the leading component of the reformist coalition that backed Khatami's policies, most are vehicles for one man's political ambitions and lack any grassroots organization. Since strong parties are absent, journals, newspapers, and increasingly websites play a key role as vehicles for discussing, formulating, and disseminating ideological alternatives.

Presidential Elections

In January 1980 Iran held its first ever presidential election, resulting in the victory of a lay Islamist, Abolhasan Banisadr. But Banisadr was impeached by Parliament and deposed by Khomeini in June 1981. His more pliant successor together with the prime minister were killed two months later by a bomb attack. The next four elections had predictable results, as close companions of Khomeini—Ali Khamenei in 1981 and 1985 and Ali-Akbar Hashemi Rafsanjani in 1989 and 1993—easily won contests in which the other candidates were minor figures. Consequently, the participation rate went steadily down, as can be seen in Figure 12.4 on electoral participation.

The pattern seemed to repeat itself in 1997. Although Rafsanjani would have liked to run again, he could not because the Constitution provides for only one immediate reelection. The mere fact that the term limit was respected shows to what an extent constitutional norms had finally come to govern Iranian politics. The speaker of Parliament, conservative cleric

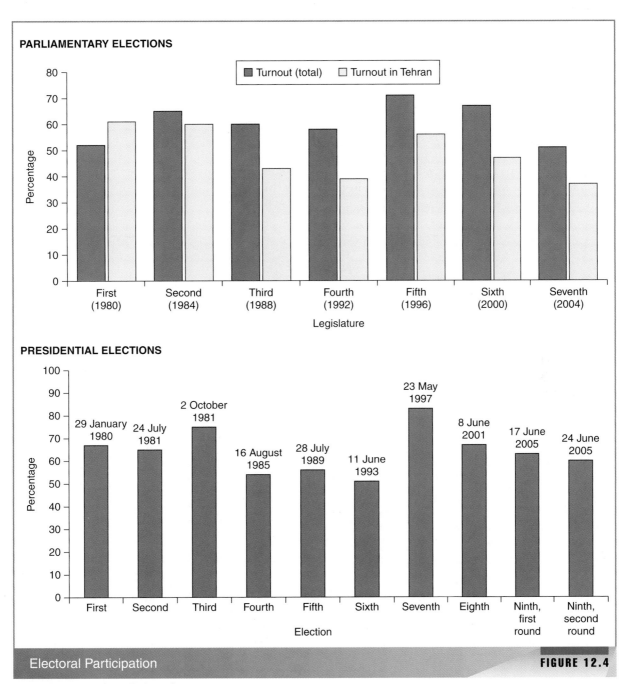

PARLIAMENTARY ELECTIONS

PRESIDENTIAL ELECTIONS

Electoral Participation

FIGURE 12.4

Source: Compiled by Arang Keshavarzian.

Ali-Akbar Nateq Nuri, was endorsed by most of the government and the politically active ulema, including the Leader, and most observers expected him to win. Instead Mohammad Khatami, a moderate cleric who had resigned as minister of culture in 1992 after conservatives gained control over Parliament, ran a modern and effective campaign by reaching out to university students and active members of the nascent civil society. He won a landslide victory. As an "outsider," Khatami appealed to all those who had been humiliated by the regime: educated people who felt that the state discriminated against them in favor of less educated but ideologically reliable Islamic activists, women who resented the legal restrictions and discriminations to which they were subjected, and young people who were tired of being harassed on a daily basis by the guardians of public morality. To all these groups Khatami promised greater cultural openness and personal freedoms. Although his reforms dwindled in 1999, he was easily reelected in 2001.

For the first time since 1981, there was no official government candidate in the 2005 presidential elections. Three allies of Khatami, four conservatives, and Rafsanjani ran for the highest elective office. No candidate having gained a majority, for the first time there was a second round, runoff election, pitting Rafsanjani against the arch-conservative mayor of Tehran, Mahmud Ahmadinejad. At around 60 percent, participation in the two rounds was lower than in the previous two elections. Ahmadinejad won an upset victory amidst allegations that Islamic Revolutionary Guard Corps (IRGC) and Basij commanders had illegally urged troops to vote for him, and perhaps even engaged them in stuffing ballot boxes to increase his share of the vote in the first round in which he placed second. In any event, Ahmadinejad's message appealed to the poor whose concerns had not been addressed by the cultural liberalization of the Khatami years (see Box 12.3).

Biography of Two Presidents and Two Generations

BOX 12.3

The biographies of Iran's last two presidents—Mohammad Khatami (1997–2005) and Mahmud Ahmadinejad (2005–present)—illustrate the changing face of Iran's political elite, from an older generation formed by the struggle against the shah and the revolution to a younger one shaped largely by the events of the postrevolutionary era. Moreover, the socioeconomic differences between Khatami and Ahmadinejad are telling.

Khatami was born in 1943 into a family of notable clerics and landowners. He is a cleric educated in the seminaries of Qom and holds a B.A. in philosophy from a secular university. He has authored several works on philosophy, is fluent in Arabic, and knows some German and English. After the revolution, he became the Minister of Culture and Islamic Guidance (1982–1992), which regulates and censors all forms of media and publications. There he was known to be a supporter of freedom of speech and the press. Khatami was able to carve out some space for his cultural activities thanks to his close relationships with Khomeini and his son, as well as with

journalists and students who would later support his presidency. Nonetheless, after growing pressure from hard-line conservatives, Khatami was forced to resign in 1992 and became the director of the National Library until he successfully ran for president.

Ahmadinejad was born in 1956 to a blacksmith and moved to Tehran at a young age. He is a product of the prerevolutionary secular education system and studied engineering. He participated in the Iran–Iraq war as a member of the Islamic Revolutionary Guard Corps. He later performed very well during his three years as governor of the newly established Ardabil Province (1993–1996). In 1997 Ahmadinejad earned a Ph.D. from a technical university and continued to teach there. In 2003 he was part of the new conservative faction of younger politicians known as the Alliance of Builders of Islamic Iran, which swept the Tehran city council elections, and he was elected as mayor.

What brings these disparate profiles and outlooks together is that both men were overwhelmingly elected president—against candidates favored by the establishment.

Sources: Wilfried Buchta, *Who Rules Iran? The Structure of Power in the Islamic Republic* (Washington, DC: The Washington Institute, 2000), 30; http://www.bbc.co.uk/persian/iran/story/2005/08/050801_pm-mv-khatami-profile.shtml; http://www.mardomyar.com/aspx2/aboutme.aspx.

Mahmud Ahmadinejad, left; Mohammad Khatami, right.

Photo courtesy of Getty Images

Parliamentary Elections

For the purpose of parliamentary elections, Iran is divided into multimember constituencies, the largest being Tehran with thirty MPs. Each voter can write down the names of as many candidates as there are seats in a constituency. The top vote-getters in each constituency are elected provided they receive over 50 percent of the total vote. If a constituency has more seats than candidates who passed the 50 percent barrier, a second round determines the remaining MPs from among the runners-up. In the second round the number of candidates is twice that of the seats that remain to be filled. In the absence of organized political parties, candidacies tend to be endorsed by a number of different political, religious, and cultural associations. This factor makes it difficult to deduce accurate figures about the relative popularity of different political groupings from the election results.

In the first legislative elections of 1980, a few National Front, LMI, and regionalist candidates were elected to Parliament. Since 1984 only candidates unequivocally committed to *velayat-e faqih* have been allowed to run. Radicals formed the majority in the second (1984–1988) and third Parliaments (1988–1992), but after Khomeini's death the conservative-dominated

Council of Guardians arrogated to itself the right to vet candidacies and proceeded to invalidate the candidacies of most radicals. Consequently, conservatives dominated the fourth and fifth Parliaments (1992–2000) with pragmatist supporters of Rafsanjani forming the minority. In the wake of Mohammad Khatami's surprise victory in the presidential election of 1997, however, a record number of reformists became candidates. Since they were unknown to the Council of Guardians, they were allowed to run for office in 2000. They swept the elections, gaining around 70 percent of the vote. Where did these reformists suddenly come from?

In the course of the 1990s many of the radicals of the 1980s had a change of heart and moderated their views. Their evolution had a number of reasons. For one, the experience of being barred from entering Parliament in 1992 brought home the importance of fair elections and political pluralism. Furthermore, the collapse of communism in the Soviet Union and Eastern Europe delegitimized the statecentric approach to social and political organization. At the same time, a group of Muslim intellectuals, some of them ulema themselves, challenged both the traditional jurisprudential approach to religion that led to the preeminence of the ulema and the survival of obsolete rules and regulations, and the ideologization of religion that led to the loss of spirituality and totalitarian government. This more liberal approach to religion created a tentative connection between Islamic reformists and social groups that had hitherto not participated in politics, boosting participation rates at elections.

For the parliamentary elections of 2004, however, the Council of Guardians disallowed about 2,000 reformist candidates, including about eighty sitting MPs, which was unprecedented. Thereupon many reformist personalities and associations called for a boycott of the elections. Although participation diminished, 50 percent of the population still went to the polls. The reason is that in many areas outside the main cities voters do not judge candidates by their ideology but by what they can do (or have done) to further the interests of their constituents. Figure 12.4 shows the evolution of electoral participation.

Local Elections

Although the Constitution of 1906 provided for elected local government councils, these bodies were never actually constituted. The similar provisions of the 1979 Constitution were first put into action in 1999, when Iranians for the first time went to the polls to elect city, town, and village councils.

Reformists won control over most councils, including Tehran. With the conservatives stymieing the reformist camp, apathy overtook voters in the new decade. Voting came to be seen by many as a futile exercise, since ultimately power rests with unelected bodies. In the second local elections in 2003 only 15 percent of the eligible voters in Tehran, mostly conservatives, bothered to vote, even though these were the freest elections in Iranian history. For the first time the Council of Guardians had not vetted candidates, and even avowed secularists were allowed to run. Consequently the nation's capital, home to about 15 percent of its total population, got a uniformly conservative city council, which elected as mayor the man who would two years later use his position as a springboard for a successful bid for the presidency. Elsewhere in the country, however, campaigns were more centered on concrete problems and participation was thus higher, testifying to a relatively high level of civic engagement of the citizenry.[23] In December 2006 the third local elections were held. Participation sharply increased, and supporters of President Ahmadinejad won only a few seats. As if to rebuke him for his incompetent management of the economy, his supporters won only three out of fifteen seats on Tehran's municipal council. They were led by his sister, Parvin Ahmadinejad.

POLITICAL CULTURE

To a large extent Iran's political culture results from its place in the international system. Iran survived the age of imperialism as a nominally sovereign state, but this independence did not prevent outside powers, mainly Great Britain and Russia, from meddling in Iran's domestic affairs and controlling its economy.[24] Their country having been a long-standing member of the international society of nations, Iranians have tended to compare themselves more readily with the dominant countries of the West than with other Third World nations; nevertheless, transforming their country's formal independence into genuine sovereignty has always been a key concern of politically conscious Iranians.

One result of foreign meddling in Iranian affairs has been the Iranians' propensity to believe in conspiracies and to interpret politics in the light of conspiracy theories (that is, theories that purport to prove that politics is dominated by the ill-intentioned and conspiratorial machinations of small groups whose aims and values are profoundly opposed to those of the rest of society).[25] Belief in conspiracies as a motor force in history is common in the rest of the Middle East as well.[26] But in the Iranian case, the plausibility of such theories is enhanced by the fact that Iran *has* indeed been the victim of conspiracies, most recently in 1953 when the U.S. and British governments conspired with Iranian conservatives to install the Shah as ruler of the country. The main reason why the seizure of the American hostages in November 1979 was so popular at the time was that it symbolically ended the era of foreign interference in Iranian affairs by allowing Iranians to occupy what most believed to be the epicenter of all conspiracies: the U.S. embassy.

System Level

Iran is not a country whose borders and statehood are a bequest of European colonialism, which helps explain why the modern polity enjoys considerable historic legitimacy among Iranians, in spite of their ethnic diversity: Iranians with different mother tongues have lived with each other for centuries. The

Iranian nationalism propagated by the Pahlavi shahs included pride in the glories of ancient Persia and in a continuous "national" history of 2,500 years. This history was interpreted as conferring upon Iranians an intrinsic nobility that neighboring peoples and states cannot match.

This intense national pride survived the revolution but changed garb. While the glories of pre-Islamic Iran are now much less emphasized than before, the new authorities and their supporters considered Iran to be the vanguard of the Islamic world's struggle against Western domination. This position fuses commitment to Islam with Iranian nationalism. In recent years, however, Pahlavi-type ethnic Persian nationalism has been making a comeback among Iranians who are disenchanted with theocratic rule.

By the same token, ethnic nationalism has become stronger among Iran's non-Persian populations. This is particularly noticeable among the predominantly Sunni Kurds, who resent not only the poverty of the Kurdish areas but also discrimination on sectarian grounds. In the most recent presidential election, for instance, a candidate who expressly addressed Sunni grievances carried the largely Sunni province of Sistan and Baluchistan. At the same time, an Azeri who emphasized his ethnicity carried the three largely Azeri-speaking provinces of northwestern Iran. In theory, there is no reason why this new ethnic assertiveness should not be compatible with a strong sense of Iranian civic nationalism, but that depends on how the central government will manage it. Repressive measures are likely to erode the identification with the Iranian state in the ethnic periphery.

One time-honored way governments shore up their legitimacy is by appealing to feelings of patriotism. In Iran the issue around which the government has recently hoped to unite Iranians is the development of nuclear technology. The Iranian leaders' insistence that Iran has a "right" to develop nuclear energy has struck a sympathetic chord among ordinary Iranians, even among many of those who oppose Islamist rule. If Americans, Europeans, Chinese, and even Indians and Pakistanis have nuclear weapons, many people ask, why should Iranians not have them too?

Process Level

One indisputable result of the Islamic revolution was the dramatic increase in the number of citizens who participated in politics. The millions of Iranians who poured into the streets to demand the departure of the Shah throughout 1978 refused to become mere subjects of a theocratic state after the revolution was over. The same cannot be said for those who opposed either the revolution or the Islamic state to which it ultimately gave rise. Many emigrated, and those who remained behind tended to consider the "Association of Militant Clerics" and the "Society of Militant Clergy" little more than Tweedledum and Tweedledee. It was these passive subjects of the Islamic Republic that Khatami had in mind when he repeatedly asserted that he wanted to be the president of *all* Iranians. They participated for the first time since the inception of the new regime, carrying electoral participation rates to new heights. In the elections of 2004 and 2005, however, many of them boycotted the elections, feeling that their participation had not brought the country nearer to a more republican and less theocratic form of government.

Another key feature of Iran's political culture is extreme individualism and lack of trust. Most observers impute this to the country's long history of despotism, which never developed a state of law that made life predictable and governed by rules rather than personal connections. The conspiracy belief mentioned earlier added to this absence of trust. Political opponents tend to accuse each other of being in league with foreign powers, making compromise (necessary for deliberative politics) very difficult, for one cannot compromise or negotiate with a "traitor." In the Islamic Republic the fact that the revolutionary credentials of the leaders of the various factions are equally strong has led to a certain mutual tolerance among those political leaders who remain faithful to *velayat-e faqih*. But even now, dissidents who question the system itself are invariably accused of doing the bidding of foreign (read: hostile) powers. The most consistent victims of this propensity to believe in conspiracies are religious minorities, especially Baha'is, who have been widely presented as agents of "Zionism." This charge is motivated by the fact that the world center of the Baha'i faith is located in Israel, which is a historic accident.

Distrust not only permeates the political elite, but is also evident among citizens. Recent results of the World Value Survey suggest that Iranians, like Egyptians, do not trust government (see Figure 12.5).[27]

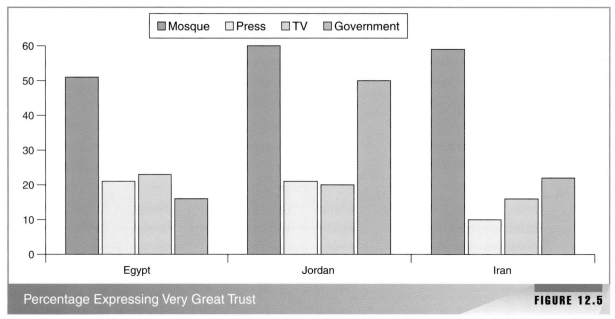

Percentage Expressing Very Great Trust

FIGURE 12.5

Source: Mansoor Moaddel and Taghi Azadarmaki, "The Worldviews of Islamic Publics: The Case of Egypt, Iran, and Jordan," in Ronald Ingelhart, ed., *Human Values and Social Change: Findings From the Values Survey* (Leiden: Brill, 2003), 81.

Since television channels are state-run and much of the press is owned by the state or heavily monitored by it, the low levels of trust in these institutions also illustrate a lack of trust in government. Meanwhile, the relatively high level of trust in the "mosque" should be interpreted with caution. As we will soon see, "the mosque" is far from a homogeneous entity and does not necessarily reflect a particular political agenda or culture.

This individualism and lack of trust are underlying causes for the absence of true political parties and the constant splits that the few parties that did come into existence have undergone. While all Iranians bemoan their inability to cooperate, it is this very inability that saved Iran from becoming a totalitarian state in the 1980s. If the ulema had the discipline and centralist organization of either the Roman Catholic Church or a Communist party, their rule would have become far more totalitarian and monolithic, and factionalism would never have been institutionalized.

A final consequence of the individualism and conspiracy belief prevalent in Iran's political culture is the periodic appearance of charismatic leaders. These leaders embody the yearning of the citizenry for overcoming the current order and the source of all problems—imperialists and autocrats. Mohammad Mossadegh, Ayatollah Khomeini, and even (to a much lesser extent) Mohammad Khatami exemplify this tendency. Some have argued that Twelver Shiism, with its expectation of the Twelfth Imam, predisposes Iranians to put their hopes in a charismatic savior figure.

Policy Level

Given the fact that the Iranian state derives most of its income from oil, Iranians have tended to expect the state to provide welfare and material well-being for everybody and alleviate the gap between rich and poor. In other words, they want their share of the oil wealth. Part of the delegitimation of the Shah's regime occurred because people thought that not enough wealth trickled down to the poorer strata.

Corruption has been endemic in Iran, and fighting it has been an aspiration of Iranians of all political persuasions. Its persistence has been blamed on the regime, which has thereby lost some legitimacy, just like the Pahlavi regime in the 1960s and 1970s.

A noteworthy feature of Iran's contemporary political culture is the suspicion of private enterprise in the industrial sector. Beginning under Reza Shah (r. 1925–1941), the state took a leading role in the development of industry. Under Reza Shah's son, this statism was supplemented by an emerging class of capitalists who contributed considerably to Iran's industrialization in the 1960s and 1970s. But they were closely connected to the Shah and his relatives, they cooperated with foreign companies whose activities were suspicious for the mere reason that they were foreign, and some of them were members of religious minorities. Consequently, both the Islamists and leftists who carried the revolutionary movement opposed them and the mode of economic development they represented, calling them exploiters. The legacy of this opposition is visible in Iran's Constitution, which puts heavy limits on foreign investment.

The populism propagated by the revolutionaries has intensified opposition to conspicuous consumption and privately owned large-scale economic activity. This has not affected rich bazaar merchants, who engage mostly in trade rather than production. Their activity is less immediately visible than that of an industrialist, as a merchant can deal in millions armed with nothing but a cell phone and sitting behind a desk in a small shop in the bazaar. In contrast, the factory and offices of an industrialist attract immediate attention.[28] The result of this general distrust of industrialists has been that citizens expect the state to be the main purveyor of development and increased living standards. The election of Mahmud Ahmadinejad in 2005 is partly due to the timid privatization carried out under his two predecessors, which aggravated income inequality.

While many Iranians thus expect the state to alleviate poverty and unemployment, others expect the state to provide an environment in which individual talent and creativity can flourish. Collectivism and individualism are both present in Iranian society, and the result is that Iran's political culture is highly conflictual. The citizenry is sharply divided over the very essence of the regime, with many, especially among the more educated, considering Islamic theocracy, if not the Islamic Republic, to be an anachronistic form of government.

POLITICAL SOCIALIZATION

The political socialization of citizens is a process simultaneously driven from above by state institutions and from below by social practices. In Iran, state-controlled institutions—such as the education system and the military—transmit many of the basic political values and norms in society and also establish the

framework for debating their meaning. Meanwhile, through their everyday practices as members of their family, neighborhood, or social group, Iranians negotiate, challenge, and even sometimes undermine these norms.

As in many postrevolutionary and postcolonial regimes, state-sanctioned political socialization in Iran has aimed at generating national unity and masking political, ethnic, and socioeconomic cleavages. Under the Pahlavi monarchy national unity was championed in the mission of creating a modern, industrial, and Western society. Under this vision the nation was presented as secular, classless, and thoroughly Persian in identity. The schools, for instance, were the primary means to educate the entire Iranian population in the official language of Persian, a critical means to distance the significant numbers of Azeri (roughly 25 percent), Kurdish (8–10 percent), and Arabic (2–5 percent) speakers from their local and ethnic loyalties. The calls for greater economic equality, ethnic inclusion, and religious observance during the Islamic revolution dramatically questioned both the notion of national homogeneity and the perception that the Iranian nation accepted this image of itself. Under the Islamic Republic, the content of the official discourse and normative agenda has changed. However, the methods of socialization and the overwhelming elite desire to limit input from citizens and ignore the pluralistic nature of society remain quite similar to the prerevolutionary regime.

Education System

The school system has been the principal "agent of socialization" for creating good Islamic citizens out of young Iranians. The school system was one of the first institutions to be Islamicized by the new regime. School curricula were changed to include a heavy dose of religious studies, yearly classes on the Islamic revolution, and an increased number of mandatory Arabic language courses. Meanwhile, textbooks were rewritten to present a state-sanctioned history of Iran, which highlighted the role of the clergy in all "popular uprisings," erased or distorted any role played by nonreligious forces (such as liberal nationalists or leftist parties), and presented the Pahlavi monarchy (and all monarchs) as equally and continually oppressive and immoral. Textbooks also depicted the state's image of the family.

Unlike the prerevolutionary textbooks that showed Iranian women as unveiled, families eating around a table, and children with non-Arabic and nonreligious names, the postrevolutionary textbooks depicted all women as veiled (even inside the home), families sitting cross-legged around a simple spread on the floor, and children with Islamic names.[29] Schoolchildren also received revolutionary doctrine by reciting chants and poems praising the greatness of Khomeini and the regime, while denouncing the Baathist regime in Iraq as well as "the imperialists," most commonly the United States.

The authorities initially emphasized the role of primary and secondary schools for creating loyal and mobilized supporters. However, a group of Islamist activists and scholars also led a charge to "cleanse" the universities of "counterrevolutionary" elements by reviewing both the faculty and the curriculum. This "Cultural Revolution" was headed by what is now known as the Supreme Council for the Cultural Revolution. University campuses being the epicenter of antiregime activism, the Cultural Revolution closed all universities for three years (1980–1983), and worked to develop links between the universities and the religious seminaries. When the universities were reopened, strict entrance requirements were established, including religious examinations, to give greater opportunities to those the regime expected would be more supportive of its ambitions. In addition, war veterans and relatives of those killed in the revolution and the Iran–Iraq war were allotted special quotas in all universities. In the meantime, the regime established new institutions to create a new set of technocrats and teachers to staff the ministries and the universities. For instance, Imam Sadeq University (on the campus of a former business school affiliated with Harvard Business School) was fashioned to produce technocrats. Another new aspect of the university system was the establishment of the "Islamic Open University," with autonomous campuses all over the country, including small towns. This university was to provide higher education to Iranians living outside of the main population centers and to provide opportunities for students who fail to pass the highly competitive entrance examination for the elite national universities or whose families would not let them move to the larger cities.

The content of higher education was transformed by the Islamic Republic with the regime promoting and funding attempts to elaborate contain fields, such as "Islamic Economics" and "Islamic Sciences," as ways to compete with what some viewed as the fundamentally distorted and anti-Islamic nature of Western social and natural sciences. Over the years, the regime has also sponsored the establishment of pro-regime volunteer organizations (**Basij**) to monitor the political activities of students and faculty and mobilize students for pro-regime activities on the campuses.

The Islamic Republic's efforts to create obedient and loyal citizens out of the "children of the revolution" seem far from successful. Many of the investigative journalists exposing government abuses and incompetence or the staunchest supporters of reform and the burgeoning civil society (such as arts organizations and women's nongovernmental organizations) are products of the state school system and its post–Cultural Revolution higher education establishments. In fact, the university that the state tried so hard to control in the wake of the revolution is again full of students publishing political journals and declarations, organizing talks challenging the regime, and flaunting and mocking the social mores and the state's policies regarding gender relations. The large student demonstrations of 1999 and 2003 are indicative of the inability of the regime to fully manage this politicized space.

The Military

Military conscription has also been a fundamental mechanism for creating national unity, at least for young men. The shared experience of basic training and interacting with the military bureaucracy was augmented by the experience of the long war with Iraq. The war was a critical historical juncture that shaped a large number of Iranian men and their families. With approximately four million to five million Iranians serving in the armed forces during the eight-year war, a very large percentage of Iranian families were directly affected by it.[30] Various public commemorations, war murals, as well as stories in cinema and fiction act to foster emotional bonds between the war generation and those who preceded and followed it.

Politically, however, the war has been divisive, with part of the ruling establishment questioning the policy to continue the war even after the Iraqi army was driven off Iranian soil in 1982.[31] Moreover, Iran's military includes the Islamic Revolutionary Guard Corps and the Basij which have become distinct institutions with growing political influence. In the parliamentary election of 2004, over 100 former members of the Revolutionary Guards won seats, and in 2005 a former member won the presidency. These institutions, largely autonomous from the regular army and police force, are under the direct supervision of the Leader, and have acquired significant economic holdings.

Religion and Religious Institutions

While most Iranians consider themselves religious and consider religious matters and practices as important aspects of their lives, results from the 2000–2001 World Value Survey project suggest a more nuanced view.[32] Table 12.2 and Figure 12.6 show that many Iranians consider themselves religious, believe religion is very important in life, and participate in religious services but at lower rates than in Jordan and Egypt. Moreover, while surveyed Iranians more often characterize themselves as "above all a Muslim" than as "above all a nationalist," about a third put nationalism first, far more than in either Egypt or Jordan.

Notwithstanding these aggregate findings, under the Islamic Republic religion and religious practice have played a more divisive than unifying role. On the surface, religion permeates daily life. Official speeches and pronouncements are peppered with religious expressions and quotations, the calendar is full of religious holidays, and religious observance is often public and conspicuous. Shiite Islam plays a central role both in official discourse and as a means to regulate who can gain high office in the state. Friday congregational prayers and commemorations of religious anniversaries are state-regulated events that bring people from all walks of life together at neighborhood public spaces. As if to underline the emasculation of Tehran University as the center of secular opposition to the Islamic regime, Tehran's official Friday congregational prayers are held on what used to be the campus's soccer field. On these occasions leading members of the government give sermons in which they passionately weave together religious and moral issues and the pressing political problems of the day.

In staging these public and mass religious meetings, the state consciously attempts to mobilize citizens in support of the regime and also to transmit political messages. These events and state-owned radio and television are dominated by the well-versed and symbolic Shiite language of martyrdom and self-sacrifice, as exemplified by the Third Imam, in the name of justice and standing up to the great powers who usurp the rights of the innocent and faithful.

It is difficult, however, to monopolize the symbols, interpretations, and ephemeral beliefs that make up a religion. Over the years the Islamic Republic has had difficulty controlling members of the political elite and clergy, let alone the hearts and minds of its citizens. Given the absence of a Shiite "pope," Iran's theocratic state has never been able fully to impose its politicized vision of Shiite Islam within Iran, let alone across the Shiite world. With the death of Khomeini and the appointment of the less religiously erudite and charismatic Khamenei, fundamental disagreements have emerged over the meaning of Islamic government and the role of religion in public life. For instance, the political faction commonly described as "reformists" has stressed the republican dimensions of the Constitution and the revolution. In contrast, the conservatives have highlighted the centrality of clerical authority and its right of oversight over the popular will. Meanwhile, lay religious intellectuals (such as Abdol-Karim Soroush) and clerics (such as Hassan Eshkevari) have called for a reformulation of the relationships among God, the individual, and political authority that explicitly challenges the basic assumptions of the current interpretation of *velayat-e faqih*.

Percentage of People Describing Self as "a Religious Person"	**TABLE 12.2**
Egypt	98
Nigeria	94
Jordan	85
Iran	82
United States	82
India	80
Turkey	75
Spain	75
Mexico	65
Russia	64
Germany	50
Sweden	33
Japan	24

Source: Mansoor Moaddel and Taghi Azadarmaki, "The Worldviews of Islamic Publics: The Case of Egypt, Iran, and Jordan," in Ronald Ingelhart, ed., *Human Values and Social Change: Findings From the Values Survey* (Leiden: Brill, 2003), 75.

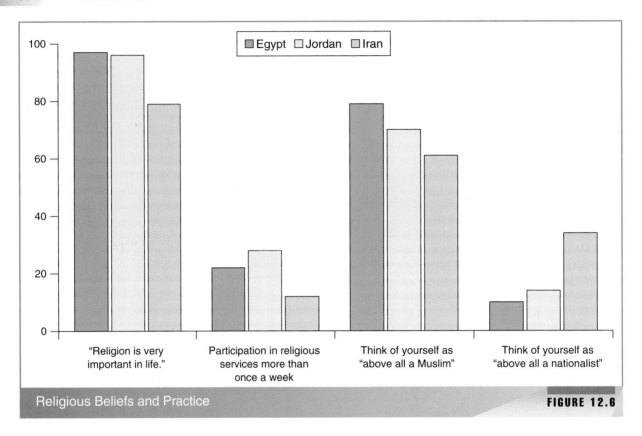

Religious Beliefs and Practice

FIGURE 12.6

These debates have not only percolated in the intellectual environments of the universities, seminaries, and magazines, but have also begun to shape more public discussions regarding the relationship between religion and politics and resonate with the philosophical and political debates of ordinary Iranians too.[33]

Finally, in more organizational terms, religious observance has always had a localized flavor. Numerous neighborhood and guild-based Koranic reading groups and religious associations cater to the spiritual needs of men and women of different regional, ethnic, and class backgrounds. These informal meetings act as grassroots and independent forums for religious practice, which by definition escape the watchful eye of those clerics who are affiliated with the regime. Sometimes escaping the attention of observers is the tension between the clerical state and the seminaries in the cities of Qom and Mashhad. With the vast majority of clergy historically shying away from politics and the seminary system historically maintaining financial independence, Khomeini's political innovation of clerical-led government has reconfigured "church"-state relations. For instance, job opportunities and income are available for clerics in the judicial system and in the ministries, and as Friday prayer leaders, the last being appointed by the office of the Leader. While the ulema, especially former students of Khomeini, have been prominent in the higher reaches of the regime, the actual running of the state has never been dominated by seminary graduates, and their presence has declined over the last quarter century. One indication is the decline in the number of clerics in the Parliament. In the very first Majles almost half of the MPs were clerics, but by the late 1990s clerics constituted less than 20 percent of MPs.

For the vast majority of clerics—who remain in the seminaries to teach, study, and interpret religious texts—the regime has in fact been intrusive. The authorities in Tehran have tried to monitor teaching in the seminaries by dictating curricula and identifying texts to be taught in Qom. In addition, the Leader has used his office and funds to support seminaries and teachers who are deemed to be "militant" and sympathetic to the regime's interpretations of Islam. The upshot is that while the mosque and state are perfectly aligned in theory, in practice the state can never be sure that the seminaries are producing appropriate clergy for the government or socializing Iranians in the official doctrine. Mosque and state remain distinct entities despite the infusion of religion and seminarians into the Constitution of the state.

Mass Media

The media play both a unifying and a divisive role in socializing Iranians. Radio and television are monopolized by the state and are one of the major means to transmit the official doctrine and to mobilize Iranians for elections and rallies across the country. Since the head of the Radio and Television Organization is directly appointed by the Leader, in recent years it has also reflected the interests of the conservative wing of the regime. The strong bias of state television was clearly demonstrated during the presidency of Mohammad Khatami (1997–2005), when news broadcasts either ignored or misrepresented many of the raging political debates.

In recent years, as satellite television has grown and the dishes have become less expensive, antiregime Persian language programming from abroad and foreign news outlets (CNN and BBC) provide greater diversity for the viewing public. In response, the state has repeatedly tried to outlaw private use of satellite dishes, although the law has not been applied consistently. The dishes can be seen on rooftops in major cities and even small towns.

The printed press has been the most diverse and fascinating form of media in postrevolutionary Iran. In the first decade of the revolution, newspapers and journals became increasingly uniform in their coverage. But as the regime began to feel more consolidated and elite competition became more open after the passing away of Khomeini, a growing number of independent newspapers and magazines appeared on the scene. These newspapers and magazines reflected specific schools of thought and critical views from intellectuals on the right and left and the more republican and the more authoritarian wings of the regime. A flourishing nonstate press and burgeoning investigative journalism constituted the backbone of Khatami's surprising election victory in 1997 and underpinned the enormous popularity of the reformist movement in his first term. The critics of the government (many of whom were part of the revolutionary establishment) and the many young journalists writing critical articles presented a new political language of accountability, civil society, and participation to the educated, urban, and young population of Iran. In doing so, these newspapers both reflected and produced deep cleavages among the ruling establishment.

During the authoritarian backlash against the reformist movement since 2000, the conservative-controlled Judiciary has gone a long way in clamping down on the most vibrant aspects of this press. Currently, journalists have turned to the Internet to distribute their reports and publish their commentaries in online newspapers or in the mushrooming collection of weblogs. Today, Persian is the fourth most widely used language in terms of numbers of bloggers, after English, French, and Portuguese. In Iran today, journalists and newspaper editors, some of whom have been imprisoned or physically attacked, have become the new political heroes of many of the youth.

The Family and Social Groups

Political socialization takes place in the private sphere as well as in the public sphere. This is particularly the case in more authoritarian contexts. In Iran, both under the monarchy and the Islamic Republic, the home has been a relatively free place to discuss politics by recounting the unofficial history of the country or debate current events with family members and friends. While patriarchy (and sometimes matriarchy) does prohibit unfettered debate in the family setting, the memory of key political episodes—such as the 1953 coup or the events leading up to the overthrow of the Shah in 1979—is transmitted in these settings. By retelling stories from earlier eras or speculating about the conspiracies behind them, older family members indoctrinate the family's younger generation in a political memory and culture that have not been sanctioned by the state and that are at variance with the official story, as contained in school textbooks and official rhetoric.

But with greater numbers of Iranians completing high school and attending universities, the family dynamic appears to have changed. Young men and women now have a certain authority as they are the first generation in their families to graduate from high school and university. It is they who are interpreting politics for their relatives by explaining differences between political factions and bringing campus politics into their homes. Over the last ten years, greater political freedoms, or at least a less fearful setting, has allowed for many of these types of discussions to take place while one waits for oven-fresh bread outside the local bakery, peruses headlines at the newspaper kiosk, or shares a collective taxi with total strangers. These ritualistic acts of resistance prevent the state from fully dominating politics, but at the same time they do not challenge the bases of regime power.

In short, political socialization under the Islamic Republic has shifted from being solely the responsibility of the state to one that is contested by counterelite and popular voices. The early revolutionary message of unity and mobilization in the name of revolutionary Islam once taught in school textbooks and recounted in Friday sermons and newspaper pages has given way to greater pluralism and contestation, intriguingly by many of the same people who read those school texts and wrote those newspaper articles in the 1980s. Whether the regime will be able to accommodate and represent pluralistic discourse or impose the single voice of unity is very much the question facing Iran's authorities. Their decision and capacity in this regard will determine whether Iran will move toward more democratic politics or authoritarianism.

RECRUITING THE POLITICAL ELITE

What kinds of people govern Iran? Under the Shah, the small class of educated and secular Iranians who could demonstrate personal loyalty to the monarch gained access to political offices. Many of the ministers came from land-owning families and attended Western high schools and universities.[34] The Shah, however, carefully monitored his court in order to prevent the rise of potential competitors with a strong personality or independent bases of support. For instance, highly competent policymakers and administrators—such as the Abol-Hasan Ebtehaj, who headed the Plan and Budget Organization—were muscled out of office as soon as the Shah sensed they were growing in stature.[35] This policy produced a highly dependent inner circle, whose members were unwilling to challenge the Shah and preferred to censor information and opinions in order not to offend His Imperial Majesty. This passive and dependent nature of the political elite prevented the Shah from

acting in a timely and decisive manner as the revolts and political challenges of 1977 and 1978 snowballed into the revolution.[36]

Under the Islamic Republic personalism has also played an important role, but in a broader sense. In the early years, political elites came from various backgrounds, but their most fundamental credentials were their revolutionary pedigrees. Those who could point to active participation in the Islamic revolution, and in particular the various groups associated with Khomeini and his students, leveraged this past experience into positions in ministries, the parastatal economic foundations, the Islamic Revolutionary Guard Corps, and various other institutions with access to state revenue. Thus, the new political elite that came to power immediately after the revolution was younger and less cosmopolitan; they were from more middle-class and lower-middle-class backgrounds, often hailing from the provinces rather than the capital.

In general, the state has expanded since the revolution. From 1976 to 1986, the number of employees in the public sector more than doubled, reaching more than 30 percent of all employed Iranians. In the 1980s, four-fifths of all new jobs created were in the public sector, and by 1986 public-sector employment accounted for 31 percent of total employment.[37] This expansion was due to a number of reasons, including the requisites of the war effort, the state-led economic development program, and the revolutionary agenda to restructure and Islamicize society from above.

Initially the clergy that were recruited into the state were trained in the seminaries in Najaf and Qom where Khomeini and his students taught during the 1960s and 1970s. The principal seminary that produced these new judges and ministers was the Fayziyeh Seminary in Qom. Over time, the Haqqani Seminary in Qom has grown in importance, in part because many of its alumni include staunch conservatives who have dominated the Judiciary, the Council of Guardians, and the security apparatus. The so-called Haqqani circle has included important figures in the conservative backlash against Khatami's attempts to institutionalize political reform and encourage active participation by civil society. In the recent parliamentary and presidential elections, the Haqqani alumni in conjunction with some elements of the Islamic Revolutionary Guard Corps have both supported social conservatives and opposed moderate conservatives and reformists.

Nonclerical parliamentarians and ministers tend to emerge from educational and military institutions. First, many attend the newly Islamicized universities, such as Imam Sadeq University or Tarbiat Modarres University. In the 1990s, think tanks and research centers were important in recruiting and producing political elites. Many of the reformists who dominated the Sixth Parliament and supported President Khatami were based in the Center for Strategic Studies. These younger elites often are too young to have significant revolutionary credentials, but their studies in these universities and institutes give them technical know-how, intellectual credentials, and the social networks to gain access to various government and state institutions.

More recently, many of the new elite have come from the ranks of the Islamic Revolutionary Guard Corps and the Basij. The current president, Ahmadinejad, the mayor of Tehran, Mohammad-Baqer Qalibaf, and many of the ministers all were military figures from these corps or worked for the research institutes connected to the IRGC. It is worth noting that the regular army, navy, and air force have not had much influence in politics. This growing militarization of politics is a new phenomenon in modern Iranian history. Unlike neighboring Pakistan, Turkey, and Iraq, which have had numerous military coups and governments headed by generals, the Iranian political establishment was overwhelmingly civilian throughout the twentieth century.

Kinship ties are commonly used to gain political and economic power. Many of the sons and brothers, and on some rare occasions, daughters and sisters, of government officials use their family ties to gain access to the state. Often their contacts are used as means for rent seeking (receiving subsidized hard currency, special import licenses, or securing subsidized loans) and personal enrichment. In addition, marriage is used as a powerful way to cement political alliances and create bonds between prominent families. For instance, President Khatami's brother, Mohammad-Reza Khatami—who was a member of the Sixth Parliament and the secretary general of the reformist Islamic Iran Participation Front—is married to Zahra Eshraqi, a granddaughter of Khomeini. Meanwhile, the daughter of the current speaker of the Parliament, Gholam-Ali Haddad-Adel, is married to the son of Ali Khamenei, the Leader. These and other kinship relations thus help integrate the elite and distinguish them from ordinary citizens.

INTEREST ARTICULATION AND AGGREGATION

The mix of electoral politics and authoritarian powers generates multiple and competing forms of interest articulation and aggregation under the Islamic Republic. The most institutionalized forms are regular presidential, parliamentary, and local elections, as discussed earlier. The least institutionalized, but probably the most prevalent and effective, is the use of personalistic ties and patron–client relations. As a consequence, representation under the Islamic Republic is highly fragmented, fluid, and contentious, although not fully pluralistic, competitive, and democratic.

Noninstitutional Forms of Interest Articulation and Aggregation

The principal means of interest aggregation in contemporary Iran is clientelism and the forging of relationships between political figures and citizens through patron-client networks. Given the state's access to external sources of revenue from the world oil market, Iranian political figures have exchanged political loyalty and support for access to such resources as subsidies, hard currency, subcontracts, and secure government jobs. This system of patronage can take a very direct form where parliamentarians, ministers, or bureaucrats dole out these resources to kin, schoolmates, and people from the same city or province. Special access to powerful figures in the office of the Leader, state-owned banks, and economic foundations have benefited these clients, while ensuring their dependence, if not loyalty, to the political system that plays more of a distributive, rather than an extractive role. Since patron–client relations are based on the goods that the patron provides the client, if the patron loses power then so do his clients.

In a less targeted manner, the Islamic Republic distributes large subsidies to ensure the loyalty of large portions of the population. Food and medicine are subsidized at an annual rate of about $2 billion and particularly to benefit the urban poor. By contrast, the annual $10 billion energy subsidy for gasoline and electricity is quite regressive because it benefits the middle and upper classes that own automobiles, homes, and electrical equipment. Obviously, this form of political aggregation undermines pretensions of institutional impartiality and meritocracy that are essential principles behind equal citizenship and participation.

Institutionalized Forms of Interest Articulation and Aggregation: Voting

Elections are regularized political events, but they do not provide complete pluralism nor necessarily entail a shift in power and policies, since the powers of the representative institutions are quite limited. Elections tend to function more as an act and measurement of regime legitimacy, and only secondarily as a means for citizens to express their interests by selecting among diverse sets of candidates with specified policy positions. Thus, except for the most recent elections, there has been more discussion about election turnout than candidates. The turnout in the nine presidential elections averaged around 63 percent (see again Figure 12.4, presidential elections) and for the seven parliamentary elections, about 60 percent.

Both the 1997 and 2005 presidential elections, however, indicated that under certain conditions elections can be moments of interest articulation and offer information regarding the preferences of citizens. In 1997, it was quite clear that the regime candidate was Ali-Akbar Nateq-Nuri, the sitting speaker of the Parliament and close confidant of the Leader. However, thanks in part to the burgeoning civil society and his low government profile, Mohammad Khatami, as "the outsider" and "nonregime" candidate, swept to victory with a surprising 70 percent of the vote. In somewhat similar fashion, although with a very different political agenda and significance, Mahmud Ahmadinejad surprised many pundits by defeating Ali-Akbar Hashemi Rafsanjani, who has been one of the cornerstones of the Islamic Republic since its establishment. These surprising outcomes indicate that in spite of the limited nature of elections in the Islamic Republic, voters are able to express their views, and these preferences can matter even when they go against the wishes of the ruling establishment or the expectations of political experts.

Given the weakness of party organizations, as mentioned earlier, political parties play no major role. The factions that contend for power and influence in Iran have not formed a clearly defined party system that would act as a mechanism for representing and aggregating the interests of constituents. Parties and political associations, such as the Society of Combatant Clergy or the Islamic Iran Participation Front, are groupings of members of the political elite that become active during elections, yet until now they have been unable to maintain party discipline with direct and formalized links to the citizenry.

Institutional Groups and Professional Organizations

While political parties are less developed, groups based in state organizations have a more corporate identity and a greater ability to shape policy, in much the same manner as controlled interest group systems. The Islamic Revolutionary Guard Corps and the volunteer mobilization corps (Basij), consisting of 120,000, and 90,000 men, respectively,[38] are two of the most prominent arms of the state that directly represent their interests in various policymaking areas, although they were established to mobilize support for the regime. These ostensibly military and security forces have also played a role in the economy through their business subsidiaries, which are involved in large-scale construction projects as well as allegedly importing consumer goods. Since the 2003 local council elections, the IRCG and Basij have taken a more visible role in politics. A number of their high-ranking figures have run for local offices, Parliament, and, most recently, the presidency. Finally, since they are in direct communication with the Leader, and not the president and Parliament, they have the ability to influence policy.

Iran does have a host of associations representing the interests of labor, business, professional groups, and industrial sectors. However, the House of Labor or the Iranian Chamber of Commerce, Industries, and Mines and other such organizations operate more as a means for state officials to manage these corporate entities rather than as vehicles to represent specific interest and shape policymaking. Only in very recent elections have professional organizations endorsed different candidates, which may signal the emergence of an independent role for these corporate groups in political competition.

In the course of the struggle against the Shah and in the years following his overthrow, neighborhood councils and guild associations sprang up all over the country as grassroots initiatives to address ordinary citizens' needs during the revolution and the war years. Over time they have become integrated into the patron-client system, and today they are either mere appendages of state officials or means for the state to penetrate society.[39] Hence, there is no clear separation between interest groups and government officials. Moreover, since the revolution the government has encouraged workers, merchants, and students to establish Islamic associations in universities, factories, and guilds as the principal means of aggregating the interests of these groups.

Nonetheless, in the 1990s and especially during the relatively less repressive administration of President Khatami, a large number of genuinely autonomous associations representing strata of society that had been largely sidelined by the revolutionary regime emerged. For instance, various women's organizations of both secular and reformist Islamist persuasion came into being and started initiatives seeking to change discriminatory laws, provide services, and raise general consciousness regarding women's issues. (Most notable is the 2003 Nobel Peace Prize Winner, **Shirin Ebadi.** She was the first woman to become a judge under the Shah, but, she lost her job when women were barred from that position following the revolution. Ebadi was active in a host of legal organizations championing and defending the rights of women, children, and political dissidents.) Simultaneously, students and secular intellectuals took advantage of these opportunities to establish or reactivate associations and publications that were independently minded and represented alternative visions of politics.

Nonassociational Social Groups

Many social strata in Iran exist without independent associations aggregating and representing their interests. Among the historically and politically important social groups without corporate representation, it is worth mentioning the bazaari merchants. Among the more recent social groups, the war veterans and the relatives of those killed in the war (referred to as "martyrs") stand out as well.

Bazaari merchants based in the historic covered bazaars of Iran, ranging from retailers and brokers to wholesalers and even international traders, have played a central role in various political episodes from the Constitutional Revolution (1905–1911) to the Oil Nationalization Movement (1951–1953) to the Islamic Revolution. Even though important differences have existed among bazaaris in terms of socioeconomic

status, political persuasion, and position in the international and national economies, they have developed a sense of solidarity because of the well-defined and vibrant physical space of the bazaar, which ensures socially embedded and crosscutting relations. Their political significance is enhanced both by their economic power and their close relationship with the ulema. Since the revolution, bazaari economic interests have been threatened by the state's domination of the economy, while the homogeneity of bazaari interests has been undermined by key pro-Khomeini bazaari families being co-opted by the new regime.

War veterans, the families of the martyrs, and those disabled in the Iran–Iraq war make up a large and politically important social group. They are ostensibly represented by various organizations and political groups, such as the Martyr's Foundation, the Foundation of the Disinherited, the Society of the Devotees of the Islamic Republic, and the Headquarters of the POWs. But these organizations have proved unable to address adequately the everyday demands of many of their constituents, and they have moved away from their original mandate of providing services to war veterans and their families. The state has also provided for this important constituency by setting up all kinds of affirmative action schemes (ranging from easier access to higher education to priority in flight reservations) and subsidizing consumer goods for veterans and relatives of both veterans and "martyrs" in order to enhance their socioeconomic standing. Yet these measures have not always worked adequately to both address the needs of this social group and suppress challenges. Some prominent war veterans and former members of the IRGC have aligned themselves with the reformist faction, calling for greater political participation and freedoms. Others have accused the regime of turning its back on the wartime principles of self-sacrifice and justice. For much of the postwar era there have been growing complaints by some war veterans that the memory of the war and respect for the sacrifices of the war generation have faded, while the veterans and relatives of the martyrs have not been sufficiently provided for. This position was given voice by some ultraconservative newspapers, certain filmmakers engaged in producing war films, and outspoken figures of a group called Ansar-e Hezbollah (Partisans of the Party of God) who have taken it upon themselves to combat moral, political, and economic corruption.

Demonstrations and Public Protests

Given the closed nature of institutional interest representation and aggregation, many social groups and political tendencies have turned to civil disobedience to express their grievances. The relatively fresh memory of the demonstrations and strikes that constituted the revolution of 1978–1979 are a model for workers, students, activist women, and the urban poor to use public collective action to make their claims. Throughout the 1990s, industrial workers, for instance, protested against privatization policies, the selling of state-owned factories, and nonpayment of their wages. One high-profile tactic has workers blocking the main expressway connecting Tehran to the industrial satellite city of Karaj. These protesters have succeeded on several occasions to block the selling of state-owned factories to private business interests they suspected of planning to lay off workers. Teachers and government pensioners in recent years have protested in front of the Parliament to draw attention to their inadequate income. On the eve of the 2005 presidential election, women's groups united to organize protests against the male bias enshrined in the Constitution. Ethnic political groups, especially Kurdish and Arab activists on the Iran–Iraq border, have vocally called for greater distribution of wealth and local authority in their provinces. Since 2003, these tensions have flared up with mysterious bombings taking place and the Iranian security forces and IRGC responding brutally.

The most dramatic protests, however, have been based in the universities and spearheaded by students. During the summers of 1999 and 2003, student organizations staged sit-ins and demonstrations to protest against authoritarian measures by the regime. In the first case they challenged the closure of a prominent reformist newspaper and in the second case the sentencing of an outspoken intellectual who had questioned clerical rule. These protests were originally based in Tehran University, but they spread to other cities and university campuses and persisted for several days. With little support or protection from reformist parties and other social groups (such as workers, bazaaris, and teachers), the volunteer forces (Basij) and police violently suppressed the demonstrators and prevented the movement from escalating.

Although these and other events demonstrate that Iranian society is not completely passive in the face of government policies, the inability for these disparate groups to unite or coordinate their localized organizational capabilities is an indication of the overwhelming social atomization in contemporary Iran. Given the pervasive use of patron–client relations and lack of trust among Iranians, collective action and alliance-building is particularly difficult. Moreover, these non-institutional forms of politics reflect the lack of efficacy of institutional politics and the belief on the part of many Iranians that their political voice cannot be heard unless it is in this form.

POLICY FORMULATION

In the Islamic Republic of Iran state policy is set by a number of bodies, some of them explicitly mentioned in the Constitution, some not. Given the mixed nature of the political system, overlaps, duplications, and even contradictions abound, and it is not rare for different policymaking bodies to work at cross-purposes.

State Institutions Mentioned in the Constitution

As befits a theocracy in which, at least in theory, no state policy may contradict Islam, those who determine what does and does not contradict Islam have a preponderant voice in setting policy. In the Islamic Republic this means first and foremost the Leader. The first Leader, Ruhollah Khomeini, on numerous occasions used his authority to determine state policy by issuing religious edicts (*fatwas*). On a few occasions these edicts broke with established religious tradition, which is not astonishing given the charismatic nature of his leadership.[40] One of the earliest examples was his ruling on caviar. According to Shiite (and Jewish) dietary laws, a fish can be eaten only if it has scales. The sturgeon, however, has no scales and traditionally its meat and, by extension, its roe (caviar) were not deemed permissible. But caviar is one of Iran's main exports, and so the matter was revisited. A specially appointed state commission concluded that the sturgeon does indeed have scales, but that they are of a peculiar shape. Taking note of this finding, in November 1983 Khomeini issued a *fatwa* declaring that caviar could be eaten. In 1988 he broke with other time-honored legal traditions by authorizing the playing of chess, provided no bets were made on the outcome, betting and gambling being forbidden in Islam. He also liberalized the early republic's stifling cultural life by relaxing the rules pertaining to music and television programming.[41]

Khomeini's interventions in the state's policy-making were often made necessary by continued deadlock between Parliament and the Council of Guardians, as mentioned earlier. To avoid paralysis, in January 1988 Khomeini amended his doctrine of *velayat-e faqih*, guardianship of the jurisprudent, by issuing an edict that gave the state, as embodied by its Leader, authority to override religious law when that is expedient. This "absolute dominion of the jurisprudent" (*velayat-e motlaqeh-ye faqih*), he averred, was the "most important of divine commandments and has priority over all derivative divine commandments . . . even over prayer, fasting, and the pilgrimage to Mecca."[42] This reinterpretation of the theocratic principle was enshrined in the Constitution when that document was revised in 1989.

Needless to say, most traditional Muslims and most members of the ulema were horrified by this subordination of religion to reason of state, as the whole purpose of setting up an Islamic state had been the exact opposite. Moreover, no person other than Khomeini could conceivably get away with disregarding religion when it was expedient for the state to do so, and as a result shortly before his death Khomeini invested the newly established Expediency Council with the authority to advise the Leader on invoking the absolute authority. As president (1981–1989), Khamenei had been a member of the conservative faction, and in his first years as Leader he more or less tried to give the impression of remaining above the fray, but with the onset of the Khatami presidency in 1997 he abandoned all pretense of neutrality and became the de facto leader of the conservatives who did their best to stymie the reformist zeal of the elected officials.

The Expediency Council has emerged as the institution in which the most vital policies of the nation are decided. For instance, in Iran's negotiations with Britain, France, Germany, and the International Atomic Energy Commission (IAEC) about its nuclear program, the top Iranian negotiator, Hasan Rowhani, did not come from the foreign ministry or the Atomic Energy Organization of Iran, but was an engineer-turned-cleric who was the secretary of the National Security Council, where foreign policy is made, and as such a member of the Expediency Council. Politically identified with Hashemi Rafsanjani, he resigned from his position as chief negotiator after the election of Mahmud Ahmadinejad to the presidency in June 2005. With Ahmadinejad's election, the old establishment became apprehensive about the new president's ultraconservative and populist policies, policies that threaten not only the domestic status quo but also Iran's security.[43] And so in October 2005 the chairman of the Expediency Council since 1997, none other than Ali-Akbar Hashemi Rafsanjani managed to extract a letter from the Leader that granted the Expediency Council broad supervisory powers over all three branches of government. Whether this move will have a moderating effect on the new administration's policymaking is impossible to tell at this point, but it shows that rivalries among institutions over policymaking powers have not disappeared now that both the presidency and Parliament are dominated by conservatives.

In the course of the 1988 revision of the Constitution, a body formed some years earlier was added to the official institutional structure: the National Security Council, whose members include the heads of the three branches of government, top military commanders, the foreign minister, the minister of information (that is, intelligence), and a few other figures named by the Leader. It has emerged as the nation's highest policymaking body in matters of foreign and security policy, which, in the case of the Islamic Republic, includes the struggle against what is officially called "Western cultural aggression."

The Council of Guardians does not have a major policymaking role, but its six lay members are present in Parliament when it is in session and have at times attempted to work with sympathetic MPs to introduce legislation. As for Parliament itself, it has been largely emasculated as a policymaking body by the unelected bodies mentioned earlier. Legislative proposals come before it either from the cabinet or from a minimum of twenty-five MPs, and while successive Parliaments have tried to create frameworks for conducting economic policies and changing the penal and civil codes, much of their activities have been stymied by the Council of Guardians.

Areas where the executive branch of government (prime minister until 1989, president since then) and Parliament have had an impact on state policy include setting the state budget, providing and regulating social and welfare services, and handling territorial administration, which includes redrawing provincial borders. Beginning in the mid-1980s, for instance, the MPs of the northwestern city of Ardabil campaigned for the creation of a new province around their city. Young men from Ardabil having died in disproportionate numbers in the Iran–Iraq war, the people of the city used the moral leverage that their sacrifices gave them to renew their demands with greater fervor after the war ended in 1988. All sorts of civic associations mobilized for the demand, which was expressed inside Parliament by the MPs. In the end, the administration of President Hashemi Rafsanjani introduced a bill in Parliament providing for the new province. The bill was hotly debated, and it finally passed in a secret vote in early 1993.[44]

The extensive powers of the Leader and the existence of such unelected decision-making bodies as the Council of Guardians, the Expediency Council, and the National Security Council severely limit the policymaking role of the elected officials: the president, the individual cabinet members named by him and approved by Parliament, and Parliament itself. Popular sovereignty is thus severely undermined.

State Institutions Not Mentioned in the Constitution

The role of elected officials is further limited by councils that are not mentioned expressly in the Constitution and that were established for the express purpose of formulating state policy in a particular field. The most prominent of these is the Supreme Council for the Cultural Revolution, which was set up by order of Khomeini in 1986 to perpetuate the policies unleashed during the Cultural Revolution of the early 1980s that purged universities of leftists and secularists. Its tasks include determining not only state policies in the realms of culture, education, and research, but also "the spread and reinforcement of the influence of Islamic culture in all areas of society." Its supremacy over Parliament can be seen from the fact that in recent years the Council of Guardians has at times vetoed legislation on the grounds that it contradicted policies determined by the Supreme Council for the Cultural Revolution, the latter having the approval of the Leader.

Power Centers and the Difficulty of Policy Coordination

Given the existence of multiple power centers, policies are often not coordinated, as some state institutions make and implement their own policies independently of the relevant ministries. This includes the Judiciary, which does not limit itself to implementing the law but in fact takes it into its own hands, and the Revolutionary Guards, who wage their own struggle against dissent and pursue a foreign policy independent of that of the foreign ministry and even the National Security Council.

The impact of these inconsistencies became particularly apparent under President Khatami, when the dispute between reformists and conservatives added an ideological dimension to the diffuse, ill-defined, and overlapping competencies of many state bodies. A few examples will illustrate this.

Under Khatami, who had been a liberalizing minister of culture between 1982 and 1992, the ministry of culture, which controls censorship and issues licenses for newspapers and journals, adopted more liberal policies, inaugurating a period of press freedom and diversity. But the Judiciary, headed by a conservative ally of the Leader, used its powers to close down newspapers and indict and jail reformist journalists and editors who had incurred the displeasure of conservatives. For every newspaper that was closed down, the ministry of culture would issue a new license and the newspaper would appear under a new name.[45] But by 2000 the most critical voices had been silenced by the Judiciary and its allies in the armed forces.

Another example comes from the security apparatus. In late 1998, six months after the commander of the Revolutionary Guards had threatened violence against opponents of the regime, a number of opposition politicians, journalists, and writers were killed in what became known as the "chain murders." Khatami insisted on an investigation and persuaded Khamenei to give his consent. Soon it became clear that the murders had been carried out by members of the ministry of information. This led to a purge in the ministry, which operates under the authority of the president and of Parliament.[46] While the ministry of information subsequently became more tolerant of dissent and respectful of the law, the Revolutionary Guards and the Judiciary proceeded to set up their own parallel intelligence organizations, replete with prosecutors and prisons, to pursue the conservatives' agenda of suppressing dissent.[47]

A final example is from foreign policy. Beginning at the end of the 1980s, a number of foreign ministry officials began calling for a policy that would privilege Iran's national interest in light of *realpolitik* rather than the pursuit of worldwide revolution. Tirelessly arguing their case and demonstrating the cost for Iran of remaining on the margins of world diplomacy, they managed to inflect foreign policy with a number of countries, except the United States and Israel. But while government officials engaged in diplomacy denied that Iran meddled in the internal affairs of other countries, various state or parastatal institutions pursued separate activist foreign policy agendas. Thus, when in 1998 the ministry of foreign affairs reached an agreement with Britain to the effect that Iran would do nothing to carry out the death penalty imposed by Khomeini in 1988 on British author Salman Rushdie, the parastatal Second of Khordad Foundation immediately increased the $2 million bounty it had put on the author's head in 1989. Although the director of this foundation is appointed by the Leader, its administrative and financial autonomy from the government enabled the latter to claim that the foundation was not a state entity.[48] Likewise, while the foreign ministry under Khatami repeatedly stated that Iran would do nothing to impede the Arab-Israeli peace process, which the Iranian government deemed doomed in advance anyway, various organizations (such as the IRGC) continue to channel funds to the Palestinian Islamic Jihad organization, which carries out suicide attacks on targets in Israel and the occupied territories. These inconsistencies have seriously damaged Iran's credibility on the international scene, as Iranian negotiators seem unable to deliver on their commitments.

Economic Policymaking

One of the most contentious topics in the postrevolutionary era is economic policymaking. From the very outset, the founders of the Islamic Republic and the new elite in the ministries and parastatal organizations had fundamentally differing views on what was the best approach to foster economic development. Initially, those who favored a more state-centered approach to development dominated policymaking through the Parliament, ministries, and such institutions as the Construction Jihad. In the 1980s the state played a critical role in rationing hard currency, setting prices for consumer goods, and using the public banking system to distribute loans to key sectors of the economy. The logic of state control found support at the time in large part due to the requirements of war, the political necessity of redistributing the assets of the numerous industrialists who had been forced into exile, and the fact that international investment had come to a standstill.

A liberal approach to development that placed greater emphasis on the private sector and market mechanisms began to dominate policymaking circles in the late 1980s. This was encouraged by the conclusion of the Iran–Iraq war and the global rise of neoliberal development agendas in the wake of the Soviet Union's demise. The major impetus to redirect economic policies, however, was the general economic recession and poor performance of the economy (see Figure 12.7 and discussion later in this chapter). Thus, both the Rafsanjani and Khatami administrations tried to restructure Iran's economy by selling state-owned assets, lifting trade restrictions, and encouraging private and foreign investment. These policy initiatives have had mixed results. Iran liberalized its trade regime, with ministries and procurement boards now playing a less pronounced role. Furthermore, private banks and industries take advantage of incentives to export goods. Nonetheless, the deregulation of the economy has also led to hardship and has therefore faced opposition. On the one hand, many state employees and those who rely on state subsidies have been hurt by economic insecurity and inflation. Many of these Iranians were probably receptive to Ahmadinejad's prowelfare and anti-inequality message, a message that harkened back to the economic approaches of the 1980s. On the other hand, the government's attempt to reform the economy has challenged the economic powers and vested interests of the large economic foundations that control large portions of Iran's commercial, industrial, and agricultural sectors, and that are largely unaccountable to the Parliament, the central bank, and development policymaking bodies.

Khatami's and the reformists' attempt to introduce greater transparency and competition into the economy was limited by the economic foundations' and parastatal organizations' autonomous and privileged access to resources and markets. Thus, any

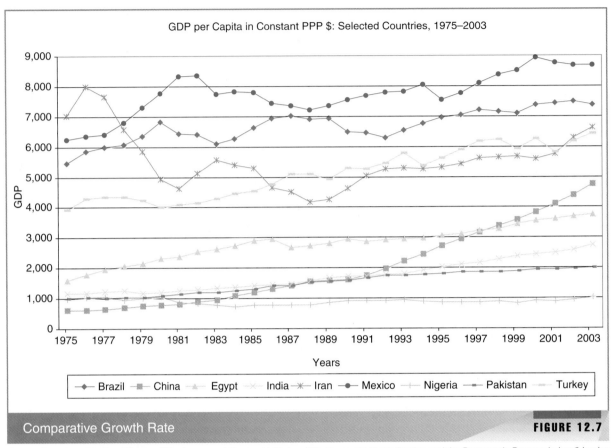

GDP per Capita in Constant PPP $: Selected Countries, 1975–2003

Comparative Growth Rate   **FIGURE 12.7**

Source: Based on data from Massoud Karshenas and Hassan Hakimian, "Oil, Economic Diversification and the Democratic Process in Iran," *Iranian Studies* 38, no. 1 (March 2005), 67–90.

attempt to reform the economy, boost productivity, or direct investment toward exports must address the inequality and inconsistencies of the parallel economy controlled by these organizations. To date, those who favor liberalizing Iran's economy have been unable to limit the power of the parastatals or even persuade large numbers of Iranians that such an economic reform would benefit them, and this policy bottleneck thus remains unaddressed in practice.

POLICY OUTCOMES

Incoherent Policies

The result of the multiplicity of policymaking bodies is frequent incoherence and sometimes paralysis. On a positive note, this incoherence has prevented the system from becoming totalitarian, as the overlapping spheres of activity of various state institutions have

made centralized control of public life well nigh impossible. To illustrate this point, let us look at one example from cultural policy, which is of supreme importance for a regime dedicated to changing the nation's culture.

Traditionally, the ulema have frowned on music, fearing that it will whet listeners' appetites for illicit pleasures, such as wine and fornication—an association not unknown in the West, as the triad "wine, women, and song" attests. After the revolution, most forms of music were officially banned in Iran. But given the impossibility of suppressing music entirely, Khomeini relaxed the prohibitions in a series of edicts. Inside the ministry of culture—whose official name is Ministry of Culture and Islamic Guidance—a general directorate for music has the task of defining guidelines for what musicians can do in public. Officially, for instance, the 6/8 rhythm, the basis of most Iranian dances, is outlawed; women may not sing solo in front of an audience that includes men; and certain poems by some of Iran's greatest poets, such as Hafez of Shiraz (1326–1390), that castigate the bigotry of the religious classes may not be sung at concerts. When musicians produce a tape, this directorate has the task of granting or withholding a license to have it distributed commercially. This arrangement would seem to give the ministry total authority over musical life, except that another organization, the Islamic Propaganda Organization operating under the auspices of the Leader, has an arts section that also contains a music department. This department issues licenses for recordings independently of the ministry of culture and operates a state-of-the-art recording studio that musicians can rent. Paradoxically, it is more liberal than its ministerial counterpart, rumor having it that the Leader is secretly a lover and connoisseur of classical Persian music. Moreover, the state radio and television monopoly maintains its own music bureaucracy, which decides independently of the other two what can be broadcast. The result is that musicians can play one bureaucracy against the other, enhancing their chances of getting around restrictions.[49]

Spreading Progress and Prosperity

The chief complaint of the revolutionaries had been that the Shah's policies failed to benefit the majority of Iranians. While succeeding administrations in the Islamic Republic have been on the whole indifferent to the interests of the educated upper middle class, they have tried to adopt policies that will improve the lot of the poor.

The state educational system is astonishingly good, given the limitations imposed by the political system. Iranian students regularly win medals at international science olympiads, and literacy rates have continued rising, reaching 84 percent for men and 70 percent for women by 2000, up from 48 percent and less than 25 percent, respectively, in 1970.[50]

After pronatalist policies in the 1980s, the government realized that birth rates had to be brought down, and it inaugurated a multifaceted policy of facilitating birth control. All forms of contraception are widely distributed and subsidized both in cities and in villages, everywhere clinics offer free sterilization to men and women, and the state actively encourages couples to have "only two children, be they boys or girls." All

over Iran couples do indeed have fewer children than their parents' generation. But for the foreseeable future Iran's population will keep rising, as the very numerous Iranians born in the 1980s are beginning to have children of their own. The current growth rate of the Iranian population is 1.3 percent, one of the lowest in the Middle East.

Health care is another area of considerable progress. Small clinics staffed by paramedics serve many villages, and there is no shortage of physicians. While the quality of medical care may not always be very high, its availability to the general population is respectable even when compared with rich Western countries. These rural social and economic development programs are successful partly because they have been spearheaded by the local communities rather than by experts from distant urban areas who typically are unaware of the local needs or social and cultural conditions.

Much effort has gone into improvements in the countryside. Paved roads now connect all towns and many villages, and many villages have clean water and electricity. But in spite of the state's efforts to create a welfare state financed by oil income, most Iranians struggle to make ends meet. To some extent this is because the middle class has grown tremendously. People whose parents were illiterate and poor peasants now aspire to a middle-class lifestyle; they expect to eat meat every day, send their children to good schools, and have decent housing. Table 12.3 compares some basic human development indicators for the year 2003 of Iran with those of a few comparable countries.[51]

The provision of basic services to the general population has been quite successful. Obviously, more than three decades of high oil income have made a difference, for in many ways the indicators for Iran are closer to those of Turkey than to those of Egypt or Pakistan. However, many Iranians are unwilling to credit the government for this, and impute it to the natural development of a country with a large oil income. It is often argued that with better planning, more competent management, and an acceptance of Saddam Hussein's offer to end the Iran–Iraq war in 1982, the situation might be much better still. Moreover, as Figure 12.7 reveals, over the last three decades Iran's overall macroeconomic performance has fallen behind the newly developing countries in Latin America or East Asia. The per capita growth rates have not kept pace with the emerging economic

TABLE 12.3

Comparison of Development Indicators, 2003

Country	Population	Population Growth	Life Expectancy	Infant Mortality (before age 1)	Access to Sanitation (%)
Iran	66 million	1.3	69	33	84
Turkey	70 million	1.5	69	33	83
Egypt	67 million	1.8	69	33	68
Pakistan	148 million	2.4	64	74	54
India	1 billion	1.5	63	63	30
China	1.3 billion	0.6	71	30	44
Mexico	102 million	1.4	74	23	77
Nigeria	136 million	2.4	45	98	38

Country	Literacy/Men	Literacy/Women	Education as Part of GNP	GNP/Capita $	GNP/PPP $
Iran	84	70	4.9	2,010	7,000
Turkey	94	79	3.7	2,240	6,710
Egypt	67	44	?	1,390	3,940
Pakistan	57	28	1.8	520	2,040
India	68	45	4.1	540	2,880
China	95	87	?	1,100	4,980
Mexico	93	89	5.2	6,230	8,980
Nigeria	74	59	?	350	900

PPP: Purchasing Power Parity.

powers of China and India.[52] In fact, Iran's growth indicators have been quite volatile, with a rather extended period of depression in the 1980s due to war, sanctions, high birth rates, and deficient economic policies. Even with the gradual improvement in per capita gross domestic product (GDP) since the early 1990s, which was largely due to the rise in oil prices, unemployment remains the number-one worry for young people, and the growth rate of the economy is not nearly enough to absorb the growing population. In fact, youth unemployment increased from 14.8 percent in 1996 to 27.5 percent in 2001.[53]

Islamicization of Society

Another motivation of much policymaking is the desire to roll back secularism and spread Islamic moral values among the population. Since the early 1980s alcohol consumption is banned except for the non-Muslim minorities; veiling is enforced in public spaces; the state is in theory committed to minimizing contact between unrelated men and women; the religious content of education is vastly expanded; and gruesome physical punishments chastise adulterers, homosexuals, and other offenders of religious morality.[54] Divine law, as interpreted by the state, also allows capital punishment, and in 2004 the number of death penalties carried out in Iran (159) was second only to China (3,400), Iran coming before Vietnam (64) and the United States (59).[55]

Outwardly, the Islamicization of society has been a success. Women cover their hair in public, people are in general more familiar with religious doctrine than before the revolution, the country has more mosques, Friday congregational prayers are routine in towns and cities, and all flights of Iran Air (the national flag carrier) begin with a prayer. Even the best hotels serve no alcohol, even to foreign guests. Underneath the surface, however, the situation is more complicated. Prostitution is rife, driven by poverty. Over two million Iranians are drug addicts. Bootlegging flourishes, often with the connivance of the forces of order, who get a cut. As education has become longer and the marriage age has gone up, young people are much more likely to have premarital sex than their parents' generation, at least in Tehran. Corruption operates at almost all levels, from the petty official who will do his job only if he is paid a bribe to the relatives of the top leaders who have enriched themselves by controlling economic life.

All of this should not be construed to mean that Iranians have become irreligious. But religious practice has become more private, as the influence of clerics over religious life has declined. One study, comparing data gathered in 1975 and in 2001, demonstrates that while levels of personal religiosity (such as frequency of prayer) have remained relatively constant, participation in organized religion (such as attendance of congregational Friday prayers) has declined, reflecting a growing ambivalence toward state-sponsored public religious practices.[56]

Iranian Islam has always contained an anticlerical strain, as believers have always criticized clerics for their greed and hypocrisy. The ulema's assumption of power in the Islamic Republic has given a new fillip to this tendency. Taxi drivers are known not to stop for clerics, many of whom have taken to wearing civilian clothes in public. Foreign observers are often astonished by how few turbaned clerics one sees in the streets of Tehran.

The rise of anticlericalism has led some of the more thoughtful members of the Shiite clergy to revisit the relations between "church" and state and to call for a separation of the two. They do so not because they advocate secularism, but out of concern for the collective reputation of the ulema. In the Muslim world advocates of the separation of "church" and state had always been secularists. In Iran for the first time *religious* arguments are being made for that separation on the grounds that coercively imposed religion harms spirituality.[57] One may even wonder whether at least some of the pious people who voted for Mahmud Ahmadinejad in the last presidential election did so in order to rebuke the ulema, many of whom—such as the losing candidate, Hashemi Rafsanjani—have joined the country's ruling class and are seen to have been corrupted by power.

Gender Relations

One of the key reproaches that Islamists addressed to the Shah's regime before the revolution was that its promotion of Western lifestyles turned women into sex objects and was generally conducive to moral corruption and sexual depravity. Hence the effort to reorder gender relations and place them on an authentic Islamic footing.

Looked at from a Western perspective, the legal status of women improved under the Pahlavi monarchy, whereas the majority of society remained more conservative than the laws governing it. After the revolution much of the legislation that reduced the gender gap was repealed. According to the Islamic penal code introduced in 1981, the value of a woman's life is half that of a man's, in the sense that the law of the talion ("an eye for an eye") instituted by that code explicitly states that the blood-money of a woman is half of that of a man.[58] In practice, this means that if a man kills another man, the relatives of the victim can either ask for the execution of the murderer or accept a legally fixed blood-money. But if a man kills a woman, her relatives can ask for the murderer's execution only if they pay half a man's blood-money. By the same token, in courts of law the testimony of one man is worth that of two women. In some cases (such as adultery, murder), a woman's testimony does not count at all. A man can easily divorce his wife, whereas in principle a woman can initiate divorce proceedings only under exceptional circumstances; polygamy is recognized under the law. To travel abroad, a wife needs the formal permission of her husband, but the latter can leave the country as he pleases. The foreign wife of an Iranian man can easily acquire Iranian citizenship, whereas an Iranian woman cannot obtain Iranian citizenship for her foreign husband and her children from that husband.[59]

In addition to these legal restrictions on women's rights, the Islamic Republic has instituted all sorts of ad hoc discriminations. Many fields of study, such as agronomy and mining engineering, were closed to female students at the universities on the assumption that they were too rough for women. Women's sports were severely restricted because the attire worn by female athletes is incompatible with veiling. This differential treatment of men and women is in stark violation of the International Convention on Civil and Political Rights, an international treaty that prohibits discrimination on religious and gender grounds. Iran acceded to the Convention in 1975 and remained a party after its regime changed. But from the point of view of theocracy, divine law obviously supercedes obligations incurred under international law.

In spite of these legal restrictions, Iranian women have continuously increased their participation in public life and their presence in the public sphere since strict Islamic law began to be enforced in the early 1980s.[60] At the same time they have challenged the logic of patriarchy. There are a number of reasons for this seemingly paradoxical development. The widespread participation of women in the mass anti-Shah demonstrations of 1978 made it unlikely that their interest in public affairs would end once the revolution was over. After the war against Iraq broke out in 1980 and millions of men were serving at the front, this situation forced many women to do jobs hitherto performed by men. Many women became their families' main breadwinners. Furthermore, the aspiration to a middle-class existence awakened by the revolution, coupled with the slow growth of the economy, has meant that women increasingly supplement their husbands' income by joining the labor force. And given the strictly enforced rules on veiling and gender interaction in the public sphere, more traditional women have felt more at ease entering the public sphere. In addition, more traditional men are less reluctant to let their wives, daughters, or sisters work outside the house. Restrictions that are deeply annoying to nontraditional women have thus had a liberating effect on religiously observant women—and these constitute, after all, a majority of the female population.

The relative strength of the antitraditional attitude toward women's roles in society is reflected in the comparative results of the World Value Survey. For instance, while only 4 percent of Egyptians and 12 percent of Jordanians disagree with the statement that "marriage has become an outdated institution," 17 percent of surveyed Iranians agree.[61] A plurality of surveyed Iranians disagree with the statement that "women need to have children in order to feel satisfied," whereas only 12 percent of Egyptians and 9 percent of Jordanians disagree with it.[62] Finally, 40 percent of Iranians agreed with the statement that "a working mother can develop intimate relationships with her children just like a nonworking mother," a rate that is double that of surveyed Egyptians and Jordanians.[63] Thus, despite the regime's initial attempts to inculcate a traditional image and role for women in the family and society, Iranian men and women seem to hold a less narrow view of women.

The visitor to today's Iran encounters women everywhere: they staff government agencies, work in offices, sell goods in shops, own and run businesses. Most dramatically, women now constitute over 60 percent of the student body at the universities, restrictions on what they can study having been gradually lifted throughout the 1990s to the point where none remain. In Persian literature, the traditional emphasis on poetry has given way to a boom in the writing of novels—and most novelists are women. In sports, a daughter of then-President Hashemi Rafsanjani took over women's sports in the early 1990s. Using her father's clout, she instituted a system whereby women compete under international rules and in normal athletic gear but at locations to which no men are admitted. This change led, incidentally, to many more women becoming coaches, referees, paramedics, and state sports officials.[64] Even veiling is now enforced less strictly, and the partial covering of the head that hardliners call "mal-veiling" has spread. None other than Khomeini's granddaughter complained in an interview with an American journalist about the state's intrusiveness in this regard.[65]

The widening gap between women's growing participation in public life and the legal system governing their society, and the many-voiced debates to which this discrepancy has given rise, have had repercussions for Islam itself in Iran. Given the impossibility of criticizing any state of affairs from a secular perspective, feminists couch their arguments in Islamic terms. This has led to the emergence of "Islamic feminism," which is espoused by both truly observant Muslim women and by secular women who have no other way of articulating their demands. Given the continued religiosity of Iranians in general, Islamic feminism has been arguably more effective in raising the gender consciousness of the average woman than secular feminism would have been. These Islamic feminists are discreetly supported by a few sympathetic clerics who have helped them to contest discriminatory policies or laws by proposing ways to circumvent them or even suggesting alternative readings of the relevant scriptural passages and legal principles. Small gains have thus been made. Take the issue of divorce. According to Islamic law, marriage is a contract whose clauses have to be agreed on freely by both husband and wife. A woman has always had the right to ask that her marriage contract include a clause giving her the right to initiate divorce proceedings, but this clause had to be added on to the standard contract issued by the state. Very few bridegrooms consented to it. Since the early 1980s, however, the standard contract includes the clause, meaning that for the woman not to get the right to divorce, bride and bridegroom have to ask for its removal—to which nowadays few educated women consent.

The greater success of women in higher education and the fact that the vast majority of Iranian drug addicts are men, coupled with the continued existence of domestic violence against women, have led Shirin Ebadi, the woman who more than any other personifies women's struggles and occasional successes, to quip that Iran does not have a "women's question" but a "men's question."

Foreign Policy

Under the Shah, Iran was an ally of the United States, but the Islamic revolution dramatically changed the foreign policy orientation of the country. Like the French, Russian, Chinese, and Cuban revolutionaries before them, Iran's Islamic revolutionaries saw themselves as the vanguard of a vast revolutionary wave that would encompass other countries as well. According to the preamble of the Constitution of 1979, the role of the army and the IRGC is not limited to "securing the borders" of the country but includes "struggling to spread the rule of divine law in the world." Managing the inherent tension between an ideological commitment to helping to overthrow or weaken other governments on the one hand, and dealing with these governments on a daily basis on the other, has posed a tremendous challenge.

Beginning in the early 1990s, "national interest" rather than "export of the revolution" came to dominate the foreign policy agenda. The best example of this trend is the discreet support Iran gave to Christian Armenia in its conflict with Muslim (and predominantly Shiite) Azerbaijan in the war that followed the breakup of the Soviet Union in the mid-1990s. But, as elsewhere in the world, there is little consensus as to what constitutes a nation's national interest, and many in Iran argue that Iran's national interest demands the solidification of its ties with the rest of the Islamic world.

Ultimately, the foreign policy of the Islamic Republic is driven by a "Third Worldist" desire to escape the hegemony of the Western world. In the parlance of Iran's leaders, Western hegemony is referred to as "world arrogance." In its struggle against "world arrogance," Iran has sought alliances, and these can be conceptualized in terms of three concentric circles. The outermost circle consists of Third World nations and in the beginning even included such groups as the Irish Republican Party (IRA) that fought British rule in Northern Ireland. The middle circle is made up of Muslim countries and movements, and the innermost one is constituted by the Shiites in West and South Asia (Lebanon, Iraq, Bahrain, Afghanistan, Pakistan).

In many Third World countries the revolution of 1979 was greeted with sympathy. However, the subsequent triumph of hard-line Islamists put a damper on pro-Iranian sympathies in non-Muslim nations. For instance, then-President Ali Khamenei's refusal to shake hands with female officials, as strict Islamic norms dictated, while on a state visit in Zimbabwe in 1986, caused a diplomatic incident. Sunni Islamists, for their part, were divided over support for revolutionary Iran. As the *Shiite* nature of the *Islamic* Republic became ever more apparent, and as Khomeini refused to accept Saddam Hussein's offer to end the Iran–Iraq war, thus causing continued intra-Muslim bloodshed, most Sunni Islamists turned away from Iran. This estrangement was encouraged by Saudi Arabia, because the Wahhabi version of Sunni Islam dominant in that country is hostile to Shiism. With American connivance, Saudi money helped create a Sunni *cordon sanitaire* around Iran to contain the spread of revolutionary Shiism in such countries as Afghanistan and Pakistan. Thus, the second Islamic state in the region, that of the Taliban in Afghanistan, was implacably hostile to the Islamic Republic of Iran. This hostility reached the point where a number of Iranian diplomats in that country were actually killed.[66] Today Iran maintains very few client movements among Sunnis, most notably the Palestinian Islamic Jihad.

This leaves Twelver Shiites as the only group among which Iranian efforts to spread the revolution have been somewhat successful. The founding of Lebanon's Hizballah in the early 1980s was facilitated by Iran, and Iran continues to support the party and its social welfare activities financially. Iran also sponsored formation in Iran of the Supreme Council for the Islamic Revolution of Iraq (SCIRI), a party that, ironically, has come to play a major role in Iraq thanks to the American intervention that led to the ouster of the Saddam Hussein regime.

In the aftermath of September 11, 2001, Iran has found itself surrounded by U.S.-installed governments in Afghanistan and Iraq and by U.S. troops and military bases in the countries to its north and south. At the same time, Al-Qaeda and other anti-Shiite groups pose a threat to the Islamic Republic's claim to constitute the vanguard of a worldwide Islamic revolution. Even within the world of Twelver Shiism, however, the Iranian theocracy may yet lose some influence. If Iraq stabilizes under Shiite hegemony, Najaf could conceivably regain its centrality and independence as a center of Shiite learning, thereby attracting Shiite scholars who do not share Khomeini's notion of *velayat-e faqih*, including even Iranians.

In its relations with the West and the Soviet bloc, the early Islamic Republic had as its motto "Neither East nor West." Iran was an American ally under the Shah, but after the revolution it joined the nonaligned movement. In practice, however, Iran's foreign policy, like that of many other Third World "nonaligned" countries, was far more anti-Western than anti-Soviet. In the case of the Islamic Republic, this stance reflects the revolutionaries' mistrust of a West that had supported the hated Shah, and the geographic proximity of the Soviet Union, whose occupation of neighboring Afghanistan in December 1979 was a constant reminder of the need for caution. The Islamic Republic has maintained cordial relations with the Soviet Union and Russia, but Iran has not had diplomatic relations with the United States since the United States severed them in response to the seizure of American diplomats as hostages in November 1979. Iranians have paid a heavy price for their government's hostility to the West. In the last stages of the war against Iraq, most Western powers discreetly assisted the Iraqi side. The United States has maintained an economic embargo on Iran. For instance, Iranian airlines have difficulty purchasing a sufficient number of modern passenger aircraft and adequate spare parts for the old ones, forcing them to keep flying old Russian planes or Boeing jets purchased before the revolution. As a result, "Iran's civil aviation sector suffers from one of the world's highest rates of accidents and incidents."[67]

After Khomeini's death, presidents Hashemi Rafsanjani and Khatami tried to lessen Iran's diplomatic isolation. Relations with Arab countries, most of which had supported Iraq in the war, improved, and Iran made an effort to mend its ties with Europe and Japan. In the 1990s, the European Union embarked on a policy of "critical dialogue" with Iran, which offered Iran concessions in exchange for improvement in the field of human rights. During the Khatami years the policies of the government did indeed become less repressive, but given the overall control of unelected bodies none of these liberalizing measures could be institutionalized.

The main issue confronting current Iranian diplomacy in its relations with the West is Iran's nuclear program. Since the days of the Shah, successive Iranian governments have declared that they are not interested in developing nuclear weapons. The official line of the government of the Islamic Republic is that all weapons of mass destruction are contrary to Islamic ethics. Iran is a signatory of the Nuclear Nonproliferation Treaty, whose Article IV grants its signatories the "inalienable right" to "research, develop, produce, and utilize" nuclear technology for peaceful purposes. On that basis, the Iranian government has embarked on a vast program to develop a self-sufficient nuclear industry by mastering the fuel cycle in which uranium is enriched to produce the fuel needed to power reactors. Western countries worry that this knowledge would also allow Iran to produce highly enriched uranium or plutonium that could be used to produce nuclear weapons. What lends this worry a certain plausibility is Iran's development of long-distance missiles to which nuclear warheads could be fitted, and the fact that some nuclear facilities and experiments were kept secret until an exiled opposition group revealed their existence in 2002. At that point, the Iranian government allowed IAEA inspectors to visit them. Britain, France, and Germany have negotiated with Iran in the hope of getting the government to suspend its enrichment program, while the IAEA has not declared Iran to be in violation of its treaty obligations. As of early 2007, the negotiations were continuing.

CONCLUSION

Iranian politics in the twentieth century were tumultuous. The century started with a constitutionalist movement seeking to make a monarchy more accountable, and ended with a reformist movement striving to make a theocracy more republican. In between these two bookends, nationalist, religious, secular, and Marxist ideologies competed for followers, while social relations were restructured by processes associated with modernization. The Pahlavi monarchy promised to usher Iran into the modern industrial age, and because of both its successes and failures in doing so, the Shah was overthrown by a mass revolution that established a republic, but one that, unlike other revolutionary regimes, incorporated the clergy.

To manage the many objectives of the revolutionaries, the Islamic Republic has created a bewildering set of institutions and organizations, many of which compete with one another and occasionally work at cross purposes. The regime has been in continuous conflict with the United States and some regional powers, such as Israel. It has provided social welfare to many of its citizens, which has resulted in outcomes that were unintended by the establishment, whose authority has increasingly been challenged. By the admission of many of its own leaders, "the economy is sick" and "social pathologies" tarnish all layers of society. Unlike most other states in the region, which have almost completely muzzled dissent, contestation is pervasive and sometimes public even among state officials.

How has a regime that faces so many challenges survived for a quarter of a century, and what are the prospects for significant change? The irony is that the same institutions that have created contestation and allowed a degree of pluralism in Iran have also contributed to the regime's survival and ability to withstand opposition.[68] The fragmented nature of the state enables differences to emerge and persist, but it is this very fragmentation that prevents the aggregation of interests. Thus, even though many of the founders of the Islamic Republic have defected from the regime or called for quite fundamental changes, they have not had the leverage to restructure the regime. Elite politics in Iran today is factional politics, not party politics encompassing debates over specific policies and specified platforms and visions of the future. Factionalism is endemic to the system: although the presidency and Parliament have been controlled by the same party since June 2005, Parliament refused to confirm the first three of the president's nominees for the important post of minister of oil.

Meanwhile, a myriad of patron-client networks, in conjunction with a robust coercive apparatus and an individualist political culture, creates a fragmented state with divisions at all levels of society. Corporate and associational interests are ill defined and undermined by personalism, and even ideologically similar groups often battle with one another over access to assets. State-society relations as they are constituted now hinder coordination and alliance-building, which are essential for mass mobilization, and prevent the emergence of public deliberation and consensus-building.

The problems faced by the Islamic Republic have reopened the debate on the proper relation between religion and politics in Iran. Going farther than revisiting Islamic law, some reformist Muslims are questioning whether religious law is as central to Islam as, say, ethics or personal experience of transcendence. These reformers impute the current preoccupation with Islamic law, *shari'a*, in Muslim governance to the prominence of the ulema in Muslim society, pointing out that the ulema are, after all, merely legal scholars. This new tendency reconnects with other important traditions within Islam, as exemplified by the beloved Persian poet Hafez of Shiraz, who wrote:

> Do what you want, but don't hurt anyone
> For that is the only sin in our *shari'a*

As we said at the beginning of this chapter, Iran was the first state in which Islamists got to exercise political power. The problems they have faced, the forces they have unleashed, and the responses they have elicited from society could have profound implications for political Islam in the rest of the world. In practice, however, Iran's experience remains of limited relevance to Islamists elsewhere. Given the Shiite nature of the Iranian state, Sunni Islamists can always brush aside the intellectual and social impasses encountered by Iran's regime in its effort to institute Islamic law in all spheres of social life by claiming that they are due to Iranians' sectarian deviation from "true" Islam.

KEY TERMS

Assembly of Experts

Basij

Council of Guardians

Ebadi, Shirin

Expediency Council

Hashemi Rafsanjani,
    Ali-Akbar

Islamists

Khamenei, Ali

Khatami, Mohammad

Khomeini, Ruhollah

Leader

Majles

Mossadegh,
    Mohammad

multiple power centers

Pahlavi, Mohammad-Reza
    Shah

parastatal foundations

Pasdaran (Islamic
    Revolutionary Guard
    Corps)

rentier states

shari'a

Sunnis

theocracy

Twelver Shiism

Tudeh Party

ulema

velayat-e faqih

SUGGESTED READINGS

Abrahamian, Ervand. *Iran Between Two Revolutions*. Princeton; NJ: Princeton University Press, 1982.

Adelkhah, Fariba. *Being Modern in Iran*. New York: Columbia University Press, 2000.

Amir Arjomand, Said. *The Turban for the Crown: The Islamic Revolution in Iran*. New York: Oxford University Press, 1988.

Amuzegar, Jahangir. *Iran's Economy Under the Islamic Republic*. London: I.B. Tauris, 1997.

Ansari, Ali M. *Iran, Islam and Democracy: The Politics of Managing Change*. London: Royal Institute for International Affairs, 2000.

Ashraf, Ahmad. "The Appeal of Conspiracy Theories to Persians." *Princeton Papers* 5 (Winter 1997): 57–88.

Ashraf, Ahmad, and Ali Banuazizi. "The State, Classes and Modes of Mobilization in the Iranian Revolution." *State, Culture, and Society* 1, no. 3 (Spring 1985): 3–39.

Atabaki, Touraj. *Azerbaijan: Ethnicity and Autonomy in Twentieth-Century Iran*. London: British Academic Press, 1993.

Azimi, Fakhreddin. *Iran: The Crisis of Democracy 1941–1953*. New York: St. Martin's, 1989.

Bakhash, Shaul. *The Reign of the Ayatollahs: Iran and the Islamic Revolution*. New York: Basic Books, 1984.

———. "The Politics of Land, Law, and Social Justice in Iran." *Middle East Journal* 43, no. 2 (1989): 186–201.

Baktiari, Bahman. *Parliamentary Politics in Revolutionary Iran: The Institutionalization of Factional Politics*. Gainesville: Florida University Press, 1996.

Bayat, Assef. *Street Politics: Poor People's Movements in Iran*. New York: Columbia University Press, 1997.

Bill, James A. *The Eagle and the Lion: The Tragedy of American-Iranian Relations*. New Haven, CT: Yale University Press, 1988.

Binder, Leonard. *Iran: Political Development in a Changing Society*. Berkeley: University of California Press, 1964.

Buchta, Wilfried. *Who Rules Iran? The Structure of Power in the Islamic Republic*. Washington, DC: Washington Institute for Near East Policy, 2000.

Chehabi, H. E. "Religion and Politics in Iran: How Theocratic Is the Islamic Republic?" *Daedalus* 120, no. 1 (Summer 1991): 69–91.

———. "The Political Regime of the Islamic Republic of Iran in Comparative Perspective." *Government and Opposition* 36, no. 1 (Winter 2001): 48–70.

Gasiorowski, Mark J. *U.S. Foreign Policy and the Shah: Building a Client State in Iran*. Ithaca, NY: Cornell University Press, 1991.

Hoogland, Eric, ed. *Twenty Years of Islamic Revolution: Political and Social Transformation in Iran Since 1979*. Syracuse, NY: Syracuse University Press, 2002.

Karshenas, Massoud. *Oil, State, and Industrialization in Iran*. Cambridge: Cambridge University Press, 1990.

Keddie, Nikki R. *Modern Iran: Roots and Results of Revolution*. New Haven, CT: Yale University Press, 2003.

Keshavarzian, Arang. "Contestation Without Democracy: Elite Fragmentation in Iran." In Marsha Pripstein Posusney and Michelle Penner Angrist, eds., *Authoritarianism in the Middle East: Regimes and Resistance*. Boulder, CO: Lynne Rienner, 2005.

———. *Bazaar and State in Iran: The Politics of the Tehran Marketplace*. Cambridge: Cambridge University Press, 2007.

Kurzman, Charles. *The Unthinkable Revolution in Iran*. Cambridge: Harvard University Press, 2004.

Maloney, Suzanne. "Agents or Obstacles? Parastatal Foundations and Challenges for Iranian Development." In Parvin Alizadeh, ed., *The Economy of Iran: Dilemmas of an Islamic State*. London: I. B. Tauris, 2000.

Martin, Vanessa. *Islam and Modernism: The Persian Revolution of 1906*. London: I. B. Tauris, 1988.

Menashri, David. *Post-Revolutionary Politics in Iran: Religion, Society, and Power*. Portland, OR: Frank Cass, 2001.

Milani, Mohsen. *The Making of Iran's Islamic Revolution: From Monarchy to Islamic Republic*, 2nd ed. Boulder, CO: Westview, 1994.

Moin, Baqer. *Khomeini: Life of the Ayatollah*. London: I. B. Tauris, 1999.

Moslem, Mehdi. *Factional Politics in Post-Revolutionary Iran*. Syracuse, NY: Syracuse University Press, 2002.

Mottahedeh, Roy. *The Mantle of the Prophet: Religion and Politics in Iran*, 2nd ed. Oxford: Oneworld, 2000.

Paidar, Parvin. *Women and the Political Process in Twentieth-Century Iran*. Cambridge: Cambridge University Press, 1995.

Parsa, Misagh. *Social Origins of the Iranian Revolution*. New Brunswick, NJ: Rutgers University Press, 1989.

Sanasarian, Eliz. *Religious Minorities in Iran*. Cambridge: Cambridge University Press, 2000.

Schirazi, Asghar. *The Constitution of Iran: Politics and the State in the Islamic Republic*. London: I.B. Tauris, 1996.

Tajbakhsh, Kian. "Political Decentralization and the Creation of Local Government in Iran: Consolidation or Transformation of the Theocratic State?" *Social Research* 67, no. 2 (Summer 2000): 377–404.

Vahdat, Farzin. *God and Juggernaut: Iran's Intellectual Encounter with Modernity*. Syracuse, NY: Syracuse University Press, 2002.

Zahedi, Dariush. *The Iranian Revolution Then and Now: Indicators of Regime Instability*. Boulder, CO: Westview, 2000.

Zonis, Marvin. *The Political Elite of Iran*. Princeton, NJ: Princeton University Press, 1971.

INTERNET RESOURCES

Iran Daily (English languages daily newspaper): **www.iran-daily.com**

Ministry of Foreign Affairs, Islamic Republic of Iran: **www.mfa.gov.ir**

Payvand (news and information portal): **www.payvand.com**

Encyclopaedia Iranica: **www.iranica.com/newsite/**

Iranian Studies Group at MIT: **www.isg-mit.org/**

The Middle East Network Information Center (MENIC), University of Texas, Austin:

menic.utexas.edu/Countries_and_Regions/Iran/

ENDNOTES

1. From Population Action International: (accessed at http://www.populationaction.org/news/press/news_042302_Youth.htm).

2. From the Washington Institute: (accessed at http://washingtoninstitute.org/templateC05.php?CID=1556).

3. All existing maps showing the linguistic and ethnic groups that make up Iran's population have to be used with caution. Census questions do not include ethnic or linguistic affiliation, and few areas have an ethnically or linguistically homogeneous population. Internal migrations and urbanization have uprooted many people from their original home area. Besides, ethnic self-identification is not equally important to all people. Among the Kurds, for instance, those who are Sunni are much more likely to identify subjectively as Kurds than those who are Shiites. We therefore dispense with a map here.

4. Abdul-Hadi Hairi, *Shiism and Constitutionalism in Iran* (Leiden: Brill, 1977).

5. Nikki R. Keddie, *Modern Iran: Roots and Results of Revolution* (New Haven, CT: Yale University Press, 2003), 123.

6. Mark Gasiorowski, "The 1953 *Coup d'Etat* in Iran," *International Journal of Middle East Studies* 19, no. 3 (1987): 261–86.

7. See James A. Bill, *The Eagle and the Lion: The Tragedy of American-Iranian Relations* (New Haven, CT: Yale University Press, 1988), 319–78.

8. Richard W. Cottam, *Iran and the United States: A Cold War Case Study* (Pittsburgh, PA: University of Pittsburgh Press, 1988), 156–69.

9. Ahmad Ashraf and Ali Banuazizi, "The State, Classes, and Modes of Mobilization in the Iranian Revolution," *State, Culture, and Society* 1 (Spring 1985): 3–39.

10. Misagh Parsa, *Social Origins of the Iranian Revolution* (New Brunswick, NJ: Rutgers University Press, 1989).

11. Ironically, even the shah himself believed in the omnipotence of the United States and Britain: after his ouster, he blamed these countries for having engineered his demise.

12. Ruhollah Khomeini, "Islamic Government," in *Islam and Revolution: Writings and Declarations of Imam Khomeini*, trans. and annotated by Hamid Algar (Berkeley, CA: Mizan, 1981).

13. See H. E. Chehabi, "The Political Regime of the Islamic Republic of Iran in Comparative Perspective," *Government and Opposition* 36 (Winter 2001): 48–70.

14. Kaveh Ehsani, "Islam, Modernity, and National Identity," *Middle East Insight* 11, no. 5 (July–August 1995): 48–53.

15. For the prerevolutionary period, see Hossein Mahdavy, "Patterns and Problems of Economic Development in Rentier States: The Case of Iran," in M. A. Cook, ed., *Studies in the Economic History of the Middle East: From the Rise of Islam to the Present Day* (London: Oxford University Press, 1970), 428–67. For the Islamic Republic, see Hootan Shambayati, "The Rentier State, Interest Groups, and the Paradox of Autonomy: State and Business in Turkey and Iran," *Comparative Politics* 26 (April 1994): 307–31.

16. Homa Katouzian, *The Political Economy of Modern Iran* (New York: New York University Press, 1981).

17. On these parastatal foundations, see Suzanne Maloney, "Agents or Obstacles? Parastatal Foundations and Challenges for Iranian Development," in Parvin Alizadeh, ed., *The Economy of Iran: Dilemmas of an Islamic State* (London: I.B. Tauris, 2000), 145–76.

18. Bahman Baktiari, *Parliamentary Politics in Revolutionary Iran: The Institutionalization of Factional Politics* (Gainesville: Florida University Press, 1996).

19. Abdol-Karim Lahiji, "Moruri bar vaz'-e hoquqi-ye Iranian-e gheyr-e mosalman," *Iran Nameh* 19 (1379–80/2001): 19. On the legal discrimination of women, see section discussing gender relations later in this chapter.

20. Mehran Kamrava and Houchang Hassan-Yari, "Suspended Equilibrium in Iran's Political System," *Muslim World* 94 (October 2004): 495–524.

21. Asghar Schirazi, *The Constitution of Iran: Politics and the State in the Islamic Republic* (London: I.B. Tauris, 1998), 134.

22. Mehdi Moslem, *Factional Politics in Post-Revolutionary Iran* (Syracuse, NY: Syracuse University Press, 2002).

23. Kian Tajbakhsh, "Political Decentralization and the Creation of Local Government in Iran: Consolidation or Transformation of the Theocratic State?" *Social Research* 67, no. 2 (Summer 2000): 377–404.

24. Before World War I, Westerners considered Iran and other non-Western but nominally sovereign countries, such as China and Thailand, to be "semi-civilized" nations, which had some but not all of the attributes of a full-fledged member of the international community. See Gerrit Gong, *The Standard of "Civilization" in International Society* (Cambridge: Cambridge University Press, 1984).

25. Ahmad Ashraf, "The Appeal of Conspiracy Theories to Persians," *Princeton Papers* 5 (Winter 1997): 57–88.

26. See L. Carl Brown, *International Politics and the Middle East* (Princeton, NJ: Princeton University Press, 1984), 233–52.

27. Mansoor Moaddel and Taghi Azadarmaki, "The Worldviews of Islamic Publics: The Case of Egypt, Iran, and Jordan," in Ronald Ingelhart, ed., *Human Values and Social Change: Findings From the Values Survey* (Leiden: Brill 2003), 81.

28. This line of reasoning is based on Azadeh Kian-Thiébaut, "Entrepreneurs privés: entre développement statocentrique et démocratisation politique," in *Les Cahiers de l'Orient* 60 (2000): 65–92.

29. Peter J. Chelkowski and Hamid Dabashi, *Staging a Revolution: The Art of Persuasion in the Islamic Republic of Iran* (New York: New York University Press, 1999), 130–31.

30. Ehsani, "Islam, Modernity, and National Identity," 51.

31. Farideh Farahi, "The Antinomies of Iran's War Generation," in Lawrence C. Potter and Gary G. Sick, eds., *Iran, Iraq and the Legacies of War* (New York: PalgraveMacmillan, 2004), 101–20.

32. Moaddel and Azadarmaki, "The Worldviews of Islamic Publics."

33. Ahmad Sadri, "The Varieties of Religious Reform: Public Intelligentsia in Iran," in Ramin Jahanbegloo, ed., *Iran: Between Tradition and Modernity* (Lanham, MD: Lexington Books, 2004), 117–28.

34. Marvin Zonis, *The Political Elite of Iran* (Princeton, NJ: Princeton University Press, 1971).

35. Frances Bostock and Geoffrey Jones, *Planning and Power in Iran: Ebtehaj and Economic Development Under the Shahs* (London: Frank Cass, 1989).

36. Khosrow Fatemi, "Leadership by Distrust: The Shah's *Modus Operandi*," *Middle East Journal* 36 (Winter 1982): 48–61.

37. Mehran Kamrava, *The Modern Middle East: A Political History Since the First World War* (Berkeley: University of California Press, 2005), 261.

38. Figures are from Wilfried Buchta, *Who Rules Iran? The Structure of Power in the Islamic Republic* (Washington, DC: The Washington Institute for Near East Policy and the Konrad Adenauer Stiftung, 2000), 68.

39. Assef Bayat, *Street Politics: Poor People's Movements in Iran* (New York: Columbia University Press, 1997).

40. In his discussion of charismatic authority, Max Weber points out that charismatic leaders oppose tradition, and he summarizes this attitude in the famous statement ascribed to Jesus: "It has been written . . . , but *I* say unto you." *Economy and Society* (Berkeley: University of California Press, 1976), 1115.

41. Schirazi, *The Constitution of Iran*, 67–68.

42. Quoted in Said Amir Arjomand, *The Turban for the Crown: The Islamic Revolution in Iran* (New York: Oxford University Press, 1988), 182.

43. In fact, Ahmadinejad belongs to a current of thought that considers the return of the Twelfth Imam imminent. This messianic expectation sets him apart from most other leaders of the Islamic Republic and may yet be the source of friction.

44. For details, see H. E. Chehabi, "Ardabil Becomes a Province: Center-Periphery Relations in the Islamic Republic of Iran," *International Journal of Middle East Studies* 29 (Spring 1997): 235–53.

45. For an inside account, see Elaine Sciolino, *Persian Mirrors: The Elusive Face of Iran* (New York: Free Press, 2000), 248–60.

46. For details see Buchta, *Who Rules Iran?* 156–70.

47. How this multiplicity of power centers affects individuals is seen in the story of Dariush Zahedi, an Iranian-American political scientist who had met with dissidents while visiting Iran one recent summer for his research. He was arrested by the ministry of information and held prisoner for two months, before being told that, as far as the ministry was concerned, he was innocent. Except that upon leaving the prison he was immediately rearrested by the intelligence agency of the Revolutionary Guards, who held him for another two months in solitary confinement and subjected him to similar interrogations as his preceding jailers, only in a less respectful tone. He was finally released and returned to the United States through the intervention of a number of Iranian diplomats after academics in the United States had publicized his plight.

48. Maloney, "Agents or Obstacles?" 149.

49. This is based on H. E. Chehabi's conversations with music officials and musicians in Iran.

50. From Earth Policy Institute: (accessed at http://www.earth-policy.org/Updates/Update4ss.htm).

51. The data are from the 2006 edition of *Der Fischer Weltalmanach* (Frankfurt/Main: Fischer, 2005), 500–15. The source of most figures is the World Bank.

52. Massoud Karshenas and Hassan Hakimian, "Oil, Economic Diversification and the Democratic Process in Iran," *Iranian Studies* 38, no. 1 (March 2005): 67–90.

53. "Youth Employment in Islamic Republic of Iran" (report prepared by the Department of International Affairs of the National Youth Organization, October 2004).

54. Mehrangis Kar, "*Shari'a* Law in Iran," in Paul Marshall, ed., *Radical Islam's Rules: The Worldwide Spread of Extreme Sharia Law* (Freedom House, Center for Religious Freedom, 2005), 41–64.

55. The numbers are from Amnesty International.

56. Abdolmohammad Kazemipur and Ali Rezaei, "Religious Life Under Theocracy: The Case of Iran," *Journal for the Scientific Study of Religion* 42, no. 3 (2003): 347–61.

57. See Mahmoud Sadri, "Sacral Defense of Secularism: Dissident Political Theology in Iran," in Negin Nabavi, ed., *Intellectual Trends in Twentieth-Century Iran* (Gainesville: University Press of Florida, 2003), 180–92.

58. Mahmud Abbasi, *Qanun-e Mojazat-e Eslami* (Islamic Penal Code) (Tehran: Hoquqi, 2002), 108.

59. Following the victory of the Mujahidin in Afghanistan, as the Iranian government became keen on repatriating Afghan refugees to Afghanistan, tens of thousands of Iranian women who had married Afghan refugee men in Iran were told by the authorities that they faced the choice of either seeking a divorce from their husbands or following him to his country.

60. Mehrangiz Kar, "Women's Political Rights After the Islamic Revolution," in Lloyd Ridgeon, ed., *Religion and Politics in Modern Iran: A Reader* (London: I.B. Tauris, 2005), 253–78.

61. Mansoor Moaddel and Taghi Azadarmaki, "The Worldviews of Islamic Publics: The Case of Egypt, Iran, and Jordan," in Ingelhart, ed., *Human Values and Social Change*, 77.

62. Moaddel and Azadarmaki, "The Worldviews of Islamic Publics," 78. Forty-five percent of Iranians agree with this statement, while 88 and 89 percent Egyptians and Jordanians agree, respectively.

63. Moaddel and Azadarmaki, "The Worldviews of Islamic Publics," 79.

64. For details, see *The International Encyclopedia of Women and Sport* (New York: Macmillan, 2001), s.v. "Iran," 586–87. For an eyewitness account by a Western journalist, see Geraldine Brooks, *Nine Parts of Desire: The Hidden World of Islamic Women* (New York: Anchor Books, 1995), 201–11, "Muslim Women's Games."

65. Asked whether she would ever "want to throw off the head scarf in public," she answered: "Do you want to issue me my death sentence?" *International Herald Tribune*, 3 April 2003, 2.

66. On this point, see Vali Nasr, "Regional Implications of Shi'a Revival in Iraq," *Washington Quarterly* 27 (Summer 2004): 7–24.

67. Najmedin Meshkati, "Iran's Nuclear Brinkmanship, the U.S. Unilateralism, and a Mounting International Crisis: Can Civil Aviation Industry Provide a Breakthrough?" *Iran News*, 26 July 2004, 14. (available at http://www.irannewsdaily.com/asp/iran_news.asp).

68. Arang Keshavarzian, "Contestation Without Democracy: Elite Fragmentation in Iran," in Marsha Pripstein Posusney and Michelle Penner Angrist, eds., *Authoritarianism in the Middle East: Regimes and Resistance* (Boulder, CO: Lynne Rienner, 2005), 63–88.

NIGERIA

POLITICS IN NIGERIA

Robert J. Mundt, Oladimeji Aborisade, and A. Carl LeVan

Country Bio

NIGERIA

Population
130 million

Territory
356,668 square miles

Year of Independence
1960

Year of Current Constitution
1979 Constitution still partially in force; draft
1995 Constitution published and revised in 1999
(the 1999 Constitution)

Head of State
President Umar Musa Yar'Adua

Head of Government
President Umar Musa Yar'Adua

Languages
English (official), Hausa, Yoruba, Igbo, and 250
other ethnic groups

Religions
Muslim 50%; Christian 40%; indigenous
beliefs 10%

In the African context Nigeria is a megastate. Even on a world scale, Nigeria is a major country. Larger than France or Britain, it claims over one-fifth of the people in Africa and has the world's largest black population. Its petroleum and its substantial standing military force guarantee its prominence in international relations; and with forty-five universities, Nigeria contains a large proportion of Africa's centers of learning and research.

For these reasons alone, one should know about Nigeria. But learning about Nigeria is also an efficient approach to learning about Africa, because Nigeria embodies much of the variety of African political experience within its borders. Its traditions include the large-scale emirates of the north and the small kingdoms and village-level republics of the south. Although both were administered by Britain, the north and south of Nigeria experienced different versions of colonial rule. Its culture is divided by ethnicity and by religion, especially between Christians and Muslims. Its history since independence includes coups, countercoups, and civil war; recently, along with many other Africans, Nigerians have been groping toward a renewal of democracy. The problems and prospects of many African ministates are found in Nigeria, but at a more daunting scale and level of complexity. To know Nigeria is not necessarily to know Africa, but to one who is well acquainted with the Nigerian experience there will be little that is surprising in politics elsewhere on the continent.

Nigeria's prominent place in the world is more potential than real, however, because in recent years Nigeria has been a *sick* giant. Its economy is in shambles and the provision of public services has broken down. This chapter examines the causes of this illness and assesses the democratic government's remedies to it.

CURRENT POLICY CHALLENGES

Of all the countries considered in this book, Nigeria might be the only one whose continued existence is currently in doubt. The country's ethnic, regional, and religious divisions have intensified in recent years, and important political actors have recently suggested breaking up the country into a weak federation or even completely independent states if political power cannot be distributed in a manner all can accept. This situation is not all that unusual: Nigeria has existed for only forty-seven years. After roughly seventy years of existence, the Soviet Union split apart over regional and policy issues, and the cohesiveness of Canada and of the United Kingdom remain open to question in some quarters today. It may be easier to explain why Nigeria is likely to fall apart in the short term than it is to specify conditions for its long-term stability.

It is against this stark reality that politics and policy must be viewed in Nigeria today. In 1999 Nigeria returned to formal civilian rule, when Olusegun Obasanjo was elected president. A few weeks later a new democratic legislature was also elected. In 2003, President Obasanjo was reelected in a landslide, and his party also captured most other important political offices. Even though Nigeria has returned to constitutional rule, that constitution will continue to be tested by Nigerians' frustration over the failure of their potentially wealthy country to provide basic human needs, education, potable water, reliable transportation and communications, and politics free of rampant corruption. Income levels per capita are barely a tenth of income in the United States or Western Europe, and among the 177 nations ranked in the United Nations' Human Development Index, Nigeria ranked number 159—among the poorest quarter of nations. Similarly, in the 2005 Corruption Perceptions Index developed by Transparency International, only five ranked worse of the 159 countries studied.

From the outset, the government has struggled to move Nigeria in a new direction. If a democratic regime cannot address these demands in reasonably short order, that regime will suffer the fate of those before it and chaos or renewed authoritarian rule will be the likely outcome. Yet, Nigerians always seem to draw on a wellspring of optimism, even as they maintain an attitude of skepticism. The following analysis will help the reader determine the degree to which that optimism is warranted.

THE EFFECTS OF HISTORY

More than forty years ago, anthropologist Clifford Geertz titled an essay on the developing nations "Old Societies and New States."[1] This title is an apt charac-terization of Nigeria, for although the concept of Nigeria dates only to 1914, and the independent state only to 1960, the cultures that compose it have ancient roots.

In one sense, then, there are "many" Nigerias. That is, there are distinct political cultures with pre-colonial origins, and there are the varied colonial experiences of north, east, and west. We will consider these causes of variety separately.

The Enduring Effects of Precolonial Events

Our images of precolonial Africa have been plagued by misunderstandings, sometimes in the form of simple ignorance, but often the result of prejudice. Many in the industrial world still view traditional Africa as "primitive," composed of a series of "tribes."[2]

A common response is that "Africa had its empires also." As we shall see, this is quite true. However, to insist that empires are a sign of advanced culture is to accept that the successful implementation of authoritarian rule over large numbers of people is "civilized." It can be argued that those peoples who at the village level developed complex systems of limitations on their rulers were at least as politically sophisticated as those who built empires. All these peoples interacted in trade, cultural diffusion, and war for many centuries before the creation of today's nation-states, and their belief systems were as complex and nuanced as any in the world.

To reiterate, there was no single Nigeria a century ago. Some of the peoples inhabiting the land that now constitutes Nigeria were organized only at the village or extended family level (for example, the **Igbo** in the southeast), while in other areas there were kingdoms and states. Where one group had subjugated the peoples around them, we can identify empires, such as that of Kanem-Bornu around Lake Chad between the eleventh and fourteenth centuries, the Oyo Empire in the western region of present-day Nigeria from the thirteenth to the eighteenth centuries, and the Fulani Empire of the nineteenth century.[3]

The **Hausa** people began forming city-states in northern Nigeria between 1000 and 1200 A.D., and came under the influence of Islam no later than the fifteenth century. By the next century, mosques and Koranic schools were flourishing, and Hausa princes were international rivals of Morocco and the

Ottoman Empire. The fortunes of these systems waxed and waned through the centuries, but they were decisively changed when non-Hausa court officials rose against them early in the nineteenth century. These officials were **Fulani,** a people with their origins in western Sudan who had entered into the Hausa lands as herders and, more importantly, as teachers, traders, and eventually court advisers. By their own accounts they were ardent Muslims who found the Hausa leaders lax in their faith and decadent. A Fulani scholar and preacher, Usman dan Fodio, inspired a religious and political revolt against the Hausa kings (he found responsive audiences to his denunciation of taxes, even among Hausa commoners). A Fulani-dominated caliphate was established in Sokoto, now northern Nigeria. This Fulani Empire controlled most of the north until the British defeated it in 1903. Sokoto retains its role as the Muslim religious capital of Nigeria to this day. The Hausa and Fulani cultures have become so intertwined, with extensive intermarriage and with Hausa the primary language of both, that the dominant culture of the north is usually referred to as **Hausa-Fulani.** The descendants of the rulers of the Hausa-Fulani kingdoms, identified by the Islamic title *emir*, continue to hold court in the major cities of northern Nigeria.

In the forest region the **Yoruba** and Bini peoples of the southwest began forming kingdoms between the twelfth and fifteenth centuries at Oyo, Ife, and Benin. In the seventeenth and eighteenth centuries the kingdom of Oyo subdued its rivals and extended its control over the entire southwestern Nigeria. These political systems developed intricate methods of limiting the powers of their rulers. For example, the ruler of Oyo, the Alafin, was chosen by a council of chiefs, the Oyo Mesi. The historian Michael Crowder recounts that "if they felt the Alafin had exceeded his powers [the Oyo Mesi] could divine that all was not well between the Alafin and his spiritual double and force him to commit suicide. . . . However, the Oyo Mesi were restrained from abuse of this power by the fact that one of their number had to die with the Alafin."[4] Clearly, limited government has other sources than the Magna Carta and comes in a variety of forms. The successors to the Yoruba kings, or *obas*, continue to act out symbolic leadership roles in many cities in southwestern Nigeria.

Because Nigeria was defined through the colonial experience, we must ask how and why the eventual British domination occurred. The immediate cause for British interest in West Africa was trade, and the first such international trade of any importance was in slaves. Coastal groups began exchanging captives for goods with European trading ships as early as the sixteenth century. Wars among the various kingdoms ensured a plentiful supply of captives, particularly in southwestern Nigeria. For the next 300 years this trade was sustained: Benin, Lagos, Bonny, and Calabar thrived as slave trade centers, exporting upward of 20,000 persons per year to the Americas. Nigeria lost some of its most able-bodied inhabitants during those "barren three centuries" of relations between Europe and Africa.

In 1807 the British Parliament outlawed the slave trade. In a remarkable turnabout, the British navy replaced British slave ships and began patrolling the West African coast to cut off the trade, which was not completely eliminated until about 1850. The established slave-trading patterns were gradually converted to other goods. British consuls established themselves on the coast and began to intervene in local politics, favoring those candidates for ruling positions who would give them commercial advantages over other European traders. The British succeeded in obtaining treaties of British protection and trade along the coast. These were treaties between unequals, increasingly favorable to the British as they first established commercial and then political control.

The Colonial Interlude (1900–1960)

With tongue in cheek, Nigerian journalist Peter Enahoro once described his nationality in this fashion: "Today, the conglomeration of tribes assembled compulsorily at the 1884 Berlin conference are assigned as Nigerians—for want of a substitute collective noun."[5] Indeed, the name "Nigeria" itself was coined by Flora Shaw, an Englishwoman who later married Sir Frederick Lugard, the architect of colonial Nigeria. Enahoro's characterization refers to the origins of Nigeria's boundaries and those of most countries of contemporary Africa. In order to avoid war resulting from the competition for colonies, the great European powers met as the Conference of Berlin in 1884–1885 and divided Africa into spheres of influence. In effect, the European powers decided to seize control of the continent rather than merely trade with its rulers and merchants. In a wave of negotiations, imperialist wars, and conquests, their efforts were successful, and by the beginning of World War I in 1914 maps of Africa showed clearly drawn lines with areas color-coded according to the European power claiming control. Thus, in 1886 the Royal Niger Company was granted a royal charter to control Nigerian trade. That charter was replaced in 1900 by the creation of the Colony of Lagos and the Protectorates of Northern and Southern Nigeria.

There was an unfortunate interaction between the colonial penetration and West Africa's natural environment: cultures tend to be affected by climate and ecology, as people adapt differently to life in the rainforest, grasslands, or desert. In West Africa, the prevailing climate and ecological zones run east and west (see Figure 13.1). However, the colonial thrust was from the coast of the Gulf of Guinea inland, and colonial boundaries were established on the coast and then extended northward, intersecting the climate zones. This virtually guaranteed that the colonies thus established would be composed of peoples coming from vastly different cultures.

Nigeria first became an entity in 1914, when the Northern and Southern Protectorates and Lagos were brought under a single colonial administration. This unifying action was largely symbolic, however, as its two parts continued to be governed separately. The Northern and Southern Provinces replaced the Protectorates, each under a lieutenant governor. Northern Nigeria remained apart as such political structures as a legislative council evolved in the south. Northerners did not sit on the Nigerian Legislative Council until 1947. Indeed, the north proved to be the perfect setting for the "indirect rule" elaborated by the governor, Lord Lugard: the British administration would not intervene directly into everyday life in its colonies, but would support the rule of traditional leaders, such as the Fulani emirs. This, Lugard argued, was the most efficient means of controlling the colonies. In southern Nigeria, however, Western-educated elites challenged the authority of the traditional rulers where they existed (as among the Yoruba); in southeastern Nigeria, among the Igbo and other peoples, there really were no traditional kings or chiefs. Attempts to create village chiefs where the concept was unknown produced results that were sometimes comical and often tragic. Novelist Chinua Achebe has an English colonial officer describe such a situation:

> Chief Ikedi was still corrupt and high-handed but he had become even more clever than before. The latest thing he did was to get his people to make him an *obi* or king, so that he was now called his Highness Ikedi the First, Obi of Okperi.

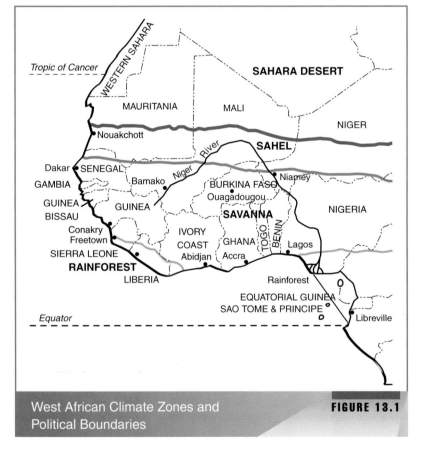

West African Climate Zones and Political Boundaries

FIGURE 13.1

This among a people who never had kings before! This was what British administration was doing among the Ibos, making a dozen mushroom kings grow where there was none before.[6]

Thus the different applicability of indirect rule served to further distinguish the political experiences of the regions.

The British colonial administration also faced the problem of incompatible objectives. In order to make the colony self-sustaining, Britain needed an export economy. However, the conversion of peasant societies from subsistence to a market orientation eroded the foundations of traditional rule. Except in the north, chiefs and kings had no traditional right to collect taxes, yet this became a central duty in the colonial system. Also, the development of a modern system of transportation and communication, necessary to stimulate commerce, encouraged the movement of people from the countryside to cities and from one part of the country to another, all under the protection of the colonial authorities. Urbanized populations and immigrants from other cultures could scarcely be expected to show deference to traditional rulers, nor did they see any good reason for paying taxes.

Along with commerce and administration, the British brought missionaries and education. Missionaries of many denominations—Anglicans, Presbyterians, Catholics, Baptists, Adventists, and others—brought the Gospels to Nigeria, although only to the south; the northern emirates had an understanding with the British that Christian proselytizing would not be permitted in their domains. Christianity spread especially rapidly in the southeast, and somewhat less so in the southwest; with it went formal schooling. As Nigerian children learned the English language and customs, they acquired the tools with which to challenge colonial rule on the rulers' own terms. However, the Western-educated elite that emerged came largely from the south. Thus, the culture is divided north and south along religious lines, but the difference has to do with much more than religion.

Modern constitutional development began within a few years of the creation of Nigeria as a single colony, with elective office first provided in 1922. An early nationalist leader, Herbert Macaulay, established a political party soon thereafter. As a Nigerian-centered political life grew up among the formally educated, other organizations arose, and the British colonial administration was pressed with demands for participation. The spirit of the times was captured by Nigerian writer Wole Soyinka as he recalled that

> Suddenly there was Oge-e-e-ed Ogendengbe (Herbert) Macaulay and there was Ze-e-e-ek (Nnamdi Azikiwe, nationalist leader). His oratory, we learnt, could move mountains. Some young, radical nationalists were being jailed for sedition, and sedition had become equivalent to demanding that the white man leave us to rule ourselves.[7]

From then on, constitutions promulgated by various governors (and named after them) were always somewhat behind the expectations of Nigerian political activists. What southern politicians judged conservative, however, was usually seen as radical by the conservative elites in the north. These differences of opinion among Nigerians resulted in 1954 in the creation of a federal system of three regions, Northern, Eastern, and Western. A single ethnic group dominated each region: The Hausa-Fulani in the north, the Igbo in the east, and the Yoruba in the west. Under pressure from their leaders, the Eastern and Western regions received self-government in 1957; the north became self-governing in 1959, a few months before national independence.

Nigerian Independence

As Nigeria approached independence, there was a general consensus that the nation should come to independence as a single country. Independent Nigeria was born on October 1, 1960.

Nigeria's independent governments at the federal and state levels experienced a very short "honeymoon." Within two years, conflict had torn apart the ruling coalition in the Western Region. The next year suspicions about the national census (as we will see later) destroyed what little trust there was among the regions. Finally, in 1965 law and order broke down in the Western Region over election-related fraud and violence, and the military ended the First Republic in a January 1966 coup.

An awareness of these experiences is critical to an understanding of political conflict in independent Nigeria. Although the colonial experience was comparatively brief, it left a legacy of political ideas that were difficult to reconcile with precolonial values and structures. Many modern Nigerians remain profoundly Yoruba or Hausa; but is there a role for obas and emirs in modern Nigeria? This is not just a clash between the "traditional" and the "modern," because there are many, perhaps hundreds of "traditions." The blending of these various influences was all the less likely given the short time allowed for political evolution prior to independence. Nigerians and other Africans are today grappling with the resultant confusion, which has produced political instability, economic woes, and constant military interventions. And the difficulties on Nigeria's road to independence are obviously related to the absence of any start in that direction prior to independence.

ENVIRONMENTAL POTENTIAL AND LIMITATIONS

Why has Nigeria's economic development been so dismal? Why are most of its people so poor? Are these conditions the result of physical environment, history, and socioeconomic context, or do they result from the Nigerian political process and the policy decisions that Nigerian governments have made?

Nigeria is counted among the world's less developed, or Third World, countries. Its gross domestic product (GDP) in 2004 was $72.1 billion or $560 per capita (we will discuss Nigeria's GDP later in this chapter, see Table 13.4 and accompanying text). This figure put it well below the United Nations criterion for "low-income countries." Previously, from 1980 to 1991, GNP per capita actually declined by 1.7 percent annually. Controlling for purchasing power parity (PPP), per capita GDP was $1,154 in 2004.

Conditions Affecting Agricultural Production and the Sale of Primary Commodities

Colonial policies not only retarded Nigeria's political development but also had profound, if mixed, effects on its economy. Since early in the colonial period, southern Nigerians have been producing cocoa, palm oil, timber, and rubber. The timber, sold mostly as tropical hardwoods for use in furniture and construction, came from the now-dwindling rainforests in the south. In the north the principal market products were cattle, hides and skins, cotton, and peanuts.

The growth of trade in these commodities was not entirely spontaneous. The British interest in Nigeria was primarily commercial, with its origins in the United Africa Company (UAC). When the UAC was granted a charter as the Royal Niger Company in 1886, it was given police and judicial power, and it was authorized to collect taxes and to oversee commerce. Not surprisingly, its policies aimed at developing the Nigerian economy to be compatible with British needs. Also, public sentiment in Britain never solidly favored creating a colonial empire, and powerful voices in Parliament favored keeping the costs of the empire to a minimum. Colonial administrations were under heavy pressure to be self-sufficient—to develop local sources of revenue to cover their costs of administration. As a result, colonial administrators pressured peasant farmers away from subsistence agriculture and into commercial farming, particularly of export crops. Furthermore, cost-efficient marketing meant emphasis on just a few of the most needed products; in Nigeria (and elsewhere in West Africa), these turned out to be palm oil, cocoa, peanuts, and cotton. Thus British raw material priorities and the need to provide a self-sufficient colonial administration distorted African economies toward dependence on the sale of a small number of primarily agricultural commodities.

The combination of population growth and the commercialization of agriculture strained relationships between agricultural techniques and the ecology that had been in place for centuries. Colonial officials sometimes assumed that productivity could be greatly increased in tropical regions with the introduction of "modern" methods without recognizing the different ecological conditions of production in a tropical setting. Lush tropical rainforest could not simply be replaced by plantations. Rainfall, temperature, and soil conditions meant that farming techniques effective in England or North America would be unsuccessful or even disastrous. Only gradually, and much later, were the efforts of agronomists applied to maximizing agricultural production in the tropics, especially to food production for local consumption. There is still a large "research deficit" between the resources expended for agricultural research in temperate zones, as opposed to that in tropical zones.

Thus, Nigeria came to independence with an economy typical of Africa and other Third World areas. It was based on the production and export of

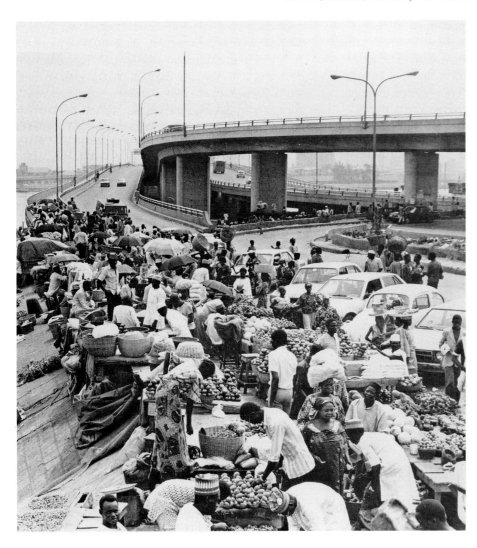

A street market bustles at an exit to the raised superhighway connecting Lagos Island to the mainland.

A. Hermann/UPI
Bettmann/Corbis

agricultural commodities, principally palm oil (of which Nigeria was the world's leading exporter) and cocoa. Because Nigeria was larger and more ecologically diverse than most African colonies, its exports showed greater diversity than in the typical case. Still, production in each of its regions was focused on one or a few commodities, and the country as a whole depended on commodity markets in the industrial countries for its foreign exchange.

Like other newly independent countries, Nigeria broke with some colonial economic development policies, especially as concerned the need to diversify production. But the need for foreign exchange meant that agriculture continued to emphasize exportable commodities, even as investment capital was largely directed toward industrialization. Economists in both the industrial and Third World countries associated industry with prosperity, and agriculture was seen as the "cash cow" from which to extract savings for investment in other areas. Also, Nigerian government officials, trained in the need to balance budgets, balanced appropriations bills with overly optimistic estimations of "expected revenue." When these fell short, the difference was made up from cash reserves accumulated by the Central Produce Marketing Board. However, "since those reserves were derived from the price differential between what was paid to the farmer and what the Board earned in export earnings . . . for close on a decade, Nigeria existed only through the exploitation of her farmers."[8]

In addition to keeping agricultural prices low to provide such reserves, Nigerian governments also tried to satisfy urban demands for cheap food by holding down the price paid to farmers in the domestic market. This action contributed to the unattractiveness of agricultural work, and enhanced the lure of the cities.

Disease

Physical illness is a part of the human condition, and the higher disease rates of poorer nations are largely explained by the lack of resources to acquire medicines, medical facilities, and personnel. But environment contributes as well: some of the most common human diseases, including malaria, can survive only in tropical climates. In tropical Africa, virtually every long-term resident carries the malaria virus, and large proportions of the population are affected by it. It is usually not fatal, but it is extremely debilitating, and it has a documented effect on labor productivity. Various river-borne diseases also account for long-term illness and fatalities, contributing especially to the high mortality rate among children. As with agricultural problems, research can attack these diseases; yet a vastly disproportionate share of the world's resources applied to health problems is focused on ailments more common to the industrialized world. In recent times, AIDS has topped the list of the most dreadful diseases in Africa. The Joint United Nations Program on HIV/AIDS reported in 2006 that 3.9 percent of all Nigerians were infected; given the country's huge population, this amounts to over 5 million people between the ages of 15 and 49. In many African countries, the AIDS epidemic is slowing down the agricultural economy in particular and national productivity in general.

Population Growth

Nothing is more striking to a visitor to Nigeria than the youth of the population; everywhere there are multitudes of children. About 45 percent of the Nigerian population is less than 15 years of age.[9] Children are considered a valuable resource in labor-intensive agricultural societies, and in a country with high infant mortality rates and no social security system, parents would be imprudent not to have enough children so that some would grow up to provide for them in their old age. This behavior becomes dysfunctional at the societal level, of course, as increasing populations struggle to survive on a limited physical environment. Table 13.2 illustrates the projected population growth through 2020. Between 1975 and 2000, the population of Nigeria grew an average of 2.9 percent annually. With slow economic growth (only about 2.4 percent annually in the 1990s), this means when measured in per capita terms, GDP growth was actually negative. During this same period, the urban population grew from approximately 23 percent to 44 percent, a major leap. In this environment of rapid population growth and urbanization, children become economic liabilities. Thus, the "dependency ratio" (the proportion of the nonworking population to the working population) has steadily risen since the early 1960s, placing a great strain on the country's underdeveloped facilities for social welfare and education.[10]

Counting the population in Nigeria has always been controversial because of its implications for the distribution of resources and political districting. There has not been a widely accepted census since 1963 (see pp. 441–442). When the government conducted its most recent census in March 2006, it eliminated questions about religion and ethnicity from the questionnaire in order to ease popular concerns and encourage participation. Instead, it asked questions about education levels, income, water supply, occupation, and access to telephones and televisions.

Nevertheless, the census encountered significant resistance, particularly from separatists in the East; about fifteen people were killed during various protests and violence. The logistical issues of surveying over one hundred million people also hampered the effort. Workers claimed they had not been paid and that not enough forms were provided, and some claimed that no one counted them. Additionally, the government asked all citizens to stay home for the weeklong duration of the census until they were counted, which many small business owners saw as a hardship. As of May 2007, the National Population Commission had released the results but the true impact of the census remains uncertain because the National Assembly had not approved the results.

Urbanization

Nigeria shares a pattern of urbanization common in Africa: Although the country is still primarily rural, it is urbanizing rapidly. Nigeria's population is projected to be over 50 percent urban by the year 2010. In the

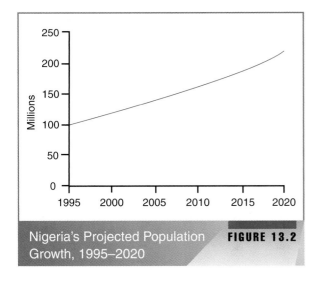

FIGURE 13.2

Nigeria's Projected Population Growth, 1995–2020

process, the development of urban infrastructure is added to the long list of demands on government. For example, the government ministry in charge of Abuja, the federal capital, announced in 2002 that the population of the city had exceeded 4 million, whereas city planners had estimated that the population would only be about 1.5 million at this stage of development.[11]

The population shift means that a smaller proportion of the labor force is available for agricultural work. That is a normal pattern of modernization, of course, but unless the productivity of agricultural workers increases, it means a drop in food production per capita. That has been the Nigerian experience: self-sufficient in food at independence, Nigeria is now heavily dependent on imports, paid for from oil revenues.

Petroleum

The magnitude of Nigeria's petroleum reserves became apparent in the 1950s with the first shipload of crude exported in 1958. Nigeria was engulfed in a bloody civil war from 1967 to 1970, which brought a halt to oil exports. At war's end, however, Nigerian petroleum production began to boom, and it grew at a dramatic rate through the 1970s. Although such a valuable mineral resource is an asset to any country, its effects on Nigeria were not all beneficial. The country's economy became distorted by the great disparity of value between petroleum and the traditional agricultural products: soon young workers were abandoning

their farms and villages and flocking to the cities and the oil fields.

Oil revenues peaked in 1979. World demand for oil decreased each year from 1979 to 1983. At the same time, oil production in countries that were not part of the Organization of Petroleum Exporting Countries (OPEC), especially Mexico, Norway, and the United Kingdom, grew substantially. Nigeria's planners were slow to realize the implications of rising supply and stagnant demand. The glory days of seemingly limitless oil revenues ended abruptly in April 1982, when production of crude oil in Nigeria dropped from 2.1 million to 0.9 million barrels per day; oil export revenues fell correspondingly, from $1.35 billion to $0.7 billion per month. In the preceding decade, Nigeria had become dependent on oil revenues for imports and large-scale development projects. As was commonly the case in the Third World, Nigeria fell behind in its debt payments, which forced the government to impose unpleasant austerity measures. A further fall in oil prices in 1986 pushed the country into a severe recession from which it has never recovered. Moreover, Nigerian fortunes became even more closely tied to oil revenues: Figure 13.3 shows that the source of Nigeria's hard currency shifted dramatically

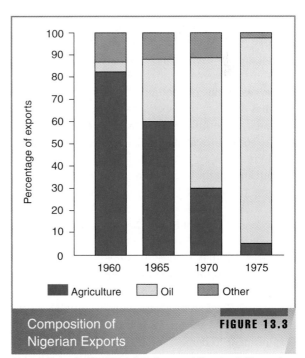

FIGURE 13.3

Composition of Nigerian Exports

Source: Peter O. Olayivola, *Petroleum and Structural Change in a Developing Country* (New York: Praeger, 1987).

from agricultural products to petroleum in the early 1970s. Since then petroleum has accounted for over 90 percent of export earnings. After world oil prices increased due to the Iraq War that began in 2003, Nigeria again began earning huge revenues, which it has applied toward its foreign debt.

The Geographic Distribution of Natural Resources: Political Effects

Nigeria's oil fields are found in the Niger delta basin, an area of 43,500 square miles, or 8 percent of the country. As a natural resource that is both geographically concentrated and far more valuable than any other, Nigerian petroleum presents a classic problem for distributive justice. To Nigerian federal governments, it is a "national patrimony." Its potential value was an important motivation behind the Eastern Region's declaration of independence as **Biafra** in 1967, and oil certainly helps explain why the rest of the country was so obstinately determined to keep the region within Nigeria. But had Biafra maintained its independence, the question of oil field ownership would not have gone away, for the people who traditionally inhabited that area were minorities in the Igbo-dominated Biafra. And even though the federal government won the civil war, local peoples continue to protest the spread of oil wealth over the whole country while their land pays the price of environmental degradation from the oil operations. Southern Nigerians in general wonder why the riches should be shared with the distant north. The oil-producing region is the least developed in Nigeria, and unrest will continue there until the Delta peoples believe they have been fairly treated.

In recent years bitter and violent combat has broken out among the youth of the various Delta peoples. Massive protests have been organized by organizations, such as the Movement for the Actualization of the Sovereign State of Biafra (MOSSOB). Hundreds of its members have been arrested for participating in peaceful rallies, prayer sessions, and even soccer matches organized to promote Igbo causes. The government's harsh response to a "stay at home" protest in August 2004 prompted criticism by human rights groups.[12] Such organizations are testing Nigeria's commitment to democratic freedoms. If these groups feel impeded from expressing themselves, they may become more militant. This seems to be the case with the **Movement for the Emancipation of the Niger Delta (MEND),** which at the end of 2006 had claimed responsibility for taking at least eighteen foreigners hostages as a protest of conditions in the oil-producing areas.

The International Environment

Nigeria, like most African countries, has been profoundly affected by its birth at the height of the Cold War, and by the sudden end of the bipolar war with the dissolution of the Soviet Union. During the Cold War, new nations were pressured to choose sides. The West and East granted foreign aid to developing nations as a reward for loyalty. Nigeria at independence was considered to be conservative and "pro-western," especially in contrast to such radical regimes as that of Kwame Nkrumah in Ghana. The prime minister at independence, Tafawa Balewa, announced the country's gratitude "to the British whom we have known first as masters, then as leaders, and finally as partners, but always as friends."[13]

Many Nigerian intellectuals equated the West's capitalism with colonialism, however, which they contended continued after independence through **neocolonial** economic ties. Political discourse through the first thirty years of Nigerian independence was often based on the ideological poles of capitalism and socialism, and relationships with the major powers involved staking a position between the two camps. In the civil war that resulted from the Eastern Region's declaration of independence as Biafra in 1967, the Soviet Union sided with the Nigerian federal government, while the U.S. government attempted to maintain a neutral position, even though the Biafran cause was widely supported by Americans. Economics finally dictated Nigeria's international position: the West was best equipped to prospect for Nigeria's oil fields, and only the West had the technology to extract and market this natural resource. Thus developed a close relationship between the Nigerian federal government and some of the world's major oil companies.

The end of the Cold War brought a new era to the relations of Nigeria and other poorer nations with the industrial world. The West's fear of the spread of communism had caused them to pay some attention to even the smallest and least-endowed countries. In the colonial period, Britain had provided virtually all foreign aid to Nigeria. In the Cold War environment at independence, Nigeria adopted a deliberate policy of diversification that diluted British influence and brought aid from the United States, Canada, the European Common Market (now the European Union), Japan, and Sweden. By the 1990s, however, those Third World countries without significant resources or with serious developmental problems were simply less interesting to the developed world; it is commonly perceived that Africa particularly has been "marginalized." In the Nigerian case, official loans and grants have not loomed large in recent years in any event, given access to oil revenues; foreign aid represented only about $2 per person in 1990.

Nigeria shared in a common Third World experience following the oil crisis of 1973 as it accumulated massive international debts. A sudden boom in oil prices resulted in huge new deposits in the world's banks. This surge in deposits without an increase in the demand for credit posed a serious problem to the lending agencies: they had to find borrowers. The increasing value of Nigeria's commodities made the nation appear extremely creditworthy. Although Nigeria's military government at the time was already busy spending the booming oil profits, there was a great demand for new infrastructure and for an expansion of public services. Banks had little difficulty convincing the Nigerian government to borrow additional sums. This borrowing seemed to make sense to all sides, given high inflation, rising prices for commodities, and the "excess liquidity" of bank deposits. Late in the 1970s commodity prices fell, however, and petroleum prices also did not remain as high as predicted. Third World debt mushroomed in the 1980s, and several governments defaulted. Nigeria's indebtedness grew from $8.9 billion in 1980 to $34.5 billion in 1991; by 1995 it represented 274.5 percent of the annual value of the country's exports, and 140.5 percent of GNP. After the transition to democracy, President Obasanjo made debt reduction a high priority for his administration and in 2000 Nigeria rescheduled $20 billion of its debt. In 2006, thanks in large part to earning from the high price of oil, Nigeria became the first African country to pay off its Paris Club debt, reducing its total debt by $30 billion. It still owes money to the World Bank and to some private lenders.

A final aspect of Nigeria's international environment is its regional context, West Africa. As an accident of colonial rule, Nigeria is entirely surrounded by former French colonies—Benin (formerly Dahomey), Niger, and Cameroon. Because France and the French-speaking West African countries have been suspicious of Nigeria's intentions and have developed close economic ties among themselves, Nigeria has had difficulty in developing the leadership role in the region that its size and strength would suggest.

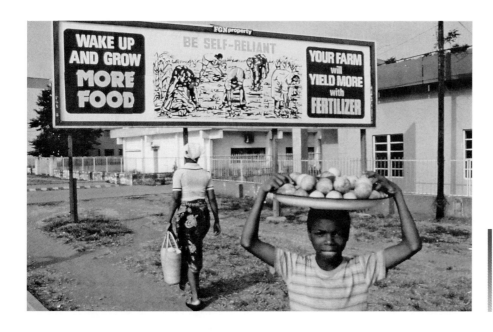

As the oil boom drained the rural workforce, signs urged Nigerians to return to agriculture.

Bruno Barbey/Magnum Photos, Inc.

POLITICAL CULTURE AND SUBCULTURES

The political culture of Nigeria is extremely heterogeneous and complex. Analysis of it must take into account a Western value system overlaid on those of its various precolonial traditions; it must assess the impact of a variety of religious beliefs and of the continuing effects of Christian and Muslim proselytizing efforts. Since the colonial experience have come new divisions based on social class and on the different experiences of urban and rural dwellers. The whole range of modern political ideologies is found among the belief systems of the politically active population. Here we will give greatest attention to the political implications of ethnic identity, religious beliefs, social and economic status, contact with urban life, and civil society.

Ethnic Identity

Because of the geographic separation of ethnic groups, Nigerians can be easily identified based on language and cultural traits. These groups vary tremendously in size, and only three of them—the Hausa, Igbos, and Yoruba—are particularly numerous and influential in the country's politics. The influence of these three major groups is a cause of great concern to the remaining minority groups. Because there has been a high degree of geographical separation of ethnic groups in Nigeria (a result of the country's policies during and since the colonial period), Nigerians can easily identify the origins of their fellow citizens by observing their dialect (or accent in English), their manner of dress (if it is traditional), and in some cases by "tribal marks," patterned facial scars that formerly were created as part of rites of passage to indicate ethnic identity. There are also differences in wealth and political awareness.

In the absence of a widely accepted census, the size of Nigerian ethnic groups can only be approximated. Approximately one-half of the country's population is in the north, and about one-fourth each in the southeast and southwest. The Hausa represent about two-thirds of the north's total population, the Igbo about two-thirds in the east, and the Yoruba about two-thirds in the west. Thus, other groups represent about one-third in each region, and one-third overall. Here we will briefly consider the three largest groups.

Hausa-Fulani The Hausa-Fulani people mostly live in the northern half of the country. As noted earlier, this hyphenated identity came from the imposition of Fulani rule over the Hausa population in the nineteenth century. The two cultures became intricately intertwined, although they have never become completely homogenized. Thus, the term "Hausa" is often used as a short form of "Hausa-Fulani." "Hausaland" actually straddles the border between Nigeria and Niger to the north, a former French colony, and the people in these two countries maintain many cultural and commercial ties. A greater proportion of Hausas engage in subsistence agriculture and live in rural villages than is true of southern Nigerians. There are sizable Hausa communities in cities all over Nigeria, where they carry on trade and commercial activities while maintaining kin and client relationships with their home region. The vast majority of Hausas (but not all) are Muslim. The Hausa heartland is itself still organized as a series of emirates: each of the major cities in northern Nigeria is the seat of an emir, one of the kings through whom the British applied their indirect rule. There is no official role for the emirs in modern Nigeria, and their unofficial role is hotly disputed, even in the north. Yet they retain great influence in their localities and, through Hausa prominence in national politics, in the rest of the country as well.

Igbo The Igbo (also spelled Ibo) occupy the southeastern part of the country, from the banks of the Niger River east. Most of the region is developed for market agriculture, with Igbo farmers growing palm products, rice, and yams. The Igbo people lived in politically independent, socially endogamous villages, usually no larger than 8,000 people and did not have a sense of common Igbo identity until the colonial period.

The Igbo are known for the enthusiasm with which they adopted Western culture. Although the encounter with British colonialism was a wrenching shock forcefully described in Chinua Achebe's novel *Things Fall Apart*, the Igbo responded enthusiastically to Western education and the missionaries who brought it, and aggressively sought advancement in modern commerce and civil service. Igbo people also emigrated widely throughout the country and seem less concerned than other groups with maintaining separate communities where they are "strangers." (In Nigeria, the term "stranger" refers specifically to a person living outside his or her "home" community.)

They are employed on the basis of their education and modern skills in all parts of the country, including the north.

Igbo officers led the first military coup in 1966, and thousands of Igbos living in northern cities were attacked and killed in reaction to that coup. The Igbos retreated to their home region. The next year they followed the call of one of their own, Lieutenant Colonel Ojukwu, in the secession from Nigeria of Igbo-dominated Biafra. The three-year civil war that ended in the defeat of Biafra in 1970 caused great hardship, but within a few years Igbos were again active in commerce (they were by then generally barred from government work in other localities) across the land. Nevertheless, the Biafran experience and the civil war left long-term mistrust between the Igbos and other Nigerians.

Yoruba The Yoruba mostly live in the southwestern part of Nigeria, including the metropolitan area of **Lagos,** the former federal capital and major urban center. Traditionally subsistence farmers, rural Yoruba people began growing cocoa and palm products for export in the colonial period. Although they share a common language, traditional religion, and myths of origin, the precolonial Yoruba were divided into a number of independent and warring kingdoms that give them separate identities today as Ijebu, Egba, Awori, Oyo, Ekiti, Igbomina, and others. The Yoruba have a long tradition of commerce, and both men and women are prominent in trade networks and markets throughout West Africa.

The Yoruba kingdoms were marked by complicated institutions that balanced power between an *oba* (king) and lineage chiefs, as in the relationship between the Alafin of Oyo and the Oyo Mesi described earlier. In their effort to impose indirect rule, the British upset these structures by supporting the obas against all challengers. In the process, the obas frequently became autocratic and lost much of their legitimacy with their own people; their influence in contemporary politics varies greatly, but is generally much less than that of the northern emirs.

Because the Yoruba had, on the one hand, a highly stratified society complete with kings and, on the other hand, were quite receptive to missionaries and their schools, they are often seen as in an intermediate position between the stratified and change-resistant Hausa and the egalitarian and innovative Igbo. In their sometimes strident assertion of their identity and interests, they also have provoked their share of mistrust among other Nigerians, as their candidates have generally been shut out of national leadership positions.

Given the ethnic-based strife so common in the world today, it should not come as a surprise that group identities are deeply rooted and emotionally charged in Nigeria as well. Ethnic rivalries often have their roots in precolonial warfare and are frequently refreshed by economic rivalries. While nationalism may serve as a cement where the feeling is shared by a country's entire population, the same feeling at a subnational level can destroy a political system. In Nigeria, these attachments are multilayered, and different levels of association can become charged at different times, as demonstrated in the Ibadan-Ijebu rivalry (see Box 13.1). Strong ethnic ties often are felt and expressed in kinship terms, and thus are often central to the definition of self. However, the Nigerian case demonstrates that ethnicity is often wrongly understood as primordial. While ethnic identity indeed has ancient roots, this does not mean that one's ethnic identity is identical with that of one's distant ancestors. In Africa, and in Nigeria in particular, we

The Ibadan-Ijebu Controversy

BOX 13.1

Ibadan is one of the two largest cities in Nigeria. An old Yoruba city, it is plagued by a historic rivalry between its two major groups, the Ibadan and the Ijebu—both claiming descent from Oduduwa (whose descendants seem as quarrelsome as Abraham's!). The Ijebu lived closest to the coast and thus were the first to enter into commerce with European traders. Their attempt to control trade with the interior—that is, with Ibadan—is said to have produced their long-standing animosity. At the same time, the animosity is not always felt at the individual level, for intermarriage between the two groups is common.

see extraordinary change, as in the bonding of two separate groups to form the Hausa-Fulani culture, in the emergence of a "Yoruba" identity over what were previously separate societies in conflict, and in the formation of an Igbo identity among villagers who previously were largely unaware of one another. Both in the colonial period and since, ethnic identities have been manipulated for political purposes.

In Nigeria some of the first associational groups were based on the perception of common ethnic bonds in "nontraditional" settings. As a student in London, the early nationalist leader Obafemi Awolowo formed the Egbe Omo Oduduwa as a cultural organization grouping expatriate Yorubas. This group was to become the basis for the Action Group, the political party Awolowo later formed.

Because the major ethnic groups are regionally based, political issues affecting such groups are often defined geographically, and Nigeria has preserved a sense of permanent attachment between a people and its "traditional" homeland to the degree that it is more difficult to become a "citizen" of another state in Nigeria than it would be for a Nigerian to acquire citizenship in many foreign countries. The ethnic exclusiveness found in each state and local authority is euphemistically referred to as Nigeria's "federal character," and it has strong effects on the nature of national policy. Thus, as Nigerians respond to educational or economic opportunities in other parts of the country, they find it necessary to organize into ethnic associations to protect and promote their interests. Hausas in the south usually live in a ghetto called the *sabo*, where they speak their language and practice their Muslim faith. Nigerians at the lowest socioeconomic level often belong to a single association, that of their ethnic group; the more educated members of these "stranger" communities will often overlay the purely ethnic associations with others in which they interact across ethnic lines.

Multiple ethnic identities even at the local level have had a fragmenting effect on political structure. Particularly since 1976, there have been numerous disputes over the site of local government headquarters, with the "loser" often petitioning to the state and federal governments for a division of the local government area. The conflict between the Ife and Modakeke in Oranmiyan local government (see Box 13.2) is but one of many examples that could be cited. Local ethnic conflict affects policy outputs as well, where local

The Conflict Between Modakeke and Ile-Ife

BOX 13.2

Early in the nineteenth century, Yorubas from Old Oyo were driven south by a Fulani invasion, and some settled in and around Ile-Ife. They were at first well received by Ile-Ife's traditional ruler, the Ooni, but soon got into a violent quarrel with the local population. The Oyo refugees were then reduced to servitude, and some were sold into slavery. Later, however, in an internal dispute, they sided with the ruler, who rewarded them with a settlement of their own, Modakeke. Strife continued between the two groups, and in an 1882 battle the Modakeke burned down the sacred city of Ife. Throughout the colonial period, the Ooni often used their conflict to play one group against the other. As independence neared, the Modakeke sought a local government independent of Ife. Also, the Ife leaders supported the Action Group (party), while Modakeke supported the National Council of Nigeria and the Cameroons (NCNC).

After independence, Ife and Modakeke were in the same local government (Oranmiyan), but they fought constantly until Oranmiyan was split in 1989. There was peace until August 1997, when the government moved one local government from an Ife to a Modakeke location and then to supposedly neutral ground. Violent conflict broke out among young men of each side. Whole villages were burned and hundreds of lives were lost. In January 1999, the Osun state administrator invited the two communities to an open meeting, at which both groups agreed to a cease-fire. The Ooni stated that he had in fact requested General Abacha to create a new state, and that Abacha had declined but had given him the new local government as a consolation prize. The traditional leader's request and the government's response inadvertently rekindled historic animosities, with tragic results. In April 2002, the federal government mandated Osun State to create an Area Office for Modakeke as part of a peace process. The Area Office was created without delay, and it is yielding some positive results within the Modakeke community.

governments build health centers or markets that are not used by some ethnic groups, thus throwing off planners' projections.

Religion

Each of the groups identified in the previous section had traditional religious institutions and beliefs in place long before the arrival of Christianity and Islam. In some cases these earlier beliefs have maintained their vigor, especially among many Yoruba. However, the missionaries brought their religion with formal education in the southern regions; most major Christian churches are well established in the south, and indigenous Christian sects have split off from them in a myriad of denominations. Not surprisingly, the Christian denominations themselves tend to be geographically and ethnically concentrated, with a higher proportion of Roman Catholics among the Igbo, a Baptist concentration among the Yoruba of Ogbomoso, the Evangelical Church of West Africa predominant in Igbomina and Kwara State, and so on. A significant proportion of Yoruba—perhaps half—are Muslim. Under the agreement between the colonial administration and the northern emirates, Christian proselytizing was barred from the north, and, except for the "strangers" living there, almost the entire population is at least nominally Muslim, and the Hausa bring their religion with them when they move south. This movement is offset by the establishment of churches in northern cities by immigrants mostly from the south.

Missionaries built and staffed the great majority of schools during the colonial period. Thus the north-south education gap, with its effect on political awareness, attitudes toward civil rights, and the like itself derives from the prohibition of missionaries in the north.

There is, then, an overlay of religion on ethnicity that intensifies the north-south cultural split, and the case can be made that the most sensitive issues now involve religion rather than ethnicity. These overlapping cleavages are more dangerous because they accentuate regional differences. Nigeria has a special problem in this regard in that the Christian–Muslim split is near fifty-fifty, whereas in almost all other African states Muslims are either the large majority of the population or compose a clear minority.

The brother of Usman dan Fodio, the leader of the nineteenth-century *jihad* (holy war) in northern Nigeria, wrote a four-volume work on the nature of legitimate Islamic government. It does not allow for the possibility of a conflict between secular concepts of justice and welfare and those in the *sharia* (Muslim religious law). These values are well rooted in the region: a survey of 686 students at Bayero University in Kano in 1983 found that 92 percent of them "believed an Islamic state was inherently superior to a secular state."[14] In the 1980s the Maitatsine Islamic movement, composed largely of young men marginalized by the socioeconomic changes of the period, rioted against the Christian presence in northern Nigeria (as well as against police repression) with loss of life estimated in the thousands. On the other side, a failed coup against the Babangida regime in 1990 is widely thought to have been a "Christian coup against the northern Muslim leadership."[15] Because fundamentalist elements in both Christianity and Islam have frequently found it unacceptable to live in a pluralist society, those seeking a basis for political stability in Nigeria must be sensitive to finding a balance between the two major faith groups. For that reason there was great distress in the south when, in 1986, President **Ibrahim Babangida** proposed that Nigeria join the Organization of the Islamic Conference (OIC), a group of more than fifty predominantly Muslim countries formed in 1970. In 1991, Babangida asserted that the membership was "in abeyance," which is perhaps the only resolution of the issue that will not exacerbate religious tensions.

The Evolution of Nigerian Nationalism

All of our preoccupation with Nigerian subcultures should not obscure the fact that the British colonial administration was responding to Nigerian nationalist forces when it granted independence in 1960. There were three major sources of nationalist sentiment. The first was a small number of freed slaves from North America and others of African descent from the Caribbean who settled on the West African coast and developed a culture unrelated to any of those indigenous to the country. Second, nationalist fervor grew out of the experience of Nigerians who fought for the British in World War II and felt frustration at the lack of recognition of their service. A third category of nationalists consisted of those Nigerians who studied in England and especially in the United States, including one of the most prominent among them, **Nnamdi**

BOX 13.3

The Story of Nnamdi Azikiwe

Although an Igbo, Nnamdi Azikiwe was born in Zungeru in northern Nigeria in 1904. He received his basic education in Nigeria, then went to the United States, where he studied at Lincoln University in Pennsylvania, Stores College in West Virginia, and the University of Pennsylvania. He also worked in the United States as a coal miner, laborer, and dishwasher. Upon his return home, he joined the Nigerian Youth Movement. His interest in self-rule led to his presence at the founding of the National Council of Nigeria and the Cameroons (NCNC) and to his founding of a pro-self-rule newspaper, the *West African Pilot*. He then moved to the Gold Coast (now Ghana), where he published an article, "Has the African a God," that resulted in a sedition charge. He won his case on appeal and went on to serve as the premier of the Eastern Region, and from 1963 to 1966 as president of Nigeria. He died in 1996 at the age of 92.

Azikiwe (see Box 13.3). Although they came from a variety of ethnic backgrounds, in their quest for independence, these activists developed a sense of Nigerian nationalism and succeeded in forming cross-ethnic alliances.

Civil war also stimulated Nigerian nationalism. The two military coups before the Biafran war were clearly ethnic in their origins. However, the Biafran conflict brought together a military force that was cross-ethnic (excluding, of course, Igbos, who were at the heart of the Biafran succession). Although the officer corps is increasingly dominated by Muslims, it has continued to recruit nationally.

A study of Nigerian political culture must focus on orientations toward national (federal) political institutions. Nigerians oriented toward public political activities can be identified by (1) exposure to formal education and (2) involvement in the modern economy. As concerns interest in public policy, many Nigerians, particularly in rural areas and in the north, are *subjects,* not *participants.* Although such people may be unaware of, and uninterested in, issues of general political concern, they still have to deal with local government officials on issues affecting themselves and their families. In Nigeria, as elsewhere in Africa and the Third World, such concerns are likely to be handled through personal interest contacting. In general, Nigerians are more likely than most to feel that the government should provide for individual needs (see Figure 3.3 in Chapter 3). A 2002 survey reported that 93 percent of Nigerians believe that it is "important or very important" for the government to provide basic necessities.[16] In most cases, such contacting is part of a *clientelist* arrangement: citizens go to an individual who is politically influential for help and expect to "pay" for help through a long-term arrangement that may include payment in kind (as in bribes), or by turning out to vote when asked to do so, even while remaining uninterested in politics. Political activity is widespread and virtually all-embracing; interest in public affairs is strongly conditioned by education and employment.

Democratic Norms and Values

In order to assess Nigeria's chances for achieving political democracy, we must first consider the distribution of norms that might support democratic institutions. The legitimacy of opposition, manifested as tolerance for criticism, opposition, and competition for control, is an obvious prerequisite for stable democracy.[17] The performance of political activists in Nigeria from 1960 on suggests problems, even under democratic civilian regimes. As single parties gained control in each region, opponents were treated very roughly, often in the physical sense, with armed thugs hired to disrupt their meetings and attack their leaders.

Nevertheless, strong support has emerged for democratic norms since the military's exit in 1999. Today 81 percent of Nigerians say "democracy is preferable to any other form of government." In addition, 83 percent say that the freedom to criticize the government is "very important or important."[18]

The Political Role of Women

In Nigeria's ethnic diversity, the position of women varies considerably. In Igbo, Yoruba, and other southern Nigerian traditions, women had considerable control over their own affairs in what anthropologists label "dual-sex" systems. That is, there were parallel systems of political and social organization for men and women. P. C. Lloyd concluded that "the Yoruba wife's status is characterized by great overt submission to her husband together with considerable economic independence."[19] Scholars of colonial history contend that women lost most of their autonomy under colonialism, because British custom at the time gave women less control of their own affairs than did the African societies they controlled. A famous case in point is the Igbo "Women's War" (referred to by the colonial government as the "Aba riots"), in which Igbo women used traditional means of protest against taxation and were harshly repressed by the colonial government (see Box 13.4).

In the north, Islamic custom greatly restricts women's roles in society. Although Hausa women have considerably more freedom than their counterparts in the Middle East, including significant roles in local production and trade, they generally were not allowed an active political role at the time of independence. Northern women voted for the first time in 1979.

The contemporary involvement of women in political leadership is similar to that of many countries: in most parts of the country, Nigerian women vote in equal numbers with men but are generally underrepresented in politics. In the 1998–1999 elections, out of 109 Senate seats, men held 106 and women held three; men held 348 seats in the House of Representatives and women twelve; men held 767 positions as local government chairmen and only seven were women; 7,665 councilors were men and seventy-five were women.

Political Corruption

A traveler on Nigerian roads meets frequent police checkpoints and barricades. Ostensibly in place to check for arms and smuggled goods, their actual function is to extort payments from travelers by uncovering various minor violations. Many Nigerians do not take offense at this behavior, noting that police officers' pay is low and often comes late.

Pervasive corruption has been a problem ever since the late colonial era; it was the central theme of Chinua Achebe's novel *No Longer at Ease,* in which an idealistic young administrator is gradually pressured by personal problems and the prevalence of corruption into accepting bribes. Achebe is only one of many Nigerians to condemn corruption; each political regime comes to power promising to eliminate the practice and punish offenders, only to fall into the same pattern. The huge sums of money that passed through officials' hands as a result of the oil boom greatly aggravated the problem: unprecedented forms of flagrant corruption appeared when oil revenues began to fill the federal treasury of General Yakubu Gowon in the early 1970s. His military governors spent large sums on openly lavish lifestyles, thus tarnishing the image of the military, which had supposedly come to power in reaction to the corruption of the First Republic. The coup against Gowon in 1975 was a direct result, as was the assassination of his successor General Murtala in 1976.[20] Achebe asserts that corruption has grown more "bold and ravenous" under each new regime.[21] It is widely believed that the deceased leader **Sani Abacha** and his family channeled enormous sums of money from petroleum revenue

---

The Igbo Women's War   BOX 13.4

"In November of 1929, thousands of Igbo women ... converged on the native Administration centers.... The women chanted, danced, sang songs of ridicule, and demanded the caps of office (the official insignia) of the Warrant Chiefs.... At a few locations the women broke into prisons and released prisoners. Sixteen Native Courts were attacked, and most of these were broken up or burned.... On two occasions, British District Officers called in police and troops, who fired on the women and left a total of more than 50 dead and 50 wounded. No one on the other side was seriously injured." The women's actions were "an extension of their traditional method for settling grievances with men who had acted badly toward them."

Source: Judith Van Allen, "'Aba Riots' on 'Ibo Women's War'? Ideology, Stratification and the Invisibility of Women," in Nancy J. Hafkin and Edna G. Bay, eds., *Women in Africa: Studies in Social and Economic Change* (Stanford, CA: Stanford University Press, 1976), 59–85.

accounts into their private coffers at home and abroad. As part of its campaign to promote transparency in government and fight corruption, the Obasanjo administration successfully recovered $2 billion from the Sani Abacha family.

In 2002, the National Assembly passed the **Economic and Financial Crimes Commission (EFCC)** Establishment Act. Its purpose is to "prevent, investigate, prosecute and penalize economic and financial crimes." Crimes within its jurisdiction include money laundering, Internet fraud, bank fraud, bribery, and misuse of public funds. To run the EFCC, President Obasanjo appointed Mallam Nuhu Ribadu, who claims credit for recovering over $5 billion and successfully prosecuting eighty-two people.

Yet the EFCC has also been widely accused of selective prosecution of the president's political enemies. For example, it launched an investigation of Vice President Atiku Abubakar in 2006, when he was running for president. The Commission's critics suspected that the charges were brought because Abubakar had opposed President Obasanjo's efforts to amend the Constitution so as to make him eligible for a third term in office.[22] The EFCC's report accused Abubakar of misappropriating $100 million in public funds. In light of the charges the People's Democratic Party (PDP) suspended him from the party for three months to prevent him from contesting the December 2006 presidential primaries. The Senate also launched an investigation into whether he should be impeached.

POLITICAL SOCIALIZATION

Nigerians develop their political beliefs and attitudes through the influence of socialization "agents," such as the family, primary and secondary groups, formal education, the media, and government-sponsored activities.[23] A caveat is necessary, however, when comparing the political socialization process in Nigeria to the established liberal democracies. Political socialization in the developed world occurs through fairly stable institutions. We treat the fluidity of party alignments in France or events such as the Vietnam War in the United States as exceptional, whereas in Nigeria people have grown up under political arrangements that shift constantly, even to their very core. Add to this the upheaval of urbanization and of the sudden and dramatic impact of petroleum on the culture and

the economy, and the need for a different perspective on socialization is apparent. Nevertheless, there is a universal quality to the importance of the agents of socialization we have identified, even as the nature of those institutions and the objects of political attitudes and values they shape may differ greatly from those in Europe or North America.

The Family

The family, whether nuclear or extended, remains the core unit of political activity in Nigeria. In many Nigerian traditions, families are identified with a particular trade or role in society. Thus, among the Yoruba a family of warriors is called *Jagunjagun,* farmers are *Agbe,* and traders are *Onisowo.* To traditionally minded Nigerians, such identification remains important to the determination of one's appropriate role in modern politics.

Many Nigerians have grown up in polygamous families.[24] There is no law preventing a man from taking more than one wife, although Muslims are theoretically limited to a maximum of four and Christians of mainstream denominations to one. All indigenous traditions in Nigeria accept polygamy, and little stigma is attached to the practice. Some Christian denominations in Nigeria enforce monogamy only on those men who hold office in the church.

The large family units that result from polygamous households and the broader definition of family give kinship special political importance. A politician may be able to count on the support of literally hundreds of actual kin, and even larger numbers if one considers clan affiliations based on a sense of kinship even where exact genealogical ties cannot be demonstrated. Kinship provides the most powerful sense of identity and loyalty to many in Nigeria and elsewhere in Africa, and it is the model (and often the real-world basis) for clientelist relationships.

Schools

In most contemporary nations, the schools play a central role in developing a sense of community. This is clearly an important mission in Nigerian schools, and balancing various loyalties is a delicate task for Nigerian educators. Also, formal education is one of the principal benefits Nigerians expect from government. The school certificate is highly regarded throughout the developing world as a means to economic and social advancement, and this is especially true in Nigeria: "It seems safe to say that by the 1930s and 1940s no people in the world placed a higher value on education or regarded its consequences more optimistically than did the inhabitants of this area."[25]

As Nigeria approached independence in the 1950s, the two southern regions invested massively in expansion of their educational systems, especially at the primary level. There is a broad consensus that primary education should be free and universal. Beyond that basic agreement, however, Nigeria has struggled with how to shape the curriculum and how to make it available.

The oil boom of the 1970s stimulated a massive wave of secondary school expansion and the university system, which grew from one in 1948 to five in 1962 to forty-five by 2002. Just between 1999 and 2002, sixteen state universities and six private ones were created. In addition to universities, the higher education system includes seventy-five polytechnics and colleges of technology and of education.

Even in the prosperous 1970s, a lack of resources threatened this educational boom, and there was a lack of properly trained instructors at all levels. With the economic collapse of the 1980s, funds for education dried up, and education suffered at all levels. Equal access has remained illusory for years, and the problem becomes more acute as one moves from the primary to the secondary and to the postsecondary level. The bias is on the one hand socioeconomic—children of the elite occupy a disproportionate share of the enrollments—and it also reflects gender. In 2002, girls constituted only about 44 percent of the students in primary schools, and this figure showed no improvement over the preceding ten years. Enrollment rates did increase dramatically after the transition to democracy, surging from 76 percent in 1998 to 95 percent in 2000. The African Development Bank reported a decline in adult illiteracy over the same years from 39 percent to 36 percent, and it has continued to drop. As a result, the level of political awareness has arguably risen too. Unfortunately other important disparities, notably those between north and south, persist.[26]

There have been indirect political effects of the education gap across regions. As the number of secondary graduates increased in the south, many of them sought jobs in the north and were embittered at northern rejection. At the same time, northerners grew alarmed at the prospect of being inundated by educated southerners. Differences in educational achievement thus contributed to the resentments that exploded in violence in 1966. Today northern political dominance in the face of higher educational achievement in the south continues to aggravate interregional political conflict.

The conference center in Abuja, the new capital.

Betty Press/Woodfin Camp & Associates

Language is an aspect of community-building that is often taken for granted, but language usage in school can have a major impact on political attitudes. As noted previously, English is the official language of Nigeria and remains the vehicle of instruction in Nigeria from primary school through the university. Furthermore, English is the language of government and, for the most part, of the mass media. Because English is a second language in most Nigerian homes, school plays an especially critical role in enabling access to the political system.

As a nation-building effort the three major indigenous languages—Hausa, Igbo, and Yoruba—are also taught through secondary school and are topics in the Senior School Certificate Examinations. Proficiency in English is required for admission to a university, where the local languages are used only in programs where they might specifically be required. The connection between English usage and government activities gives added weight to the usual relationship between education and political efficacy.

Whatever the effect of intentional socialization in the schools, studies of political culture invariably affirm the effect of education on political participation. This is especially true in less developed countries, where the cultural gap between those with and without formal education is especially great. Data from the 1999 World Values Survey in Nigeria finds that only 25 percent of illiterate Nigerians are very interested in politics, compared with 46 percent among the most educated.

The Mass Media

The presence of a lively and politically independent press goes back at least to Azikiwe's *West African Pilot*. By the time of independence a considerable number of competing newspapers existed in Nigeria (virtually all published in Lagos, then distributed nationwide). Yet the current combined circulation of daily newspapers is only about 2.7 million, or about twenty-four per 1,000 people.

The political effect of the press is naturally limited in a country where one-third of the adults are illiterate. A 2000 survey found that approximately 30 percent of Nigerians get their news from newspapers at least once a week. That same survey reported that 64 percent of Nigerians are somewhat or very interested in politics, and 65 percent say they discuss politics and the

government with people "sometimes" or "often."[27] Today, newspaper readership includes all politically active Nigerians, and the perspectives in the press undoubtedly have a wide word-of-mouth circulation.

Most Nigerians get their news from radio and 60 percent of Nigerians list television as a source of news at least once a week. Radio and television have always been state-controlled and thus are faithful purveyors of the government's "spin" on political events. Shortwave broadcasts from the BBC, Voice of America, and other outside sources have been available as independent sources for decades, however. In recent years, indigenous television competes with satellite news services and since 1999 new independent media outlets have opened. In the year 2000 alone, Nigerians saw several new newspapers launched and six new privately operated radio stations. Although only a tiny proportion of the country's population have access to satellite telecasts or the Internet, such advanced communications technology permits outside views of Nigerian events to be introduced into the country, then spread by word of mouth or reflected in the print media.

The authoritarian regimes imposed a substantial number of restrictions on the media. According to the Center for Free Speech, a Nigerian watchdog organization, the military issued twenty-one decrees between 1966 and 1995, limiting press freedoms or even proscribing particular publications outright. There was a high level of tension between military governments and the press, and the life of a journalist was not easy. Many journalists were arrested, and in 1986 a prominent critic of the government was killed by a letter bomb.

The Constitution promulgated in 1999 reversed many restrictions instituted under General Sani Abacha and previous military rulers. Article 39 states: "Every person shall be entitled to freedom of expression, including freedom to hold opinions and to receive and impart ideas and information Without interference." Although this article guarantees broad freedom for the media, journalists can still face criminal punishment for defamation of public officials, and a 1999 decree requires them to be accredited by a government-run media council. In other ways journalists are still subject to harassment. Reporters without Borders lists Nigeria as one of the countries in Africa where violence against journalists is "routine" and goes unpunished; twenty journalists suffered physical attacks in 2005 and "scores" of others were imprisoned for what they wrote. One newspaper publisher was detained without charge after running a negative story on the First Lady.[28]

The State

The Nigerian government has at its disposal the modern means of mass communication that oil revenues have allowed it to develop. Periodically it launches propaganda campaigns on one issue or another, as in Operation Feed the Nation and Free Primary Education (in the 1970s), the War Against Indiscipline (in the 1980s), or the more recent Road Safety Operation, for which the government recruited author Wole Soyinka as director.

As part of its "transition program" to democracy (between 1986 and 1993), the regime of General Ibrahim Babangida inaugurated the Directorate for Social Mobilization, also known as MAMSER (Mass Mobilization for Self-Reliance, Economic Recovery and Social Justice). MAMSER's ostensible purpose was to shape a mass political culture that would be congenial to democracy. The government devoted considerable resources to this effort, although many questioned its effectiveness and some its sincerity. In 1995, the Abacha regime replaced it with a smaller organization intended to work through local governments. In 1990, the Babangida regime also established the Center for Democratic Studies (CDS) in Abuja, to conduct research on democratization and present seminars on that topic for government officials. In 1996, it too was closed by Abacha.

Nigerian political attitudes are far more likely to be affected by everyday contact with the state than by the state's direct, intentional efforts to shape attitudes. In Nigeria's federal system, direct contact comes largely through local officials. Rural residents without English-language proficiency find that, even at the local level, officials are much more educated than they and generally expect and get deference. Government is remote and must be approached through some form of informal mediation. For those with formal education, contact with local government is relatively simple; furthermore, because Nigerian policy is to hire civil servants from their home areas, there is neither a social nor a cultural difference between the educated citizen and the public servant. Nigerians expect to pay for expeditious service, and while they are aware of norms of honesty and ethics that are higher than the behavior they perceive, they are not scandalized by the difference. Perceptions of policymakers are not usually the result of direct contact.

Nigerians generally express great cynicism about the motivations of policymakers at all levels, civilian or military, but for the most part this results from media accounts of venality and corruption. Whether through direct contact or media portrayal, they most often get what they expect from governmental officials, which of course becomes a self-fulfilling prophecy:

> The Complete Nigerian civil servant unlike his predecessor is not self-effacing behind an array of coded titles. You meet him here, you see him there, and you talk to him yonder. He is eager to make your acquaintance. He takes you into little corners to confide in you. For instance, he tells you how much it would cost you to have your file speeded up, which I think is very nice.[29]

One would expect that the unhappy experience with military rulers would leave Nigerians cynical and disillusioned. There certainly have been such effects, but there is a remarkably abiding faith in the importance of politics, especially among the educated. There is an impact here of the oil economy. Profits from the sale of petroleum have flowed through the central government, so that the stake in access to those in government, especially at the top, is high. For many intellectuals, however, the knowledge that important resources will be distributed through the government is offset by the uncertainty of the outcome of any attempt to become involved. They tend, thus, to leave the political field to a collection of seasoned politicians, those who have assembled a voter base every time a regime has offered the prospect of new elections.

Contact with Urban Life

Massive population movement from the countryside to the cities is a nearly universal characteristic of less developed countries. Today over 46 percent of Nigeria's population lives in urban areas, reflecting an urbanization trend that began in the 1970s with the oil boom, when the massive infusion of wealth stimulated employment opportunities in construction and other areas. From 1970 to 1995, Nigeria's urban population increased from 20 to 39 percent of the total. The subsequent economic downturn left many of the new urban residents in an economically marginal position that was all the more precarious because they were removed from the possibility of subsistence production, the usual option of peasants when profits from marketed goods are low. In such an environment, urban residents are "available" for political mobilization; they are physically close to political institutions that might be held responsible for their problems, and communication about political events can spread quickly. Political unrest in Nigeria's most populous city, Lagos, was an important consideration in the military regime's decision in the 1970s to move the federal capital to Abuja, a city much farther to the north.

Religion

Given the importance of religion in many Nigerians' lives, it is not surprising that religious institutions and religious leaders affect political orientations. According to the 2000 survey mentioned earlier, nearly 80 percent of all Nigerians say they belong to religious associations, and half of those say they are active members. A dramatic example is the activity against political authorities in northern Nigeria inspired by religious leader Alhaji Mohammed Marwa Maitatsine. In the 1970s, the rapid urbanization of the country produced a marginalized stratum of youth in the towns and cities of northern Nigeria. Fundamentalist Muslim reformers were active at the time, with financial support from Saudi Arabia and other Arab countries. The fundamentalist message, especially as preached in the Izala movement—an acronym for the Society for the Removal of Heresy and Reinstatement of Tradition—proved appealing to the young urban migrants and directed them religiously and politically against the dominant leadership in the north. They were thus mobilized into the region's political factionalism:

> Religion is a powerful instrument of mobilization in Northern Nigeria . . . ambitious politicians and local notables supported the creation of the Izala movement . . . support for a religious movement by a politician offers political rewards. This is all the more so given the fact that religious leaders mediate between the politicians and the civil society. Moreover, with the pledge by the military to hand over power in 1979, and with the heightened inter- and intra-party competition, one observed an intensification of contacts between politicians, local notables and religious leaders.[30]

With the return of democracy in 1999, Nigeria has experienced a new wave of religious tension, especially in the north where several states have declared their intention to implement Sharia, or Islamic law. Christian associations have opposed these changes and the conflicts have sometimes been dramatic: more than 10,000 people have been killed in religious conflicts between 1999 and 2003. The ongoing sensitivity over Islam in Nigeria was brought to the world's attention in one unfortunate incident in 2002. When the Miss World Beauty Pageant took place in Abuja, a newspaper suggested that the contestants were so beautiful that the religion's founding prophet would have chosen one of them. Over 200 people died when tensions between Christians and Muslims flared up.[31] At the same time, scholars such as John Paden maintain that Islam also provides cultural frameworks that northern Nigerians draw upon in order to resolve potential conflicts.

POLITICAL RECRUITMENT

All the chief executives of Nigeria since independence are identified in Table 13.1. Several conclusions are apparent. First, northerners have dominated the leadership of the country under both civilian and military rule, in the first case because the population of the north is about the same as in the east and west combined, and in the case of the military regimes, because of increasing dominance of the officer corps by northerners.

In the early years of independence, a military career lacked prestige, especially among educated southerners. In an effort to speed the replacement of remaining British officers, the Balewa government actively recruited university graduates into the officer ranks. One result was the introduction of large numbers of educated Igbos into officer ranks; another was the politicization of the army. Three of the first six university graduates to enter the army led the first coup.

Because the military controlled the country between 1983 and 1999, an officer's commission has come to be seen as the most regular path to political power. It seems that the ethos of the military has changed in this regard. The first coup leaders in 1966 professed great regret at the necessity to intervene and promised that their stay would be temporary. They were removed and killed in the second 1966 coup before their sincerity could be tested. The longevity of General Gowon's regime was made necessary by the need to prosecute the civil war, and then to lay a constitutional framework for civilian rule. When

				TABLE 13.1
Nigerian Chief Executives, 1960–2007				

Dates	Name	Title	Ethnicity	Cause of Departure
1960–Jan. 1966	Tafawa Balewa	Prime Minister	Hausa-Fulani (North)	Coup (killed)
1963–Jan. 1966	Nnamdi Azikiwe	President [appointed]	Igbo (East)	Coup (removed)
Jan.–July 1966	Agusi Ironsi	Military Head of State	Igbo (East)	Coup (killed)
July 1966–1975	Yakubu Gowon	Military Head of State	Tiv ("Middle Belt")	Coup (removed)
1975–1976	Murtala Muhammed	Military Head of State	Hausa-Fulani (North)	Coup (killed)
1976–1979	Olusegun Obasanjo	Military Head of State	Yoruba (Southwest)	Handed power to civilian government
1979–1983	Shehu Shagari	President	Hausa-Fulani (North)	Coup (removed)
1983–1985	Muhammed Buhari	Military Head of State	Hausa-Fulani (North)	Coup (removed)
1985–1993	Ibrahim Babangida	Military Head of State	Gwari (North)	Forced out of office
Aug.–Nov. 1993	Ernest Shonekan	Interim Head of State [appointed]	Yoruba (South west)	Forced out of office
Nov. 1993–June 1998	Sani Abacha	Head, Provisional Ruling Council	Kanuri (North)	Died in office
May 1998–May 1999	Abdulsalami Abubakar	Head, Provisional Ruling Council	Gwari (North)	Handed power to civilian government
May 1999–May 2007	Olusegun Obasanjo	President	Yoruba (Southwest)	Civilian-to-civilian transfer
May 2007–present	Umar Musa Yar'Adua	President	Hausa-Fulani (North)	

Gowon seemed inclined to settle in for the long term, he was removed, and General Obasanjo set and abided by his 1979 deadline. Thus, through the first period of military rule, although there was serious profit-taking on the part of many military leaders, none of them expected to have long-term political careers.

The second round of military power (1983 to 1999) produced a gradual change in the perspectives of at least some military officers. Many observers have wondered about the military leadership's annulment of the 1993 presidential election results and the abolition of state and local elective offices already filled. Most feel that if the presumed winner, Moshood Abiola, had been allowed to assume power, he would have been unable to deal effectively with the country's problems, would quickly have lost an already dubious legitimacy, and would thus have prepared the way for a return of the military with acceptance by the population. As it was, the Abacha regime faced massive resistance and was able to rule only on the basis of force, at least in much of the south. Many assume that Abacha's actions, while certainly supported by elements in the north that could not stomach a Yoruba president, also reflected the strong desire of a new generation of military officers to

enjoy the fruits of power that come from oil revenues and from the potential profits that flow from the corruption of public office. The country witnessed open jockeying for positions as state governors or "chairmen" of local governments, which were allocated according to military rank. National-level offices were usually filled by generals, brigadiers, or colonels; state governors were mostly colonels; and local chairmen were lieutenant colonels and majors, often retired from active service. Politics in Nigeria is still largely a game of money; therefore, the retired military, the business group, and some retired civil servants dominate the elective positions while a few academics have political appointments, like minister, commissioner, and the foreign service.

Nigerian universities produce large numbers of trained public administrators, and they follow long-term careers in federal, state, or local administration that usually are not affected by changes at the top. An analysis of the educational backgrounds of the "administrative class" (assistant secretaries to permanent secretaries) just before the restoration of civilian rule in 1979 showed that all but 11 percent of them held university degrees.[32] An appropriate educational level had come to be expected in the civil service.

There has been some upheaval in the civil service following regime changes: an estimated 11,000 administrators were removed when Murtala Muhammed came to power in 1975 and took vigorous action against corruption. But to the degree that the administrative system continues to function through the many regime changes, it does so because of the permanence of the civil service.

Recruitment into political positions at the local and state levels generally exclude "strangers," even though they may be long-time residents of a community and, of course, Nigerian citizens. There are some exceptions: where "strangers" are sufficiently numerous, they can run and win. In most places, however, regulations have expressly limited candidacy to indigenous candidates. In addition to simple democratic fairness, the advantage of creating a multiethnic council is that it stimulates identity and participation in the community on the part of populations that are otherwise excluded. The overriding characteristic of recruitment into political or administrative office, however, is the effort faithfully to "reflect the federal character of Nigeria"—that is, to fill positions to have a government that is an ethnic microcosm of the locality or state it controls.

In the past, appointments of military personnel to government posts also reflected the country's "federal character": northern officers were appointed in the northern states, Yorubas and others from the southwest to states in that region, and so on, although Abacha introduced a pattern of more random assignments, placing southern officers in the north and vice versa. However, the highest military positions have come from the combat arms, which recently are dominated by northerners; without the northern preponderance in these positions, Abacha's control of the country could not have been maintained.

Even northerners have not always been reliable: Press reports claimed that a majority of junior officers had voted in 1993 for the southern civilian, **Moshood Abiola.** Abacha's support base was narrowed even further when, in March 1995, he arrested former head of state **Olusegun Obasanjo** and one of the most prominent senior northern military leaders, Shehu Musa Yar'Adua. Obasanjo was released by Abubakar after Abacha's death in 1998; Yar'Adua died in prison in December 1997. The same month, Abacha arrested the chief of the general staff, General Oladipo Diya, on the charge of plotting a military coup, and thus removed

the most senior Yoruba officer. Ethnic politics are still very much dominating the politics of Nigeria. However, President Olusegun Obasanjo has made use of the zoning structure, which breaks Nigeria into six divisions for the purpose of appointments and the distribution of infrastructures, but the minority—especially in the Delta areas of the oil-producing region—would want more functional roles in government. On many occasions, the oil-producing regions have usurped the laws and frictions developed between them. The federal government had to break it up. It is to be noted that the oil-producing regions have been neglected even by other administrations.

POLITICAL STRUCTURE

It is open to question whether we can realistically describe the "structure" of the decision-making process in a country that has experienced five successful coups, three civilian constitutions, and a particularly amorphous arrangement from President Babangida's annulment of the 1993 elections to the election of Obasanjo in February 1999. It is, however, useful to be familiar with the range of constitutional arrangements the country has known and the patterns in their evolution.

The first political institution in which Nigerians participated as Nigerians was the legislative council mandated by the Clifford Constitution of 1922, which provided for elected representatives from Lagos. Elections were introduced in this way and stimulated political activity. Through successive constitutional changes in the 1940s and 1950s, elective office was extended to local and regional governments and the first provisions for a federal structure were introduced.

The Development of the Constitution of 1999

As Babangida postponed the return to civilian rule in 1993, his standing with the population, and even within the military, moved ever lower. When he delayed announcing the outcome of the June 12, 1993, presidential election, apprehensions grew, for it was popularly believed that Moshood Abiola had won. Two days after the election, initial results released by the National Election Commission (NEC) showed that Abiola had won in eleven of fourteen states. Later, a private human rights coalition, the Campaign for

Democracy, published election results indicating that Abiola had won in nineteen of the thirty states. A few days later, the military government declared the election invalid. At the same time, Babangida promised new elections, and once again promised a return to civilian rule. He appointed a transition committee chaired by a Yoruba, Ernest Shonekan, and Babangida vacated the capital without fanfare—in a technical sense meeting his deadline for the restoration of civilian rule. However, Shonekan had virtually no support and was pushed aside by General Sani Abacha three months later in November 1993. General Abacha maintained the myth of a return to civilian government and created the Constitutional Conference to draft yet another governing document. The Constitutional Conference was inaugurated on June 27, 1994, but two weeks earlier, on the anniversary of the annulled election, Moshood Abiola had declared himself president. Abiola was arrested on June 23, 1994, and charged with three counts of treason. One count stated that he "solicited, incited, addressed, and endeavored to persuade people to take part in unconstitutionally overthrowing the head of state," an ironic indictment from a government whose leader seized control by force. Abacha seemed to manipulate the system to remain president, but his strategy was aborted by his death of a reported heart attack in May 1998. Meanwhile, Abiola had maintained his claim from prison, but he also died of a reported heart attack two months after Abacha, just as he was negotiating his release with Abacha's successor, Abdulsalami Abubakar. The succession of deaths, first of Shehu Yar'Adua in prison (November 1997), then Abacha (May 1998), and Abiola (July 1998), was seen by many Nigerians as an entirely improbable set of events. Even though the departed represented an extreme range of political positions, conspiracy theories have since then been widely floated.

From 1983 to 1999, politics in Nigeria took the form of a succession of military regimes that constantly planned a return to democracy. Administrative and judicial proceedings continued as though a constitutional structure were in place. The 1995 Constitution was widely discussed and even cited as the basis for election procedures in 1997 and 1998—yet the document was only officially promulgated by General Abubakar in May 1999 as he handed power over to a civilian regime. The overall structure of the current Constitution is outlined in Figure 13.4.

Federalism

In a country as vast and complex as Nigeria, many political decisions are not made at the national level. A federal system was established as Nigeria moved to independence in 1954. In a uniquely Nigerian scenario, two of the regions, the Eastern and the Western, gained self-governing status in 1957; the north followed in 1959. Thus a very decentralized federal system was already in effect at independence. The Constitution of 1960 was explicitly federal, dividing responsibilities between the federal government and the three regions. Federalism has been a constant in the three constitutions (1963, 1979, and 1989) since that time, and in the constitution developed but never promulgated under Abacha in 1995, which Abubakar used as the basis for his return of the country to civilian rule in 1999. Indeed, it is difficult to imagine a stable political structure that would not allow a considerable devolution of power to leaders of the three major ethnic groups at least. There have been two attempts to impose a unitary system: in the first coup in 1966, General Ironsi attempted to end the autonomy of the regions, and there seemed to be a similar thrust in the aborted coup of 1990. In each case, reactions to the suggestion of a unitary system were decidedly cool.

In the face of formal federalism, however, stands a fiscal condition that calls the federal concept into question: all levels of government derive the largest portion of their revenues from the national oil monopoly, distributed through the national government. Beyond this fiscal fact of life, there has been the control of Nigeria by military governments for twenty-nine of forty-seven years of independence. It is difficult to define federalism under a military chain of command. Nonetheless, any permanent civilian constitution will undoubtedly be genuinely federal. As political activists in the south have become convinced that northerners are bent on dominating any central government in Nigeria, they have argued for greater state or regional autonomy. Moreover, with the emergence of militant groups, such as MOSSAB and MEND (see page 406), the federal government has had to confront an increasingly visible and viable secessionist movement in the south.

Some southerners even call for separate military forces for the major regions. We can be certain that defining state and local government boundaries will continue to be a central issue confronting any regime, civilian or military.

The Structure of Government Under the 1999 Constitution

FIGURE 13.4

In our discussion of culture, we noted the effect of ethnic fragmentation on local government boundaries. When the federal military government created 301 local government administrations (LGAs) in 1976, boundary lines were drawn in Lagos with minimal consultation locally, and communities were not allowed to change them. When the country returned to civilian rule in 1979, however, elected officials were much more receptive to demands for subdividing local government areas. Within a year there were 716 local governments, an increase of 238 percent. Naturally, such a large number of local administrations placed a heavy burden on a country with limited financial and human resources. Since the local governments themselves had little potential for generating revenue,

they were unable to provide the services demanded by local populations. Interethnic competition to ensure responsive government produced units that were unable to respond to those who had "won" their own local governments.

The next military government addressed this situation. After seizing power on December 31, 1983, it returned the country to 301 local governments, plus three in the new Federal Capital Territory. Even the military was susceptible to local demands, however: the number again began to grow, and now at the "grassroots" there are 774 LGAs, a new high.

State-level politics has often been dominated by local ethnic rivalries, as states are called upon to settle local government boundary disputes and to decide on the competence of various traditional institutions. Pressures analogous to those at the local level have led to an expansion of the number of states. The three colonial regions, which became the states of federal Nigeria, quickly became four. With the outbreak of civil war in 1967, the country was divided into twelve states, a number that was increased to nineteen in 1976, to thirty in 1991, and to thirty-six in 1996 (plus the Federal Capital Territory; see Figure 13.5).

All these tensions finally converge at the national level, the source of most government resources. Recent federal governments have attempted to calm the ethnic struggle with a Nigerian version of affirmative action based on the country's "federal character." Various regions (and thus ethnic groups) are guaranteed a proportionate share of federal positions. This is an application of the consociational model, a common solution where countries are deeply divided by religion or ethnicity.[33] If appointments were made on competence alone, the educational advantage of the southernmost populations would result in their having a disproportionate share of civil service jobs. The major exception to apportioning positions according to federal character may be an indication of priorities. The Nigerian national football (soccer) team is not selected with attention to geographic representation!

Both the 1979 and 1989 Constitutions describe a three-level federalism. In such other large federations as the United States, Canada, and Australia, the constitution focuses on the federal–state relationship, with local government principally in the domain of the state or province. The fact that Nigerian constitutions have specified a uniform structure and common functions for local government is rather unusual. While there are no doubt advantages to this uniformity of structure and function, it does not allow for local governments to reflect the diversity of local cultures present in the country, nor is experimentation possible of the sort that has produced the manager and commission systems at the local level in the United States. Since colonial times, however, local government has really been little more than local administration of federal policy, a situation unlikely to change until local governments acquire independent sources of revenue. Clearly, in an oil-centralized system the demand for local governments cannot be explained by the control of decision making. Rather, ever more local government is attractive because of the formula-driven allocation of funds that supports local activities. In 1981, the Second Republic's National

Assembly decided to allocate 10 percent of federal revenues and 10 percent of state revenues to the localities. However, not only were state governments unwilling to abide by this mandate, but they frequently tapped for their own purposes the federal allocation that was transmitted to them for distribution at the local level. To remedy this situation, the 1989 Constitution provided direct payment of the federal allocation to local governments; in 1990 that allocation was increased to 15 percent, and a few years later to 20 percent of federal revenues, where it stands as of 2007.

The process of subdividing administrative and political units has fueled a growth of the public sector. Employment in the public service is an indicator of the growth of government. At independence, there were 71,693 employees of federal and regional government; by 1974 there were about 630,000, not counting the 250,000 in military service. A study of local governments in 1978 and 1979 found another 386,600 positions at that level, not counting general laborers or district or village heads. The drop in oil revenues in the mid-1980s brought an end to government growth. However, the Buhari administration imposed a 15 percent across-the-board personnel reduction that started a long period of stability in government employment.[34] Since 1999 competition among states for the distribution of federal revenues is acute in two arenas: first in disagreements between the president and the National Assembly over the amount of money that should be returned to the oil-producing areas, or what Nigerians refer to as the "derivation formula." Second, the controversy has played out between the states and the federal government in a series of major Supreme Court decisions in 2002 concerning states' entitlement to off-shore oil revenues and the federal government's right to exempt certain expenses from funds distributed under the derivation formula.

Some suggest that a genuine federalism would help to cure Nigeria's political problems, which almost always involve the tremendously large stakes in the oil-rich nation's federal government. Perhaps a national government with limited resources would result in a federation that is not viewed as a high-stakes zero-sum game.

Parliamentary vs. Presidential Government

Without exception, British colonies came to independence with a parliamentary system based on the mother country's Westminster model. Initially, Nigeria

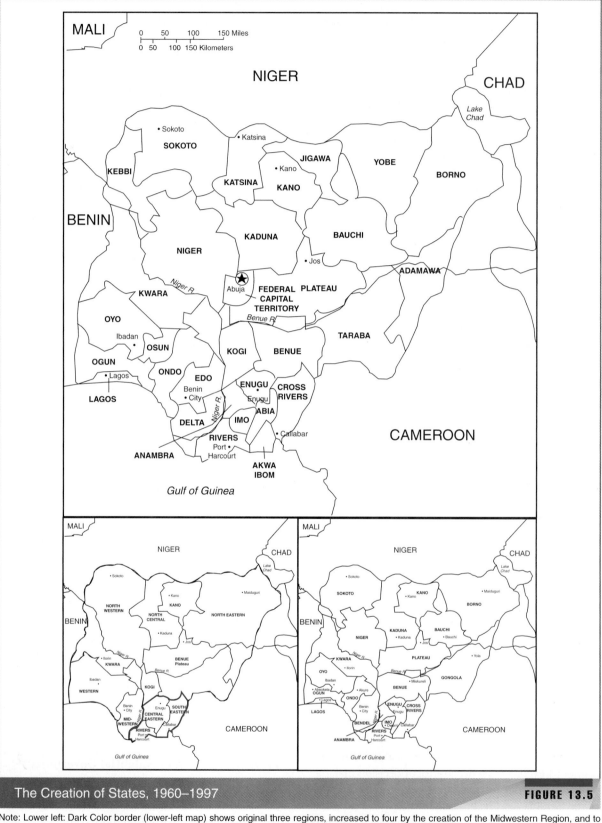

The Creation of States, 1960–1997

FIGURE 13.5

Note: Lower left: Dark Color border (lower-left map) shows original three regions, increased to four by the creation of the Midwestern Region, and to twelve in 1967. Lower right: Nineteen states, 1976–1991. Above: 30 states, 1991–1997. (Current 36 states are shown at the beginning of the chapter.)

followed the Commonwealth pattern, with a ceremonial governor-general named by the British monarch. In 1963, the formal structure was redesignated a republic, with Nnamdi Azikiwe as president with mostly ceremonial powers; the parliamentary system was maintained, with a prime minister as head of government. Because Nigeria's first experience with civilian rule ended disastrously in 1966, it is not surprising that the previous system was called into question as a new constitution was being framed in the 1970s. The 1979 Constitution of the Second Republic was unabashedly modeled on the U.S. presidential model: an independently elected president was balanced against a two-house National Assembly at the federal level, with governors and legislatures following the same model at the state level. The disorder in the Second Republic might have brought presidentialism into disrepute as well, but the principal aspects of the presidential system were maintained in the 1989 and 1995 Constitutions.

The 1999 Constitution provides for an independently elected president and a dual chamber National Assembly at the federal level. Governors and single-house legislatures follow the same basic model at the state level. The speaker of the house presides over the House of Representatives, while the president of the Senate, who is in the line of presidential succession after the vice president of the republic, presides over the upper chamber. Each of Nigeria's thirty-six states has three senators (plus one for the Federal Capital Territory of Abuja), while population determines the number of constituencies in each state for a total of 360 representatives. Senators and representatives serve four-year terms and are elected at the same time, rather than in staggered elections. One legacy of the long years of military rule is that many of the legislators elected in 1999—nearly 80 percent in each chamber—had no previous legislative experience. There are about sixty standing committees in each chamber with jurisdiction over different issues. Committees are still getting accustomed to their role in the legislative process, and many bills are not amended or debated until they reach the floor for debate. As permitted by the Constitution, the Executive Branch introduced the federal budget and other major pieces of legislation, and how much the National Assembly can or should modify these bills has been a hotly contested issue since the transition to democracy. Differences of opinion between the two branches of government have been dramatic, even though the president's party has consistently enjoyed a majority in both legislative chambers since 1999.

Nigeria's problems with achieving stable constitutional rule have made it an important case study in arguments over the relative advantages of the two systems in conditions of cultural pluralism. On the face of it, the fault may seem to lie with defects in the various constitutional frameworks, but the problem may actually be the intractable nature of Nigerian pluralism. A constitutional document cannot succeed at papering over a lack of trust among the country's subcultures. The lack of trust has led to suggestions of a "zoning" arrangement, which would require that the presidency and other top posts rotate automatically among the various geographical "zones" in the country, such that every major group could have a turn. The Constitutional Conference of 1995 gave a general endorsement to zoning at all levels of government—that is, for governorships of states and chairmanships of local governments as well as at the federal level. The National Assembly proposed similar constitutional reforms in 2001. But would such a plan really inspire trust, or would it inspire officeholders to even more rapacious rent seeking, knowing they would be in a given office only for one term?

The Judiciary

Nigeria came to independence with a well-established legal system that included a court system and a thriving legal profession in the British tradition. The federal and state courts are integrated into a single system of trial and appeal courts. Thus the 1999 Constitution provides a Supreme Court, a Court of Appeal, and state and federal High Courts with original and appellate jurisdictions. Traditional authorities maintain their greatest influence in their judicial powers, for states are explicitly allowed to constitute customary and Sharia (Muslim Koranic law) courts, both original and appellate. Ten northern states maintain Sharia courts, a point of contention between Muslim authorities and those who see such official recognition as divisive.

It has been one of the greater anomalies of Nigeria's often chaotic politics that the independent judiciary has survived, even through military regimes that rule by decree. The final blow to judicial independence may have come, however, under the Abacha regime, which showed no inclination to respect any semblance of legal system autonomy. It reacted to court orders by changing the rules—even constitutional provisions—that might be used against it. It also established special military tribunals for robbery and firearms violations, for the trial of Ken Saro-Wiwa and others in Ogoniland, and for those accused of supporting coups against Abacha in 1995 and 1997.

INTEREST ARTICULATION

There are at least two aspects of political influence in Nigeria. First is the effect of organized interest groups, such as unions and trade associations and religious bodies. The second involves the more informal channels of participation through individual relationships often described by the term "clientelism."

Nigerian author Wole Soyinka describes how some of the first formal interest groups formed during the colonial period out of previously nonpolitical associations:

> Much later, we heard of the formation of the Nigerian Women's Union. The movement of the *onikaba*, begun over cups of tea and sandwiches to resolve the problem of newly-weds who lacked the necessary social graces, was becoming popular and nation-wide. And it became all tangled up in the move to put an end to the rule of white men in the country.[35]

The activities of formal associations and institutions often offer the most vigorous expression of societal independence from a government. Characteristically, voluntary associations were either brought under control or abolished in the authoritarian regimes that took hold in Africa soon after independence. This was not, however, the case in Nigeria, where even during military regimes organizations such as the Nigerian Women's Union have maintained an independent existence, even as their political influence was reduced.

Ethnic and Religious Associations

Many of the first formal associations in Nigeria had an ethnic base. The Igbo Federal Union (later the Igbo State Union) was "inaugurated by politically conscious representatives of the Igbo intelligentsia."[36] The Egbe Omo Oduduwa was organized among young, urban, Yoruba professionals. Minority groups especially found comfort in formal associations such as

the Ibibio State Union, the Edo National Union, the Urhobo Renascent Convention, and others. These associations often formed the organizational base for parties, and contributed to the latter associations' ethnic orientations. In the north, where individual clientelist ties are relatively stronger, associations even of the ethnic type have played less of a role. An ethnic association of contemporary significance is the Movement for the Survival of the Ogoni People (MOSOP), founded by **Ken Saro-Wiwa.** MOSOP claims to speak for the 500,000 Ogoni people whose land is now occupied by Shell Oil drilling rigs. The Ogoni complain that they have borne the brunt of the inconvenience of Nigeria's oil industry and have received little in return. By the early 1990s they had begun to disrupt production, and Saro-Wiwa was arrested. He won his freedom and continued to campaign overseas against Shell Oil and the Nigerian government. When four Ogoni chiefs were murdered by young militants, Saro-Wiwa was again placed under arrest (along with fourteen other Ogonis) and charged with murder for inciting the youths. In October 1995, he and eight codefendants were convicted by a military court. In November they were hanged, despite pleas of clemency from around the world. After five years in the grave, in July 2002, the federal government allowed their families to exhume bodies of Ken Saro-Wiwa and others for a proper burial.

As in many other countries, religious institutions and associations play an important part in Nigerian politics. These groups are especially durable and resilient, because when political activity is repressed they remain organized around denominational objectives, and where an ethnic association might have to play a less obvious role, neither Christian nor Muslim religious groups and leaders find it necessary to camouflage their identities. As in other countries, religious-based interest groups take several forms: the formal institutions (churches, Koranic schools), leadership roles such as bishops, pastors, and *mallams* (Muslim teachers and learned men), and voluntary denominational associations. The effectiveness of religious institutions in articulating concerns to government has been reduced by intergroup conflicts, most frequently between Christians and Muslims, that put the government in the role of mediator.

Not surprisingly, associational life is most active in the south; however, the north is home to an Islamic "mystic brotherhood," the Tijaniyya, which is particularly influential among lower-class Hausa Muslims and is looked on with suspicion by the representatives of orthodox Islam (another brotherhood, the Khadiriyya, is identified with the traditional elite of the north). The existence of such groups blurs the distinction between "modern" associations and "traditional" institutions. A new breed of ethnic organizations has emerged under democracy, with groups such as the Arewa People's Congress, which declares its mission as "defending northern interests," and the Odua People's Congress militating for its version of Yoruba interests in the southwest.

Associational Groups

In the more urban and industrialized areas of the country, one encounters a range of associational interest groups common to the politics of any modern nation. Trade unions have played a role in Nigerian politics since the colonial period, sometimes collectively through the Nigerian Labor Congress (NLC) and its seventeen affiliated unions. However, labor action is organized more frequently by sector. Groups representing the petroleum workers can have an immediate impact on the national economy and consequently have the potential for great political influence, as was demonstrated in 1994 strike actions by the **National Union of Petroleum and Gas Workers (NUPENG)** and the Petroleum and Natural Gas Senior Staff Association (PENGASSAN). Groups such as the Nigerian Union of Local Government Employees (NULGE) are especially influential because of their immediate impact on government.

Professional organizations—such as the Nigerian Bar Association, the Nigerian Medical Association, and especially the Nigerian Union of Journalists—are politicized as issues concern them directly. Military governments periodically force the dissolution of such groups by arresting their leaders. After the NLC met in Kaduna in July 1994 and voted a general strike, the Abacha government arrested Frank Kokori, secretary of NUPENG, and most members of the petroleum industry unions eventually returned to work. (Kokori was one of the first political prisoners released by General Abubakar following the death of Abacha.)

The universities are another modern sector that has a tradition of political activism. Faculty (the term "staff" is used in Nigeria), as well as students, were some of the earliest critics of military rule, and military governments have tried to marginalize their

role in the country. Strikes by staff and students are common, and the campuses were the most vocal opponents of Abacha's continuation of military rule. However, because recent military regimes have been content to let the universities deteriorate, campus political activities have not had the impact on policy as have parallel actions of, say, petroleum workers.

The National Democratic Coalition (NADECO) and the Campaign for Democracy (CD) are groupings of civil rights and democracy activists that are particularly influential in intellectual circles and among students. In 1994 they were at the front of much anti-Abacha activity. These groups played leading roles criticizing General Abubakar's approach to a return to civilian rule.

During the long periods of military rule, politicians at all levels who were turned out by the military have constituted an interest group united around their desire to be allowed back into the circles of power. They were a force pushing for the return to civilian rule, even as many of them were content to be "co-opted" into administrative service under the military.

Nonassociational Groups

A clear Nigerian example of the nonassociational interest group, but shadowy in its definition, is the famous **"Kaduna Mafia."** Hardly any informal conversation on Nigerian politics fails to mention this network of powerful northern leaders who are said to maintain strong influence over the military and Nigerian politics. Richard Joseph offers this description:

> In a general sense [Kaduna Mafia] refers to members of the northern intelligentsia who assumed positions of political and social influence during the decade of military rule after the civil war. These individuals are, on the whole, better educated than their predecessors in the emirate North who held similar positions in the first decade after independence. [They also] were less dependent on the patronage of the traditional rulers to advance in their careers.[37]

This group was highly influential in the Babangida years, but Sani Abacha distanced himself from it, and the arrest and death in prison in 1997 of General Yar'Adua, a leading figure in the Kaduna Mafia, suggests that the organization has lost its influence, at least temporarily.

Given that most of Nigeria's labor force is involved in agriculture, one expects to find strong associational activity among farmers. However, the ethnic divisions in the country have prevented the formation of any national-level farm organizations. Those groups that do exist are usually engaged in local cooperative activities and are not active beyond the regional level. More commonly, the interest articulation activities of farmers are of the anomic protest variety (that is, spontaneous and unorganized), or take the form of clientelism (as we will discuss later).

Finally, one institution is far more than an interest group: the military itself. We will address its political role later. The Nigerian military is not a cohesive interest, as was demonstrated in the transition from Abacha to Abubakar. The enlisted personnel and lower ranking officers have not seen any direct benefit from military rule, and many supported efforts to return to civilian rule. Also, the country's ethnic divisions are reflected in the military as well, although they compete there with a well-ingrained military professionalism. The military rank-and-file were originally drawn mostly from northern non-Hausa minorities. Later recruitment drew from all over the country, but the minorities, especially from the "Middle Belt," remain disproportionately numerous. The early preponderance of Igbo officers ended with the second coup and the Biafran civil war, which resulted in the northern dominance in the officer corps that is present today. However, there is wide ethnic diversity among the officers, and ethnicity is only one factor in the complex disputes within the military. There is a constant possibility that new factions will emerge to challenge the current leadership, to forestall or delay the return to civilian control. The Abacha regime cited a conspiracy to that end when, in March 1995, it ordered the arrest of "a group of over-ambitious and misguided officers and civilians." According to then second-in-command General Oladipo Diya, the coup plotters included "a cross-section of the country, officers from all parts of the country." Ironically, Diya himself was arrested as part of an alleged coup plot two years later.

The role of a vital civil society as a balance to political authority was played by a range of interest groups in the wake of General Sani Abacha's seizure of power in November 1993. Trade unions and unions of the academic staff at secondary schools and the universities engaged in a series of strikes against the Abacha regime. These activities were designed to force Abacha to release Moshood Abiola from prison, to agree to political activity on Abiola's part, and to turn over power to a civilian regime. Their strike stimulated an increase in world prices of raw crude oil and in pressing shortages in refined petroleum products in Nigeria. Abacha responded by arresting the union leaders and replacing them with his handpicked successors. Many Nigerians thought that strike and demonstration action would force Abacha out, but he stubbornly clung to power until his death.

Abacha's regime was not without substantial support. An organization called the Association for a Better Nigeria, formed under Babangida, went to court to seek an injunction against certification of the 1993 election. This and other associations represented those in the country who profited from the existing arrangement and were not eager for a new constitutional regime, and so continued their vocal support of the Babangida and Abacha regimes both in Nigeria and abroad. These elements were largely discredited after Abacha's death, and a number of their leaders made public pleas for forgiveness.

Patron-Client Networks

An alternative structure for interest representation is found in the **patron-client network.** Powerful Nigerian political figures are able to mobilize support through personal "connections" with subordinates, who may themselves serve in a corresponding role of "patron" for a yet-lower set of "clients." **Clientelism** was an integral aspect of political life in the larger-scale precolonial systems of the Hausa, the Yoruba, and others. Those who are not represented by formal associations may be able to take advantage of their connections to achieve political ends, particularly at the local level, and where traditional rulers and their political systems maintain some influence. Furthermore, the pattern of personal contacts is ingrained in the culture and thus remains important as an approach to powerful modern figures independent of any local traditional context.

Resting on these patron-client networks in Nigeria is a patronage system in which a ruler or an official gives a public office to an individual client in return for his loyalty in delivering political support at some lower level. The prevalence of such a system in Nigeria is not dependent on particular regimes, civilian or military.[38] Their durability makes the "restructuring" of Nigerian administration difficult when regimes are under pressure to develop an "austerity" budget.

POLITICAL PARTICIPATION

The forms of action that Nigerians take in pursuit of political goals cover the whole spectrum of possibilities, from voting to participating in the terribly violent civil war of 1967–1970. Given the lack of either good census data or reliable voter registration figures, it is difficult to be precise about voter turnout figures, but estimates are in the range of 40 to 60 percent in some earlier elections, an impressive level for a majority poor and illiterate populace. Some of the explanation is found in the prevalence of patron-client systems, the "machine politics" that ties ordinary voters into the electoral process through personalistic ties with political activists.

Interest in elections, even in the mobilization of patron-client networks, declined during the long transition to civilian rule, but it rose again with the return to civilian rule. In the presidential election of February 1999, turnout was estimated at 52 percent. Voter turnout for the 2003 election was an estimated 69 percent.

Violence also is employed frequently, from the use of "thugs" by political parties in both republics to the confrontations with police in Lagos and the southwest during the last days of the Babangida regime and in the challenges to Abacha's seizure of power. Violence by the state, although less common than in many authoritarian regimes, has played a major role in Nigeria politics: upward of fifty people were executed for participating in the failed coups of 1986 and 1990; death sentences against those accused in 1995 were not carried out, only because members of the PRC could not agree among themselves on whether to do so. The greatest example of political violence was, of course, the Biafran civil war in 1969 to 1996. Nigeria has experienced over 2 million deaths in wars from 1960 to 1992, the vast majority of them during the civil war.

Nigeria has been a highly politicized country ever since independence, although alienation and frustration with the failure to develop stable, honest, and responsive institutions are increasingly evident.

PARTIES AND ELECTIONS

After the Babangida government voided the national elections of 1993 and Abacha came to power, party activities were banned in Nigeria. The exception was the artificially created five-party system that contested local and state elections under Abacha; these parties were allowed to exist only if they refrained from any criticism of the regime, and they leaned so far in the other direction that all five named Abacha their presidential candidate! In 1998 the Abubakar regime allowed new parties to be formed and contested the 1998–1999 elections. The rebirth of party activity is evidence that the evolution of political parties and their effect on Nigerian politics are worthy of attention.[39]

The first modern party was formed by Herbert Macaulay in Lagos in 1923. Several such movements contended for power at the local level under the colonial regime, and a diverse nationalist movement emerged in 1944, under the leadership of Macaulay and Nnamdi Azikiwe, the National Council of Nigeria and the Cameroons (NCNC).[40] This organization advocated increased representation in the Nigerian colonial government. Chapters were established across Nigeria. However, when the British introduced a more democratic and decentralized constitution in 1951, the NCNC broke up along ethnic lines. The 1951 Constitution mandated indirect assembly elections in the three regions; Lagos was in the Western Region, where the Yoruba were in the majority. An opposition party, the Action Group (AG), emerged under the leadership of a young Yoruba lawyer, Obafemi Awolowo, with an initial organizational base in the Egbe Omo Oduduwa, a Yoruba cultural society. Although Azikiwe's NCNC won in multiethnic Lagos, the AG won the majority of seats in the Western Region. The NCNC won overall in the Eastern Region, where Azikiwe's own Igbo ethnic group was in the majority.

From the beginning there were forces within both the NCNC and the AG arguing for movement in a multicultural, issue-based, cross-regional direction. The AG was especially split along liberal (cross-regional, pushing for quick movement toward independence) and conservative (ethnic-based, evolutionary) lines. Elected offices were first established regionally, and only later (in 1957) at the national level. This favored the forces of regionalism. Azikiwe particularly was committed to action at the national level, but it became clear that a regional power base was essential, and Azikiwe also was constrained to center his party on its strength in the east. Thus the NCNC came to be identified with that region and the Igbo people (see Table 13.2).

In the north, Britain's successful application of indirect rule had resulted in an alliance between the

This is President Olusegun Obasanjo in a full Yoruba Agbada dress campaigning to the Yoruba people of the southwest—his own ethnic group—for his second term. In 1999, he did not get good support from the Yoruba. But in the election of 2003, the Yorubas gave him overwhelming support, because he had proved himself as a worthy leader.

AP Images

Ethnic Distribution of Party Leaders, 1958			TABLE 13.2
Party*	Igbo	Yoruba	Hausa-Fulani
NCNC	49.3	26.7	2.8
AG	4.5	68.2	3.0
NPC	—	6.8	51.3

*NCNC: National Council of Nigeria and the Cameroons; AG: Action Group; NPC: Northern People's Congress.

Source: Richard Sklar and C. S. Whitaker, Jr., "Nigeria," in James S. Coleman and Carl Rosberg, eds., *Political Parties and National Integration in Tropical Africa* (Berkeley: University of California Press, 1964).

colonial administration and the traditional emirs that impeded the formation of modern political movements. Whereas in the south such movements had arisen among a Western-educated elite outside the control of any traditional authority, in the north the only youth to receive a modern education came from the families of the traditional elites. Although reformist political organizations were formed—notably the Northern Elements' Progressive Union (NEPU) under Mallam Aminu Kano—they operated only at the margins and tension points of the emirates. A more conservative movement, the Northern Peoples' Congress (NPC), was taken over by the Sardauna (a traditional title) of Sokoto and a Hausa commoner, Abubakar Tafawa Balewa. The NPC, the traditional

emirates, and the preindependence administrative structure were intertwined such that young administrators could run successfully for public office, but only if they had the support of their administrative superiors and of the local traditional elite. This political structure grew up among a population that was not as educated (less than 15 percent were literate) as in the south, and that was much more loyal to their traditional authorities. In the 1959 Northern House of Assembly, 24 percent of NPC delegates were sons of incumbent or former emirs, and over a third were blood relatives of emirs. The elite origins of the party's officers and candidates were de-emphasized through both communal (ethnic) and religious (Islamic) appeals to the electorate. Not surprisingly, the NPC did not give high priority in its program to achieving national independence. The NPC was challenged in northern elections, but with only occasional success. Unlike the NCNC and AG, neither the NPC nor its northern rivals even tried to obtain political support outside their own region.

When General Ironsi assumed power following the breakdown of political order in the Western Region and the first coup, one of his first moves was to abolish all parties and a large number of political associations. The country remained without formal parties from 1966 until the preparations for a return to civilian rule in 1979. General Yakubu Gowon (head of state from 1966 to 1975) had considered the creation of a one-party state in Nigeria, with himself as leader of a "national movement." Nigeria's diversity and the plurality of its power bases made that concept impossible to achieve: to northern leaders, it suggested southern domination, while to the politicians waiting for the return of civilian rule, it meant the end of their ambitions. Gowon was unable to decide on a course of action and was deposed before any plan had been adopted.

After taking power, Murtala Muhammed set in motion a process to return to civilian rule. The military regime established the Constitution Drafting Committee, and in his address to its opening session, Murtala Muhammed laid down several principles relating to parties. He encouraged them to "discover some means by which Government can be formed without the involvement of political parties," but otherwise that they should draft a plan to guarantee "genuine and truly national political parties," while striving to work out "specific criteria by which their number would be limited."[41] The drafters responded with a constitution that was carefully crafted to promote national parties. It specified that to be elected president, a candidate would have to poll at least 25 percent of the votes cast in each of at least two-thirds of the states. Elections were to be controlled by the Federal Election Commission (FEDECO), with which all parties must register. Parties were to offer membership to any Nigerian, and party governing boards were to reflect the country's "federal character"—specifically, coming from at least two-thirds of the states. The Electoral Decree was published in 1978; in that same year political parties were again made legal, and they came in a flood—some 150 were formed.

The elections of 1979 and 1983 are difficult to analyze because five parties competed for president, Senate and House seats, and state assemblies with varying degrees of success. Looking at the Senate, House, and state assemblies overall, most states were controlled by a single party. Awolowo's United Party dominated five of the nineteen states, all in the Yoruba west and the midwest (a "minority" area). Azikiwe's NPP carried three states, two of which were in the Igbo-dominated east. Aminu Kano's northern opposition party carried only its leader's own state, Kano, in the north. The GNPP won two states in the northeast, home region of its presidential candidate. However, the ethnic factor was complicated by the success of the NPN in building cross-regional alliances. The NPN

controlled eight states; five of these were in the north, but three were in the southeast.

In order to participate in the elections of 1998 and 1999, parties were required to demonstrate a nationwide organization. On the basis of the cases they submitted, nine parties were qualified to compete in the local elections of December 1998. The three parties that received the highest number of votes in the 774 local governments were then allowed to compete in the state and national elections of 1999. The People's Democratic Party (PDP) won in 389 local governments, the All People's Party (APP) in 182, and the Alliance for Democracy (AD) in 100, with other parties winning in the remaining 103. As the presidential elections of February 1999 approached, the APP and AD negotiated to present a single candidate—in other words, the normal effect of a winner-take-all situation pushed toward the creation of a two-party system. There were ultimately just two candidates, Olusegun Obasanjo representing the PDP and Olu Falae leading the APP. Obasanjo won with 62.8 percent compared with Falae's 37.2 percent. The **Independent National Election Commission (INEC)** created by the Abubakar regime for this election declared Obasanjo the winner.

In 2003, Obasanjo ran for reelection. The APP, which had in the meantime renamed itself the **All Nigeria People's Party (ANPP),** selected Muhammed Buhari, another former military ruler, as its presidential candidate. Despite the internal tensions in the PDP, the party increased its majority in both houses of Congress and won twenty-eight out of thirty-six governorships. Obasanjo was reelected by a landslide, winning almost twice as many votes as Buhari. He and the PDP particularly improved their position in the southwest, where they captured five governorships from the AD. Table 13.3 shows the results of the 2003 elections. At every level, the PDP consistently demonstrated its dominance. Because of the very public tensions between President Obasanjo and Vice President Atiku Abubakar, the future of the PDP is uncertain. The party expelled Abubakar in 2006 following the corruption charges against him, but he continued to campaign for president. The broader party system is also in flux, as INEC has registered a score of new parties. The PDP secured majorities in the House and Senate again in 2007, and won most of the governorships. But many results are being contested and elections will be re-run in several states.

	PDP (%)	ANPP (%)	AD (%)	Others (%)
TABLE 13.3 — Results of 2003 National Elections				
Presidential vote	61.9	32.2	Did not contest	5.9
National assembly vote (seats)	54.5 (213)	27.4 (95)	9.3 (31)	8.8 (7)
Senate vote (seats)	53.7 (73)	27.9 (28)	9.7 (6)	8.7 (0)

Note: PDP: People's Democratic Party; ANPP: All Nigeria People's Party; AD: Alliance for Democracy.

Source: The Independent National Electoral Commission, preliminary results. http://www.inecnigeria.org.

Ethnic Solidarity and Party Loyalty

Figure 13.6 shows the formation of Nigerian political parties, notably their reemergence with the same ethnic bases after suppression by military regimes. Governments, especially the military ones, have tried to force Nigerians to express their will through cross-ethnic parties. However, because ethnicity drives much of the political organizing in the country, political leaders have succeeded in subverting the goal of truly national parties through their calls to ethnic identity. A political career is started in a local community on an ethnic basis, and a cross-ethnic party is, in that situation, nothing more than a coalition of ethnic interests. The Hausas have been most successful in this situation; they captured the presidency each time this national office was filled by election until Obasanjo's victory in 1999. With envy and bitterness, many political activists in the south were convinced that the Hausas knew they could assemble an electoral majority under their control and that they act accordingly. Many charged that Obasanjo, although not Hausa, could not have won without their support and was in effect the "northern" candidate.

The NPN won the ultimate prize, the presidency, in 1979, essentially on the basis of a combination of northern voters and minority voters in the southern regions. The most significant difference for parties between the First and Second Republics turned out to be the carving up of the original three regions into nineteen states. Ethnic groups other than the "big three" were dominant in a number of these states and had thus broken free of regional ethnic dominance. Party strategists henceforth combined a strong base in one of the main ethnic group areas with a successful appeal for support among minorities and potentially among dissident groups in the home bases of the other two major groups.

The same five parties remained in existence through the four years of the Second Republic, and contested again in 1983 for the presidency, seats in the Senate and House, and state-level positions. However, the smallest parties, the PRP and the GNPP, had been weakened by their lack of access to resources. And, as is normal in a presidential system where the ultimate prize, the presidency, is a winner-take-all election, there were pressures on the two major opposition parties to combine against the incumbent. Such cooperation proved impossible, however, when neither Azikiwe nor Awolowo would defer to the other as presidential candidate. In a campaign marked with violence and vote-rigging, the NPN won a solid victory, recording gains against the opposing parties in their home areas.

The NPN victory was short-lived. Three months into its second term it met an early demise at the hands of Nigeria's fourth military coup. Party financing in the 1983 elections was based on unprecedented political corruption, even as the country's financial situation had greatly deteriorated, and was among the reasons offered by the military for again abolishing the country's political parties. The public's acceptance of that action was rooted in the civilian government's failure to address in policy the issues raised during the campaign. For example, both the UPN and the NPP promised full employment and free education at all levels. These promises were beyond the regime's fiscal capacity and showed a serious lack of responsibility; it is not surprising that they contributed to voter cynicism.

The two-year reign of Muhammadu Buhari (1983–1985) presented no timetable for a return to electoral politics. However, Buhari's successor, Ibrahim Babangida, began outlining conditions for a return to civilian rule in 1986 that revealed his view of the country's problems. Babangida announced that forty-nine politicians convicted of corruption would be banned

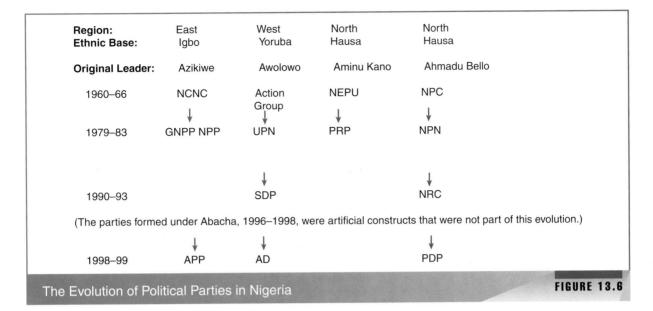

Region:	East	West	North	North
Ethnic Base:	Igbo	Yoruba	Hausa	Hausa
Original Leader:	Azikiwe	Awolowo	Aminu Kano	Ahmadu Bello
1960–66	NCNC	Action Group	NEPU	NPC
1979–83	GNPP NPP	UPN	PRP	NPN
1990–93		SDP		NRC

(The parties formed under Abacha, 1996–1998, were artificial constructs that were not part of this evolution.)

| 1998–99 | APP | AD | | PDP |

The Evolution of Political Parties in Nigeria   **FIGURE 13.6**

from politics for life. Between 1987 and 1989, a series of decrees created the National Election Commission (NEC) to replace the defunct FEDECO in managing the electoral process. The NEC provided for nonpartisan local council elections in 1987; set a timetable for the creation of political parties and the sequential election of legislators and executives at the local, state, and national levels; and promulgated a constitution to come into effect in 1992.

The NEC was entrusted with the task of establishing guidelines for party formation that would result in the emergence of a de facto two-party system. In 1989 the ban on party activities was lifted and associations were invited to form, with the proviso that they have a national following and an internally democratic structure. Some fifty parties sprang up overnight.

The effect of forcing a two-party system on this political chaos was not clear. Some feared it would lead to a polarization along north-south, Christian-Muslim lines. Such a polarization would imply the papering over of serious splits among northerners and between powerful interests in the southeast and southwest; in this context, the emergence of two monolithic political movements would not automatically occur. Thirteen groups eventually petitioned the NEC for recognition. After careful scrutiny, the NEC certified five parties to the Armed Forces Ruling Council (AFRC). The AFRC response was extremely innovative: all thirteen associations, including those certified

by the NEC, were dissolved, and two parties were established by the military government, perhaps the only time in history that an authoritarian leadership had imposed a two-party system!

Babangida charged the NEC to examine the various documents of the dissolved parties and synthesize them into two discrete philosophies, one for a party "a little to the left," the other to fit a party "a little to the right" on the political spectrum. However, they were to have identical constitutions, providing for the choice of candidates by primary election. Even the parties' names were assigned by the government: the party on the left would be the Social Democratic Party, that on the right the National Republican Council. The impact of the American model on Nigerian constitution-making had never been more obvious.

The government built headquarters buildings for both parties at each local government and provided generous "take-off grants" to sustain their organizing efforts. In a first round of elections, party officials at all levels were elected. However, powerful politicians had naturally formed parallel organizations and set about using their clientelist networks to capture one or the other party at various levels.

Nigerians reacted to these developments with a mixture of cynicism and hope. It was difficult for intellectuals to accept a "democracy" based on parties and elections mandated by an authoritarian government; yet it was the "only game in town" and promised to bring the country back to civilian rule, however constraining the new rules might be. Many participated in the 1990 elections of local government secretaries and councils under the two party labels. The next year saw the election of state governors and legislators and a National Assembly. And the process was inevitably building to the election of a president, in 1992, at which time the military would hand over power.

The process was set back late in 1992, when the regime nullified the results of the parties' efforts to produce presidential candidates. The process had indeed been so poorly handled as to justify a postponement of the process. Yet Nigerians were ever more skeptical as to whether the military really intended to leave, or were just playing an elaborate game to buy time.

Babangida scheduled a new election for June 1993, ordered the parties to produce new candidates, and set August 27, 1993, as the date for turning over power to the civilian government. Under more careful control, the parties reconvened their national conventions and nominated new candidates. The National Republican Council selected a relatively unknown figure, Bashir Tofa (a Kanuri from the northeast), while the Social Democrats nominated a rich businessman from the southwest, Moshood Abiola. Abiola was inexperienced in politics but, like Tofa, had close ties to the military hierarchy. He seemed to have an ideal combination of identities for Nigeria's plural culture: although a Yoruba, he, like his opponent, was also a Muslim. Significantly, both had been active supporters of the NPN in the Second Republic.

The election finally took place on **June 12, 1993.** Nigerian and international observers reported that it was a generally fair election, certainly the cleanest Nigeria had ever seen; the NRC had not announced any plans to contest the outcome. Perhaps equally as important as its relative fairness, the election produced a unifying outcome that was everything advocates of a two-party system could have desired. Abiola, from the south, appeared to have won a majority of the votes in nine northern states, including his opponent's home state of Kano. The results seemed to suggest that, under a two-party system, factionalism in each region and state could be exploited to prevent a strictly regional outcome.

The 1993 results were never officially announced, however, and two weeks later Babangida annulled the election. "June 12" became a term forever etched into

Nigerian memory, particularly for political activists in the southwest who claimed the Yoruba had been denied the presidency. Party politics, even the contrived variety invented by the Babangida regime, had once again proved to be an exercise unacceptable to the military leadership and their allies. The Abacha regime announced guidelines for the creation of new parties in June 1996, and political entrepreneurs immediately began forming alliances, even though NADECO and other opposition groups denounced the exercise as a sham. We have seen that the five parties certified for local elections in March 1997 all nominated Abacha for the presidency.

On July 20, 1998, Abubakar announced the dissolution of the five parties, the nullification of the local and state elections, and a new start toward democracy with freely formed parties and a promise to hand over power to an elected president on May 29, 1999. A new organ, the Independent National Electoral Commission, was created to supervise the electoral process. Of the nine parties originally certified in October 1998, the three that survived the local elections represented some degree of continuity with earlier party formations—each with a base among one of the three major ethnic groups. However, because of the requirement to have a national base and for other strategic considerations, the candidates of each party were not necessarily of the ethnic group presumably dominant in it. Most importantly, even though the PDP is said to have its base in the north, its leaders threw their support for the presidential nomination to General Obasanjo, who had only recently been released from Abacha's prison. As both a southerner (both he and his principal opponent Olu Falae were Yoruba) and a former military ruler, Obasanjo was seen by many both inside and outside the country as the individual most likely to provide effective leadership in the postmilitary state. However, some of those active in the various human rights and democracy movements were dubious that a former authoritarian leader was an appropriate president for a democratic state, and his northern backing raised doubts among many southerners. And the question still remained: Would the military be ready to return to the barracks? The answer came with the inauguration of Obasanjo as president on May 29, 1999.

For Nigeria's third attempt at democracy to succeed, President Obasanjo's administration will have to tackle significant problems, including a depleted treasury, a bureaucracy in need of retraining, ethnic and religious conflict, economic stagnation, and widespread corruption. Even though the president's party holds a majority in the National Assembly, there have been significant tensions between the executive and legislative branches. Since 1999, corruption investigations have resulted in two changes of leadership in the Senate and one in the House. In 2002, PDP members in the Assembly responded with an impeachment campaign against President Obasanjo.

The elections of April 19, 2003, in Nigeria, were the first civilian-conducted elections in twenty years. This development represents a big step toward establishing an enduring democracy in Nigeria. It was the first election in Nigeria where three retired army generals contested for the presidency. President Olusegun Obasanjo won with 62 percent of the votes to Muhammed Buhari's 32 percent; other candidates had 6 percent, including Odumegu Ojukwu, the former seccessionist leader of Biafra (1967–1970). Olusegun Obasanjo's PDP captured most of the governorships, and supermajorities in the House and Senate. Election observers reported significant irregularities, concluding they "severely limited and even denied in some parties of the country, the ability of Nigerians to express their franchise" during both the legislative and presidential elections. The National Democratic Institute's observation report continued: "The cumulative effect of these problems seriously compromised the integrity of the elections where they occurred." Despite these flaws, Obasanjo was widely accepted as the winner and the international community interpreted the elections as a step toward democracy.

Umar Musa Yar'adua, the governor of Katsina State, emerged as the winner of the 2007 presidential contest. The election marked the first civilian-to-civilian transfer of power in the country's history, although power remained firmly entrenched in the ruling People's Democratic Party. It also marked the return of power to the north, since Yar'adua comes from a traditional Hausa-Fulani background.

International observers and domestic monitors criticized election preparations and the conduct of voting even more harshly than in 2003. The major national civil society coalition, the Transition Monitoring Group, called for the results to be cancelled outright. The European Union's Observation Mission said the "State and Federal elections have fallen far short of basic international and regional standards for democratic elections." A report issued immediately after the elections noted "significant

evidence of fraud" and concluded that the elections "cannot be considered to have been credible." In some states where little or no voting took place, INEC pledged to hold special elections. In 2007 many candidates, including the defeated Vice President Atiku Abubakar, promised to challenge results using election tribunals and the courts. Other politicians, including the defeated ANPP candidate Muhammadu Buhari, expressed little confidence in these procedures given the sluggish dispute resolution process following the 2003 elections. In sum, the peaceful transfer of power is historic but the new government must also overcome lingering doubts about its legitimacy and its commitment to democratic procedures.

POLICY FORMATION AND IMPLEMENTATION

Many people have stopped bothering themselves with classifying African regimes as democratic or otherwise. They instead keep asking: How much do the regimes address themselves to the needs and aspirations of the people? I am one, I tell you, all these noises about democracy and democratic are mere luxuries to the sufferers.[42]

In comparing Nigeria's various civilian and military regimes, the ultimate question must always be their *performance.* This is certainly the "bottom line" for Nigerians, whose support of these various regimes is based on the quality of life they experience under them. This section thus focuses on the *decisions* governments have made, particularly in raising revenues, dispersing funds, and implementing programs; it will also discuss some background issues, such as planning and conducting the federal census, the results of which underlie all policy; and finally it presents the constraints imposed on Nigerian decision making by the outside world, particularly in the World Bank–supported **Structural Adjustment Program (SAP).** Dealing with "SAP," as the economic restructuring program is commonly called, leads us back to the discussion of environment with which we began. Policy relating to Nigeria's international economic situation has responded to initiatives from other African countries, world powers, international organizations, and multinational firms. Here we consider the critical constraints that the world economy puts on the choices available to a Third World country, even one as large and resource-rich as Nigeria.

Extractive Performance

> The tax people brought this paper, they say that, because I have a large farm, I am to get a special assessment. They say that I am *Gbajumo* (well-to-do) because I have a large farm, but they say nothing about the thirteen children and four women who depend on the farm for gari [food], no. They say I am *gbajumo* with a large farm.[43]

Nigeria inherited a fiscal system in 1960 that depended mainly on taxes on international trade. Indirect taxes provided 64 percent of total revenues, direct taxes only 16.5 percent, and other revenues 19 percent. The colonial system had developed a revenue system that operated through agricultural marketing boards. Ostensibly created to provide price stability to farmers, marketing boards accumulated surplus funds in good years that tempted government officials with development projects in mind. Peasant farmers also paid direct taxes, of which they were much more aware: widespread tax riots broke out in the Western Region in 1968 and 1969, a period during which tax collection was halted, eventually to be replaced by a lower, much simpler flat tax.

In the First Republic and under the Gowon administration, the state governments collected the personal income, sales, and poll taxes. Tax collections generally declined as new states were created, without fiscal institutions in place and with smaller tax bases than the old regions. At the same time, rising oil revenues strengthened the fiscal position of the federal government (and those states with oil fields).

Oil production began in earnest in 1958. At independence, the federal government was collecting modest royalties from private Western oil companies. In 1971, within a few years of the Biafran civil war, Nigeria joined the **Organization of Petroleum Exporting Countries (OPEC),** and also formed the **Nigerian National Oil Corporation (NNOC)** to participate directly in oil production. NNOC acquired a one-third interest in the AGIP Company and Elf, both French-controlled firms. At the time, this was seen as retribution for French support of the Biafran separatist effort, but within a few years the government had acquired a majority interest in all oil-production activities. The NNOC was merged with the Ministry of Petroleum Resources to form the Nigerian National Petroleum Corporation. Over this same period (the mid-1970s), petroleum prices had risen dramatically, from $3.30 per barrel in 1972, to $21.60 in 1979. Thus the sale of crude oil directly by the Nigerian federal government to multinational oil companies came to provide the greater part of federal government revenues and, through the federal system, of state and local revenues as well.

In a pattern typical of Third World oil-exporting countries, Nigeria today depends almost entirely on the revenues from this single industry. Since there is no indication that the world's appetite for oil will diminish in the near future, it is a reliable revenue source that substitutes for the various forms of taxes on private income. Nigerians are fortunate that they have not been directly burdened with the cost of supporting government programs; they are perhaps unfortunate that governments, especially authoritarian military regimes, can tap this vast wealth without risking the wrath of taxpayers. The exceptions to this general rule are enterprises and property owners in Lagos state, which has a large share of the country's modern enterprises and generates over half its revenues, and the Ogonis and other peoples who inhabit the oil-producing region, who do not feel they benefit from the natural resources of their home area.

Given their control of vast petroleum reserves, Nigerian regimes have not actively sought large amounts of direct foreign aid. Whereas low-income countries received an average of $10.20 per capita ($24.50 excluding China and India) in 1991, Nigeria's per capita aid totaled only $2.60 that year—a mere 0.8 percent of GNP. At the same time, Nigeria used its oil reserves as the collateral for massive borrowing from foreign and international banks in the 1970s and 1980s. The funds supported massive capital expenditures, and gave Nigeria an enormous external debt, which rose from 10 percent of GNP to 140.5 percent between 1980 and 1995. Oil wealth did not bring the country financial independence; quite the contrary, the debt gave international lenders a predominant voice in Nigeria's allocation of public funding. With the debt payoffs in 2005 and 2006, Nigeria will now be substantially insulated from such outside influences.

Distributive Performance

As a producer of high-grade petroleum, Nigeria has an unusually great potential to move out of the ranks of the less developed into the middle-income nations. In the 1970s, impressive projects, such as road development and irrigation projects as well as the launching of Abuja as the nation's capital, were signs that potential might become reality.

Unfortunately, political corruption grew apace, and probably began consuming a higher proportion of national wealth than in the pre-oil period. When oil revenues suddenly began their decline in 1980, "corruption and mismanagement prevented any kind of disciplined adjustment," and "the economy was plunged into depression and mounting international indebtedness. . . . Sucked dry of revenue by the corruption, mismanagement, and recession, state governments became unable to pay teachers and civil servants or to purchase drugs for hospitals, and many services (including schools) were shut down by strikes."[44]

In spite of the country's raw material advantage, Nigerians have not seen their lives improve in recent years. The United Nations Development Program publishes the Human Development Index based on three factors: life expectancy at birth, adult literacy, and per capita GDP. Table 13.4 shows some development rankings for Nigeria, its immediate neighbors (Benin, Niger, and Cameroon), and a sample of other countries. Nigeria has a rank of 159 out of 177 countries on the HDI, and a rank of 157 on per capita GDP alone. It is not surprising to find the less developed countries low on these listings. However, GDP per capita is a good measure of distributive potential; thus the comparison of per capita GDP and the HDI ratings can be an indicator of how well a country has done for its people compared with other countries with similar capacity. Although the Nigerian data are comparable to those of its neighbors and to Africa as a whole, these data suggest that the Nigerian advantage in oil revenue has had little noticeable impact on the overall quality of life.

Budgetary priorities are important in analyzing distributive performance. In the case of a country ruled by the military for most of the last decade, one might expect that military expenditures would loom especially large. This is not the case in Nigeria, where published sources put the 2000 military budget at $234 million. At the peak of General Abacha's rule, the per capita expenditure on the military was only $2 per annum, for a rank of 154 out of 160 countries. However, there are believed to be significant additional military expenditures that are not publicly reported. Extremely modest in size at independence, Nigeria's armed forces grew to 250,000 at the height of the Biafran civil war. Then the Gowon regime began a program of gradual attrition that reduced the force to about 100,000 in the mid-1980s. Further shrinkage since then has resulted in a total force of 77,000. This still leaves Nigeria a major military force, and despite

TABLE 13.4

Nigeria's Ranking on GDP per Capita and Human Development Index (HDI)

Country	Life Expectancy at Birth, 2004	Adult Literacy Rate (%) 2004	Real GDP per Capita 2004*	Human HDI 2004	Rank in per Capita GDP, 2004	Rank by HDI	Per Capita GDP-HDI
United States	77.5	99.0	39,676	.948	2	8	−6
Japan	82.2	99.0	29,251	.949	18	7	11
Britain	78.5	99.0	30,821	.940	10	15	−5
Mexico	75.3	91.0	9,803	.821	60	53	7
Botswana	34.9	81.2	9,945	.570	58	131	−73
Indonesia	67.2	67.2	3,609	.711	116	108	8
China	71.9	90.9	5,896	.768	90	81	9
Cameroon	45.7	67.9	2,174	.506	131	144	−13
Nigeria	43.4	66.8	1,154	.448	158	159	−1
Benin	54.3	34.7	1,091	.428	161	163	−2
Niger	44.6	28.7	779	.311	170	177	−7

*Note: These figures are in U.S. dollars converted at purchasing power parity (PPP) rates.

Source: United Nations Development Program, *Human Development Report 2006.*

its use as a springboard to political power, Nigeria's army remains one of the more professional on the continent. As we will discuss later, Nigerian leaders have used this military strength to maintain a high profile in West Africa.

Nigerians have a great enthusiasm for education, and parties and regimes have promised universal access to it. Some progress can be noted. In 1964 Nigeria ranked twenty-ninth among African nations in enrollments, with 5 percent of the school-age population in primary school; it was nineteenth in secondary enrollments, with 5 percent of the appropriate age group in school. Ten years later, 24 percent of the school-age population was in school, and Nigeria was fifteenth in Africa on this measure. In 1990, 60 percent of the school-age population was in primary school, an impressive accomplishment given population growth in that period; but it had fallen back to nineteenth in rank on the continent. Current information about primary and secondary enrollment is scarce, but youth literacy was 87 percent in 2000, up from 65 percent in 1985.

The Nigerian government's performance in the area of health has been mediocre. The 1990 expenditure of $906 million was only $9 per capita, compared with a continent-wide average of $24. Part of this poor performance is seen in the low foreign assistance component in Nigeria's effort. Only 6 percent of its health expenditure came from that source, the third lowest proportion in Africa. But here again there has been progress in outcomes: Nigeria's infant mortality rate has dropped from 185 in 1960, to 139 in 1970, 114 in 1980, and 98 in 2003. However the under-age-5 mortality rate per 1,000 births is now 198, meaning nearly 20 percent of Nigerian children do not reach age 5. This trend reflects an unfortunate and perhaps surprising increase over the last several years.

With petroleum firmly established as the major source of foreign exchange in Nigeria, and with that industry under government control, the distribution of wealth is heavily influenced by policy decisions. Private consumption surged as oil revenues multiplied in the 1970s, about 8 percent per year. This average figure conceals tremendous increases in wealth at the top; the lower 40 percent of the population benefited very little. Government expenditure grew at an even greater rate than private consumption, both in absolute terms and as a proportion of GDP.[45] This aspect of expenditure, of course, includes sums lost in corrupt payments to individuals. Nigeria should have reaped another windfall during the Gulf War, as petroleum prices temporarily shot up, but increased revenues never showed up in national accounts. In 1994, economist Pius Okigbo examined the books of the Central Bank of Nigeria; he reported (as he left the country) that $12.6 billion were not accounted for. The skimming of oil profits had indeed reached astronomical proportions.

Income distribution is also affected by inflation, which followed from the rapid increase in the money supply during the 1970s oil boom and continued apace later on, as governments followed a time-honored approach to balancing budgets when revenues decline: they printed money. The result was continuous inflation, a problem that became especially serious in the 1990s, as shown in Figure 13.7. The case study (see Box 13.5) shows the effect of this inflation on individual income. Inflation has fluctuated since the return of democracy, ranging from about 4 percent in 2002 to nearly 27 percent in 2005.

Governments have attempted to deal with inflation by enforcing an official exchange rate for

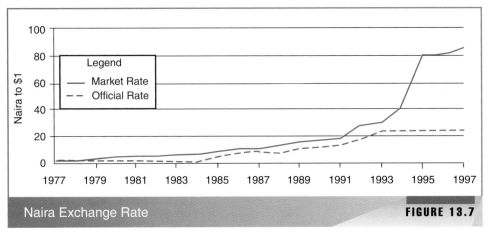

Naira Exchange Rate   **FIGURE 13.7**

The Effects of Inflation: A Case Study

BOX 13.5

A young graduate with a new doctoral degree won a position as an instructor at a Nigerian university in 1977. His salary and benefits totaled 6,000 naira per year. At that time, one naira equaled $1.50, so his salary was the equivalent of $9,000—modest by industrial-world standards but very comfortable in Nigeria. Twenty years later, this same man achieved the rank of full professor, at a salary of 51,000 naira per year, with fringe benefits raising his total annual compensation to 90,000 naira. However, at the parallel market exchange rate of 80 naira to the dollar, his salary was the equivalent of $1,125 per year, a figure not taking into account

the effect of inflation on the purchasing power of the dollar since 1977. In 1998, a national review of faculty salaries increased the professor's salary to the equivalent of $5,000 per year. This discussion implies that salaries are regularly paid. However, in early 1999, the Abubakar government was in such financial straits that it failed to provide salary payments at all. In 2000, President Obasanjo improved the workers' pay generally and moved university teachers' pay to 130,000 naira per month, the equivalent of $1,000 dollars per month. He did this to discourage brain drain in Nigeria and to promote high-level productivity in all sectors.

the **naira**—Nigeria's national currency. The result was a huge divergence in official and market exchange rates, causing chaos in the financial system. That chaos dried up investments and stimulated corruption, since anyone with access to foreign exchange at the official rate can then sell the foreign currency "on the street" for a large profit. Since 1999, the government has reduced its role in stabilizing the currency, allowing the value of the naira to be largely determined by forces of supply and demand.

As a policy issue, distribution in a large country such as Nigeria is also seen as a geographic question, not just one of policy priorities. Nigerians have a fondness for referring to the national budget as the "national cake," and they see state and local governments as the major recipients of slices. The federal government now spends between two-thirds and three-fourths of public monies, and also has great control over how the money distributed to state and local governments will be spent. On the contentious question of how to distribute resources as the number of states and local governments expanded, governments settled on relatively straightforward formulas, a combination of equality (across-the-board distributions to all states) and population. States other than Lagos now depend on the federal Revenue Allocation System (RAS) for 70 to 90 percent of their recurrent revenues. In order to fund local governments, the RAS was extended to cover them directly in 1981. Beginning in 1982, federal revenues were shared according to set

percentages among the three levels of government. Given the set formulas in the RAS, it is not surprising that regions and localities strive for statehood and local autonomy, and that population counts loom large as a political issue.

Dealing with Debt and Structural Adjustment

Nigeria's recent debt repayments are historic—both for the country and for Africa. It solves a problem that began with fiscal indiscipline during the 1970s oil boom, when the government paid insufficient attention to the lack of productivity of public spending. Much of the money was applied to an increase in welfare expenditures, to developing an unprofitable steel industry, and to building the new capital at **Abuja.** Late in the 1970s, commodity prices fell, while oil prices remained high; African governments borrowed at an even faster pace, and the continent's total indebtedness increased between 1978 and 1982 from $27 billion to $72 billion. As African governments became unable to make debt payments, international financial institutions, principally the International Monetary Fund (IMF) and the World Bank, were called in to monitor a restructuring and rescheduling of the debt. Nigeria's total indebtedness continued to increase in the 1980s, from $8.9 billion in 1980 to $34.5 billion in 1991; by 1991 it represented 257 percent of the annual value of the country's exports and 109 percent of GNP. The annual cost of servicing the debt consumed

25 percent of the value of exports (up from 4 percent in 1980); the weight of this burden almost ensured that the debt would continue to grow. Throughout the past decade, the question of how to deal with the external debt was a principal focus of political discussion in Nigeria.

The debt problem that began under military rule became much more acute during the Second Republic (1979–1983). The Buhari regime approached the IMF for relief in the form of new loans and more favorable repayment terms but rejected the severe conditions the IMF attached to its help. The naira would have to be devalued, trade restrictions would have to be dropped, and subsidies for domestic gasoline consumption ended. These and similar measures have been the issues involved in Nigeria's Structural Adjustment Program (SAP). It was clear to the military leadership that such measures would be extremely unpopular with the Nigerian public and would lead to outbursts of political violence. When Ibrahim Babangida seized power in 1985, he opened a "national debate" on the issue. He claimed to fashion a Nigerian version of structural adjustment (while at the same time negotiating with the IMF). As the program's austerity measures began to be felt, the SAP became extremely unpopular. In his parallel program of moving back toward civilian rule, Babangida forbade candidates to criticize the program, but at the same time he eased off on the necessary austerity measures. The net result was that, although Nigerians were suffering from the country's poor position in international finance, the SAP did not reduce the debt or reform the financial system. Rather than allow the naira to float as urged by the IMF, the Abacha regime maintained the official exchange rate of 22 naira to the dollar, a decision certainly supported by those who were able to take advantage of it. In 1995 the exchange rate was partially opened to market forces, but the N22 to $1 exchange rate was maintained for government transactions. This neither stabilized the economy nor satisfied the international sector. The total external debt reached almost $8 billion, and the Nigerian National Petroleum Corporation owed over $1 billion to its foreign partners. In responding to gasoline shortages, however, the government lowered the subsidy on petroleum products. Nigeria once had the lowest fuel prices in the world, but in 1994 gasoline prices were raised 400 percent—still at the lower end of the range of prices in the world. Holding the price down had

deprived the country of gasoline, as stocks were spirited over the borders to fetch higher prices or sold along the roadside at "unofficial" prices. However, the sharp price rise seemed one more hardship to endure for those on low and fixed incomes, already suffering from rapid inflation. The discomfort increased when extreme fuel shortages reappeared in 1997. Long lines at official stations prompted a black market rate of up to 80 naira ($3.60) per liter (about one quarter gallon), or about seven times the normal price; the shortage was attributed to deteriorating conditions in Nigeria's four refineries as well as to mismanagement and diversion of maintenance funds and to massive smuggling of petroleum out of the country for personal profit by high-placed government officials.

There could hardly be a more dramatic demonstration of policy failure: a country rich in petroleum incapable of providing its citizens with fuel. In 1998 the Abubakar government imposed a variety of measures to remedy the situation, from severe penalties for fuel diversion to emergency funds to repair refineries and pay for increased imports of refined petroleum. The government also raised the price at the pump from 11 to 25 naira per liter. At the same time, the government and its partner oil companies were bedeviled by increasing unrest and violence in the oil-producing areas and against the pumping operations themselves. By late 1998 these disruptions were having a serious impact on Nigerian oil production, a situation that complicated the inauguration of a stable civilian government. After President Obasanjo was inaugurated in May 1999, he tried to bring calm to the situation by voiding all contracts awarded in the six months prior to his administration. Since then, each attempt by the government in 2000, 2001, and subsequent years to raise the price at the pump has been met with the return of lines at filling stations. Efforts to reduce government spending by eliminating the petroleum subsidy for domestic consumption remain highly controversial because those efforts impact not only the cost of public transportation but also food and other daily essentials.

Regulative Performance

At independence in 1960, the Nigeria Police Force was essentially regionalized. Because the police were frequently mobilized for political purposes during the rough and tumble politics of the 1960s, the military regime decided to consolidate the police function at the national level. It is this national police force that now enforces traffic laws and other government legislation. However, it is often still the case that "law and order" is maintained in individual communities—especially in rural areas—through traditional institutions and norms. Traditional leaders not only prevent deviant behavior but also take responsibility for the welfare of the "strangers" who, in accord with accepted procedures, have taken up residence in their communities.

Although Nigeria was under military rule from 1983 to 1999, the average citizen has not felt oppressed by an authoritarian state. That citizen is aware of the police presence at checkpoints along the country's highways, but fear of authority does not restrict the citizen's actions to any degree. As in most Third World countries, there simply are not the resources available to the Nigerian government to keep close tabs on its large population.

Nigeria's judicial system remains vigorous, and until the advent of Abacha's reign it had been surprisingly diligent at following a rule of law through the various informally constituted regimes. Still, military regimes intruded on that rule of law. The regime imposed the State Security (Detention of Persons) Decree in 1984, which allows detention without trial of those "suspected of posing a threat to national security." State officials seemed to intervene with increasing frequency into the judicial system where political questions are involved.

Freedom of expression was reduced even further as Sani Abacha held onto power. Repression touched members of the political and military elite and internationally famous figures who hitherto had appeared to be safe. In 1994, writer Wole Soyinka was prevented from leaving the country by air, and his passport was seized. (He later slipped across the border and criticized the regime from abroad until after Abacha's death.) Prominent political prisoners under Abacha included former head of state (and future president) Olusegun Obasanjo and Moshood Abiola and former presidential candidate Shehu Yar'Adua. Abacha showed himself to be unconcerned about international opinion in allowing the execution of Ken Saro-Wiwa in the face of an international outcry and in ignoring Pope John Paul II's plea for release of political prisoners during a 1998 visit.

The Census Issue One policy issue has overshadowed all the others since independence, because the outcome often determines how political goods will be distributed. A minor policy issue in some countries, in Nigeria population counts have been fraught with conflict. In a country where federal subsidies make up the lion's share of budgetary allocations at all levels, the distribution of population directly affects the distribution of resources. (Americans will recognize a similar issue that arose concerning undercounting of some ethnic groups and the homeless after the 1990 census in the United States, and in the debate over whether to use representative samples rather than the whole population in some aspects of the 2000 census.)

After a false start in 1962, a national census was conducted in 1963. It reported a total population of 55.6 million, making Nigeria the tenth largest country in the world. However, it found a majority of that population (30 million) to be in the north, a finding that was then and is always questioned by southern Nigerians, who maintain that a flyover or drive through the north and south will easily demonstrate that population densities are higher in the latter (although it is also true that the area of the north is much larger). Nevertheless, the 1963 census, or straight-line projections from it, remained the official source of population statistics for almost twenty years. At the same time, voices are continually raised in favor of a new "fair" count in the regions that perceive themselves undercounted.

In 1973, General Gowon's Supreme Military Council attempted a census update, and ordered that enumerators be accompanied by unarmed soldiers. With the prestige and integrity of the armed forces behind the count, the resulting figures presumably could be trusted, and used for economic planning, electoral preparation, and military disengagement. Gowon's optimism was misplaced. The 1973 census figures, when finally released, appeared as politically manipulated and inflated as the discredited results of a decade earlier. . . . Apparent overcounting in certain areas, especially in the north, revived the latent fears of regional domination that periodically roil Nigerian politics.[46]

After almost two additional decades of continued reliance on the 1963 figures, the Babangida government commissioned a new census to be conducted by a

National Population Commission. Following methodical pretesting and sampling, a census in November 1991 put the country's total population at 88.5 million, a substantial downward revision from estimates that had exceeded 100 million. According to this census, the highest population concentrations were in the states of Bauchi, Kaduna, Kano, Katsina, and Sokoto in the north, and Lagos, Oyo, and Rivers in the south. The census caused new consternation in the south, where feelings ran high that the figures had again been "cooked" to favor the north. As mentioned earlier, the recent 2006 census effort fared only slightly better, and its results had not been approved as of early 2007.

Conclusions on Performance

While our judgments on performance should be nuanced given the complexity of Nigeria's political environment and the problems it faces, an overall conclusion emerges unfailingly. In comparison to other countries with equivalent natural resources, skilled human resources, and size, Nigeria has not done well.

That outcome caused Chinua Achebe to write *The Problem With Nigeria,* in which he concluded that the "problem" was leadership. Until Nigerians can settle on a constitutional arrangement that provides responsive leadership from the national to the local levels, the country will continue to fall far short of its potential. Although the Second Republic failed, it was a significant improvement over the first in reining in the politicization of ethnicity. There was reason to be optimistic that the Constitution developed in the later years of the Babangida regime would introduce another increment of correction. Although Abubakar was able to move the country to civilian rule, his decision to base the transition on the poorly articulated Constitution drafted under Abacha in 1995 did not inspire confidence in most Nigerians that the new regime would be based on the rule of law. Democracy cannot be "delivered" by a military regime; indeed, further progress in democratization will depend on the formation and maintenance of a coalition with the strength to force the country in that direction.

A fatal flaw in political culture may have developed in Nigeria since independence, and it is part of the "curse of oil": public policy is often seen in Nigeria as the "national cake," and the unfortunate analogy suggests that "they"—the government—bake a cake that is distributed in slices sized to match the political influence of various constituencies. At least at the mass level, constituencies are defined in ethnic terms, and politics becomes a competition among ethnic groups for larger slices of cake. The analogy could of course be used to describe the politics of many countries, but not to the extreme degree that it applies in Nigeria. There, communities look to the government to provide for them. A successful Nigerian constitution must not only provide responsive leaders; it must also shift responsibility so that extractive and distributive performance come from the same budget, and so that there is some relationship between the amounts one pays into and receives from the public sector. Public goals based on community effort were the norm in most Nigerian traditions; that norm must be rediscovered.

NIGERIA IN AFRICA AND IN THE WORLD

Nigeria (now along with South Africa) has the population and resource base to be a regional power, and it has stimulated hopes and fears among its neighbors concerning that potential. Under the First Republic (1960–1966), Nigeria generally focused inward and played a rather minor role in the continent's turbulent politics. But then came the civil war over Biafra in 1966; Nigeria's army grew from 10,000 to 250,000, the country's oil potential became known, and, as we have seen earlier, world powers took an interest in the war's outcome.

Some West African governments offered clear support to Biafra, a support Nigerians suspected grew from a desire to see their country divided up and thus reduced in influence. This was thought especially to be the case with Cote d'Ivoire (the Ivory Coast) under President Houphouet-Boigny, who favored Biafra with French support. When the war ended, relations among these countries were, as might be expected, strained.

Subsequently, Nigeria under General Gowon took a leading role in establishing, in 1975, the **Economic Community of West African States (ECOWAS),** hoping both to bring Nigeria closer to other West African countries while at the same time countering French influence in the region. The Ivoirian government had taken the lead in forming the Economic Community of West Africa, an exclusively French-speaking organization, and was wary of the predominant position that Nigeria might play in a wider regional organization. But Nigeria was successful in first approaching Togo, Benin, and Niger, the French-speaking countries with which it already had close ties, offering attractive economic inducements that included special petroleum prices. With this group in hand, Nigerian diplomats cast their net wider, and the representatives of sixteen West African governments signed the Treaty of Lagos. The ECOWAS treaty specified a two-year phase during which intracommunity tariffs would be frozen, followed by an eight-year period that would end with the removal of duties on trade among members. Finally, a common external tariff wall would be created.

Thus, West Africa under Nigerian leadership is partaking in the worldwide movement toward free-trade zones. As elsewhere, however, progress has been difficult. Ten years after its creation, ECOWAS reported that it had not made "tangible progress in practical terms," and by 1989 the member governments were $80 million in arrears in their contributions to the organization. The proportion of intracommunity trade in the member countries' total international trade has not changed since 1980. At the same time, ECOWAS has had better success as a regional political organization, especially in mediating disputes among member states, and in 1990 a Nigerian proposal was approved that created a standing mediation committee.[47]

Nigeria has played a prominent role in the region through commitment of its substantial military capacity, notably in supplying the leadership and the majority of troops for ECOMOG, the ECOWAS-sponsored peace-keeping force in Liberia. That operation was viewed a success, with armed conflict halted and elections held. Nigerian troops have also been stationed in Sierra Leone to protect that country's borders from incursions of Liberian rebels, and have confronted a Sierra Leonean military junta that overthrew an elected civilian government, an action more than a bit ironic, given the origins of the Abacha regime. Nigeria has participated in wider ranging United Nations operations in Lebanon, Rwanda, the former Yugoslavia, and Somalia. However, as in other countries, these overseas deployments are seriously questioned at home, given the country's financial difficulties.

Because of its prominence on the continent, Nigeria's international financial problems have been especially embarrassing. Forced along with other African nations to accept stringent structural adjustment planning from the World Bank and International Monetary Fund, Nigeria has reacted with frustration and anger. It has led the region's governments in their critique of international lenders' policies, hosting the meeting that led to the Lagos Plan of Action as a response to international debt-structuring proposals.

Of all the world powers, France plays the most prominent role in West Africa. Although the French interest focuses on its own former colonies, in recent years the French believe that Nigeria's size and potential wealth should not be overlooked, and France actively promotes closer economic ties with Nigeria, a move that upsets Nigeria's French-speaking neighbors. The Western powers, especially Britain and the United States, were openly critical of Nigeria's military rulers and supported the country's return to civilian rule, especially during the Babangida regime and once again with Abdulsalami Abubakar. The United States and Britain condemned Babangida's 1993 election annulment, and they suspended aid as a result. However, this relationship was not important enough to Nigeria's rulers to modify their behavior. Presumably an embargo on purchases of Nigerian oil would have had that effect, but the industrial nations' governments did not have the will to take such a drastic step. Most observers saw the Abacha regime's treatment of dissenters as a calculation of how far it could silence opposition without provoking more severe international sanctions. In contrast, many Nigerians were critical of what they saw as the West's premature enthusiasm over actions that until then were only *promised* by Abubakar in 1998. Western support returned with enthusiasm upon Obasanjo's inauguration.

PROSPECTS FOR DEVELOPMENT

Nigeria's political and economic setbacks do not equal the tragedies of Rwanda, Sudan, or Somalia, but the frustrations are nonetheless deep and enduring. Billions of desperately needed naira have been wasted, a few have grown rich at the expense of the poor, and accountability in government has proved highly elusive. Poet Tanure Ojaide captured this frustration in "No Longer Our Own Country," written in 1986:

> We have lost it,
> the country we were born into.
> We can now sing dirges
> of that commonwealth of yesterday—
> we live in a country
> that is no longer our own.[48]

In much of the world, the attraction of democracy has been its association with prosperity. Like other people, Nigerians are more interested in the outcome of the political process than in the process itself. Calls for better leadership and the welcome initially extended to some military regimes suggest that Nigerians' highest priorities are economic security and the rule of law. If these could be provided by generals, the country would probably accept an authoritarian system. However, at least since Plato we have known that benevolent authoritarianism is an elusive concept. Western democracies have developed on the premise that democracy is a necessary, if not sufficient, condition for accountable leadership. And Nigerians have had enough opportunities to compare the results of military rule with their expectations so that a majority of them are ready for another try at elective civilian rule. Perhaps another constitutional correction will be enough to usher in the long-term political stability for which they have hoped.

We have focused this discussion on those aspects of the Nigerian situation most amenable to correction. There remain several rather intractable problems that will be overcome only with truly revolutionary change. Larry Diamond has identified as a central problem for Nigeria the relationship between the economy and the state. In his words, "Stable democracy is associated with an autonomous, indigenous bourgeoisie, and inversely associated with extensive state control over the economy. In Nigeria, and throughout much of Africa, the swollen state has turned politics into a zero-sum game in which everything of value is at stake in an election, and hence candidates, communities, and parties feel compelled to win at any cost."[49] The answer appears to be the emergence of a vigorous private sector less dependent on government subsidies and freed from the kinds of patronage costs that have drained the initiative and resources of the private sector. In West Africa and the world, Nigerians have a reputation for entrepreneurship. The challenge is to reduce the role of government to that of providing necessary infrastructure and public welfare safety nets so that Nigerian entrepreneurial initiative can thrive. Oil revenues remain critical. As the sense of public duty among some of the military elite declined from Gowon and Murtala to Babangida and Abacha, a subculture developed among officer ranks that can be identified as "when do I get my turn?" Such corruption of values is common, but the availability of oil revenues means that authoritarian leaders need not seek their rents directly from the populace. Rather, they have learned that all they must do is control the spigot and the narrow slice of the population that operates and protects it, and opponents will be helpless. The oil workers' unions and the people whose homelands are located where the drilling is done must be neutralized; the rest could safely be ignored.

Mancur Olson observed that "resolute autocrats can survive even when they impose heinous amounts of suffering upon their peoples. When they are replaced it is for other reasons (e.g., succession crises) and often by another stationary bandit." He then concluded that democracy appears under "historical conditions and dispersions of resources that make it impossible for any one leader or group to assume all power."[50] These conditions are not close at hand for Nigeria, with its economy overwhelmingly dependent on oil and the state's resources controlled directly by the regime. In this situation, interactions among the military become supremely important. Abubakar proved not to be "another stationary bandit," but instead represented a faction of military leaders with no taste for politics and a desire to reprofessionalize the military services. Had he and his supporters not taken a longer-term view than Abacha, the continued existence of Nigeria as a single state would have been in doubt. After inheriting a fifteen-year legacy of continuous military rule and misgovernment, there is some indication that the Obasanjo administration was able to achieve some successes. For example, privatization achieved success in the areas of telephone and domestic transportation. Other areas in which progress has been made are water, housing, and electricity. Nigeria is gradually becoming a service-oriented country but profound political and social challenges remain.

KEY TERMS

Abacha, Sani

Abiola, Moshood

Abuja

All Nigeria People's Party (ANPP)

Azikiwe, Nnamdi

Babangida, Ibrahim

Biafra

clientelism

Economic and Financial Crimes Commission (EFCC)

Economic Community of West African States (ECOWAS)

Hausa, Hausa-Fulani

Igbo (Ibo)

Independent National Election Commission (INEC)

Kaduna Mafia

Lagos

Movement for the Emancipation of the Niger Delta (MEND)

naira

National Union of Petroleum and Gas Workers (NUPENG)

neocolonial

Nigerian National Oil Corporation (NNOC)

Obasanjo, Olusegun

Organization of Petroleum Exporting Countries (OPEC)

patron-client network

Saro-Wiwa, Ken

Structural Adjustment Program (SAP)

Yar'Adua, Umar Musa

Yoruba

SUGGESTED READINGS

Abernethy, David B. *The Political Dilemma of Popular Education: An African Case.* Stanford, CA: Stanford University Press, 1969.

Achebe, Chinhua. *A Man of the People.* New York: Doubleday-Anchor, 1967.

———. *The Trouble With Nigeria.* Enugu: Fourth Dimension Press, 1983.

Beckett, Paul, and Crawford Young, eds. *Dilemmas of Democracy in Nigeria.* Rochester, NY: University of Rochester University Press, 1997.

Coleman, James S. *Nigeria: Background to Nationalism.* Berkeley: University of California Press, 1958.

Crowder, Michael. *The Story of Nigeria,* 4th ed. London: Faber & Faber, 1978.

Diamond, Larry. *Class, Ethnicity, and Democracy in Nigeria: The Failure of the First Republic.* Syracuse, NY: Syracuse University Press, 1988.

———. "Nigeria: Pluralism, Statism and the Struggle for Democracy." In Larry Diamond et al. eds., *Democracy: Africa.* Boulder, CO: Lynne Rienner, 1988, 33–91.

Diamond, Larry, Anthony Kirk-Greene, and O. Oyediran, eds. *Transition Without End: Nigerian Politics and Civil Society Under Babangida.* Boulder, CO: Lynne Rienner, 1997.

Dudley, Billy. *An Introduction to Nigerian Government and Politics.* Bloomington: University of Indiana Press, 1982.

Gordon, David F. "Debt, Conditionality, and Reform: The International Relations of Economic Restructuring in Sub-Saharan Africa." In Thomas M. Callaghy and John Ravenhill, eds., *Hemmed In: Responses to Africa's Economic Decline.* New York: Columbia University Press, 1993, 90–129.

Graf, William D. *The Nigerian State: Political Economy, State Class and Political System in the Post-Colonial Era.* Portsmouth, NH: Heinemann Educational Books, 1988.

Guyer, Jane I. "The Spatial Dimensions of Civil Society in Africa: An Anthropologist Looks at Nigeria." In John W. Harbeson, Donald Rothchild, and Naomi Chazan, eds., *Civil Society and the State in Africa.* Boulder, CO: Lynne Rienner, 1994, 215–29.

Joseph, Richard A. *Democracy and Prebendal Politics in Nigeria: The Rise and Fall of the Second Republic.* Cambridge, England: Cambridge: University Press, 1987.

Kane, Ousmane. "The Rise of Muslim Reformism in Northern Nigeria: IZALA (The Society for the Removal of Heresy and Reinstatement of Tradition)." In Martin Marty and Scott Appleby, eds., *Accounting for Fundamentalisms.* Chicago: University of Chicago Press, 1994.

Koehn, Peter H. *Public Policy and Administration in Africa: Lessons From Nigeria.* Boulder, CO: Westview, 1990.

Lewis, Peter M., Pearl T. Robinson, and Barnett R. Rubin. *Stabilizing Nigeria: Sanctions, Incentives, and Support for Civil Society.* Washington, DC: Brookings Institution Press, 1998.

Metz, Helen Chapin, ed. *Nigeria: A Country Study* 5th ed. Washington, DC: U.S. Government Printing Office, 1992.

Nafziger, E. Wayne. *The Economics of Political Instability: The Nigeria-Biafran War.* Boulder, CO: Westview, 1983.

Normandy, Elizabeth. "Nigeria." In Mark W. Delancey, ed., *Handbook of Political Science Research on Sub-Saharan Africa.* Westport, CT: Greenwood Press, 1992.

Ogbondah, Chris W. *Military Regimes and the Press in Nigeria, 1966–1993.* Lanham, MD: University Press of America, 1994.

Ohiorhenuan, John F. E. *Capital and the State in Nigeria.* New York: Greenwood Press, 1989.

Olagunju, Tunji, Adele Jinadu, and Sam Oyovbaire. *Transition to Democracy in Nigeria (1985–1993).* Ibadan, Nigeria: Safari Books, 1993.

Olayiwola, Peter O. *Petroleum and Structural Change in a Developing Country: The Case of Nigeria.* New York: Praeger, 1987.

Oyediran, O., ed. *Nigerian Government and Politics Under Military Rule 1968–79.* London: Macmillan, 1979.

Oyewole, Anthony. *Historical Dictionary of Nigeria.* Metuchen, NJ: Scarecrow Press, 1987.

Paden, John. *Muslim Civic Cultures and Conflict Resolution.* Washington, DC: Brookings Institution Press, 2005.

Publius: The Journal of Federalism 21, no. 4 (Fall 1991) [special issue on Nigeria].

Soyinka, Wole. *AkÈ: The Years of Childhood. Ibadan, Nigeria:* Spectrum Books, 1968.

Suberu, Rotimi T. *Federalism and Ethnic Conflict in Nigeria.* Washington, DC: U.S. Institute of Peace, 2001.

INTERNET RESOURCES

National Orientation and Public Affairs: **www.nopa.net/**

Federal government of Nigeria: **www.nigeria.gov.ng/**

Current information on Nigeria, including news from the major daily papers in Lagos, can be obtained through the Nigeria

page of *Africa South of the Sahara: Selected Internet Resources:* **www-sul.stanford.edu/depts/ssrg/africa/guide.html**

ENDNOTES

1. Clifford Geertz, *Old Societies and New States: The Quest for Modernity in Asia and Africa* (New York: Free Press of Glencoe, 1963).

2. Because Africans have frequently referred to their ethnic groups as "tribes" and to the conflicts among those groups as "tribalism," these terms seem appropriate to our discussion of ethnicity in Nigeria. The problem from an outside perspective is that the term "tribe" has been applied indiscriminately to small groups of villages or whole empires, and often in conjunction with the adjective "primitive." Thus "tribe" has lost any specific meaning and imparts prejudicial notions. One may ask whether, if the Yoruba or Igbo of Nigeria are tribes (of 30 million or 40 million), are not the less numerous peoples known as Norwegians or Irish also tribes? What is the distinction? And if ethnic conflict in Africa is "tribalism," the same phenomenon in Yugoslavia, Britain, Germany, or the United States deserves the same label.

3. This discussion relies principally on A. Oyewole, *Historical Dictionary of Nigeria* (Metuchen, NJ: Scarecrow Press, 1987); Michael Crowder, *The Story of Nigeria,* 4th ed. (London: Faber & Faber, 1978); James S. Coleman, *Nigeria: Background to Nationalism* (Berkeley: University of California Press, 1958).

4. Crowder, *The Story of Nigeria.*

5. Peter Enahoro, *How to Be a Nigerian* (Ibadan, Nigeria: Caxton, 1966), 2.

6. Chinua Achebe, *Arrow of God* (Garden City, NY: Anchor Books, 1967) 65.

7. Wole Soyinka, *AkÉ: The Years of Childhood* (Ibadan, Nigeria: Spectrum Books, 1981) 200.

8. Billy Dudley, *An Introduction to Nigerian Government and Politics* (Bloomington: University of Indiana Press, 1982), 230.

9. World Bank, "World Development Indicators," in *World Development Report 2006* (Washington, DC: World Bank, 2006).

10. Patrick Smith, "Economy," in *Africa South of the Sahara 1994* (London: Europa 1994), 660.

11. "Abuja Faces Population Explosion Crisis," *This Day,* 12 September 2002.

12. "Government Cracks Down on Biafra Secessionist Movement," IRIN, 19 April 2005 and "More Than 100 People Arrested at Separatist Biafra Rally," IRIN 10 May 2005.

13. E. Wayne Nafziger, *The Economics of Political Instability: The Nigeria-Biafra War* (Boulder, CO: Westview, 1983), 73.

14. Barbara J. Callaway, *Muslim Hausa Women in Nigeria* (Syracuse, NY: Syracuse University Press, 1987), 93.

15. Naomi Chazan and Victor Lavine, "Africa and the Middle East," in John Harbeson and Donald Rothchild (eds.) *Africa in World Politics* (Boulder: Westview 1991), 202–27.

16. Afrobarometer Round 1: Compendium of Comparative Data From a Twelve Nation Survey (March 2002). For earlier evidence of this same pattern, see Sidney Verba, "The Parochial and the Polity," in Sidney Verba and Lucian Pye, eds., *The Citizen and Politics: A Comparative Perspective* (Stamford, CT: Greylock Publishers, 1978), 3–28.

17. Robert A. Dahl, *After the Revolution* (New Haven, CT: Yale University Press, 1971); see also the discussion in Billy Dudley, *An Introduction to Nigerian Government and Politics* (Bloomington: Indiana University Press, 1982), 80–83.

18. Afrobarometer Round 1.

19. P. C. Lloyd, "The Yoruba of Nigeria," in James L. Gibbs, Jr., ed., *Peoples of Africa* (New York: Holt, Rinehart & Winston, 1965), 565.

20. See the discussion in Dudley, *An Introduction to Nigerian Government,* 80–83.

21. Chinua Achebe, *The Trouble With Nigeria* (Enugu, Nigeria, Fourth Dimension Press, 1983), 42.

22. BBC News, "Nigerian Leaders 'Stole' $380 billion," 20 October 2006; BBC News, "Nigeria Governors in Graft Probe," 28 September 2006; BBC News, "Obasanjo Accuses Deputy of Fraud," 7 September 2006.

23. The discussion that follows draws on Crawford Young's treatment of socialization in his chapter on "Politics in Africa" in earlier editions of this book.

24. In anthropological usage, polygamy is a general term for marriage to more than one spouse. Polygamy is preferred to describe the marriage of one man to more than one woman (and polyandry for the reverse). However, polygamy is the term in general use in Nigeria and elsewhere in English-speaking Africa.

25. David B. Abernethy, *The Political Dilemma of Popular Education* (Stanford, CA: Stanford University Press, 1969), 18.

The description of education development that follows draws on this same source.

26. *A Handbook of Information on Basic Education 2003* (Abuja: Federal Ministry of Education and UNESCO 2003).

27. Afrobarometer Survey, "Attitudes Toward Democracy and Markets in Nigeria," 2000; U.S. Department of State, "Country Reports on Human Rights Practices: Nigeria," 4 March 2002; Committee to Protect Journalists, Attacks on the Press in 2001 (Washington, DC: Brooking Institution, 2002).

28. Reporters Without Borders, *Annual Report 2006;* "Publisher Under Arrest After 'Greedy Stella' Obasanjo Story," IRIN, 9 May 2005.

29. Peter Enahoro, *The Complete Nigerian* (Lagos: Malthouse Press, 1992), 121.

30. Ousmane Kane, "The Rise of Muslim Reformism in Northern Nigeria," in Martin Marty and Scot Appleby, eds., *Accounting for Fundamentalism* (Chicago: University of Chicago Press, 1994).

31. Associated Press, "Hundreds Flee Nigerian City Swept By Riots," 25 November 2002.

32. Peter H. Koehn, *Public Policy and Administration in Africa* (Boulder, CO: Westview, 1990), 16.

33. As noted in Chapter 5, the concept of consociational arrangement comes from Arend Lijphart, *Democracy in Plural Societies* (New Haven, CT: Yale University Press, 1977).

34. Keohn, *Public Policy and Administration in Africa,* (17–18) cites various sources for these totals.

35. Soyinka, *AkÉ* 199–200.

36. Richard Sklar and C. S. Whitaker, Jr., "Nigeria," in James S. Coleman and Carl G. Rosberg, Jr., eds. *Political Parties and National Integration in Tropical Africa* (Berkeley: University of California Press, 1964), 636.

37. Richard A. Joseph, *Democracy and Prebendal Politics in Nigeria* (Cambridge: Cambridge University Press, 1987), 133–34.

38. Joseph, *Democracy and Prebendal Policy in Nigeria.* Joseph calls the Nigerian version of patronage prebendalism, "patterns of political behavior which rest on the justifying principle that such offices should be competed for and then utilized for the personal benefit of officeholders as well as for their reference or support group. The official public purpose of the office often becomes a secondary concern, however much that purpose may have been originally cited in its creation or during the periodic competition to fill it" (8).

39. This account of party development through the first years of independence is taken from Sklar and Whitaker, "Nigeria."

40. "Cameroons" here refers to the English-speaking portion of the contemporary country of Cameroon (French Cameroun) on Nigeria's eastern border. The former German colony of that name was divided into League of Nations Trust Territories after World War I under British and French control. The NCNC was meant to include members from the British trust territory as well as from Nigeria, but in a pre-independence plebiscite, the English-speaking Cameroonians opted for incorporation into Cameroon. The NCNC then was renamed the National Convention of Nigerian Citizens.

41. Address of Brigadier Murtala Muhammed, reprinted as the preface to the *Report of the Constitution Drafting Committee* (Lagos: Ministry of Information, 1976), quoted in Dudley, *Introduction to Nigerian Government,* 127.

42. Letter to the editor, *Lagos,* 1983; quoted in Joseph, *Democracy and Prebendal Politics in Nigeria.*

43. Wole Soyinka, *AkÉ,* 201.

44. Diamond, "Nigeria," 53.

45. I. William Zartman, with Sayre Schatz, "Introduction," in I. William Zartman, ed., *The Political Economy of Nigeria* (New York: Praeger, 1983), 13. The military figures cited here come from Ruth Sivard, "World Military and Social Expenditures 1996" (Leesburg, VA: WMSE Publications, 1996), and "The Military Balance 2001–2002" (London: Oxford University Press, 2001).

46. Claude E. Welch, *No Farewell to Arms?* (Boulder, CO: Westview, 1987), 10.

47. The preceding treatment of the formation of ECOWAS is drawn from Carol Lancaster, "The Lagos Three: Economic Regionalism in Sub-Saharan Africa," in John W. Harbeson and Donald Rothchild, eds., *Africa in World Politics* (Boulder, CO, Westview Press, 1991), 249–67.

48. Tanure Ojaide, *The Blood of Peace and Other Poems* (London: Heinemann, 1991), 9.

49. Diamond, "Nigeria," 69.

50. Mancur Olson, "Dictatorship, Democracy, and Development," *American Political Science Review* 87 (September 3): 573.

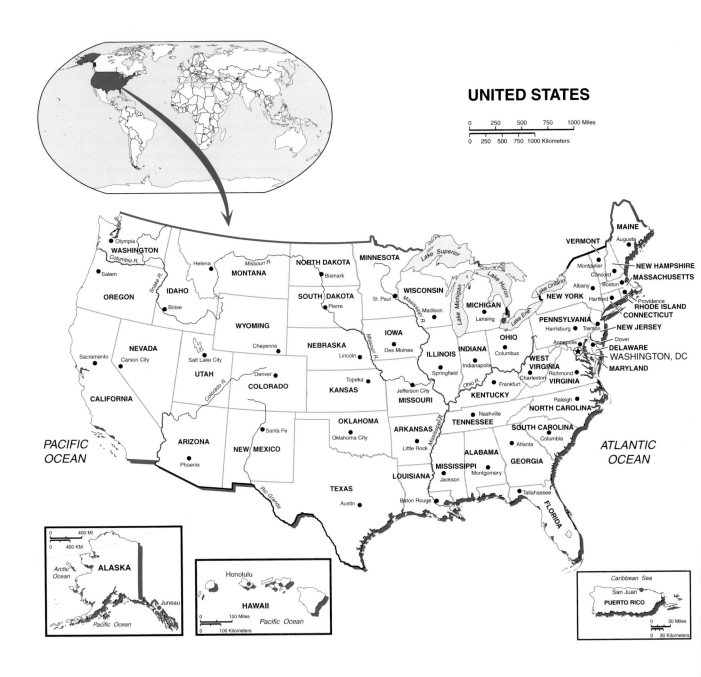

UNITED STATES

0   250   500   750   1000 Miles

0   250   500   750   1000 Kilometers

Olympia • WASHINGTON
Columbia R.
Salem •
OREGON
IDAHO
Boise •

Helena •
MONTANA
Missouri R.

Snake R.

NORTH DAKOTA
Bismark •

MINNESOTA

Lake Superior

St. Paul •
WISCONSIN
Madison •
Mississippi R.

MAINE
Augusta •
VERMONT
Montpelier • NEW HAMPSHIRE
Concord •
Albany • Boston • MASSACHUSETTS
NEW YORK Hartford • Providence
RHODE ISLAND
CONNECTICUT

SOUTH DAKOTA
Pierre •

WYOMING
Cheyenne •

NEBRASKA
Lincoln •

Missouri R.

IOWA
Des Moines •

Lake Michigan
Lansing •
MICHIGAN

Lake Huron

Lake Erie

Lake Ontario

PENNSYLVANIA
Harrisburg • Trenton •
NEW JERSEY
Dover •
DELAWARE

NEVADA
Sacramento •
Carson City •

Salt Lake City •

UTAH

Denver •
COLORADO

Topeka •
KANSAS

ILLINOIS
Springfield •

OHIO
Columbus •

INDIANA
Indianapolis •

WEST
VIRGINIA
Richmond •
Charleston •

Annapolis
WASHINGTON, DC
MARYLAND

VIRGINIA

CALIFORNIA

Colorado R.

Santa Fe •

Jefferson City •
MISSOURI

KENTUCKY
Frankfort •
Ohio R.

Raleigh •
NORTH CAROLINA

ARIZONA
Phoenix •

NEW MEXICO

OKLAHOMA
Oklahoma City •

ARKANSAS
Little Rock •

TENNESSEE
Nashville •

SOUTH CAROLINA
Columbia •

PACIFIC
OCEAN

Mississippi R.

ALABAMA

GEORGIA
Atlanta •

ATLANTIC
OCEAN

TEXAS
Austin •

Rio Grande

LOUISIANA
Baton Rouge •

MISSISSIPPI
Jackson •
Montgomery •

Tallahassee •

FLORIDA

0   400 MI
0   400 KM
Arctic
Ocean
ALASKA

Juneau

Pacific Ocean

Honolulu

HAWAII
0   100 Miles
0   100 Kilometers
Pacific Ocean

Caribbean Sea
San Juan
PUERTO RICO
0   30 Miles
0   30 Kilometers

POLITICS IN THE UNITED STATES

Austin Ranney and Thad Kousser

Country Bio

UNITED STATES

Population
300 million

Territory
3,475,031 square miles

Year of Independence
1776

Year of Current Constitution
September 17, 1787, effective March 4, 1789

Head of State
President George W. Bush

Head of Government
President George W. Bush

Languages
English, Spanish (spoken by a sizeable minority)

Religions
Protestant 52%; Roman Catholic 24%; Muslim 1%; Mormon 1%; Jewish 1%; none or not stated 21%

And what should they know of England
Who only England know?

RUDYARD KIPLING[1]

Why a chapter on the United States in a book on comparative politics? One reason is that most of its readers are Americans,[2] and politics in the United States affects our lives far more than politics in any other country. Moreover, however feeble we may feel is our personal power to influence the actions of our government, it is certainly greater than our personal power to influence the actions of other nations' governments.

The question Rudyard Kipling asked about the English in the quotation above can be asked with equal relevance about Americans. There are, of course, many excellent textbooks on the American political system written by American authors and intended for American students. But most of them make few references to, let alone systematic comparisons with, other political systems. Thus, viewing American politics with a special focus on how it resembles and differs from politics in other nations will help us better meet our version of Kipling's challenge. It may even give us some

insight into how the distinctive ways of American politics are likely to affect our country's ability to meet the enormous challenges it will face in the years ahead.

CURRENT POLICY CHALLENGES

The policy challenges facing the United States were radically altered by the events of September 11, 2001 (see Box 14.1). The day after the terrorist attacks President George W. Bush announced that they had been planned and executed by members of Al Qaeda, an international terrorist organization of radical Muslim fundamentalists led by Osama bin Laden (described further in Chapter 1). Bush declared that the attacks "were more than acts of terror, they were acts of war." He added that the "war against terror" would be resolutely fought by the United States and its friends not only against Al Qaeda but also against any nation-state that sheltered terrorists, financed them, or supported them in any way.

The new war was unlike any other in American history. The enemy was not another nation-state, such as Nazi Germany or Imperial Japan in World War II, or

BOX 14.1

September 11, 2001

At 8:45 A.M. on that fateful Tuesday, a hijacked American Airlines Boeing 767 was flown into the north tower of the World Trade Center in New York City, setting it on fire. At 9:03 A.M. a hijacked United Airlines Boeing 767 was flown into the Center's south tower, setting it on fire. At 9:43 A.M. a hijacked American Airlines Boeing 757 was flown into the west side of the Pentagon outside Washington, D.C. And at 10:10 A.M. a hijacked United Airlines Boeing 757 crashed in a rural area near Pittsburgh (it is believed that the plane was targeted on the White House or the U.S. Capitol, but that some passengers' efforts to recapture the plane deflected its course). At 10:05 A.M. the Trade Center's south tower, its structural steel fatally weakened by the fire's intense heat, collapsed from the top down, followed at 10:28 A.M. by the north tower.

The deaths totaled nearly 3,000, including the airplanes' hijackers, passengers, and crews, and the people caught in the burning buildings. This was the most killed in any peacetime disaster in the nation's history and far more than those slain in any other terrorist attack anywhere.

---

even a seceding section of the United States, like the Confederacy in the American Civil War. Consequently, there were no organized armies to be defeated in battle by the U.S. armed forces, no enemy governments to acknowledge defeat and sign peace treaties, indeed, no way to tell when the war was over and whether the United States had won. Instead, the enemy was an unknown number of shadowy, hard-to-find secret cells of terrorists dedicated to attacking American civilians, who had no way of knowing what "victory" would be and how we would recognize it. So the United States now faces a long and difficult twilight struggle in which most of its other policy challenges will take second place.

Nevertheless, many such challenges will remain. In domestic affairs, the problem of the economic and social status of African-Americans—some version of which has bedeviled the nation from its beginnings—remains high on the agenda. While African-Americans today are in many respects better off than they were a generation ago, they still lag behind whites in many areas, including family incomes, crime and imprisonment rates, formal education, housing quality, family stability, vulnerability to such diseases as AIDS and prostate cancer, and life expectancy. The nation's attention was focused on many of these inequalities after Hurricane Katrina flooded and destroyed many areas of New Orleans, a heavily African-American city, in August 2005. The lack of planning for this frequently-predicted emergency and the agonizingly slow response to it by all levels of government led many, both black and white, to question whether the race and poverty of New Orleans' residents put them especially at risk.

In the new millennium, our nation of immigrants will once again debate immigration policy and the nature of U.S. citizenship. The acceleration in recent decades in the ethnic and linguistic diversity of nearly every state, along with a rise in the number of illegal immigrants, has led to demands for a more inclusive citizenship policy as well as calls for increased border security. During the spring of 2006, Latino activists led a series of demonstrations in favor of a more open immigration policy that echoed the civil rights marches of the 1960s in their scale, fervor, and level of controversy. Conflicts over immigration policy, affirmative action, and the use of languages other than English will surely continue well into the twenty-first century.

Other, equally familiar domestic policy challenges will continue, including such diverse matters as the "war on drugs," measuring national standards of educational achievement by uniform tests, reconciling environmental protection with economic growth, and addressing the bitter conflict over abortion between pro-choice and pro-life forces.

In the early years of the twenty-first century, the American economy, the largest in the world, was struggling with a brief recession, a weakening dollar, and a stock market that from 2000 to 2003 lost over 40 percent of its value. While the market and the economy overall recovered quickly, long-term economic worries remain. The steep rise in oil and thus gas prices in 2006 raised fears of inflation and concerns about America's reliance on foreign energy sources.

Unfunded liabilities in social security and particularly in the Medicare system threaten to consume much of the federal government's budget and dampen economic growth in future decades. While the United States stands today as the world's economic leader, the expanding economies of China and India promise to threaten its position eventually.

In foreign policy, the unchallenged position of the United States as the world's most powerful nation and leader of the forces supporting democratic governments will certainly continue in the early twenty-first century. But national hubris is not warranted, for such a position carries perils in international affairs.

Perhaps the biggest issue is whether the United States should conduct its foreign policy mainly or solely through the structures and procedures of the United Nations (UN) or do what the U.S. president thinks is imperative even if the UN votes against it. This policy choice arose starkly in 2002–2003 in the debate over the Bush administration's intention to invade Iraq and remove its dictator, Saddam Hussein, without the clear authorization of a resolution by the United Nations, over the strong protests of public opinion in most nations, and over the determined opposition of such traditional allies as France and Germany.

The rationale underlying the Bush administration's choice is known as the "Bush doctrine." First enunciated by President George W. Bush after the Al Qaeda attacks of September 11, 2001, the doctrine declares that the United States should no longer wait to be attacked before it acts. It should, with the help of allies if possible but alone if necessary, take preemptive military action against any nation or terrorist group that possesses weapons of mass destruction that might be used against the United States. It was intended to replace such earlier policies as the Truman doctrine (containment of hostile regimes), the Reagan doctrine (support all Freedom Fighters), and the Clinton doctrine (always act multilaterally).

The doctrine guided the Bush administration's decision in March 2003 to invade Iraq despite the U.S. failure to win endorsement from the UN Security Council. The war was quick, and Baghdad fell within weeks. Yet winning the peace has proved much more difficult than winning the war, as it has become clear that the United States committed too few troops and was too optimistic in its hopes to be welcomed as a liberator. The ongoing conflict with insurgents who oppose the American presence in Iraq has intensified,

and more than 3,300 American soldiers had been killed in Iraq by May 2007. Even after the first democratic elections in January 2005 and the formation of a cabinet in May 2006, it appears that continued U.S. presence in Iraq is required to maintain order. Perhaps most damaging to America's international prestige, President Bush's domestic approval, and the prospects for future use of the Bush doctrine, no weapons of mass destruction have been found in Iraq. When American voters turned over control of Congress to the Democratic Party in 2006, many did so as a rejection of Bush's Iraq policies.

This brief sketch of some of the high-priority domestic and foreign policy challenges facing the United States in the new century underlines the gravity, and in some cases the intractability, of its problems. Let us see how well or poorly its political system is equipped to deal with them.

THE UNITED STATES AMONG THE WORLD'S NATIONS

History

The world today is divided among more than 190 nations. The great majority of them are "new nations," that is, nations that have recently broken away from older countries and become independent sovereign nations. Indeed, 73 percent of all modern nations have achieved their independence since the end of World War II in 1945.

Some of these nations have established political systems capable of meeting enough of their citizens' needs that their polities have remained relatively stable and peaceful. Unhappily, however, many of them have changed their political systems with some frequency since independence and have yet to find one that works well enough to stay in business very long (Cambodia, Ethiopia, Rwanda, Somalia, and Yugoslavia are among the sadder examples).

Seymour Martin Lipset has argued that the United States was the world's "first new nation," in the sense that the problems it faced in its efforts to establish a stable and principled political system after winning its independence from Great Britain in 1783 were in many respects similar to those faced by the nations created after 1945.[3] Thus, the United States, which is so often described as a young nation, is actually an old one—not as old as, say, Great Britain, France, or Japan, but much older than most other modern nations. The United States has the world's oldest written constitution still in effect. It can fairly claim to have become a democracy well before any other large modern nation. In the 1790s, it developed the world's first modern political parties, and today's Democratic Party is generally recognized as the world's oldest active political party.

We will touch on several developments in American history throughout this chapter, but here we will emphasize only that the Civil War (1861–1865) is the United States' great historical watershed. Before 1861 it was a much-disputed question whether the United States was merely a convenient alliance among independent sovereign states, which had every right to secede whenever they wished, or an indissoluble sovereign nation whose people chose to divide power between the national government and the state governments. After 1865, in both law and fact, it was established that the United States was, as every American schoolchild is drilled to know, "one nation, indivisible," and not a federation of sovereign states.

Before 1861 many Americans, especially those in the eleven southern states that seceded to form the Confederacy, felt that they were first and foremost citizens of their states and derived their American citizenship from the membership of their states in the union. (The most famous example was Robert E. Lee: he strongly opposed both slavery and secession, and yet when Virginia seceded he refused command of the Union Army and cast his lot with Virginia because he felt he owed his primary loyalty to his state, not his nation.) The Fourteenth Amendment to the Constitution, ratified in 1868, removed all doubt by declaring: "All persons born or naturalized in the United States and subject to the jurisdiction thereof, are citizens of the United States and of the State wherein they reside." In short, all Americans are now primarily citizens of the United States, and derivatively become citizens of the state in which they reside. (Interested readers can see the broader discussion of federalism in Chapter 6.)

Geography

The United States has jurisdiction over a territory totaling 3,475,031 square miles. This makes it geographically the fourth largest nation in the world, smaller only than Russia (6,592,800 square miles), Canada (3,849,674 square miles), and the People's Republic of China (3,696,100 square miles).[4] The United States is bounded by the Atlantic Ocean on the east, the Pacific Ocean on the west, Canada on the north, and Mexico on the south. This secure location—great oceans on two sides, militarily weak nations on the other two sides—made feasible the foreign policy of isolation from alliances and wars with foreign countries that the United States pursued until the end of the nineteenth century. In these days of intercontinental ballistic missiles, orbiting spy satellites, and international terrorism, however, no nation, including the United States, can count on its geographical location to keep it isolated from world politics.

Population

The U.S. Bureau of the Census estimated that the total population in the United States surpassed 300 million in 2006. This makes it the third most populous nation in the world, behind China with 1.3 billion and India with 1.1 billion.[5] The U.S. rate of population increase has been impressive. The first census in 1790 reported a total population of 3.9 million, and so the 2004 figure represents a staggering increase of 7,413% percent in 214 years. Over 50 million people have moved from other parts of the world to the United States—a phenomenon characterized by the British analyst H. G. Nicholas as "the greatest movement of population in western history."[6] Accordingly, one of the most important facts to recognize about the United States is that, more than any other nation in history, it is a nation of immigrants. The census classifies only 1.8 percent of the population as being of Native American or Hawaiian ancestry;[7] the rest are immigrants or descendants of immigrants from all over the world.

Most immigrants came in one or the other of three historic waves: first, 1840–1860, mainly from Western Europe and Scandinavia; second, 1870–1920, mainly from Asia and Eastern Europe; and third, 1965–to the present, mainly from Latin America and Asia. In the 1920s, Congress imposed a ceiling on the number of immigrants allowed, and the immigration rate dropped sharply. It rebounded after the Immigration and Nationality Act was amended in 1965 to eliminate caps on the number of people who could migrate from each country. Today, about 700,000 to one million *legal* immigrants continue to arrive in America every year. In addition, an estimated seven million *illegal* immigrants—those who are foreign born and enter the country without inspection or

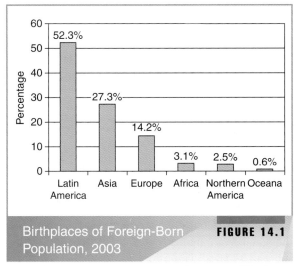

Source: *Statistical Abstract of the United States: 2006* (Washington, DC: Bureau of the Census, 2006), Table 44, 45.

violate the terms of a visa—reside in the United States.[8] Figure 14.1 divides up America's foreign-born population (including both legal and illegal immigrants) according to places of birth.

Thus, from its beginnings the United States has received far more immigrants than any other nation in history, and it has the most ethnically and culturally diverse population the world has ever seen (only India comes close). Later, we will consider some of the consequences for American politics.

Economy

At the end of the 1990s the United States had the world's largest economy. In 2003, its gross national product (GNP), or the total value of all the goods and services it produced, was calculated at $11.0 trillion, compared with Japan's $4.4 trillion and Germany's $2.1 trillion.[9] The American dollar continues to be the world's basic monetary unit; the value of most nations' currencies is customarily measured by how many euros, pounds, rubles, yen, and other units it takes to exchange for part or all of a dollar.

Some economists believe that American economic dominance has ended. The United States, which for many years was the world's greatest creditor nation, has become the world's greatest debtor nation, in part because Americans continue to buy billions of dollars more of foreign goods than foreigners buy of American goods, and in part because of the longstanding enormous deficits in the federal government's budget. From

1980 through 1997, the federal government spent a total of $3.1 trillion more than it took in, then ran modest surpluses from 1998 to 2001, but has returned to record-setting deficits since then. By 2005, the accumulated gross national debt was more than $8 trillion.[10]

America has long been regarded as the citadel of capitalist economic ideas and institutions, and the main antagonist of people and nations who believe in socialism. If we measure the degree of capitalism in an economy by the proportion of economic enterprise that is privately owned and operated for profit, that characterization is correct. Even so, American economic institutions and practices have never come close to meeting the standards for completely free enterprise laid down by such laissez-faire economists as Adam Smith in the eighteenth century and Milton Friedman in the twentieth. These economists advocated the barest minimum of government interference in economic affairs, including no government regulation of the operations, profits, and wages paid by successful businesses and no government subsidies or "bailouts" for unsuccessful businesses.

Yet American governments have always subsidized American businesses in many ways. They do expensive research on materials, design, production, and marketing in a variety of areas and make their findings available to private businesses free of charge. State, local, and federal governments work together to provide public goods, such as education and a transportation infrastructure. Federal tax law subsidizes the pensions and health plans that businesses offer to their employees, creating a hybrid public/private safety net that works something like a European welfare state, though only for those who get a job with good benefits.[11] Congress imposes tariffs and import quotas on certain foreign manufactured goods so as to prevent them from undercutting American manufacturers. Federal laws guarantee that all workers will be paid a certain minimum wage regardless of what they would get in a truly free market—and so on. Most of these goodies have come from political pressure by business associations, labor unions, and other pressure groups. Thus, it seems fair to say that, while most Americans say they believe in free enterprise, they prefer to practice safe enterprise.

America's Position in World Politics

Until the end of the nineteenth century the United States followed an isolationist foreign policy and was only a minor player in world politics. The changeover began with the Spanish-American War (1898), Theodore Roosevelt's mediation of the Russo-Japanese War (1905), and America's belated entry (1917) into World War I (1914–1918). Since 1918 America has been a leading player on the world stage.

From 1945 to 1989, world politics was dominated by the "Cold War" between the two great superpowers and their allies: the United States, leading an alliance of Western capitalist/democratic nations, and the Soviet Union, leading an alliance of Eastern communist/authoritarian nations. The Cold War came to an end in the early 1990s when the Soviet Union was formally dissolved (see Chapter 9) and Eastern European nations established their independence.

In the first years of the new millennium, the United States continues to be the world's most powerful nation, but a new international order is emerging. Whatever its final shape may be, the United States will continue to play a leading role, though that role is bound to be different from what it was during the Cold War.

THE CONSTITUTIONAL SYSTEM

As in most modern nations (Great Britain and Israel are two notable exceptions), the basic structure of the American system of government is set forth in a written constitution—the Constitution of the United States, a document drawn up in 1787, ratified in 1788, and inaugurated in 1789. It is the world's oldest written constitution still in force.

Of course, the Constitution of the 2000s differs from that of 1789 in a number of important ways. It has been formally amended twenty-seven times, the most recent being the 1992 amendment, which provided that no law changing the compensation for members of Congress shall take effect until an election of members of the House has been held.[12] Among the most important amendments are the following. The first ten, known collectively as the **Bill of Rights,** list the rights of individuals that the national government is forbidden to abridge (see Box 14.2).

The Fourteenth Amendment, ratified just after the Civil War, makes national citizenship legally superior to state citizenship, and prohibits the states from violating the "privileges and immunities" of U.S. citizens—which, by judicial interpretation, has come to mean nearly all the rights guaranteed against the national government by the first ten amendments. Other major amendments have outlawed slavery (the Thirteenth), guaranteed the right to vote to former slaves (the Fifteenth) and women (the Nineteenth), limited presidents to two elective terms (the Twenty-Second), and spelled out the conditions under which an incapacitated president can be replaced (the Twenty-Fifth). Even with these amendments, most of the basic elements of the 1789 Constitution have remained in force, whereas the written constitutions in

---

The U.S. Bill of Rights   BOX 14.2

1. Freedom of religion, speech, press.
2. Right to bear arms.
3. Freedom from quartering soldiers without owner's consent.
4. No unreasonable searches and seizures.
5. Trial of civilians only after indictment by a grand jury; no double jeopardy; prohibition against compelled self-incrimination; no deprivation of life, liberty, or property without due process of law; no taking of private property for public use without just compensation.
6. In criminal prosecutions, right to speedy and public trial by an impartial jury; defendant must be informed

of the nature and cause of accusations; defendant has power to compel testimony by witnesses in his or her favor; right to assistance of counsel.
7. Guarantee of trial by jury where the amount in controversy is over twenty dollars.
8. No excessive bail, no excessive fines, no cruel and unusual punishments.
9. Enumeration of certain rights in the Constitution shall not be construed to deny or diminish others retained by the people.
10. Powers not delegated to the national government nor prohibited to the states are reserved to the states or to the people.

many other countries and in most of the American states have been replaced altogether several times. Thus, if durability is a mark of constitutional strength, the Constitution of the United States is one of the strongest in history.

Yet the words in the Constitution do not tell all there is to be told about the basic structure of the American constitutional system. A number of customs, usages, and judicial decisions have significantly altered our way of governing without changing a word in the Constitution. Examples are the addition of judicial review, the development of political parties, and the conversion of the presidential selection process from a closed process by small cliques of insiders to popular elections open to all citizens. We will say more about each of these changes below.

Taken together, the provisions of the written Constitution of the United States and their associated customs and usages add up to a constitutional system that has three distinctive features: federalism, separation of powers, and judicial review.

Federalism

Federalism is a system in which governmental power is divided between a national government and several subnational governments, each of which is legally supreme in its assigned sphere. This system has some ancient precursors, notably the Achaean League of Greek city-states in the third century B.C. and the Swiss Confederation founded in the sixteenth century A.D. But the men who wrote the American Constitution established the first modern form of federalism. They did so because they had to. The 1787 convention in Philadelphia was called because its members felt that the new nation needed a much stronger national government than the Articles of Confederation provided, but the representatives from the small states refused to join any national government that did not preserve most of their established powers. The framers broke the resulting stalemate by dividing power between the national and the state governments, and gave each state equal representation in the national Senate. Only thus could the large and small states agree on a new constitution.

Even so, some of the framers regarded federalism as more than a political expedient. James Madison, for example, believed that the greatest threat to human rights in a popular government is the tyranny of popular majorities that results when one faction seizes control of the entire power of government and uses it to advance its own special interests at the expense of all other interests. He saw a division of power between the national and state governments, combined with separation of powers, as the best way to prevent such a disaster.

Federalism has been widely praised as one of the greatest American contributions to the art of government. A number of nations have adopted it as a way of enabling different regions with sharply different cultures and interests to join together as one nation. The clearest examples of such nations today are Australia, Canada, Germany, and Switzerland, but significant elements of federalism are also found in systems as disparate as those of Brazil, India, and Mexico.

The American federal system divides government power in the following principal ways:

- Powers specifically assigned to the federal[13] government, such as the power to declare war, make treaties with foreign nations, coin money, and regulate commerce between the states.
- Powers reserved to the states by the Tenth Amendment. The main powers in this category are those over education, marriage and divorce, intrastate commerce, and regulation of motor vehicles. However, the federal government often grants money to the states to help them build and operate schools, construct and repair highways, make welfare payments to the poor and the sick, and so on. The states do not have to accept the money, but if they do they also have to accept federal standards governing how the money is to be spent and federal monitoring to make sure it is spent that way.
- Powers that can be exercised by both the federal government and the states, such as imposing taxes and defining and punishing crimes.
- Powers forbidden to the federal government, mainly those in the first eight amendments, such as abridging freedom of speech, press, and religion, and various guarantees of fair trials for persons accused of crimes.
- Powers forbidden to the state governments. Some of these are in the body of the Constitution, but the main ones are the Fourteenth Amendment's requirements that no state shall "abridge the privileges or immunities of citizens of the United States; nor shall any State deprive any person of life, liberty, or property without due process of law; nor Deny to any person within its jurisdiction the equal protection of the laws." A series of

U.S. Supreme Court decisions have interpreted these phrases to mean that almost all the specific liberties guaranteed against the federal government in the first eight amendments are also guaranteed against the state governments by the Fourteenth Amendment.

When all is said and done, however, perhaps the most important single point to note about the nature of American federalism is made in Article VI of the Constitution:

> This Constitution, and the laws of the United States which shall be made in Pursuance thereof; and all Treaties made, or which shall be made, under the Authority of the United States, shall be the supreme Law of the Land; and the Judges in every State shall be bound thereby, any Thing in the Constitution or Laws of any State to the Contrary notwithstanding.

In short, while the federal government cannot constitutionally interfere with the powers assigned exclusively to the states, whenever a state constitution or law is inconsistent with a law or treaty the federal government has adopted in accordance with its proper powers, the conflicting state constitution and law must yield. Moreover, it is the Supreme Court of the United States, an organ of the federal government and not of the state governments, that decides which acts of the federal government and the state governments are within their respective powers. Thus, to the extent that the American federal system is a competition between the national government and the states, the chief umpire is a member of one of the two competing teams.

Separation of Powers

Since most analysts of the American system maintain that separation of powers is the most important single difference between the U.S. system (which is called a **presidential democracy**) and most other democratic systems (which are called *parliamentary democracies*), let us be clear on the institution's main features.

Separation of powers means the constitutional division of government power among separate legislative, executive, and judicial branches (see Figure 14.2).

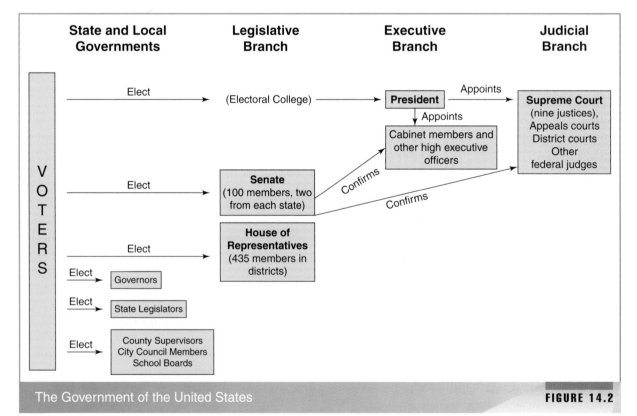

The Government of the United States

FIGURE 14.2

Source: *The United States Government Manual 2005/2006* (Washington, DC: U.S. Government Printing Office, 2005), 21.

The Constitution of the United States specifically vests the legislative power in Congress (Article I), the executive power in the president (Article II), and the judicial power in the federal courts, headed by the Supreme Court (Article III).

The three branches are separated in several ways, the most important of which is the requirement in Article I, Section 6: "No Person holding any Office under the United States, shall be a Member of either House during his Continuance in Office." This provision means that each branch is operated by persons entirely distinct from those operating the other two branches. Thus, for example, when Representative Norman Mineta was appointed Secretary of Transportation in 2001, he had to resign his seat in the House before he could take up his new post. This, of course, is the direct opposite of the fusion-of-powers rule in parliamentary democracies, such as Great Britain and Germany, which require the head of the executive branch to be a member of Parliament.

The persons heading each branch of the U.S. government are selected by different procedures for different terms. Members of the House of Representatives are elected directly by the voters for two-year terms, with no limit on the number of terms they can serve. Members of the Senate are elected directly by the voters for six-year terms without term limits, and their terms are staggered so that one-third of the Senate comes up for election or reelection every two years.[14]

The president is elected indirectly by the **electoral college** (which is selected by direct popular election) for a four-year term, and is limited to two full elected terms. All federal judges, including the members of the Supreme Court, are appointed by the president with the approval of a majority of the Senate, and they hold office until death, resignation, or removal by Congress.

The other main devices ensuring the separation of powers are the **checks and balances** by which each branch can keep the other two branches from invading its constitutional powers. For example, the Senate can disapprove top-level presidential appointments and refuse to ratify treaties. The two chambers of Congress acting together can impeach, convict, and remove the president or federal judges from office. They can (and often do) deny the president the legislation, appropriations, and taxes he requests. The president, in turn, can veto any act of Congress, and the Constitution requires a two-thirds vote of both chambers to override the veto. The president also makes the initial appointments of all federal judges. Presidents have normally nominated judges who are likely to agree with their political philosophies and policy preferences, but once appointed and confirmed judges rule without political supervision.

The Supreme Court, through its power of judicial review, can declare any act of the president or Congress null and void on the ground that it violates the Constitution. Such a decision can be overturned only by a constitutional amendment or by the Court, usually with new members, changing its mind.

Some scholars believe that the American system is more accurately described as a system of "separated branches exercising shared powers," since getting government action usually requires some kind of joint action by the Congress and the president, with the acquiescence of the Supreme Court. Separation of powers is what most political scientists have called this feature of the system since the time of the *Federalist Papers*. Whatever it is called, this constitutional feature, more than any other, makes the American system different from most other democratic systems.[15]

Judicial Review

Judicial review can be defined as the power of a court to render a legislative or executive act null and void on the ground of unconstitutionality. All American courts, including the lower federal courts and all levels of the state courts, exercise this power on occasion. But the final word on all issues involving an interpretation of the national Constitution (which, as we have seen, is "the supreme law of the land") belongs to the U.S. Supreme Court.

Although every democracy has to determine who has the final word on what its constitution allows and prohibits, the United States is one of the few democracies in which that power is given to the top appellate court of the regular court system. Some countries, such as Italy, give the final word to special tribunals rather than to bodies in their regular court systems, while in others (such as Mexico and Switzerland) the power includes only the "federal umpire" power, and not the power to override decisions of the national executive and legislature. Thus, judicial review is a prominent but not exclusive feature of the American constitutional system.

POLITICAL CULTURE AND SOCIALIZATION

The American constitutional system, though important to how Americans make political decisions, is not the whole story. To a considerable degree, the American political system functions as it does because it is operated by Americans rather than by Britons, Italians, Mexicans, or Iraqis, and it does what it does because Americans have a distinctive political culture that underlies, animates, and shapes all of the formal institutions we have reviewed.

Two of this book's editors say that "a **political culture** is a particular distribution of political attitudes, values, feelings, information, and skills" that "affects the conduct of [a nation's] citizens and leaders throughout the political system."[16] Chapter 3 discusses political culture and socialization in a comparative perspective, and America's unique political culture deserves close attention.

Melting Pot or Patchwork Quilt?

Most Americans are immigrants or descendants of immigrants who came from many different cultures in Africa, Asia, Western and Eastern Europe, and Latin America. Thus, throughout most of its history the United States has had to deal with how best to fit the immigrants and their different cultures into American economic, social, and political life.

Throughout our history, two visions of how immigrants should become incorporated into society have clashed in intellectual discourse, policy debates, and actual practice. One vision is of a **"melting pot"** that blends all the different cultures of immigrants into one uniquely American culture, which was to be expressed and passed on in one language, the American version of English. Some room was left for such special ethnic folkways as Polish weddings, Irish wakes, and Mexican food, but the paramount task given to the educational system was to turn everyone into an English-speaking American imbued with the main values and attitudes of the nation's political culture.

A contrasting vision sees America as a true cultural **"patchwork quilt"** (the phrase is Jesse Jackson's)—an array of the languages, history, customs, and values of each of the nation's major ethnic groups, each receiving the same attention, respect, and importance as every other, with none dominant. This view rejects the melting pot idea that the ancient and distinct cultures of immigrant groups should be homogenized into one prevailing national culture—a culture which, they say, is not truly a blend of all cultures but rather the culture of Western Europe, especially Great Britain. While the patchwork quilt metaphor was recently coined and is today associated with some leaders among the African-American, Latino, and Asian communities, members of various immigrant groups have sought to cling to their cultural identities and native languages for over a century. Italian, Irish, and especially German immigrants often resisted melting into America's customs and language, and reshaped the mainstream culture and even the English language.

Among the policies advocated by adherents to the patchwork quilt vision are bilingual education (educating minority-group children in their native languages rather than forcing them to learn English as their primary language); printing ballots and other official documents in languages other than English; and broadening school curricula so as to give full and fair attention to the contributions of African, Asian, and Latin cultures as well as of British and Western European cultures.

Some opposition has set in against this movement. One manifestation is the laws adopted by several states and the May 2006 vote by the U.S. Senate declaring English to be the official language. Political scientist Sam Huntington's book, *Who Are We? The Challenges to America's National Identity*, offered a controversial defense of the Anglo-Protestant culture against a threatened erosion by today's wave of immigration from Latin America. The clash between the competing melting pot and patchwork quilt visions of immigrant assimilation will likely continue throughout the twenty-first century.

Main Elements of the Traditional American Political Culture

The first dimensions of political culture that political scientists usually consider are called trust in institutions, and trust in government and/or trust in leaders. How do Americans compare with other peoples on these dimensions? Some of the answers are presented in Table 14.1, which compares the levels of popular trust in government in the United States and four Western European nations.

	United States	Great Britain	France	Germany	Italy
TABLE 14.1					
Trust in Government in Five Western Nations (in percentages)					
Most elected officials are trustworthy	44	39	30	32	26
Elected officials care what people like me think	41	43	26	20	15
Government is really run for the benefit of all the people	48	57	52	30	16
Trust the government	40	57	33	41	35
Average	43	49	35	31	23

Source: *1997 Deconstructing Distrust Survey*, Pew Research Center for the People and the Press.

Table 14.1 shows that significantly greater proportions of Americans than of British, Germans, French, or Italians believe that most elected officials are trustworthy. On the other hand, fewer Americans than Britons or French believe that government is really run for the benefit of all the people. Averaging the answers on all four trust-in-government questions shows that Americans rank above the French, Germans, and Italians, but below the British. These findings do not support the charge made by some commentators that Americans are exceptionally "alienated" from their government. Moreover, other studies have shown that more Americans say they are very proud of their country (80 percent) and are willing to fight for it (71 percent) than the citizens of Great Britain, Spain, Italy, France, and Germany say about their countries (where the proportions range from 55 and 62 percent in Great Britain down to 21 percent and 35 percent in Germany.)[17]

Thus, while fewer Americans may trust their government to do what is right than some Western Europeans do, they are nevertheless more proud of being Americans and more willing to fight for America than the Western Europeans are for their countries. How can we explain this paradox?

The answer may lie in the fact that throughout history most Americans have strongly held two ideas that may be logically (but not emotionally) inconsistent. One is the idea that ordinary Americans are good, solid, reliable folks with plenty of common sense, and that America is a wonderful country. Conversely, they feel that the *government*, which is not the same thing as the country, is, as former President Ronald Reagan put it, "the problem, not the solution," and they feel that the professional politicians who fill its offices, lead its parties, and conduct its business are self-seeking lightweights more interested in winning votes and getting reelected than in making courageous and forward-looking policies to solve the nation's problems. Thus many Americans love their country but distrust the politicians who run its governments.

Another dimension of political culture is the degree to which ordinary people believe that their preferences significantly influence public officials. One of the findings of the first major comparative study of political cultures was that Americans score higher on this dimension than people in Great Britain, Germany, Italy, and Mexico, and that in all five countries better educated people score higher than less educated people.[18] Subsequent studies have confirmed that Americans generally feel more "politically efficacious" in this sense than do the citizens of most other nations.

Political scientists usually think of ideology as a comprehensive and strongly held set of convictions about how governments ought to make their decisions and/or what those decisions ought to be. The ideologies that receive the most attention in discussions of the political cultures of other nations are socialism and capitalism, with the Left (leaning more toward socialism) and the Right (leaning more toward capitalism). Considerable attention is also paid to democracy and authoritarianism, and constitutionalism and totalitarianism. Almost every comparative study of political cultures concludes that ideology plays a smaller role in American political culture than in many others, with only handfuls of Americans supporting such classically European ideologies as socialism, communism, or fascism.[19]

Another exceptional feature of our nation is the depth of the conviction among most Americans—black and white, women and men, young and old—that they have certain basic rights and that often the best way to make sure they get their rights is not to wait for executives, legislatures, and bureaucrats to do the right thing but to file lawsuits to force public officials—and other private individuals—to honor their rights. The **litigiousness** of Americans—that is, their tendency to file law suits against government officials and other private citizens for violating their rights—gives the courts a central role in America. American legal scholar Robert Kagan argues that litigation in the United States accomplishes (at a much higher cost) the same things that European nations accomplish through regulation.[20] America has pursued this different path most likely because of the notion, espoused by populists like President Andrew Jackson, that the common man has enough wisdom to supervise everything, even his government.

Political Socialization

Political socialization is the process by which children are introduced to the values and attitudes of their society, shaping their notions of what the political world is like and which people, policies, and institutions are good and bad. That process in America is much the same as in every other modern populous industrialized democracy. Political socialization begins in children as young as age 3 or 4 and continues until old age and death. Children typically begin by perceiving some political figures, notably the president and the local policeman, as important persons outside their own families. As they grow older their perceptions broaden and deepen, and they learn about political parties, legislators, judges, and public policies and issues.

The main agencies shaping Americans' political socialization are their families (especially their parents), schoolteachers, friends, schoolmates, work associates, and the mass communications media. Most recent studies agree that parents continue to have the most powerful impact on most people's political socialization. However, as the influence of the mass communications media has increased in recent years, parents' impact has lessened. This should not surprise us, for most analysts of political life in America and the other large-scale industrial democracies agree that the mass media, especially television, have become one of the most important forces—many would say *the* most important force—affecting people's political socialization, attitudes, and behavior.

The term **mass communications media** includes all the devices used to transmit information, thought, or feeling to a mass audience that does not see the communicator face-to-face. They fall into two categories: the print media (newspapers, magazines, books, and pamphlets) and the electronic media (radio, broadcast television, cable and satellite television, and the Internet).

The relative political importance of these media in America and three European democracies is shown in Table 14.2. It demonstrates that television is the most important source of information about politics for most Americans, as well as for most Britons, Germans, and French, with newspapers a distant second in all four nations. In all four nations the other media, such as direct communications among people, are less important. Note that the figures on Internet usage, taken from surveys conducted in 2000 and 2003, likely understate its growing importance.

Most Important Source of Political Information (in percentages)				TABLE 14.2
	United States **2000**	**Great Britain** **2003**	**Germany** **2003**	**France** **2003**
Television	70	54	75	66
Newspapers	39	44	59	40
Radio	15	28	38	36
Internet	11	18	14	15
Magazines, other print media	4	16	24	23
Personal discussion	—	18	20	25
Other	1	33	14	19

Source: Russell J. Dalton, *Citizen Politics: Public Opinion and Political Parties in Advanced Industrial Democracies*, 4th ed. (Washington, DC: C.Q. Press, 2006), Table 2.1, 23.

The United States, like most other industrialized democracies, has a mixture of publicly owned and privately owned television and radio stations and networks. The privately owned media are much more important than the publicly owned in America: there are three times as many private as public broadcasting stations, and the public stations usually have only about 10 percent of the viewers. Additionally, nearly all high-circulation newspapers, magazines, and websites are privately owned and supported by advertising revenues and subscribers.

The political content produced by print media outlets is almost entirely unregulated by government because of the First Amendment's protection of freedom of the press (see again Box 14.2). About the only restrictions on what is printed are libel and slander laws, but in the landmark case of *New York Times v. Sullivan* (1964), the U.S. Supreme Court held that public officials and public figures cannot collect damages for remarks made about them in the print media unless those comments are (1) knowingly false or made with a "reckless disregard" for their truth and (2) made with proved "malice" as a deliberate attempt to damage the victim's public reputation and standing—a change that is very difficult to prove.[21]

By contrast, radio and television stations are much more closely regulated than the print media. They can broadcast only if they are granted a license by the Federal Communications Commission (FCC). That license requires that the political content of programs meet certain standards. For example, the stations must make available to all candidates for a particular political office an equal opportunity to make their appeals; they do not have to *give* any of them free time, but if they do give time to one candidate they must give it to all. If they sell time to one candidate, they must sell it to all at the same rates and offer comparably desirable times. They cannot charge political advertisers higher rates than they charge commercial advertisers.

The U.S. Supreme Court has consistently upheld the government's power to impose such restrictions on the electronic media while denying government any comparable power over the print media. The reasons have to do with what is generally called the **scarcity doctrine:** the Court has found that there is no limit, other than economic, on the number of newspapers, books, magazines, or pamphlets that can be printed and circulated. But there is a physical limit on the number of television or radio stations that can operate in a given portion of the broadcast spectrum. Accordingly, said the Court, broadcasting is a public resource, much like the national parks or navigable rivers; this gives the government the right not only to allocate frequencies, but also to set standards to ensure that their use will promote "the public convenience, interest, or necessity."[22]

Perhaps the most liberated media outlets are independent Internet sites, which are not subject to licensing requirements, do not have to stay in the good graces of a large range of advertising clients, and have little reputation to lose if they publish news reports that become discredited. Web logs, or "blogs," authored by activists from every part of the ideological spectrum play an increasingly important (and often-criticized) role in campaigns, with their ability to spread fact, rumor, and baseless accusation across the cyberspace with unchecked speed. Because of the Internet's rising importance in politics, regulation of its political content is an evolving area of policy and jurisprudence.

POLITICAL PARTICIPATION AND RECRUITMENT

Participation by Voting

Since voting in elections is the main way in which ordinary citizens in all democracies actually participate in their nations' governing processes, most political scientists believe that **voting turnout**—the percentage of all the people eligible to vote who actually do so—is one of the most important indicators of any democratic system's health. Studies of voting turnout in the world's democracies, like that in Table 14.3, usually find that the turnout is lower in the United States than in any other democracy except Switzerland.

Many commentators in America have also pointed to figures suggesting that voter turnout has declined dramatically here over the past few decades as signs of a deep sickness in U.S. politics. They have claimed, variously, that it is a symptom of too much negative campaigning, too few good candidates, the rising role of money in campaigns, the diminishing role of parties in grassroots politics, and many other ills. However, recent research shows that these are false diagnoses of what turns out to be a healthy patient: turnout has remained fairly stable in America over the past thirty years.

Average Voting Turnout in Elections to Lower House, 1961–1999	TABLE 14.3

Nation	Average Turnout
Australia[†]	95
Belgium[†]	92
Italy[†]	90
Sweden	88
New Zealand	87
Germany	86
Canada	75
United Kingdom	75
France	75
Japan	69
India	59
United States	52*
Switzerland	52

[†]Compulsory voting law
*Presidential elections

Source: Adapted from Mark N. Franklin, "The Dynamics of Electoral Participation," in Lawrence LeDuc, Richard G. Niemi, and Pippa Norris, eds., *Comparing Democracies* 2 (Thousand Oaks, CA: Sage 2002), Table 7.1, 150.

The conventional wisdom that turnout had dropped was wrong because it relied on a misleading approximation of turnout, which calculated the percentage of those old enough to vote who actually did so. The problem with this measure is that many people who are old enough to vote in the United States are not eligible to cast a ballot, some because they are not citizens and some because they are convicted felons living in states that bar them from voting. As the percentage of Americans who are noncitizens (including both legal and illegal immigrants) or felons has grown in recent decades, a smaller portion of the voting age population has been eligible to vote. Scholars who counted up these groups and correctly calculated the percentage of eligible voters who participate found that turnout in presidential elections has remained steady at 55–60 percent since 1972 (after the Twenty-Sixth Amendment gave 18-year-olds the right to vote, and turnout in fact dropped).[23]

Further scrutinizing what goes into these turnout figures makes America look better compared to the rest of the world, and points out a key obstacle to voter participation here. When voting turnout is counted in exactly the same way in the United States as it is in other democracies—as a percentage of registered voters—the

American record looks much better. In America, as in most of the world's other democracies, citizens' names must appear on voting registers before they can legally vote. But the United States differs from other nations in one important respect: in most other countries, getting on the register requires no effort by the voter. Public authorities take the initiative to get all eligible citizens enrolled, a job often made easier in countries that have a national list of residents. As a result, almost every citizen of voting age is registered to vote.

In the United States, by contrast, there is no list of residents, and each state regulates **voting registration.** In most states, would-be voters must make an effort to get on the register; no public official will do it for them. Moreover, in most democratic countries when voters move from one part of the country to another, they are automatically struck off the register in the place they leave and are added to the register in the place they move to, all with no effort on their part. In contrast, when people move from one U.S. state to another they are not automatically added to the register in their new state.[24] One study that compared turnout of registered voters in the United States, which averages 86.8 percent, with turnout of registered voters in twenty-four other democracies found that the United States ranks eleventh highest on this measure.[25]

This ranking is still lower than many might expect from the world's self-described citadel of democracy. Another explanation for America's low voting turnout arises from the fact that American voters are called on to cast far more votes than the citizens of any other country (only Switzerland comes close). In the parliamentary democracies, the only national elections are those for the national parliament, in which voters normally vote for one candidate or for one party. They also vote periodically for a candidate or a party in the elections for the city or rural district in which they live. In the federal systems, they also vote for a member of their state or provincial parliament. Hence, in most democracies other than the United States and Switzerland, the typical voter makes a total of only four or five voting decisions over a period of four or five years.[26]

In the United States, the combination of separation of powers, federalism, the direct primary, and, at the state and local levels, the initiative and referendum means that citizens may be faced with several *hundred* electoral decisions in a period of four years. At the national level, voters are called on to vote in the presidential primaries of their parties, and in the general election to decide (mostly) between the Democratic and Republican candidates. They are also expected to vote in primary elections and general elections every two years for members of the House of Representatives and twice in every six years for members of the Senate. At the state and local levels not only are the leading executive officials (governors and mayors) and members of the legislatures nominated in primary elections and elected in general elections, but in most states and localities a considerable number of other offices that are appointed positions in most other democracies—for example, state secretaries of state, attorneys general, treasurers, superintendents of education, judges, school superintendents, and members of local school boards, sanitary commissions, park commissions, and so on—are selected by much the same primary-plus-general-election procedures.

Direct democracy processes, such as the **direct initiative** (a proposal for a new law that goes before voters if enough of them sign a petition), and the **popular referendum** (a vote on whether or not to keep an existing law), give many Americans even more choices to make at the ballot box. Although the U.S. federal government has never held a direct democracy election, twenty-four states and many local governments make the initiative process available, meaning that about 70 percent of Americans live in a city or state with the initiative.[27] This sometimes adds as many as thirty complex policy choices to a ballot.

Thus American citizens are called on to vote far more often and on more questions than those of any other country except Switzerland (where voters in many cantons also have direct democracy). Surely the opportunity to vote in free, fair, and competitive elections is a *sine qua non* of democratic government, and therefore a good thing. Yet a familiar saying is that there can be too much of a good thing, and many Americans leaving their polling places after casting their ninetieth (or more) vote of the year are likely to conclude that the sheer number of voting decisions in America is a case in point.[28]

Participation by Other Means

Voting, of course, is only one of several ways citizens can participate in politics. They can also serve in office; work in political parties; donate money to candidates, parties, and causes; attend rallies; take part in street demonstrations; send letters, telegrams, faxes, and e-mail messages to their elected representatives; write letters and op-ed pieces to newspapers; call radio and television talk shows; try to persuade families and friends; file lawsuits against public officials; and so on. These other forms of participation have not been studied as extensively as voting, but Russell Dalton has collected some interesting comparative data on conventional and unconventional forms of participation in the United States and some Western European countries (see Table 14.4).

TABLE 14.4

Nonvoting Forms of Political Participation in Four Democracies (in percentages)

Activity	United States	Great Britain	Germany	France
Voting				
Voted in national election	53	72	74	61
Campaign Activity				
Attempt to convince others how to vote	49	—	28	29
Attend meeting/rally	8	3	5	6
Work for party/candidate	3	3	7	7
Communal Activity				
Sign a petition	81	81	47	68
Membership in public interest group	33	8	8	6
Protest Activity				
Participate in lawful demonstrations	21	13	22	39
Join in boycott	25	17	10	13
Participate in unofficial strike	6	9	2	12

Source: All figures are from Russell J. Dalton, *Citizen Politics in Western Democracies*, 4th ed. (Washington, DC: C.Q. Press, 2006). Voting figures are taken from p. 40, campaign activity from pp. 44–46, communal activity from p. 49 and p. 68, and protest activity from p. 68.

The responses in Table 14.4 show that citizens of France are more likely than citizens of the United States, Great Britain, or Germany to participate in demonstrations and political strikes, whereas Americans are more likely than the others to persuade other people how to vote and to work with citizen groups.

Several other studies have found that the form of participation most frequently claimed by Americans is voting in elections (53 percent), followed by stating their political opinions to others (32 percent), contributing money to campaigns (12 percent), displaying political bumper stickers and signs (9 percent), and attending political meetings or rallies (8 percent). Only 4 percent report belonging to a political club or working for a political party.[29]

In short, Americans participate in politics in ways other than voting in elections as much or more than the citizens of the other Western democracies for whom we have reliable information. These data certainly do not support the conclusion that Americans are in any way more alienated or lazier than the citizens of other democracies.

RECRUITMENT OF LEADERS

Recruitment is the process whereby, out of the millions of a nation's citizens, emerge the few hundreds or thousands who hold elective and appointive public office, play leading roles in parties and pressure groups, decide how the mass communications media will portray politics, and, within the limits permitted by the general public, make public policy.

Many scholars have studied leadership recruitment in many countries and have found certain general tendencies that are also evident in American politics. For instance, American leaders, like leaders in other countries, are drawn disproportionately from the middle and upper ranges of wealth and status. The reason lies not in the existence of any conspiracy to oppress the lower classes but in the kinds of knowledge and skills a person must have to win the support needed for selection as a leader. These skills are more likely to be acquired and developed by well-educated rather than poorly educated people. For example, people's chances to climb in a political party or a pressure group, to be selected for public office, or to be appointed to higher administrative offices, are considerably enhanced if they have the ability to speak well in public, and, for elected officials increasingly, to look and sound good on television.

The federal and state governments choose most of their administrative employees by procedures and standards other than the unabashed political patronage that prevailed until the late nineteenth century. In today's system, initial selection is made according to the applicants' abilities to score well on standardized examinations or possession of other abilities and experience desired by their employers, and salary increases and promotions depend on job performance rather than on party connections. Since the merit system was established in 1883, more and more federal positions have been placed under it or under the "general schedule" category, and today only about 1 percent are available for purely political appointments.

Accordingly, in most respects elite recruitment in the United States differs very little from its counterparts in other advanced industrialized democracies. But in one aspect of that process—the nomination of candidates for elective office—the United States is unlike any other nation in the world.

The Unique Direct Primary

We can divide the process of electing public officials into three parts: (1) *candidate selection*, the process by which political parties decide which people to name as their standard-bearers and campaign for; (2) *nomination*, the process by which public authorities decide which people's names will be printed on the official ballots; and (3) *election*, the process by which the voters register their choices among the nominees.

Many political scientists believe that candidate selection is the most important of the three processes. After all, the recruitment of public officials is essentially one of narrowing the choices from many to one. For example, in 2000 about 130 million Americans satisfied all the constitutional requirements for being elected president. Theoretically, all 130 million names could have been printed on the ballot and each voter could have had an absolutely free choice among them. But, of course, no voter can possibly make a meaningful choice among 130 million alternatives, and so a practical democratic election requires that the choices be narrowed down to a manageable number. The same is true for elections to office in all democratic countries.

In the United States, as in every other democracy, the narrowing process is accomplished mainly by the political parties. Each party chooses its candidates, gives their names to the election authorities, and those names appear on the ballot.[30] Accordingly, in 2004 the Democrats chose John Kerry to be their presidential candidate over Howard Dean, Wesley Clark, John Edwards, Al Sharpton, Carol Moseley Braun, Bob Graham, Dick Gephardt, Dennis Kucinich, and Joe Lieberman. President George W. Bush did not face any serious contenders for the Republican Party's nomination. These nominations made it relatively easy for the voters to make the final choice between Bush and Kerry.

Given the crucial role of candidate selection in democratic elections, it is important to recognize that the United States is the only nation in the world that makes most of its nominations by direct primaries. In nearly all the parliamentary democracies, the parties' candidates for parliament are chosen by the parties' leaders or by small groups of card-carrying, dues-paying party members. A few countries, such as Germany and Finland, require the parties to choose their candidates by secret votes of local party members in procedures that resemble but, strictly speaking, are not direct primaries. Consequently, in every nation except the United States the candidates are selected by only a few hundred, or at most a few thousand, party insiders.[31]

In the United States, nominations for almost all major elective public offices[32] are made by **direct primaries,** in which candidates are selected directly by the voters in government-conducted elections rather than indirectly by party leaders in caucuses and conventions. Moreover—and this is the key difference between America's direct primaries and the primary-like procedures in other countries mentioned earlier—public laws, not party rules, determine who is qualified to vote in a particular party's primary. In 2002, twenty-seven states held **closed primaries,** in which only persons preregistered as members of a particular party could vote in that party's primary. Eleven states held **crossover primaries,** which are the same as closed primaries except that voters do not have to make a public choice of the party primary in which they will vote until election day. Nine states held **open primaries,** in which there is no party registration of any kind, and voters can vote in whichever party primary they choose (they can, however, vote in only one party's primary in any particular election) with no public disclosure of their choice.[33] In its 2000 *California*

Democratic Party v. Jones decision, the U.S. Supreme Court prohibited California's **blanket primary** (which allowed voters to switch back and forth between the parties in voting for nominees for particular offices) on the grounds that it violated a party's First Amendment right to free association. This decision, which also caused Alaska and Washington to alter their primary systems, makes clear the extent to which nomination procedures are formal, regulated by the government, and structured by the Constitution.

Direct primaries make candidate selection in the United States by far the most open and participatory in the world. As noted earlier, in all other countries only a few thousand dues-paying party members at most participate in choosing candidates; in the United States they are chosen by any registered voter who wants to participate, and millions do in every election cycle. To give just one example: although American presidential candidates are formally selected by national nominating conventions, a great majority of the delegates to both conventions are chosen by direct primaries. In 2004, a grand total of 24,227,443 votes were cast in the Democratic and Republican presidential primaries.[34]

The American system for choosing its presidents may be wiser or more foolish than the ways other democracies select their top political leaders, but it is far more participatory.

INTEREST ARTICULATION: PRESSURE GROUPS AND PACS

As we have seen throughout this book, every society has a number of different and conflicting political interests,[35] and the more advanced the economy and the more heterogeneous the society the more individuals and groups there are with interests that to some degree conflict with other interests. The inevitable clash of these interests generates the political process, which consists of two main parts: (1) interest articulation, by which the persons and groups make known their desires for government action or inaction; and (2) interest aggregation, by which various demands are mobilized and combined to press for favorable government policies. That is why many political scientists agree with Harold D. Lasswell that the essence of government is deciding "who gets what, when, and how."[36]

In most democracies interests are articulated mainly by pressure groups and political parties, and the governing parties also aggregate interests in formulating and implementing their programs. In the United States, however, the political parties are much weaker and less cohesive than those in most other democratic systems. Consequently, pressure groups play a major role in both interest articulation and aggregation in the United States.

Many foreign observers of America's peculiar politics have been especially struck by the great variety and power of our organized political groups.[37] Today they are even more numerous and important than in the past. They take two main forms, each of which specializes in a particular technique for influencing government: (1) political action committees and campaign contributions, and (2) pressure groups and lobbying.

PACs and Campaign Contributions

Strictly speaking, a **political action committee (PAC)** is any organization that is not formally affiliated with a particular party or candidate and spends money to influence the outcome of elections. PACs differ from political parties in two main respects. First, unlike parties, they do not nominate candidates and put them on ballots with PAC labels; rather, they support or oppose candidates nominated by the parties. Second, PACs are interested mainly in the policies public officials make, not in the party labels those officials bear. Hence, they often support candidates of both major parties who are sympathetic to the PACs' particular policy preferences.

Such organizations have operated in American politics at least since the Civil War, and some of them have had considerable success. For example, the Anti-Saloon League was founded in 1893 to support both Democratic and Republican candidates for Congress pledged to support a constitutional amendment outlawing the manufacture and sale of alcoholic beverages. Most historians believe that it deserves much of the credit (blame?) for the adoption of the Eighteenth Amendment (prohibition) in 1919. One of the most powerful organizations in the second half of the twentieth century was the Committee on Political Education (COPE) of the AFL-CIO, which has supplied millions of dollars and thousands of election workers for candidates (mostly but not entirely Democrats) sympathetic to organized labor.

The greatest increase in the number and activity of PACs in American history has come since 1974 as an unanticipated (and, by many, unwanted) consequence of that year's amendments to the Federal Election Campaign Act. The amendments set low limits on the amount of money individuals could contribute to a candidate or a party, but considerably higher limits on what organizations could contribute. They also stipulated that although labor unions and business corporations could not directly contribute money to election campaigns, they could sponsor PACs and their PACs could make campaign contributions as long as the funds came from voluntary contributions by sympathetic individuals rather than by direct levies on union and corporate funds.

In ruling on the constitutionality of these rules, the Supreme Court upheld the limits on direct contributions, but said that limiting the amounts of money that an individual or an organization can spend on behalf of a candidate (that is, by broadcasting or publishing ads *not* controlled by candidates or parties) was a violation of the First Amendment's guarantee of free speech.[38]

These changes in the substance and interpretation of the campaign finance laws led most politically active interests to conclude that forming a PAC was the best way to influence election outcomes, and that is just what they have done. In 1974, only 608 PACs operated in national elections; by 2006 the number had exploded to 4,210 (see Box 14.3).

At present, each PAC must register with the Federal Election Commission and periodically report its receipts (who contributed and how much) and its expenditures (to what candidates it gave contributions and how much, and how much it spent on its own independent campaigning). A PAC can contribute $5,000 to a particular candidate in a primary election and another $5,000 in the general election. Yet there is no limit on the total amount it can contribute to all candidates and party committees. There is also no limit on the amount it can spend on behalf of a particular candidate or party as long as its beneficiaries have no say in how the money is spent. The enactment in 2002 of the McCain-Feingold bill prohibited all "soft money" contributions—formerly unlimited contributions that were made to federal, state, and local political parties. However, a perceived loophole in this law has allowed "527 Committees" (a name that comes from their categorization in the tax code) to play the

Top Ten PACs in Overall Spending, 2003–2004

BOX 14.3

Rank	PAC Name	Overall Spending
1	MoveOn PAC	$30,043,750
2	Emily's List	26,051,693
3	America Coming Together	15,154,735
4	American Federation of State, County & Municipal Employees-PEOPLE, Qualified	14,056,945
5	United Auto Workers Voluntary Community Action Program	13,336,541
6	National Rifle Association Political Victory Fund	12,772,488
7	Service Employees International Union Committee on Political Education	12,461,614
8	Democratic Republican Independent Voter Education PAC for International Brotherhood of Teamsters	10,468,934
9	Republican Issues Campaign	7,959,860
10	Voice of Teachers for Education/Committee on Political Education of New York State United Teachers	7,634,014

Source: Harold W. Stanley and Richard G. Niemi, *Vital Statistics on American Politics, 2005–2006* (Washington, DC: Congressional Quarterly, 2006), Table 215, 107–08.

role that parties formerly played by collecting the same sorts of unlimited contributions and spending them independently to influence campaigns.

Although many PACs take some part in presidential election campaigns, the federal government finances most of the costs of those campaigns. Thus, most PACs make most of their contributions to House and Senate campaigns. It is estimated that they now contribute about 28 percent of all the funds for those campaigns.[39]

The most important PACs can be classified in one of three main categories:

1. *Narrow material interest PACs.* These are PACs concerned mainly with backing candidates who will support legislation that favors a particular business or type of business (for example, Chrysler, Coca Cola, General Electric, General Motors, Texaco), and many other corporations have their own PACs, as do many labor unions, including the Air Line Pilots Association, the American Federation of State, County & Municipal Employees, and the American Federation of Teachers. In addition, a number of PACs represent the interests of whole industries, such as the Dallas Energy Political Action Committee (oil), Edison Electric Institute (electric power), and the National Association of Broadcasters (radio and television).

2. *Single, nonmaterial interest PACs.* These PACs promote candidates who favor their positions on a particular nonmaterial issue. For example, the National Abortion Rights Action League (prochoice) and the National Right to Life Committee (antiabortion) are concerned with the abortion issue and the National Rifle Association (anti-gun-control) and Handgun Control, Inc. (procontrol) focus on the gun control issue.

3. *Ideological PACs.* Finally, a number of PACs support candidates committed to strong liberal or conservative ideologies and issues. Liberal PACs include MoveOn, the National Committee for an Effective Congress, and the Hollywood Women's Political Committee. Conservative PACs include the Republican Issues Campaign and the Conservative Victory Committee.

Pressure Groups and Lobbying

Another tactic that PACs use to advance their interests is **lobbying** through their Washington representatives. This stratagem concentrates on inducing public officials already in office to support government action (including administrative and judicial rulings as well as legislative acts) the groups favor and to block those the groups oppose.

In the bad old days, pressure groups often used straight bribes in the form of cash payments or guarantees of well-paid jobs after retirement. Sadly, bribes are still occasionally offered and accepted, but the laws against them are strict and the mass media's investigative reporters love to expose bribe-taking. In a recent example, the San Diego *Union-Tribune*'s 2005 investigation of Congressman Randall "Duke" Cunningham for accepting over $2 million in bribes in exchange for influencing defense contracts led to an eight-year prison term for Cunningham, as well as a Pulitzer prize for the newspaper. Congress reacted to the Cunningham scandal and the investigations that forced the resignation of House Majority Leader Tom DeLay and sent former lobbyist Jack Abramoff to jail by considering new ethics legislation. These scandals played a major role in the Democratic surge in the 2006 congressional elections (see Box 14.5). Calls for reform are likely to fade, though, as the scandals pass. Such was the case with the "Teapot Dome" influence-peddling scandal of the 1920s, which caused huge outrage at the time but is now a quaint historical footnote. Bribery is quite rare in everyday American politics, since most interest groups and public officials have decided that giving or taking bribes is either too immoral, too risky, or both.

The main tactic of lobbyists is now *persuasion*—convincing members of Congress (and their staffs, who play key roles in making most members' decisions) that the legislation the lobbyist seeks is in the best interests of the nation and of the member's particular district or state. After all, almost all members of Congress feel that their job is to do the best they can for the interests of their particular constituents. Since it is those constituents rather than the rest of the nation who determine whether or not the members will get reelected, their likely reactions must be the members' first concern.

Accordingly, lobbyists for all interests use the most persuasive evidence and arguments they can to convince a particular member that the actions their groups want will be in everyone's best interest—the voters in the particular district or state, the member's, and the nation's. Lobbyists who work for interest groups that also have PACs may sometimes hint that the PAC will be contributing to the campaigns of legislators who see the light on their issues. Surprisingly, however, most lobbyists and PACs work quite independently of one another, and a great volume of studies by political scientists have failed to provide any

clear evidence that campaign contributions influence the votes cast by legislators. Contributions may ensure access to politicians, scholars have found, but it does not buy votes.

Although American interest groups most frequently employ electioneering and lobbying, they sometimes use tactics that are more widely used in other countries, such as mass political propaganda, demonstrations, strikes and boycotts, nonviolent civil disobedience, and sometimes even violence. There is one tactic, however, in which the United States leads the world: the use of **litigation** for political purposes. Tocqueville wrote in 1835, "Scarcely any political question arises in the United States that is not resolved, sooner or later, into a judicial question."[40] Political scientists Benjamin Ginsberg and Martin Shefter note that from 1955 to 1985 the number of civil cases brought in federal district courts increased from 50,000 a year to over 250,000 a year. One of several reasons for that enormous increase, they say, is the fact that a growing number of interest groups that have done poorly in both elections and lobbying have filed suits in the courts to reverse their losses in other arenas:

> Civil rights groups, through federal court suits, launched successful assaults on Southern school systems, state and local governments, and legislative districting schemes. . . . Environmental groups used the courts to block the construction of highways, dams, and other public projects that not only threatened to damage the environment but also provided money and other resources to their political rivals. Women's groups were able to overturn state laws restricting abortion as well as statutes discriminating against women in the labor market.[41]

Conservative groups have countered by trying to ensure that **conservatives** rather than liberals or feminists are appointed to the Supreme Court and other federal judgeships. Liberal groups have also organized campaigns to influence appointments and confirmation battles in order to populate the judicial branch with those who are sympathetic to their goals. Ever since Democrats in the Senate failed to confirm President Ronald Reagan's nomination of Robert Bork to the U.S. Supreme Court in 1987, nearly every appointment to the nation's highest court has been fought with intense lobbying, public pressure, and even with avalanches of television ads. The fact that interest groups are involved in judicial battles far more in America than in any other democracy should not surprise us, because the popularity of pursuing one's individual rights through litigation is one way in which the political culture of America differs significantly from the political cultures of most other countries.

The most important special trait of interest articulation and aggregation in the United States, however, is the very different party environment in which they take place. In most of the democracies discussed in this book most interests operate closely within political parties. (Indeed, in several instances particular interest groups are formally associated with particular parties, such as the trade unions with the British Labour Party.) Their main tactic is to persuade the parties with which they are associated to give their demands prominent places in the parties' programs and actions in government.

In contrast, American political parties are so much weaker and so much less important players in the policymaking process that the interest groups operate largely outside the parties and are little concerned about whether they are helping or hurting the parties. In 1980, for example, the National Organization for Women (NOW) fought for a rule in the Democratic Party to prevent the party from helping to elect any Democratic candidate who opposed the Equal Rights Amendment. In 1984 NOW said that it would refuse to support the party's national ticket unless a woman was nominated for the vice presidency (and, indeed, Geraldine Ferraro was nominated). In the 2004 election, Emily's List, a PAC supporting women candidates, spent a total of $26,051,693 to help women's campaigns, the second-largest amount spent by any PAC.[42]

The same observation applies to the Republican Party. For some time before 1994 many business PACs contributed much more campaign money to incumbent Democrats than to their Republican challengers even though the Republican political philosophy is much closer to that of business. The national leaders of the Republican Party complained bitterly about what they regarded as treason to the party and to conservatism, but Doug Thompson, the leader of the National Association of Realtors, rejected the Republicans' complaints and has spelled out his PAC's political priorities:

> We are a special interest group. Our interest is real estate and housing issues; it is not Contra aid, it is not abortion, it is not the minimum wage.... Our members are demanding a lot more accountability. Gone are our free-spending days when we poured money into a black hole called "challenger candidates." Our marching orders on PAC contributions are very clear: Stop wasting money on losers.[43]

Since the Republicans won control of Congress in the 1994 election there have been more Republican than Democratic incumbents, and Republicans have received more PAC contributions than Democrats. (This may change after the 2006 elections handed control of Congress back to Democrats.) In short, interest articulation and aggregation are in many respects different in the United States because its political parties are in most respects very different from those in any other democracy.

THE SPECIAL CHARACTERISTICS OF AMERICAN POLITICAL PARTIES

A Two-Party System

The American party system is usually a nearly pure two-party system; that is, one in which two major parties are highly competitive with one another and taken together win almost all the votes and offices in elections.[44] The most notable exception since the 1930s came in 1992, as Figure 14.3 shows, when independent H. Ross Perot won 19 percent of the popular votes for president (Democrat Bill Clinton won 43 percent and Republican incumbent George H. W. Bush won 38 percent). After the election Perot founded the Reform Party and ran as its presidential candidate in 1996, but, as the figure shows, his vote share fell to 8.6 percent. He did not run in 2000, but his party's presidential candidate, Pat Buchanan, got less than 1 percent of the votes.[45]

In 2004, in addition to Republican George W. Bush and Democrat John Kerry (see Box 14.4), there were presidential candidates from twenty-three other parties on the ballot in at least one state. However, all these other parties polled a combined 1.3 percent of the popular vote. In addition, nearly all the members of the House and Senate for the past several decades have been affiliated with one of the two major parties. The United States is one of the most distinctive two-party systems in the world.

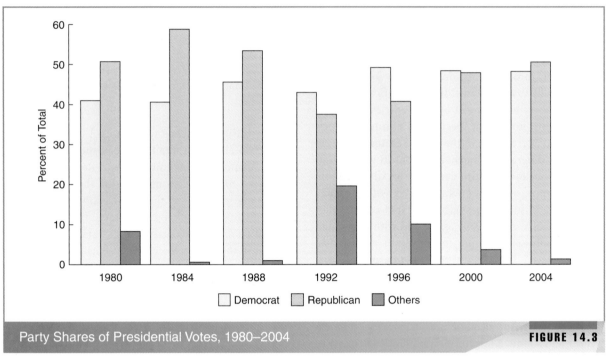

Party Shares of Presidential Votes, 1980–2004   **FIGURE 14.3**

Source: *Statistical Abstract of the United States: 2006* (Washington, DC: Bureau of the Census, 2006), Table 384, 247.

The "Americanization" of Electioneering

Electioneering—what parties and candidates do in campaigns to maximize their votes in elections—has changed considerably in most democratic nations since the 1950s, and the United States is generally credited with (or blamed for) leading the way. Before the 1950s electioneering in democracies was conducted mainly by party leaders and workers. The party workers made direct contacts with their candidates' known and potential supporters, and used the mass media mainly to publish newspaper advertisements and to print pamphlets and flyers for the party workers to distribute.

Since the 1950s, American parties and candidates have replaced the old techniques. They now depend mainly on paid television advertisements and broadcasters' interviews and talk shows to showcase their candidates and policies to the voters. They employ experts to conduct frequent polls of the voters to test how well their strategies are working. They canvass voters by telephone rather than by ringing doorbells. They store and analyze information about the demographics and past electoral behavior of election districts in computerized databases. They also have

transferred control of electioneering from party politicians to paid professional campaign consultants trained in advertising agencies rather than party organizations. They have made televised debates among the candidates the most important events in campaigns.

Party leaders and candidates in other democracies have watched U.S. electioneering. Many have deplored it, and some have vowed never to "Americanize" (their term) their own campaigns. Nevertheless, campaigners in most democracies have adapted some or all of the high-tech American methods for their own uses. For example, the United States held its first nationally televised debates between presidential candidates in 1960. Similar debates among leading parties and candidates are now regularly held also in Brazil, Chile, Denmark, France, Germany, Mexico, Norway, Sweden, and Venezuela. Most parties in most democracies now hire professional campaign consultants, some of them American or trained in America, to plan their campaigns. They use private polls to assess the effectiveness of their campaigns, and they use the mass media, especially television, as their main device for soliciting the voters' support. They have followed America's lead by increasingly using negative advertising to sharpen the contrasts between candidates or to ruin an opponent's reputation. In short, while the "Americanization" of electioneering may or may not be a healthy development, it has happened to some degree in all democracies and to a considerable degree in many.[46]

Differences Between the Major Parties

Throughout the 1950s and 1960s, foreign observers (and many Americans) saw few differences between the Democratic and Republican parties. Their nominees were sometimes likened to "Tweedle Dee and Tweedle Dum" twins, and their members were internally

divided on issues such as civil rights and the Vietnam War. Today, however, the split between the two major parties is sharp and meaningful. There is a vast gap between the views of Democratic and Republican voters on President Bush's job performance, on the Iraq War, and on many policy issues. In Congress, the Democratic caucus has moved further and further to the left since 1970, just as Republicans have become increasingly conservative.[47] Thus, the level of mass and elite **partisan polarization** in America is now quite high, as it is in most European nations.

This does not mean that there is no one left in the middle of the American political spectrum: indeed, most

---

The Presidential Election of 2004

BOX 14.4

Candidate	Popular Votes	Electoral Votes
George W. Bush, Republican	61,872,711	286
John Kerry, Democrat	58,894,584	251
Others	1,582,185	1

Like the presidential election of 2000, the race in 2004 was a close contest in which a razor-thin margin separated two candidates who espoused widely different governing philosophies, with neither winning a certain victory when most Americans went to bed on election night.

But unlike in 2000, they awoke the next day to a concession speech from Democratic nominee John Kerry when it became clear that Republican President George W. Bush had carried Ohio by a percentage margin of 51–49, giving him the electoral votes he needed to secure reelection. Bush won in both the Electoral College and in the popular vote, a feat he had not managed four years before, and the nation was spared another long, drawn out legal battle over the presidency. Yet despite the relative clarity of the final election result, Bush's prospects for reelection were in doubt throughout the campaign, and his narrow win left him far short of the mandate that he, like nearly all political victors, quickly claimed.

After receiving high approval ratings for his job performance in the wake of the terrorist attacks, on September 11, Bush began to lose popularity throughout 2002 as Democratic voters objected to his domestic

policy stances and confrontational approach to Iraq. After the United States invaded Iraq in March 2002, voters rallied to their Commander in Chief. As the success of the initial strike into Baghdad gave way to the more difficult task of stabilizing and rebuilding an entire country, the war began to lose its popularity and opposition to it galvanized many Democratic activists. Yet the party's voters were divided on their support for the war, as was their party's nominee.

Senator John Kerry, a decorated Vietnam War veteran who had voted for a resolution supporting President Bush's tough stance toward Iraq, emerged as the party's mainstream choice to challenge Bush. Throughout the summer of 2004, though, Kerry's equivocal positions on the war stalled his campaign. At the Democratic convention, he had difficulty explaining why he had voted against a bill authorizing $87 billion to continue to fund the Iraq War, and his Vietnam War record came under fire from the dubious charges of a group (financed by conservative activists) calling itself "Swift Boat Veterans for Truth." President Bush remained consistent in his prowar position, even as "Texans for Truth" (started by a Democratic political consultant) criticized his stateside service in the National Guard during the Vietnam Era. With Iraq and terrorism remaining the top issues throughout the campaign, the candidates traded slight leads during the summer and fall of 2004. By November, 52 percent of registered voters remained in favor of the war, 48 percent approved of the president's performance overall, and he survived by winning 50.6 percent of the vote.

Americans see themselves as moderates who lean only slightly in the liberal or conservative direction. Instead, the increase in partisan polarization reflects the fact that Americans today have sorted themselves into the party that most accurately reflects their ideology.[48] No longer are there many conservative Democrats in the South or liberal Republicans in New England or the Midwest.

This sorting has taken place among elected officials, party activists, and ordinary voters alike. Because of it, the parties now differ significantly in both the social composition of the voters who identify with them and the policy positions taken by their elected leaders.

As is shown in Figure 14.4, Americans are almost evenly divided among Democrats (35 percent), Republicans (36 percent), and independents (29 percent). (It should be noted, though, that most of these independents lean toward one party and vote for its nominees quite loyally.[49]) Democrats have greater support among women than men, among blacks than whites, and among people with lower incomes and educations than upper-status people. Other research shows that the link between income and party affiliation has grown in recent decades: "The relatively poor are increasingly Democratic and the rich Republican."[50] Thus, as income inequality has increased in America, the gap between the two parties has widened. Finally, the parties now differ more than ever in how religious their members are, with Republican presidential candidates doing better among regular churchgoers than Democrats.[51]

These rising differences in each party's social base help to explain why Democratic

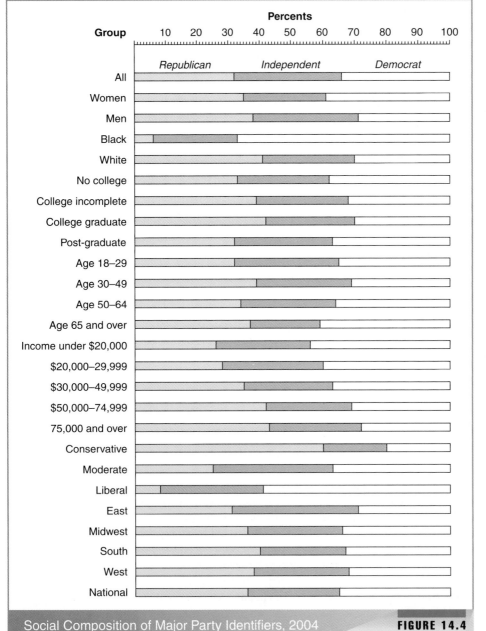

Social Composition of Major Party Identifiers, 2004   **FIGURE 14.4**

Source: Harold W. Stanley and Richard G. Niemi, *Vital Statistics on American Politics, 2005–2006* (Washington, DC: CQ Press, 2006), Table 3–2, 119.

and Republican members of Congress increasingly take different policy positions. Table 14.5 explores these divisions by looking at roll call votes on some significant issues before the House and Senate from 1993–2003. It shows that there are significantly more liberals than conservatives among the Democrats in both houses of Congress and significantly more conservatives than liberals among the Republicans—although on most issues some Democrats vote for conservative positions and some Republicans vote for liberal positions.

Generally, Democrats tend to believe that government should take a major and active role in dealing with the nation's problems, while most Republicans tend to agree with Ronald Reagan that "big government *is* the problem." Thus, compared with Republicans most Democrats favor higher levels of government spending on aid for the poor and homeless, education, medical care, public housing, and the like. On the so-called social issues, Democrats tend to favor less government intervention in people's moral, religious, and intellectual lives, while Republicans favor policies that allow greater government involvement in such matters as limiting or outlawing abortions, prohibiting the exhibition of obscene films and art, and encouraging prayer in the public schools.

Democrats also tend to be more egalitarian than Republicans. That is, Republicans tend to support measures for equal opportunity (giving every citizen an equal chance to engage in fair competition for material riches and the other good things in life), while Democrats tend to support measures for "equal conditions" (giving all citizens a guaranteed minimum of the good things in life even if they cannot earn them by their own efforts).

Although there are some issues on which legislators from both parties agree—in fact, many bills in Congress are passed by unanimous votes—a number of contentious issues reveal a split between the parties in America that is deep and growing.

Selected Votes in Congress, 1993–2003						**TABLE 14.5**
	Republicans			**Democrats**		
	Liberal	Conservative	Cohesion Index*	Liberal	Conservative	Cohesion Index*
House						
Lift ban, leave gays-in-military issue to Clinton	101	157	22	163	11	88
Welfare reform	30	165	70	226	4	96
Impeach Clinton for perjury	5	223	98	200	5	98
Bush-proposed tax cut, 2001	0	219	100	197	10	91
Iraq War	6	215	95	126	81	22
Partial-birth abortion ban	4	218	96	137	63	37
Bush-proposed tax cut, 2003	1	224	99	198	7	93
Senate						
"Brady bill" for handgun control	8	47	70	28	16	28
Welfare reform	1	51	96	23	23	0
Bush-proposed tax cut, 2001	0	50	100	38	12	52
McCain-Feingold campaign finance reform	12	38	52	47	3	88
Iraq War	1	48	96	21	29	16
Partial-birth abortion ban	3	47	88	30	17	28
Bush-proposed tax cut, 2003	3	48	88	46	2	92

*The cohesion index is a measure of the extent to which members of a particular party in a legislature vote alike on matter of public policy. The percentages of the members voting each way are calculated, and the smaller percentage is subtracted from the larger. If they all vote alike the index is 100. If they split evenly the index is 0. If they split 75–25 the index is 50.

Source: *Congressional Quarterly Reports, 1993–2003.*

Decentralized Organization

Most political parties in most democracies are organized as **hierarchies,** with a national leader and national organization at the top holding the power to supervise the activities of local and regional party organizations. In sharp contrast, the American Democratic and Republican parties are organized, in Samuel Eldersveld's apt phrase, as "**stratarchies.**"[52] That is, their organizations at the national, state, and local levels have little power, legal or extralegal, over the organizations at the other levels. Moreover, within each level most parties have an executive organization and a legislative organization, and neither has any power over the other.

At the national level, for example, the Democrats and Republicans each have a **presidential party** and a **congressional party.** For the party that holds the presidency, the presidential party consists of the president, the national committee, the national chairman, and the national nominating conventions. The party that does not hold the presidency has no single person as its universally acknowledged leader.

Each party in each house of Congress has a caucus, consisting of all the party's members in the particular chamber (and thus equivalent to what in most democracies is called the parliamentary party). A floor leader is selected by the caucus to serve as the main coordinator of the party's legislative strategy and tactics. A policy committee, chosen by the caucus, advises the floor leader and the caucus on matters of substantive policy and legislative tactics. The whips are chosen by the caucus to serve as channels of communication between the leaders and the ordinary members. The campaign committees are chosen by the caucus to raise money and distribute it among the campaigns of selected candidates for the particular chamber.

We should emphasize, however, that the presidential party has little formal connection with the congressional party, and that any effort by the president (to say nothing of the national committee or the national chairman) to intervene in the congressional party's selection of its leaders or the determination of its policies or strategy is resented and rejected as "outside interference." On the other hand, in the 1998–1999 impeachment and trial of Democratic President Clinton, most Republican members sought his **impeachment,** conviction, and removal from office, while most Democrats supported him.

At the state level, both parties usually have a gubernatorial party and a legislative party. The gubernatorial party consists of the governor (the other party has no single, acknowledged leader), the state central committee, the state chair, and the state conventions. The legislative parties, like the congressional parties, usually have caucuses, elected floor leaders, policy committees, and whips. But each state's gubernatorial and legislative parties have no power over one another, and the national parties have no power over any part of the state parties. The national and state parties are simply different strata, not higher and lower levels in a chain of command headed by the national agencies.

At the various local levels there are congressional district committees, county committees, city committees, ward and precinct committees, and others too numerous to list here. In most states the local party committees and conventions are, both in law and in fact, independent of the state and the national party agencies. Hence, they constitute a third stratum, which is just as independent from the state agencies as the state agencies are from the national agencies.

Far more than almost any major party in any other modern democratic nation, then, American party organizations are agglomerations of hundreds of different leaders and committees distributed among various organizational strata, each of which has little or no power to command or obligation to obey any other agency in its own stratum, let alone any agency in any other stratum. Former Georgia governor and Senator Zell Miller's speaking career exemplifies this. A moderate Democrat from a state with many such voters, he delivered the keynote address to the Democratic National Convention in 1992. After growing disenchanted with national Democrats and supportive of President Bush, Miller gave the keynote at the Republican National Convention in 2004, but remains a Democrat.

Low Cohesion

The parliamentary parties in most modern democratic nations have high **party cohesion,** a term that denotes the degree to which the members of a legislative party vote together on issues of public policy. Abstentions and even votes against the party leaders' wishes are not unknown in those parties, and in some countries their frequency has increased, though very slowly, in recent years. But these are, at most, minor deviations from the norm that all the members of parliamentary parties in other countries vote solidly together in most parliamentary votes.

By sharp contrast, the only matters in either chamber of Congress on which all Democrats regularly vote one way and all Republicans vote the other way relate to "organizing" the chamber—that is, selecting the speaker of the house, the president pro tem of the Senate, and the chairs of the leading standing committees. On all other issues they rarely vote unanimously, though most usually vote together.

On the issues shown in Table 14.5, party cohesion was generally higher among House Democrats than among Senate Democrats, and even higher among House and Senate Republicans. On some issues one party or the other approached the cohesion levels of most major parties in other democracies. For example, the House Democrats' opposition to President Clinton's impeachment was very high, while House Republicans had perfect cohesion for President George W. Bush's tax cut proposal in 2001. On the other hand, House Democrats split more evenly on gays in the military and Bush's tax cut.

Consequently, the congressional parties have some party cohesion. It is especially high on such issues as higher spending for social welfare measures and greater regulation of business—with the Democrats usually voting predominantly, but not unanimously, Yes; and the Republicans usually voting predominantly, but not unanimously, No. On the other hand, on issues that cut sharply across party lines—especially moral issues such as abortion, capital punishment, and the regulation of pornography—both parties regularly split relatively evenly. Thus, in comparison with the major parliamentary parties in most other democratic nations, the American congressional Democrats and Republicans have low cohesion on most issues.

This situation has important consequences for the role of American parties in the policymaking process, which we will consider later. It also has several causes, the most important of which is the fact that, compared with most other democratic parties, the leaders of the Democrats and the Republicans have very weak disciplinary powers.

Weak Discipline

The leaders of most major parties in the world's democracies have a number of tools to ensure that the legislators bearing their parties' labels support the parties' policies in the national legislatures. For one, they can make sure that no unusually visible or persistent rebel against the party's positions is given a ministerial position or preferment of any kind. If that fails to bring the fractious member into line, they can expel him or her from the parliamentary party altogether. Many parties in many countries give their leaders the ultimate weapon: the power to deny the rebel reselection as an official party candidate at the next election.

In sharp contrast, in the United States any person who wins a party's primary for the House or Senate in any congressional district or state automatically becomes the party's legal candidate for that office, and no national party agency has the power to veto the nomination. On one notable occasion, called by historians "the purge of 1938," Franklin D. Roosevelt, an unusually popular and powerful national party leader, tried to intervene in the primary elections of several states to prevent the renomination of Democratic senators who had opposed his New Deal policies. He failed in twelve of thirteen attempts, and most people have since concluded that any effort by a national party leader to interfere in candidate selection at the state and local levels is bound to fail.

To be sure, presidents and their parties' leaders in Congress can and often do plead with their fellow partisans to support the president's policies for the sake of party loyalty and/or to increase the party's chances at the next election or to keep the party from looking foolish. If persuasion does not work, leaders can (but rarely do) promise to provide future campaign funding to a reluctant member or grant a hearing to a stalled bill authored by that member. Unless they have some strong reason to do otherwise, most members of Congress go along. However, unlike the leaders of most parties in most other countries, neither the president nor his party's congressional leaders have any effective disciplinary power to compel their members in Congress to vote in ways contrary to their consciences—or to what they perceive to be the interests and wishes of their constituents.

A Special Consequence: Divided Party Control of Government

In a pure parliamentary democracy, one party cannot control the legislature while another party controls the executive. If the parliament refuses a cabinet request, the cabinet either resigns and a new cabinet acceptable to the parliament takes over, or the parliament is dissolved, new elections are held, and a new cabinet is formed that has the support of the new parliamentary majority. There can never be more than a short interim period in which the parliamentary majority and cabinet disagree on any major question of public policy.

In the United States, in contrast, separation of powers and the separate terms and constituencies for the president, the members of the House, and the members of the Senate make it possible for one party to win control of the presidency and the other party to win control of one or both houses of Congress. How often does it actually happen? From the election of 1832 (when most historians say the modern electoral and party systems began) through the election of 2000, there have been a total of eighty-seven presidential and midterm elections. Each of these elections could have resulted in either divided party control or unified party control. In fact, fifty-five (63 percent) produced unified control, and thirty-two (37 percent) produced divided control.

Even more noteworthy is the fact that since the death of Franklin D. Roosevelt in 1945, **divided party control** has occurred so frequently that many observers feel it has become normal, not exceptional. From 1946 to 2006 there have been thirty-one elections. Only twelve (39 percent) have produced unified control (nine with Democratic presidents and congresses, and three with a Republican president and congresses), and nineteen (61 percent) have produced divided control (see Figure 14.5).

The election of 2000 initially produced unified Republican control, with President George W. Bush joining the Republican-controlled Congress. But it didn't last long: in 2001, Senator James Jeffords of Vermont announced that he was leaving the Republican Party to become an Independent, and that he would vote with the Democrats. That gave the Democrats only a 50–49 margin, but with Jeffords' support they regained control of the Senate and once again became part of a divided government. In 2002, the voters restored control of both houses to the Republicans, but then delivered both the Senate and the House of Representatives to Democrats in 2006 (see Box 14.5).

The most obvious cause for this situation, which is both unknown and impossible in parliamentary democracies, is the fact that the chief executive and the members of both houses of Congress are, as we have

Year	Congress	President
1946	Republicans	
1948	Democrats	Harry S Truman, Democrat
1950	Democrats	
1952	Republicans	Dwight D. Eisenhower, Republican
1954	Democrats	
1956	Democrats	
1958	Democrats	
1960	Democrats	John F. Kennedy, Democrat
1962	Democrats	
1963	Democrats	Lyndon B. Johnson, Democrat
1964	Democrats	
1966	Democrats	
1968	Democrats	Richard M. Nixon, Republican
1970	Democrats	
1972	Democrats	
1973	Democrats	Gerald R. Ford, Republican
1974	Democrats	
1976	Democrats	James E. Carter, Democrat
1978	Democrats	
1980	S–R, H–D	Ronald W. Reagan, Republican
1982	S–R, H–D	
1984	S–R, H–D	
1986	Democrats	
1988	Democrats	George H. W. Bush, Republican
1990	Democrats	
1992	Democrats	William J. Clinton, Democrat
1994	Republicans	
1996	Republicans	
1998	Republicans	
2000	S–D, H–R	George W. Bush, Republican
2002	Republicans	
2004	Republicans	
2006	Democrats	

FIGURE 14.5

United/Split Party Control of the Presidency and Congress, 1946–2006

seen, elected separately by overlapping constituencies and with different terms. The constitutional structure thus makes it possible for American voters to do something that voters in most parliamentary democracies cannot do, namely, "split their tickets"—that is, vote for a member of one party for president and for a member of the other party for Congress.

Ticket-splitting explains the increasing frequency of divided party control. Figure 14.6 shows the changing percentages of respondents in the National Election Studies of all presidential elections from 1952 through 2004 who reported voting for the presidential candidate of one party and a candidate of another party for the House of Representatives. This figure shows that split-ticket voting rose steadily from 1952

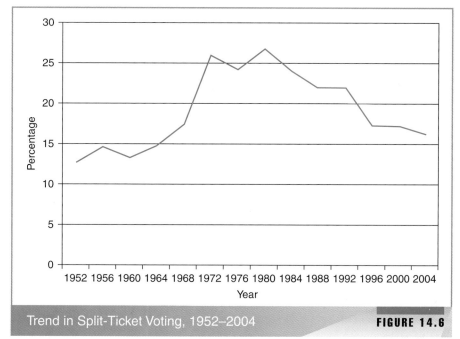

Trend in Split-Ticket Voting, 1952–2004   **FIGURE 14.6**

Source: American National Election Studies, Inter-University Consortium for Political and Social Research, University of Michigan, compiled by Gary Jacobson. Data points are the percentage reporting a different vote for the presidential and House of Representatives elections; third-party candidates are excluded from the calculations.

and implementing effective, coherent, and forceful national policies was not their prime goal.

They believed that government should never be regarded as some kind of benevolent mother, doing whatever is necessary to keep all her children well fed and feeling good. We should never forget, they warned, that government is a powerful and dangerous institution created by fallible human beings. Its prime objective—indeed, its only legitimate reason for existing and being obeyed—is to secure every person's God-given right to life, liberty, and property. Anything that government does beyond that, they believed, is not only less important but not even acceptable if it in any way abridges those basic rights.

The best way to make a government strong enough to secure the rights of its citizens without becoming so powerful that it overrides them, they believed, is to disperse its power among many different agencies—among the federal and state governments by federalism, and within the federal government by separation of powers. The power should be so divided, they held, that no single faction would likely ever get control of the whole power of government and promote its interests at the expense of all the others.[54]

Accordingly, they did not think that policy deadlocks, in which the government cannot act because one of its parts blocks action by other parts, are some kind of terrible failure that should be avoided wherever possible and unblocked as soon as possible. Rather, they regarded such deadlocks as highly preferable to any government action that rides roughshod over the interests and objections of any significant part of the community. Consequently, whenever a deadlock blocks today's government from making effective policies to deal with budget deficits, mounting national debt, crime, health care, campaign finance, the war on terror, or any other public problem, the

until 1980. It has fallen since then, as partisan polarization in the electorate has increased, but in 2004 it was still higher than it was in 1952.

However, divided government apparently does not significantly weaken (or strengthen) the federal government's ability to make public policies. David Mayhew's careful study of the most important pieces of legislation passed from 1946 to 1990 shows that the rate of production was about the same in periods of divided party control as in periods of unified control.[53]

THE POLICYMAKING PROCESS IN AMERICA

When we consider the policymaking process in the United States, we must first understand that the constitutional framework within which the process operates was carefully designed to keep government from doing bad things, not to make it easier for it to do good things. To be sure, in writing the Constitution the men of Philadelphia hoped to get a more effective national government than that provided by the Articles of Confederation. But making

BOX 14.5

The Congressional Elections of 2006

Voters dissatisfied with President Bush's handling of the Iraq War and with the Republican congressional leaders' handling of a multitude of scandals gave Democrats a landmark victory in the 2006 midterm elections. The Democratic Party captured thirty-one new seats, to take control of the House of Representatives for the first time since 1994. It also picked up six Senate seats, securing its first majority in the upper house since 2002. These gains were not limited to Washington, D.C.: Democrats won six new governorships and retook control of four state legislatures.

What brought about this sharp turn to the left across the nation? The results of the national exit poll conducted by the Edison/Mitofsky firm indicate that it represented a rejection of Republican policies and performance, more than an embrace of the Democratic platform. The 57 percent of voters who disapproved of George W. Bush's handling of his job voted overwhelmingly for congressional Democrats, as did the 61 percent of voters who thought Congress was performing poorly. A majority of voters disapproved of the war in Iraq, and 92 percent said that corruption and scandals in government were important in their decision about how to vote in their district's congressional race. The

influence-peddling scandals that led to jail terms for lobbyist Jack Abramoff and Republican Congressman "Duke" Cunningham, and to the resignation of Republican Majority Leader Tom DeLay, greatly wounded the party. The fatal blow came just weeks before the election when Mark Foley, a Republican Congressman from Florida, resigned in disgrace after journalists reported sexually explicit instant messages that he had sent to teenaged boys serving as congressional pages. Voters who disapproved of the way that Republican leaders handled the scandal voted three-to-one for Democrats.

The Democratic surge put former Minority Leader Nancy Pelosi into power as the first female Speaker of the House of Representatives. Because the Democrats did not set forth a clear and united policy on Iraq, Pelosi will face the tough task of leading a party and a House that is divided over how to improve the situation there. Still, this is nothing new in American politics. The historical record of landmark congressional elections shows that the largest swings have come after wars, scandals, and economic downturns. Just as in 2006, they are more often a rejection of past performance than a clear prescription for future policies.

least we can say is that the policymaking process is operating as the framers intended.

Traditional Ways of Avoiding Deadlocks

Alexis de Tocqueville wrote: "I have never been more struck by the good sense and the practical judgment of the Americans than in the manner in which they elude the numberless difficulties resulting from their Federal Constitution."[55] He had a point. From the opening of the First Congress in 1789 to the twenty-first century, Americans have found that, however dangerous to human rights it may be, the government of the United States has to make and implement at least *some* policies. It has to regulate interstate and foreign commerce, increase or decrease the supply of money, conduct relations with foreign nations, levy taxes, make appropriations, and so on. As Tocqueville rightly observed, Americans have developed ways of getting

policies made despite the constitutional system's many roadblocks and general tendency toward inertia. One set of ways has been traditionally used in ordinary times, and the other set has been called on in times of great crisis.

In ordinary times, public policies in America have been made mainly by putting together ad hoc, issue-specific coalitions of interests by bargaining and cutting deals among their representatives. The main coalition builders have included public officials of all kinds, including presidents and their chief political aides in the Cabinet and the Executive Office of the President; members of Congress and their professional staffs; political heads and permanent civil servants in the executive departments and the independent agencies; and federal judges and their clerks. At least as active and often as powerful as these inside players are the outside players, especially the lobbyists representing the major organized interest groups that feel they

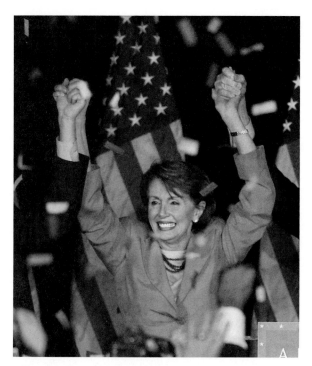

Democratic leader: Nancy Pelosi celebrates after the 2006 elections.

J. Scott Applewhite/AP Images

have major stakes in the policy outcomes. The usual result is that, while each contest over each policy produces winners and losers, it never produces total victory or total defeat for any highly involved interest. Each contestant gets something of what it wants but never all; and each manages to stave off total disaster.

Many commentators, past and present, have been highly critical of this process. They claim that it usually takes far too long to get anything done, and that what is done is usually messy, full of inconsistencies, self-defeating, and in constant need of repair. They are also struck by how difficult it is to get closure on any major policy: typically, when a coalition loses in the presidency, it tries in the Congress; when it loses in the Congress, it tries in the bureaucracy; when it fails to persuade incumbent elected and appointed officials, it tries to replace them; and when it loses everywhere else, it turns to the courts to upset or water down policies made by the other agencies.

In recent years, for example, environmentalists have increasingly focused their efforts on lobbying the federal agencies that implement natural resources legislation rather than only the members of Congress

who pass it. As another example, when civil rights advocates in the 1950s failed to get Congress to abolish racial segregation in the schools, they turned to the U.S. Supreme Court and won their victory in the landmark decision of *Brown v. Board of Education* (1954). Those who today advocate same-sex marriage rights have found success in several court cases while they have generally lost in legislative fights and in initiative battles.

Without doubt the ordinary-times process falls far short of the neat, orderly, and swift policymaking process that parliamentary democracies usually enjoy because of their fusion of powers and the consequent impossibility of prolonged deadlock between the executive and the legislature. Yet the American process has undeniably produced a large number of major national policies, many of them quite successful: for example, the establishment of Alexander Hamilton's economic development program in the 1790s, the western expansion of the country in the nineteenth century, the absorption of millions of immigrants, the Progressive reforms of the early 1900s, the New Deal, the constant (though to some too slow) advance in the status of African-Americans since the end of slavery, the Great Society welfare and health care programs of the 1960s, the drastic overhaul of the tax system in 1986, and so on. Even at its best, however, the ordinary-times process has always taken a lot of time to produce results, and there have been occasions in American history when the danger that it would not work fast enough to meet the needs made the nation turn to a less rigid but more controversial type of policymaking process: unilateral action taken by presidents.

When the Southern states started seceding in 1861, Abraham Lincoln took a number of steps that were far outside the ordinary policymaking process. By executive proclamations he suspended the writ of *habeas corpus;* called for volunteers to join the Union Army; spent government money to buy them food, uniforms, and weapons; and made the fateful decision to provision Fort Sumter even though he expected the action would start a civil war. Then, after having done all this, he summoned Congress into session, told them what he had done, and asked for retroactive authority—which they had no choice but to give him.

Since then, presidents have often taken the view that when the national interest requires prompt action, they either should do it on their own, as Lincoln did, or persuade Congress to rush through their radical reform measures, as Franklin D. Roosevelt did in the 1930s when it seemed clear that in the absence of extraordinary measures the economy would collapse under the stress of the Great Depression.

Presidents usually exert these extraordinary powers in foreign rather than domestic crises, as when Truman ordered American troops into Korea in 1950; Kennedy and Johnson followed suit in Vietnam in the 1960s; the first Bush ordered troops to Panama, the Persian Gulf, and Somalia in the 1980s and early 1990s; Clinton sent troops to Haiti in 1994 and to Bosnia in 1995; and the second Bush in 2001–2002 sent American soldiers and airmen to Afghanistan to overthrow the terrorist-sheltering Taliban government, and in 2003, sent the armed forces to invade Iraq and depose Saddam Hussein. The War Powers Act of 1974 was designed to limit the president's power to take this kind of action without congressional approval, but in fact it has restrained presidents very little. No one doubts that in any future crisis, especially in foreign affairs, presidents will again bypass the ordinary policymaking process and do what they feel needs to be done.

Recent experience, however, makes it clear that the **presidential-dictatorship** escape valve does not stay open indefinitely. When a military action drags on for months and years with huge expense, many casualties, and little hope of a clean-cut final victory—Korea and Vietnam are so far the leading examples, and Iraq seems to be taking its place on the list—the president eventually loses popular and then congressional support, and the nation returns to the ordinary process. In any case, a leader who is held to account for his actions in free elections every four years is no dictator.

He can also be checked by the courts and by the press, which has happened to President George W. Bush with increasing frequency. The *New York Times* revealed in December 2005 that the National Security Agency, at the president's request, was conducting surveillance on domestic and international telephone calls without obtaining court warrants as proscribed by the Foreign Intelligence Surveillance Act (FISA). The Bush administration argued that the presidency's inherent powers justify going around this congressional act during a time of war, but the president has faced tough questioning on this issue from reporters and from some members of Congress. In June 2006, the U.S. Supreme Court ruled that detainees held at

Guantanamo Bay could not be put on trial before secretive military commissions, in part because the commissions were created without congressional authority. This landmark case points out the limits of executive power, even in wartime.

POLICY PERFORMANCE

Tax Policies

When considering policy performance in the United States, it is important to remember that we are dealing with the outputs of many governments, not just the one in Washington, D.C.[56] In 2002, there were over 87,000 governmental units in America, including the federal government, 50 states, 3,034 counties, 19,429 municipalities, 16,504 townships, 13,306 local school districts, and 35,052 special districts—each of which had some constitutional or statutory power to make policies.[57]

Of these 87,576 authorities, the federal government extracts the greatest share of revenues: it collects 62 percent of all taxes and 57 percent of revenues from all sources. Its share is, of course, smaller than the shares taken by the national governments of unitary nations—such as Great Britain, Japan, and Sweden—but it is larger than those taken by the national governments in any of the federal systems except Austria.[58]

Table 14.6 displays the main types of taxes as percentages of total revenue in the United States and eight other industrialized nations in 2000. This table shows that the United States relies more on personal income taxes than any other nation. Social security taxes paid by employees in America are higher than average. The United States relies less on sales and other taxes on consumption than any other country. Part of the reason is that, unlike most European governments, the U.S. national government has never levied a sales tax or a value-added tax, although most American states levy sales taxes as well as income taxes. Accordingly, the tax structure in the American federal system as a whole is more progressive (in the sense of placing the heaviest burden on people with the greatest ability to pay) than that in most but not all other nations.

Americans frequently complain about the heavy tax burden they bear, and Republican presidents Ronald Reagan, George H. W. Bush, and George W. Bush all made cutting taxes the cornerstones of their economic programs. Just how great is the tax burden

Tax Sources as Percentages of Total Revenue, 2000						**TABLE 19.6**
	Personal Income	Corporate Income	Employees' Social Security	Employers' Social Security	Sales and Consumption	Specific Goods
Great Britain	29.1	9.8	6.9	9.6	18.3	12.4
Canada	37.0	11.2	5.7	8.0	14.3	8.7
France	18.0	6.9	9.0	24.8	16.9	8.2
Germany	25.3	4.8	17.2	19.2	18.4	8.8
Italy	25.7	7.5	5.4	19.8	15.8	10.0
Japan	20.2	13.2	13.9	18.2	8.7	7.7
United States	42.4	8.5	10.2	11.8	7.5	6.3

Source: *Statistical Abstract of the United States: 2006* (Washington, DC: Bureau of the Census, 2006), Table 1336, 878.

of Americans compared with that borne by the residents of other industrialized democracies?

The answer depends on what measure is used. Expressed as a percentage of gross domestic product (GDP), American taxes take a total of 25.6 percent, the lowest figure among the major industrialized nations (Sweden, at 50.6 percent, is the highest). Moreover, its take from GDP has increased at a slower rate than in any other industrialized democracy since 1980. (Again, Sweden leads with the highest rate of increase.[59]) In summary, compared with the tax systems of most other industrialized countries, the American system is one of the more progressive in its structure but takes a smaller proportion of the GDP than any of the others.

Distributive Performance

Figure 14.7 gives an overview of how the federal government spent its $2.5 trillion budget in 2005. This figure shows the federal government spent 64 percent of its budget on domestic welfare and education functions, 20 percent on defense-related functions, 7 percent for interest on the national debt, and 9 percent in other areas.

Among the world's other democratic governments, only Israel spends as high a proportion of its budget on defense as the United States. (Some developing countries, such as North Korea, Oman, and Saudi Arabia, spend even higher proportions.) Some Americans argue that defense spending is far too high, especially now that the Cold War has ended. Others counter that the events of September 11, 2001, demonstrate that the world is still a dangerous place, and

America needs to spend whatever it takes to win the **war on terror.** Whatever the merits of these positions, the trend up to 2001 was toward lower proportions of federal spending on defense, but defense spending then climbed from 2002 through 2005.

Other international comparisons show that U.S. per capita expenditures on health care are by far the highest in the world, followed at some distance by Switzerland and Germany.[60] And in proportion of the GDP spent on education, the United States (with 7.3 percent) ranks second behind South Korea (8.2 percent) and ahead of Denmark (7.1 percent), Iceland (6.7 percent), and Sweden (6.5 percent).[61]

Regulatory Performance

Like all modern industrialized democracies, the United States is a welfare state in the sense that many of its policies proceed from the conviction that government has an obligation to guarantee certain minimum levels of life's basics to all its citizens, especially to those who cannot provide them for themselves. However, nations differ markedly both in the particular items of basic needs that government should provide and the levels at which they should be provided. In this section we briefly review the major policies adopted by American governments in three main problem areas.

Social Insurance The United States was among the last of the modern industrialized nations to embrace the goals of the welfare state, and today the proportion of the nation's GDP spent on public welfare programs

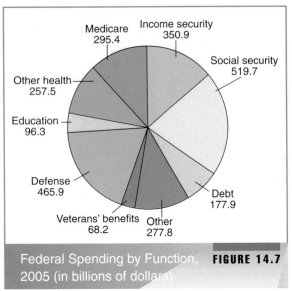

Medicare
295.4

Income security
350.9

Social security
519.7

Other health
257.5

Education
96.3

Defense
465.9

Veterans' benefits
68.2

Other
277.8

Debt
177.9

Federal Spending by Function,
2005 (in billions of dollars)   **FIGURE 14.7**

Source: *Statistical Abstract of the United States 2006* (Washington,
DC: Bureau of the Census, 2006), Table 463, 319.

is lower than that in most industrialized nations. Even so, the federal, state, and local governments together have a wide range of policies intended to put a floor beneath the income and living conditions of the poor. For that purpose they use two main instruments: social insurance and public assistance.

Social Insurance and Welfare This category includes programs to protect citizens against the risk of loss of income due to old age, retirement, sickness, industrial accidents, and unemployment. The basic federal legislation is the Social Security Act of 1935, which established a fund from mandatory contributions by employees and employers from which all wage earners are entitled to receive cash payments at retirement or on reaching a certain age. Since the benefits are available to all who contribute, most Americans regard its benefits as entitlements, not handouts. No stigma attaches to receiving social security checks, and most Americans of all income levels approve of the program.

Public Assistance This category includes both direct cash and in-kind payments to poor people, such as cash aid to families with dependent children, food stamps, free milk for young children, and day care for children of working mothers with low incomes. Unlike Social Security, these programs are noncontributory and thus constitute obvious income transfers from upper-income people to lower-income people. As a result, some social

stigma does attach to receiving public assistance benefits, and these welfare programs are much more controversial than the social insurance programs.

For years, there were many complaints that the welfare system, especially Aid for Families With Dependent Children (AFDC), was removing recipients' incentives to work and making them into lifelong dependents on government handouts. Then, in 1996, the Republican Congress passed and President Clinton signed a bill for **welfare reform.** The new law ended the federal guarantee of direct AFDC payments to all eligible families. Instead, the federal government gave $16.4 billion in block grants to the states to develop and fund their own new welfare programs, *provided* that the states impose work requirements for welfare recipients, develop job training programs for them, and put time limits on welfare benefits (thereby replacing welfare with "workfare" according to the new law's advocates).[62]

Education In the United States as in other industrialized nations, education is provided mainly by schools financed and operated by the government, although there are more privately owned and operated schools, especially universities (including such famous institutions as Columbia, Harvard, Princeton, Stanford, and Yale), in America than in most other countries (they are also important in Japan and Great Britain).

What sets the American school system apart from systems in other countries is its high degree of decentralization. Most schools, from kindergartens through universities, are financed and regulated by state and local governments, although the federal government provides considerable subsidies for many special programs, each of which carries restrictions on how the money is to be spent. For example, in awarding federally funded scholarships and other forms of financial aid for students, schools may not discriminate against applicants because of their race or gender. The local financing and regulation of schools has many consequences, not the least of which is the fact that schools in poor states and poor districts generally spend considerably less money per pupil than schools in richer states and districts.

Whatever the consequences of these differences, the United States, as Table 14.7 shows, still has a higher proportion of its population with secondary or university degrees than any other nation. It also has the second highest proportion (after Japan) of 17-year-olds in secondary schools, the highest proportion

Educational Attainment, Ten Top Nations (11 with a tie), 2002 (percent of persons 25 to 64 years old)			**TABLE 14.7**
Rank	Nation	Secondary Education (%)*	University Education (%)
1	United States	87	29
2	Norway	86	28
3	Denmark	80	23
4	Netherlands	66	22
5	Canada	83	21
6	Japan	84	20
7	Australia	61	20
8	Iceland	59	20
9	Great Britain	64	19
10	Sweden	82	18
10	South Korea	71	18

*Included in university education.

Source: *Statistical Abstract of the United States 2006* (Washington, DC: Bureau of the Census, 2006), Table 1326, 872.

of 21-year-olds in colleges and universities, and the highest proportion of college graduates going on to graduate and professional schools.[63]

A number of industrialized nations operate on the theory that higher education should be reserved for only the most talented and accomplished students. They therefore require that only those students who do well in demanding nationally administered tests after finishing one level may advance to a school at the next higher level. The United States, in contrast, operates on the theory that as many people as possible should be given a chance at a college education. As educational sociologist Martin Trow sums it up, "If Europe's slogan for higher education has been 'nothing if not the best,' America's has been 'something is better than nothing.'"[64] Consequently, it is much easier for American 18-year-olds to enter some kind of postsecondary education—a four-year college or university, or a two-year community college—than for their peers in any other country, and many more do so. In 2002, 29 percent of Americans between the ages of 25 and 64 had university educations—a higher proportion than in any other industrialized democracy.

What about the *quality* of American education? Many scholars, school administrators, and politicians in America have long and inconclusively debated that question, and the literature on the subject is far too vast and complicated to survey in detail here. We will note only that U.S. students score just above the mean for industrialized countries on a combined reading scale and just below the mean on math and science scales.[65]

Environmental Protection Of the policy areas considered here, environmental protection is the most recent to take center stage, not only in the United States but in most other industrialized nations as well. From the beginning of the Industrial Revolution in the late eighteenth century until well after World War II, one of the highest goals of every nation was economic growth—constantly increasing the nation's production of goods and services, both for home consumption and for sale abroad.

For many purposes that goal remains highly desirable today, since economic growth allows governments to reach a diverse set of policy goals, including boosting their military strength and diplomatic clout; providing more food, shelter, and medical care for the poor; or increasing the coverage and improving the quality of health and education. In recent years, however, policymakers in many nations, including the United States, have come to realize that economic growth, especially unrestrained and rapid growth, has great costs. Nowhere is this cost greater than in the area of toxic emissions and solid wastes that have been the by-products of large-scale industrialization.

As a result, policymakers in the United States and elsewhere have become increasingly aware that they must grapple with environmental problems. Some nations, especially Japan and Great Britain, have approached these problems less by relying on government regulations than on encouraging corporations and labor unions to work together to develop their own plans for dealing with pollution. Early in the era of environmental policy, the United States took a quite different approach. It enacted a series of stringent laws, beginning with the Clean Air Act of 1970. These laws require manufacturers to reduce sharply their emissions that pollute the air and water by installing expensive devices (such as smoke scrubbers and water purifiers) to recycle solid wastes, and to clean up, mostly at their own (and/or their insurance companies') expense, the toxic waste dumps they have previously created. The federal government established a special agency, the Environmental Protection Agency (EPA), to make sure that these laws are strictly enforced.

More recently, U.S. policymakers have moved away form stringent regulations and toward incentives, voluntary industry goals, and tradable permits that seek to reduce pollution in the most cost-effective way possible. Perhaps the clearest indication that the United States has moved away from the forefront of environmental regulation is the federal government's refusal to ratify the Kyoto Protocol, an international agreement designed to stave off global warming by reducing emissions of "greenhouse gases," such as carbon dioxide. Opponents have argued that abiding by the protocol's targets would slow down economic growth in the United States, and that it places too much of a burden on industrialized nations while putting much looser limits on developing countries. Still, the United States and Australia now stand alone in opposing an environmental treaty that had been signed by 163 countries by 2006.

AMERICAN EXCEPTIONALISM: MYTH OR REALITY?

The Idea in History

During much of its history, many of the United States' leaders and citizens—and some foreign commentators and many of the millions of immigrants who left their native countries to become Americans—have regarded the United States as not just another polity in a world of many polities, but as significantly different from other political systems. Some have viewed it as a great social experiment from which all political systems can

and should learn lessons relevant to founding and reforming their own systems.

Thus in his first Inaugural Address, George Washington said, "The preservation of the sacred fire of liberty, and the destiny of the republican model of government, are justly considered as deeply, perhaps as finally staked, on the experiment intrusted to the hands of the American people."[66]

In December 1862, when the very existence of the American system was at stake in the Civil War, Abraham Lincoln said to the Congress, "We of this Congress and this administration, will be remembered in spite of ourselves.... The fiery trial through which we pass, will light us down, in honor or dishonor, to the latest generation.... We shall nobly save, or meanly lose, the last, best hope of earth."[67]

How True Is It?

It seems altogether fitting and proper that we should end this chapter by asking not whether the idea of **American exceptionalism** is noble or vainglorious, but rather how true it is. That is, in what respect and to what degree does the American system resemble and differ from the world's other political systems? Our conclusions are summarized in Table 14.8.

How the American System Closely Resembles Other Systems It is a government that has jurisdiction over a certain territory and peoples. It makes laws governing their behavior and enforces them with means up to and including capital punishment.

American society is composed of many different groups with different interests, and its political process is essentially a contest among them to advance their interests. Few if any policies benefit all groups and interests equally, and most political decisions have, relatively speaking, some winners and some losers.

In addition, this book's basic theoretical scheme for comparing governments is as applicable to the United States as to any other nation.

How the American System Resembles a Few Nations But Differs from Most As Table 14.8 notes, the United States is a democracy along with other democracies. It is based on the principle of constitutionalism. Its society is diverse in the ethnic and religious makeup of its residents.

The United States is a presidential democracy rather than a parliamentary democracy, based on the

The new immigrants: Mexicans crossing the Rio Grande to enter the United States.

J.P. Laffont/Sygma

separation of powers rather than on their fusion. The head of government is elected rather than hereditary. Furthermore, the roles of chief of state and head of government are performed by the same official.

The United States is also unusual because it is a federal system rather than a unitary system.

The legislative system also displays differences from other systems. The presiding officers of its legislative chambers are partisan rather than neutral. Its legislative committees play a critical role in the legislative process. And American legislators are largely free of party discipline and control their own votes.

The U.S. legal system is based on the English common law rather than on the continental European civil law. This means that our legal precedents are derived from the prior decisions of judges rather than from an extensive codification of principles constructed by legislative or executive branch officials. Also, its highest court has the power to declare acts of other government officials and agencies unconstitutional and thereby render them null and void.

U.S. elections use the single-member, plurality system rather than proportional representation. Because of this, they are almost always contested by only two major parties. Not only can different parties control different branches of government at the same time, but they often do. American elections are held on

Republican leaders: Vice President Cheney, President Bush, former House Speaker Hastert.

AP Images

	TABLE 14.8
The U.S. Compared with Other Nations: A Summary	

Characteristic	How the U.S. Is Like Other Nations	How the U.S. Resembles a Few Nations But Differs from Many	How the U.S. Is Unique or Nearly So
Society	Consists of many different groups with different interests	Large population of immigrants and descendants of immigrants High religious diversity	
Political System	Has a government, which makes and enforces laws	Is a democracy	
Structure of Government		Based on principles of constitutionalism Federal system	Extensiveness of system of checks and balances
Executive Branch	Has a chief executive	Presidential system rather than parliamentary system Chief of state and head of government roles performed by same person President is directly elected through an electoral college	
Legislative Branch	Has a national legislature	Both houses of the legislature are directly elected	Legislative committees play a critical role
Judicial Branch	Courts settle civil and criminal disputes	All national judges appointed; some state and local judges elected Most courts have power of judicial review	Many political issues settled by courts rather than by parties or legislatures
Parties and Elections	Has regular elections	Has a two-party system Elections use single-member districts and plurality decisions Elections held on fixed dates; no power of dissolution Parties closely regulated by law Executive and legislative branches can be and often are controlled by different parties	Candidates selected by direct primaries Voter registration is decentralized and responsibility of voter Voters have many elections and many choices at each Party leaders have no power to admit or expel party members Parties are decentralized and largely undisciplined and uncohesive

fixed dates, and there is no power of dissolution. The practice is well established by law and custom that members of the national legislature must live in the states and districts they represent. Particularly in some states and localities, though not at the national level, there is extensive use of popular initiatives and referendums.

How the United States Is Unique or Nearly So Finally, Table 14.8 highlights many of the unique aspects of the American political system. For instance,

committees within Congress are more powerful and autonomous than committees in nearly every other national legislature.

American political parties choose most of their nominees for office by direct primaries conducted and regulated by public law, not by party rules. Many of its executive officers, particularly at the state and local levels, are directly elected and nominated by direct primaries; consequently, the U.S. voter faces more frequent elections and more decisions to make at each election than voters in any other democratic nation except Switzerland. In addition, America's systems for registering voters are largely decentralized and put most of the burden on the voters.

Political parties are closely regulated by law. But political parties do not control who can become and remain their members, and the parties are, compared with those in other democratic systems, uncohesive, undisciplined, and decentralized.

Because candidates run as individuals rather than as local representatives of national party teams, and because no publicly financed free media time is given to parties or candidates, the raising and spending of large amounts of money are more important in American elections than in most other democracies.

The court system is also unusual. A higher proportion of political issues are settled in the courts than in any other democracy. Consequently, lawyers play a more important role in the American political system than in any other.

CONCLUSION

It seems fitting to end this chapter comparing the American political system to the world's other systems with a quotation from one of its greatest foreign observers, the English scholar and statesman, Lord Bryce:

> All governments are faulty; and an equally minute analysis of the constitutions of England, or France, or Germany would disclose mischiefs as serious . . . as those we have noted in the American system. To any one familiar with the practical working of free governments it is a standing wonder that they work at all. . . . What keeps a free government going is the good sense and patriotism of the people . . . and the United States, more than any other country, are governed by public opinion, that is to say, by the general sentiment of the mass of the nation, which all the organs of the national government and of the State governments look to and obey.[68]

REVIEW QUESTIONS

- Why is voter turnout lower in the United States than it is in most democracies?

- How has immigration policy changed over the past century? What effect has this had on American political culture?

- What impact has the direct primary had on the power of political parties in the United States? Why?

- How has America's traditional approach to environmental issues differed from the strategies pursued in Europe? In what ways has our approach changed recently?

- On which areas of government does the United States spend more than the rest of the world does?

KEY TERMS

American exceptionalism
Bill of Rights
blanket primary
checks and balances
closed primaries
congressional party
conservatives
crossover primaries
direct initiative
direct primaries
divided party control

electoral college
federalism
hierarchies
impeachment
judicial review
liberals
litigation
litigiousness
lobbying
mass communications
    media

melting pot vs. patchwork
    quilt
open primaries
partisan polarization
party cohesion
political action committee
    (PAC)
political culture
popular referendum
presidential democracy
presidential dictatorship

presidential party
scarcity doctrine
separation of powers
stratarchies
ticket-splitting
voting registration
voting turnout
war on terror
welfare reform

SUGGESTED READINGS

Abraham, Henry J. *The Judiciary: The Supreme Court in the Governmental Process*, 10th ed. New York: New York University Press, 1996.

Ansolabehere, Stephen, Roy Behr, and Shanto Iyengar. *The Media Game: American Politics in the Television Age.* New York: Macmillan, 1993.

Bryce, James. *The American Commonwealth*, 2nd ed. London: Macmillan, 1889.

Davidson, Roger H., and Walter J. Oleszek. *Congress and Its Members*, 7th ed. Washington, DC: Congressional Quarterly Press, 2000.

Delli Carpini, Michael S., and Scott Keeler, *What Americans Know About Politics and Why It Matters.* New Haven, CT: Yale University Press, 1996.

Epstein, Leon D. *Political Parties in the American Mold.* Madison: University of Wisconsin Press, 1986.

Fiorina, Morris P. *Culture War? The Myth of a Polarized America.* New York: Pearson-Longman, 2005.

Ginsberg, Benjamin, and Martin Shefter. *Politics by Other Means: The Declining Importance of Elections in America*, rev. ed. New York: Basic Books, 1999.

Hamilton, Alexander, James Madison, and John Jay. *The Federalist Papers*, ed. Clinton Rossiter. New York: New American Library, 1961.

Jacobson, Gary C. *A Divider, Not a Uniter: George W. Bush and the American People.* New York: Pearson-Longman, 2007.

Jones, Charles O. *Separate but Equal Branches: Congress and the Presidency.* Chatham, NJ: Chatham House Publishers, 1995.

King, Anthony S., ed. *The New American Political System.* Washington, DC: American Enterprise Institute, 1978.

———. *Running Scared: Why American Politicians Campaign Too Much and Govern Too Little.* New York: Martin Kessler Books, 1997.

Mayhew, David R. *Divided We Govern: Party Control, Lawmaking, and Investigations, 1946–1988.* New Haven, CT: Yale University Press, 1991.

McCarty, Nolan, Keith T. Poole, and Howard Rosenthal, *Polarized America: The Dance or Ideology and Unequal Riches.* Cambridge: MIT Press, 2006.

McClosky, Herbert, and John Zaller. *The American Ethos: Public Attitudes Toward Capitalism and Democracy.* Cambridge, MA: Harvard University Press, 1984.

Neustadt, Richard E. *Presidential Power and the Modern Presidents: The Politics of Leadership From Roosevelt to Reagan.* New York: Free Press, 1990.

Nicholas, Herbert G. *The Nature of American Politics*, 2nd ed. New York: Oxford University Press, 1986.

Peltason, Jack W. *Corwin & Peltason's Understanding the Constitution*, 14th ed. Fort Worth, TX: Harcourt Brace 1997.

Polsby, Nelson W. *Congress and the Presidency*, 4th ed. Englewood Cliffs, NJ: Prentice Hall, 1986.

Robinson, Donald L., ed. *Reforming American Government: The Bicentennial Papers of the Committee on the Constitutional System.* Boulder, CO: Westview Press, 1985.

Rourke, Francis E. *Bureaucracy, Politics, and Public Policy.* Boston: Little, Brown, 1984.

Schlozman, Kay Lehman, and John T. Tierney, *Organized Interests and American Democracy.* New York: Harper & Row, 1986.

Tocqueville, Alexis de. *Democracy in America*, 2 vols. Henry Reeve text, revised by Francis Bowen, edited by Phillips Bradley. New York: Alfred A. Knopf, 1945.

Wildavsky, Aaron. *The New Politics of the Budgetary Process*, 2nd ed. New York: HarperCollins, 1992.

INTERNET RESOURCES

White House: **www.whitehouse.gov**

U.S. Senate: **www.senate.gov**

U.S. House of Representatives: **www.house.gov**

U.S. Courts: **www.uscourts.gov**

Library of Congress: **lcweb.loc.gov**

National Political Index: **politicalindex.com**

ENDNOTES

1. "The English Flag," in *Barrack-room Ballads and Other Verses* (London: Methuen, 1892), stanza 1.
2. Strictly speaking, "America" means all the nations located in North and South America, including Canada and the countries in Central America, the Caribbean, and South America. Yet, for better or worse, most people around the world use "American" to label anything connected with just one of those nations, the United States of America. With apologies to the citizens of other Western Hemisphere nations, we will use this common, though technically incorrect, label in this chapter.
3. Seymour Martin Lipset, *The First New Nation: The United States in Historical and Comparative Perspective* (New York: Basic Books, 1963).
4. *The World Almanac and Book of Facts 2002* (New York: World Almanac Books, 2002), 782, 804.

5. *Statistical Abstract of the United States, 2006* (Washington, DC: U.S. Census Bureau, 2006), Table 1314, 836.

6. H. G. Nicholas, *The Nature of American Politics*, 2nd ed. (New York: Oxford University Press, 1986), 4.

7. *Statistical Abstract of the United States, 2006*, Table 13, 15.

8. See *Statistical Abstract of the United States, 2006*, Table 5, 9, for figures on legal immigration, and Table 7, 10, for estimates and definition of illegal (or unauthorized) immigration.

9. *Statistical Abstract of the United States, 2006*, Table 1327, 873.

10. *Statistical Abstract of the United States, 2006*, Table 459, 317.

11. See Jacob Hacker, *The Divided Welfare State: The Battle Over Public and Private Benefits in the United States* (New York: Cambridge University Press, 2002).

12. The Twenty-First Amendment repeals the Eighteenth (prohibition) Amendment, so there are, in effect, only twenty-five amendments. The resistance to amending the Constitution even with quite popular provisions was demonstrated in June 2006, when an amendment that would have given Congress the power to ban flag burning fell one vote short of gaining the required two-thirds majority in the U.S. Senate. See Johanna Neuman and Faye Fiore, "Flag Measure Fails by 1 Vote," *Los Angeles Times*, 28 June 2006.

13. A word about this usage: strictly speaking, the government in Washington, DC, is the "national" government, and the whole divided-powers system of national and state government is the "federal" government. However, most Americans use the terms "national" and "federal" interchangeably to mean the government in Washington, DC. We will do the same, but the reader should be aware of the ambiguity of this usage.

14. Fifteen states have term limits for members of their legislatures. A number have also tried to impose similar limits on their members of Congress, but the U.S. Supreme Court ruled in 1995 (*U.S. Term Limits, Inc. v. Thornton*) that the states have no constitutional power to limit the terms of national legislators.

15. In recent years an old dispute has been revived by a number of political analysts who argue that presidential democracy is inherently inferior to parliamentary democracy, and the United States should convert to a system of parliamentary democracy similar to Great Britain's. Other analysts reply that, judging by the results—effective policies, loyal citizens, and stability—the American system has done at least as well as the parliamentary systems. See Chapter 2 for a discussion of the issues and arguments in the dispute's current version.

16. Gabriel A. Almond, G. Bingham Powell, Jr., and Robert J. Mundt, *Comparative Politics: A Theoretical Framework* (New York: HarperCollins, 1993), 55.

17. James Q. Wilson and John J. DiIulio, *American Government*, 6th ed. (Lexington, MA: D. C. Heath, 1995), Table 4.3, 81.

18. Gabriel A. Almond and Sidney Verba, *The Civic Culture: Political Attitudes and Democracy in Five Nations* (Princeton, NJ: Princeton University Press, 1962), 186.

19. See, for example, Seymour Martin Lipset, *Political Man: The Social Bases of Politics*, 2nd ed. (London: Heineman, 1983); and Angus Campbell et al., *The American Voter* (New York: John Wiley, 1960).

20. Robert A. Kagan, *Adversarial Legalism: The American Way of Law* (Cambridge: Harvard University Press, 2003).

21. *New York Times v. Sullivan*, 376 U.S. 254 (1964).

22. The two key cases are *National Broadcasting Co. v. United States*, 319 U.S. 190 (1943), and *Red Lion Broadcasting Co. v. Federal Communications Commission*, 395 U.S. 367 (1969).

23. See Michael P. McDonald and Samuel Popkin, "The Myth of the Vanishing Voter," *American Political Science Review* 95, no. 4 (December 2001), 963–74.

24. In 1993 Congress passed the "Motor Voter" act, which was intended to make registration much easier and thereby increase voting turnout. The legislation requires the states to allow citizens to register when applying for a driver's license, to permit registrations by mail, and to provide registration forms at public assistance agencies, such as those distributing unemployment compensation and welfare checks. While most political scientists applaud the new law, its effectiveness is not yet clear. Turnout of eligible voters, which stood at 61 percent in the 1992 presidential election, *dropped* to 53 percent in 1996. It rose to 56 percent in 2000, and then to 61 percent in 2004.

25. David Glass, Peverill Squire, and Raymond E. Wolfinger, "Voter Turnout: An International Comparison," *Public Opinion* (December 1983/January 1984), 49–55.

26. Russell J. Dalton, *Citizen Politics*, 2nd ed. (Chatham, NJ: Chatham House, 1996), 45–47.

27. See John G. Matsusaka, *For the Many or the Few: The Initiative, Public Policy, and American Democracy* (Chicago: University of Chicago Press, 2004).

28. One distinguished foreign observer of American politics argues persuasively that American public officials, such as members of the House of Representatives, face elections far more frequently than do their counterparts in other democracies. Consequently, he says, they have to spend large parts of their time in office raising money, touring their districts, appearing on television, and otherwise preparing for the next election. These necessities leave them less time than is needed for the careful study of public issues and the formulation of good public policy. See Anthony S. King, *Running Scared: Why America's Politicians Campaign Too Much and Govern Too Little* (New York: Martin Kessler Books, 1997).

29. Robert S. Erikson, Norman R. Luttbeg, and Kent L. Tedin, *American Public Opinion*, 4th ed. (New York: Macmillan, 1991), Table 1.2, 5.

30. In the United States, as in many democratic countries, voters can write names other than the parties' nominees on their ballots, but few voters do so and write-in candidates almost never get more than a handful of votes. An exception came in the 2004 mayor's race in San Diego, when write-in candidate Donna Frye came within a few hundred votes (and a disputed vote tabulation procedure) of getting elected mayor of the nation's seventh largest city.

31. See Reuven Y. Hazan, "Candidate Selection," in *Comparing Democracies 2*, ch. 5.

32. The exception to this rule is the presidential "caucus-convention," to which all party registrants or loyalists are invited and which selects a nominee after debate, persuasion, and many rounds of voting by attendees. In the 2004 presidential contest, at least one of the major parties used a caucus to select its nominee in 20 states, according to Harold W. Stanley and Richard G. Niemi, *Vital Statistics on American Politics 2005–2006* (Washington, DC: CQ Press), 69–70.

33. William J. Keefe and Marc J. Hetherington, *Parties, Politics, and Public Policy in America*, 9th ed. (Washington, DC: CQ Press, 2003), 61–63.

34. Federal Election Commission, *Election Results for the U.S. President, the U.S. Senate and the U.S. House of Representatives* (Washington, DC: Federal Election Commission, 2005).

35. We take the term *political interest* to mean something of value to a person or group, to be gained or lost by what government does or does not do.

36. Harold D. Lasswell, *Politics: Who Gets What, When, How* (New York: Meridian Books, 1936).

37. See, for example, Alexis de Tocqueville, *Democracy in America*, Vol. 1, pp. 191–93; and Michel Crozier, *The Trouble With America*, translated by Peter Heinegg (Berkeley: University of California Press, 1984), 81.

38. *Buckley v. Valeo*, 424 U.S. 1 (1976).

39. Marjorie Randon Hersey, *Party Politics in America*, 11th ed. (New York: Pearson Longman, 2005), 222.

40. *Democracy in America*, Vol. 1, 280.

41. Benjamin Ginsberg and Martin Shefter, *Politics by Other Means: The Declining Importance of Elections in America* (New York: Basic Books, 1990), 151–52.

42. Harold W. Stanley and Richard G. Niemi, *Vital Statistics on American Politics 2005–2006* (Washington, DC: Congressional Quarterly, 2006), Table 2–15, 107–08.

43. *New York Times*, 21 November 1988.

44. Arend Lijphart puts the United States at the top of his list of democratic nations with the smallest number of effective legislative parties, closely followed by New Zealand, the United Kingdom, and Austria: *Democracies: Patterns of Majoritarian and Consensus Governments in Twenty-One Countries* (New Haven, CT: Yale University Press, 1984), Table 7.3, 122. Austin Ranney's ranking of "two-partyness," based on the somewhat different measure of "party fractionalization," which includes both the number of effective parties and the closeness of electoral competition between them, ranks the U.S. parties second behind New Zealand (although in 1995 New Zealand adopted proportional representation, and since then it has had a multiparty system): *Governing: An Introduction to Political Science*, 8th ed. (Englewood Cliffs, NJ: Prentice Hall, 2001), Table 8.6, 181.

45. Richard Scammon, Alice McGillivray, and Rhodes Cook, *America Votes, 24* (Washington, DC: Congressional Quarterly Press, 2001), 8.

46. For a recent survey of changes in electioneering in the United States and other democratic nations, see David Butler and Austin Ranney, eds., *Electioneering: A Comparative Study of Continuity and Change* (New York: Oxford University Press, 1992).

47. Gary C. Jacobson, *A Divider, Not A Uniter: George W. Bush and the American People* (New York: Pearson-Longman, 2007), chs. 1–2.

48. Morris P. Fiorina, *Culture War? The Myth of a Polarized America* (New York: Pearson-Longman, 2005) 18, 5.

49. Bruce E. Keith et al., *The Myth of the Independent Voter* (Berkeley: University of California Press, 1992).

50. Nolan McCarty, Keith T. Poole, and Howard Rosenthal, *Polarized America: The Dance or Ideology and Unequal Riches* (Cambridge, MA: MIT Press, 2006), 12. But note that the very rich often vote for and contribute to Democrats, making the 90210 ZIP code in Beverly Hills a top fundraising area for the Democratic Party.

51. Morris P. Fiorina, *Culture War? The Myth of a Polarized America*, 70.

52. Samuel J. Eldersveld, *Political Parties in American Society* (New York: Basic Books, 1982), 133–36.

53. David Mayhew, *Divided We Govern* (New Haven, CT: Yale University Press, 1991).

54. The fullest exposition of this philosophy is, of course, *The Federalist Papers*, especially the tenth paper, by James Madison. See Clinton Rossiter, ed., *The Federalist Papers* (New York: New American Library, 1961).

55. *Democracy in America*, Vol. 1, 167.

56. Hundreds of books have been written comparing American public policies with their counterparts in other nations. We have drawn heavily on two: Arnold J. Heidenheimer, Hugh Heclo, and Carolyn Teich Adams, *Comparative Public Policy*, 3rd ed. (New York: St. Martin's Press, 1990); Harold Wilensky and Lowell Turner, *Democratic Corporatism and Policy Linkages* (Berkeley: Institute of International Studies, University of California, 1987).

57. *Statistical Abstract of the United States, 2006*, Table 415, 272.

58. *Comparative Public Policy*, Table 6.5, 198.

59. OECD, *Revenue Statistics 1965–2004* (Washington, DC: OECD, 2005), Table 3, 68.

60. *Statistical Abstract of the United States, 2006*, Table 1323, 871.

61. OECD, *OECD in Figures, OECD Observer 2005/Supplement 1* (Washington, DC: OECD, 2005), 66–67.

62. For the law's details, see *Congressional Quarterly Almanac, 1996* (Washington, DC: Congressional Quarterly Press, 1997), 6–13 to 6–24.

63. *Comparative Public Policy*, Table 2.1, 30.

64. Quoted in *Comparative Public Policy*, 29.

65. OECD, *OECD in Figures, OECD Observer 2005/Supplement 1* (Washington, DC: OECD, 2005), 67–68.

66. *The Addresses and Messages of Presidents of the United States*, compiled by Edwin Williams (New York: Edward Walker, 1846), Vol. 1, 32.

67. Address to Congress, 1 December 1862, in Roy P. Basler, ed., *The Collected Works of Abraham Lincoln* (New Brunswick, NJ: Rutgers University Press, 1953), Vol. 5, 537.

68. *The American Commonwealth*, Vol. 1, 300–301.

INDEX